The Worship Of The Dead

Or, The Origin And Nature Of Pagan Idolatry And Its Bearing Upon The Early History Of Egypt And Babylonia

John Garnier

Alpha Editions

This Edition Published in 2020

ISBN: 9789354306280

Design and Setting By
Alpha Editions
www.alphaedis.com
Email - info@alphaedis.com

PREFACE

THE intimate relation of the ancient Paganism to the early history of mankind, and its influence on the fate and fortunes of the human race, gives no little interest and importance to any inquiry into its origin and nature, and many learned men, during the last sixty years, have carefully collected and compared the traditions and archæological remains relating to it in various countries. But, although their works form a valuable literature on the subject, they are not only too voluminous to be consulted by the ordinary reader, but they fail to supply a succinct and comprehensive history of its origin, development and exact nature, without which its true character and significance cannot be fully recognised.

In the present work the author has endeavoured to supply this want, and, while availing himself of the researches of previous writers, has endeavoured to compress into a moderate compass and readable form, the facts and archæological discoveries which show the relation of the gods and religious systems of various nations to each other, and to point out the significance and interpretation of the ancient traditions and mythological stories, and their bearing on the events of actual history.

Attention is called to the fact that the numerous testimonies referred to by the author are not those of one people and one age, but of many individuals living in different ages, and of different nationalities; and that one and all are without the slightest evidence of artificial construction or systematic purpose. They are, for the most part, the statements of persons without relation to each other, who simply record the statements and opinions of the people of other countries, or briefly allude to the general belief current in their own. They form, therefore, a number of perfectly independent witnesses, whose testimony is all the more valuable because they are often entirely unaware of the import and significance of their own evidence.

It will be seen, also, that their statements mutually explain and confirm each other, while their very mistakes and misconceptions, due to their ignorance of the matters to which they refer, are a guarantee of the genuineness of the statements themselves, and often help to explain their significance.

In the face of this total absence of all evidence of design and system on their part, it might be thought that their testimony would be regarded as valid and conclusive. But of late years a school of criticism has arisen, which seeks to discredit this testimony, and boldly asserts it to be mere invention and forgery. This is especially the case with regard to the evidence which proves that the originals of the Pagan gods were human beings who had once lived upon the earth. These critics say, without the slightest justification, that this is merely an invention of the later Pagan writers, and assert, equally without a shadow of real evidence for the assertion, that every testimony in support of it is a forgery.

This kind of destructive criticism has indeed been extended, more or less, to all ancient history and tradition, including that of the Old Testament. But it will be observed that it mainly depends upon mere assertions and plausible suggestions, such as those which represent the prophecies of Scripture to be merely the utterances of imaginative and patriotic men, whose wishes were fathers of their thoughts, or that certain prophecies were so exactly fulfilled, that they must have been written after the event.

This school of criticism also seizes upon every point and feature in sacred and profane tradition which is out of the common, or difficult of explanation, to impugn the veracity of the whole. In the case of sacred history, most of these attacks have been fully replied to, and shown to be without foundation, although they continue to be repeated. But in the case of ancient profane history and tradition, it is evident that, while fable and exaggeration would be almost certain to collect round the memories of celebrated persons, yet they are no proof that these persons never existed. This is the case with the fables which have collected round the history of the celebrated Arthur, King of the Silures, and which have afforded an excuse for saying that he never existed. But Gibbon, sceptic though he was, warmly repudiates such a conclusion, which is quite unwarranted.

Niebuhr, again, rejected the whole history of the kings of Rome as fabulous, but without any sufficient reason for so doing; and recent researches have confirmed the history and proved this hypercriticism to be false.

There are also people who assert that Herodotus, "the father of history," was the very "father of lies." Yet every page of his chronicles bears the impress of a man who is honestly and faithfully relating exactly what he saw and heard. But because some of his stories—which he simply relates as he was told them, and, as was natural of the age in which he lived, often believed himself—were mythological fables, therefore he himself is stigmatised as a liar, as if he had been the inventor of them! Such assertions only illustrate the superficiality and injustice which characterise much of this destructive criticism. Moreover, some of the myths related by Herodotus are probably of no little value, as indicating actual facts concealed beneath the allegorical language of mythology.

In the case of those who assert that every testimony in support of the human origin of the Pagan gods is an invention or forgery, it may be asked, "What possible reason or motive could there be for such inventions and forgeries?" It is quite inconceivable that Pagans, whose writings evince their reverence for their religion, should invent a theory, the only tendency of which was to belittle their own gods by bringing them down to the level of human beings. For it was this very thing, that the Pagan gods were only deified men, which the early Christian apologists cast in the teeth of their Pagan opponents; and the latter could not deny it.

Moreover, if it was an invention unfounded on fact, how could the inventors have persuaded the rest of the Pagan world to accept a belief so opposed to its previous convictions? Is it not certain that many would have opposed it, and that full records of the controversy would have existed? But there are no such records. The later Pagan and early Christian writers, who have summarised or have referred to the general belief of their day, never give the smallest hint of a suspicion that it was an invention, and it is impossible that they should not have been aware of it, if it had been the case, and equally inconceivable that they should not have noticed or referred to it.

It was the secret teaching also of the most solemn feature in the Pagan religion, "The Mysteries," and it is impossible to suppose that the very priesthood combined to support an invention which tended to diminish the mystery and solemnity which surrounded their gods, and on which their own influence depended.

The Greek and Latin testimony in support of it is also corroborated by similar evidence from Egyptian, Phœnician, Assyrian, Hindu, and other sources. It is absurd to suppose that the people in these different countries, and in different ages, all combined to fabricate it.

Even the monumental evidence corroborates it, and we find the kings of Babylon, Egypt and India claiming to be descended from these gods whom they speak of as their ancestors or forefathers.

But when, in addition to this, we see that the testimony in proof of the human origin of the gods is not only consentient, but entirely devoid of the method and artificialities which characterise invention, we may ask why should there be such hostility to the evidence in its favour? Why, when no just grounds for the assertion can be given, should these evidences be declared to be inventions and forgeries, when we have before our eyes the fact that the worship of the dead, or of men celebrated for their power, wisdom or piety, has always, and in all ages, been one of the predominant tendencies of human nature?

In the face of these considerations, the reader may reasonably ask for some better evidence than the mere assertion or suggestion that these testimonies are fabrications and forgeries, before rejecting them.

It will be seen that much of the force of the conclusions arrived at in the course of our inquiry, especially those connected with the human origin of the gods, depends on the evidence in proof of the identity of the various gods and goddesses, and it will be observed that the evidence is accumulative. For instance, the identity of A with B may be shown, and that of B with C, and of C with D, and of D with E, and from this the identity of all might be fairly inferred. But when, in addition to this, the identity of A with C, D and E, and the identity of B with D and E, and that of C with E is shown, the force of the conclusion is enormously increased.

But although the identity of the various Pagan gods and goddesses with each other is the general conclusion arrived at by all the most learned men who have studied the subject, yet, as might be expected, it is strongly opposed by some who, in spite of the accumulative evidence referred to above, seize upon every superficial point of difference in the character of the gods as a reason for rejecting it.

Now it is quite evident that certain differences and local names and accretions would naturally gather, in time, round the gods of those nations who originally obtained them from other nations. This is the case with the gods of Greece and Rome, who obtained most of their gods and religious ideas from Egypt, Phœnicia and Babylon. They not only misunderstood the allegorical language, and misinterpreted the symbolism which revealed their true characteristics, but they naturally attributed to them many of the characteristics of their own race and country. But, this being recognised, it is manifestly absurd to make these local and generally superficial differences a reason for rejecting the far stronger and broader proofs of the original identity of these gods, nor is it probable that any unprejudiced person will do so, in the face of the accumulative force of the evidence in support of that identity.

To some readers the details of this evidence may seem to be tedious, but a certain degree of acquaintance with it will be found to be necessary for the proper understanding of the general argument and the conclusions which follow from it.

Much of the interest of the inquiry will be the light which it appears to throw upon the early history of Egypt and on the identity of the mysterious Shepherd kings, and it will be seen that the conclusions arrived at are confirmed by the monumental records of that country, which have been hitherto rejected for the uncertain testimony of the Greek records of Manetho. The inquiry also into the occult aspect of the Pagan gods, and the true nature of Pagan magic and sorcery, and their relation to the phenomena of modern Buddhism and Spiritualism, will be of interest to many, while the author's analysis of the true moral aspect of the Ancient Paganism may be worth the attention of the thoughtful Christian.

In the Appendices the author has examined Sir Gardner Wilkinson's view of the Egyptian gods and religion; certain modern theories respecting the antiquity of the human race, the Deluge and the Glacial Period; the ancient Accadians and Turanians and their religion, the Cushite Empire of Nimrod, the monumental records of that monarch, the distribution of peoples after the Deluge, the early influence of the Semitic race, and the authenticity of Sanchoniathon's history.

CONTENTS

PART I.

The Pagan Gods and Goddesses.

xi

PART II.

ORIGIN AND NATURE OF PAGAN IDOLATRY.

CHAPTER VIII.—THE TEACHING OF HERMES—MAGIC, NECROMANCY, ETC. Cush and Nimrod did not originate their own worship, but the Idolatry instituted by them was the same in principle as that afterwards established—Chief characteristics of the primitive Idolatry—Magic and demon worship—Buddhist countries the chief seat of modern Hermetic teaching—The books of Buddha—Claim of supernatural powers — Modern Theosophy — Intuitional memory — Previous astral existence—Clairvoyance—Power over forces of nature—Projection of soul through space — The Divine Essence — Incantations — Powers of magicians of Egypt—Agency of spirits—Pagan gods were devils or daimonia—The Delphic Oracle—Its celebrity—The Pythoness possessed by a god or spirit—Pagan gods supposed to be spirits of the dead—

State of the dead—Pagan gods stated by Scripture to be daimonia similar to those cast out by Christ, and whose chief was Satan—Power claimed by the latter—Theosophy—Intercourse with spirits—Testimony of Cyprian and Clement—Temples of health—Remarkable cures—Theomanteis—Daimonia leptoi—Enthousiastai—Dreamers of Dreams—The prophetic faculty—Capacity for receiving impressions from spiritual agencies—Physical conditions—Similar to those inculcated in the foretold apostasy from Christianity which commenced with the worship of the dead—Explanation of dreams and visions—Instances of these—Real nature of intuitional memory—Spiritualism—Number of its adherents—Testimonies to reality of phenomena—Mixed up with trickery—The spirits personate the spirits of the dead—Similar belief of Pagans—Description of Spiritualistic phenomena — Analysis of — Levitation—The same in Paganism—Roman Catholic Saints—Magical power of Pagan Idols—Proof that phenomena of Spiritualism due to spirits—Clairvoyance and Mesmerism due to same agency—Use of Mesmerism by Pagan priests for consulting the gods—Part played by the Mesmeriser—Self Mesmerism — Indian Fakirs — Colonel Townshend — Electro Biology and Hypnotism due to same agencies — Mesmeric power independent of force of will—Powers of adept due to possession by a spirit—Phenomena of Electro Biology not due to Biologist—Similar Phenomena of Hypnotism—Pagan divination by table-turning—The Trinity of Theosophy same as that of Paganism—Supernatural phenomena which are not due to daimonia—Distinction between the two classes of phenomena—Other phenomena—Haunted houses and localities under a curse—"The Doune murderers"—Modern efforts to revive intercourse with spirits—Spiritualism, Theosophy and Romanism only a revival of Paganism   .   .   .   .   .   pages 147-181

CHAPTER IX.—THE NEPHILIM. Description of Oannes and the Annedoti before the Deluge—The antediluvian Chrysor or Hephæstus the first Hermes—Distinct from the first Oannes—Chrysor or Hephæstus one of the gods of the postdiluvians—Postdiluvian Idolatry a revival of antediluvian—The buried writings—Tradition of Berosus, Manetho, Josephus—The Indian traditions—The books of Vishnu, Buddha, Mahabad, Menu, Prydain—Interpretation of these traditions, and other mythological stories—Fanciful fables of Greeks due to their ignorance of the esoteric meaning of Pagan allegory and symbolism—Correspondence between Pagan traditions and the Scriptural account —The ten antediluvian kings—The giants of Gothic, Celtic, Indian, Chinese, Buddhist and Greek mythology—Scriptural account—The "Sons of God"—Meaning of the term—The giants or Nephilim—Meaning of *Nephilim*, the "Fallen Ones"—Intercourse with women—Testimony of ancient writers—Iranian tradition of Djemschid—Reference to the Nephilim by St Peter—Nature of their sin—Hindu tradition that the

b

PART III.

OVERTHROW OF THE PRIMITIVE PAGANISM AND ITS RELATION TO THE EARLY HISTORY OF BABYLON AND EGYPT.

thrower of Osiris (Nimrod)—Titan (Shem), the overthrower of Saturn (Cush)—Set the real name of Typhon—Set a synonym of Shem or Sem —Set also called Semu—Sem the Greek form of Shem—Set worshipped as a god until time of the Rameses, and after that called Typhon, the principle of evil, as the enemy of Osiris—Means taken by Shem to overthrow Osiris — Shem a prophet of God—His warning against Nephilim worship, which had brought about the destruction of the antediluvian world — Set symbolised by a Boar—Tusks of a Boar emblem of the power of the mouth, or of words—Sem or Shem, the Egyptian Hercules, called also "*Chon,*" "the Lamenter"—Hercules *Ogmius,* "the Lamenter," and the god of Eloquence—Set or Typhon said to be the father of the Jews and builder of Jerusalem—General tradition of Jews that Shem was Melchisedek, king and priest of Jerusalem—The Sha emblem of Set—Set worshipped as "*Set Nubti,*" "Set the Golden"—Subsequent hatred of Set and his identification with Typhon, the evil spirit—Symbolised by a Red Ass—Red or ruddy complexion of Set—Men of similar complexion sacrificed to the black Osiris—Christ called Typhon in Egypt and symbolised by an Ass—Set as the god Bes—The power of words by which Typhon overcame Osiris represented as horrid yells and shrieks—Similar misrepresentation of Christians in after times—Story that when gods were overthrown by Typhon they assumed the shapes of animals by the advice of Pan, and went to Egypt—This refers to the secret resuscitation of Idolatry in that country—Shem, or Titan, said to be assisted by his brother Titans in his war against Saturn—Implies general co-operation of other descendants of Noah against the Cushites—War of giants against the Pagan gods refers to the same event—Its distinction from the war of the Titans against Cœlus (Heaven), which was headed by Saturn— The giants represented with the long hair and beards distinctive of the Semitic Patriarchs—Chaldean legend of the war of the wicked gods against the Moon god (Cush)—Scandinavian tradition of the death of Balder by Loki the spirit of evil—Indian tradition of the overthrow of the gods by Durga—Exact similarity to the story of Typhon—Similar stories of Mahesha and Ganesa.

Set, or Typhon, identical with the Shepherd king Set or Saites— The latter called Set Nubti in the reign of Rameses II., and given same titles as the god Set or Typhon—Proofs that the Shepherd king Set was Typhon—City of Avaris built by him called Typhonian city, and the zone in which it was built the Sethroite zone—Story of the overthrow of Idolatry by the Shepherds identical with that of the overthrow of Osiris by Typhon—Description of Shepherds as "Wandering Phœnician kings" exactly descriptive of Semitic Patriarchs— Reason for building Avaris by Shepherd king Set—Same hatred to Shepherds as to Typhon—Identification of the Shepherds as the same race as the Israelites by Manetho—Shepherds called "Our Ancestors"

PART IV.

RESUSCITATION AND DEVELOPMENT OF THE PRIMITIVE IDOLATRY.

APPENDIX A.
SIR GARDNER WILKINSON ON THE EGYPTIAN RELIGION.

APPENDIX D.

THE ACCADIANS.

Accadian magic and nature gods similar to those of the Turanian races—
Accadian language also similar to that of Turanians—Later Chaldean
language, Semitic—Hence it is argued that the Cushite language was
Semitic—Language of Canaanites in later times also Semitic—Dis-
tinction drawn between Cushite and Accadian religion—Argument by
M. Lenormant that Accadians were Turanians and not Cushites—
Replies to these conclusions:—

(1). Evidence that inhabitants of Chaldea before Cushite conquest
were Turanian—Impossibility that Turanians could have imposed their
language and religion on their conquerors, and probability that they
adopted the language and religion of the Cushites and carried it with
them in their subsequent migrations to the east and north—Accadians
were the authors of cuneiform writing, possessed high civilisation and
knowledge of Astronomy, and were the originators of the learning and
civilisation of the Chaldees—This wholly inconsistent with Turanian
character—This is the argument of M. Renan—The force of it shown.

(2). The question of language—Semitic races in the valleys of Tigris
and Euphrates must have outnumbered the Cushites—Evidence of the
decline of the Cushite power in the days of Abraham—Early Cushite
migration to India—Consequent predominance of the Semitic people
and language in the days of Amraphel and his successors.

The language of Canaan—Powerful influence of Semitic peoples,
and the conquest and dispersion of Hamitic Canaanites sufficient to
account for its later Semitic character—Previous language similar to
Accadian—The Hittites—The northern Amorites probably Aramæans
—Cuneiform writing used at first by Israelites.

(3). Distinction by M. Lenormant between the Babylonian and
Accadian religions—Nothing known of Accadian religion as distinct
from that of the kings of Ur—Absence of outward forms among
Turanian races is what might be expected.

(4). Assertion that there was never a Cushite conquest of Babylon—
"The Nimrod Myth"—No mention of Nimrod on monuments—
"Nimrod" only a soubriquet, not his real name—Identity of "*Sargani Sar
Ali*," king of Accad, with Nimrod—Nimrod must have been first king of
Accad, Erech, Ur and Babylon—*Lugal Saggisi*, king of Erech, is "The
king Sargani"—Inscriptions describing him identify him with Nimrod
and show him to be King of Accad, Erech and Ur—Called son of
Bel (Cush), and king of the children of Bel (Cushites)—Shown to have
been deified—"*Lugal Kigub*," king of Ur, and "Kienge Accad" is also
Nimrod—"*En Sag Saggani*," king of Kienge, should probably read "*En
Sar Sargani*"—"*Sumu Abi*" and "*Sumu la Ilu*," first kings of Babylon—
Their probable identity with Cush and Nimrod—Their successor "*Zabu*,"
or "*Zamu*," is probably the "*Zames*" of the Greek lists—Correspondence

Notes on Chronological Table.

APPENDIX E.

" History of Sanchoniathon."

PLATES.

List of the Principal Works Consulted or Quoted, and Notices of any Particular Editions Used.

Aglio—Mexican Antiquities.
Ammianus Marcellinus—History.
Apuleius—Opera.
Asiatic Researches.
Augustine—De Civitate Deo.
    Do.   Citie of God; translation by J. Healy. 1642.

Baldwin—Prehistoric Nations.
Bancroft—Native Races of the Pacific Coast of North America.
Barker and Ainsworth—Lares and Penates of Cilicia.
Beal—Catena of Buddhist Scriptures.
Belzoni—Operations and Discoveries in Egypt and Nubia.
Berosus—From Cory's Fragments.
Betham (Sir W.)—Gael and Cimbri.
    Do.   Etruscan Literature and Antiquities.
Birch (Samuel)—History of Egypt.
Brown (R.)—Great Dionysiac Myth.
Brugsch—History of Egypt.
Bryant—Plagues of Egypt.
    Do.   Ancient Mythology.
Bunsen—History of Egypt.

Cæsar—Commentaries.
Catlin—North American Indians. Edition 1876.
    Do.   The Uplifted and Subsided Rocks of North America.
Cicero—De Natura Deorum.
    Do.   Tusculan Disputations.
Colebrook—Religious Ceremonies of the Hindoos.
Coleman—Indian Mythology.
Colquhoun—Isis Revelata: Enquiry into Animal Magnetism. 1836.
    Do.   Magic and Witchcraft. 1851.
Computation of the Number 666—Nisbet. 1891.
Conder (Colonel R. E.)—The First Bible.
Cory—Ancient Fragments.
    Do.   Do.   Edited by Hodges.

Crabb—Mythology.
Crichton—Ancient and Modern Scandinavia.
Cumberland—History of Sanchoniathon.
Cunningham (Major-Gen. Alexander)—Stupa of Bharhut.

Davies—Celtic Researches.
  Do.   Mythology and Rites of British Druids.
Deane—Worship of the Serpent.
Diodorus Siculus—Bibliotheca.
Donnelly, Ignatius—Atlantis.
Dryden's Virgil.
Dupuis—Origin of Religions; translation by Partridge.   Burns.
Dymock—Classical Dictionary.

Edkins—Chinese Buddhism.
Elliot—Horæ Apocalypticæ.
Eusebius—Præparationes Evangelicæ.

Faber—Origin of Pagan Idolatry.
Ferguson—Tree and Serpent Worship.

Gall—Primeval Man Unveiled.
Gibbon—Decline and Fall.   One   Volume   Edition.   Ball,
          Arnold & Co.   1840.
Gill—Myths of the South Pacific.
Gray (Mrs Hamilton)—Sepulchres of Etruria.   1843.

Hales' Chronology.
Herodotus.
Hislop—Two Babylons.   7th Edition.
Howarth (Sir H. H.).—The Mammoth and the Flood.
          Do.   The Glacial Nightmare.
Humboldt—Researches on the Ancient Inhabitants of America.
Hurd—Rites and Ceremonies.

Josephus—Whiston's.

Kennedy—Hindu Mythology.
Kennett—Roman Antiquities.
Kenrick—Egypt under the Pharaohs.
Kinns—Moses and Geology.
Kitto—Illustrated Commentary.

Lang—Origin and Migrations of the Polynesian Nation.
Layard—Nineveh and its Remains.
  Do.   Nineveh and Babylon.
Lemprière—Classical Dictionary.
Lenormant—Ancient History of the East.
  Do.   —Chaldean Magic and Sorcery.
Lillie—Buddha and Early Buddhism.
Lynam—Roman Emperors.

Macrobius—Opera.
Maimonides—More Nevochim.
Mallet—Northern Antiquities.
Mankind, their Origin and Destiny.
Maurice—Indian Antiquities.
Moor's Hindu Pantheon.

Nash—The Pharaoh of the Exodus.
Newman (Cardinal)—Development of Christian Doctrine.
Newton (Benjamin Wills) — Reflections on the Spread of
                         Spiritualism. Boulston & Sons.
Nimrod.

Osburn—Monumental History of Egypt.
Ovid—Opera.

Pember—Earth's Earliest Ages.
Perfect Way (The). 1882.
Peter Martyr—De Orbe Novo.
Petrie (Flinders)—History of Egypt.
Piazzi Smyth—Life and Work at the Great Pyramid.
Plato—Opera.
Pliny—Natural History. Bohn. 1855.
Plutarch—De Iside et Osiride.
Pococke--India in Greece.
Pompeii.
Poole—Horæ Egypticæ.
Potter and Boyd—Grecian Antiquities.   In one Volume.
               Griffin & Co. 1850.
Prescott—Conquest of Mexico.   In one Volume.   Routledge.
  Do.   Conquest of Peru.   Do.   do.
Purchas—Pilgrimages.

Quarterly Review, 1877.

Ragozin—Stories of the Nations: Chaldea.
Rawlinson (G.)—Egypt and Babylon.
       Do.   Five Great Monarchies of the Ancient East.
       Do.   Herodotus.
Rhys Davis—Buddhism.
Russell—Egypt, Ancient and Modern.

Salverte (Eusebe)—Sciences Occultes.
Sanchoniathon—History: from Cory's Fragments.
Saville—Truth of the Bible.
Sayce—Fresh Light from the Ancient Monuments.
  Do.   Early Israel and the Surrounding Nations.
  Do.   Races of the Old Testament.
Secret Doctrine (The)—By H. P. B.   2nd Edition.   1888.
Sharon Turner—Anglo-Saxons.
Smith—Dictionary of the Bible.
  Do.   Classical Dictionary.
Smith (George)—Chaldean Account of Genesis.
Stukeley—Stonehenge and Avebury.
Strabo—Bohn
Suggestive Inquiry into the Hermetic Wisdom.

Tacitus—Manners of the Germans.
Taylor—New Zealand and Its Inhabitants.
Tertullian—Opera.
Toland—History of the Druids.
Tylor—Researches into the Early History of Mankind.

Vaux—Nineveh and Persepolis.
Virgil.
Vyse (Colonel Howard)—Pyramids of Egypt.

Wild—Spiritual Dynamics.
Wilkins—Hindu Mythology.
Wilkinson—Manners and Customs of the Egyptians.   6 Vols.
                                      1841.
   Do.   do.   Edited by Birch.   1878.

Yule—Marco Polo.

PLATE I.

GROUP OF SHEPHERDS

PLATE II.

SHEPHERD—ENLARGED VIEW

215 Sphinx Hyksos / Musée Ghizeh

TANIS SPHINXES

PLATE IV.

"SHEFRA" OR "NUM SUPHIS"

PART I

THE PAGAN GODS AND GODDESSES

A

The Worship of the Dead

CHAPTER I

INTRODUCTORY—THE DELUGE

THERE are some modern writers who have represented the various
religious superstitions and idolatries of different nations as being the
spontaneous invention of each race, and the natural and uniform
outcome of human nature in a state of barbarism. This is not the
case; the theory is wholly opposed to the conclusions of those who
have most fully studied the subject. The works of Faber, Sir W.
Jones, Pococke, Hislop, Sir G. Wilkinson, Rawlinson and others
have indisputably proved the connection and identity of the
religious systems of nations most remote from each other, showing
that, not merely Egyptians, Chaldeans, Phœnicians, Greeks and
Romans, but also the Hindus, the Buddhists of China and of Thibet,
the Goths, Anglo-Saxons, Druids, Mexicans and Peruvians, the
Aborigines of Australia, and even the savages of the South Sea
Islands,[1] must have all derived their religious ideas from a common
source and a common centre. Everywhere we find the most startling
coincidences in rites, ceremonies, customs, traditions, and in the
names and relations of their respective gods and goddesses.

There is no more convincing evidence of this fact than the common
tradition in all these nations of the Deluge, as collected by Mr Faber,
and more lately by the additional traditions of the Mandan and other
North American Indians, in Mr Catlin's interesting work on those

[1] Mr Lang quotes Sir Stamford Raffles and Marsden as stating that there was
one original language common to the South Sea Islands and to Sumatra, New
Guinea, Madagascar and the Philippines. He says that the language of the
Polynesians has also a remarkable resemblance to that of the Chinese, and that
their religious customs are similar to those of the Mexicans, Peruvians, Phœnicians
and Egyptians, the name even of their Sun god being "Ra," as in Peru and
Egypt (Lang's *Polynesia*, pp. 19, 20, 41-44. *See* also Taylor's *New Zealand* and
Gill's *Myths of the South Pacific*.)

tribes,[1] showing that, with the exception of the Negro races, there is hardly a nation or tribe in the world which does not possess a tradition of the destruction of the human race by a flood; and the details of these traditions are too exactly in accordance with each other to permit the suggestion, which some have made, that they refer to different local floods in each case. Now Mr Faber has exhaustively shown in his three folio volumes that the mythologies of all the ancient nations are interwoven with the events of the Deluge and are explained by it, thereby proving that they are all based on a common principle, and must have been derived from a common source.

The force of this argument is illustrated by the fact of the observance of a great festival of the dead in commemoration of the event, not only by nations more or less in communication with each other, but by others widely separated, both by the ocean and by centuries of time. This festival is, moreover, held by all on or about the very day on which, according to the Mosaic account, the Deluge took place, viz., *the seventeenth day of the second month*—the month nearly corresponding with our November.

The Jewish civil year commenced at the autumnal equinox, or about September 20th, and the seventeenth day of the second month would therefore correspond with the fifth day of our month of November; but as the festival was originally, as in Egypt, preceded by three days' mourning, it appears to have been put back three days in countries where one day's festival only was observed, and to have been more generally kept on November 2nd.

Mr Haliburton says :—"The festival of the dead, or feast of ancestors, is now, or was, formerly observed at or near the beginning of November by the Peruvians, the Hindus, the Pacific Islanders, the people of the Tonga Islands, the Australians, the ancient Persians, the ancient Egyptians and the northern nations of Europe, and continued for three days among the Japanese, the Hindus, the Australians, the ancient Romans and the ancient Egyptians.

"Wherever the Roman Catholic Church exists, solemn Mass for *All Souls* is said on the 2nd November, and on that day the gay Parisians, exchanging the boulevard for the cemetery, lunch at the graves of their relatives and hold unconsciously their 'feast of

[1] Faber, *Pagan Idolatry*, book iii. chap. vi. vol. ii.; Catlin, *North American Indians*. A general summary of these traditions has also been collected by Sir H. H. Howorth in his work, *The Mammoth and the Flood*.

ancestors' on the very same day that savages in far-distant quarters of the globe observe, in a similar manner, their festival of the dead. Even the Church of England, which rejects All Souls as based on a belief in purgatory and as being a creation of Popery, clings devoutly to All Saints."[1]   Again, with reference to the Peruvian festival of the dead, Mr Haliburton writes:—"The month in which it occurs, says Rivers, is called 'Aya Marca,' from '*Aya*,' a 'corpse,' and '*Marca*,' 'carrying in arms,' because they celebrated the solemn festival of the dead with tears, lugubrious songs and plaintive music, and it was customary to visit the tombs of relations, and to leave in them food and drink. It is worthy of remark that this feast was celebrated among the ancient Peruvians at the same period and on the same day that Christians solemnise their commemoration of the dead —2nd November."[2]

Again, speaking of the festival of agriculture and death in Persia, Mr Haliburton says, "The month of November was formerly called in Persia 'the month of the angel of death.' In spite of the calendar having been changed, the festival took place at the same time as in Peru;" and he adds that a similar festival of agriculture and death, in the beginning of November, takes place in Ceylon.[3]   A like ceremony was held in November among the people of the Tonga Islands, with prayers for their deceased relatives.[4]

The Egyptians began their year at the same time as the Jews, and on the seventeenth day of their second month commenced their solemn mourning for Osiris, the Lord of Tombs,[5] who was fabled to have been shut up in the deep for one year like Noah, and whose supposed resurrection and reappearance was celebrated with rejoicing.[6] The death of the god was the great event in Paganism, as we shall explain later, and all the religious rites were made to centre round it.

In Mexico "the festival of the dead was held on the 17th November, and was regulated by the Pleiades. It began at sunset, and at midnight, as that constellation approached the zenith, a human victim, says Prescott, was offered up to avert the dread calamity which they believed impended over the human race. They had a tradition that, at that time, *the world had been previously destroyed*, and they

---

[1] "The Year of the Pleiades," by R. G. Haliburton ;—from *Life and Work at the Great Pyramid*, by Piazzi Smith, vol. ii. pp. 372-73.
[2] *Ibid.*, p. 388.   [3] *Ibid.*, p. 390
[4] *Ibid.*, p. 387.   [5] *Ibid.*, pp. 382-391.
[6] Hislop, *Two Babylons*, p. 136; Plutarch, *De Iside et Osiride*, vol. ii. p. 336.   D.

dreaded that a similar catastrophe at the end of a cycle would anni-hilate the human race."[1]

In Rome the festival of the dead, or "Feralia," called "Dii Manes," or "the day of the spirits of the dead," commenced on February 17th, the second month of their year. In more ancient times, the "festival of the spirits," believed to be the souls of deceased friends, was called "Lemuria," and was held on May 11th. This also was the seventeenth day of the second month of the year at that time; for the old Latin year commenced April 1st, which month consisted of thirty-six days, so that May 11th was exactly the seventeenth day of the second month.[2]

A feast called the "Anthesteria" was also celebrated at Athens on February 11th-13th, in honour of Bacchus, who was identical with the Egyptian Osiris, and there can be little doubt that it referred to the same event, the time being transferred to the second month of their year.

A similar variation in the period of the festival occurred some-times in more modern times, but by far the most general period among the majority of nations is the beginning of November.

Mr Haliburton has some interesting arguments to prove that the festival in many nations was fixed by the first rising of the Pleiades above the horizon. There are certainly strong grounds for connecting the two events, and the very name Pleiades, from *Pleo*, "to sail," and the belief that their rising marked the best time to start on a *voyage*,[3] is suggestive of the event to which the feast referred.

But the Pleiades, as their other name, "Vergiliæ," implies, are spring stars in the Northern Hemisphere, whereas the Deluge com-menced in the autumn; nor does it appear that the festival of the dead, among the nations of the Northern Hemisphere, was ever con-nected with the *rising* of the Pleiades. If their festival was in any way regulated by them, it must have been by their *setting*. Never-theless there was another event in the Mosaic account of nearly equal importance, which would be exactly marked by the rising of the Pleiades in the Northern Hemisphere, namely, the seventeenth day of the *seventh* month, when the ark rested on Mount Ararat. This also, being the commencement of the summer, would be the best time for starting on a voyage.

In the Southern Hemisphere, where the seasons are the reverse of ours, Mr Hull, speaking of the Australian Aborigines, says, "Their

[1] Haliburton, from *Life and Work*, vol. ii. p. 390.
[2] *Ibid.*, p. 396, and Hales, *Chronology*, vol. i. p. 44.
[3] Lemprière, *Pleiades*.

grand corroborees are held only in the spring (our autumn), when the
Pleiades are generally most distinct, and their corroboree is a worship
of the constellation which announces spring." Mr Fyers says that
" they dance and sing to gain the favour of the Pleiades (Mormodellick),
the constellation worshipped by one body as *the giver of rain.*" Mr
Haliburton adds, " Now the Pleiades are most distinct in the spring
month of November, when they appear at the horizon in the evening
and are visible all night." He further says, " We are told by one
gentleman examined by the Committee, that all the corroborees of the
natives are associated with a worship of the dead and last three
days." [1]

The Society Islanders also held a festival of the dead, and a first-
fruits celebration in the month of November, connected with the
rising of the Pleiades, called by them " Matarii i nia," or " The Pleiades
above," which marked the commencement of their year, or rather the
first season of their year, the second being called " Matarii i raro," " The
Pleiades below." This festival of the dead and of the first-fruits is
evidently that referred to by Ellis as taking place " at the ripening,
or completing of the year." He says, " The ceremony was viewed as
a national acknowledgment to the gods. When the prayers were
ended, a usage prevailed resembling much the Popish custom of Mass
for souls in purgatory. Each one returned to his home or family
Marae, there to offer special prayers for the spirits of departed
relatives." [2]

It is clear from these remarks that one or other of the two great
events in the history of the Deluge, namely, the commencement of
the waters and the beginning of their subsidence, were observed
throughout the ancient world, some nations observing one event and
some the other. It would also appear probable that the observance
of this festival was intimately connected with, and perhaps initiated,
that worship of the dead which, as we shall see, was the central
principle of the ancient idolatry. So also the uniform character of
the festival, the three days' mourning which preceded it, and the
identical day on which it was held by nations separated from each
other by periods of probably several thousand years, are evidences of
the unity of the religious system from which it emanated. It shows
also that nations like the Aborigines of Australia, the South Sea
Islanders and others, now sunk in barbarism, were probably off-shoots
from one or other of the highly-civilised nations of antiquity.

Finally, the observance of this festival at, or about, the seventeenth

[1] Haliburton, from *Life and Work*, pp. 384-386.   [2] *Ibid.*, pp. 386-387.

day of the second month of the recognised year in exact accordance with the Mosaic account, by almost every race and nation of the earth, in commemoration of a world-wide cataclysm in which a few survivors saw all their friends and relations swept away by a mighty flood of waters, is overpowering evidence of the reality of the Flood and of the truth of the Bible; although for that very reason, in accordance with the spirit of the present day, modern criticism and modern science have done what they can to discredit it.

The point, however, which we have to consider at present is this: that the similar religious rites and beliefs of different nations so widely separated from each other, in all of which the tradition of the Deluge is so deeply interwoven, could not have been the separate invention of each race. Speaking of all the various systems of Pagan idolatry which he examines, Mr Faber writes:—"There is such a minute and regular accordance between them, not only in what is obvious and natural, but also in what is arbitrary and circumstantial, both in fanciful speculation and in artificial observance, that no person who takes the pains of thoroughly investigating the subject can avoid being fully persuaded that they must have all sprung from some common origin."[1] This is also confirmed by Scripture, which likens the effect of the idolatry to drunkenness, and states:—"Babylon hath been a golden cup in the hand of the Lord to make all the earth drunken. The nations have drunken of her wine, therefore are the nations mad" (Jeremiah li. 7). It is further confirmed by the researches of modern writers who uniformly regard Babylon and Assyria as the cradle of the ancient Paganism, Egypt receiving her religion from Chaldea, Greece from Egypt and Phœnicia, and Rome, partly from the Etruscans, an Asiatic colony from the same original centre, and partly in later ages from Greece.

Egypt, as will be shown later on, was one of the first countries conquered by Nimrod, the founder of the Babylonian Empire. Speaking of the sciences of arithmetic and astronomy, Zonares writes:—"It is said that these came from the Chaldees to the Egyptians and thence to the Greeks,"[2] and as the astronomy of the Chaldees was inseparable from their religion, and the very names they gave to the stars were the names of their gods, these facts imply that the religion of Egypt and Greece came from the same source.

This is also the conclusion of Bunsen and Layard. Bunsen concludes that "the religious system of Egypt was derived from Asia and the primitive Empire in Babel." Layard also says, "Of

[1] *Origin of Pagan Idolatry*, vol. i. p. 59.   [2] Zonares, lib. i. vi. p. 34.

the great antiquity of this primitive worship, there is abundant evidence, and that it originated among the inhabitants of the Assyrian plains we have the united testimony of sacred and profane historians. It obtained the epithet of 'Perfect,' and was believed to be the most ancient of religious systems, having preceded that of Egypt. The identity of many of the Assyrian doctrines with those of Egypt is alluded to by Porphyry and Clemens."[1]

Birch also on the Babylonian inscriptions writes:—"The Zodiacal signs show unequivocally that the Greeks derived their notions and arrangements of the Zodiac, and consequently their mythology, which was intertwined with it, from the Chaldees."[2] Ouwaroff, in his work on the Eleusinian mysteries, says that "the Egyptians claimed the honour of having transmitted to the Greeks the first elements of Polytheism," and concludes his inquiry in the following words:— "These positive facts would sufficiently prove, even without conformity of idea, that the mysteries, transplanted into Greece, and there united with a certain number of local notions, never lost the character of their origin, derived from the cradle of the moral and religious ideas of the universe. All these separate facts, all these scattered testimonies, recur to that fruitful principle which places in the East the centre of science and civilisation."[3]

Herodotus also states that the names of almost all the gods came from Egypt to Greece.[4]

Much of the religion of Greece was introduced by Cadmus the Phœnician, who, it is said, taught the Greeks the worship of Phœnician and Egyptian gods and the use of letters,[5] and according to Macrobius the Phœnicians derived the principal features of their religion from the Assyrians.[6] The fact also that Cadmus built Thebes in Bœotia, calling it after the Egyptian city of that name, which was the chief centre of Egyptian idolatry, and especially entitled Diospolis (the city of the gods), shows that his religion was also obtained from Egypt. Manetho, the Egyptian historian, also speaks of colonies which migrated from Egypt to Greece, and which would naturally bring their religion with them.[7]

---

[1] Bunsen's *Egypt*, vol. i. p. 444 ; Layard's *Nineveh and Its Remains*, vol. ii. p. 440.

[2] Layard's *Nineveh*, vol. ii. pp. 439, 440.

[3] Ouwaroff's *Eleusinian Mysteries*, sect. ii. p. 20.

[4] Herodotus, ii. 50.

[5] *See* Lemprière, *Cadmus*.

[6] Macrobius, *Saturnalia*, lib. i. cap. xxi. p. 79.

[7] *See* Manetho's *Dynasties* ; Cory's *Fragments*.

Professor Rawlinson remarks:—" The striking resemblance of the Chaldean system to that of the Classical Mythology seems worthy of particular attention. The resemblance is too general and too close in some respects to allow of the supposition that mere accident has produced the resemblance. In the Pantheons of Greece and Rome and in that of Chaldea the same general grouping is to be recognised; the same genealogical succession is not unfrequently to be traced; and in some cases even the familiar names and titles of classical divinities admit of the most curious illustration and explanation from Chaldean sources. We can scarcely doubt but that, in some way or other, there was a communication of beliefs,—a passage in very early times from the shores of the Persian Gulf to lands washed by the Mediterranean, of mythological notions and ideas." [1]

The religion of Rome, although in later times partly borrowed from Greece, was primarily obtained from the Etruscans, to whom their patrician youth was sent for instruction, and whose coins and monumental remains intimately connect them with both Chaldea and Egypt.[2] Colonel Conder, R.E., quotes Dr Isaac Taylor (*Etruscan Researches* and *Etruscan Language*) as showing that the Etruscan language was remarkably similar to the ancient Chaldean or Accadian. "Tarkon," or "Tarquon," the name of the first great Etruscan king and hero, which is repeated in "Tarquin," king of Rome, is frequently found both in the ancient Hittite language and in Turkish, signifying "a chief," and both these languages are intimately allied to the ancient Chaldean.[3]

This seems to indicate that the Etrurians were an ancient colony from Chaldea. In short, long before the foundation of Rome, Virgil represents his hero Æneas as finding on the site of that city, on either side of the Tiber, the ruins of two cities, called Saturnia and Janicula, or the cities of Saturn and Janus, two names of the deity known as the "father of the gods," and Saturn was certainly of Chaldean origin.[4] This shows that the ancient Paganism was established at a very early date in Italy, and in confirmation of this, there is the fact that Italy in most ancient times was called "the Saturnian Land," or Land of Saturn.[5]

The above constituted the principal civilised nations of ancient

[1] Rawlinson's *Five Great Monarchies of the Ancient Eastern World,* vol i. chap. vii. pp. 111, 112.

[2] *See* Mrs Hamilton Grey's *Etruria.*

[3] *The First Bible,* p. 72., and note 7 p. 207.

[4] *Æneid,* lib. viii. lines 467, 470, vol. iii. p. 608.

[5] Lemprière, *Saturnia.*

Paganism, and we shall see, in the course of our inquiry that the religions of other more remote nations, such as the Hindus, the nations of Eastern Asia, the ancient Germans, Celts, and the Mexicans and Peruvians of America, are intimately related to the religion of Babylon, Egypt, Greece and Rome, and must have originally been derived from the same source.

Babylon having been the centre from which the ancient Paganism originated, the names, in other countries, of many of the gods, and of terms connected with religion, must have had a similar origin, and the meaning and etymology of these names and terms ought not, therefore, to be sought from the language of those countries, but from that of Babylonia and Assyria, viz., either the Semitic Assyrian or the ancient Chaldean.[1] This is the more important, because the most ancient language of Babylonia, viz., that of the Sumerians or Accadians, the founders of the city of Accad, was regarded as the sacred language. It was carefully preserved, and used for their incantations and magical sorceries by the Assyrians, and the sanctity thus attached to it would naturally lead those nations who received their religion from Babylonia and Assyria to preserve the names of many of the gods when adopted by them.

Moreover, the invention of letters and writing is universally attributed to the Babylonians and Egyptians, and as it was simultaneous with the origin of their religion, the latter would necessarily exercise considerable influence on their language. Hence, instead of explaining the names of gods by the meaning of words in common use, it is probable that, in many cases, the words originated from some particular attribute of one or other of the gods. This is the case even with modern English, in which the word "vulcanise" is derived from the supposed characteristics of the god Vulcan, and this may have been much more commonly the case with the ancients.

[1] The language known in later times as Chaldean was an Aramæan or Semitic dialect, and distinct from the ancient Chaldean or Accadian. *See* Rawlinson's *Five Great Monarchies*, vol. i. pp. 44, 45.

CHAPTER II

IN considering the origin and nature of the ancient Paganism, the first point to be determined is what, and who, were the gods worshipped. This point, indeed, is the key to the whole subject, and has been fully examined by the authors referred to in the last chapter. But their learned works are too voluminous and tedious for perusal by the general reader, and it is important therefore to present a condensed summary of their researches. Limits of space prevent more than a brief reference to their explanations and conclusions, especially in the case of the etymologies of words and names, for a fuller explanation of which the reader is referred to the authorities quoted. The subject in itself is an abstruse one, but its discussion is necessary for the proper understanding of the conclusions based on it, which are of no little historic and religious interest.

Our sources of information respecting the ancient Paganism are the mythological traditions of Phœnicia, Greece and Rome, the notices of ancient historians, and the researches of modern archæologists among the monumental remains of Assyria, Egypt, etc.

It is of importance to notice first, that all the various gods and goddesses of the ancients, though known by many names and different characteristics, can yet all be resolved into one or other of the persons of a Trinity composed of a father, mother and son; and that this fact was well known to the initiated. It should also be observed that the father and the son constantly melt into one; the reason being that there was also a fabled incarnation of the son, who, although identified with him, was yet said to be his own son by the goddess mother. Hence being the father of this supposed incarnation of himself, he was naturally sometimes confused with the original father of the gods, the result of which was that both father and son were sometimes called by the same name.

It has been concluded by those who have studied the subject that the gods best known among the ancient Greeks, Romans, Egyptians and Babylonians, such as Cronus, Saturn, Bel, Il, Thoth, Hermes, Bacchus, Mercury, Osiris, Dionysius, Thammuz, Apollo, Horus, Mars, Hercules and Jupiter, are all one and the same god, each being the separate deification of him under different aspects and attributes; and Mr Faber quotes the statement of a multitude of ancient Pagan and mythological writers to this effect, viz., "that all the gods are ultimately one and the same person."[1] But a close examination shows that though father and son are, as explained, constantly confused with each other, yet they may be generally recognised as two distinct persons, related to each other as father and son, as sage and conqueror, and as counsellor and great king; while some, as Apollo and Horus, are more distinctively the titles of the supposed incarnation of the son.

The great goddess, however, is always one, and for this reason was called "*Dea Myrionymus*"—"the goddess with ten thousand names."[2]

The names of the gods varied also in some degree according to the various languages of the nations, as well as according to the particular attribute under which the god was recognised; and the poetry of Greece still further multiplied and gave personality to each of these attributes. Nevertheless, the initiated were well acquainted with the fact that all the different gods or goddesses were but different manifestations of the same god and goddess, or of their son.

The question is, however—What was the origin of the Pagan gods?

It has been argued by some, that the great gods of the heathen were simply the powers of nature and the sun, moon and stars deified. This is so far correct. Sun worship and nature worship constituted the essence of the Pagan system; but there is, nevertheless, the strongest evidence to show that the first originals of the Pagan gods were *men* who after death were deified; that this was the real foundation of the Pagan system; and that these spirits of the dead, according to their different attributes, were subsequently identified with the sun, moon and stars, etc., which were regarded as their habitations, and which received their distinctive names from them.

The evidence of the Pagan writers on the subject is conclusive.

Hesiod, who was the contemporary of Homer, says that "the gods were *the souls of men* who were afterwards worshipped by their posterity, on account of their extraordinary virtues."[3]

[1] Faber, *Origin of Pagan Idolatry*, vol. ii. bk. iv. chap. i.
[2] Wilkinson's *Egyptians*, vol. iv. p. 179.
[3] Hesiod, *Opera et Dies*, lib. i. verses 120-125.

The writer who adopts the name of "Hermes Trismegistus" asserts that "Æsculapius, Osiris and Thoth were all *holy men*, whose souls were worshipped after their death by the Egyptians." [1]

Plutarch states that the Egyptian priests expressly taught "that Cronus, Osiris, Horus, and all their other principal deities were once *mere men*, but that after they died their souls migrated into some one or other of the heavenly bodies, and became the animating spirits of their new celestial mansions." [2]

Similarly, it is said by Sanchoniathon, that Il, or Cronus, was once *a man*, that he was deified by the Phœnicians after his death, and that his soul was believed to have passed into the planet which bears his name,[3] viz., Saturn, who was the same as Cronus.

Diodorus Siculus says that "Osiris, Vulcan, and other cognate deities were all originally *sovereigns of the people* by whom they were venerated." [4]

Cicero employs the same argument to the person with whom he is disputing :—"What, is not almost all heaven, not to carry on this detail any further, *filled with the human race*? But if I should search and examine antiquity, and go to the bottom of this affair from the things which the Greek writers have delivered, it would be found that even those very gods themselves, who are deemed *Dii Majoram Gentium* (the greater gods) *had their originals here below*, and ascended from hence into heaven. Inquire to whom those sepulchres belong which are so commonly shown in Greece. Remember, for you are initiated, what you have been taught in the mysteries." [5]

Cicero also quotes Euhemeros, who lived about three centuries B.C., as testifying to the same thing :—"What think you," he says, "of those who assert that *valiant and powerful men* have obtained divine honours after death, and that *these are the very gods now become the object of our adoration ?* Euhemeros tells us when these gods died, and where they were buried." [6]

The testimony of Euhemeros, like every other ancient testimony which tends to bring into contempt, or cast discredit upon, the Pagan system, has been held up to scorn by certain modern writers, more

---

[1] Herm. Apud. Mede's *Apost. of Later Times*, pt. i. chap. iv.
[2] Plutarch, *De Iside*, p. 354.
[3] Euseb., *Præp. Evan.*, lib. i. chap. x.
[4] Diodorus, *Bibl.*, lib. i. pp. 13, 14, 15.
[5] Cicero, *Tusc. Disp.*, lib. i. chaps. xii., xiii.
[6] *De Nat. Deor.*, lib. i. chap. xlii.

especially, for obvious reasons, by those with Roman Catholic proclivities, and "Euhemerising" is used by them as a term of contempt for those who support the human origin of the Pagan gods. Had Euhemeros been the only authority for that origin, there would have been some reason for questioning it, but his testimony is supported by that of every other Pagan writer who has referred to the matter, and his statements must therefore be regarded as a valuable and unquestionable expression and explanation of the general belief and opinion of those who were best acquainted with the subject.

Alexander the Great also wrote to his mother that, "Even the higher gods, Jupiter, Juno and Saturn and the other gods, *were men*, and that the secret was told him by Leo, the high priest of Egyptian sacred things," and required that the letter should be burnt after it had been revealed to her.[1]

Eusebius says that, "The gods first worshipped are the *same persons, men and women*, even to his time received and worshipped as gods."[2] In short, the Christian apologists in their arguments with the Pagans taunted the latter with worshipping gods who were only *deified men*, showing that the fact was generally admitted by the Pagans.[3]

This is equally admitted by the Hindus of their gods,[4] as, for instance, of their Menu, or Vishnu, who is regarded as having two aspects, the one as Vishnu in his character of the sun, the other as Menu Satyavrata, a *human being*.[5] The supreme god of the southern Buddhists is likewise recognised to have been a man born about five centuries B.C.

Hence the sun, moon and stars were regarded as "wise and intelligent beings, actuated by a divine spirit"; and Posidonius represents the stars "as parts of Jupiter, or the sun, and that they were all living creatures with rational souls."[6]

Maimonedes also declares that "The stars and spheres are every one of them animated beings, endued with life, knowledge and understanding."[7]

[1] Augustine, *De Civ. Dei*, chap. v.
[2] Euseb., p. 31, from Bp. Cumberland's *Hist. of Sanchoniathon*, pp. 8, 9.
[3] Clem. Alex. Cohort., p. 29 ; Arnob., *Adv. Gent.*, lib. vi. ; Jul. Firm., *De Error. prof. rel.*, pp. 4, 13 ; Faber, vol. ii. pp. 224, 226.
[4] Moor's *Hind. Panth.*, p. 14 ; *Asiatic Researches*, vii. pp. 34, 35 ; viii. p. 352.
[5] *Asiatic Researches*, vol. vi. p. 479 ; Faber, vol. ii., p. 228.
[6] Zen. apud Stob ; Posid. apud Stob ; Augustine, *De Civ. Dei*, lib. iv. chap. xi.
[7] *Jesude Hattorah*, chap. iii. p. 9. *Apud Cudw. Intell. Syst.*, p. 471.

The Platonists held that all the superior gods were aspects or manifestations of the sun, and that the inferior gods were *deified heroes* who dwelt in the stars.[1] Thus Ovid, speaking of the death of the great warrior and hunter Orion, says, " He was *added to the stars* "—that is to say, he was identified with that particular constellation which now bears his name.[2]

It is thus abundantly evident that, although the gods of the ancients were identified with the sun, moon and stars, they were also supposed to be the spirits of dead heroes and ancestors who inhabited those planets ; that this was especially revealed to those who were initiated into the mysteries, and that it was the primary foundation of the Pagan system. The evidence of this will be seen to accumulate as we proceed.

Diodorus Siculus, the Pagan historian, who flourished about 44 B.C., and who took especial care in collecting and recording the traditions of Pagan mythology, says, " Osiris (the principal god of the Egyptians) having married Isis, in many ways promoted the good of that kingdom (Egypt), but especially by building the chief city thereof, called by the Greeks Diospolis (Thebes), but called by the Jews ' Hamon No,' and erected a temple to his parent, whom the Greeks call Zeus and Hera, but the Egyptians Ammon, and the Jews Hamon and Ham." [3]   Ham, or Ammon, was the principal Sun god of the Egyptians, and was worshipped under the name of Jupiter Ammon. This fact is a clear proof that Ham was the human original of the Sun god of Egypt, although in later times Osiris held that position. It also shows that the Egyptian god Osiris was a son, or grandson, of Ham, and that the gods of the ancients were therefore the immediate descendants of the patriarch Noah. When, therefore, these gods had been identified with the Sun, the Egyptian kings who could claim descent from them took the title of " Sons of the Sun," which, without such claim, would have been absurd and unmeaning.

Cedrenus gives an account of the manner in which the worship of ancestors arose in other nations :—" Of the tribe of Japhet was born Seruch, who first introduced Hellenism and the worship of idols. For he and those who concurred with him in opinion, honoured their predecessors, whether warriors, or leaders, or characters renowned during their lives for valour or virtue, with columnar statues, as if

---

[1] Plot. *Ennead.*, ii. lib. ix.
[2] Ovid, *Fasti*, lib. v. lines 540-544.
[3] Quoted by Cumberland, *Hist. of Sanchoniathon*, p. 99.

they had been their progenitors, and tendered them a species of religious veneration as a kind of gods, and sacrificed. But after this their successors, overstepping the intention of their ancestors, that they should honour them as their progenitors and inventors of good things with monuments only, honoured them as heavenly gods, and sacrificed to them as such." [1]

Epiphanius, a Christian bishop of the fourth century, who translated the Greek histories of Socrates, Sozomon and Theodoret, testifies to the same origin of idolatry among the Greeks, and he adds:— "The Egyptians, Babylonians, Phrygians and Phœnicians were the first propagators of this superstition of making images and of the mysteries, from whom it was transferred to the Greeks from the time of Cecrops downwards. But it was not until after (their death), and at a considerable interval, that Cronus, Rhea, Zeus, and Apollo, and the rest, were esteemed and honoured as gods." [2]

Eupolemus, quoted by Eusebius, writes:—" For the Babylonians say that the first was Belus, who is the same as Cronus (the father of the gods among the Greeks), and from him descended a second Belus, and Chanaan, and this Chanaan was the father of the Phœnicians" (Phœnicia being the name given to the land of Chanaan by the ancients). He adds:—"Another of his sons was Chum, the father of the Æthiopians and brother of Mistraim, the father of the Egyptians." [3] Chum, the father of the Æthiopians, is clearly Cush, "Cushite" and "Æthiopian" being synonymous. Belus, or Cronus, the father of Canaan and Cush, is therefore Ham, but Belus is more usually identified with his son Cush. For, owing to the tendency, before alluded to, of the father of the gods and his son to blend into each other, Ham sometimes took the place of Cush. Ham appears to have been worshipped in Egypt only.

The most ancient portion of the Sibylline Oracles, the authority of which as an historical record was appealed to by both the Pagans and early Christian apologists in their controversies,[4] speak of Cronus, Japetus and Titan as the three sons of the patriarch Noah.[5] Here, again, Cronus is Ham, and as Japetus is Japhet, Titan is clearly Shem, and all were regarded as gods.

Similarly, in the Hindu mythology, "Sama," "Chama" and "Pra

[1] Cedrenus, from Cory's *Fragments*, p. 56.
[2] Cory, pp. 54, 55.
[3] Euseb., *Præp. Evan.*, lib. ix. ; Cory, p. 58.
[4] *See* article in *Quarterly Review*, 1877, on the age and authority of this portion of the Sibylline Oracle.
[5] Cory, p. 52.

B

Japeti" are said to be born of Menu, and to be the human names of the gods " Vishnu," " Siva " and " Brahma." [1] " Pra Japeti " means " the Lord Japhet," and the final " a " in Sama and Chama being quiescent, it is clear that Chama is only a form of Cham or Khem, the Egyptian name of Ham, and that Sama is Sem, the Greek form of Shem.

Greek mythology also speaks of Cronus, Japetus and Typhon as the principal sons of Ouranos, or Cœlus, who must therefore be Noah ; and Euhemeros, quoted by Eusebius, states that in his travels he visited the Island of Panchrea, where "there was a temple of Zeus (Jupiter), founded by him when he ruled over the habitable world, while he was yet *a resident among men.*" In the temple stood a golden column, on which was a regular history of the actions of Ouranos, Cronos and Zeus. He relates that "the *first king* (of the world) was Ouranos, a man renowned for justice and benevolence, and well conversant with the motion of the stars," and that "he was the first *who honoured the heavenly gods with sacrifices,* (a probable allusion to the statement in Gen. viii. 20), on which account he was called Ouranos" (Heaven). He represents Cronos as the son of Ouranos and father of Zeus, and says that the latter went to Babylon, "where he was hospitably received by Belus, and afterwards passed over to Panchea, where he erected an altar to Ouranos, his forefather. From thence he went into Syria to Cassino. Passing from thence into Cilicia he conquered Cilix, and having travelled through many nations, he was honoured by all and universally acknowledged as god." [2]

The objection made by modern writers to the human origin of the Pagan gods has no valid support. The only reason for this objection is that, if these gods were sun and nature gods, they could not be men. But it is not a question of what they could, or could not, be, but what they were believed to be. The Pagans believed many absurdities, and the consentient testimony of Pagan writers, and of those who lived when the Pagan system was still in existence, and had every means of ascertaining its nature and characteristics, is that the gods were believed to be men who had lived upon the earth, and who, after death, were supposed to inhabit the sun, moon and other planets, and to be their animating spirits. In all ages mankind have shown a tendency to worship their dead relatives, or pious and celebrated men, as is the case in Romanism and Spiritualism at the present day ;

---

[1] *Asiatic Researches*, vol. viii. p. 255 ; Moor's *Hind. Panth.*, p. 173.

[2] Euseb., *Præp. Evan.*, ii., as quoted from Diodorus Siculus, *Ecl.*, p. 681 ; Cory's *Fragments*, by Hodges, pp. 172-174.

and this was equally characteristic of the ages succeeding the Deluge.

Professor Rawlinson remarks that, though in one aspect the religion of ancient Chaldea was astral, or the worship of the sun, moon and stars, "it is but one aspect of the mythology, not by any means its full and complete exposition. The Æther, the Sun, the Moon, and, still more, the five planetary gods, are something above and beyond those parts of nature. They are *real persons* with a life and history, a power and an influence, which no ingenuity can translate into a metaphorical representation of phenomena attaching to the air and to the heavenly bodies. It is doubtful indeed whether the gods of this class are really of astronomical origin, and not rather primitive deities, whose characters and attributes were settled *before the notion arose of connecting them with certain parts of nature.* They seem to represent *heroes* rather than celestial bodies, and they have all attributes quite distinct from their physical or astronomical character." [1]

Both Scripture and profane historians agree in attributing the origin of the Pagan system to Babylon and Assyria, and there is the strongest evidence to prove that the first originals of the gods were the founders of the Babylonian or first great empire of the world, Cush and his son Nimrod.

In short, *Belus,* the chief god of the Assyrians and Babylonians, is represented in the dynasties of Berosus and others as the *first king* of Babylon. [2]

Castor says, " *Belus* was the first king of the Assyrians, and after his death was worshipped as a god." [3]

Megasthenes, quoted by Abydenus, records a speech of Nebuchadnezzar, king of Babylon, in which he refers to Belus and Beltis, the god and goddess of Babylon, as " *my ancestors.*" [4] In like manner the Egyptian priest and historian Manetho, in the dedication of his History to Ptolemy, calls the Egyptian god Hermes " *our forefather.*" [5] From this it is clear that both the Egyptians and the Babylonians held the belief that their gods were human beings from whom they were descended.

Eupolemus also states, " The Babylonians say that the first of

[1] Rawlinson's *Five Great Monarchies,* vol. i. chap. vii. p. 111.
[2] Chaldean Dynasties, Cory's *Fragments,* pp. 70, 71.
[3] Castor, Cory's *Fragments,* p. 65.
[4] Cory's *Fragments,* p. 44.
[5] *Ibid.,* p. 169.

their kings was Belus," [1] showing that this was not a mere invention of the Greeks, but the belief of the Babylonians themselves.

The classical writers in the centuries immediately preceding the Christian era speak of " Cepheus, the *son of Belus*," as the first king of the Ethiopians, or Cushites, and Cepheus, they say, was, after his death, placed among the stars—that is, worshipped as a god. [2] This shows that it was the general belief of the civilised world at that time that the father of the king of the Cushite race, who under Nimrod were the founders of the Babylonian empire, was the human original of the Babylonian god Belus, and that both he and his son were deified after death.

The inscriptions show that there were two god-kings of the name of Belus, the first of whom is called by Sir H. Rawlinson " Bel Nimrod the lesser," and it was his son, the second Belus or Bel Nimrod, who was by far the most important person in the Babylonian worship, and who, as we shall see, is especially identified with Nimrod.   This would make his father, the first Belus, to be Cush.

Nimrod was the first king of the Babylonian *empire*, " the first who began to be mighty on earth," but it would appear that his father Cush had previously been the ringleader in the attempt to build the Tower of Babel, and was the first founder of the city, which was commenced at the same time, [3] and is therefore recognised in the dynastic lists as the first king, under the name of Bel or Belus.

In strict conformity with the Assyrian inscriptions, we have seen that Eupolemus says that Belus is the same as Cronus, the Greek name of Saturn, [4] and that from him descended a *second* Belus. [5]

Sanchoniathon, the Phœnician, also states that Cronus begat a son called Cronus. [6]

In the monumental inscriptions the two Bels, or Belus's, are called, according to the reading of Sir Henry Rawlinson, "*Bilu Nipru*," and they are associated with a goddess called "*Bilta Niprut*."   Bil, Bilu, or Bel signify " The Lord," and Bilta " The Lady," while Niprut is suggested to be a variation of the name " Nimrod."   " P " and " b " are interchangeable letters in ancient languages, and so also are " t "

---

[1] Eupolemus, Cory, p. 58.

[2] Smith's *Class. Dict.*, "Cepheus."   *See* also Lemprière, who refers to Pausanias, Apollodorus, Ovid, Cicero, etc.

[3] Genesis xi. 4-8.   See *infra*, p. 32, on the part taken by Cush in the building of Babel.

[4] Lemprière, *Chronus*.   [5] Eupolemus, Cory, p. 58.   [6] *History*, Cory, p. 13.

and "d," and Niprut might therefore be read Nibrud, and having practically the same phonetic value, might be so spelt by foreigners ; while as there is much uncertainty regarding the vowels intended by the inscriptions, which would also vary in different dialects, Niprut, or Nibrud, might be regarded as the same name as *Nebrod*, the name of Nimrod among the Greeks, and the name by which he is called in the Septuagint version of the Old Testament.[1] Bilu Nipru and Bilu Niprut would therefore be equivalent to The Lord and Lady Nebrod, or Nimrod, and both Sir Henry and Professor Rawlinson therefore speak of the former as "*Bel Nimrod.*"[2]

Sir H. Rawlinson remarks in confirmation of this that Babylon, which was the beginning of Nimrod's kingdom, is called in the inscriptions "The City of Bilu Nipru," and that this was the case as late as the reign of Nebuchadnezzar, although the latter rebuilt the city. Bilu Nipru and Bilta Niprut are also called "The Lord and Lady of Nipur, or Niffer," and, according to an Arabian tradition before the time of Islam, when Arabia was a Cushite country,[3] Niffer was the ancient Babylon, the seat of the Tower of Babel,[4] and beginning of Nimrod's kingdom.

Nimrod was also a mighty hunter, and Bilu Nipru and Bilu Niprut are "The Hunter and Huntress," and the latter is represented as presiding over, and the protector of hunters.[5]

But while this tends to identify Bilu Nipru with Nimrod, it would seem that the etymology of the names Nipru and Nimrod is different. "*Nimrod*" is later Chaldean, and means "The subduer of the leopard," from *nimr*, "leopard," or "spotted one," and *rad*, "to subdue," in commemoration of him as the first to use the hunting leopard, or cheetah, for the chase of deer, etc.[6] On the other hand, "*Nipru*," which is the same as "*Nipru*," called also "*Nipra*," the chief seat of his worship, would seem to be derived from *napar*, "to pursue," and to be the name given to him as "god of the chase."[7]

Much uncertainty exists with regard to the phonetic value of the

---

[1] In Egypt, where the Septuagint was translated, "m" and "b" were often convertible (Bunsen, vol. i. p. 449), and Nimrod would thus become Nibrod or Nebrod in Egypt, and the Greeks no doubt adopted the name from the Egyptians Hislop, p. 47, note.

[2] Rawlinson's *Herodotus*, vol. i. essay x. pp. 594, 596.

[3] See *infra*, chap. iv., on Arabia as the first home of the Cushite race.

[4] Rawlinson's *Herod.*, vol. i. pp. 596, 597.

[5] *Ibid.*, p. 598.

[6] Hislop, p. 44, note.

[7] Rawlinson's *Five Great Monarchies*, vol. i. pp. 117, 118.

cuneiform inscriptions, and alternative readings of these names have been suggested, while the ancient Chaldean or Accadian equivalent of Bel or Bilu is "*Mulge*" or "*Enge.*" But for the purpose of identification, it will be preferable to retain the name "Bel Nimrod" in the following remarks, as being that used by both Sir Henry and Professor Rawlinson.

It is not likely, however, that Nimrod would have been deified under his own name, but under a name or names expressive of some divine attribute, that is to say, not as being himself the mighty hunter, or the subduer of the leopard for hunting, but as the god or protector of hunters. Hence, as the voice of antiquity testifies to the fact that the originals of the Pagan gods were human beings, and that the gods of ancient Babylon were the first monarchs of that empire, the identification of the gods with those monarchs must be expected rather from their attributes than their names. When, therefore, we see that the attributes and relationships of those gods agree with the characteristics of those monarchs, it is what we might expect, and it confirms the testimony of the ancient writers.

We have referred to the fact that the various gods of Paganism represent merely the different deified characters or attributes of, at the most, two original gods. This is fully recognised by those who have studied the question, and it is especially the case with the Egyptian Pantheon as pointed out by Sir Gardner Wilkinson,[1] and Professor Rawlinson refers to the same feature in the gods of Babylon. In short, the Pagan goddess was called "*Dea Myrionymus*," "the goddess with ten thousand names," implying that they were all one and the same being, worshipped under many different aspects. Therefore, as every god had a goddess associated with him,[2] it follows that these gods must also be different aspects of one and the same original being. The conclusion is, however, so far modified by the fact that the goddess is the wife of one set of gods, and both wife and mother of the other. This was the case with the Babylonian goddess,[3] and the latter incestuous union, which will be more fully referred to hereafter, is therefore one of the distinguishing marks between the two sets of gods.

Of the two gods called Belus, or Bel Nimrod, the first is spoken of by Sir H. Rawlinson as "*Bel Nimrod the lesser,*" and he is the father of the second or greater Bel Nimrod. This first Bel Nimrod is shown by Sir Henry Rawlinson to be the same as a god called "*Hea,*"[4] and

---

[1] See *infra*, p. 51.　　　　　　　　[2] Rawlinson's *Herod.*, vol. i. p. 589.
[3] *Ibid.*, vol. i. p. 625, 626.　　　　[4] *Ibid.*, pp. 599, 601.

Hea is also shown on the inscriptions to be the father of a god called "*Nin*," or "*Nin-ip*," who is especially represented at Nipur to be the husband of Bilta Niprut.[1]   Now, as Bilta Niprut was the wife of Bel Nimrod, and they were the Lord and Lady of Nipur, this tends to identify Nin with Bel Nimrod, and as Nin was the son of the first Bel Nimrod, he must be the second Belus, or Bel Nimrod the greater, *i.e.*, Nimrod.   Nin is the same name as the *Ninus* of the Greeks with the Hellenic termination, and in accordance with the above Castor says that Belus, the first king of the Assyrians, was succeeded by Ninus and Semiramis, and the latter queen would therefore correspond to Bilta Niprut.[2]   Velleius Paterculus in his *History* also represents Ninus and Semiramis as the first rulers of the Babylonian empire, and they would therefore be Nimrod and his queen.[3]

The characteristics given to Nin on the Babylonian inscriptions tend to confirm this.   He is called "Lord of the Brave," "The Champion," "The Warrior who subdues Foes," "The Destroyer of Enemies," "The First, or Chief of the Gods," "The God of Battle," "He who tramples upon the wide world."[4]   All this is strictly descriptive of him who "first began to be mighty upon the earth."

He is also called "The Eldest Son," and, as we shall see hereafter, it was in his aspect as "The Son" that the second person of the Pagan Trinity was especially worshipped.   This also is the meaning of his name.   He was likewise called "*Bar*"; and *Nin*, or *Non*, is the later Chaldee, and *Bar* the Semitic for "a son."[5]   So also, like Nimrod the mighty hunter, and "Bel Nimrod the greater," he is the god of the chase as well as the god of war,[6] and he must be regarded, therefore, as another deified aspect of Nimrod.

Nimrod, moreover, is said to have been a giant, and in the Septuagint he is called "Nimrod the Giant."   So also Nin is the Assyrian *Hercules*,[7] and is represented as a giant hunter overcoming by sheer strength a lion and a bull (*see* woodcut).   This Hercules is also identified by Barker with Dayyad *the hunter*.[8]   Hercules is identified with Belus by Cicero, who says that Hercules Belus is the most ancient Hercules.[9]   There can be little doubt, therefore, that Nin or Hercules is simply another aspect of the second Belus or Bel Nimrod the greater, and his characteristics correspond exactly with

[1] Rawlinson's *Herod.*, p. 599, and *Five Great Monarchies*, vol. i. p. 121.
[2] Castor, Cory's *Fragments*, p. 65.   [3] *Ibid.*, p. 66.
[4] Rawlinson's *Herod.*, vol. i. p. 618.   [5] Hislop, p. 223, note.
[6] Rawlinson's *Herod.*, vol. i., p. 619.   [7] *Ibid.*, pp. 601, 624.
[8] Barker's *Lares and Penates of Cilicia*, p. 131; Hislop, p. 34, note.
[9] Maurice, *Ind. Antiquities*, vol. iii., p 53.

those of Nimrod. It thus appears that Nimrod was the original of the Hercules of the ancients, whom the Greeks turned into a sort of knight-errant, and associated with so many fanciful legends.

Birch also says that "the identity of Nimrod with the constellation Orion is not to be rejected."[1] Now *Orion* was a giant and a mighty hunter who boasted that no animal could compete with him, on which account he was killed by the bite of a scorpion, and, says Ovid, "added to the stars"[2]— that is, regarded after death as that constellation and worshipped as a god.

In a woodcut, given by Layard, of a Babylonian cylinder,[3] Nin, the Assyrian Hercules, represented as a giant, is shown first attacking

Babylonian Cylinder, in green Jasper.

and killing a bull, and then, crowned with the bull's horns as a token of his prowess, is represented attacking a lion and killing him.

This is exactly in keeping with the character of the mighty hunter Orion. It will also be noticed that there is a fawn at the feet of the Assyrian Hercules, and as this was a usual way of symbolising the person represented, it is a further evidence that Hercules, or Nin, was Nimrod; for a spotted fawn was one of Nimrod's distinctive symbols, and in Greece, where Nimrod was known as "*Nebrod*," the fawn, as sacred to him, was called "*Nebros*."[4]

The feat of strength by the Assyrian Hercules is probably, as pointed out by Mr Hislop, the origin of the significance of a horn as a symbol of power and sovereignty throughout the world.[5] It is also probably the origin of the gigantic *man-bulls* in the Assyrian sculptures representing Assyrian deities. This is further confirmed by the fact that the Chaldean "*Tur*" means both "bull" and

[1] Layard's *Nineveh*, pp. 439-340.
[2] Lemprière, *Orion*, and Ovid, *Fasti*, lib. v. lines 540-544 ; Hislop, p. 57, note.
[3] *Babylon and Nineveh*, p. 605.   [4] Hislop, p. 47 and note.
[5] *Ibid.*, pp. 33-35.

"prince" or "ruler," and "*Tur*" without the points becomes in Hebrew "*Shur*," a word having the same double significance.[1] Thus the horned man-bulls are simply symbols of The Mighty Prince, a title well expressive of him who "first began to be mighty on earth" (Genesis x. 8). This also explains the meaning of the title "*Cronus*" given to Belus, or Bel; for Cronus, or Kronos, is derived from *krn* "a horn," and thus means "the horned one."[2] The Latin *corona*, "a crown," has evidently a similar derivation, and indicates the origin of the points, or "horns," by which crowns are surmounted. We are also told by Pherecydes that Saturn (*i.e.*, Cronus or Belus) was "the first who wore a crown."[3] Saturn, however, was the *first* Belus, the father of Nin, or Nimrod, and was generally represented as the first king of the Babylonian empire.

Apollodorus, a famous Pagan writer on mythology about 115 B.C., emphatically asserts the identity of Ninus with Nimrod. "Ninus," he says, "is Nimrod."[4]

Trogus Pompeius says, "Ninus, king of the Assyrians, first of all changed the contented moderation of the ancient manners, incited by a new passion, the desire for conquest. He was the *first* who carried on war against his neighbours, and he conquered all nations from Assyria to Lybia, as they were as yet unacquainted with the art of war.[5] This can only apply to Nimrod, who first "began to be mighty on the earth."

Similarly, Diodorus Siculus says, "Ninus, the *first* of the Assyrian kings mentioned in history, performed great actions. Being naturally of a warlike disposition, and ambitious of glory that results from valour, he armed a considerable number of young men that were brave and vigorous like himself, trained them up a long time in laborious exercises and hardships, and by that means accustomed them to bear the fatigues of war and to face dangers with intrepidity."[6]

Mr Hislop has also pointed out that the words in Genesis x. 11, descriptive of the acquirement of empire by Nimrod, viz., "out of that land went forth Ashur and builded Nineveh," are forced and unnatural, for they appear, without any previous introduction, to represent another great monarch setting up a kingdom in the immediate neighbourhood of Nimrod. Moreover, the Semitic Assyrians, the

---

[1] Hislop, p. 33, note.   [2] *Ibid.*, p. 32, note.
[3] Tertullian, *De Corona Militis*, cap. vii. vol. ii. p. 85 ; Hislop, p. 35.
[4] Appollodori, *Fragments*, 68 ; Müller, vol. i. p. 340 ; Hislop, p. 40.
[5] Justin's *Trogus Pompeius*, Hist. Rom. Scrip., vol. ii. p. 615 ; Hislop, p. 23.
[6] Diodorus, *Bibl.*, lib. ii. p. 63 ; Hislop, p. 23.

descendants of Ashur, did not rise into prominence until many centuries afterwards. For this reason some have proposed to render the passage—"Out of that land he went forth into Assyria and builded Nineveh;" but the original will not bear this translation, and Mr Hislop remarks that the word "ashur" is the passive participle of a word which in its Chaldee sense means "to make strong." [1] This would make the passage, "Out of that land, *being made strong*, he (Nimrod) went forth and builded Nineveh." Now if Nimrod built Nineveh it further identifies him with Ninus, for the word *Nin-neveh* means "the habitation of Nin." [2]

There are two other gods in the Babylon Pantheon who must be regarded as deified aspects of Nimrod. One of these is "*Bel Merodach*," or "*Meridug.*" He is constantly spoken of by the Assyrians under the name of "Bel" only, and was worshipped under that name in the great temple of Belus at Babylon,[3] which indicates that he was the particular form of the god Belus worshipped by the Assyrians. At the same time he is spoken of in connection with another Bel as "Bel and Merodach." [4] We must therefore conclude that Bel Merodach was one of two gods known as Belus or Bel Nimrod, and, as he is stated on the tablets to be the son of Hea, or Bel Nimrod the lesser,[5] he must be the second Belus, or Bel Nimrod the greater. This is confirmed by his title "The firstborn of the gods," [6] which is synonymous with that of "The eldest son," the title of Nin, or Bel Nimrod the greater. He is also the star Jupiter, and Jupiter was the son of Saturn, who, we have seen, to be the first Cronus, or Belus, and father of the gods.[7] He was also the husband of a goddess called "*Zerbanit*," who is stated to be the queen of Babylon,[8] and must therefore be another aspect of Bilta Niprut, the wife of the first Bel Nimrud, and mother and wife of the second. This relationship to the latter seems to be indicated by her name Zerbanit—from *Zer*, or *Zero*, "seed," or "son," and *banit*, "genetrix," [9] *i.e.*, "mother of the son," the "first-born of the gods."

[1] Chaldee Lexicon in Clavis Stockii, verb "asher"; Hislop, p. 24 and note.

[2] Hislop, p. 25.   [3] Rawlinson's *Herod.*, vol. i. p. 629.

[4] Rawlinson's *Five Great Monarchies*, vol. ii. p. 13.

[5] Rawlinson's *Herod.*, vol. i. p. 630.   [6] *Ibid.*, p. 628.

[7] Assyriologists have suggested that Nin was represented by the planet Saturn, but there is no direct proof of this, as in the case of Merodach and Jupiter, Nebo and Mercury, Nergal and Mars, etc., and as the classical authors always recognise Saturn as the same as Cronus or Belus, the father of the gods, we must conclude that they had strong grounds for doing so.

[8] *Ibid.*, p. 630.   [9] Hislop, p. 18 and note.

"*Nergal*," like "Nin," is the god of war and of hunters. He is called "The Great Hero," "King of Battle," "Champion of the gods," and "God of the Chase." His character is thus precisely the same as that of Nin and Bel Nimrud the greater, and he is also the titular god of Babylon. He is identified with the planet Mars, and must therefore be regarded as the original of the Roman god of war. Professor Rawlinson considers him to be a deified form of Nimrod.[1]

The tendency of the Pagans to invoke each god under various titles descriptive of his different attributes is illustrated by the case of Crœsus referred to by Herodotus, who represents him as thus invoking Jupiter.[2] This would naturally lead to the worship of the god under different titles, and in the case of nations who adopted the gods of another nation, the original identity of the god would soon be lost sight of. This was no doubt the case with the Assyrians, who adopted the Babylonian gods.

It is not necessary to refer particularly here to other gods of the Babylonians, such as "*Shamash*," the sun, and "*Iva*," or "*Bin*," the god of the wind, etc., and who may be expected to be merely aspects of one or other of the gods mentioned. In short, all the principal Pagan gods were eventually recognised as The Sun, as in the case of Belus, whose temple at Babylon was the Temple of the Sun.[3]

We may here refer to a remark of Mr George Smith which expresses the difficulty many learned writers have experienced in recognising the human origin of the Pagan gods. He says, "The idea that Nimrod was Bel or Elu, the second god in the great Babylonian triad, is impossible, because the worship of Bel was much more ancient, he being considered one of the creators of the universe and the father of the gods. Similar objections apply to the supposition that Nimrod was Merodach, the god of Babylon, and to his identification with Nergal, who was the man-headed lion. Of course Nimrod was deified, like other celebrated kings; but in no case was a deified king invested as one of the supreme gods and represented as a creator; such a process could only come if a nation entirely forgot its history and lost its original mythology."[4]

To this it may be replied that the historical archives were deposited with the priesthood, who alone had access to them, and, as is always the case, the common people had little or no knowledge of the past history of their country. Nimrod was certainly not deified at

[1] Rawlinson's *Herod.*, vol. i. pp. 631, 632.   [2] Herodotus, lib. i. cap. xliv.
[3] Rawlinson's *Herod.*, vol. i. pp. 627-629.
[4] *The Chaldean Account of Genesis*, p. 181.

first as The Creator. He was simply worshipped as a hero. But there is a constant tendency in religion to *development*,[1] and for the priesthood to magnify and exalt the powers and attributes of their gods. Everything points to the fact, as we shall see hereafter, that the ultimate aspect of the ancient Paganism was arrived at by a process of gradual development continued from age to age. The gods as first worshipped were not what they afterwards became. Their human origin was merely a stepping-stone to their ultimate aspect, and after it had served its purpose that origin was carefully kept out of sight, or revealed only to the initiated. Moreover, when the chief god had come to be regarded as the Creator and Life-giver whose manifestation was The Sun, the belief that he had once become incarnate, had reigned as a king on earth, and had been slain for the good of mankind by the principle of evil only enhanced the reverence in which he was held.

Therefore, while it would have been absurd and impossible to have represented Nimrod immediately after his death as The Creator, there is nothing incompatible with this in the fact that he should have ultimately *developed* into the Sun god and Creator—a development which was natural and inevitable among a priesthood who, in order to recommend their religion, did everything to enhance the power and glory of their gods.[2]

Turning now to the father of Nin, or Ninus, viz., the first Belus, or Bel Nimrod the lesser, it is evident that if Nin, or Bel Nimrud the greater, is Nimrod, then Bel Nimrud the lesser, or Hea, is *Cush*. It is indeed stated by the Sibylline Oracles, that the first Cronus, or Belus, was the son of Noah and brother of Japetus and Titan (Japhet and Shem), which would make him Ham. But this is an error arising from the identity of name of the first and second Belus, which caused them to be sometimes confounded together as one individual, and led later writers to regard the first Belus as Ham. As we shall see, there is accumulative evidence to show that the first Belus was Cush. It is also to be observed that the ancients called all the direct descendants of a person his *sons*, and Cush, whose fame quite eclipsed his father Ham, would thus be the most prominent " son " of Noah in that family.

Nimrod, as the human original of the different gods representing

---

[1] This is illustrated by the present religion of the Roman Catholic Church, between which and that of primitive Christianity there is little resemblance. But, as Cardinal Newman has elaborately argued, the former has been developed out of the latter—*Development of Christian Doctrine.*

[2] *See* description of this development, *infra*, chap. xv.

the various attributes under which he was deified, was the most prominent and important deity in the Pagan mythology, and Cush, as the father of these gods, was therefore known as "Cronus," or "Saturn," the "father of the gods." But he also held another equally important position.

We have seen that the elder Belus, or Bel Nimrod the lesser, was called "Hea," and Hea is described as the source of all knowledge and science. He is "The Intelligence," and is called "The Lord of the Abyss or Great Deep," "The Intelligent Fish," "The Teacher of Mankind" and "The Lord of Understanding."[1] In these respects he appears to be identical with "*Nebo*," the prophetic god and "god of writing and science," and both gods are equally symbolised by the wedge or arrow head which was the essential element of cuneiform writing, as if both had been inventors of writing.[2] Nebo, like Hea, is entitled "He who Teaches," "He who possesses Intelligence," "The Supreme Intelligence," "He who hears from afar," and is called "The glorifier of Bel Nimrod."[3] The latter title may mean that he was the counsellor or instructor of Bel Nimrod the greater, through which the latter obtained his power, and this, as we shall see, is the particular relation which the elder god bears to the younger.

Moreover, the wife of Nebo is the goddess "*Nana*," which was the Babylonian name of "*Ishtar*."[4] Now Ishtar corresponds in all respects to Bilta Niprut. Bilta is called "The Great Goddess," and "Mother of the great gods." Ishtar is called "The Great Goddess," and "Queen of all the gods." Bilta is "The Queen of heaven." Ishtar is called "The Mistress of heaven." Bilta is the goddess of generation or fecundity. Ishtar is the same. Bilta is "The Lady of Babylon." Ishtar is also "The Lady of Babylon." Bilta is the goddess of war and the chase, and so also is Ishtar.[5] Ishtar must therefore be another aspect of Bilta, the Beltis of the Greeks, and although worshipped under a different name, it is quite impossible that the identity of the two goddesses should not have been recognised by the initiated. But if so, Nebo, the husband of Ishtar, must be either the first or second Belus, and as his characteristics are identical with those of the first Belus, or Hea, we may conclude that he is another form of that god.

---

[1] Rawlinson's *Herod.*, vol. i. p. 599, 600 ; Lenormant, *Chaldean Magic and Sorcery*, p. 114.

[2] Rawlinson's *Herod.*, vol. i. p. 601.

[3] *Ibid.*, p. 637 ; Lenormant, *Chaldean Magic*, p. 69.

[4] Rawlinson's *Herod.*, vol. i. p. 635.

[5] *Ibid.*, p. 635, and *Five Great Monarchies*, vol. i. pp. 120 and 138, 139.

These characteristics of the elder Belus, viz., as the god of wisdom and teacher of mankind, distinguish him from the second Belus, the god of war and hunting, and they appear to be alluded to by Stephanus of Byzantium, who says that " Babylon was built by Babilon son of *the all-wise Belus*." [1]   Now, as Nimrod was the founder of Babylon, it is clear that his father, " The all-wise Belus," was Cush, the first Belus or Hea, " The Lord of Understanding " and " Teacher of Mankind."

Nebo appears to have taken the place of the Babylonian Hea in the Assyrian Pantheon.   For although Hea is invoked in the incantations in the old Chaldean language, Nebo, coupled with Bel, who in this case must be Bel Merodach, are the gods ordinarily invoked as the two principal gods by the Assyrian kings. [2]   This is also implied by the passage in Isaiah xlvi., " Bel boweth down, Nebo stoopeth."

" *Sin*," the moon god of the Assyrians, requires a brief notice. He is called " The King of the gods," " God of gods," titles which were peculiar to Hea, the father of the gods, or the first Belus, who was Cronus or Saturn.   Sin is also called " Lord of spirits," and this was the particular attribute of Hea, who was always appealed to as the ruler of the spirits good and evil. [3]   This would imply that Sin, the moon god, was another aspect of Hea and Nebo, *i.e.*, Cush, and we shall see that there is further evidence that this was the case.   Sin is also stated to have been the first divine monarch who had reigned upon earth, which can only apply to the first Belus or Cush. [4]

It is true that both Sin and Nebo are sometimes represented as sons of Hea, but, as Professor Rawlinson remarks, " the relationships are often confused and even contradictory." [5]   This is what might be expected among a people who adopted the gods of another people. Hea was so evidently a god of the first importance, and being known as the father of the gods, it was natural that the Assyrians, when they did not fully recognise the identity of gods like Sin and Nebo, should regard them as sons of Hea.

We may also refer to " *Dumuzi*," mentioned on the Izdubar tablets.   The name might be written " *Tummuz*," and he is generally recognised to be the Babylonian and Phœnician god " *Tammuz*," for whom yearly lamentations were made.   He was the husband of Ishtar, and must therefore be one of the gods known as Belus or Bel

[1] Quoted by Baldwin, *Prehistoric Nations*, p. 201.
[2] Rawlinson's *Herod.*, vol. i. pp. 637, 638.
[3] Lenormant, *Chaldean Magic*, pp. 42, 43, 59, 158, etc.
[4] *Ibid.*, p. 208.   [5] *Five Great Monarchies*, vol. i. p. 113.

Nimrod. The legends refer to his having suffered a tragic death and to the sorrow of his wife Ishtar, and this, as we shall see, was the fate of the younger god, which was always represented as being lamented by the goddess, besides being celebrated in every nation by annual lamentations.[1] He was also known by the title of "The Only Son," which also tends to identify him with Nin, or Bar, "The Son," or "Eldest Son," and with Bel Merodach, "The First-born of the gods." We shall refer to him again later on.

The intimate relation of the gods and religion of Babylon and Egypt is generally recognised, and we shall show later on that the Egyptians, as distinguished from the Mizraimites or descendants of Mizraim, were a Cushite race who at a very early period introduced their religion and gods into Egypt. This being the case, it suggests the identity of the gods Hea and Nebo with the Egyptian "*Thoth*" or "*Hermes*," who was also the god of writing, science and intellect, and the great teacher of mankind. Hermes, or Thoth, was "The god of all Celestial Knowledge,"[2] who, Wilkinson says, was "The god of Letters and Learning; the means by which all mental gifts were imparted to men, and he represented the abstract idea of intellect."[3] He is described as "The Thrice Great Hermes, the inventor of letters and arithmetic";[4] "the god of writing and science, who first discovered numbers and the art of reckoning, geometry and astronomy, and the games of chess and of hazard";[5] "Thoth, famous for his wisdom, who arranged in order and in a scientific manner those things which belong to religion and the worship of the gods, first vindicated from the ignorance of the lower classes and the heads of the people."[6] There seems strong grounds, therefore, for concluding that Thoth, or Hermes, famous for his wisdom, the god of intellect and the first instructor of men in religion and science, is identical with "The all-wise Belus," Hea, "The Intelligence," "The Lord of understanding and instructor of mankind," and with the prophet Nebo, "The Supreme Intelligence" and the god of writing and science. In short, Gensenius identifies Hermes with the Babylonian Nebo as the prophetic god.[7] Moreover, Nebo was represented by the planet *Mercury*,[8] and Hermes was the Greek name of Mercury.

---

[1] As in the case of the Israelitish women weeping for Tammuz (Ezekiel viii. 14).
[2] Wilkinson's *Egyptians*, vol. ii. chap. xiii. pp. 9, 10.
[3] Wilkinson's *Egyptians*, by Birch, vol. iii. p. 168.
[4] Wilkinson's *Egyptians*, vol. v. p. 3.
[5] Rawlinson's *Herod.*, vol. i. pp. 599-602.
[6] *Sanchoniathon's History*, Cory's *Fragments*, by Hodges, p. 21.
[7] Hislop, p. 26.   [8] Rawlinson's *Herod.*, vol. i. p. 637.

Again *Hermes* means "the son of Her,"[1] *i.e.*, of Ham, for "*Her*" is synonymous with "*Ham*," both meaning "the burnt one,"[2] and the first Belus or Hea, was Cush the son of Ham. On these grounds, which are confirmed by other relationships referred to later, we may conclude that Thoth or Hermes was the Egyptian form of the Babylonian Hea and Nebo.

If then Cush was Hermes or Mercury, he would seem to have been, not only the teacher of mankind and originator of the ancient idolatry, or worship of the gods, but also the ringleader in the enterprise undertaken to build the Tower of Babel, in order to "reach unto heaven" (Genesis xi. 4). This tower was not intended, as some have supposed, to be a place of refuge in case of a second Deluge, but as a central temple for the worship of the gods in order to keep the human race together and under the influence of these gods, "lest we be scattered abroad upon the face of the whole earth."[3] Now Hyginus says, "For many ages men lived under the government of Jove without cities and without laws, and all speaking *one language*. But after Mercury *interpreted* the speeches of men (whence an interpreter is called 'Hermeneutes') the same individual distributed the nations. Then discord began."[4] There is an evident contradiction here in saying that Mercury *interpreted* the speeches of men when they were all of *one language*; but, as pointed out by Mr Hislop, the Chaldee *peresh*, meaning "to interpret," was pronounced by the Egyptians and Greeks in the same way as the Chaldee *peres*, "to divide,"[5] and the Greeks, knowing Hermes as "the *interpreter* of the gods," substituted the word "*interpreted*" for the word "*divided*." Thus the tradition, correctly rendered, would mean that Mercury, or Hermes (that is Cush), "divided the speeches of men," or was the cause of the confusion of tongues and subsequent "scattering abroad" or "distribution of the nations" which followed the building of the Tower of Babel; that, in short, he was the ringleader in that enterprise, and the consequent *cause of discord* or *confusion*. This is also

---

[1] *Ms* or *Mes*, "to bring forth, or be born"; Bunsen, vol. i., *Hieroglyphic Signs*, App. B. 43, p. 540, and Vocab. App. i. p. 470. Thus *Thothmes*, "the son of Thoth," *Rameses*, "the son of Ra." The "m" seems to be omitted in certain cases, as in *Athothes*, "the son of Thoth," and who by Eratosthenes is called "Hermogenes," *i.e.*, "born of Hermes," or Thoth.

[2] Hislop, p. 25, note.

[3] Genesis xi. 4. As a place of refuge the tower would only have accommodated a few hundred persons, and the low-lying plains of Babylon would have been the last place chosen for such a refuge. It was, as described by Herodotus for the worship of the gods.—Herodotus, lib. i. cap. 181-182.

[4] Hyginus, Fab. 143, p. 114 ; H., p. 26.   [5] Hislop, p. 26.

confirmed by Gregory Turonensis, who represents Cush as the ring-leader in that apostasy.[1]

It would appear also that, as the cause of discord, his name became synonymous with "confusion," for, whatever the original meaning of the word, "Bel" came to signify "the confounder."[2] Hence the significance of the passage in Jeremiah l. 2, "Bel is confounded," which might be paraphrased "The confounder is confounded." In one of his deified aspects he was also known as "the god of confusion." As Cronus, or Saturn, he was "The father of the gods," and the father of the gods was also known as "*Janus*," who was called "The god of gods," from whom the gods had their origin.[3] Now, Ovid makes Janus say of himself, "The ancients called me *Chaos*,"[4] and "Chaos" was the Greek god of confusion.

It seemed highly probable, as suggested by Mr Hislop, that the very word "chaos" is a form of the name "Cush," for Cush is also written "Khus," the "sh" in Chaldee frequently passing into "s," and Khus in pronunciation becomes "Khawos," or without the digamma "Khaos" or "Chaos."[5]

On the reverse of an Etruscan medal of Janus[6] a club is shown, and the name of a club in Chaldee is derived from the word which signifies to "break in pieces" or "scatter abroad,"[7] implying, according to the usual symbolism of Paganism, that Janus was the cause of the human race being "scattered abroad." The title on the medal, "Bel Athri," also points to its Babylonian origin. Its meaning is "Lord of spies, or seers," an allusion to his character as "all-seeing Janus," for which reason he is represented on the medal by two heads, back to back, looking in all directions.[8] This is also the character of Hea, the "Lord of understanding," Hermes, "The god of all celestial knowledge," and Nebo, "The prophetic god," or god of seers.

Another form of the "father of the gods" was Vulcan, who was called "*Hephaistos*," which has a similar signification to the club of Janus, for it is derived from *Hephaitz*, "to scatter abroad," Hephaitz becoming in Greek "Hephaist."[9] This also is, no doubt, the

[1] Gregory Turonensis, *De Rerum Franc.*, lib. i; Bryant, vol. ii. pp. 403, 404.
[2] Hislop, p. 26.
[3] Macrobius, *Saturn.*, chap. ix. p. 54 ; Col. 2. H ; Bryant, vol. iii. p. 82 ; Hislop, p. 26.
[4] Ovid, *Fasti*, lib. i. ver. 104 ; vol. iii. p. 19.   [5] Hislop, pp. 26, 27, note.
[6] From Sir William Betham's *Etrusc. Lit. and Ant.*, plate ii. vol. ii. p. 120.
[7] Hislop, p. 27, note.   [8] *Ibid.*
[9] As in the case of Mestraim for Mitzraim, etc., Hislop, p. 27, note.

C

meaning of the *hammer* shown in the hands of Vulcan, meaning that he was "the breaker in pieces" or "scatterer abroad," although the Greeks, as in the case of other gods adopted by them from Babylon and Phœnicia, being ignorant of their original characteristics, supposed the hammer to mean that Vulcan was simply a forger of metals.

Vulcan, or Hephaistus, was the chief of the Cyclops, and this further identifies him with Cronus and Bel, for the former was also king of the Cyclops,[1] who are called "the inventors of tower building," or the first who built towers,[2] thus identifying them and their king with the builders of Babylon and the Tower of Babel.

Again, Vulcan was the god of fire, and as the word "Cyclops" (Greek, *Kuklops*) is probably of Chaldean origin, it would mean "kings of flame," from *khuk*, king, and *lobh*, flame.[3]

This tends to identify Vulcan with *Moloch*, the god of *fire*, to whom children were sacrificed by *burning*. "Moloch," or "Molk," signifies "king," and it seems probable that "Mulkiber," the Roman name of Vulcan, is derived from the Chaldee *Molk*, "king," and *gheber*, "mighty."[4]

To both Moloch and Baal human sacrifices were offered, and it was the universal custom for the priests to partake of the sacrifice offered, as in the case of the Jewish ritual to which the Apostle Paul refers,[5] thus implying that, in the rites of the heathen gods, this was also the custom of the Pagan priests. In fact, the Cyclops, of whom Cronus was king, were said to be *cannibals*, and "to revive the rites of the Cyclops" meant to revive the custom of eating human flesh.[6] This is still part of the religious rites of many of the Hamitic races of Africa. Mr Hislop also remarks that the word "cannibal," our term for eaters of human flesh, is probably derived from *Cahna bal*, "the priest of Bel"; *Cahna* being the emphatic form of *Cahn*, "a priest."[7]

Cannibalism appears to have been initiated by Cronus, *i.e.*, Saturn or Cush. For we are told by Sanchoniathon that Cronus was the originator of human sacrifices:—"It was the custom among the

[1] Hislop, p. 32 and note.   [2] Pliny, lib. vii. chap. lvi. p. 171.
[3] Hislop, note, p. 229.   [4] *Ibid.*, pp. 32, 33, 229.   [5] 1 Cor. x. 17-21.
[6] Ovid, *Metam.*, xv. 93, vol ii. p. 132 ; Hislop, p. 232 and note.
[7] Hislop, p. 232 and note. "Cannibal" is said by some to be derived from *Carib*, the name of the people of the Caribbean Islands. But the derivation is very forced and unnatural. Shakespeare used "cannibal" as a well-recognised term in his time for eaters of human flesh, and as the West Indies had only been discovered ninety to a hundred years before, and the name "Carib" was not known until much later, it could hardly have been corrupted into "cannibal," nor is there the slightest evidence that such a forced and unlikely corruption ever took place.

ancients in times of great calamity, in order to prevent the ruin of all, for the rulers of the city or nation to sacrifice to the avenging deities the most beloved of their children as the price of their redemption. They who were devoted for that purpose were offered mystically, for Cronus, whom the Phœnicians call Il, and who after his death was deified and installed in the planet which bears his name (Saturn), when king, had, by a nymph of the country called Anobret, an only son, who, on that account, was styled Ieoud, for so the Phœnicians call an only son; and when great dangers from war beset the land he adorned the altar, and invested this son with the emblems of royalty and sacrificed him." [1] It would also appear that he partook of the sacrifice thus offered, for Saturn is represented as devouring his own children. [2] From this we may conclude that Cush was the originator of human sacrifices and of cannibalism, and identical with Vulcan, the chief of the cannibal Cyclops.

It has been said that the characters of "the Father of the Gods" and his son constantly blend, and Nimrod also appears, like Vulcan, to have been worshipped as the "god of fire." Nimrod is stated to be the first who initiated the worship of fire; [3] and Apollodorus says that Ninus was the first who taught the Assyrians to worship fire. [4] This identifies Nimrod with "*Zoroaster*," the head of the fire-worshippers. But this Zoroaster, called also *Zeroastes*, meaning "fire-born," from *Zero*, "seed," and *ashta* "fire," [5] was not, as pointed out by Mr Hislop, the Bactrian of that name who lived in the time of Darius Hystaspes, and adopted the title, but the Chaldean Zoroaster who is stated by Suidas to have been the founder of the Babylonish idolatry. [6]

We have seen that Nimrod would seem to be identical with Tammuz. Tammuz, called also "Baal Tammuz," was, like Nimrod, the Fire god. Fire was regarded by the Pagans as the great spiritual purifier, from which arose the practice of passing children through the fire in the rites of Moloch in order to purify them, and *Tammuz* means the "perfecting fire," from *tam*, "to make perfect," and *muz*,

---

[1] *Hist. of Sanchoniathon*, Euseb., *Præp. Evan.*, lib. i. c. x.; lib. iv. c. xvii.; Cory's *Fragments*, pp. 16, 17.

[2] Lemprière, *Saturnus*. [3] Johannes Clericus, tom ii. p. 199, and Vaux, p. 8.

[4] Müller, *Fragment*, 68, vol. i. p. 440.

[5] Hislop, pp. 18 and 59, note. Zero passes naturally into Zoro, as in the case of the name Zerubbabel, which in the Greek Septuagint is Zorobabel. The name Zoroaster is also found as Zeroastes.—Johannes Clericus, tom. ii; *De Chaldæis*, sect. i. c. ii. p. 194; Hislop, p. 59.

[6] Wilson's *Parsee Religion*, p. 398, note. Suidas, tom. i. p. 1133; Hislop, p. 59, note.

" fire," or " to burn."[1]   Again, in a Persian legend it is stated that
" Hoshang, the father of *Tahmurs*, who built Babylon, was the
first who bred dogs and *leopards* for hunting ";[2] a reference which,
although it makes the father of Nimrod the great hunter, identifies
Nimrod himself with Tammuz.

The name "Nimrod," which means " the subduer of the leopard, or
spotted one," tends to further identify that monarch with the younger
Babylonian god.   For one of the names of the son of the Babylonian
goddess was "*Moumis*," and *Moumis*, like *Nimr*, means " the spotted
one."[3]

Again, a distinctive title of Nin, or Bar (the Son), who was the son
of the elder Belus, or Hea, was " the eldest son," while Bel Merodach,
who was also the son of Hea, is called "the first-born."   So also
Moumis is called " the only son,"[4] and this was likewise the distinctive
title of Tammuz.[5]

Nimrod also appears to have been the human original of the
Egyptian "*Osiris*."   Osiris was the son of Saturn,[6] *i.e.*, of the first
Belus, who was the father of Ninus, or Bel Nimrud the greater, which
tends to identify Osiris with Nimrod.   Again, Thoth, or Hermes,
who is universally known as " the counsellor " of Osiris, the god-king
of Egypt, is stated by Plato to be " the counsellor " of " Thamus,
king of Egypt,"[7] thus identifying the Babylonian Tammuz, and
therefore Nimrod, with the Egyptian god Osiris.   The intimate
connection of Nimrod and his father with Egypt will be shown
hereafter.   Tammuz is also the same as Adonis " the hunter,"
as stated in his commentary on Ezekiel by Jerome, who lived in
Palestine where the rites of Tammuz were still celebrated.[8]   These
rites were the same as those of Osiris, and the lamentations for
Tammuz (Ezek. viii. 14) were also the same as those for Adonis and,
Osiris.[9]   Thus it would appear that " Nimrod, the mighty hunter,"
was the original of " Adonis, the hunter," whom Lenormant identifies
with the Sun god " Baal Tammuz," called also " Adon " (the lord), and
concerning whom he says, " This famous personage, who to the Greeks
was a simple Syrian hunter, was, to the Phœnicians, the Sun god
himself."[10]

[1] Hislop, p. 245, note.   [2] Sir W. Jones's works, vol. xii. p. 400 ; Hislop, p. 45.
[3] Hislop, p. 47.   [4] Damascius, Cory's *Fragments*, p. 318.
[5] See *ante*, p. 31.   [6] Lemprière, *Osiris*.
[7] Wilkinson's *Egyptians*, vol. v. p. 3 ; and chap. xiii. p. 10.
[8] Jerome, vol. ii. p. 353 ; Hislop, p. 314.
[9] Lucian, *De Dea Syria*, vol. iii. p. 454 ; Bunsen, vol. i. p. 443.
[10] Lenormant's *Anc. Hist. of the East*, vol. ii. pp. 218, 219.

The rites of "*Bacchus*" were also identical with those of Tammuz, Adonis and Osiris, and Herodotus always speaks of Osiris as Bacchus, which implies that Bacchus was another title of the deified monarch Nimrod. We have seen that the latter's name means "the leopard subduer," and in the rites of Bacchus leopards were trained to draw his car, while his priests, who were always representatives of the god, were clothed with leopard skins, or, when these could not be obtained, with spotted fawn skins.[1] The name of the *spotted fawn* in Greece is also significant. It was "Nebros," and the name by which Nimrod was known in Greece was "Nebrod." The spotted fawn was in fact

ASSYRIAN GOD.

a symbol of the god as "the subduer of the spotted one," and in the rites of Bacchus a spotted fawn was torn in pieces in commemoration of the death of the god,[2] the history of which death will be dealt with hereafter. This further identifies Bacchus and Osiris with Nimrod. Pliny also states of Bacchus what is said of Cronus, viz., that he was "*the first who wore a crown.*"[3]

The spotted fawn, the emblem of Nimrod, appears to have been the usual symbol of the deified monarch, as in the case of the bas-relief portraying the exploits of Nin, the Assyrian Hercules, where the fawn shown at the feet of the god is evidently introduced for the purpose of identifying him. This is also the case with the Assyrian god in the accompanying woodcut,[4] which must, therefore, be regarded as a representation of Nimrod ; for the branch in his left hand is a conventional one, and is the usual symbol for a son or child, and hence symbolic of "the Son," or "Nin," the distinctive aspect under which Nimrod was deified, while the spotted fawn with horns further identifies the god with the mighty hunter.

The name "Bacchus" is of Chaldean origin and means "the lamented one," from *bakkha*, "to lament," and Hesychius says, "Among

[1] Hislop, p. 46.   [2] Photius, *Lexicon*, pars. i. p. 291 ; Hislop, p. 56.
[3] Pliny, lib. xvi. p. 317.
[4] Vaux, *Nineveh and Persepolis*, chap. viii. p. 233.

the Phœnicians Bacchos means weeping." [1]   Lamentations for the god
were a principal feature of his worship, as in the case of Tammuz,
Adonis and Osiris, and "the lamented one" is evidently another form
of the same god.   Again, "Cush," says Eusebius, "is he from whom
the Æthiopians came," [2] while Epiphanius calls Nimrod "the son of
Cush, the Æthiop." [3]   Now Dionysius, one of the names of Bacchus, is
called "Æthiopais," *i.e.*, the son of Æthiops, [4] which further identifies
Bacchus with Nimrod.   Bacchus is also connected with the Chaldean

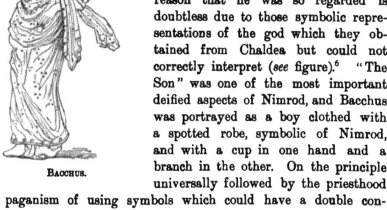

Zoroaster, "the Fire - born," by the
titles "Pyrisporus" and "Ignigena,"
meaning "Fire-born." [5]

The identity of Nimrod with Bacchus
admits of still further proof.   By the
Greeks, Bacchus was regarded merely as
the god of wine and revelry, and the
reason that he was so regarded is
doubtless due to those symbolic representations of the god which they obtained from Chaldea but could not
correctly interpret (*see* figure). [6]   "The
Son" was one of the most important
deified aspects of Nimrod, and Bacchus
was portrayed as a boy clothed with
a spotted robe, symbolic of Nimrod,
and with a cup in one hand and a
branch in the other.   On the principle
universally followed by the priesthood

BACCHUS.

of paganism of using symbols which could have a double construction, this meant to the initiated, "the Son of Cush;" for the
Chaldee for "cup" is *khus*, a form of "Cush," and a branch is
the recognised symbol for a son. [7]   Bacchus was worshipped in Rome
under the name of the "Eternal Boy." [8]

[1] Hesychius, p. 179; Hislop, p. 21.   It is possible, however, that, in accordance
with the mystery used by the Pagan priesthood by means of the double meaning
of words, the name Bacchus had a twofold signification, and that while "the
lamented one" was its outward or exoteric meaning, its secret or esoteric meaning
to the initiated was "the son of Cush," from *Bar*, "son," and *Chus*, a common
form of "Cush."

[2] Euseb., *Chronicon*, vol. i. p. 109.

[3] Epiphanius, lib. i. vol. i. p. 7.   [4] Anacreon, p. 296 ; Hislop, p. 48.

[5] See *ante*, p. 35, "Zoroaster," and Hislop, p. 59, note.

[6] From Smith's *Class. Dict.*, p. 208.

[7] Hislop, p. 48.   [8] Ovid, *Metam.*, iv. 17, 18 ; Hislop, p. 73.

The relationship of Bacchus to Cush is further shown by one of the names of the former, viz., "*Kissos*." Kissos is the Greek for ivy, and ivy in consequence was always present in the worship of Bacchus, and was sacred to him. Now Strabo, speaking of the inhabitants of Susa, the people of Chusistan, or land of Cush, says, "the Susians are Kissioi," that is, the people of Kissos, or Bacchus. Æschylus also calls the land of Cush "Kissinos."[1]

We have said that the rites of Bacchus and Osiris were identical, and that the lamentations for each were the same as those for the

HIGH PRIEST OF OSIRIS.
(Wilkinson, vol. iv. p. 341.)

OSIRIS.
(Wilkinson, plate xxxiii.)

Babylonian Tammuz, whose identity with Osiris and with Nimrod has already been pointed out. Like the priests of Bacchus, the Egyptian High Priest of Osiris had to be clothed in a leopard's skin (*see* figure). "Leopard skins," says Wilkinson, "were worn by the High Priest at all the most important solemnities, and the King himself adopted it when engaged (as High Pontiff) in the same duties."[2] Leopard's skins were the insignia of the god, and Osiris himself, like Bacchus, is represented as clothed with a leopard's skin (*see* figure), while the

[1] Strabo, lib. xv. p. 691 ; Æschylus, *Pers.*, v. 16. ; Hislop, p. 49.
[2] Wilkinson's *Egyptians*, by Birch, vol. iii. p. 361.

sacred Apis, or bull calf, symbolic of the god, was similarly clothed.[1] This further identifies Osiris with Nimrod, the "leopard subduer" and "spotted one." The figure of Osiris, given by Wilkinson, is described by him as Asar, or Osiris, son of Seb, the father of the gods, whom he identifies with Cronus, the Saturn of the Greeks, *i.e.*, Cush, the father of Nimrod.[2]

Bacchus, the Greek Osiris, was the son of Æthiops, and Plutarch records the tradition that Osiris was black,[3] and therefore an Æthiopian or Cushite, the black colour being peculiar to the Cushite race as implied by the prophet Jeremiah, " Can the Æthopian (Cushite) change his skin" (Jer. xiii. 23). The features of Osiris in the woodcut are evidently those of a negro. The sacred bulls Apis and Mnevis are also stated to have had black hair,[4] and both were sacred to Osiris.[5] Apis especially was worshipped as Osiris himself.[6] Ælian also says that at Hermonthis the Egyptians worship a black bull, which they call "Onuphis,"[7] and Onuphis, according to Plutarch, was a title of Osiris.[8] Macrobius calls the sacred bull of Hermonthis "Bacchis," which further tends to connect Osiris with Bacchus.[9]

The land of Egypt was called Khemi or Khami ; and Khami signifies black.[10] Herodotus always speaks of the Egyptians as black, and particularly remarked the thickness of the skulls (a negro characteristic) of those who fell in battle against the Persians.[11] The monuments show that there were two races in Egypt, which is what we might expect from the distinction made in the historical records between "Misraimites" and "Egyptians."[12] Egypt or Ægypt was not the original name of the land of Misraim, but was given to it after " Ægyptus, *the son of Belus*."[13] Now as Belus was Cush, Ægyptus must be Nimrod, or Osiris, the latter being the son of Saturn, who is the same as Belus. In short, Diodorus Siculus states, "The Ethiopians, *i.e.*, the Cushites, say that the Egyptians are a colony drawn out of them by Osiris," and that the laws, customs, religious

[1] *See* figure of the Apis from copy made by Col. Hamilton Smith from the French Institute of Cairo ; Hislop, p. 46.

[2] *Wilkinson*, by Birch, vol. iii. pp. 59-62.

[3] *De Iside et Osiride*, vol. ii. p. 359.

[4] Herod., lib. iii. cap. xxviii.   [5] Diodorus, i. 21.

[6] *Wilkinson*, by Birch, vol. iii. pp. 86-91.

[7] Ælian, *Nat. An.*, xii. 11.

[8] *De Iside*, s. 35 ; *Wilkinson*, by Birch, vol. iii. pp. 69, 70.

[9] *Wilkinson*, by Birch, vol. iii. p. 307.

[10] *Ibid.*, vol. iii. p. 198.

[11] Herod., *Thalia*, lib. iii. cap. xii.

[12] *Infra*, chap. iv.   [13] *Lemprière, Ægyptus.*

observances and letters of the ancient Egyptians closely resembled those of the Ethiopians, "the Colony still observing the customs of their ancestors."[1]

Ninus, like Nimrod, is stated to have conquered all Asia, Egypt, and part of Europe. Osiris is also said to have done the same. An inscription found on certain ancient monuments reads as follows:—
"Saturn, the youngest of all the gods, is my father. I am Osiris, who conducted a large and numerous army as far as the deserts of India and travelled over the greater part of the world, and visited the streams of the Ister (Danube) and the remotest shores of the ocean, diffusing benevolence to all the inhabitants of the earth."[2] Here Osiris, like Ægyptus, is stated to be the son of Saturn, or Belus, i.e., Cush. Moreover, the circumstantial account of his conquests is the strongest evidence that, although afterwards deified and identified with the Sun, the original of Osiris was a human king. Finally the same expedition and conquests are attributed to Bacchus or Dionusus, to the Indian "Deonaush" (who we shall see is identical with the Greek Dionusus), and to Ægyptus and to Hercules.

The identity of Osiris with Ninus or Nimrod, and the intimate relation of the early history of Egypt and Babylon, will be more fully demonstrated in Chapter IV.

"Jupiter," called "Diespiter," "Heaven Father," which is regarded as the original etymology of the name, seems to have been peculiar to the Aryan nations, the descendants of Japhet, and to have been the name of their god. The name may also possibly be a corruption, or adaptation, of the name of their ancestor Japetus, who, we know, was deified under the title of "Pra Japeti." When, however, the Cushite idolatry was introduced among them they appear to have called the chief divinity of that idolatry by the name of their god and regarded him as the son of Saturn, or Belus, and identified him with the planet Jupiter, which would make him the same, therefore, as Ninus, Bel Merodach, Osiris, etc. Jupiter was also identified with Bacchus, the Greek Osiris, both having the surname of "Sabavius."[3]

The god "Mars," or "Ares," seems to be likewise identified with Nimrod. For we have seen that Nergal, the Babylonian god of war and of hunting, who was regarded as the planet Mars, was probably a

[1] Diodorus, quoted by Baldwin, *Prehistoric Nations*, pp. 275, 276.
[2] Lemprière, *Osiris*. Shem, Ham and Japhet were, as we have seen, worshipped as gods, which may account for Cush, the son of Ham, when he had been deified as Saturn, being called the *youngest* of the gods.
[3] Faber, vol. ii. p. 292.

deified form of Nimrod, and his identity with the younger Belus, or Bel Nimrod the greater, and Bel Merodach, who have also been shown to be deified forms of the same king, is confirmed by the name given to the wife of Mars. The death of the gods under whose names Nimrod was deified (Osiris, Tammuz, Bacchus, Adonis, etc.) was yearly lamented, and these lamentations were the principal feature in their worship, and their wives are specially represented as lamenting their death. Now the wife of Mars was "*Bellona*," a name which signifies "the lamenter of Bel" (from *Bel* and *ohnah*, to lament),[1] which connects Mars with the second Belus, who is the same as Osiris, Tammuz, etc. The name also by which Mars was known by the Oscans of Italy was "*Mamers*," which signifies "the rebel," or "causer of rebellion"; and the name of the Babylonian god "Bel Merodach" appears to have the same meaning, viz., "Bel, the rebel" (from *Mered*, to rebel),[2] which was probably given him as the champion of the gods against their opponents.

"The god of the dead" worshipped under the name of "*Anu*" or "*Ana*" at Babylon appears to be another deified form of Nimrod. Anu was the Lord of Urka, the city of the dead, and Beltis, or Bilta Niprut, is associated with him as the Lady of Bit Ana, the temple of Anu at Urka. Sargon II. also associates Ishtar, or Astarte, with Anu, as his wife,[3] and as Beltis and Ishtar are forms of the same goddess who was the wife of the two Bel Nimruds, we may conclude that Anu is a form of one or other of those gods, and the evidence seems to show that he must be the younger god, or Nimrod.

Anu was also called "*Dis*," which identifies him with "*Pluto*," the Greek god of the dead, who was called by the Greeks "*Dis*,"[4] and Pluto is identified with Osiris, who was the Egyptian god of the dead, by numerous Greek inscriptions which are dedicated "To Pluto, the Sun, the great Sarapis";[5] Sarapis being a combination of "*Asar*," a name of Osiris, with "*Apis*," the sacred bull by which Osiris was represented.[6] Therefore as Osiris has been shown to be Nimrod, Anu or Pluto must be a deified form of the same monarch.

The Greek god "*Pan*" appears to be a deified form of Cush. Pan was the chief of the Satyrs[7] (Greek "*Saturs*"), which is derived

[1] Hislop, p. 44, note.　　　　[2] *Ibid.*
[3] Rawlinson's *Herod.*, vol. i. pp. 592, 593.
[4] Lemprière, *Pluto.*
[5] *Wilkinson*, by Birch, vol. iii. p. 97.
[6] *Ibid.*, p. 87—woodcut 519 of Osiris as *Asarapis.*
[7] Lemprière, *Pan.*

from the Chaldean "Satur," whence the name "Saturn," who must be
the chief of Satyrs and therefore identical with Pan. Pan is also
the god of generation, or fecundity, like Mercury or Hermes, another
form of Cush, and was represented under the form of a goat.[1]
Wilkinson identifies Pan with "*Khem,*" the Egyptian god of Generation.[2] According to Herodotus, Pan was the same as the
Egyptian god "*Mendes,*" who, he says, was also represented with the
head and legs of a goat, and that Pan and a goat were both called
Mendes in Egypt.[3] Wilkinson dissents to this because he can find
no monuments of this god thus represented;[4] but this fact does not
invalidate the more ancient testimony of Herodotus. The goat, the
ram and the bull were all emblems of the principle of Generation, and
Plutarch says the Mendesian goat had the name of "Apis," the sacred
bull of Memphis,[5] while Diodorus states that the goat was chosen as
the emblem of Generation.[6] Birch says that, according to the
inscriptions, Mendes was represented "with the head of a sheep, or
goat," and that "the goat of Mendes was the living spirit of the Sun,
the life of Ra, the generator, the prince of young women, the original
male power of the gods." He was also represented under the form
of a ram and as ram-headed.[7] We must, therefore, conclude that he
was a form of Khem, the god of Generation, and identical with Pan
and Mercury. Pan is further identified with Saturn by the Orphic
poet, who calls him "the Universal father and the Horned Zeus or
Cronus," *i.e.,* Saturn.[8]

"*Æsculapius,*" the god of Medicine, may more or less be identified
with both the Babylonian gods, who, as pointed out, sometimes blend
into one. The symbol of Æsculapius was a snake, which represented
him as the "life restorer," because the snake, which obtains a new
skin every year, was thus supposed to constantly renew its life.[9]
Now "Hea," or "Heya," one of the names of Bel Nimrud the lesser,
is the Arabic word for both "life" and "serpent,"[10] and the god
was represented by a serpent.[11] The etymology of the name

[1] Lemprière, *Pan.* [2] *Wilkinson*, by Birch, vol. iii. p. 186.
Herod., book ii. chaps. 42, 46.
[4] *Wilkinson*, by Birch, vol. iii. p. 187. Apparently no representation at all of
Mendes has been discovered, so that the evidence in support of Wilkinson's
objection is wholly negative.
[5] *De Iside,* s. 73. [6] Diodorus, i. 88.
[7] *Wilkinson*, ed. by Birch, vol. iii., p. 186; note by Birch.
[8] Faber, vol. ii. p. 406. [9] *Sanchoniathon's History;* Cory, *Fragments*, p. 18.
[10] Rawlinson's *Herod.*, vol. i. p. 599.
[11] Lenormant, *Chaldean Magic*, p. 232.

Æsculapius tends to further identify him with "Hea," for "Aish shkul ape" (which would be written "Aishkulape," and "Æsculapius" in Greek), means "the man instructing serpent," from *aish*, "man," *shkul*, "to instruct," and *ape* or *aphe*, "serpent."[1] Similarly "Hea," the serpent god, is called "The Teacher of Mankind, the Lord of Understanding,"[2] etc., and, like Æsculapius, he is "The Life-giver."[3]

But Æsculapius is represented as the child of the Sun,[4] like Osiris and other Sun gods, or their supposed reincarnations as Horus, Apollo, etc. The Greek myth of the birth of Æsculapius is also identical with that of Bacchus. His mother was consumed by lightning and he was rescued from the lightning which destroyed her, just as Bacchus was rescued from the flames which consumed his mother.[5] Æsculapius also is said to have died a violent death. He is stated to have been killed by lightning for raising the dead.[6] This identifies him with Nimrod rather than with his father, the violent death of the former constituting a most important feature in the Pagan mythology.

The characteristics, however, of Æsculapius and the etymology of his name tend to associate him more especially with Bel Nimrud the lesser, Hea, the prophet Nebo, "the all-wise Belus," Thoth, or Hermes, etc., and it is probable that the Greeks, confusing father and son, applied some of the traditions of the latter to the former.

Cush, or Bel Nimrud the lesser, seems to be the human original also of "*Dagon*," the Fish god of the Babylonians and Canaanites. One of the titles of Bel was "Dagon,"[7] and under his name "Hea," Bel Nimrud the lesser is called "The God of the Great Deep," "The Intelligent Fish." This tends to connect Hea with another Fish god, viz., "*Oannes*," who is regarded as identical with Dagon. Oannes is represented as teaching the Babylonians science and religion, and is described as having a fish's head over his own head, and a fish's tail behind his legs.[8] Dagon was represented in a similar way.[9] M. Lenormant also identifies Hea with Oannes.[10]

Berosus, in his history, mentions several forms of Oannes, who were sea monsters with the reason and speech of men, but with a

---

[1] Hislop, p. 278, note.   [2] *Ante*, p. 29.
[3] Lenormant, *Chaldean Magic*, pp. 114, 115.
[4] Ovid, *Metam.*, lib. xv. ll. 736-745.   [5] Lemprière ; Hislop, p. 236.
[6] *Æneid*, lib. vii., ll. 769-773, pp. 364-365 ; Hislop, p. 236.
[7] Rawlinson's *Five Great Monarchies*, vol. ii. p. 14.
[8] Berosus ; Cory, *Fragments*, pp. 22, 23.
[9] Layard, *Babylon and Nineveh*, p. 343 ; and Hislop, p. 215
[10] Lenormant, *Chaldean Magic*, p. 157, and Appendix I. p. 201.

fish's head above a man's head and a fish's tail behind a man's legs. The first of these beings, he says, "appeared out of the Erythræan Sea where it borders on Babylonia," and "taught the Babylonians to construct cities, to found temples, to compile laws, and explained to them the principles of geometrical knowledge."[1] Following him appeared a second, very similar in form to the first, whom he calls a "sea dæmon," and after this one, "four double-shaped personages' appeared, and finally, "another having the same complicated form between a fish and a man,"[2] whose name was "Odacon," which is equivalent to "O'Dagon"—"the Dagon" or "the Fish."[3] All this, however, is described as occurring during the reign of ten kings previous to the Deluge, of whom the last was Xisuthrus, or Noah, whose escape from the Deluge he describes very similarly to the account in Genesis. These ten kings correspond with the ten generations mentioned in Genesis, and with the earliest history of things which has been preserved in other nations, all of which describe ten kings, or generations, before the Deluge. Berosus further says that Xisuthrus was directed by the deity to write the history of things, which would, of course, include the knowledge obtained from the various sea dæmons, and to bury it at the City of the Sun at Sippara. These writings, he says, were found after the Deluge, at Sippara, upon which "they built cities and erected temples, and Babylon was inhabited again."[4]

This story of the sea dæmons has, at first sight, the appearance of little more than fanciful fable, but it will be found as we proceed that many of the mythological traditions of the ancients, which have a similar appearance of fable, can be shown to be a record of real events, concealed indeed beneath allegorical language, and often encrusted with fabulous additions, but the meaning of which is plain when compared with other traditions and known historial facts. We shall have to refer to the above statements of Berosus again; but, for the present, the point to be noticed is that these sea dæmons, who were said to be teachers of a certain knowledge to mankind, were the original "Oannes" and "Dagon," and that their names were probably given to Hea, that is to say, Bel Nimrud the lesser, or Cush, because he also was Nebo, the false prophet, and great teacher of the primitive idolatry.

Nimrod, in his character of Bacchus, was also called "*Ichthys*"

---

[1] Berosus, from *Polyhistor;* Cory, pp. 22, 23.
[2] Berosus, from *Apollodorus and Abydenus*; Cory, p. 30-33.
[3] Dag or Dagon is the Chaldee for fish ; Faber, vol. ii. p. 378.
[4] Berosus, from *Polyhistor;* Cory, pp. 27-29.

"the Fish,"[1] but he was so called for a different reason from that which gave to his father the titles of Oannes and Dagon. His death was the great event commemorated in the later form of idolatry, when he and his father were worshipped as gods, and the enemy of the god who compassed his death was called "Typhon," the name, among the Egyptians, of the evil principle. The ocean which destroyed the human race at the Deluge was also called Typhon, and the enemy of the god was thus identified with the ocean. Bacchus is therefore represented as plunging beneath the waves of the ocean in order to escape from his enemies, from whom he was rescued by Thetis.[2] Hence his name "Ichthys."

A similar story is told of Osiris, the Egyptian Bacchus, but in this case the god is identified with Noah. He is represented as being shut up in his coffin and set afloat on the waters of the ocean on the seventeenth day of the second month of the Egyptian year, *i.e.*, the day on which the Deluge commenced, and to have remained there, as did Noah, for exactly one year.[3] The coffin or ship in which he was preserved was called "*Argo*," "*Baris*," and "*Theba*," the latter being the word used for the ark of the Deluge by Moses.[4] Thetis also, who received Bacchus, is shown by Faber to be identified with the ark,[5] and just as Noah was, as it were, born again in a new world out of the ark, so Bacchus is called "*Thebe genus*," "Arkborn," and his heart was supposed to be carried in a box called "the ark" at his festivals.[6]

The reason why Bacchus and Osiris were thus identified with Noah was, firstly, to obtain for the god the veneration in which the father of the human race was held, and secondly, to associate his worship with the memory of the Deluge which had so solemn and profound an effect on the postdiluvians, that, as we have seen, it is to this day yearly commemorated in almost every nation under the sun.[7] The latter event had also a particular bearing on the origin of Paganism, which will be duly noticed hereafter.

It does not appear that "*Ham*," or "*Ammon*," was worshipped as a god except by the Egyptians. He was venerated by them under the name "Amon," or "Amen," at Thebes,[8] which in Scripture is called "No Amon," or the abode of Amon. He was identified with the Sun as "Amenra," and is represented with a ram's head surmounted by the

---

[1] Hesychius, *Bacchus*, p. 114 ; Hislop, p. 114.

[2] Homer, *Iliad*, vi. v. 133 ; Bryant's *Mythology*, vol. iv. p. 57 ; Hislop, p. 142.

[3] Plutarch, *De Iside*, ii. p. 336, D ; *Apollodorus*, lib. iii. cap. xiv.

[4] Faber, vol. i. pp. 21, 360-371.

[5] *Ibid.*, vol. iii. book v. chap. iii.

[6] *Ibid.*, vol. ii. pp. 265-267.

[7] See *ante*, chap. i.

[8] *Ante*, p. 16.

disk of the Sun to symbolise the generative power of the Sun.[1] Under this aspect he is identified with "Khem," "Cnoubis," or "Cnouphis," and Osiris, all of whom represented the generative principle. "Khem," or "Kham," whom Wilkinson identifies with the Greek god Pan,[2] is the Egyptian name of Ham, and therefore the same god as Amen in a different aspect, and he is represented by exactly the same figure as Amen.[3] Cnoubis is also represented, like Amenra, with a ram's head,[4] and by the Romans was known as Jupiter Amon Cnoubis.[5] Birch says that the hymns of the eighteenth dynasty represent Amenra as the creator of men, animals and plants; that they identify him with Khem, and ally him in all respects with the Sun, while in the time of Darius he is identified both with Ra, the Sun, and with Osiris.[6] Khem was also regarded as the generating influence of the Sun, and in one of the hieroglyphic legends is called the Sun.[7] Cnouphis likewise represents the Creative spirit in Nature.[8] The god "*Phthah*" also represented the Creative power, and was identified by the Greeks with Vulcan, the father of the gods, and Phthah, like Vulcan, was the father of the gods.[9] He was represented by the Scarabæus beetle, which was an emblem of the Sun as being "the type of the Creative power, self-acting, and self-sufficient."[10]

"*Seb*," like Phthah, was also the father of the gods, and identical with Saturn,[11] and must therefore be Cush, but with these exceptions, and that of Thoth, or Hermes, Cush does not appear to have been otherwise worshipped in Egypt, and Ham seems to have taken his place under the forms of Kneph, or Cnouphis, Amen, and Khem, as the god of Generation, like the Mercury and Pan of the Greeks. But it is evident that the different gods blend into each other, or, as Wilkinson says, "take each other's characters and attributes."[12] Ammon, in short, as "Jupiter Ammon," was ultimately identified with Jupiter, the son of Saturn, and therefore with Osiris, and in Manetho's Dynasty of Gods Ammon is classed as merely a demi-god, showing that he had lost his position in later times, when Osiris had

[1] *Wilkinson*, by Birch, vol. iii. p. 9—pl. xix.   [2] *Ibid.*, p. 186.
[3] *Ibid.*, compare pl. xix. p. 8, and woodcut p. 25.
[4] *Ibid.*, pl. xviii. p. 3.
[5] *Ibid.*, p. 2.
[6] *Ibid.*, p. 13, note by Birch.
[7] *Ibid.*, p. 26.
[8] *Ibid.*, p. 2. Wilkinson here tries to idealise the character of Cnouphis by calling him "the Spirit," but the ram's head and other characteristics given to him shows that he was the Phallic god, the supposed author of natural life and generation.
[9] *Ibid.*, p. 17, note by Birch.   [10] *Ibid.*, p. 15.
[11] *Ibid.*, p. 62.   [12] *Ibid.*, pp. 9, 10.

become the chief god of the Egyptians and was identified with the Sun.[1]

We have seen that the Egyptian Thoth, or Hermes, was "the God of letters and learning, the means by which all mental gifts were imparted to men, and he represented the abstract idea of intellect."[2] Now the Egyptians regarded the heart as the seat of intellect, and Horapollo describes the Egyptian Hermes as "the president of *the heart*."[3] The significance of this will be evident when it is remembered that Hermes has been identified with Belus, or Bel, and that "Bel" is the Chaldee for "heart." Thoth is called by Jamblicus "the God of all Celestial Knowledge,"[4] *i.e.*, celestial knowledge according to the Pagan idea of it, which well accords with the character of Cush as the teacher of mankind and the originator of Pagan idolatry. These characteristics also tend to identify Thoth with Phthah, who is called "Intellect, the Lord of Truth,"[5] that is of truth in the Pagan sense. In short, Phthah was the "father of the gods," and therefore the same as Saturn or Cush.[6] In the rites of Osiris, Thoth is represented as his scribe and counsellor, and was called "Hermes Trismegistus," or "Thrice Great Hermes."[7]

The god "*Anubis*" appears to be especially identified with Thoth, Hermes and Mercury, and therefore with Cush. Apuleius speaks of him as the interpreter of the gods, like Mercury or Hermes. He is also the god of the dead like Mercury, while, like Mercury, he is represented as holding the "*caduceus*," in his hand.[8] His office, as god of the dead, would seem to connect him with the Babylonian god of the dead Anu, Dis, or Pluto (*i.e.*, Nimrod). But the two deities were gods of the dead in different ways, Mercury, or Hermes, and Anubis being the *conductors* of the dead, while Pluto, Osiris, etc., were *judges* of the dead.[9]

There are one or two other gods who were regarded as re-incarnations of Osiris and other forms of the same god, and they are practi-

---

[1] *See* Manetho's "Dynasty of the Gods"; Cory, p. 94.
[2] *Wilkinson*, by Birch, vol. iii. p. 168.
[3] *Ibid.*, p. 324.   [4] *Ibid.*, p. 168.
[5] *Ibid.*, p. 15.   [6] *Ibid.*, p. 17.
[7] *Wilkinson*, by Birch, vol. iii. p. 169. Wilkinson makes another god out of Hermes Trismegistus because he is found with the additional title of "Lord of Pantnouphis." But considering the variety of titles given to the gods and kings of Egypt, the reason has little weight as compared with the great unlikelihood of two gods being given exactly the same name.
[8] *Wilkinson*, by Birch, vol. iii. p. 160.
[9] *Ibid.*, p. 159; *Anubis*, p. 67; Lemprière, *Osiris, Pluto, Mercury*.

cally identical with him. Osiris himself was recognised as the Sun god, and both "*Horus*" and "*Apollo*" are represented as sons of the Sun and as the Sun himself; for when the god, as Osiris, was identified with the Sun, the incarnation of himself became both the Sun and the son of the Sun. Thus "*Isis*," the goddess mother and wife of Osiris, and mother of Horus, is represented as saying, "No mortal hath raised my veil. The fruit which I have brought forth is the Sun."[1]

"*Cupid*," another incarnation of the god, is similarly identified with his father, but he is the son of the god and goddess from a different point of view. He is represented to be, as might be expected from the identity of so many gods and goddesses, the son of many of them, and this also accounts for the various genealogies given in Greek mythology to the different gods. Cupid, however, is more especially the son of *Venus*, in whose arms he is represented, just as Horus, under the name of "*Harpocrates*," is represented in the arms of Isis.[2] Cupid is also portrayed with a heart in his hands, or else with the heart-shaped fruit of the Persea,[3] which caused the Greeks to regard him as the god of the heart, or god of love, just as the representation of Bacchus caused them to regard him as the god of wine. But in both cases the real significance of the symbol was misunderstood. For the Chaldee for "heart" is "Bel,"[4] which, on the principle of the double signification of words adopted by the Pagan priesthood to conceal the true meaning from the uninitiated, denoted that the child was the son of Bel, or Cush; while he is further identified with "the mighty hunter" by the bow and arrows.

For the same reason the heart contained in an ark was carried by the priests in procession at the festivals of Bacchus,[5] to identify him with the Babylonian god. The Roman youths also used to wear a heart-shaped amulet suspended round their necks, called the "Bulla,"[6] which had evidently the same significance. Cupid, known also as "*Eros*," was lamented by the Egyptians, like Osiris and Tammuz, under the name of "*Maneros*," who, they said, was "*the only son of their first king.*"[7] This first king, we shall see, was Thoth, or the elder Belus, which also identifies Maneros, or Cupid, with Osiris, or

[1] Lemprière, *Isis*.
[2] Harpocrates means, as shown by Bunsen, "Horus the child"; Hislop, p. 188. note.
[3] *Pompeii*, vol. ii. p. 177 ; Hislop, p. 189.   [4] Hislop, p. 190.
[5] Jul. Firm., *De Error., prof. rel.*, pp. 14, 15 ; Arnob., *Adv. Gent.*, lib. v. Faber, vol. ii. p. 265.
[6] Kenneth's *Atiquities*, pp. 300, 301 ; Hislop, pp. 189, 190.
[7] Herod., lib. ii. cap. lxxix.

D

Nimrod. Now Osiris was worshipped by the Greeks as Bacchus, and Herodotus states that he was greatly surprised at the fact that the dirge which they used in lamenting Maneros was exactly the same as the dirge of *Linus*, who was identical with Bacchus.[1]

In spite of this necessarily brief examination, the consentient evidence of so many ancient writers is practically conclusive of the fact that the originals of the gods of Babylon, Egypt, Greece and Rome were human beings, the first great monarchs of the world, viz., Cush and his son Nimrod, the founders of the Babylonian empire. This is also confirmed by the very names of some of the gods; by their characteristics; by their having been the originators of fire worship and the first teachers of idolatry; by their history as human kings, as in the case of Osiris, Bacchus and Ninus, which so exactly agree with that of Nimrod; by the fact that they are represented as reigning both in Babylon and Egypt; by the claim of the kings of those countries to be their descendants; by various independent and undesigned references to them; and by the accumulative evidence of the identity of the various gods with each other. This evidence will be found to be still more accumulative when we come to speak of the gods of other nations, and of the relations of the great goddess in her various forms to the different gods.

The latter evidence is also confirmed by the testimony of ancient and modern writers to the intimate connection of the religious systems of each country, and to the fact that Egypt, Phœnicia, Greece and Rome obtained their religion either directly from Babylon and Assyria, or from each other.

The intimate connection of these religious systems is also shewn by the fact that the Grecian mythology speaks of half a dozen or more Cupids, and various Apollos, Mercurys, etc. This, on the face of it, would be inexplicable, for we cannot suppose that they invented so many gods of the same name, and all with similar attributes. But it is at once explained when it is considered that the Greeks obtained their religion from Babylon through Phœnicia, and Egypt. For it would necessarily follow from this, that each Cupid or Apollo would be represented to them as the son of various gods and goddesses, and not recognising that the latter were merely the deified attributes of one original God and Goddess, they would naturally suppose that the sons of each god and goddess were different persons, although of the same name.

Herod., and Hislop, p. 22, note.

Wilkinson, speaking of the gods of Egypt, says, "I have stated that Amunre and other gods took the form of different deities which, though it appears at first sight to present some difficulty, may be readily accounted for when we consider that each of those whose figures or emblems were adopted, was *only an emanation or deified attribute of the same great Being*, to whom they ascribed various characters according to the several offices he was supposed to perform."[1]

Bunsen also says, "Upon these premises we think ourselves justified in concluding that the *two series of gods* were originally identical, and that in *the great pair of gods* all these attributes were concentrated, from the development of which, in various personifications, that mythological system sprang which we have already been considering."[2]

Owing to the fact of the same names, such as "Cronus," "Belus," or "Bel," being given to both father and son; to the fact that both were regarded as gods of fire, and taught or enforced the worship of fire and idolatry; and also to the fact that both had a claim to be founders of Babylon,—because Babel (the design of Cush), and the city, which was commenced at the same time (Gen. xi. 5, 8), were the *beginning* of Babylon, which Nimrod completed,—the distinction between the two has often been lost sight of.

But the distinction is of great importance, and in spite of a trifling confusion at times, due to the above causes, may be readily recognised.

Thus we have seen that the elder "Cronus," the elder "Belus," or Saturn, who was the father of Ninus, Osiris and Ægyptus, was "Cush the Æthiop," the father of Bacchus; and that he is more especially identified with "Vulcan," "Hephæstus," "Chaos," "Janus," "Pan," the Egyptian "Phthah," and "Seb," as the *"father of the gods"*; and that he is represented as the ringleader, or principal actor, in the building of the Tower of Babel; while under the names of "The Prophet Nebo," "Hea, the Lord of Understanding," "Thoth," "Hermes," "Taautus" (the counsellor both of "Osiris" and "Tammuz"), "Mercury," "Anubis," "Æsculapius," "Oannes" and "Dagon," he appears to have been the teacher of mankind and initiator of the Pagan religion.

Similarly, Nin, or Ninus, the younger "Cronus," and the younger "Belus," or "Bel," or "Bel Nimrud the greater," Bel Merodach, etc., is Nimrod the Great King and Conqueror, who is more especially identi-

---

[1] Wilkinson's *Egyptians*, vol. iv. p. 245.
[2] Bunsen's *Egypt*, vol. i. p. 418.

fied with "Hercules," the giant hunter "Orion," "Adonis," "Adon," "Baal Tammuz," "Osiris," "Ægyptus," "Bacchus," "Jupiter," "Mars," "Anu," "Dis," "Pluto," etc.

It is to be observed, however, that although the distinction between the two sets of gods is more or less clear, all were regarded by the ancients as the Sun, which was a consequence of the intimate relation to each other of the two sets of gods, viz., the relation of father to son, and the tendency of the one to blend into the other. Mr Faber quotes a number of ancient mythologists who assert the identity of the different gods with the Sun.[1]

Thus Saturn, or Cronus, is declared to be the Sun by Macrobius and Nonnus.

Jupiter is declared to be the Sun by Macrobius, Nonnus, and the Orphic poet.

Pluto, or Aidoneus, is said to be the Sun by the Orphic poet.

Bacchus, or Dionusus, is said to be the Sun by Virgil, Ausonius, Macrobius, Sophocles and the Orphic poet.

Priapus is said to be the Sun by the Orphic poet.

Apollo is said to be the Sun by Macrobius, Nonnus, the Orphic poet, Ovid, and by his own oracular responses.

Janus is said to be the Sun by Macrobius.

Pan, or Phanes, is said to be the Sun by Macrobius and the Orphic poet.

Hercules is said to be the Sun by Nonnus and Macrobius.

Vulcan, or Hephæstus, is said to be the Sun by the Orphic poet.

Æsculapius is said to be the Sun by Macrobius.

Mercury is said to be the Sun by Macrobius.

Osiris, Horus, Serapis, are each said to be the Sun by Diodorus Siculus, Macrobius, an ancient oracle of Apollo, and the Horapolline hieroglyphics.

Belus is said to be the Sun by Nonnus.

Adonis, or Attys, is said to be the Sun by Macrobius.

The Hindus, in like manner, assert that Vishnu is the Sun at night and in the west; that Brahma is the Sun in the morning and in the east; and that Siva is the Sun from noon to evening.[2]

Mr Faber gives the names of other gods who were regarded as the Sun, but the above are sufficient to show the general character

[1] Faber, *Pagan Idolatry*, vol. ii. bk. iv. chap. i. pp. 206-214.
[2] Moor's *Hindu Pantheon*, pp. 6, 9, 13, 33, 277, 294; *Asiat. Res.*, vol. i. p. 267; vol. v. p. 254.

of the Pagan belief, and the subject will be more fully considered in future chapters.[1]

Thus, although these gods can be identified with human originals, this in ancient times was known only to the priesthood and to the initiated; while to the common people the gods were merely beings possessed of certain powers and characteristics, whose material manifestations were the sun and certain planets, and whose spirits were supposed to inhabit certain images and temples. The truth only became gradually known as the influence of, and veneration bestowed on, idolatry began to decay, and our present knowledge is due to the facts thus revealed by ancient authors, and to the careful comparison by modern students of ancient myths and traditions.

In conclusion we may refer to the legend of "*Izdubar*," translated by Mr George Smith from the Assyrian Tablets, as it would seem to be an indubitable evidence that the human originals of the Babylonian gods were Nimrod and Cush.

Mr Smith identifies Izdubar with Nimrod. Izdubar, like Nimrod, is a mighty leader, a man strong in war. Like Nimrod, he is called "the mighty giant." Like Nimrod, he is a mighty hunter who slays by sheer strength the most formidable wild animals. In his time the whole of the Euphrates Valley was divided into petty kingdoms, and Izdubar, like Nimrod, establishes his dominion over them, the centre of his dominion being in the region of Shinar at Babylon, Accad, Ereck and Nippur, exactly corresponding with that of Nimrod.[2] Moreover, Izdubar speaks of Noah as *his father*, a term of relationship which would be equally applied to one who was his grandfather or great-grandfather. For Hasisadra,[3] his father, is the person who, in the Chaldean Tablets of the Deluge, is preserved with various animals and beasts of the field in an ark, and who at its termination sends forth a dove and a raven to see if the waters had abated.[4] His relationship, therefore, to Noah, together with his characteristics and

[1] *See* chap. x., "Sun, Serpent, Phallic and Tree Worship."
[2] *Chaldean Account of Genesis*, pp. 174 and 203, ll. 44, 45.
[3] Ha Sisadra is evidently the Noah of Berosus's *History of the Deluge*, the name being translated by the Greeks, "Xisuthrus" or "Sisithrus." The Greeks constantly substituted "th" for "d," as in "Theos" for "Deus," and always gave a Greek termination to names. Ha Sisadra would therefore become "Ha Sisathrus," or without the prefix, "Sisathrus."
[4] *See* Izdubar legend, *Chaldean Account of Genesis.*

exploits, makes it impossible to doubt that the legend is a romance founded on the history of Nimrod.

But although Izdubar is undoubtedly Nimrod, he is, as shown by M. Lenormant, the god of fire, and the personification or incarnation of the Sun, while the twelve tablets on which his enterprises are recorded appear to symbolise the Sun god passing through the twelve signs of the Zodiac, and is probably the origin of the twelve labours of Hercules.[1] In short, just as Nin, the Assyrian Hercules, was the husband of the Assyrian goddess Bilta, or Beltis, so Izdubar is the lover and husband of Ishtar, another form of the same goddess.[2]

We have also seen that the two Pagan gods are associated together in the respective characters of king and counsellor, hero and sage, warrior and prophet, as in the case of Thoth and Osiris, Thoth and Tammuz, Bel and Nebo, Ninus and Oannes, Nin and Hea. In like manner, Izdubar is associated with a wonderful sage named " *Hea-bani*," " *famed for his wisdom in all things and his knowledge of all that is visible and concealed*," and whose name and characteristics therefore exactly correspond with those of Hea. The suffix *bani* signifies " to make,"[3] and as one signification of the name " Hea " is " life,"[4] *Hea-bani* would signify " life-maker," or " life-giver," which was the particular attribute of Hea, Æsculapius, etc.

Again Hea-bani helps Izdubar in his exploits and the two are represented on a Babylonian cylinder (*see* woodcut) in exactly the

Izdubar and Hea-bani.

---

[1] Lenormant, *Chaldean Magic*, pp. 188, 189.
[2] Izdubar Tablets.   [3] *Chaldean Account of Genesis*, p. 185.
[4] Rawlinson's *Herod.*, vol i. p. 600. Hea was " the life-giver "; Lenormant, *Chaldean Magic*, pp. 114, 115.
[5] Copied from *The Chaldean Account of Genesis*, by the permission of Messrs. Sampson, Low, Marston & Co.

same style and manner as the Assyrian Nin, or Hercules,[1] while the fawn, the particular symbol of Nimrod, at the feet of Izdubar also identifies Izdubar with Nin, and both with Nimrod. M. Lenormant also identifies Izdubar with the god Bar or Nin.[2]

M. Lenormant speaks of the legend as "a god transformed in epic poetry into a terrestrial hero, and not an historical king as Mr Smith would have him considered."[3] But it is clear that Mr Smith is correct and that the legend is a romance founded on the history of the great king and giant hunter Nimrod, who was afterwards deified and eventually transformed into the Sun and Fire god of the Babylonians. It is the story of a terrestrial hero transformed into a god, and not the story of a god transformed into a hero.

The legend, in short, is a further and conclusive evidence that the originals of the Babylonian gods, and of the gods of other nations who received their religion from Babylonia and Assyria, were the two first kings of the first great empire of the world, Nimrod and his father Cush. For while it is clear that Izdubar is Nimrod, it is equally clear that he is the Babylonian Sun god, and Nin the Assyrian Hercules and god of war and hunting, and that his friend and counsellor Hea-bani is the god Hea.

Mr Smith gives a portrait of Izdubar from a Khorsabad sculpture (*see* woodcut,)[4] and he remarks:—"In all these cases and in every other instance where Izdubar is represented he is indicated as a man with masses of curls over his head, and a large curly beard. So marked is this and different in cast to the usual Babylonian type that I cannot help the impression of its being a representation of a distinct and probably Ethiopian type."[5] But the Cushite type is not only displayed in the crisped hair. It is seen also in the flattened and distended nostrils, and in the thick, turned-out sensual lips, and it is just what we might expect to find in the progenitor of the black or negro race. This portrait, therefore, also tends to identify Izdubar with the Cushite monarch, and the sculpture is probably a fair likeness of the giant hunter Nimrod.

It will be seen that he is represented as not only strangling a lion, but as carrying in his right hand a dead serpent. This, as will be pointed out in another chapter, was the peculiar characteristic of the

[1] Compare *ante* woodcut, p. 24.
[2] *Chaldean Magic*, p. 189.
[3] *Ibid.*, p. 188.
[4] Copied from *The Chaldean Account of Genesis*, by the permission of Messrs Sampson, Low, Marston, & Co.
[5] *Chaldean Account of Genesis*, p. 194.

various forms of the god under which Nimrod was deified. They were represented as the slayer of the serpent.

IZDUBAR STRANGLING A LION (from Khorsabad Sculpture).

There is much uncertainty regarding the phonetic value of the signs which Mr George Smith has translated by the name Izdubar or Isdubar.[1] M. Lenormant has pointed out that "*bar*" signifies fire, and considers the name "Izdubar" to mean "mass of fire"; but "*bar*" is also the Semitic for "son," which is such a prominent feature in the titles of the younger Babylonian god. Again, the symbols for "s" and "sh" are often the same in Egyptian hieroglyphics, and this is also the case with those of Babylon, in which case the first syllable of the name might perchance be read as "*Ish*," or "*Isha*," signifying the "woman," the root of the name "Ishtar." It may also be remarked that "d" and "t" are generally interchangeable, as in the case of "Dumuz," who was generally known as "Tammuz." Is it not possible, therefore, that the name may be a combination of the name of the Babylonian goddess *Ishtar* with the term "*bar*," or "son," added, signifying "the son of Ishtar," which would represent Izdubar to be both the son and the lover, or husband, of the goddess?

This, as already pointed out, was the particular relationship of the younger god to the goddess. He was called "the son and husband of the mother," and considering the evident identity of Izdubar with the god Nin, or Bar, there seems to be a possibility at least that this may be the correct meaning of the name.

[1] Later writers have translated the name as "*Gilgames*," but little dependence can as yet be placed on the interpretation.

CHAPTER III

THE GREAT GODDESS

It is necessary now to point out briefly the identity of the principal goddesses with each other and with the Babylonian Queen.

The usual title of the goddess in Babylonia, Assyria, Egypt and in classical mythology is "The Great Goddess Mother" or "The Mother of the Gods," but she is represented as being both the mother and wife of the gods, and as it is the uniform testimony of the ancients that the various goddesses were all one and the same person, it is a further evidence that the originals of the various gods were only two persons bearing the relation to each other of father and son.

These two originals we have seen to be Cush and his son Nimrod, and the goddess would therefore seem to have been the wife of Cush and the mother of Nimrod. But, as we shall see, she was not only the wife of the former, but both the mother and the wife of the latter, and she is more generally represented as the wife of the younger god.

As it seems clear that Nimrod is the Nin, or the second Bel Nimrod, of the monuments, and the Ninus of history, it follows that "*Semiramis*," the wife and queen of Ninus, must have been the wife of Nimrod, and that as he was the human original of the younger god, so was she the human original of the great goddess, Bilta Niprut, Beltis, Ishtar, etc., who are clearly different aspects of the same goddess.

Both Justin and Castor state that Ninus was the second king of Babylon and the son and successor of Belus, and that, after the death of Ninus, his wife Semiramis succeeded him on the throne of Babylon.[1] This is also testified to by Eusebius and Africanus in their dynasties of Assyrian kings.[2] There was a second Semiramis who lived about the time of the Trojan war, and Sir. H. Rawlinson has found the records of this later queen at Babylon, and on this ground, but with-

[1] Justin, *Historia*, p. 615 ; Castor, Cory's *Fragments*, p. 65.
[2] Cory, pp. 70, 71.

out sufficient reason, has questioned the existence of the first Semiramis. Nothing was more common than for later sovereigns to take the name and endeavour to surround themselves with some of the glory of a celebrated predecessor. We are also told by both Diodorus Siculus and Athenagoras that Semiramis after her death was worshipped by the Babylonians and throughout the East as "*Rhea*," "the great goddess mother."[1] She was also known in Greece as "*Ammas*,"[2] which is the Hellenic form of the Chaldee *Ama*, "the mother." This certainly could not apply to the later Semiramis.

Cronus, *i.e.*, Belus, was king of the Cyclops, who are called "the inventors of tower building,"[3] the first tower being that of Babel. Babylon also was surrounded by a wall with towers at intervals, and, according to Ovid, Justin and others, it was Semiramis who surrounded Babylon with a wall.[4] This is equally ascribed by Megasthenes to Belus,[5] but, as we shall see, Semiramis finished what the second Belus, or Nimrod, had commenced, and she was even more famous as a builder than her husband. It was in consequence of this that so many of the goddesses are represented wearing a mural crown, or crown of towers. Thus Rhea, known also as "*Cybele*," is represented with a turreted crown, and Ovid says that the reason why she wore this crown was because "she was the first who erected towers in cities,"[6] which further identifies her with Semiramis.

Rhea is usually represented as the wife of Saturn, the elder Belus, or Cush, rather than the wife of Nimrod, and we shall see that there are grounds for concluding that Semiramis was the wife of the father before she became the wife of the son, which may have been the primary reason of the title given to the latter, viz., "The Husband of the Mother."[7]

Like Rhea, or Cybele, "*Diana*," or "*Artemis*," is also represented, with a turreted crown,[8] and a scholiast on the *Periergesis* of Dionysius makes Semiramis the same as the goddess "Artemis Despoina."[9] The title "*Despoina*" is the Greek for "the lady" and "*Domina*," "the

[1] Diodorus Siculus, lib. ii. p. 76 ; Athenagoras, *Legatio*, pp. 178, 179 ; *Paschal Chronicle*, vol. i. p. 65.

[2] Hesychius, *sub. voce*, "Ammas."   [3] Pliny, lib. vii. cap. lvi.

[4] Ovid, opera *Metam.*, lib. iv. fab. 4. l. 58, vol. ii. p. 177 ; Hislop, p. 308.

[5] Megasthenes, Cory, pp. 45, 46.

[6] Ovid, op. vol. iii. ; *Fasti*, iv. 219-221 ; Hislop, p. 30.

[7] Bunsen's *Egypt*, vol. i. pp. 438, 439, and Rawlinson's *Herod.*, vol. i. essay x. pp. 625, 626.

[8] *See* figure from Kitto's *Commentary*, vol v. p. 205 ; Hislop, p. 29.

[9] Layard's *Nineveh*, vol. ii. p. 480, note.

lady," was the common title of Rhea or Cybele in Rome,[1] as was "Bilta," or "Beltis," "The Lady," of the goddess in Babylon.

Semiramis is also identified by Athenagoras and Lucian with the Syrian goddess,[2] and the Syrian goddess has been shown by Layard to be the Phœnician *Astarte*,[3] whose name "Astarte," or "*Ashtart*," was in Hebrew "*Ashtoreth*," and Astarte and Ashtoreth are the Phœnician and Hebrew forms of the Babylonian goddess Ishtar.[4] Mr Hislop remarks that it is generally admitted that the last syllable, "*tart*," of the Phœnician "Ashtart," is derived from the Hebrew *tr*, "to go round, surround, or encompass"; the masculine *tor* being used for a border or row of jewels round the head (Parkhurst, *sub voce* No. 11, and also Gensenius). Hence as "*Asha*" is woman, Ashtart and Ashtoreth would mean "the woman who encompasses," alluding to her surrounding cities with walls and towers.[5] This is further confirmed by the fact that Astarte, like Diana and Rhea, is depicted standing on a lion, with a turreted crown,[6] while Diana was called "*Tauropolos*," from *tor*, "a tower," and *pol*, or *poleo*, "turn round," or "surround with towers or fortifications."[7] If, as seems evident, both from the etymology and the turreted crown, this is the meaning of the names "Ashtart" and "Ashtoreth," we may conclude that it is also the meaning of "Ish*tar*," the goddess of war, "who defends from attacks,"[8] for "*Isha*," like "*Asha*," signifies "woman."

Astarte, according to Sanchoniathon, was the Babylonian *Aphrodite*, or *Venus*,[9] and Ishtar was identified by the Babylonians with the planet Venus.[10] Pausanias also, speaking of the temple of Vulcan at Athens, says, "Near this is the temple of the celestial Venus who was first worshipped by the Assyrians and, after them, by the Paphians of Cyprus, and the Phœnicians who inhabited the city of Ascalon in Palestine."[11] Under the name of "*Mylitta*," virgins were prostituted to her in Babylon, and the same was done in Cyprus in honour of Venus.[12]

Bel, under the title of "*Beel Samen*," was called "The Lord of

---

[1] Ovid, *Fasti*, lib. iv. p. 340 ; Hislop, p. 30.

[2] Athenagoras, *Leg.*, vol. ii. p. 179 ; Lucian, *De Dea Syria*, vol. iii. p. 382 ; Hislop, p. 307.

[3] Layard, *Nineveh*, vol. ii. p. 456.

[4] *Five Great Monarchies*, vol. i. p. 138.   [5] Hislop, pp. 307, 308.

[6] Layard, *Nineveh and Its Remains*, vol. ii. p. 456.   [7] Hislop, p. 308.

[8] Rawlinson's *Five Great Monarchies*, vol. i. p. 139.

[9] *Sanchoniathon*, Cory, p. 14.   [10] Rawlinson, *Herod.*, vol. i. pp. 619, 620.

[11] Pausanias, lib. i. *Attica*, cap. xiv. ; Hislop, p. 157.

[12] Herod., lib. i. cap. cxcix.

Heaven," [1] Ishtar was called "The Mistress of Heaven," while Beltis, under the name of "*Melkat Ashemin*," was known to the Babylonians and Jews as "The Queen of Heaven." [2] This was also the title of the Egyptian "*Isis*," who in later Egyptian mythology was identified with the moon, as was Osiris with the sun. Isis is, in fact, the Greek form of *Isha*, "the woman." [3]

Isis also is the same as "*Ceres*," [4] and the rites of Isis and Ceres were similar, [5] as were those of "Rhea," or "Cybele," and "Astarte." [6]

Thus we have "Rhea," "Cybele," "Diana," "Astarte," or "Ashtoreth," "Ishtar," "Venus," or "Aphrodite," "Isis" and "Ceres," all more or less identified with Semiramis and the Babylonian goddess, and with each other, and the relationship of Rhea to Saturn, of Venus to Adonis, Isis to Osiris, etc., still further confirms this identity.

We have seen that Baal Tammuz was also called "Adon," "The Lord," who was the Greek Adonis, and Adon with the points is pronounced in Hebrew "*Athon*." Now, speaking of local names in the district of Laodicea, Eustathius states that "Athan is God." [7] The feminine of Athan is "*Athana*," which, in the Attic dialect, is "*Athena*," which signifies "The Lady," as does "Adon," or "Athan," "The Lord." [8] This identifies "*Minerva*," whose name in Athens was "Athena," with the wife of Adon, or Tammuz, viz., Ishtar, and therefore with Beltis, whose name also signifies "The Lady." Minerva was the "*Neith*" of the Egyptians, the goddess of Sais, and was called "the mother of the gods," [9] like Rhea, Isis and others. The Minerva of the Egyptians was also the mother of Apollo, [10] who was the same as Horus, which shows that Minerva, or Neith, was identical with Isis, the mother of Horus.

The name of the goddess "*Juno*" is derived from the Chaldee *D'Iune*, which, without the article, becomes "June" or "Juno." "Diune," or "Dione," was a name given to Venus, and Ovid uses the title for the Babylonian Venus, [11] while Julius Firmicus also identifies Venus with Juno. He says, "The Assyrians and part of the Africans wish 'the air' to have the supremacy of the elements, for they have

---

[1] Hislop, p. 165.
[2] Jeremiah, vii. 18 ; Parkhurst, *Hebrew Lexicon*, pp. 402, 403 ; Hislop, p. 264.
[3] Hislop, p. 103, note.　　　[4] Lemprière, *Isis*.
[5] *Ibid.*　　　[6] Hislop, p. 304.
[7] Eustathius, *Periergesis* of Dionysius, iv. 915 ; Apud Bryant, vol. iii. p. 140.
[8] Hislop, pp. 20, 21, note.
[9] Wilkinson, vol. iv. p. 285 ; Hislop, p. 21 ; Lemprière, *Neith*.
[10] Lemprière, *Minerva*.
[11] Ovid, *Fasti*, lib. ii. pp. 461-464 ; vol. iii. p. 113.

consecrated the same under the name of Juno, or the virgin Venus."[1]

Diune is the Chaldee for "dove."[2] Doves were sacred to Juno, and in a medal given by Layard[3] the Babylonian goddess is represented with two doves on her head, while on the reverse there is a dove bearing an olive branch in its mouth. In another case[4] the goddess Cybele, or Rhea, is represented with a conventional branch in her hand, both representations symbolising the goddess as "the branch bearer" (*see* woodcuts). Now the name "Semiramis" signifies "the branch bearer," being derived from *Se*, "the," *emir*, "branch,' *'amit*, "bearer," the word in its Greek form becoming Semiramis;[5] and, according to Hesychius, Semiramis was the name given by the Greeks to wild pigeons or doves.[6] This further tends to identify Semi-

LAYARD.   BRYANT.

ramis with Juno, Rhea and Venus, and there can be little doubt, therefore, that Semiramis was a name or form of the Pagan goddess.

It is not to be supposed, however, that "Semiramis" was the original name of the Babylonian queen, any more than "Ninus" was the original name of the Babylonian king. Even the very name "Nimrod," "the leopard subduer," could not have been given him until after he had signalised himself as a great hunter; while the name "Nin," or "Ninus," "The Son," could not have been given him until after his death, when, for reasons which will be noticed hereafter, he was deified under the title of "The Son." So also with the name "Semiramis," "the branch bearer." The branch is the recognised symbol of "a son," and olive branches in particular are, to this day, a term for children; the name was therefore given to the deified queen as "The Mother, or Bearer of The Son." She had also a similar name given to her in Babylon as the wife of

[1] Jul. Firm., *De Errore*, cap. iv. p. 9.
[2] Hislop, pp. 78, 79.
[3] Layard, *Nineveh and Babylon*, p. 250.
[4] Bryant, vol. iii. p. 84.
[5] Hislop, p. 79.   [6] Hesychius, *Semiramis.*

Bel Merodach, viz., "*Zerbanit*," signifying "The Mother of the Seed," from *Zero*, "seed," and *banit*, "genetrix." [1]

In accordance with the genius of Paganism, the symbol of the dove bearing an olive branch had a double meaning. It is evidently taken from the incident in the history of the Deluge, the events of which, as before remarked, are so intimately interwoven with every ancient mythology, and, as is well known, the olive branch was the symbol of peace throughout the ancient world. The symbol, therefore, as applied to the goddess, signified that she was not only the mother of the seed, but the goddess of peace and mercy. Hence she was called "*Aphrodite*," the "wrath subduer," from *aph*, "wrath," and *radah*, "to subdue," *radite*, being the feminine emphatic.[2] So also she was "*Mylitta*," "the Mediatrix;" "*Amarusia*," "the mother of gracious acceptance," from *ama*, "mother," and *rutza*, the active participle of *retza*, "to accept graciously"; "*Bona Dea*," "the good goddess," etc., upon whose altars no bloody sacrifices were allowed to be offered.[3]

Other forms of the goddess might be mentioned, but the above is sufficient to identify the deified queen of Babylon with the principal goddesses of the great nations of antiquity, and to show their connection with each other. Rawlinson, speaking of the Great Goddess Mother, says, "She was Astarte in Phœnicia (*Cic nat Deorum*, p. 3) who is even said by Sanchoniathon to have had a cow's head, like Athor, the Venus of Egypt, whence called Astoreth Karnaim.[4] She was Venus Urania, said by Pausanias to have been chiefly honoured by the Assyrians." He also identifies her with "Anaitis, with Ceres, with The Queen of Heaven, The Moon, Rhea, or Cybele, Juno, Diana, Lucina, Isis and Athor, the Phœnician Tanith, Minerva and the Egyptian Neith." [5]

Apuleius, when he was initiated into the mysteries, says that Isis revealed herself to him in the following words, "I am nature, the parent of all things, mistress of all the elements, the beginning of ages, Sovereign of the Gods, queen of the manes, the first of

[1] Rawlinson's *Herod.*, vol. i. p. 630.

[2] Hislop, p. 158, note. The Greeks supposed the name to be derived from their word *aphros*, "foam," and hence said that Venus was born from the foam of the sea, but such a derivation is unmeaning, and, like other Greek explanations of the characters of their gods, is based on ignorance of the original meaning, which should be sought from the language of Chaldea.

[3] *Ibid.*

[4] Karnaim, "horned," the word having the same derivation as *kronos*.

[5] Rawlinson's *Herod.*, vol. ii. essay i. pp. 537-539.

heavenly beings; my divinity, uniform in itself, is honoured under numerous forms, various rites and different names. The Phrygians call me Pessimuntca, 'mother goddess'; the Athenians, 'Autochthones,' the Cecropian 'Minerva'; the people of Cyprus, 'Paphian Venus'; the arrow-armed Cretans, 'Diana Dictyana'; the Sicilians, 'Stygian Proserpine'; the Eleusinians, 'Ancient Ceres'; others, 'Juno,' 'Bellona,' 'Hecate,' 'Rhammusia'; but the sun-illumined Ethiopians and the Egyptians, renowned for ancient lore, worshipping me with due ceremonies, call me by my real name, 'Queen Isis!'"[1]

It is worthy of note that this revelation especially speaks of the Ethiopians, or Cushites, and the Egyptians, who were largely composed of the same race, as the true centres of the ancient idolatry.

This revelation is also in accordance with a passage in the Acts, where Diana is said to be "She whom all Asia and the world worshippeth,"[2] which could not mean that she was universally worshipped under the name of Diana, but that it was recognised that she was the same goddess who was worshipped under a variety of names, and called in consequence "*Dea Myrionymus*," "the goddess with ten thousand names."

The history of Ninus and Semiramis by Ctesias corroborates much that has been deduced from other sources, and explains, among other things, why so many forms of the great goddess are represented with a mural or turreted crown. It also throws some light on other points which have to be referred to hereafter.

The objection which has been raised against the history of Ctesias, viz., that Ninus and Semiramis can be clearly identified with the Babylonian god and goddess, is the same objection which Wilkinson has raised to the fact of Osiris having had a human original.[3] But the consentient evidence, showing that the originals of the great god and goddess were a human king and queen, is conclusive, and cannot be set aside, or explained away. We might as well say that there was no such king as Nimrod, because he can be identified with various Pagan gods, or that the sons of the patriarch Noah, because they were deified, never existed!

The worship of ancestors and deification of heroes have been characteristic of mankind in all ages, and the actions ascribed to the gods are essentially those of human beings, while the conquests of Ninus, of Bacchus and of Osiris are those of a human king, and in

---

[1] *Wilkinson*, by Birch, vol. iii. p. 99.   [2] Acts xix. 27.
[3] *See* Appendix A, where the nature of these objections is considered.

exact accordance with those of Nimrod. The history of Ctesias, in short, is in strict keeping with the rest of the evidence and corroboratory of it, and against that evidence nothing can be offered except the mere assertion that the originals of the Babylonian gods could not have been a human king and queen. It is said, indeed, that the Assyrian monuments make no mention of Ninus and Semiramis as a human king and queen; but considering the secrecy with which the human origin of the gods, who were subsequently identified with the sun, moon and stars and the powers of nature, was kept, it would have been a wonder if anything had been thus openly recorded which would have betrayed it. For the same reason we may be sure that the Chaldean priesthood would not have revealed to Herodotus the secret; but it is significant that they ascribe some of the principal works of Babylon, attributed by Ctesias to Semiramis, to two queens, Semiramis and Neitocris [1] (Neith, the victorious),[2] the names respectively of the deified queen in Babylon and in Egypt.

Finally, the fact that so many of the goddesses are represented with turreted crowns, and the reason given for this, viz., that they first erected towers in cities, implies not only a human original, but associates that original with the first builders of fortified cities, Nimrod and his queen. In short, if the human original of the Pagan god known as Ninus, Bel Nimrud, etc., was Nimrod, we must conclude that the goddess associated with him was his queen.

Ctesias was physician of Artaxerxes Memnon, and had therefore access to the Babylonian archives, which, according to custom, had been in the charge of the Chaldean priesthood, and it is far more probable that he obtained the story, hitherto kept secret, from those archives, than that, without a shadow of reason for so doing, he invented it.[3]

The objection is made to his history that it is composed of Arian, Semitic, Egyptian and Greek appellations.[4] But nothing was more common among the ancient writers when they understood the signification of names, to translate them into their own language, as in the case of Eratosthenes' list of Egyptian kings, which is largely composed of Greek appellations. This is no more evidence of forgery

---

[1] Herod., lib. i. caps. clxxxiv-clxxxviii. It seems clear that Herodotus confused the original Semiramis with the later queen of that name.

[2] Eratosthenes translates "Neitocris," by "Minerva the victorious," Minerva being the Neith of the Greeks (Wilkinson's *Egyptians*, vol. iv. p. 47).

[3] Lenormant, *Anc. Hist. of East*, vol i. p. 369.

[4] Rawlinson's *Five Great Monarchies*, vol. i. p. 165, note.

E

than the fact that English writers translate into English the soubriquets of foreign kings—such as " Charles the Bold." Ctesias, no doubt, sometimes did this, leaving at other times the Semitic Assyrian names; but it is far more probable that the Greek transcribers are responsible for the Hellenic names, the Greeks having always been the chief offenders in this respect. Ctesias may have made mistakes, especially in his dates, which might be expected from the fact that he had to interpret the Babylonian records without the aid of the Chaldean priesthood, but it does not invalidate the general truth of his history.

The objections, therefore, to his history have no real weight, while the fact that Ninus and Semiramis can be identified with the god and goddess of Babylon is only in accordance with the evidence which shows that Nimrod and his queen were the human originals of those deities and it is the strongest proof of the authenticity of his history.

M. Lenormant has suggested that Ctesias obtained his history from the Persians and that it is a Persian tradition.[1] There is nothing to support this and no trace of it in Persian records, although, if it was the tradition of a people living in such close contiguity to Babylonia, there would be every reason to believe that it was founded upon fact. But the Persians, as remarked by M. Lenormant, were no historians, and this history is exact, detailed and circumstantial. The fact that it was questioned by Aristotle, who opposed everything connected with mythology and was yet generally accepted as true by the Greeks, is an evidence that its authenticity could not be shaken at the time. Moreover, the Greeks had heard of " Ninus, the son of Belus," the first king of Babylon before the time of Ctesias,[2] and therefore Ninus was neither an invention of Ctesias nor of the Persians.

Had M. Lenormant and others recognised the accumulative force of the evidence which proves that the originals of the great god and goddess of Paganism were a human king and queen, they would hardly have questioned the general truth of the history of Ctesias.

But both the history of Ctesias, and all that we have hitherto deduced, will be remarkably confirmed when we come to consider the origin, rise and subsequent development of the ancient idolatry.

Ctesias represents Ninus as first attacking and subduing the people of Babylonia with the aid of an Arab chieftain, who, like himself, was jealous of the power of the Babylonians, *i.e.*, the people who

[1] *Anc. Hist. of the East*, vol. i. p. 368.   [2] Herod., lib. i. cap. vii.

then occupied Babylonia, who were probably Medes, or people of Turanian origin.

Ninus is said to have taken the king of Babylonia and his children and put them to death. Thence he marched on Assyria, and, having terrified the inhabitants by the sack of some towns, compelled them to submit. Thence he marched on Media, took the king prisoner and crucified him, and in seventeen years made himself master of the countries between the Mediterranean Sea and the Indus.

After these conquests ("being made strong"[1]) he built Nineveh and called it by his name,[2] making it the capital of his dominions and surrounding it with a wall and towers of vast extent. It appears to have been at first simply an enclosed tract of country for defensive purposes, and its dimensions, as given by Ctesias, accord with the description of it in the Bible, viz., "an exceeding great city of three days' journey" (that is round it); a day's journey being twenty miles, which would make it about sixty miles in circumference.[3] Similarly Ctesias describes it as eighteen miles long by ten miles in breadth, and its circumference would thus be fifty-six miles. Hence it was capable of containing everything necessary for the lengthened support of the army and people of Ninus, with their families and their flocks and herds. This accords with the fact that at the time of the prophet Jonah it contained "120,000 children who knew not their right hand from their left (representing a population of about 600,000), and also much cattle"; which shows that it was even then more of the character of an enclosed track of land than a closely-built city.

It will be seen that the history so far strictly accords with the scriptural history of Nimrod.

After this, Ninus attacked Bactria. In this war he met with Semiramis, the wife of *Oannes*, governor of Syria, which is the name by which the ancients spoke of *Assyria*. Ninus took Semiramis from her husband and married her. Shortly afterwards he died and left her sole mistress of the empire.

Now "Oannes" was a name given to Cush as the great teacher, and it would appear from this that Ninus, or Nimrod, took his father's wife and married her. This is in exact accordance with the

---

[1] See *ante*, p. 24.

[2] Nin-neveh, "the habitation of Nin, or Ninus." The chief part of its ruins are called "Nimrod" to this day (Layard's *Nineveh*, vol. i. p. 7).

[3] Smith, *Dict. of the Bible*, "Nineveh."

story of Vulcan and his wife Venus, who was taken from him by Mars.[1] For, as we have seen, Vulcan was Cush, Mars was Bel Merodach, or Nimrod, and Venus was Semiramis. Other traditions, to be noticed later, confirm this conclusion.

The first thing that Semiramis did on the death of Ninus was to build, or complete, the building of Babylon, and the account proceeds to give the well-known dimensions of the city, with its walls and towers. The history also gives a detailed account of the vast works within the city, describing the method of architecture, and the temporary diversion of the River Euphrates which flowed through it, in order to form a tunnel beneath the bed of the river. Ctesias also says that two gates of bronze which closed either end of the tunnel were in existence at the time of the Persian conquest. Semiramis then made an expedition against the Medes, who had revolted, and both there and in Persia constructed various vast works, making roads and canals for the supply of cities. She is also represented as subduing Egypt and Ethiopia, although this was really the act of her husband. Finally she made an expedition against India, in which she was completely defeated with the total loss of her army, after which she devoted herself to the completion of her great building works.[2]

Alexander the Great found her name inscribed on the frontiers of Scythia with the inscription:—" I ruled the Empire of Ninus, which reaches eastward to the River Hinaman (Indus), southward to the land of incense and myrrh (Arabia), northward to the Saces and Sogdians. Before me no Assyrian had seen a sea; I have seen four that no one had approached, so far were they distant. I compelled the rivers to run where I wished and directed them to places where they were required. I made barren lands fertile by watering them with my rivers. I built impregnable fortresses. With iron tools I made roads across impassable rocks. I opened roads for my chariots where the very wild beasts had been unable to pass. In the midst of these occupations I have found time for pleasure and love."[3] It is well known that Semiramis was famous for her beauty and immorality, and was a fitting original for the goddess " Venus Aphrodite."

---

[1] Lemprière, *Vulcan.*

[2] Lenormant, *Anc. Hist. of East,* vol. i. pp. 364, 367.

[3] Recorded by Polyænus, Lenormant, vol. i. p. 367. M. Lenormant discredits this statement of Polyænus, but to accuse every ancient author of deliberate and motiveless falsehood when his statements do not agree with the author's own theories is wholly unjustifiable. Polyænus states as a fact what it is inconceivable he should, without object or reason, have invented, and his statement is therefore the strongest confirmation of the history of Ctesias.

The history concludes by saying that Semiramis abdicated in favour of her son, and disappeared, being changed into a dove (the symbol of Juno), and was worshipped as a goddess.

These accounts are confirmed by Strabo, who says that Ninus built Nineveh, which he describes as much larger than Babylon, and that Semiramis built the latter city. "These sovereigns," he says, "were masters of Asia. Many other works of Semiramis besides those at Babylon are extant in almost every part of the continent, as, for example, artificial mounds which are called the mounds of Semiramis, and walls and fortresses with subterranean passages, cisterns for water, roads to facilitate the ascent of mountains, canals communicating with rivers and lakes, roads and bridges."[1]

[1] Strabo, vol. iii. lib. xvi. chaps. ii. and iii.

CHAPTER IV

THE GOD KINGS OF EGYPT AND BABYLON

WE now propose to show more fully the identity of the God Kings of Egypt and Babylon, and the intimate relations of the early history of the two countries.

We have seen that Cush, the first Belus or Cronus, was not only the father of the gods, but was " Hea, the Lord of Understanding and Teacher of Mankind," " The All-wise Belus," Hermes, or Thoth, " The God of all Celestial Knowledge," " The God of Intellect," who " first arranged in order and in a scientific manner those things which belong to religion and the worship of the gods," etc.; which implies that he must have been the first originator of idolatry. This idolatry differed indeed from its subsequent form, inasmuch as he and his son were not then deified; but it appears to have been the same in substance. It would also appear that his son Nimrod, who conquered the habitable world, was the chief propagator of this idolatry.

One of the chief features of the subsequent idolatry was the obscene Phallic worship, and Osiris, Bacchus and other forms of the deified king were pre-eminently Phallic gods, or gods of generation, a huge figure of the Phallus being carried in the processions made in their honour; [1] from which it would appear that Nimrod was the first propagator of this worship. He seems also to have been the first propagator of the Sabæan worship, which consisted of the worship of the sun, moon and stars, and was intimately connected with Phallic worship; the sun being regarded as the great creative power and source of life and generation, of which the Phallus was the manifestation in the animal world.

Speaking of Tammuz, one of the forms of the deified king,—Maimonides, who was deeply read in the learning of the Chaldeans, says,—" When the false prophet named Thammuz preached to a certain king that he should worship the seven stars and the twelve signs of the zodiac, that king ordered him to be put to a terrible death. On the night of his death all the images assembled from the

[1] Herod., lib. ii. cap. xlviii.

end of the earth unto the temple of Babylon, to the great golden image of the sun, which was suspended between heaven and earth. That image prostrated itself in the midst of the temple, and so did all the images around it, while it related to them all that had happened to Thammuz. The images wept and lamented all night long, and then in the morning they flew away, each to his own temple again to the ends of the earth. And hence arose the custom every year, on the first day of the month Thammuz, to mourn and weep for Thammuz." [1]

This, of course, is the allegorical account of Pagan mythology; but the violent death of Thammuz, Osirus, Ninus, Bacchus, and other forms of the deified monarch, is amply attested, and the memory of it formed the chief feature in the subsequent Pagan worship.[2]

The account, however, implies that the religion originated by Cush and propagated by Nimrod consisted of the worship of the sun, moon and stars, which were regarded as the origin of the powers of nature. It would seem also that they were the originators of the ancient magic and necromancy which was one of the principal features of the ancient Paganism, and which received the name of "Accadian" from "Accad," one of the first cities built by the Cushite monarch.

That they were the originators of these superstitions is confirmed by other traditions; but before referring to them it is necessary to point out the original home of the Cushite race.

The land of Cush, or Æthiops, was Æthiopia, and the word which in the Old Testament is translated "Æthiopia" is in the original "Cush," and "the Æthiopian" is "the Cushite." Now it is supposed by many people that Æthiopia was only the country of that name in Africa. But in Gen. ii. Æthiopia, or Cush, is said to be encompassed by one of the four rivers which branched off from each other at the site of the Garden of Eden, one of which was the Euphrates and another the Tigris. The Æthiopia there referred to must, therefore, have been in Asia, and as shown by the author of the article "Eden" in Smith's *Dictionary of the Bible*, included Arabia and also Susiana, or Chusistan, to the east of the Euphrates, which, as its name implies, was also the land of Cush.[3] The names, "*Havilah*" and "*Seba*," two of the sons of Cush, and "*Dedan*," his grandson, were the names respectively of portions of Northern, Southern and Eastern

---

[1] More *Nevochim*, p. 426.

[2] See *infra*, chap. xii., "The Death of the Pagan God."

[3] Smith's *Dict. of the Bible*, "Eden"; *see also* Hale's *Chron.*, vol. i. pp. 354, 379.

Arabia, implying therefore that Arabia was the first home of the Cushite race. The reason why the African Æthiopia is best known to us is that the Asiatic Æthiopia was absorbed in the Babylonian Empire, which was not the case with African Æthiopia ; and the inhabitants of the latter, and probably many of those of the interior of Africa, are, to this day, the best representatives of the once great Cushite race.

Strabo says that the ancient Greeks called the whole of the Southern nations toward the Indian Ocean "Æthiopia," adding that "if the moderns have confined the term to those who dwelt *near Egypt* this must not be allowed to interfere with the meaning of the ancients."[1] Again he says, "The Æthiopians were considered as occupying all the south coasts of both Asia and Africa, and were divided by the Arabian Gulf, or Red Sea, into Eastern and Western, Asiatic and African."[2] So also Stephanus of Byzantium says that "Æthiopia was the first established country on earth" (*i.e.*, it was the kingdom of Nimrod), and that "the Æthiopians were the first who introduced the worship of the gods and established law."[3] The old Sanskrit geographers also speak of two lands of Cush, or Æthiopias, which they called "Cusha dwipa within" and "Cusha dwipa without." The first extended from the shores of the Mediterranean and mouths of the Nile to Serhind on the borders of India, and they make it one of the seven great dwipas, or divisions of the world. The other sub dwipa, or "Cusha dwipa without," was beyond the Straits of Bab-el-Mandeb, that is, Upper Egypt, or African Æthiopia.[4]

Arabia is generally considered the home, and Arab the name, of the descendants of Ishmael. But Professor Baldwin has pointed out that there were two races in Arabia, viz., an old race called "Aribah," from whence Arabia received its name, and those of Mahomet's race called "Moustaribes," who, according to tradition, were grafted on to the original stock by a marriage of Ishmael with a princess of the Cushite race. The language of the old race has been discovered, and is called "Himyaric." A remarkable inscription written in this language has been deciphered. It was found in the tomb of a Himyaric queen, and proves to be of the time of the great famine during the governorship of Joseph in the land of Egypt.[5] The language was still extant a century or two before Christ, and other inscriptions of that time have been found and deciphered. Professor Baldwin says, "It is found also in the ruins

---

[1] Strabo, book i. chap. ii. § 28.   [2] Strabo, book i. chap. ii. §§ 22-26.
[3] Baldwin's *Prehistoric Nations*, pp. 61, 62.   [4] *Ibid.*, p. 64.
[5] *See* text of inscription given by Saville, *Truth of the Bible*, p. 270.

of Chaldea, and in remote antiquity it seems to have been spoken throughout most of Western Asia, and also in Hindustan, where it is probably represented at the present time, in a corrupted form, by the group of languages called 'Dravidian.'[1] It cannot properly be classed with the Arabic, but is closely related to the old Egyptian.[2] In the terminology of linguistic science this language is called Æthiopic, Cushite, and sometimes Hamitic."[3] It appears therefore to have been the same as that known as "Accadian," or ancient Chaldean, which is the language found in the ruins of Chaldea, and which was that of the primitive inhabitants of Babylonia.

Sir H. Rawlinson confirms this. He says that the Himyaric language is closely allied to the Ethiopian, or Cushite, and is believed to be Cushite. He further says that the most ancient records of Babylonia are written in a language, viz., that of the *Accadians*, which presents an affinity to the dialects of Africa, and that it is more Hamitic than Semitic.[4] Canon Rawlinson says that "this language is predominantly Cushite in its vocabulary," and that "its closest analogies are with the Ethiopian dialects, such as the Mahra of Arabia, the Wolaitsa of Abyssinia, and the ancient language of Egypt."[5]

Modern writers have proposed to call this language "Sumerian," because in later times it was confined to the people of Sumer, or Southern Babylonia, while the language of the people of Accad, or Northern Babylonia, had then become Semitic. But we shall retain the name "Accadian" as being better known, and because, as will be pointed out, it was probably the original language both of Accad and Sumer.[6]

This language, although a dead language in the time of the later Assyrian Monarchy, was still used by them for magical incantations, being regarded as a sacred tongue and of divine efficacy,[7] which implies that the Accadians were the originators of that magic. It

[1] The languages known as "Dravidian" belong to Lower and Central India, which are the chief seats of the Phallic worship, the origin of which can be clearly traced to the first Cushites, and where also exist those Cyclopean temples or other buildings which were so characteristic of that people. (*See* chap. v.)
[2] There were two races in Egypt, the "Mizraimites," or descendants of Mizraim, and the "Egyptians," who we shall see were Cushites. The ancient Egyptian would therefore be closely related to the Cushite language.
[3] Baldwin, *Prehist. Nations*, p. 75.
[4] Rawlinson's *Herod.*, vol i. p. 646, note 655-660.
[5] Rawlinson's *Five Great Monarchies*, vol. i. p. 61.
[6] *See* Appendix D, "*The Accadians and Nimrod.*"
Lenormant, *Chaldean Magic*, chap. i. p. 2.

would seem also that the Aribah, the ancient Cushite inhabitants of Arabia, were of the same race as the ancient Accadians.

These ancient Cushites of the Arabian peninsula originally consisted of twelve tribes—Ad, Thamoud (probably so named after Thamus or Tammuz), Tasm, Djadis, Amlik (Amalek), Oumayim, Abil, Djourhoum, Wabar, Jasm, Antem and Hashem. From this it would appear that the Amalekites who occupied the country to the extreme north of Arabia and the south of Palestine were of this race.[1] According to the Arabian tradition, the father of this old race was a king called "*Ad*," who built a great city that became rich and powerful, but it was destroyed on account of the unbelieving wickedness of the people. "Old as Ad" is a term used in Arabia for remote antiquity,[2] implying therefore that he was the first of the race and probably Cush himself. It may also be remarked that *Ad* is an Accadian word meaning "father,"[3] which would be just the name which would be given to the progenitor of these Cushites, and it further tends to identify them with the Accadians.

Another account speaks of these Adites as very powerful, that they were *giants*, and that their king, *Sheddad Ben Ad* (the son of Ad), *reigned over the whole world*.[4] This exactly accords with the character of Nimrod, who was himself a giant. "These traditions," says Professor Baldwin, "quoted as authentic by all Mahommedan writers on Arabia, represent the Adites, Thamoudites and their contemporaries as enterprising, rich and powerful; that they had great cities and wonderful magnificence, and declare that they finally disappeared from the earth under the curse of heaven for their pride and arrogant idolatry."[5]

All this accords with the character of the Cushite or Ethiopian race, who, by all traditions, are represented to be the founders of the primitive idolatry. To this day the ruins of mighty cities are found in the interior of Arabia, and Professor Baldwin says that the Arab traditions speak of the Adites, or Aribah, as "wonderful builders," a characteristic peculiar to the Cushite founders of the mighty cities of

[1] Amalek was also the name of one of the sons of Esau, but as the Bible speaks of the Amalekites as quite distinct from the Edomites, and as the Israelites were told to destroy the Amalekites, but not to meddle with the Edomites, we must conclude that the Amalekites were the Cushites of that name. (*See* Deut. ii. 5, 6; xxiii. 7; and Smith's *Dict. of the Bible*, "Amalekites".)

[2] Baldwin, *Prehistoric Nations*, p. 108, p. 72, note.

[3] Lenormant, *Chaldean Magic*, p. 300.

[4] Arabian account quoted by Col. Howard Vyse; *Pyramids of Ghizeh*, vol. ii., App., p. 135.   [5] Baldwin, *Prehist. Nations*, p. 104.

Babylon and Nineveh, the colossal temples of Karnac and Luxor in Upper Egypt, the chief seat of the Cushite Egyptians, and those of Salsette, Ellora, etc., in India. Such buildings are spoken of as "Cyclopean," the Cyclops being regarded as the great builders of antiquity, and, as we have seen, must be identified with the Cushite race. These traditions also speak of the Aribah as having magnificent cities and sumptuous palaces, and the architecture of the ruins of some of these cities is identical with that of ancient Egypt. The Greeks called the country " *Saba*," and the people " *Sabœans*," and the Sabæan idolatry was instituted by the Cushite race. *Saba*, or *Seba*, was a son of Cush (Gen. x. 7), and the ruins of an ancient city of that name has been discovered in the interior of Yemen.[1]

The Cushite race, as we have seen, were the original founders of the sciences of mathematics and astronomy, and the wisdom of the Chaldees was of world-wide renown. It is also well known that much of our knowledge of these sciences has been derived from the Arabians, who, we may presume, received it from the ancient Aribah, or Cushite, race.

It would therefore appear that the Aribah or Adites, the ancient inhabitants of the Arabian peninsula, previous to the arrival of the Semitic Arabs, were the Cushite founders of the first Babylonian Empire; and that Arabia, lying midway between African and Asiatic Æthiopia, was the first home of the Cushite race. Hence in the account of Ctesias, it is said that Ninus was accompanied by an Arab, *i.e.*, Aribah, or Cushite, chieftain (probably one of the other sons of Cush), when he started on his conquests, which also implies that he started *from* Arabia.

This accords also with the Arab and Iranian traditions of " *Djemschid* " and " *Zohak*." The Iranian tradition speaks of the reign of Djemschid, when there was a tendency "to build large cities and to organise religious worship with a tendency to natural-ism," or nature worship. Djemschid is also stated to have established idolatry, and the description, therefore, would perfectly apply to Cush. Immediately after this, the country, *i.e.*, Iran, the original seat of the Bactrians, Medes, and other races conquered by Nimrod, was con-quered by an Arabian, *i.e.*, an Aribah, or Cushite, conqueror called Zohak, who is described as a sanguinary tyrant, a corrupter of manners, and a teacher of a monstrous and obscene religion (Phallic worship) involving human sacrifices.[2]

---

[1] Baldwin, *Prehist. Nations*, pp. 78, 80-84.
[2] Lenormant, *Anc. Hist. of East*, vol. ii. p. 22.

All this exactly agrees with the character of Ninus, or Nimrod, who crucified his prisoners, and was the propagator of the religion of his father, who originated human sacrifices. M. Lenormant considers that the tradition refers to the conquests of Nimrod.

Zohak is called "the Tasi," and Taz is said to have been the father of the Tasis.[1] Now "Tasm," which is the plural of Taz, was one of the Adite tribes, and Zohak must therefore have been an Adite or Cushite.

The Arabs have a similar tradition of Zohak. They say that his conquests extended eastward from Arabia, the home of the Cushite race, to the borders of Hindustan, which was equally the boundary of the conquests of Ninus. Moreover, they say that he and his successors ruled the empire for a period of 260 years.[2] This is nearly exactly the period assigned by Berosus to the first Chaldean kingdom, which, of course, was that founded by Nimrod.[3]

It is also stated that he dethroned Djemschid and married his sister, a story which has the appearance of being a slightly altered version of the account given by Ctesias of the relations of Ninus, or Nimrod, Oannes, or Cush, and Semiramis.[4]

Making allowances for the slight inaccuracies and misrepresentations which are involved in all traditions of long standing, there seems to be little doubt that these traditions refer to the history of Nimrod and that he was the Aribah or Adite king Zohak, and that Djemschid was Cush.

It seems clear, therefore, that Arabia was the first seat of the Cushite race and that they were the ancient Adites or Aribah from whom Arabia received its name, and that under Nimrod, who appears to be the same as Shedad-ben-ad and Zohak, they issued from Arabia and conquered the whole of Western Asia, including the peoples inhabiting the Tigris and Euphrates valleys.

It appears to be equally clear that these Cushites were the same people as the Accadians or ancient Chaldeans. Accad, in short, was one of the cities founded by Nimrod at the beginning of his kingdom (Gen. x. 10), the name in later times being extended to a considerable district of country. Everything also points to the fact that Hea, *i.e.*, Cush, was the originator of the magic, necromancy and sorcery which formed the principal feature of the worship of the gods, and the fact that the forms of this magic and sorcery were carefully preserved

[1] Baldwin, pp. 108, 109.
[2] "Chronicle of Tabiri," Baldwin's *Prehistoric Nations*, p. 108.
[3] *See* chap. xiv.   [4] See *ante*, chap. iii. pp. 67, 68.

in the Accadian language implies that it was the language of the originator. Moreover, this language was the same, or similar, to the Himyaric, which was the language of the ancient Cushites of Arabia.

Cush also, in his deified forms as Hea and Nebo, was the god of writing and science, and the symbol of both these gods was the wedge or arrow-head, the distinctive sign of the cuneiform writing, indicating that Cush was the inventor of that writing, and as this writing is universally admitted to have been of Accadian origin, the Accadians must have been Cushites. Hea, in fact, was an essentially Accadian deity, and the general voice of antiquity attributes the origin of Paganism and the worship of the gods, which archæology traces to the Accadians, to the Cushite race and to Babylon, the beginning of Nimrod's empire.

But although on these grounds we must conclude that the ancient Accadians were the people of Cush and Nimrod, there are those who assert that the Accadians were not Cushites, but of Turanian race, while some even go so far as to deny that there was ever a Cushite conquest of Babylonia and Assyria. The facts, however, on which these conclusions are based are capable of a very different explanation, and as the question is of some importance it is more fully considered in an appendix.[1]

We will now proceed to point out the intimate connection of the Cushites with the early history of Egypt.

Sir Henry Rawlinson and other writers have noticed the close resemblance of the gods of Egypt to those of Babylon, the similarity of their alphabets and vocabularies, and the fact that the origin of letters and writing is attributed to each. The cuneiform writing of the ancient Accadians or Cushites of Babylonia was used all over Western Asia and in Egypt before 1500 B.C., and Colonel Conder has shown strong reasons for concluding that it was even used by the Israelites at the time of their Exodus from Egypt.[2] The term "Ra," the ancient Chaldean, *i.e.*, Cushite, equivalent of the Semitic "*Il*," "God," was also the name of God in Egypt, who in that country was especially identified with the Sun, and the Accadian or Cushite term, "*Ka ra*," "gate of God," was the ordinary suffix to the titles of the Egyptian kings, and signified "proceeding from God" (an evidently cognate meaning), and hence "born of" or "son of the Sun god." In short, as previously pointed out, the ancient Accadian or Cushite

---

[1] Appendix D, "*The Accadians and Nimrod.*"
[2] Conder, *The First Bible*, pp. 5, 93 *et seq.*

language was closely allied to the early Egyptian and to the Ethiopian dialects of Africa.[1] It is also worthy of note that among the ancient Chaldean remains, figures, apparently of priests wearing a mitre, have been found holding in their hands the "*crux ansata*," which in Egyptian sculptures is always shown in the hands of gods and kings as a symbol of their authority.[2]

We have also seen that Osiris was black, or of Cushite race, and this was the characteristic of the Egyptians. Herodotus speaks of the Egyptians generally as black and woolly haired, and in speaking of a certain woman who was called a dove, he says, "But in saying that the dove was *black* they show that she was Egyptian."[3]

There were two races in Egypt, viz., the Mizraimites who first colonised the country, and the black Egyptians, the latter receiving their name from "*Ægyptus*," the son of Belus, *i.e.*, Cush. So also it is stated by Diodorus Siculus that "the Egyptians were an Æthiopian (Cushite) colony brought there by *Osiris* (who was also the son of Saturn or Belus), and that the laws, customs and religious observances of the ancient Egyptians resembled those of the Cushites, the colony still retaining the customs of their ancestors;" also that "the *Egyptian* letters were called by ancient writers *Ethiopian* letters, and Hermes, or Thoth, an *Ethiopian*" (or Cushite).[4]

This, therefore, is a further confirmation of the evidence which shows that Hermes or Thoth was the Egyptian form of the Babylonian Hea, the elder Bel Nimrod or "All-wise Belus," who was Cush the first king of Babylon and father of Ninus or Nimrod.

We have also seen that Bacchus was the son of Æthiops or Cush, the father of the Æthiopians, but Bacchus is the same as Osiris, the son of Saturn or Belus, *i.e.*, Cush, which confirms the statement of Diodorus that Osiris was a Cushite, and also shows that Thoth, the counsellor of Osiris, was really his father.

There can be little doubt, therefore, that Ægyptus, the father of the *black* Egyptians and son of Belus, is the same as the *black* Osiris, who led the Egyptians into Egypt, and who was also the son of Belus. Moreover, Ægyptus is stated to have been "*the first king* of Kham*" (Ham), and therefore Nimrod, and that "*he reigned in Egypt also.*"[5] So likewise Belus, the father of Egyptus, although repre-

[1] *Ante*, p. 73.
[2] Rawlinson's *Five Great Monarchies*, vol. i. p. 106.
[3] Herod., lib. ii. caps. lvii., civ.
[4] Diodorus Siculus, quoted by Baldwin, *Prehistoric Nations*, pp. 275, 276.
[5] Pasch., *Chron.*, p. 48 ; Faber, vol. ii. p. 473.

sented as the first king of Babylon, is stated to have been *king of Africa also*,[1] which we shall see was the case.

But if Ægyptus was the same as Osiris or Nimrod, then the famous conqueror "*Sesostris*" was also Osiris or Nimrod. For Egyptus was the same as Sesostris, and the Greeks, who incorrectly attributed the deeds of Sesostris to Rameses II., called him both Sesostris and Egyptus,[2] while Josephus, speaking of Rameses, whom he calls *Sethosis*, a corruption of Sesostris, says, "The country of Egypt took its name from Sethosis (Sesostris), who was also called Ægyptus.[3]

M. Lenormant has shown how mistaken the Greeks were in attributing the name and actions of Sesostris to Rameses II., who, with the usual self-glorification of the Egyptian kings, probably adopted the name of that great conqueror.

It is stated in the traditions of Sesostris that his father ordered all the children in his dominions to be trained for war with his son, so that when the latter came of age he had a band of warriors devoted to him. He then divided Egypt into thirty nomes and marched at the head of a numerous army to the conquest of the world. Ethiopia was the first country he conquered. He then invaded Asia, subdued Syria, Mesopotamia, Assyria, Persia, Bactria and India. He then subdued the Scythians as far as the Tanais, and established the colony of Colchis in the country between the Black and Caspian Seas; then, passing into Asia Minor, he crossed the Bosphorus and subdued the Thracians.[4]

All this was attributed by the Greeks to Rameses II.; but M. Lenormant remarks that it represents Rameses as conquering Ethiopia, which was already subject to Egypt, and as marching over countries where Egyptian armies had never been seen.[5] In fact, contemporary history shows that such a conqueror could not have existed, either in the time of the Rameses, or in that of the twelfth dynasty of Theban kings, where the third king is also called Sesostris and the same conquests attributed to him, although the Theban kings at that period were only vassals, or viceroys, of the Memphite kings of Lower Egypt and had not then obtained the power which they afterwards acquired in the eighteenth and following dynasties.

On the other hand, the conquests of Sesostris are precisely the

[1] Lemprière, *Egyptus.*
[2] Lenormant, *Anc. Hist. of East*, vol. i. p. 246; compare the Armenian and Syncellus lists of Manetho's eighteenth dynasty; Cory, p. 142.
[3] Josephus, *Contr. Appion.*, lib. i. chaps. xiv., xv.
[4] Lenormant, *Anc. Hist. of East*, vol. i. pp. 246-247; Lemprière, *Sesostris.*
[5] Lenormant, vol. i. p. 247.

same as those of Ninus, Osiris, Hercules and Dionusus,[1] and, in particular, the story of a number of youths being trained for war with him during his youth is precisely the same as the story of Ninus.[2] In short, Wilkinson regards Sesostris and Osiris as the same,[3] and the whole evidence confirms this conclusion.

Sesostris, moreover, is said to have erected pillars in the countries he conquered to commemorate his conquests, just as Hercules did, and Herodotus speaks of seeing some of these pillars of Sesostris in Scythia. It is clear from the account of Herodotus, that these were Phallic pillars,[4] which implies that, like the Arabian king Zohak, he was the institutor of the Phallic worship.

Herodotus also says that the Colchians, the colony established by Sesostris, were evidently *Egyptian*, not only because they had similar customs, but because they were black and curly headed, which shows that they were Cushites.[5] This statement of Herodotus is therefore a further proof that Sesostris and his followers who founded the Colchian colony were Osiris and his Ethiopians, *i.e.*, Nimrod and the Cushites.

Again Herodotus says that he had seen two images of this king carved on rocks in Ionia, that they both represented a man four and a half cubits high with an equipment partly Egyptian and partly Ethiopian, and that from one shoulder to the other, across the breast, extended sacred Egyptian characters engraved, having the meaning, "I acquired this region by my own shoulders."[6] M. Lenormant says that he has seen one of these images and that it has no appearance of Egyptian art.[7] If it had, however, we might confidently conclude that it was not a product of the time of Osiris ; for Egyptian art and sculpture began with the Pyramid builders, and attained its greatest perfection under them. Mr Sayce has also remarked with regard to this figure, that the characters by the side of a sculpture on the face of a rock in the Pass of Karabel, which is supposed to be one of these figures (*see* woodcut),[8] are Hittite characters, and concludes therefore that Herodotus was in error in saying that the writing he saw was Egyptian.[9] But the characters referred to by Mr Sayce are *by the side* of the figure, whereas the sacred Egyptian characters seen by Herodotus were "*across the*

---

[1] *Ante*, p. 41.   [2] *Ante*, pp. 25, 66, 67.   [3] Wilkinson's *Egyptians*, vol. i. p. 69.
[4] Herod., lib. ii. cap. cvi. ; Faber, vol. ii. p. 474.
[5] Herod., lib. ii. cap. civ.   [6] *Ibid.*, cap. cvi.
[7] Lenormant, *Anc. Hist. of East*, vol. i. p. 247, note.
[8] From Rawlinson's *Herod.*, vol. ii. p. 174.
[9] Sayce, *Fresh Lights from Ancient Monuments*, p. 90.

breast," and may have since been obliterated by time, or by design, and the Hittite characters added. Moreover, the mode of engraving inscriptions across the body of a figure is essentially Babylonian, which is an additional proof that these figures were those of the

Rock Sculpture at Nimfi, near Smyrna.

Babylonian monarch.[1] It may also be remarked that the Hittites used the cuneiform writing of the Cushite Accadians and that their language was closely allied to the Accadian, so that the supposed Hittite characters may really be Cushite in its earliest and rudest form.[2]

[1] Rawlinson's *Herod.*, vol. ii. pp. 148-150 and note. Mr Rawlinson remarks that the portion about the shoulders is much *weatherworn*. The figure is of the same height as that described by Herodotus, viz., two and a half metres nearly, or four and a half Egyptian cubits of twenty-one inches.
[2] *See* Colonel Conder, *The First Bible*, pp. 70-72.

F

There is no reason, therefore, to doubt the statement of Herodotus that these figures really were erected by the great Egyptian conqueror Sesostris, which appears to have been the Egyptian name of the great Cushite conqueror Nimrod; Herodotus records many fables generally believed in his time, yet it is evident that he truthfully records them just as they were told to him, and in simple statements of fact he may be relied upon. His history bears the impress of being a truthful and exact record of the things he saw himself, or heard from others, told with an almost childlike simplicity.

These figures may therefore be regarded as one of the few existing records of the time of Sesostris, or Osiris, and the words across their shoulders imply that he by his own personal strength had subdued the country, and that his strength lay in his shoulders. Now we know that Nimrod, the original of the Assyrian Hercules and of Orion the Hunter, was a giant whose strength was so vast that he is represented as slaying a bull and a lion unarmed, while Orion boasted that no creature on earth could cope with him.[1] In Manetho's second dynasty there is also a giant like that one mentioned by Herodotus, who is stated to be five cubits high and three cubits across the shoulders. Manetho, or his Greek transcribers, call him "*Sesochris,*" and give him the same length of reign, viz., forty-eight years, that they give to *Sesostris* of the twelfth dynasty, who is also described as a giant of about four and a half cubits.[2] These striking points of similarity indicate that they are one and the same individual.

These names, " Sesochris " and " Sesostris," are the Greek forms of the original name, and Josephus, who confounds Rameses II. with the same hero, calls him "Sethosis," which is probably more nearly the correct form of the name. Mr Rawlinson says, " The frequent habit of putting a double ' S ' as a prefix to the Egyptian names makes it probable that Sesochris, Sesorthus and Sesostris are all forms of O'siris, or He'siris, whose name is found with the sign signifying a double S beginning it."[3] He also thinks that the name " *Soris,*" or " *Sesoris,*" of the fourth dynasty is another form of the same name, and this, as we shall see, may also be concluded on other grounds. " *Sethosis* " is probably a corruption of " *Sethothes,*" which would

[1] *Ante.* p. 22.
[2] Four cubits, three palms, two fingers. Manetho's *Dynasties,* Armenian. *See* Cory, p. 111.
[3] Rawlinson's *Herod.,* vol. ii. pp. 342-351.

naturally pass into "*Sethoses.*"   Now the prefix "*Se*" before the name is merely an emphatic substituted for the article "O," or "He," and signifies "the great," or "the illustrious," or "the well-known," and the termination of "Sethoth*es*" would appear to be the Greek genitive signifying "of," or "proceeding from," as in the case of "Athoth*es*," which Eratosthenes says signifies "Hermogenes," *i.e.,* "born of," or "proceeding from," "Hermes," or "Thoth," or in other words, "The Son of Thoth."   Similarly *Se Thothes* would mean "The Great Son of Thoth."

The termination "*chris*" of Sesochris would be the Hellenised form of the Egyptian "*chre,*" meaning "impersonation" or "incarnation," and Sesochris might thus very well be a corruption of "*Se,*" "*Soro,*" and "*chre,*" signifying "the great incarnate seed," which is one of the principal aspects of the younger Pagan god.

There is reason to conclude, therefore, that both Sesochris and Sesostris are the same individual, and as no such conqueror as Sesostris existed since Osiris, that they both refer to the giant hero Nimrod or Osiris.   In short, Africanus states of the Sesostris of the twelfth dynasty that "the Egyptians say that he is *the first after Osiris,*" [1] which, as Osiris was only recognised as a god by the Egyptians, would make Sesostris the first mortal king of Egypt, *i.e.,* Osiris himself, or Nimrod.

The height of the giant Sesochris or Nimrod, measured by the Egyptian cubit of twenty-one inches, would be eight feet nine inches, and considerably inferior to some of the giants of Canaan ; [2] but the proportionate breadth across the shoulders of three feet, makes it probable that his actual muscular strength may have been superior to theirs, and it tends to identify him with the original of the images described by Herodotus, whose strength lay in his shoulders.   It was not to be expected that the Egyptian priests would altogether ignore the vast human powers of their hero god, and as the powers would not have been striking in a god, they introduced him into the list of their mortal kings.

Sesostris was also the most famous king in the Egyptian annals,

[1] Cory, p. 110.

[2] Goliath of Gath was six cubits and a span, and as the Hebrew cubit was twenty-five inches, he would be about thirteen and a half feet high ; while the bed of Og, king of Bashan, was nine cubits "of a man" long, and four cubits broad, or fifteen feet nine inches by seven feet wide, implying a man of from fourteen to fifteen feet high ; which agrees with the description of the giant of Canaan by the prophet, " whose height was like the height of the cedars, and he was strong as the oaks " (Amos ii. 9).

so that when the Persian conqueror Darius wished to place his statue before the statues of Sesostris in front of the temple of Vulcan, the priest of Vulcan refused to allow him to do so, because, great as had been his conquests, they were inferior to those of Sesostris; and Darius, it is said, admitted the force of the objection.[1]

Who then could this great conqueror have been whose conquests exactly correspond with those of Ninus, Osiris, Bacchus, etc.,—of conquests there is no record in later Egyptian and contemporaneous history,—but Nimrod, the founder of the first great empire of the world?

It may also be remarked that the story told of Sesostris, exactly corresponds with that of Osiris. Both are said to have first established the government and laws of Egypt before departing on their expeditions. Moreover, just as Typhon, the *brother* of Osiris, is represented as having conspired against Osiris, while the latter was absent on his expeditions, and on his return captured him and put him to death, so the *brother* of Sesostris is represented as having conspired against Sesostris while he was absent on his expeditions, and on his return captured him with the intention of putting him to death. The only difference in the two stories is that the priests represented to Herodotus that Sesostris managed to escape the death prepared for him.[2]

It seems clear, therefore, that Sesostris, or Ægyptus, the son of Belus, and the father of the Cushite Egyptians, is the same as the Cushite Osiris, the son of Belus and leader of the Cushite Egyptians into Egypt, and the same as the Cushite monarch Ninus or Nimrod, the son of Belus or Cush.

We have also seen that Hermes or Thoth, the counsellor of both the Egyptian Osiris and the Babylonian Tammuz, is the same as Belus, and therefore the father of Sesostris, or Osiris, *i.e.*, Nimrod. Now, Belus, although the first king of Babylon, is represented as king of Africa also, and this is confirmed by the history of Sanchoniathon. Sanchoniathon represents Cronus as the ruler of the world, and, like Ninus, Osiris, etc., to have visited all its habitable parts, and he must therefore be the *second* Cronus or Nimrod. He says of him, that while on his expeditions, "he gave all Egypt to the god Taautus (the Phœnician name of Thoth or Hermes) to be his kingdom."[3] Exactly the same action is related of Osiris, who after establishing

---

[1] Herod., lib. ii. cap. cx.
[2] Compare Lemprière, *Osiris*, and Herod., lib. ii. cap. cvii.
[3] *Sanchoniathon's History*, Cory, p. 16.

his rule in Egypt, and before proceeding on his expeditions, is said to have left Hermes, *i.e.*, Taautus, in charge of the kingdom.[1]

It would thus appear that both Nimrod and his father Cush were kings of Egypt, and that while Nimrod was the establisher of the laws and constitution of the kingdom, his father was king in his absence, and the first actual ruler. In all probability, the Cushite occupation of the country of Mizraim was not so much the result of conquest as of peaceful submission on the part of a people closely related to the Cushites, and who bowed down before the wisdom of the father and the military fame and abnormal strength of the son.

In further evidence that these two monarchs were the first two kings of Egypt as well as of Babylon, we find that just as Belus was succeeded by *Ninus* and *Semiramis* on the throne of Babylon, so in Manetho's list of the god kings of Egypt, Cronus, *i.e.*, Belus, is succeeded by *Osiris* and *Isis*, Isis being the Egyptian name of the goddess queen of Babylon.

But the evidence that both Nimrod and his father were the first kings of both Babylon and Egypt admits of still more decisive proof.

Both in Manetho's dynasties and on the monumental lists, "*Mena*" (written by the Greeks *Menes*) and "*Athoth*," or "*Athothes*," are always represented as the first two human kings of Egypt.

But who was Menes? Menes has, indeed, been supposed by writers both ancient and modern to be "Mizraim," because the latter was the father of the Mestraoi, the original people of the country, and the early conquest of the country by the Cushite Egyptians, under Osiris, *i.e.*, Nimrod, has not been taken into consideration by them. But by no ingenuity can Menes be made into a corruption of Mizraim.

"Menes," it is said by Diodorus, "instituted the worship of the gods"—that is to say, he was the originator of idolatry.[2] He adds that a curse was inscribed in the temple of Amun Ra, at Thebes, by Tnephachtus, the father of Bocchoris the Wise, against Menes, for having changed the original simple manners of the Egyptians.[3] But it was Thoth, or Hermes, *i.e.*, Cush, appointed king over Egypt by Nimrod, who "first arranged those things which belonged to religion and the worship of the gods."[4] So also it was Hermes Trismegistus whom Manetho, the Egyptian priest, calls *our forefather—i.e.*, he from whom the *Cushite Egyptians* were descended—who "wrote the sacred books which were translated from the writings which were deposited

[1] Lemprière, *Osiris.*
[2] Diod. Sic., i. cap. xxxvii.
[3] *Ibid.*, cap. xlv.
[4] See *ante*, p. 31.

by the first Hermes in the land of Siriad."[1]   So also Jamblicus says that "the Egyptian Hermes was the god of all celestial knowledge, which being communicated by him to his priests, authorised them to inscribe their commentaries with the name of Hermes;" and that "he taught men the proper mode of approaching the Deity with prayer and sacrifice."[2]   The principal books of this Hermes, according to Clemens of Alexandria, were treated by the Egyptians with the most profound respect, and carried in their religious processions.[3]

If, then, Hermes and Menes were both the first instructors of the Egyptians in religion and the worship of the gods, and both were the forefathers from whom the Egyptian kings claimed descent, it is clear that they were one and the same person.

The very name "Mena" confirms this.   The symbol used on the monuments for the last vowel of the name, represents both *i* and *a*, and the name may properly read "*Meni.*"   Now Hermes was worshipped in Egypt as "*the Lord Moon,*"[4] and "*Meni*" or "*Men*" was the name given to the Moon god throughout Asia Minor[5] and by the ancient Saxons also, with whom the moon was the male deity, he was called in the Edda "*Mane*" and in the Voluspa "*Mani.*"[6]   This is a further evidence that "Sin," *the Moon god* of the Assyrians, was a form of the first Belus or Cush who has been identified with Hermes.

Meni is the Chaldee for "*numberer*" (Hebrew *Mene*),[7] and it was said to be given to Hermes as the Lord Moon, because the moon *numbers* the months.[8]   But it was evidently given to him also because he was "the inventor of letters and *arithmetic,*" "who *first discovered numbers and the art of reckoning,* geometry and astronomy."

Meni is a cognate term to the Latin "*Mens,*" or "*mind,*" and to the term "*men*" given to the human race as distinguishing them from the animals by the possession of *mind,* or the power of thought and calculation; and Hermes or Cush was "The God of all Celestial Knowledge," "Thoth, famous for his wisdom," "The God of Letters and

---

[1] Manetho, Cory's *Fragments*, pp. 168, 169.

[2] Wilkinson's *Egyptians*, vol. v. chap. xiii. pp. 9, 10.

[3] Clem. Alex., *Strom.*, lib. vi. vol. iii. pp. 214-219 ; Hislop, p. 209, note.

[4] Champollion, *Egyptian Pantheon*, pp. 152, 153 ; Pl. 30A ; *Wilkinson*, by Birch, vol. iii. pp. 165, 166.   In later times the Egyptians identified Isis with the moon, and hence Plutarch (*De Iside*, s. 43) remarks that the Egyptians regarded the moon as both male and female.

[5] Lenormant, *Chaldean Magic*, p. 133.

[6] Mallet, vol. ii. p. 24, and supplement to Ida Pfeffer's *Iceland*, pp. 322, 323.

[7] Hislop, p. 94.   [8] Wilkinson, vol. i. p. 11.

Learning, the means by which all mental gifts were imparted to man, and he represented the abstract idea of *intellect.*" [1] Hermes has also been identified with "The All-wise Belus," "Hea," the "Lord of Understanding" and "Teacher of Mankind."

As Belus, Cronus, Saturn, Hea, etc., Cush was deified as the father of the gods, and according to Proclus, "*Mind*" or "*Mens*" is the same as Saturn, or Belus, the father of the gods,[2] while Wilkinson remarks that some considered "*Number*" to be the father of the gods and men.[3] Wilkinson also mentions the fact, that *Pan*, another form of the father of the gods, or Cush, although identified by the Greeks with Kham, was likewise considered by them to be Menes.[4]

Meni is also referred to in Isa. lxv. 11 in conjunction with *Gad*, as the two gods to whom the Israelites paid idolatrous worship. For the words translated "troop" and "number" should be respectively "*Gad*" and "*Meni*" (*see* margin). The name "*Gad*" means "the assaulter,"[5] and would represent the god of war, that is either Nergal or Bel Merodach, and the names "Gad" and "Meni" would thus be the two Babylonian gods who are generally coupled together in Scripture, as in the case of the passage, "Bel boweth down, Nebo stoopeth" (Isa. xlvi. 1.)

If then Meni was one of the names of the father of the gods in Babylon, it would explain the true meaning of the duplicated "*Mene, Mene*" in the handwriting which appeared on the wall at the feast of Belshazzar. The king, being both the representative and high priest of the god, was identified with him, and called by his name, as in the similar case of the kings of Egypt, who constantly took the name of one or other of the gods. Hence, in accordance with the interpretation of the prophet, the prediction would read "the *Numberer* is numbered"—that is, as Daniel said, "God hath numbered thy kingdom and finished it."

It is thus quite evident that Mena, or Meni, the first human king of Egypt, was identical with Hermes, or Meni, the Lord Moon, and with "Meni," "number," or "mind," the father of the gods, *i.e.*, Saturn or Cush. But all doubt of the identity of Menes and Hermes or Thoth must cease when we consider the name of the *son* and successor of Menes, viz., *Athothes*, which is simply the Greek genitive of the first declension of *Athoth*, the monumental name of the king, and Athothes thus means "proceeding from," *i.e.*, "born of, Thoth." In short,

---

[1] *Ante*, chap. ii. p. 31   [2] Faber, vol. ii. p. 172.
[3] Wilkinson, vol. iv. p. 196.   [4] *Wilkinson*, by Birch, vol. iii. p. 13.
[5] Hislop, p. 94 and note.

Eratosthenes, in his canon of the kings of Egypt, says that Athothes, the son of Menes, is called by interpretation "Hermogenes," *i.e.*, born of Hermes,[1] and Menes and Hermes, or Thoth, are therefore one and the same person.

It follows from this that Athothes, the son of Menes or Hermes, *i.e.*, Cush, is Osiris or Ægyptus, *i.e.*, Nimrod, and that Cush and Nimrod were both the first two kings of Babylon and the first two kings of Egypt.

It is also to be observed that Scaliger, speaking of the Babylonian kings, says that "Belus reigned sixty-two years, Ninus fifty-two years, and Semiramis, called Rhea, on account of her manifold atrocities, forty-two years."[2] In accordance with this, we find in the list of Egyptian kings, that both Manetho and Eratosthenes give Menes, like Belus, a reign of sixty-two years, and Athothes, who must be the same as Ninus, is given a reign of fifty-seven years by the former and fifty-nine years by the latter.[3]

Belus is represented as the first king of Babylon, because he was the originator of the Tower of Babel, and the first founder of the city of Babylon, which was commenced at the same time (Gen. xi. 5-8), and it is probable, therefore, that his sixty-two years date from that period, and not from the beginning of Nimrod's empire, which must have been some years later.

This first Cushite dominion in Egypt was of short duration, and its overthrow was accompanied by the death of Nimrod and the flight of Cush, the circumstances connected with which will be fully considered in another chapter.

[1] Eratosthenes, Cory, p. 84.
[2] Scaliger, Cory, p. 76.
[3] *Egyptian Dynasties*, Cory, pp. 84, 94.

CHAPTER V

THE GODS OF INDIA

IN any consideration of the gods of those nations more or less removed by distance and intercourse from the original sources of idolatry in Babylon and Egypt, it is to be expected that the confusion, which at times exists between the various gods identified with Cush or Nimrod, would be more pronounced. Making allowance for this, however, it will be found that there is ample data to identify the gods of other nations with those of Babylon, Egypt, etc., and with their human originals.

The Aryan races of Bactria, Persia and India seem to have escaped, or to have thrown off in no small degree, the influence of the Cushite idolatry. We have said that Nimrod was overthrown, and that the commemoration of his overthrow and death were special features in the Pagan worship. This also seems to be referred to in the Iranian tradition of Zohak, which states that he was overthrown by a blacksmith named Caveh, who headed a revolt against him. It is also added that he was succeeded by a grandson of Djemshid, who, if Djemshid was Cush, therefore continued the Cushite empire.[1] But it would appear that the Aryan races eventually recovered their independence, and rejected much of the Cushite idolatry, the Medes and Persians of later times being the most determined opponents of that idolatry.

In India, the bulk of whose inhabitants are of Aryan origin, a purer religion at one time prevailed, and the fact that Semiramis was defeated in her attempt to conquer India after the death of Nimrod, and that Stratobatis, the king, threatened to crucify her if he was victorious,[2] are evidences of the strongest hostility on the part of the inhabitants of that country, who were presumably Aryans, to the Cushites.

M. Lenormant quotes the Vedas to show that the Aryans of

[1] *Anc. Hist. of East*, vol. ii. p. 22.

[2] *Hist. of Ctesias;* Lenormant, *Anc. Hist. of East*, vol. i, p. 367. India here referred to does not mean Hindustan, but is the name given by the ancients to the countries north of the Indus.

India had primarily a belief in a one and only God.[1]   Nevertheless, as admitted by him, the purer religion was subsequently darkened by a debasing polytheism, although, as we have seen, the first human originals of the Hindu triad—Brahma, Vishnu and Siva—were not the Cushite kings of Babylon, but "Pra-Japetus," "Sama" and "Cama," *i.e.*, Japhet, Shem and Ham.[2]   These, however, were eventually displaced by the influence of the Cushite gods.

We find in India "Isis" and "Osiris," or Isiris, under the names of "*Isi*" and "*Iswara*," and in the same relation; for just as Osiris, in his re-incarnation as "Horus," is represented as a babe at the breast of Isis, so is "Iswara" shown at the breast of "Isi"; and just as Osiris is called the son and husband of the mother, so is the child "Iswara" stated to be the husband of "Isi."[3]   Iswara also, like Osiris, was the Phallic god, or god of the "Phallus," or "*Lingam.*" The "Lingam" was his symbol, and was on his altars when they burned incense to him, while he himself was worshipped under the title of "*Ek Linga.*"[4]

He is also identified by Mr Faber with the Indian "Deonaush," who, like Osiris and Bacchus, subdued the world, and who is evidently identical with Dionusus, the surname of Bacchus, the Greek Osiris, who made similar conquests.[5]

"*Siva*" is identical with Iswara, which was one of his most common appellations.[6]   He is the god of destruction and is worshipped with bloody rites, like Moloch, Baal and Saturn, and the name "*Laut*," given to his image in the temple of Sumnaut, is a synonym of the Chaldee "*Lat*" and "*Satur*" or "*Saturn*," both *Lat* and *Satur* meaning "the hidden one."[7]   Like Bacchus and Osiris, Siva wears a tiger's skin, and in his hand holds a small spotted deer or fawn[8] in the same way as the figure of the Babylonian god given by Vaux.[9] Moreover, just as Osiris and Bacchus were Phallic gods, and the worship of the Phallus one of the most important in their rites, so the identical worship of the "Linga" or "Lingam" was followed in the rites of Siva or Shiva.[10]

---

[1] Lenormant, *Anc. Hist.*, vol. ii. p. 11.   [2] See *ante*, pp. 17, 18.
[3] Kennedy, *Hindu Mythol.*, p. 49, and p. 338, note.
[4] Col. Tod's *Rajasth*, vol. i. p. 79, from Pococke's *India in Greece*, p. 224.   *See* the account by Herodotus of Osiris, the Egyptian Bacchus, as the Phallic god —Herod., lib. ii. cap. xlviii.
[5] *Asiat. Res.*, vol. vi. p. 503.   [6] Faber, vol. ii. p. 274.
[7] Borrow's *Gypsies in Spain or Zincali*, vol. ii. p. 113 ; Hislop, p. 270, note.
[8] Nightingale's *Religions and Ceremonies*, p. 365.
[9] See *ante*, p. 37.   [10] Nightingale's *Religions and Ceremonies*, p. 365.

Thus Siva, although originally identified with Ham as one of the sons of the Patriarch,[1] was subsequently identified with his more famous grandson Nimrod or Osiris; for not only were the bull and lingam his symbols, but he is also identified with Iswara or Osiris by the titles "Iswara" and "Mahe shwara," or "Maha Ishwara," "The Great Iswara."[2] So also, like Osiris, who was fabled to be shut up in an ark for one year, Siva is represented as making a voyage during the Deluge on the ship *Argha*.[3] He is, moreover called "*Baghis*,"[4] which is probably the Indian form of ",Bacchus."

Siva, in short, like Jupiter in Greece and Rome, eventually became, as his title "Maha deva," *i.e.*, "Great God," implies, the greatest of the gods, and although, as Siva, he is "the Destroyer," yet he is identified with "Brahma" and "Vishnu" "as Creator" and "Preserver."[5] It is taught, however, that he is superior to Vishnu and Brahma, and Brahma, who is Pra Japeti, is little worshipped.[6]

The fact that the claims of Brahma and Vishnu were eventually overshadowed by those of Siva, and that the latter was identified with Osiris or Nimrod, instead of Ham, points to a revolution in religion at some time; and also to the fact that, before that revolution, the worship of the dead was a recognised part of religion. Now Nimrod and his father were not deified under their numerous appellations until long after their death, and not until they had been deified could this revolution have taken place. But the worship of ancestors seems to have been a part of the idolatry propagated by Nimrod, for we are told that Osiris built a temple in Egypt to his grandfather Ham, and, if so, he would inculcate a similar worship on the peoples he conquered. In the case of the Aryans who came under his influence, this would naturally be the worship of their ancestor, Japhet, who would be to them "Brahma," "The Father," with whom were associated Sama or Vishnu,[7] and Cama or Siva, as the other sons of the Patriarch.

It would seem, however, that the bulk of the Aryan population of India did not arrive there until after the Cushite race had firmly established themselves in that country. Professor Rawlinson says that "linguistic research shows that a Cushite or Ethiopian race

[1] See *ante*, chap. ii. pp. 17, 18.
[2] Faber, vol. i. pp. 181, 182.
[3] Wilkins' *Hindu Mythol.*, pp. 229, 230.
[4] Wilkins' *Hindu Mythol.*, p. 235.
[5] *Ibid.*, vol ii. p. 292.
[6] *Ibid.*, pp. 88-90, 229.
[7] Vishnu, as one of the triad, would naturally be identified with Shem. But Vishnu is really the Sanskrit form of the Chaldee, "Ishmuh," "The man of rest," or "The man Noah"; while "Indra." the god of *rain*, another form of the same god, is also called "Ishnu."—Hislop, p. 135.

extended along the shores of the Southern Ocean from Abyssinia to India; that the whole of India was peopled by this race previous to the Aryans (*i.e.*, previous to Hindus and Brahmins), and that the cities on the Northern shore of the Persian Gulf are shown by brick inscriptions to belong to this race."[1] Euphorus likewise states that the Ethiopians occupied all the Southern Coasts of both Asia and Africa.[2] Signor Gorrisco, the translator of the Ramayana, says that the Ante-sanskrit people of Southern India were of a Hamitic origin, that they had serpents, dragons, and other symbols peculiar to the Cushite religion, and Siva was their principal god. He also states that Siva was not a Vedic god, but adopted by the Brahmins.[3] Professor Stevenson similarly states that neither Siva, nor the Phallic worship, were Aryan; that the Lingayats, or Phallic worshippers, have a bitter hatred to the Brahmins, and that the Brahmins call them " Pakhundi" or heretics. The Aryans called the old inhabitants " Dasyus," " Raksharas," " fiendish creatures, demons and monsters."[4]

The above extracts, quoted by Professor Baldwin, show that the Aryan immigration and Brahminism were subsequent to that of a Cushite race more or less hostile to them and to their religion. Professor Baldwin further quotes General Briggs and Professor Benfey, who consider it certain that a nation of high civilisation preceded the Sanskrit race in India,[5] and this is eminently characteristic of the Cushite race, who, wherever they went, left stupendous buildings and temples as memorials, which have received the name of " Cyclopean " from the Cyclops, " the inventors of tower building," whose king " Cyclops " has been identified with Cronus or Cush. Colonel Forbes Leslie writes:—" It will not be disputed that the primitive Cyclopean monuments of the Dekkan were erected prior to the arrival of the Hindus." Such are the famous rock temples at Salsette, Ellora and Elephanta, the latter name suggesting some intimate connection with Elephantine in Upper Egypt, the stronghold of the Cushite Egyptians. Now there are no rock temples to Brahma and Vishnu; the temple of Salsette is a temple of Siva, and the Lingam and Yoni appear everywhere in its internal recesses, and Siva, the Phallic god, is also the only god worshipped at Ellora.[6]

We find Aryan traditions speaking of themselves as white, and the Dasyus as *black*—*i.e.*, Cushite; they call them " demons and devil worshippers, and lascivious wretches who make a god of the *Sisna*,

[1] From Baldwin's *Prehistoric Nations*, vol. i. p. 220.   [2] *Ibid.*, p. 219.
[3] *Ibid.*, p. 221.   [4] *Ibid.*, pp. 221, 222.
[5] *Ibid.*, p. 227.   [6] *Ibid.*, pp. 228, 233.

i.e., the Lingam or Phallus.[1] The translator of Ferishta's *Mahom-medan India* says, "There is every day stronger reason to believe that the worship of the Bull, Linga, and Yoni, is the same as the Phallic worship of Egypt, and as that of the call and pillar, emblematic of Baal and the Sun, by the nations surrounding the Israelites; that this worship was founded on Sabaism, and that the emblems are types of fructification (generation). Abundant proof exists of the antiquity of Tauric and Phallic worship over that of idolatry and demi-god heroes. All the temples of the latter are modern compared with those of Mahadeva,"[2] *i.e.*, Siva.

The Sanskrit books also speak of "Divodesa, king of Cusha dwipa within" (*i.e.*, Asiatic Ethiopia), as reigning over the Western districts of Asia from the Mediterranean to the Indus. Another tradition speaks of "Charvanayanas," king of Cusha dwipa within, who had a son called "Capeyanas," who had a *passion for arms and hunting*, that he became a heroic warrior, was supreme ruler of Cusha dwipa, and made great conquests and ruled a vast kingdom with great glory. Similarly Deva-Nahusha or Deonaush (Dionusus) is mentioned as living at a time when Indra (*i.e.*, Ishnuh or Noah) was king of Meru, and as having conquered the seven dwipas, and led his armies through all known countries, and made his empire universal.[3] Another legend represents him as having attained the sovereignty of the three worlds, but that intoxicated by pride he became arrogant to the Brahmins and was changed into a serpent,[4] which is probably the mythical way of saying that he became a god worshipped under the form of a serpent, the special symbol of the Pagan god.

All these accounts, corresponding as they do with the traditions of Ninus, Osiris and Bacchus, and the Arabian and the Iranian account of Zohak, plainly refer to the establishment of the first great empire of the world by Nimrod, and with it the first form of idolatry at a period long anterior to the Aryan immigration to India. It would thus appear that the Sun and Phallic worship taught by Nimrod was firmly established in India previous to the Aryan immigration. Moreover, since Osiris, Belus and the other gods were not worshipped until long after the death of their human originals this must have been equally the case with the Phallic god of India, Siva or Iswara, whose worship was nevertheless firmly established at the time of the Hindu invasion.

[1] Baldwin's *Prehistoric Nations*, vol. i. p. 248, 249.
[2] *Ibid.*, pp. 224, 225.
[3] *Ibid.*, pp. 281, 282, 287.
[4] *Ibid.*, p. 291.

On the other hand, the Indian conquests of Nimrod did not extend farther than the Indus, beyond which it was supposed there were deserts, while a few years later Semiramis received a severe check from the king of that country. It is therefore evident that the arrival of the Cushite race in India was subsequent to this, that a large number of them afterwards left Chaldea and emigrated to India and spread southwards over the whole peninsula, carrying with them the religion of their ancestors. The consequent diminution of their numbers in Chaldea would partly account for the later predominance of the Semitic language in that country.

The fact of the Cushite race having been in India previous to the Hindu invasion explains the reason of the strange mixture of Aryan and Cushite ideas in the religion of India. The former, as in the case of the Persians, were Sun and Fire worshippers, but modern Brahmanism, according to Stevenson, quoted by Professor Baldwin, is a combination of Brahmanism, Buddhism, and the ante-Brahman or Cushite religion. He says that the worship of Siva was an aboriginal superstition, and that the Brahmans adopted it to gain influence with the old race, but that the amalgamation is not perfect. He also states that no Brahman officiates in a linga temple in the Marathi country, where Saivas prevail, and that the same is the case in the Dekkan. Siva worship has its chief seats in those places where the Sanskrit has been weakest, namely, in the South and South-East, where the worshippers of Siva greatly exceed those of Vishnu.[1]

We find also an intimate connection between the mythology of Egypt and that of India. Moreover, just as "*Ra*" is the Sun in Egypt, and "*Rameses*," the name of several Egyptian kings, means "the Son of Ra, or the Sun," so Colonel Tod, speaking of India, observes, "From *Rama* all the tribes named the Surya Vausa, or race of the Sun, claim descent."[2] He also says that Rama was chief of the Suryas and that his two sons were *Cush* and *Sova*.[3] It seems probable, however, that the genealogy has been confused, and that "Rama" and "Sova" are "Raamah" and "Seba," the two sons of Cush (Gen. x. 7). For "*v*" and "*b*" are interchangeable letters, and "Seba" would therefore easily pass into "Sova." But, just as the Sun god Osiris displaced the Sun god Ham and became the chief god of Egypt, so Rama, as the chief Sun god of India, was regarded as the father of the Surya race.

[1] Baldwin, *Prehist. Nations*, pp. 258, 259.
[2] Pococke, *India in Greece*, chap. xiii. p. 165.   [3] *Ibid.*, chap. xiv. p. 183.

It would seem also that the ultimate development of the Cushite idolatry in Egypt, although partly due to the Ethiopians of Upper Egypt, received a wave of influence from the Ethiopians of India, who came to Egypt at the latter part of the eighteenth dynasty, when, for the first time, the Pharaohs adopted the Indian title of " Rameses," and the worship of Osiris was substituted for that of Set.[1] The Hindus also have a tradition that their four sacred books were taken to Egypt.[2]

The principal gods of the Vedas were "*Indra*," the god of rain, "*Surya*," the Sun, and "*Agni*," the god of fire,[3] and Max Müller says that these gods were not represented by idols. Ultimately, however, they were more or less identified with the Cushite gods. Surya is represented, like the Sun god in Greece, as drawn by a chariot and horses.[4] He is identified with Agni, the god of fire, and the latter, like Vulcan, the Roman god of fire, was represented as old and deformed,[5] and just as Vulcan, king of the Cyclops, was represented to be an eater of human flesh, so also was Agni.[6] Siva, although not mentioned in the Vedas, is by the Puranas declared to be "*Rudra*," who is the same as Agni.[7]

Fire also was recognised as having the same purifying efficacy as in other forms of the Cushite idolatry. The Suttees, who devoted themselves on the funeral pyres of their husbands, were considered to become pure by burning,[8] and a worshipper is represented, according to the sacred books, as addressing the fire, " Salutation to thee, O Fire, who dost seize oblation, to thee who dost shine, to thee who dost scintillate, may thy auspicious flame burn our foes, mayest thou, the purifier, be auspicious to us." [9]

With regard to other Indian gods, it is evident that "Dyauspiter" ("Heaven Father"), the god of lightning, is identical with Jupiter, the god of lightning, who was also called "Diespiter."[10] "*Juggernaut*" is the Indian Moloch, and, like him, required human victims. Again, although Saturn was the father of the gods in Greece and Rome, he was said to be the son of "Cœlus" and "Terra," "Heaven" and "Earth," while Cronus was similarly represented to be the son of the

---

[1] *Egypt. Dynasties*, by Syncellus ; Cory, p. 142.
[2] *Asiat. Res.*, vol. iii. p. 75. [3] Wilkins' *Hindu Mythol.*, p. 7.
[4] *Ibid.*, pp. 26, 27. [5] *Ibid.*, p. 16.
[6] *Ibid.*, p. 23. [7] *Ibid.*, pp. 220, 221.
[8] Moor's *Pantheon*, "*Siva*," p. 43 ; Hislop, p. 315.
[9] Colebrooke's "Religious Ceremonies of Hindus" in *Asiatic Researches*, vol. vii p. 260.
[10] Lenormant's *Anc. Hist. of East*, vol. ii. p. 12.

same parents by their Greek appellations, "Ouranos" and "Ge." Similarly the Indian "*Dyaus*" and "*Prithivi*," "Heaven" and "Earth," are said to be the parents of all the gods.[1]

"*Krishna*" is the Indian Apollo or Horus, and, as we shall see later on, is represented as taking the same part in the ultimate development of idolatry as Horus and Apollo. He is a herdsman like Apollo. He is represented with a flute, as Apollo is with a harp, is an archer like Apollo, and, like Apollo, is the destroyer of the serpent.[2]

"*Cama deva*" is a youth like Cupid, and, like Cupid, is the son of the Indian Venus, "Luksmi." Like Cupid, he carries a bow and arrows, and with his arrows creates desire, and, as the god of desire, is invoked by brides and bridegrooms. He is represented as sitting on a deer to show his swiftness.[3]

"*Parvati Dvorgu*" is the Indian Minerva. She derived her surname from the giant "*Dvorgu*," whom she slew, just as Minerva obtained the name of "*Pallas*" from the giant "*Pallas*" whom she slew.[4] "*Luksmi*" is the Indian Venus. She springs, like Venus, from the froth of the sea, and, as in the case of Venus, her beauty is so great that all the gods are enamoured of her, while, like Venus, no bloody sacrifices are allowed on her altars.[5] "*Yuni*" is the Indian Juno or June, and the symbol, the "Yoni," worshipped with the "Lingam," is evidently derived from her name. She is identified with the ship *Argha* (the Ark), and with *the dove* called "*Capoteswari*,"[6] as in the case of Juno and Semiramis.

The gigantic bulls of Babylon and Assyria were, we know, symbols of their great god, and the same symbol existed in Egypt in the forms of the bulls Apis and Mnevis, the symbols of Osiris or Horus. Thus in a dedicatory inscription, in the temple of Luxor, to Amenhotep III., who, as vice-regent of the god, was identified with him,[7] it is said, "I am Horus, the strong bull, who rules by the sword and destroys all barbarians." He is "king of Upper and Lower Egypt,

---

[1] Wilkins' *Hindu Mythol.*, p. 10.

[2] Nightingale's *Religions and Ceremonies*, chap. x. p. 373, and Lemprière, *Apollo*.

[3] Nightingale, chap. x. p. 375.

[4] *Ibid.*, p. 370.   [5] *Ibid.*, p. 372.

[6] Faber, vol. i. p. 372 ; vol. iii. pp. 31, 32.

[7] Lenormant remarks, "The Egyptian monarchs were more than sovereign pontiffs, they were real deities. They styled themselves 'The Great God,' 'The Good God,' they identified themselves with the great deity Horus, for as one inscription says, 'The king is the image of Ra, the Sun god among the living.'" He also quotes Diodorus Siculus as saying, "The Egyptians respect and adore their kings as the equal of the gods."—*Anc. Hist. of East*, vol. i. p. 294.

absolute master, son of the Sun."[1] Like the sacred bull "Apis" in Egypt, the sacred bull "*Nanda*" was similarly the symbol of the god in India. His altar is attached to all the shrines of Iswara and of Siva.[2]

The wife of Siva, "*Cali*," is a form of the goddess "Parvati Dvorgu," "Doorga" or "Durgu,"[3] the Indian Minerva. The wife of Siva is also known as "*Uma*," who, like Minerva, is the goddess of Wisdom.[4] Doorga is also known as *Maha Maia*, the Great Goddess Mother, who, like Minerva, is represented as slaying the giants who rebelled against the gods.[5] This episode, of which there are many traditions in the mythology of India, and which are in very exact correspondence with the similar traditions of Egypt and Greece, will be more fully noticed hereafter.

The Indian "*Yama*" seems to be another form of Osiris. Like the latter, he is the judge of the dead, and weighs their good actions against their bad actions, in order to decide their fate. He is also the Indian Pluto, or Dis, the king of Hades, another form of Osiris, Nin, etc., and, like Pluto, has two dogs to guard the road to his abode.[6]

The Indian Cupid, "*Cama*," is represented as having been seized by a demon, Sambara, and put into a box and cast into the ocean, where he is discovered by his wife "*Reti*," *who was also his mother*, and who brought him up until he acquired strength to destroy the demon.[7] In like manner Osiris was killed by Typhon, the evil spirit of the Egyptians, and shut up in the ocean for one year, when he comes to life again as Horus, and by his aid his mother, Isis, who is also his wife, overcomes Typhon. The identity of *Cama*[8] with Horus and Osiris is additionally confirmed by a remark of Plutarch, who says that the elder Horus, *i.e.*, Osiris, was the god "*Caimis*," and that his wife was "*Rhytia*,"[9] who are manifestly the same as Cama and Reti. So also Cama, like Osiris, dies and is shut up in the ship *Argha*, and is lamented by "*Reti*,"[10] just as Osiris was lamented

---

[1] Lenormant, *Anc. Hist. of East*, vol. i. p. 237.

[2] Pococke, *Ind. in Greece*, pp. 224, 225.

[3] Faber, *Pag. Idol.*, vol. i p. 375 ; Wilkins, *Hind. Myth.*, p. 257-264.

[4] Wilkins, *Hind. Myth.*, p. 240.

[5] *Ibid.*, pp. 247-250.

[6] *Ibid.*, pp. 67-74.

[7] Faber, vol. ii. pp. 407, 408.

[8] Cama was originally Kham or Ham, but, as in other cases, was ultimately identified with his grandson Nimrod.

[9] Faber, vol. ii. p. 408.

[10] *Ibid.*, pp. 408-411.

G

by Isis, which further emphasises the identity of Cama with Osiris and Horus.

From these remarks it is clear that the mythology and gods of India are practically identical with the mythology and gods of Babylon, Egypt, Greece and Rome, and must have been derived from the same original source.

CHAPTER VI

Buddhism

THE religion of the nations of Eastern Asia is known as Buddhism, and its followers are said to number nearly five hundred millions of the human race. For this reason, and because it has certain features which distinguish it from the religions of other Pagan nations, it requires particular notice.

The principal representatives of this religion are the Chinese and people of Thibet, and its founder is generally spoken of as "Sakya Muni," or "Gautama," a Brahmin of India, who is supposed to have lived about 500 B.C. But whatever influence Sakya Muni may have had upon the religion of these countries, it is quite clear that he did not originate it. In most of its salient features it is similar to other systems of Paganism, with an elaborate ritual, and, like them, it has orders of priesthood, gods and goddesses, idols, worship of the dead, etc. Sakya Muni, on the other hand, was a reformer, opposed to ritual observances, priestly castes, sacrifices, and, as some assert, to the worship of the gods, although the latter point is doubtful.

He taught a severe asceticism and the necessity of subduing every natural desire, not only those which are unlawful, but those which are lawful, requiring his followers to abstain from marriage, wine and animal food, and to relinquish all their worldly goods; the ultimate object being the attainment of "Nirvana," or a state of placid indifference to everything, which was supposed to be accompanied by certain magical powers. His moral teaching included some excellent precepts of kindness to men and animals, together with others which were false and extravagant; but, with the exception of abstaining from taking any form of animal life, his moral principles have had very little influence on his professed followers.

Sakya Muni is called "*Buddha.*" But "Buddha" is a title which was in existence before it was applied to him. It was a title of the Supreme God, similar to such titles as "The Almighty," "The Self-Existent," and meant "The Omniscient" or "All Wise"; and the old

Buddhist, Amirta Nanda Bandhya, told Mr Hodgson that the name in esoteric Buddhism always meant "God."[1]

Sakya Muni, after a long course of asceticism, is represented to have *become* "Buddha," or "enlightened," *i.e.*, he had attained to the wisdom of God, or had become as God, with a knowledge of good and evil.[2]   He is represented to be one only of the seven mortal Buddhas, *i.e., Avatars*, or incarnations of the supreme Buddha, and in a statue in South Kensington Museum, Buddha is represented with seven heads,[3] while in the "Stupa of Bharhut," the oldest monument of Buddhism in existence, being constructed in the time of King Asoka, 250 B.C., the seven sacred trees and thrones of the seven Buddhas are portrayed.[4]

In the Chinese ritual the worshipper says, " All hail, Buddhas of the ten quarters ! " and in the Ceylon ritual,[5] " I worship continually the Buddhas of the ages that are past, I worship the Buddhas All-Pitiful."[6]   Sakya Muni himself, in short, is represented in " *The White Lotus of Dharma* " as acknowledging these other Buddhas; he promises to appear before them when he has attained complete " Nirvana "; and, in another passage, says that " He will execute what those sages, the Buddhas, have ordered ; " while in another passage he " calls to witness the beatified Buddhas that exist."[7]   Again, in the " *Lalita Vistara*," which is considered to be the oldest life of Sakya Muni, his various temptations which he has to go through before he attains " Nirvana " are described, and in the final one, when he is attacked by the demon host, he calls upon ." Brahma Prajapati, lord of creatures, and to all the Buddhas that live at the ten horizons to disperse them."[8]   Finally, he is represented as repudiating his human parentage and claiming to be descended from the prophets, or " Buddhas," of old.[9]

It would appear that all these Buddhas are regarded as " Avatars," or incarnations, of one and the same supreme Buddha.   Thus, on the birth of Sakya Muni, it is pretended that an aged *rishi* (saint) called Asita, who, being possessed of the five classes of transcendental knowledge, recognises that the child is Buddha, takes him in his arms, and says, " The Buddha Bhagavat " (that is, The Supreme

[1] Lillie, *Buddha and Early Buddhism*, pp. 20, 21.
[2] Rhys Davis, *Buddhism*, p. 40.   [3] Lillie, p. 12.
[4] *Stupa of Bharhut*, by Gen. A. Cunningham, p. 108.
[5] Beal's *Catena of the Buddhist Scriptures*, p. 409.
[6] *Pattimokkha*, pp. 5, 7 ; Lillie, pp. 27, 28.
[7] Lillie, p. 128.
[8] *Ibid.*, p. 108.   [9] Rhys Davis, p. 65.

Buddha) "comes to the world only after many kalpas" (ages), and then declares that the child will be Buddha.[1]

Sakya Muni was born a Brahmin, and we see him acknowledging Brahma as the Supreme God. The Cingalese priests say there is a Supreme Being above all others, and although there are many gods, yet there is one who is God of the gods. This god is Brahma, but that when a Buddha was upon earth he became the Supreme God.[2] This is the teaching of modern Buddhism in Ceylon, but it is evident that the ancient doctrine of the Vedas made Brahma the one Supreme God. Sakya Muni, in becoming an ascetic, merely followed the example of the *Rishis* of Vedaism, who sought to subdue their lower natures by vigils, fasting, chastity and asceticism, their object being by these means to obtain "a knowledge of Brahma, a knowledge of the universal self, and the universal soul."[3] This was just what Sakya Muni did, and what he thought he attained when he became "a Buddha," or "enlightened." In short, he called his followers "Brahmanas," or seekers after Brahma.[4] But he did what the Rishis of Vedaism did not do—he opposed, or rather denied, the utility of a ritual and priesthood, and asserted that a person could attain "Nirvana" by his own efforts, or asceticism, without their aid. This, of course, was a blow to the influence of the Brahminical priesthood; and accordingly Sakya Muni, instead of being regarded as Buddha by Brahminism, is to this day looked upon as a heretic, and his followers as infidels, with the result that a great hostility exists between the Brahmins and those Buddhists who acknowledge Sakya Muni as the Supreme God.[5]

Nevertheless, the Brahmins acknowledge *a* Buddha, who is represented to be an Avatar of Vishnu, and in an ancient inscription at Buddha Gaya he is invoked by the sacred name "O. M.," or "A. U. M.," and declared to be the same as the triple god Brahma-Vishnu-Mahesa (Siva).[6] The Chinese traveller Fa Hian, who lived in the fourth century A.D., also states that some of the Buddhist sects of India, near Savrasti, refused to acknowledge Sakya Muni, and only reverenced the three previous Buddhas, claiming to be followers of "*Deva Datta*."[7]

The religion of Guatama was introduced into China subsequent

[1] *Lalita Vistara*, Lillie, p. 76.
[2] *Statement of Cingalese Priests*, Lillie, p. 122.
[3] Lillie, pp. 4, 5.   [4] *Ibid.*, p. 116.
[5] *Asiat. Res.*, vol. vii. pp. 55, 56 ; vol. viii. pp. 532, 533 ; Faber, vol. ii. p. 328.
[6] *Ibid.*, vol. i. pp. 284, 285 ; Faber, vol. ii. p. 328.   [7] Rhys Davis, p. 181.

to the Christian era,[1] but previous to this they had worshipped a Buddha under the name of "*Fo*" from the beginning of their national existence, and this "Fo" is shown by Sir William Jones to be identical with the primitive Buddha of Hindustan.[2]

From these facts it is abundantly plain that there was a Buddha and Buddhism distinct from the worship of Sakya Muni.

In Nepaul, on the borders of Thibet, and in Thibet, this Buddha is "*Amitabha*," or "*Amida Buddha*," called also "*Adi Buddha*." "*Amida*" in Sanskrit denotes "immeasurable";[3] he is the Buddha of Buddhas, and quite distinct from Sakya Muni. He is said to be "without beginning, revealed in the form of flame or light, the essence of wisdom and absolute truth. He knows all the past, he is omnipresent. He is the creator of all the Buddhas. He is Iswara, the Infinite,"[4] etc.

In Thibet, the constant chant of the Llamas is, "I adore Tathagata Amitabha, who dwells in the Buddha region Devachan."[5] Mr Edkins says that the name of "Amitabha" is constantly on the lips of the Chinese and Thibetan priests, and is seen everywhere painted on walls and carved on stone, and that he is worshipped assiduously by the Northern Buddhists, although unknown in Siam, Burmah, and Ceylon.[6] In the Chinese liturgy he is addressed, "One in spirit, respectfully we invoke thee. Hail, Amitabha Lokafit of the world;" and again, "O, would that our teacher Sakya Muni, and our merciful father Amitabha would descend to this sacred precinct, and be present with us. . . . May the omnipotent and omniscient Kwanyin (the goddess) . . . now come amongst us, reciting these divine sentences."[7] Here Sakya Muni is clearly distinguished from Amitabha, the great father, and Kwanyin, the goddess mother, to whom we shall refer later.

In "*The White Lotus of Dharma*," one of the most important Buddhist works obtained by Mr Hodgson from the Buddhist Amirta Manda Bandhya, the omnipotence of Amitabha is dwelt on in some gathas:—"He sits on the Lotus throne in the centre of heaven, and

[1] *Asiat. Res.*, vol. i. p. 170;　l. vi. p. 262; vol. ix. p. 41; Faber, vol. ii. p. 242.

[2] Faber, vol. ii. pp. 342, 343.

[3] *Asiat. Res.*, vol ii. p. 374; Faber, vol. ii. p. 342.

[4] From old Sanskrit works by Karanda Vyûha and Nama Sangiti, quoted by the Buddhist Amirta Nanda Bandhya to Mr Hodgson; Lillie, pp. 14, 15.

[5] Schlagintweit, *Buddhism in Thibet*; Lillie, p. 13.

[6] Edkins' *Chinese Buddhism*, p. 171.

[7] Beal, *Catena of Buddhist Scriptures.* p. 403; Lillie, pp. 13, 14.

guides the destinies of mortals," while Sakya Muni occupies "a subordinate position, and is a saint and not a god." [1]

In China, Adi Buddha, or Amitabha, is called "*Omito Fo,*" and his mother, the Sanskrit "*Maya,*" is called "*Moyo,*" the "o" in both cases being substituted for the "a." It should also be noted that in Boutan and Thibet, Buddha is called "*But,*" "*Put,*" "*Pot,*" "*Pout,*" and "*Poto*"; in Cochin, "*But,*" and in Siam, "*Pout,*" while in the vernacular of Siam, "*Pout,*" or "*Pot,*" is pronounced "*Po,*" the "t" being quiescent as in the French. In China the "p" is aspirated and becomes "*Pho*" or "*Fo.*" [2] In the Tamulic dialect the name is pronounced "*Poden,*" or "*Pooden.*" [3] Mr Edkins gives some of the curious changes of pronunciation, as follows:—"*Fuh,*" old sound "*But*"; in Amoy, "*Put*"; in Nanking, "*Fuh*"; in Peking "*Fo.*" [4] In Japan, Buddha is called "*Budso,*" "*Amita Fo,*" "*Toka Daibod,*" or "*Deva Bod*" (the Divine Bod), and "*Ab buto,*" or "Father Buto." [5]

Buddha is also known as "*Heri Maha,*" "The Great Lord"; [6] as "*Datta,*" "*Deva Tat,*" and "*Deva Twashta*"; [7] as "*Mahi-man,*" [8] "man" being probably the same as *mens,* mind, or intelligence, as in "*Menu,*" or "*Men Nuh.*" "Mahi-man" would thus mean "the great Mind," which is exactly the character given to Buddha. He is also known as "*Ma Hesa*" and "*Har Esa,*" "The Great Hesa," and "Lord Hesa." [9]

There are other Buddhas represented in the Chinese temples, in addition to Amita, or Omito, viz., "*Yo shi Fo,*" who is the Buddha of the Eastern Paradise, and "*Milo Fo,*" or "*Maitreya Buddha,*" who is the Buddha to come. Then there is the ancient Buddha "*Jang ten,*" the instructor of Sakya Muni in a former "Kalpa," or age, and "*Kwanyin,*" the male deity corresponding to the goddess "Kwanyin." This male Kwanyin is called "*Chin Fo,*" "the ruling Buddha," although Sakya Muni Buddha is regarded as the Buddha reigning in the present age or "Kalpa." [10]

Professor Baldwin says, "Buddhism was much older than Gautama, or Sakya Muni, the Buddha of the Ceylonese records. He was only

[1] *Lotus,* pp. 266, 268 ; Lillie, pp. 128, 129.
[2] *Asiat. Res.,* vol. ix. p. 220 ; vol. vi. p. 260 ; vol. i. p. 170 ; Faber, *Pag. Idol.,* vol. ii. p. 342.
[3] Faber, vol. ii. p. 349.   [4] Edkins, p. 413.   [5] Faber, vol. ii. p. 348.
[6] *Asiat. Res.,* vol. ix. pp. 212, 215 ; Faber, vol. ii. p. 350.
[7] *Ibid.,* vol. v. p. 261 ; vol. vi. pp. 263, 483 ; vol. x. p. 59.
[8] *Ibid.,* vol. iii. pp. 195, 201.
[9] *Ibid.,* vol. i. pp. 284, 285 ; Faber, vol. ii. p. 350.
[10] Edkins, pp. 240, 246, 261.

one of its prophets. A passage in the *Raja Taringini*, a religious history of Kashmir, translated by Mr Turnour, shows that in China, Thibet, and Nepaul, six Arhatas, or mortal predecessors of Gautama, are recognised, and this accords with the fact that the Jainas, whose religious system originated in Buddhism, celebrate '*Kasyapa*,' one of their predecessors, as their great prophet, claiming that the Buddhists themselves followed him before Gautama appeared." Again he says, "Buddhism was the growth of many ages preceding that in which Sakya Muni appeared. Its system of doctrine and practice was completely developed before his time, and the fact explains why the various Buddhist sects have differed and disputed so much concerning the date of his appearance," which "varies from 2470 B.C. to 453 B.C." [1]

It would thus appear that in Ceylon, Burmah and the south, where Amitabha Buddha is unknown, Sakya Muni is recognised as the chief god, but that throughout the north, in Thibet, Nepaul, China, and by the Brahmins of India, Amitabha is the supreme deity, although in Thibet and China, Sakya is recognised as a great teacher and an Avatar, or incarnation, of Buddha. It is plain also that the Buddhists of the south sprang out of Brahminism, for they more or less acknowledge the Vedic gods, although they place them in a subordinate position—Brahma, Vishnu and Siva being represented in some of the temples, and also in China, as disciples of Sakya Muni.[2] This, no doubt, is because the Brahmins regard Sakya Muni as a heretic, and the consequent hostility between them and the followers of Sakya Muni has led the latter to elevate their prophet above the Vedic gods in retaliation for the charge of heresy.

Everything, therefore, seems to point to the fact that the seat of the worship of the original, or mythological, Buddha Amitabha was in the north, especially in Thibet, where it has all the aspect of a perfected system, and where the magical powers of the priesthood are most famous. This is further corroborated by the fact that the Chinese recognise and reverence the Grand Llama of Thibet, who claims to be the living incarnation of Fo, or Buddha. The more remote Tartars regard him as the Deity, and call him God, the Everlasting Father of Heaven, and even the Emperor of China, who is Pontifex Maximus, or chief ecclesiastic, in China, pays him religious homage, acknowledging him as his ecclesiastical superior and great

[1] *Prehistoric Nations*, pp. 254, 255.   [2] Edkins, pp. 214, 215.
[3] Nightingale, *Rites and Ceremonies*, pp. 443, 448 ; *Asiat. Res.*, vol. i. pp. 207-220 ; vol. vi. pp. 483, 484 ; Le Compte, *China*, p. 332 ; Faber, *Pag. Idol.*, vol. ii. p. 341.

spiritual Father, or the living representative of his own god " Fo," or Buddha.[1]

As before remarked, the religious system of the great Buddhist countries, China and Thibet, resembles that of other forms of Paganism, and must be supposed to have a similar origin and antiquity. It has its Great Father, its Goddess Mother, and their Son, or incarnation, and these are represented by numerous idols to whom its followers pray. The Trinity consists of Amitabha Buddha, the goddess Dharma, or Kwanyin, and their son,[3] the latter occupying precisely the same position as in other Pagan systems, which, we have seen, consists of the father of the gods, known as Belus, Bel Nimrud the lesser, Saturn, Cronus, Janus, etc.; the goddess mother "with ten thousand names"; and their son, known as Bel Nimrud the greater, Ninus, Osiris, Horus, Bacchus, Apollo, Tammuz, etc.

The Buddhist Trinity is usually expressed as " Buddha," who in Northern Buddhism is "Amitabha," the goddess "Dharma," and "Sangha." King Asoka, who lived about 250 B.C., expresses his faith in Buddha, Dharma and Sangha as personal deities, and at the initiation of the Buddhist novice he recites the following text, " I salute Buddhanath, Dharma, and Sangha, and entreat them to bestow on me the Pravrajya."[2] In later times in the South the personality of Dharma and Sangha were ignored, in consequence of the doctrines of Sakya Muni, which made salvation and the attainment of Nirvana to depend entirely upon a person's own subjugation of his natural passions and desires, and dispensed with the assistance and the worship of the gods involving the ritual and priesthood to which Sakya Muni was opposed. It is clear, however, that in the earliest times, as in the case of Asoka, they were regarded as personal deities and worshipped as such.

The following prayers to Dharma are given by Mr Lillie: " I salute Dharma, who is Prajna Paramita (Prajna, wisdom),[3] pointing out the way of perfect tranquillity to all mortals, leading them into the path of perfect wisdom, who by the testimony of the sages produced all things, who is the mother of all the Bodhisatwas" (holy men nearly emancipated).—(*Baptismal Service in Natal*).[4]

" And thou ever present Kwan Shi Yin Bodhisatwa (our mother), who hast perfected wondrous merit, and art possessed of great mercy,

[1] Lillie, p. 5.   [2] *Ibid.*, pp. 56, 60.
[3] Edkins, p. 40. "*Paramita*" appears to mean "complete measure" or "attainment," "perfection."
[4] Hodgson, p. 142.

who in virtue of thine infinite power and wisdom art manifested throughout the universe for the defence and protection of all creatures, and who leadest us to the attainment of boundless wisdom," etc. (*Chinese Liturgy*).[1]

"Those Buddhas who are merciful and the teachers of the world, all such Buddhas are thy children. Thou art all good, and the universal Mother." (*Ashta Sahasrika*).[2]

"Upon a lotos of precious stones sustaining a moon crescent sits Prajna Paramita." (*Bhadra Kalpa Vadana*).[3]

"The external and internal diversities belonging to all animate nature are produced by her, Buddha Matra." (*Pancha Vinsati Sahasrika*).[4] *Matra* in the Sanskrit means "mother," and "matter," i.e., "the earth."

"Hitherto we have gone astray but now we return. Oh, that the merciful Kwanyin would receive our vows of amendment." (*Termination of a Chinese General Confession*).[5]

"I bow my head to the ground and worship Dharma. May Dharma forgive me my sin." (*Cingalese Version of the Pattimokkha, or Ritual of Confession*).[6]

"Hail, mother of the seven Kotis of Buddha." (*Chinese Invocation*).[7]

From the above, it is clear that Dharma, or Prajna, is a personal deity the goddess of wisdom, like Minerva, and is identical with Kwanyin. But modern Buddhism has substituted for this personal source of wisdom and knowledge, wisdom and knowledge itself, as taught by Sakya Muni, and Dharma has become a name for "*Canon law*"—i.e., the teaching of Sakya Muni. The original character of the goddess is, however, plain enough. She is not only the goddess of wisdom, but the great mother, and is identified with matter, or the earth. She is called the mother of Buddha, and also given the title of the goddess in other Pagan systems, viz., "The Queen of Heaven," and like them is addressed by the title of "Our Lady."[8]

Sangha is said to be born from the union of "*Upaya*," a name of God, i.e., of Amitabha Buddha, and "*Prajna*." As "*Padmapani*," the son of Amitabha, he created the world, and is called "The Lord of the World."[9] He is called also "*The Voice of the Dragon*,"[10] that is to

[1] Beal, *Catena*, p. 403.   [2] Hodgson, p. 86.   [3] *Ibid.*, p. 85.
[4] *Ibid.*   [5] Beal, *Catena*, p. 408.
[6] Dickson's translation, p. 6.
[7] Beal, *Catena*, p. 413 ; Lillie, pp. 21, 22.   [8] Beal, *Catena*, p. 412.
[9] From the Scriptures of Nepaul, Hodgson, p. 88.
[10] Max Müller, chap. i. p. 263 ; Lillie, p. 22.

say, just as Christ is said to be "The *Word* of God," *i.e.*, "the expression" or "manifestation" of God, by His words and life as man, so Sangha, as the incarnation of the supreme god and goddess, was regarded as "the voice" or "expression" of the dragon, or serpent, with whom, as we shall see, the Pagan "father of the gods" was identified. The symbols of Sangha were the Sun and the Elephant,[1] both of which are also the particular symbols of Buddha.

Sangha is, moreover, one of the seven great prophets or Buddhas, but in Southern Buddhism he represents " *The body of dead and living saints.*"[2]

Sangha in Northern Buddhism is thus the incarnation of the supreme god, and, as in other Pagan systems, takes the position of a false Christ, and is practically a mystical aspect of Buddha himself, while in Southern Buddhism Sangha represents all the saints of Buddhism, and, in order to get rid of him as a personal deity, he is called "*Congregation.*" But, as Mr Lillie remarks, the prayers addressed to him and Dharma become absurd when these terms are substituted for their names, as in the Ceylon ritual, in which the following prayers occur :—

"May Sangha (*congregation*) forgive me my sin." "I have no other refuge ; Dharma (*canon law*) is my refuge." "I bow my head to the ground and worship Dharma (*canon law*), Sakya Muni is the best refuge." "May Dharma (*canon law*) forgive me my sin."[3]

Amitabha Buddha, Dharma and Sangha may thus be regarded as the original or mythological Trinity of Buddhism.

When, therefore, Sakya Muni was recognised as Buddha, he was naturally incorporated into the system and recognised as the son of the supreme god and goddess, and, indeed, as Buddha himself in mortal form. Therefore, in Southern Buddhism, which knew nothing of the original or mythological Buddha Amitabha, he became the supreme god to the exclusion of other deities.

All the Pagan gods, as we have seen, were identified with the Sun, which was regarded as the Great Father, the generator of all life, while the goddess was the Earth, or matter, the passive source of generation. Their son, or incarnation, was the human expression of the Father, as manifested to man, and was therefore also regarded as the Sun. Hence it was fabled of Sakya Muni, after he had been worshipped as Buddha, that the Sun in the form of a white Elephant (the particular symbol of the Sun) entered

[1] Lillie, p. 22.   [2] *Ibid.*, p. 23.
[3] *Pattimokkha*, pp. 3-5 ; Lillie, pp. 24, 25.

into his mother Maya's side, and the result was the birth of Sakya Muni. Hence also his birthday was said to be on December 25th, the time of the winter solstice, when the sun first begins to regain its power.[1] This was the birthday of all the Sun gods, and was celebrated in Pagan Rome as "Natalis invicti Solis," "the birthday of the un-conquered Sun."[2]

In short, Mr Beal says that, "The ordinary representation of Buddha is *the rising sun*. His jewelled crest is called the 'rasmi culamani,' that is, the ray jewel crest, and the Ceylonese figures of him are generally provided with his crown of triple rays."[3]

Sakya Muni thus took the place of Sangha in his aspect as the great prophet or teacher, the incarnation of the Sun, and as "the Voice of the Dragon."

All the Pagan gods were eventually identified with the Serpent, which was also regarded, like the Sun, as the Great Father, and was a symbol of the Sun. The Serpent, in short, was regarded both as the source of life, and also of wisdom and knowledge, and as the instructor of men, as in the case of Æsculapius and the Babylonian Hea, the "Lord of Understanding" and "Teacher of Mankind," both of whom are represented by serpents. The name *Hea* also means "serpent," and this deity is identified by Sir Henry Rawlinson with the star "Draco," or "the dragon."[4]

The terms "dragon" and "serpent" were practically synony-mous in ancient times, and the Dragon god of Greece and the Dragon standards of Rome are really serpents.[5] The Dragon standard was adopted by the Emperor of Constantinople from the Assyrians,[6] and it was an especial object of worship by the Babylonians.[7] It was also worshipped both in China and Japan. The great Chinese Dragon was, as in Rome and Babylon, the banner of the Empire, and indicated everything sacred.[8] Just also as the serpent was the

---

[1] *See* account, Lillie, pp. 71, 73. He was born, according to the fable, on the eighth day of the second month, which, as the first day of the Hindu year was Nov. 17th, would be Dec. 25th ; Lillie, pp. 71-73.

[2] Gieseler, *Eccles. Hist.*, p. 42, note.

[3] Beal, *Buddhist Lit. in China*, p. 159, and frontispiece.

[4] Rawlinson, *Herod.*, vol. i. p. 600 ; Lenormant, *Chaldean Magic*, pp. 232, 233. *See* also *infra*, chap. x., on the worship of the Sun and the Serpent.

[5] *See* Pl. "Dragon Standard," Elliot's *Horæ Apocalypta*, vol. iii. p. 14.

[6] Vossius, *De Idol*, lib. iv. cap. liv., citing Codinus ; Deane's *Serpent Worship*, p. 46.

[7] "In that same place was a great dragon which they of Babylon worshipped." —*Bel and the Dragon*.

[8] Stukeley's *Abury*, p. 56.

insignia of royalty and dominion in Egypt, so the dragon was "the stamp and symbol of royalty in China, and is sculptured in all temples."[1] "The Chinese," writes Cambry, "delight in mountains and high places, because there lives the dragon upon whom their good fortune depends. They call him 'the Father of Happiness.' To this dragon they erect temples shaded with groves."[2] "The dragon," says Mr Lillie, "represents the Indian cobra as a symbol in China for the supreme god."[3] He is called the "Dragon King," and prayers are regularly offered to him.[4]

Therefore, although the dragon is not actually identified with Amitabha, or Adi Buddha, yet it is plain that he occupies a similar position, and Sangha being at once "the voice, or manifestation, of the dragon," and the incarnation of Amitabha, an intimate connection between the two is implied. This also is the case with Sakya Muni when he takes the place of the mythological Sangha. He is called "the King of the Serpents," "the Tree of Knowledge and the Sun,"[5] thus occupying, as Buddha, apparently the same position as the Babylonian Hea, or the prophet Nebo.

Nor is this the only thing connecting Buddha with the Babylonian Hea, who, as we have seen, is identified with the Egyptian Hermes or Mercury. For the "*Tri-Ratna*" of Buddhism, which is called "the three precious symbols of the faith," consisted of two serpents twining round a staff (*see* sketch), and forming a circle and a crescent, symbolic of the sun and moon, in exactly the same way as the "*Caduceus*" of Hermes or Mercury, the only difference in the Caduceus being that the staff is placed below the serpents. Mercury was the Phallic god, and the whole emblem, the male and female serpents, and the Sun god and Moon goddess, are symbols of generation, the staff, or tree, being symbolic of the Phallus. It occupies the same position as the centre stroke in the letter Φ, which had a similar symbolism.[6]

TRI-RATNA.

[1] Maurice, *Hist. Hind.*, vol. i. p. 210.
[2] Cambry, *Monuments Celtiques*, p. 163 ; Deane, pp. 69, 70.
[3] Lillie, p. 31.   [4] Edkins, p. 207.
[5] *Lalita Vistara*, Lillie, p. 26.
[6] *Vide infra*, chap. x., "Sun, Serpent, Phallic and Tree Worship," where a figure of the "Caduceus" is given.

These, and other features of Sun and Serpent worship, show that it must have existed in China and in Thibet, as it did in India and throughout the world, from the earliest ages, and that when Sakya Muni had been acknowledged as Buddha, he became incorporated into the system, and received many, if not all, the attributes of Amitabha, such as "Heavenly Father," "God of Gods," "King of Kings," "The Omniscient," "The Self-existent."[1] This was only natural, if a mythological Buddha with these attributes already existed, and Sakya Muni was regarded as his incarnation; for, both being Buddhas, whatever was said of the one would be said of the other; as, for instance, the daily prayer throughout China, viz., "May Buddha forgive my sins,"[2] must have applied originally to Amitabha, or Omito Fo, the supreme Buddha, but would also be applied to Sakya Muni when he was recognised as Buddha.

From the fact that the ecclesiastical superiority of the Grand Llama of Thibet is recognised by the Chinese, and even by the Emperor himself, it seems evident that the religious system of Thibet is of the greatest antiquity. It is also the most elaborate and complete. The Grand Llama occupies precisely the same position as the Pontifex Maximus, or Chief Priest of the hierarchies of Babylon, Egypt and Rome. They were always the King, or Emperor, who, like the Grand Llama, were regarded as divine, and as representative of the Divinity on earth. They were addressed as "Your Holiness," and their feet kissed by their subjects.[3] The Llama also wears the fish-headed mitre, similar to that of the Babylonian Fish god Dagon.[4] The Emperor of China, when, as High Priest of the nation, he blesses the people once a year wears the same mitre.[5] There is also in Thibet and China an established priesthood with regular orders, like those of the other Pagan nations, living apart from the rest of the community, and, like the priests of Isis in Egypt, and the priesthoods of Pagan Greece and Rome, vowed to celibacy.[6]

The priesthood of Buddhism is also distinguished by the "*tonsure*," which was the particular symbol in other Pagan nations of the

[1] *See* Lillie, p. 118.   [2] *Ibid.*, p. 25.

[3] Wilkinson's *Egyptians*, vol. ii. p. 68 ; Layard, *Nineveh and Its Remains*, vol. ii. pp. 464, 472, 474 ; Gaussen on Daniel, vol. i. p. 114 ; *see* also Hislop, pp. 211, 212 and note.

[4] Nightingale, *Religions and Ceremonies*, p. 453 ; Layard's *Babylon and Nineveh*, p. 343.

[5] Bryant, vol. v. p. 384.

[6] *See* Lemprière, *Isis* and *Osiris ;* Potter and Boyd, *Grecian Antiq.*, bk. ii. chap. iii. pp. 208, 209.

priesthoods of the Sun god. "The ceremony of tonsure," says Maurice,[1] "was an old practice of the priests of Mithra (the Sun god of Persia), who in their tonsures represented the solar disk." The priests of Isis likewise shaved their heads,[2] so did those of Osiris;[3] so did those of Pagan Rome.[4] "The Arabians," says Herodotus, "acknowledge no other gods but Bacchus and Urania, the Queen of Heaven, and they say their hair is cut in the same way as Bacchus' is cut. Now they cut it in a circular form, shaving it round the temples.[5] Sakya Muni is said to have shaved his head, and directed his disciples to do so in obedience to a command of Vishnu.[6] Hence their title, "The shaved heads." The antiquity of the custom is shown by the commands given to the Israelites forbidding it.[7]

It may be noticed also that the heads of all the images of Buddha, Kwanyin and other deities are surrounded by the "*aureole*," or "*halo*," which was also a particular symbol of the Sun god in other nations. It was placed round the heads of the images of the gods and heroes in Rome and Greece, and also round the heads of the Roman Emperors, to whom divine honours were paid after death. It was regarded as the token of the divinity of the person represented, that is to say, of his being a son of the Sun god, as implied by the lines :—

> "Twelve golden beams around his temples play,
> To mark his lineage from the *god of day*." [8]

The author of *Pompeii* notices it in a painting of Circe and Ulysses, and says it is defined by Servius as "the luminous fluid which encircles the heads of the gods." [9]

Considering then that the Sun is Buddha's special emblem, that he is called "The Sublime Sun Buddha whose widespread rays brighten and illumine all things," and that he is reported to have said that bowing to the East (the usual act of adoration to the Sun god) was "the paramita of charity," that is, the perfection of righteousness,[10] it is very evident that the ancient Buddhism, like other Pagan systems, was founded on Sun worship, and that the

[1] Maurice, *Ind. Antiq.*, vol. vii. p. 851.   [2] Lemprière, *Isis* and *Isiaca*.
[3] Macrobius, lib. i. cap. xxiii.
[4] Tertullian, vol. ii., *Carmina*, pp. 1105, 1106.
[5] Herod., lib. iii. cap. viii.
[6] Kennedy, *Buddha in Hindu Myth.*, pp. 263, 264 ; Hislop, pp. 221, 222.
[7] Leviticus xix. 27, 28 ; Deut. xiv. 1.
[8] Dryden, *Virgil*, book xii. pp. 245, 246 ; vol. iii. p. 775 ; Hislop, p. 237.
[9] On *Æneid*, lib. ii. ver. 616 ; vol. i. p. 165 ; Hislop, p. 87.   [10] Lillie, p. 193.

original or mythological Buddha, whose attributes were given to Sakya Muni, was, like the other Pagan gods, a Sun god.

The character of the goddess "Kwanyin" also corresponds with that of the goddess in other systems, who, known by many names indicative of her various attributes, or aspects, was yet one and the same deity. Just as Buddha is "the Sun," so is Kwanyin, "matter," or "the earth,"[1] and these were the principal aspects of the god and goddess throughout Paganism. Just also as the god was called "Lord of Heaven," so was the goddess called "Queen of Heaven," and this, as we have seen, was equally the title of Kwanyin. Like Minerva, she is the goddess of wisdom.[2] Like *Venus Mylitta,* "The Mediatrix," *Aphrodite,* "The Wrath Subduer," *Bona Dea,* "The Good Goddess," the title of Ceres in Rome, and other forms of the great goddess, the character of Kwanyin is always one of mercy. She is called "the goddess of mercy," and this is the attribute especially applied to her in the Chinese liturgy, and in Buddhism "no person holds so large a place in saving mankind as Kwan shi yin."[3]

Finally Kwanyin is represented with a child in her arms,[4] and in China the Holy Mother, "Shing Moo," who is probably a form of Kwanyin, is represented in the same way.[5] Now this peculiar mode of representing the goddess and her son was common throughout Paganism. In Egypt, she was represented as Isis with the child Osiris or Horus in her arms. In India, as Isa and Iswara. In Asia, as Cybele and Deoius. In Rome, as Fortuna and the boy Jupiter. In Greece as Ceres with a babe at her breast, or as Irene with the boy Plutus.[6]

[1] *See* Prayer, *ante,* p. 106.   [2] *Ibid.*

[3] Edkins, pp. 382, 385. Dr Edkins seems to think that Kwanyin was once a male deity, and that his sex has been changed. But this is unlikely, and it is more probable that, as was constantly the case in Paganism, there was a god and goddess of the same name, the latter being the feminine counterpart of the former and possessing similar attributes. The male Kwanyin was really a form of Buddha and called Chin Fo. The ancient liturgies clearly address Kwanyin as a goddess.

[4] Edkins, p. 242.

[5] Crabb's *Mythology,* p. 150 ; Davies, *China,* vol. ii. p. 56 ; Hislop, p. 21 and note.

[6] *See* Hislop, woodcuts of goddess and child from Babylon and India, pp. 19, 20. In Mr Edwin Long's picture "Anno Domini," there is a golden figure of Isis with Horus in her arms, carried in a long procession of priests from an Egyptian temple, while in the foreground is the infant Jesus with Mary and Joseph. It is the meeting of the true and false Christs, for, as we shall see, everything was done to identify the Pagan god with the promised "seed of the woman."

But while this indicates the intimate connection of Buddhism with other Pagan systems at some previous period, it is yet evident that the period must have been very remote, for the Chinese have altogether lost the real significance of the mother and child; Kwanyin being now simply regarded as "the giver of sons."[1]

It is possible that Sun worship and the distinctive features of Western Paganism were never fully received by Eastern Asia, and were probably in part derived from the mythology of India.

There are, however, many points of identity between the two systems. Tree worship, for instance, is as characteristic of Buddhism as it was of Western Paganism, in which the Grove worship, so constantly referred to in the Old Testament, and the worship of certain sacred trees, were prominent features.[2] Buddha is represented as sitting under a tree, and the same homage was paid to the tree as to Buddha himself. In the edicts of King Asoka, veneration to the Holy Fig-tree is strongly inculcated, and the *Stupa of Bharhut* represents the Bodhi trees of the seven Buddhas, each being worshipped. General Cunningham quotes Quintus Curtius as saying that the companions of Alexander the Great noticed the fact that "the Indians reputed as God whatever they held in reverence, specially trees, which it was death to injure."[3]

The worship of the dead was, as we have seen, the distinguishing feature in Western Paganism. This was not merely the case in the worship of the greater gods, but also in the worship of minor deities, who were illustrious men, and called "hero gods." It is still more characteristic of Buddhism, in which, besides the Buddhas and goddesses, there are a multitude of Bodhisat was, or holy men, whose images are also worshipped after their death. In short, the heads of the Cingalese monasteries assert that their main rites are "saint worship."[4] There is also a special day set apart for the worship of their ancestors by the Chinese, viz., the fifteenth day of their seventh month,[5] which therefore nearly exactly corresponds with the date on which the festival of the dead was held in many other nations, viz., the seventeenth day of the seventh month.[6]

There are also prayers for the dead as in Egypt, where large sums were paid for the celebration of prayers and sacrifices for the dead;

---

[1] Edkins, p. 383.   [2] See *infra*, chap. x.
[3] *Stupa of Bharhut*, by Gen. Cunningham, pp. 106, 109, 113-116.
[4] Upham's *Sacred and Historical Books of Ceylon*, p. 161 ; Lillie, pp. 27, 43, 45.
[5] Edkins, p. 268.   [6] Gen. viii. 4 ; see *ante*, chap. i.
[7] Wilkinson's *Egyptians*, vol. ii. p. 94 ; vol. v. pp. 383, 384.

H

and as in Greece, where the greatest and most expensive sacrifice was the mysterious sacrifice called "*Telete*," offered for the sins of the living and the dead.[1]   In India the service of the "*Sraddha*" for the repose of the dead was equally costly.[2]   It was the idea among the Pagans that the dead went to a purgatory which Plato describes as a subterranean place of judgment, where they underwent various sufferings until they were cleansed from their sins,[3] and these sufferings were supposed to be shortened by the prayers and services held by the priesthood. Similar services called "*Kungte*" (merit) are performed by the Buddhist priests for the dead.   They profess to have the power to save the soul, and by their mediation to "redeem the deceased person from the punishment due to his sins."   This is expressed by the phrase "*Shu tsui*," "redeem from guilt."[4]

The Pagans of the West consecrated their images and believed that, by so doing, the god they represented entered into them and dwelt there.[5]   The Buddhist idols are also consecrated by a ceremony called "opening to the light," and directly the crystal eyes are put into an image the spirit of the god, or departed saint, is supposed to animate it.[6]

There are other minor points of resemblance, as, for instance, the rite of initiation, similar to that of "The Lesser Mysteries" in Egypt and Greece, by which, after a confession and a baptism of water, the initiate was supposed to be reborn and forgiven all his sins.[7]   In Buddhism the initiate is also baptised after a confession of his sins and certain vows, and is considered regenerated, the change being called "the white birth."[8]   A sutra of Sakya Muni Buddha entitles it "The baptism that rescues from life and death, and confers salvation."[9]

But the feature in which Buddhism most closely resembles the Paganism of the West, and especially that of Assyria and Egypt, is its *demonology* and *magic*.   M. Lenormant has collected from the cuneiform inscriptions of Western Asia a number of incantations and spells used by the Chaldean priesthood, by which they invoked the aid of a multitude of beneficent spirits, to defeat the actions of evil

[1] Plato, vol. ii. pp. 364, 365 ; Suidas, vol. ii. p. 879.
[2] *Asiat. Res.*, vol. vii. pp. 239, 240.
[3] Dryden's *Virgil*, book vi. ll. 995-1012 ; vol. ii. p. 536 ; Plato, *Phædrus*, p. 249.
[4] Edkins, pp. 385, 386.
[5] Arnobius, lib. v. caps. ix. and xvii.   [6] Edkins, p. 252 ; Lillie, p. 39.
[7] Tertullian, *De Baptismo*, vol. i. pp. 1204, 1205 ; Gregory Nazianzen, *Opera*, p. 245.
[8] Lillie, pp. 55, 57.   [9] *Journ. Asiat. Soc.*, vol. xx. p. 172.

spirits, and dispel the effects of sorcery, disease, misfortune, etc.[1]
The extreme antiquity of these incantations is shown by the fact
that they are expressed in the ancient Accadian language, which it
was thought gave them greater efficacy. So with Buddhism. "It
was plainly," says Mr Lillie, " an elaborate apparatus to nullify the
action of evil spirits by the aid of good spirits."[2] Even the liturgical
prayers of the Buddhists are incantations. Mr Edkins says, "They
are chanted by the priests," and "consist of extracts from sutras, or
special books, containing charms. They are not prayers in our
sense. They work a sort of magical effect."[3] The Tanists, a
Buddhist sect,[4] "occupy themselves with writing charms for driving
demons out of houses, and with reading prayers for the removal of
calamities." The Tanist magician "will undertake to drive
out a demon from the body of a madman, and from a haunted
house, to cure the sick by magic, and to bring rain in time of
drought."[5]

Mr Edkins remarks that the present popularity of Buddhism
certainly does not rest on the doctrines of the faith, but on the
supposed magical powers of the priests, "because the people believe
in the magical efficacy of Buddhist prayers."[6] These powers were
due to "*necromancy*." The aid of beneficent spirits was sought
"through the instrumentality of the corpse, or portion of the corpse,
of the chief aiding spirit." "A saint dies, and is buried in a tumulus,
or under a tree, and under this tree, by-and-by, sits another holy man
who periodically gets obsessed by the dead saint, and in that state
exhibits the various marvels of clairvoyance, fortune-telling," etc.[7]
"The Buddhist temple," says Mr Lillie, " the Buddhist rites and the
Buddhist liturgy all seem based on this one idea, that a whole, or
portion, of a dead body was necessary."[8] Hence "a portion of the
relics of Buddha was a *sine qua non* in each of its temples. This was
plainly for magical purposes. When Yung Shin, the Chinese
pilgrim, visited the King of Oudeyana he gave such a flattering
picture to that monarch of the divination, alchemy, medicine and
magic practised by the Buddhists of China that he made the king
eagerly desire to visit that land of marvels. To this day the
Buddhist temple is the home of marvels; and in front of many
statues of Buddha there is a table in China on which an apparatus

[1] Lenormant, *Chaldean Magic.*   [2] Lillie, p. 47.
[3] Edkins, p. 257.   [4] *Ibid.*, chap. xxiv.
[5] *Ibid.*, p. 382.   [6] *Ibid.*, pp. 380, 381.
[7] Lillie, pp. 37, 47.   [8] *Ibid.*, p. 47.

similar to a planchette is used for ghostly communications. This planchette has been known for many hundred years." [1]

The magical powers exercised by the Buddhist priest are attributed to asceticism. "Six supernatural faculties were expected of the ascetic before he could claim the grade of *Arhat*. He had to rise into the air, to rain down water and then fire from his body, to make that body expand and then grow indefinitely small; the sixth exploit was to disappear in the heavens and return to earth and then rise once more aloft." [2]

The *Samanna Phala Sutra*, which is said to have been written by Sakya Muni, enlarges upon the exact object of the ascetic. "Man," he says, "has a body composed of the four elements. It is the fruit of the union of his father and his mother. In this transitory body his intelligence is confined. The ascetic therefore directs his mind to the creation of the Manas. He represents to himself in thought another body created from this material body. This body, in relation to the material body, is like the sword and the scabbard, or a serpent issuing from a basket in which it is confined. Then the ascetic, when purified and perfected, commences to practise supernatural faculties. He finds himself able to pass through material obstacles—walls, ramparts—and he is able to throw his phantasmal appearance into many places at once; he can walk upon the surface of the water, and fly through the air. Another faculty is now conquered by the force of will. He acquires the power of hearing the sounds of the unseen world as distinctly as those of the phenomenal world. By the power of the Manas he is able to read the most secret thoughts of others. Then comes the faculty of 'divine vision,' and he sees all that men do on earth and after they die, and when they are again reborn. Then he detects the secrets of the universe," etc. [3]

The name given to these ascetics was "*Shamanas*," or "*Shramanas*," a word meaning "quieting of the passions," [4] the object of asceticism being the complete subjugation of every natural desire as a means to the attainment of these supernatural powers. Mr Lillie remarks, "The marvels of the Shaman are so well known to readers of travels in Buddhist countries that they need not be dwelt on here. Messrs Huc and Gabet report that they saw a Bokté rip open his own stomach in the Great Court of the Lamaserai of Rache Tchurin, in

---

[1] Beal, *Buddhist Pilgrims*, p. 190; *Strange Stories from a Chinese Studio*, vol. ii. p. 295; Lillie, pp. 38, 39.

[2] *The Lotus*, p. 270, Appendix, p. 476; Lillie, p. 45.

[3] Quoted by Lillie, pp. 45, 46.　　　　　　[4] Edkins, p. 89, note.

Tartary. After a copious flow of blood had deluged the court, the Bokté closed and healed the wound with a single pass of his hand. 'These horrible ceremonies,' say the good fathers, 'are of frequent occurrence in the Great Lamaserais of Tartary and Thibet, and we do not believe there is any trick or deception about them; for from all we have seen and heard we are persuaded that the devil has a great deal to do with the matter.'"[1]

In Yule's *Marco Polo* there is also reference to the magical powers of the Buddhist priesthood in Tartary. The Khan is described as favourably disposed to Christianity, and it is added, "Since he holds the Christian faith to be best, why does he not attach himself to it and become a Christian? Well, this is the reason that he gave to Messer Nicolo and Messer Maffeo when he sent them as his envoys to the Pope, and when they sometimes took upon them to speak to him about the faith of Christ, he said—'How would you have me to become a Christian? You see that the Christians of these parts are so ignorant that they achieve nothing, whilst you see the idolaters can do anything they please, inasmuch that when I sit at table the cups from the middle of the hall come to me full of wine, or other liquor, without being touched by anybody, and I drink from them. They control storms, causing them to pass in whatever direction they please, and do many other marvels, whilst, as you know, their idols speak and give them predictions on whatever subjects they choose. But if I were to turn to the faith of Christ and become a Christian, then my barons and others who are not converted would say, "What has moved you to be baptised and take up the faith of Christ? What powers or miracles have you witnessed on His part?" You know that the idolaters here say that their wonders are performed by the sanctity and power of their idols. Well, I should not know what answer to make, so they would only be confirmed in their errors, and the idolaters, who are adepts in such surprising arts, would easily compass my death."[2]

These powers, if they were real, did not exceed those of the sorcerers and magicians of Egypt, who, up to a certain point, were able to imitate, by their enchantments, the miracles performed by Moses and Aaron in the presence of Pharaoh, and we may presume that the Chaldean priesthood, whose wisdom was as famous as that of the Egyptian priests, had similar powers, the knowledge

[1] Lillie, p. 47.
[2] Ramusis' edition of *Marco Polo*; Yule's *Marco Polo*; bk. ii. chap. vi. vol. i. p. 339.

of attaining which had been handed down from the ancient
Accadians.

The Buddhist doctrine is that by asceticism and intense self-
absorption and mystic meditation, it is possible to attain a mental
state by which six kinds of supernatural wisdom called "*abhinna*,"
and ten supernatural powers called "*Iddhi*," are acquired; and there
are four stages, or "*Jhanas*," of this self-induced mystic ecstasy
before the perfect state is attained. In addition to this, there
is the state of "*Samadhi*," or self-induced mesmeric trance, which is
supposed to be a proof of superior holiness, and of which there have
been well-authenticated instances.[1] Similar states of extasia and
mesmeric trance were customary with the Greek prophets and
diviners, and the devotees of Brahminism.[2]

Mr Lillie says, "The Buddhists are the great adepts of
mesmerism. To this day the ministrations of Buddhist monks outside the Viharas are almost exclusively confined to this magnetic
healing. '*Akasa*,' the mesmeric fluid, and the spirit of God, are one
in the East."[3]

Mesmerism was equally used by the Egyptian priesthood to produce a state of trance, or extasia, in which the spirits of the gods
were supposed to enter into the person and speak by him.[4]

The knowledge and powers, however, obtained by means of
mesmerism were distinct from, and supplementary to, those possessed by the ascetic himself, the conditions for acquiring which
were celibacy and abstinence from wine and meat, combined with
solitude and self-absorption. The reason given, according to the
teaching of Sakya Muni, for abstaining from meat is that flesh "pre-
vents charms and other magical devices from taking effect,"[5] and we
may presume that the other forms of abstinence were considered to
be equally necessary. This, however, will be more fully considered
in another chapter.

It is clear that the magic and sorcery used by the priests of
Buddhism are similar to those made use of by the priesthoods of
Chaldea and Egypt, and by the necromancers, wizards, sorcerers and
magicians of the Canaanitish nations, and to the magic, divination,
and other methods used by the Greeks for consulting the gods.[6]   The

[1] Rhys Davis, *Buddhism*, pp. 174, 175.
[2] *See* Potter and Boyd, *Greek Ant.*, book ii. chap. xviii.   [3] Lillie, p. 140.
[4] See *infra*, chap. viii.   [5] Edkins, p. 204.
[6] These are more fully described in chap. viii.   *See* also Potter and Boyd, *Greek
Ant.*, book ii. chaps. vii.-xviii.

original source of this magic, as shown by M. Lenormant, is to be traced to the Accadian race, the primitive Cushite inhabitants of the Euphrates and Tigris valleys, as is clear from the fact that the later Chaldeans used the Accadian language as a sacred tongue, which they regarded as of special efficacy for their charms and incantations. Moreover, M. Lenormant has pointed out that the Turanian and Mongolian races use the same magic, and that the Ugric and Altaic tribes have their "*Shamanas*" like the Buddhists, and and that a similar magic existed among the people of Media.[1] It may also be remarked that the priesthoods of Persia and Bactria are also called "*Samaneans*,"[2] the name given by Strabo and Porphyry to the Buddhists of India,[3] and by which, as we have seen, the followers of Sakya Muni were called. This is the name now given by German philosophers to all who believe in an intercourse with the spirit world.

M. Lenormant has also pointed out the intimate relation of the Accadian language to that of the Turanian, or Ugric—Altaic races,[4] implying therefore that the Mongolian people of Northern Buddhist countries, Thibet and China, were at some remote period intimately associated with the Accadians.[5]

It is also worthy of remark that in the Chaldean demonology there were two classes of *demi-gods*, one of which was called in the Accadian language "*Llamma*," and in Assyrian "*Lamas*," meaning "*giant*,"[6] the name by which the Nephilim and Nephilim races, of which we shall speak hereafter, were known, and which would be equally applied to those who claimed either descent from them, or the possession of their powers. Considering therefore the connection of the Accadian and Mongolian languages, we have probably here the origin of the name "*Lamas*," who are the Buddhist priests and magicians of Thibet.

Taking these things into consideration and the fact that Shamanas and Shamanism, which are the principal features of Northern Buddhism, exist in countries where Sakya Muni is unknown, together with other points of identity between Buddhism and the religious systems of Western Asia, it is clear that the religion of Northern Buddhism and of the Turanian or Ural-Altaic races must have been

---

[1] *Chaldean Magic*, chaps. xiv., xv., and chap. xviii., pp. 263, 265.

[2] Cyril, *Opera*, lib. ii. p. 133 : Clem. Alex., *Strom.*, lib. i. p. 305.

[3] Strabo, lib. xv., pp. 712-714 ; *Porph. de Abstin.*, lib. iv. p. 17 : Faber, *Pag. Idol.*, vol. ii. pp. 351, 353.

[4] *Chaldean Magic*, chaps. xviii, xxiii.

[5] *See* Appendix D, *The Accadians.*   [6] *Chaldean Magic*, chap. ii. p. 23, 24.

derived from the same source as that of Babylon, Egypt, Phœnicia, etc., but that having separated from the peoples of those countries at an early period, it had only partially adopted their later and more complicated mythological developments.

If so, we must look for the origin of the primitive or mythological Buddha from the same source. We may also presume that the colossal images by which Buddha is represented, and those by which he is shown as a triple deity, like the Buddha of Brahminism, who is the mysterious *A. U. M.*, and which appear to be quite incongruous with the character of the teacher and reformer Sakya Muni, were originally representative of the mythological Buddha, although they were subsequently identified with Sakya Muni. The same may be said of the gigantic impression of Buddha's foot which is shown in various places, and his gigantic teeth (probably the fossil teeth of a mammoth or mastodon) which are treasured as relics. They are quite inconsistent with the character of an ascetic and teacher, and are evidently the rude expression of a belief in a being of abnormal power.

The Arabs, who are not Buddhists, have also a god, the impression of whose gigantic foot is treasured as a sacred object in the Caaba of Mecca. They worship him as the great father and call him " *Theuth-Ares*," or " *Thoth-Ares*," and they also call him " *Wudd*," or " *Budd*," and no doubt he is the primitive mythological Buddha.[1]

It would appear that Sakya Muni, beyond being recognised as an Avatar of Buddha, has had little or no influence on the religion of Northern Buddhism. Its priesthood and ritual, its magic and sorcery, are probably the same now as when first derived from the ancient Accadians, while the moral teaching of Sakya Muni is not only without effect upon the people of these countries but, as Mr Edkins remarks, the books containing his teaching " are never, or almost never, read in the liturgical services, and as to trying to be good, the Buddhists (of China) do not evince much indication that this aim is vital and vigorous among them."[2] Asceticism, or the denial of every natural and legitimate desire, does not appeal to the majority of mankind, nor will a barbarous and cruel race, or indeed any race, consent to forego any form of retaliation on those who injure them, even to the extent of forgiving criminals, as taught by Sakya Muni. It is only a few who will even undertake the self-denial required to enable them to attain those magical powers which are believed to be associated

[1] Maxim. Tyr., *Dissert.*, chap. xxxviii. p. 374 ; *Asiat. Res.*, vol. ii. pp. 8, 9 ; vol. iii. pp. 304, 305; Faber, vol. ii. p. 390.
[2] Edkins, p. 381.

with it, and it may be safely asserted that the teaching of Sakya Muni would have had little or no influence had it been without the promise of those powers. Mr Edkins says that Buddhism (not the teaching of Sakya Muni) is believed in by the people because they "believe in the magical efficacy of Buddhist prayers and in moral causation, or, in other words the law of moral retribution which Buddhism teaches." What that morality is he explains:—"It is on these accounts that money flows into the Buddhist treasury for the erection and repair of temples and pagodas, and for the support of innumerable priests. If I give money to gild sacred images, the law of causation will give me back happiness."[1] In other words, it is the morality which the priesthoods of Paganism have taught in all ages, viz., the promise of salvation to those who support the priesthood and temples of the gods.

Mr Rhys Davis rather deprecates the idea that his hero, Sakya Muni, should have believed in, and advocated, magic, because it might seem to be inconsistent with the supposed high morality of his teaching.[2] But that teaching, although certain of its features are not unlike the precepts of Christianity, is in spirit diametrically opposed to it, for it appears to make man the author of his own salvation, which, when supposed to be attained, can only exalt the pride and self-confidence which is so opposed to the spirit of Christ, while the adulation and worship which these supposed holy men receive from their followers cannot fail to conduce to the same result. Nor can that result be altered merely because self-righteousness is condemned and humility enjoined. The humility in such cases will only be affectation, the pride that apes it.

Moreover, certain features of this morality, or righteousness, taught by Sakya Muni are a travesty and exaggeration of that of Christianity, and condemned by it, while the asceticism he enjoined is identical with that of the apostasy from Christianity foretold by St Paul, the authors of which are described as condemning marriage, and commanding to abstain from meats; "teaching" which, the Apostle says, is that "of seducing spirits and doctrines of devils" (daimonia).—(1 Tim. iii. 1-3). It would seem indeed that this abstinence is a necessary qualification for attaining those powers wielded by the priesthood and magicians of Paganism, and which powers are not of God.

Without doubt, Sakya Muni was not the originator of the methods for attaining these magical powers, which clearly existed

[1] Edkins, p. 381.   [2] Rhys Davis, *Buddhism*, p. 177.

before his time, but there is not only no evidence that he ever opposed them, but it is impossible to believe that he could have attained the influence he has had, if he had made no claim to them.

Remusat, quoting from a Japanese Encyclopædia, says that, " Buddha (Sakya Muni) before his death committed the secret of his mysteries to his disciple Maha Kashiapa. The latter was a Brahmin born in the kingdom of Magadha in Central India. To him was entrusted the deposit of the esoteric doctrine called ' *Chen fa yen tsang*,' the pure secret of the eye of right doctrine." [1] Mr Edkins says that the symbol of this esoteric principle communicated orally

without books is   卍   " *man*," or " *wan*," and implies the posses-

sion of ten thousand perfections. It is usually placed on the heart of Buddha in images and pictures of that divinity. It is sometimes called " *Sinyin*," " heart's seat." It contains within it the whole mind of Buddha. In Sanskrit it is called " *Svastika.*" " It was the monogram of Vishnu and Shiva, the battle-axe of Thor in Scandinavian inscriptions, an ornament on the crowns of the Bonpa deities of Thibet, and a favourite symbol with the Peruvians." [2]

Here, then, is evidence of the existence of an occult doctrine distinct from the moral teaching of Sakya Muni, and shown by the " Svastika " to be connected with the mysteries of other Pagan nations, and which, we may presume, was the secret of attaining the magical powers which constitute the chief feature of Buddhism, and are the real source of its influence.

It is probable that this secret doctrine was originally that of the primitive mythological Buddha, and that, like other characteristics of the latter, it was afterwards attributed to Sakya Muni, when he was recognised as Buddha. It seems certain, as we shall see, that such occult teaching concerning magical powers was attributed to the primitive Buddha, but as Sakya Muni could never have had the influence he has had by his moral teaching only, we may presume that his reported association with these occult and magical powers is correct.

Sakya Muni was a product of Brahminism, the devotees of which followed a similar asceticism, and laid claim to similar magical powers. He acknowledged the Vedic gods and advocated the worship of the *Chaityas*,[3] and we must presume that his teaching

---

[1] Quoted by Edkins, p. 62.   [2] Edkins, pp. 62, 63.
[3] *Chaityas*, sacred trees, images, etc. ; See *Stupa of Bharhut*, pp. 108 109.

and asceticism were the product of his religious environment, viz., of Brahminism and the Northern Buddhism of Nepaul and Thibet, which, as we have seen, was acknowledged and honoured by the Brahmins, Buddha being regarded by them as identical with the triple deity Brahma, Vishnu and Siva, and known by the sacred and mysterious name A. U. M.[1]

Professor Baldwin quotes Eugene Bournouf as saying that, "he found it difficult to understand the intimate connection that existed between Buddhism and Siva worship."[2] But the difficulty is removed when, as we shall see, both are found to have originated from the same source, and were recognised therefore by the Brahmins as merely different aspects of the same religious system.

Sakya Muni's influence is paramount in Southern Buddhism, which sprang out of Brahminism. In Southern Buddhism he holds the position that Amitabha holds in Northern Buddhism, and the reason of this is, no doubt, because his teaching was anathematised by the Brahmins, and his followers excommunicated, which led them to repudiate the Vedic gods and exalt Sakya Muni to the position of the supreme God.

It is clear, however, that Buddha and Buddhism existed before Sakya Muni; that the characteristics of the supreme, or mythological, Buddha are similar to those of the sun and serpent gods of other Pagan nations; that the Buddhist Trinity of Father, Mother and Son is similar to their Trinities; that the principal features of the religion of Northern Buddhism are identical with those of other Pagan systems, and that their origin must therefore be sought for in a remote antiquity.

The question is—Can we identify and ascertain the origin of the primitive and mythological Buddha?

The Buddhists of Thibet insist that their religion has existed from the beginning, and that it has remained unchanged for the last 3000 years;[3] and the fact that the name of their Pontifex and priesthood, viz., "*Lamas*," who wield such remarkable magical powers, is the same as that of the demi-gods of the Accadians, the originators of magic, suggests the common origin of both.

The Buddha of the Chinese, "Fo," called also "Fo Hi," *i.e.*, "Fo, the Victim," is stated to be "the first Emperor, who was manifested on the mountains of Chin, immediately after that great division of time which was produced by the Deluge;" that "he carefully bred

---

[1] *Ante*, p. 101.   [2] *Prehistoric Nations*, p. 255.
[3] Faber, vol. ii. pp. 329, 343; Nightingale, *Rites and Ceremonies*, p. 445.

seven different kinds of animals which he used to sacrifice to the Great Spirit of heaven and earth," and that he was "born of a rainbow."[1] Here he is evidently identified with Noah, and his sacrifice is clearly an allusion to the sacrifice by Noah of the different kinds of clean animals which he took into the Ark by sevens, while the rainbow is an allusion to the covenant made by God with Noah and his descendants. The events of the Deluge were, as shown by Mr Faber, incorporated into the mythologies of all the Pagan nations, while their gods, though subsequently identified with Cush and Nimrod, were primarily identified with Noah, as in the case of Osiris, who was fabled to have slept a year on the deep, just as Noah was shut up in the Ark for that period.

The title "Fo, the Victim," tends to identify him with Brahma, also called "the Victim," who was decapitated, and also with Belus, who was likewise decapitated, and with Osiris, the search for whose head was yearly commemorated,—the death of each being represented as having been undergone for the good of mankind.[2]

In the story of Menu Satya Vrata, translated by Sir William Jones from the *Bhagavat*, there is the account of the great Deluge, and the preservation of Menu with seven saints in an Ark sent by Brahma in the form of a great fish, called "*Maya.*"[3] Menu (*Men Nuh*, or "the mind Nuh"), like Fo Hi, is, of course, Noah; and Vishnu, who is the same as Ish-Nu, the man 'or mind Nu, or Nuh, is the same person, and is represented issuing from the mouth of a fish,[4] which is a symbol of the Ark. So also Buddha is called "*Narayana*," or "Buddha dwelling in the waters," and is called by the Hindus "*Machodar Nath*," or "The Sovereign Prince in the belly of the Fish."[5]

The Mother of the gods and men is constantly identified with the Ark, as that out of which they were, so to speak, born again in a new world, and the great fish which saved Menu and out of which, in his character as Vishnu, he was born, was called Maya, and Maya is said to be the Mother of Universal Nature and of all the inferior gods—that is to say, she is the same as the goddess mother of Paganism, who was identified with the Ark.[6]

So also the mother of Buddha was called "*Maha Maya*," "The

[1] Faber, vol. ii. pp. 343, 344.

[2] *Asiat. Res.*, vol. v. pp. 379, 386 ; vol. vii. pp. 251, 252 ; Moor, *Hind. Panth.*, p. 102 ; Berosus, *Apud. Bunsen*, vol. i. p. 709 ; Faber, vol. i. pp. 210, 211, 491-495.

[3] *Asiat. Res.*, vol. i. pp. 230, 234 ; Faber, vol. ii. pp. 113, 116.

[4] Maurice, *Hist. Hind.*, vol. i. p. 507.

[5] *Asiat. Res.*, vol. vi. pp. 479, 480 ; Faber, vol. ii. p. 117.

[6] Faber, vol. i. p. 223.

Great Maya." This was also the name of Parvati, the mother of Siva. The author of *Amaracosha* says that Buddha was the son of the Lunar god, and that he married Ila, and Ila was also both the daughter and wife of Menu.[1] Both Buddha and Menu are also called " *Dharma Rajah*," " King of Justice," and it is thus clear that Buddha and Menu are regarded as different aspects of the same god in Indian mythology, and that their character as Noah is the same as that of the Chinese Fo Hi.

As many of the gods of Western Paganism were at first more or less identified with Noah, this does not reveal the real human original of Buddha, but it tends to show that it was similar to theirs. Buddha, as we have seen, is also identified with the triple deity— Brahma, Vishnu, Siva—and is especially called " Iswara," who has been identified with Osiris.

We have seen that some of the Buddhists of India who refuse to acknowledge Sakya Muni, worship Buddha under the name of *Deva Datta*, " The Divine Datta";[2] and Buddha is known also by this title in China, as in a Buddhist temple at Pekin wherein is shown the impression of the foot of Buddha, and it is called the impression of the foot of Datta.[3]

We have also seen that the sacerdotal orders of the Persians and Bactrians were entitled " Samaneans "—the general name given to the priesthood of Buddha—and " Samaneans " must therefore be another name for the Persian " *Magi*." The name, in their *Zend Avesta*, of the first sacred Man-bull (which was a representative of the Pagan god in Babylon, Egypt and India) was " *Aboudad*," which, like the Abbuto of the Japanese, is plainly *Ab-boud dad*, " Father Boud Dat," or " Datta," the " d " and " t " being interchangeable. The name also of their second Man-bull was " *Taschta*," which is plainly a form of another title of Buddha, viz., *Twashta*.[4] So likewise, according to the Dabestan of Mohsan, they held that the first monarch of Iran and of the whole world was " *Mahabad*," and that there were, or would be, fourteen Avatars of this Mahabad. Sir William Jones remarks that " Mahabad " is Sanskrit, and he identifies him indisputably with Menu, who also was supposed to have fourteen Avatars, and has been identified with Buddha. This identifies Mahabad with Buddha, and his name " Mahabad " is evidently " The

[1] *Asiat. Res.*, vol. vii.
[2] *Ante*, pp. 101, 103.
[3] *Asiat. Res.*, vol. ii. pp. 482, 483 ; Faber, vol. ii. p. 347.
[4] Faber, vol. ii. p. 353.

Great Bad," or "Bud." [1]   The head also of the priesthood in Persia and Bactria, who was always the earthly representative of the Pagan god, is called "The Chief Bad" or "Bud." [2]

Now, as Nimrod's was the first great empire of the world, and included the country called "Iran," this would make Maha Bad to be Nimrod, and the name given to Buddha, viz., Datta, or Tatta, and Deva Tat, or "The Divine Tat," is evidently the same as "*Tat*," the name given by Manetho to the son of Hermes. [3]   This would represent Buddha, or Datta, to have been Nimrod; but the characteristics of father and son so constantly blend that they are often confused together, and we shall see that there is strong evidence to identify Buddha with the gods known as Thoth, Hermes, Mercury, Hea, Nebo, and with the various forms of the father of the gods whose human original was Cush.

There were two great sects among the Pagan nations of the West, one of whom regarded the Sun as their chief god and the Moon as the goddess, and the other with whom the Moon was a male deity and their chief god.   The former was represented by the nations of Western Asia—the Assyrians, Phœnicians, etc.—and by the Egyptians, Greeks and Romans, who represented the more civilised nations of ancient times, and the latter by the ancient Germans, the Celts and by the Arabians.

These two sects existed together in India, and are noticed by Strabo and Porphyry.   They were called the Solar and Lunar races, and constituted the two great dynasties in that country, viz., the *Surya Vansa*, or Solar dynasty, and the *Chandra Vansa* or Lunar Dynasty; Rama being regarded as the great head of the Solar race, and Buddha of the Lunar race. [4]   It is true that in later times Buddha was regarded as a Solar deity, through his association with the Vedic gods; but in the more distant Buddhist races, such as the Kalmuck Tartars, Buddha was believed to live in the moon, [5] and there seems to be little doubt that the *Woden* of the ancient Germans and Anglo-Saxons (with whom the moon was the chief diety) is identical with *Poden* or Buddha. [6]   The Arabs also worshipped a god called Wudd, or Budd, and have the impression of his foot in the Caaba of Mecca, just as the impression of Buddha's foot is shown in

[1] *Asiat. Res.*, vol. ii. pp. 58, 60 ; Faber, vol. ii. pp. 353, 354.
[2] Vallancey's *Vindic. Apud Collect. de reb. Hibern.*, vol. iv. No. 14, pp. 429, 437 ; Faber, vol. ii. p. 454.
[3] Cory, *Fragments*, p. 173.
[4] Pococke, *India in Greece*, chap. xiii. pp. 160, 161 ; chap. xiv. p. 183.
[5] Rhys Davis, p. 197.   [6] See *infra*, chap. vii.

Buddhist countries.[1] All these, together with the Celtic Gauls, constituted those races with whom the Moon was a male deity and their chief god.

But it has been shown that Hermes, or Thoth, was the Moon god, and that he was worshipped in Egypt and throughout Asia Minor as Meni, The Lord Moon, while his name among the Anglo-Saxons was Mane or Mani. He was thus the Moon god of the Lunar races, and it would therefore appear that Buddha, the head of the Lunar race in India, was the same god, viz., Thoth or Cush. In short, one of the names of Buddha, or Budd, among the Arabs was *Thoth-Ares*.[2] This conclusion is confirmed by other evidence.

The Latin writers state that the chief god of the German and Celtic nations was Mercury or Hermes. He was called by the Goths " *Tuisto* " and " *Teut*," and by the Gauls " *Teutates* "[3]—names which are evidently forms of *Taut* or *Taautus*, one of the names of Thoth or Hermes—and the name *Twashta* (*Tuasta*), one of the titles of Buddha, would easily pass into *Tuisto*. The mother of Hermes or Mercury was Maya, or Maia,[4] and this was also the name of the mother of Buddha. The fourth day of the week was called " Mercury's day " by the Celtic nations, as it is now by the French " Mercredi," and by German nations " Wodensday " or " Wednesday."[5] In Buddhist nations the same day is called " Boodwar," or " Buddha's day."[6] The star Mercury is also called " Buddha " by the Hindus.[7] Mercury was represented by a conical black stone: Buddha is likewise represented by similar black stones.[8]

Mercury was the conductor of the dead. So also Buddha, in his character as *Naravahana*, is represented as conveying the souls of the dead over the river of Hell,[9] and Menu Satyavratta, who is identified with him, is also depicted as the god of funeral obsequies.[10] Again, the sacred symbol of Buddha, the *Triratna*, composed of two serpents

[1] *Ante*, p. 120.   [2] *Ibid.*

[3] Lucan, *Pharsal*, lib. i. vers. 444, 446 ; Lactant, *Instit.*, lib. i. cap. xxi ; Faber, vol. ii. p. 361.

[4] Lemprière, *Mercury.*

[5] Iceland, *Wonsdag;* Swedish, *Odinsdag;* Dutch, *Woensdag;* English, *Wednesday*—Junii, *Etymol. Anglic,* fol. 1748.

[6] *Asiat. Res.*, vol i. p. 162 ; vol. iii. p. 562 ; Maurice, *Hist. Hind.*, vol. ii. p. 481.

[7] *Asiat. Res.*, vol. i. p. 162 ; vol. ii. p. 375 ; vol. iii. p. 258 ; Faber, vol. ii. pp. 359, 360, note.

[8] Maurice, *Hist. Hind.*, vol. ii. p. 481 ; *Ind. Ant.*, vol. iii. p. 31 ; Faber, vol. ii. pp. 339, 340.

[9] *Asiat. Res.*, vol. ix. p. 173 ; *Ramayun*, bk. i. sect. 5.

[10] Faber, vol. ii. pp. 119, 298, 299.

making a circle and a crescent, is evidently a slightly different form of the *Caduceus* of Mercury, which is also two serpents forming a circle and a crescent.

The title "Buddha" is synonymous with "prophet," "teacher," "sage," and it signifies "wisdom," "intellect," "mind,"[1] and has therefore the same significance as "*Mens*," "Mind" or "Intellect," the "*Men*" of "*Menu*," and as "*Meni*," "the Numberer," the title of the Moon god Thoth or Hermes, who, like Buddha, was the great instructor and prophet. Buddha was also called "*Mahi Man*," "the great man or Mind," and this was exactly the character of Hermes, celebrated for his wisdom, the god of science and intellect, the great mind of the ancient Paganism. Hea, the Babylonian form of the same god, called also "the All-Wise Belus," has the same character. He is the instructor of mankind, the "Lord of Understanding," "The Intelligent Fish," and his special symbol was *a serpent.*[2] So also Buddha is called "The King of the *Serpents*," "The Tree of Knowledge,"[3] and his special symbol is *the serpent.*[4]

"Hea," "The Intelligent Fish," is also identified with the Fish god "Oannes,"[5] called by Berosus "O'dacon," *i.e.*, "The Dagon," or "The Fish On," from the Chaldee "*Dag*," a fish, and "*On*," the name of the sun,[6] and he is clearly the same as the Fish god Dagon. Now some of the temples of Buddha are called the temples of Daghope and Dagon.[7] In Pegu there is a temple of Kiaki, who is the same as Dagun, and this Dagun is represented by a gigantic figure sixty feet long, in a sleeping posture,[8] just as Buddha is represented by a sleeping figure of nearly the same length in one of the temples of Ceylon.[9] It is clear, therefore, that Dagun, or Dagon, is a title of Buddha. The names Buddha Narayana, or "Buddha dwelling in the Waters," and Machodar Nath, "The Sovereign Prince in the belly of the Fish,"[10] and the name of Buddha in Thibet, viz., *Dag Po, i.e.*, *Dag Buddha*, or "The Fish Buddha,"[11] further identifies Buddha with the Babylonian Dagon and Oannes, or Hea.

[1] Edkins, p. 413.   [2] *Ante*, pp. 43, 44, 108.
[3] *Ante*, pp. 107-109.
[4] Colonel Tod, *Rajast*, vol. i. p. 250 ; Pococke, *India in Greece*, p. 189.
[5] Lenormant, *Chaldean Magic*, appendix i. p. 201.
[6] Faber, vol. ii. p. 378.
[7] *Asiat. Res.*, vol. vi. p. 451 ; *Purch. Pil.*, bk. v. chap. iv. p. 468.
[8] Hamilton, *Acc. of East Ind.*, vol. ii. p. 57 ; Syme's *Embassy to Ava*, vol. ii. p. 110 ; Faber, vol. ii. p. 379.
[9] *Asiat. Res.*, vol. iii. p. 451.
[10] *Ibid.*, vol. vi. pp. 479, 480; Faber, vol. ii. p. 117
[11] Faber, vol. ii. p. 379.

Hea was also the god of Magic, the source of the Chaldean magical powers, whose assistance was always sought in times of need. "He alone possessed the inviolable secret, the magic word by which he could restrain the powers of the abyss."[1] So also Buddha was the god who was the supreme source of the magical power of the Samanean priesthood, and the possessor of "five holy Scriptures which give the power of knowledge and retrospection, the ability of accomplishing desires of hearts, and the means of carrying words of the mouth into effect,"[2] or, in other words, the knowledge of magic and magical incantations.

These holy Scriptures are said to have been received by him from above. In like manner Menu is said to have left a book of regulations or divine ordinances, which the Hindus hold equal to the Vedas, and the language of which they believe to be that of the gods.[3] Mahabad, "The Great Bud," the first king of Iran, is also said to have received from the Creator a sacred book in heavenly language which he promulgated among men.[4]

Brahma is said to have lost the sacred books while he slumbered at the close of a prior world, that is during the year in which he was shut up in the Ark at the close of the antediluvian world. Vishnu, therefore, became incarnate in a fish, under which form (*i.e.*, the Ark), he preserved Menu while the whole world was inundated by a Deluge, and when the waters retired he recovered the holy volumes from the bottom of the ocean.[5] Hu, or Prydain, the British god, was also the author of the sacred writings, and he, as we shall see, was called *Budd, Budwas* and *Menu;* and Taliesen, speaking of these Scriptures, says that "should the *waves* disturb their foundation he would again conceal them deep in the cell, a holy sanctuary there is upon the margin of the flood."[6]

In the history of Berosus, the Fish god Oannes, whom M. Lenormant identifies with Hea, "The Intelligent Fish,"[7] is said to have instructed the antediluvians in letters and science, and the construction of cities and temples, or the worship of the gods, and that Xisuthrus was directed before the Deluge to bury the records of this knowledge at the city of the Sun at Sippara, by Cronus, and after the Deluge to search for them at Sippara when they were made

[1] Lenormant, *Chaldean Magic*, pp. 108, 158, etc.
[2] *Asiat. Res.*, vol. ii. p. 386.
[3] *Ibid.*, p. 59.   [4] *Ibid.*
[5] From first Avatar of Vishnu, Faber, vol. ii. p. 150.
[6] *Taliesen, Min. Dinbych. Apud Davies;* Faber, vol. ii. pp. 131, 132.
[7] Lenormant, *Chaldean Magic*, chap. xiii. p. 183 ; and Appendix I. p. 201.

I

known to all mankind.[1] Finally, the sacred writings of the first Thoth, or Hermes, before the Deluge were said to be recovered by the second Hermes and deposited in the penetralia of the temples of Egypt,[2] and this second Hermes, or Thoth, was he who first "arranged in order, and in a scientific manner, those things which belong to religion and to the worship of the gods," that is to say, the principles of that magic and sorcery by which the aid of the gods was sought.

Thus we have an exact correspondence in the characters of Buddha, Menu, Mahabad, Hu, or Budd, with those of Oannes, Hea and Thoth, or Hermes, whose human original was Cush.

We have seen that the particular symbol of Buddha, the teacher of magic, and of Hea, the great teacher of mankind and god of magic, was a serpent. Now the serpent was deemed "symbolical of divine wisdom and power and creative energy, and of immortality and regeneration."[3] "It was the general opinion in Hindustan," says Maurice, "that the serpent was of a *prophetic* nature,"[4] and Deane remarks that the same word which denotes "*divination*" in Hebrew, Arabic and Greek, also denotes "*a serpent*."[5] Consequently Apollo, the god of the Delphic oracle, was worshipped under the form of a serpent, and the Dragon or serpent Python, according to Hyginus and Ælian, formerly uttered the oracles at Parnassus,[6] while the tripod of the Pythoness, called by Athenæus the "Tripod of Truth," was formed of a triple-headed serpent of brass.[7]

The Celtic Hu, or Budd, was also called "*The Dragon Ruler of the World*," his car was drawn by serpents, and his priests were called "*Adders*."[8] In short, the Druids called themselves "prophets and serpents,"[9] and in the rites of Uther Pendragon (the Dragon god) *i.e.*, Hu, he was invoked under the name of "*The Victorious Beli*,"[10] which tends to identify him with "The All-Wise Belus," another form of the same god of whom we are speaking.

In Canaan, the priesthood of which constituted the magicians,

[1] Berosus, from *Alex. Polyhistor*; Cory's *Fragments*, pp. 23, 27, 29.
[2] Writings of Manetho from *Syncellus Chron.*, p. 40, and Euseb., *Chron.*, p. 6 ; Cory, pp. 168, 169. We shall see, chap. ix., that the *first* Hermes was an antediluvian.
[3] Bryant, *Plagues of Egypt*, p. 200 ; Deane, p. 127.
[4] Maurice, *Hist. Hind.*, vol. v. p. 343 ; Deane's *Serpent Worship*, p. 66.
[5] Deane, p. 228.
[6] Hyginus, *Fab.*, 140 ; Ælian, *Var. Hist.*, lib. iii. cap. i ; Deane, pp. 209, 210.
[7] Herod., ix. 81 ; Deane, pp. 211, 212.   [8] Davies, *Druids*, pp. 116, 122, 210.
[9] *Taliesen*, from Deane, p. 254.   [10] Deane, p. 256.

wizards, necromancers and sorcerers, alluded to in Scripture, the name of the sacred serpent was *Aub, Ob, Oph* and *Op*, which is the word used for wizards and persons having familiar spirits in Levit. xx. 27, Deut. xviii. 11, and the witch of Endor is likewise called an *Ob*, or *Oub*;[1] while in Africa, which to this day is the home of magical marvels, the serpent is the great object of worship and the worshippers are called *Obi*.[2]

It is thus plain that the serpent was regarded as the source or symbol of prophetic and magical power, and as the symbol, there- fore, of those gods who represented the great prophet of Paganism, *i.e.*, Hermes, or Cush, who was the teacher of those magical powers. The serpent is also the especial symbol of Buddha, while the *caduceus* of Hermes, formed of intertwined serpents, is evidently identical with the *triratna* of Buddha.

Again, Janus, the father of the gods, who has been identified with those gods of whom Cush was the original, is called "The All-seeing Janus," or "The Seer," indicative of his prophetic character, and he was also worshipped in Phœnicia under the form of a serpent.[3] It is, moreover, to be noted that Buddha is called "*Cala*," or "Time,"[4] which is the equivalent of the title "Cronus," or "Time," given to the father of the gods (*i.e.*, Cush) in Greece and Rome.

The primitive or mythological Buddha is, therefore, identified with the prophetic god, and the author of magic and sorcery of Western Paganism, known under the name of Thoth, Taautus, Hermes, Mercury, Hea, Oannes, "The All-wise Belus," and the British Hu, or Budd, whose human original was Cush. The evidence of this identification is, it will be seen, accumulative, while the fact that the origin of magic is traceable to the early Cushite inhabitants of the Euphrates and Tigris valleys, whose language is so intimately allied with that of the Turanian and Mongolian races who worship Buddha, leaves little doubt that he is the same as the prophetic god of the primitive Cushites, or Accadians.

But there is yet another reason why Buddha must be identified with those gods whose human original was Cush, the great prophet and teacher of the ancient Paganism, the father of the *black* or *Ethiopian* race, whose son Nimrod established, shortly after the Deluge, the first great empire of the world in the valleys of the Tigris and Euphrates.

[1] Deane, pp. 81-84.
[2] *Ibid.*, pp. 160-178. He quotes Bossnan on *Guinea Acta Erud.*, Leips., 1705, p. 265 ; *Purchas. Pil.*, part i. p. 768 ; Lander's *Records*, pref. and vol. ii. p. 198, etc.
[3] Macrobius, lib. i. cap. ix.
[4] *Asiat. Res.*, vol. i. pp. 239, 240 ; Faber, vol. ii. p. 393.

Buddha, although the chief god of the *yellow* race, is constantly represented as *black*, with woolly hair and negro features. "The representative of Buddha at the period of Chrishna," says Colonel Tod, "was Nema Nath; he is of black complexion, and his statues exactly resemble in feature those of the young Memnon. His symbol was the snake."[1] "It has ever," says Ferguson, "been one of the puzzles of the people of Buddhism that the founder of their religion should always have been represented in sculpture with woolly hair, like that of a negro."[2] "Buddha Jain, or Mahiman," says Mr Faber, "is perpetually represented by his Oriental worshippers with the complexion, the features, and the crisped hair of an African negro, so that many have argued that *Buddha must have been an Egyptian, or Ethiopian*." "The Brahmins," he says, "who highly reverence Buddha, although they esteem his votaries (the Southern Buddhists) as heretics, are not a little offended when this resemblance to the African race is pointed out. When the crisped hair of their god was pointed out to them by Mr Mackenzie, with the inquiry whether it was meant to represent the hair of an Abyssinian, the priests answered in the negative with abhorrence. But, as Mr Wilford justly remarks, no evasions respecting the hair will account for the flat noses and thick lips of many of the ancient statues which occur in Hindustan, for these are clearly the well-known features of the genuine African negro."[3]

There is but one explanation, viz., that the human original of Buddha was the same as the human original of the god who was the great prophet, teacher and magician of Paganism, worshipped under the forms of Thoth, Hermes, Hea, Oannes, the prophet Nebo, and the all-wise Belus, *i.e.*, Cush, the Ethiopian, the father of the *black* race.

[1] *Rajast*, vol i. p. 250; Pococke, p. 189.
[2] *Tree and Serpent Worship*, p. 122.
[3] Faber, vol. ii. pp. 463, 464.

CHAPTER VII

THE GODS OF OTHER NATIONS

Ancient Germans, Celts, Mexicans and Peruvians

IN the Gothic mythology "an impious race of *giants*" (*see* Gen vi.) are represented as having perished at the great Deluge, with the exception of one man who escaped in his boat; also that at that time a great cow begot *Bore*, or *Bure*, who begat *Woden, Vile* and *Ve.*[1] Now the mystic word for "cow" was "*theba*," and "*thebh*" is also the word used in Scripture for the Ark of Noah, and, as the incidents of the Deluge were interwoven with the Pagan mythology, the great goddess mother was identified with the Ark, and a cow became her symbol, just as the bull was the symbol of the great god.[2] Bore, therefore, and his three sons are simply the Patriarch Noah and his three sons born out of the Ark.

But the result of thus representing the goddess mother as the mother Ark is to make her the mother both of the Patriarch and of his sons, and his wife also, as in the case of Osiris, who is called the husband of the mother and is also represented as floating on the ocean for a year in a ship called *Argo, Baris* and *Theba.*[3] Hence the Egyptian and Babylonian god is sometimes confused with his father, grandfather and even great-grandfather, and we shall find that Woden, though here represented to be one of the sons of the Patriarch, is more especially identified with his grandson Cush.

Thus Tacitus says that the chief god of the Germans, who was *Woden*, was Mercury or Hermes.[4] Woden also, like Hermes and Buddha, is represented as the author of the sacred writings, the inventor of letters, and the god of Magic.[5] Like Mercury and Buddha, he receives the souls of dead warriors, and conducts them to the

---

[1] *Edda*, Fab. iii.; Faber vol. ii. p. 356.
[2] Faber, vol i. pp. 19-21.
[3] Plut., *De Iside*, p. 359; Faber, vol. i. pp. 370, 371.
[4] Tacitus, *Manners of the Germans*, chap. ix.
[5] Mallet, *North. Ant.*, chap. xiii. pp. 371, 372; Faber, vol. ii. pp. 357, 358.

133

mansions of the Blessed.[1]   Just also as the fourth day of the week is called Mercury's day and Buddha's day, so it is also Woden's day, and the name of the Gothic god Tuisto, or Teut,[2] is evidently the same as Taautus, or Taut, the Phœnician name of Thoth, Hermes or Mercury.   Woden is also identified with the same god in his aspect as father of the gods.   For he is the husband of *Freya*, or *Frea*, who, like the Babylonian Rhea, wife of Saturn the father of the gods, is Mother Earth and mother of the gods.[3]

The Tamulic pronunciation of Buddha, or Bodhi, is *Pooden*, or *Poden*, and as the B of the one dialect is the P of another dialect, and W and P are identical letters in Sanskrit,[4] the Budd, or Poden, of one people would easily become the Wudd, or Woden, of another people. Moreover, *Twashta*, one of the titles of Buddha, would just as easily pass into *Tuasta*, or *Tuisto*, one of the titles of the German god.

It is well known that Woden is the same as the *Odin* of the Scandinavians, who are a branch of the great Scythian nation from whom the ancient Germans sprang.   The sons of the Patriarch in the Scandinavian tradition are *Odin*, *Vile* and *Ve*, instead of *Woden*, *Vile* and *Ve*, and Wednesday is called in Scandinavian *Odinsday*, instead of *Wodensday*.   It would also appear that Woden, or Odin, who seems to be identified with those gods of whom Cush was the human original, had a son "*Balder*," who was slain by Loki, the spirit of evil, just as Osiris was slain by Typhon, the spirit of evil.   Just also as the deaths of Osiris, Bacchus, Thammuz, etc., are lamented, so is Balder lamented by his mother, Freya or Frigga, who was told by Hela, the goddess of Hell, that he would be restored to life if everything on earth wept for him.[5]   Again, just as the war god Mars or Nergal was another manifestation of the younger Babylonian god, so "*Thor*," the war god of the Scandinavians, was another son of Odin, the name "Thor" being probably, as suggested by Mr Hislop, a cognate term to the Greek *Thouros*, "the seed,"[6] a title particularly characteristic of the younger Pagan god.   Odin, Freya and Thor, in short, are the Scandinavian Trinity, corresponding to the Egyptian Trinity, Osiris, Isis and Horus, and other forms of the same Trinity, and, like Horus, Apollo and Chrishna, Thor is represented as bruising the head of the serpent.[7]

[1] *Edda*, Fab. vii. ; Faber, vol. ii. p. 357.   [2] Faber, vol. ii. p. 361.
[3] *Edda*, Fab. v. ; Faber, ii. p. 357.
[4] Professor Holmboe quoted by Lillie, *Buddha and Early Buddhism*, chap. xiv. p. 231.
[5] *Scandinavia*, vol. i. pp. 93, 94 ; Hislop, pp. 57, 58.
[6] Hislop, p. 312.   [7] Wilkinson's *Egyptians*, vol. iv. p. 395.

Mr Lillie quotes Professor Holmboe, as proving many remarkable similarities between the worshippers of Odin, or Woden, and those of Buddha. He shows that the principle on which the Scandinavian "*haughs*" are constructed is precisely the same as that of the Buddhist "*topes*," that they contain the same relics, that their origin is attributed to Woden in the one case and to Buddha in the other, and that the Buddhist symbols, the "*Svastica*" and "*Nandavasta*," are constantly found in them,[1] while the Svastica, according to Mr Edkins, is constantly found in Scandinavian inscriptions.[2]

Moreover, the Indian cobra, which was the representative of the great Father, or creative power, in Eastern religions, is represented on almost every sword and bracelet of the worshippers of Woden. This snake in China was the dragon, and the dragon was also the symbol of the Scandinavian great Father, and was the figure-head of their warships, as it is of the Chinese war-junks.[3] In short, just as it was the stamp and symbol of royalty in China,[4] so it was the royal standard of the Danes, Normans and the English kings.[5]

It is easy to understand how these nations received their religion. They called themselves "*Asas*," and came from Northern Asia, from the shores of the Euxine and Caspian, where they were in intercommunication with the Tartar races, and also with the Bactrians and Persians, races which, as we have seen, were more or less of the same religion as the Buddhists, the Magi of the Persians being evidently the same, and known by the same name, as the Samaneans of Buddhism. The only difference between Woden and the Southern Buddha is that the former is a war god in accordance with the martial character of his worshippers, while the followers of the Southern Buddha are supposed to be peaceable and gentle. This, however, they are not, and we may well believe that the Buddha of Northern Buddhists, such as the warlike Bactrians, was of a very different character.

We are told by Cæsar that the Germans only worshipped the Sun, the Moon and Fire, and that they knew of no other deities,[6] and with them, as with other nations who worshipped the god whose original was Cush, the Moon was the male deity and the Sun female.[7] Their Yule Day or "Child's Day,"[8] on the 25th of December was, therefore,

[1] Lillie, chap. xiv. pp. 230, 235.   [2] Edkins, p. 63.
[3] Lillie, p. 356.   [4] Maurice, *Hist. Hind.*, vol. i. p. 210.
[5] Deane, *Serpent Worship*, pp. 70, 249, 269.
[6] Cæsar, *Com.*, book vi. chap xxi.
[7] Sharon Turner, *Anglo Saxons*, vol. i. p. 213.
[8] "Yule," probably from the Chaldee "*Eol*," pronounced "Yeol," "an infant"; Hislop, p. 93, note.

with them the birthday of the Moon, instead of being, as in other Pagan nations, the birthday of the Sun, and this day, as we have seen, was also the birthday of Buddha.

This was also the case with the Arabs, with whom the Sun was female, and the Moon god Meni was the chief diety. They kept December 24th as his birthday.[1] We must conclude, therefore, that Woden, the chief god of the German nations, was the Moon, and that this was the case also with the Arabian god Wudd, or Budd, who is evidently Buddha, and who, like Buddha and Mercury, was represented by a square stone.[2]

The identity of the *Druidical* religion with that of Babylon and Phœnicia is generally admitted. It differed considerably from that of the Scythian races, the Scandinavians and ancient Germans, and was more especially the religion of the Celtic nations who preceded them in their emigration to Western Europe. The Celts, unlike the Germans, paid great respect to sacrifices, and had many images of their chief god,[3] who is stated by Cæsar and others to have been the same as the German god, viz., Mercury, and was called *Teutates*,[4] a name which, like the German *Teut*, is evidently a form of the Egyptian *Taut*. They also worshipped *Hesa*, called by the Latins *Hesus*,[5] which is the same as *Ma Hesa*, "the great Hesa," a title of Buddha. Cæsar says that they also worshipped Apollo, Mars, Jupiter and Minerva.[6] Dionysius also says that the rites of Bacchus were celebrated in the British Islands,[7] and Strabo, quoting Artemidorus, says that there is an island near Britain (Ireland) in which they performed sacrifices to Ceres and Proserpine in the same fashion as they did in Samo Thrace.[8] It is well known that the Phœnician element was largely represented among the Celtic Irish.

The Phœnician gods, *Baal Thammuz, Baal Moloch, Baal Zebub,* and *Baal Samen*, required human victims, and the human sacrifices of the Druids, like those of the Phœnicians, were by fire and of the most bloody nature. Speaking of these sacrifices at Carthage, M. Lenormant writes, " These barbarous sacrifices took place every year and were frightfully multiplied on the occasion of public calamities

---

[1] Stanley, *Hist. Phil.*, p. 1066, col. i. ; Sharon Turner, vol. i. p. 213.

[2] Maxim. Tyr., *Dissert.*, xxxviii. p. 374.

[3] Cæsar, *Com.*, bk. vi. chaps. xvii., xxi.

[4] Cæsar, bk. vi. chap. xvii. ; Minucius Felix. Octav., p. 293 ; Livy, *Hist.*, lib. xxvi. chap. xliv. ; Lucan, *Pharsal.*, lib. i. vers. 444, 446 ; Faber, vol. ii. pp. 36, 362.

[5] Faber, vol. ii. pp. 361, 363. "*Hesus*" is the Latin form of "*Hesa*."

[6] Cæsar, bk. vi. chap. xvii.

[7] Periergesis, v. 565.   [8] Strabo, lib. iv. chap. iv. c. ?

to appease the wrath of the gods "; he also says that " in every place where the Phœnicians carried their trade and their arms, not only at fixed periods, but at all critical conjunctures, their fanaticism celebrated these horrible sacrifices." [1] So also Cæsar, speaking of the Druidical religion in Gaul, says, "They who are engaged in battles and dangers, either sacrifice men as victims, or vow that they will sacrifice them, and employ the Druids as the performers of these sacrifices, because they think that unless the life of a man be offered for the life of a man, the mind of the immortal gods cannot be propitiated, and they have sacrifices of that kind ordained for national purposes. Others have figures of vast size, the limbs of which formed of osiers they fill with living men, which being set on fire, the men perish enveloped in the flames." So also he says that at their funerals, like the similar practice of Suttee in India, "all things, including living creatures, and slaves, and dependents, which they suppose to have been dear to them when living, are burnt together with them." [2]

Toland says that the Druids offered sacrifice by fire on the 1st of May, in order that the harvest might prosperously grow, and at Midsummer on June 24th, to obtain a similar blessing. [3] The remains of these rites still exist in some parts of Britain, where men and women assemble round a fire at an ancient Druidical circle of stones ; after casting lots, one has to jump through the fire. The fact that this takes place on May 1st, which is still known as *Beltane* [4] is a clear proof of the Babylonian origin of the Druidical religion. Similar Baal fires take place still in Ireland on June 24th, as described by Charlotte Elizabeth, on which occasion the peasantry pass through the flame and children are thrown across it. [5] The day chosen for doing this also confirms the Babylonian origin of the Druidical rite, for June 24th is the first of the month of Tammuz, the god of fire, on which the principal festival of that god was celebrated. [6] The Celtic Gauls offered their human sacrifices to Teutates and Hesa, or Hesus, [7] that is, Mercury or Taautus, who was another form of Saturn or Cronus, the father of the gods, or Cush, and who appears to have been the originator of such sacrifices. [8]

[1] *Anc. Hist. of East*, vol. ii. p. 280.   [2] *Commentaries*, lib. vi. caps. xvi.-xix.
[3] Toland's *Druids*, p. 107 ; Hislop, p. 116.
[4] Lord John Scott, quoted by Mr Hislop, pp. 104, 105.
[5] *Wayside Pictures*, p. 225 ; Hislop, pp. 115, 116.
[6] Stanley's *Sabæan Philosophy*, p. 1065 ; Hislop, p. 113.
[7] Faber, vol. ii. p. 361.
[8] *Sanchoniathon's History*, Cory's *Fragments*, by Hodges, pp. 20-22.

It is clear also that the Druids regarded the Sun as a deity, and fire as having a divine efficacy, as in the worship of Tammuz and Moloch. Thus, in the Druidical hymn to the Sun, it is said, "They celebrated the praise of the Holy One in the presence of the purifying fire which was made to ascend on high."[1] It is worthy of remark, moreover, that while "*El*" is the Hebrew for God, "*Al*" the Semitic, and "*Il*" the Chaldee, so "*Haul*" is the Welsh for "fire," "*Hil*" the Maeso Gothic for the Sun, and "*Ell*" the Gothic for "fire."[2] The "Grove worship" of the Druids is a further evidence of the Babylonian origin of their religion, and so is their worship of *the cross* with which it was combined, for throughout Paganism the latter emblem was the sacred symbol of their god.[3] "The Druids in their grove worship were accustomed to select the most stately and beautiful tree as an emblem of the deity they adored, and having cut off the side branches they affixed two of the largest of them to the highest part of the trunk in such a manner that the branches extended on each side like the arms of a man, and together with the body presented the appearance of a huge cross, and on the bark in several places was also inscribed the letter Thau" (or T).[4]

Considering that the Scythian or German ancestors of the British only recognised some of the primary features of the old idolatry, any remains of the Druidical worship are, as might be expected, principally found at the present day in the southern and western parts of England, to which the previous Celtic inhabitants were driven by the Belgic British and other German invaders, and in those parts which were easily accessible to the Phœnician traders. These remains are of the same character as the memorials of the Cushite race in India. Colonel Forbes Leslie, speaking of the Cushite or "Cyclopean excavations in mountains of rock, Cyclopean fanes, barrows containing human remains, stone circles, cromlechs, dolmens," etc., says, "they are incontestably of the same character as those of Syria and Western Europe. These monuments in the Dekkan are found in all the varied forms in which they are found in France and Britain."[5] Professor Baldwin also remarks that among the Cushite races of Southern India, where the Dravidian dialects prevail, the word "*mag*," like the Celtic "*mac*," means "son."[6]

[1] Davies, *Druids*, pp. 369, 370.
[2] Rawlinson's *Herod.*, vol. i. p. 546.　　[3] *See* chap. x.
[4] Maurice's *Indian Antiquities*, vol. vi. p. 49.
[5] Baldwin, *Prehistoric Nations*, i. p. 227.　　[6] *Ibid.*, p. 240.

In Ireland also where the Celtic (and probably Phœnician) population seems to have been in excess of the German Belgae, and other tribes of similar origin, there are more evidences of the former prevalence of the religion of Babylon and Phœnicia. General Vallancy says that the ancient Irish were worshippers of Buddha. "*Bod*," or "*Bud*," was their god who presided over *marriage* and was probably the phallic god like Mercury. He was also known as "*Tath*," or "*Tait*," and his identity with "*Tat*," or "Buddha," and with "*Taautus*," or "Thoth," is clear from the fact that the 1st of August, which was the beginning of the Egyptian month of Thoth, was called by the Irish, "*la Tat*," *i.e.*, Tat's day.[1] "*Samano*," a title of Buddha, is also evidently the Irish "*Saman*," or "*Shamma*," who, like Buddha, was the god of the dead and judge of departed spirits, while the festival of Shamna, or Shony, was a festival of the dead, held in November, at the same time as the feast of All Souls, in both Ireland and the Western Isles of Scotland. At this festival peasants waded into the sea to search for the head of the god, just as in the lamentations of Osiris, and other forms of the god, there was a search for a lost portion of his body.[2]

It was also said by Demetrius, quoted by Plutarch, that the islands of Scotland were inhabited by the gods of the natives. Now Bute, Arran, Islay, Iona, Skye, etc., may very well be synonymous with "*Bud*"; "*Arhan*," a title of Buddha; "*Ila*," his wife; the Indian "*Yune*," "*Ione*," or "*Juno*"; and "*Sakya*," one of the most general titles of Buddha.[3]

Again, "*Hu*," the god of the Celtic nations, was also called "*Budd*," "*Budher*" and "*Budwas*," and just as we have seen that Buddha was identified with Menu, so the Celtic Hu was also called "*Manon*," "*Menu*" and "*Menroad*."[4] Like the gods also of Babylon and Egypt, the symbols of Hu were the bull and serpent, and he is called "The Bull of Flame" and "The Solar Bull."[5]

The Pagan Irish likewise worshipped Bacchus under the title of "*Ce Bacche*," and that he was the same as the Bacchus of Greece and Rome is evident from his title "*Broum*," for both the Greek and Latin Bacchus was called "*Bromus*" or "*Brumus*."[6]

These facts show that the Celtic religion, while clearly from the

[1] *Collect de reb. Hibern.*, vol. iii. No. 12, pp. 469, 470; vol. iv. No. 13, p. 43; Faber, vol. ii. p. 365.
[2] Faber, pp. 449, 460. [3] Plut., *De Defect Orac.*, Faber, vol. ii. p. 366.
[4] *Mythology of Brit. Druids*, pp. 116, 118, 176, 228, 364, 428, 468, 557, 568, 584; Faber, vol. ii. pp. 363, 364.
[5] Faber, vol. ii. pp. 304-306. [6] *Ibid.*, p. 279.

same original source as the other branches of Paganism, yet differed considerably, especially in the names of its principal gods, from the Phœnician religion, the gods of which were Baal Tammuz, Baalzebub, etc., and that the Celts therefore did not, as some have supposed, obtain their religion wholly from the Phœnicians, similar as the latter religion was to that of the Druidical. It is clear also that, like the rest of the nations at a distance from Babylon and Egypt, the chief god of the Celts was Buddha, *i.e.*, Mercury, or Thoth, the human original of whom was Cush.

The Gods of Mexico and Peru.

Turning now from the old world to the new, we find, according to Mr Kennedy, that the language of the Mexicans was largely Phœnician.[1] Like the ancient British, they had a god called "Hu the Mighty," while the names of others of their gods were compounds of Baal or Bel, viz., *Balan Quitze, Balan Agal,* etc.[2] Their bloody human sacrifices, amounting, it is said, to fifty thousand a year, were also in strict keeping with those of the Celts, Phœnician and the Canaanitish nations, and, like them, they sacrificed children. The remarkable custom also of the sacrificing priest tearing out *the heart* of the living victim and holding it up as an offering to the Sun god,[3] who in Chaldea was Bel, is a further proof of the origin of the Mexican religion; for the "heart," which in Chaldee is "*bel*," was, as we have shown, especially sacred to the Pagan gods.[4]

The Mexicans had also pyramids, not like those of Egypt, but constructed in exact conformity to the tower of Belus at Babylon, viz., with a winding ascent outside and resting-places, while just as the temple of Belus was at the top of the great tower of Babylon, so on the top of the Mexican tower was their temple, and the altar on which they sacrificed their victims,[5] while the features of the image of the god to whom they were sacrificed were *black*, indicating its Cushite origin.[6] The Mexicans also worshipped the cross. The Spaniards found it as a sacred symbol in the Mexican temples, and,

---

[1] *Vide* Kennedy's *Atlantis*, chap. vii., in which he points out this identity of language.

[2] *Ibid.*, chap. iv.

[3] Prescott's *Conquest of Mexico*, bk. i. chap. iii. pp. 24-26.   [4] See *ante*, p. 49.

[5] Herodotus, lib. i. cap. 181 ; Humboldt's *Mexican Researches*, vol. i. p. 82, and Prescott's *Conquest of Mexico*, book iii. chap. vi. p. 167 ; bk. iv. chap. xi. p. 213.

[6] Prescott, bk. iii. chap. vi. p. 168.

as in other Pagan nations, it was a general object of adoration.[1] So also, just as in the Lesser Mysteries of Paganism, which consisted of a baptism of water, the initiate was pronounced "regenerated and forgiven all his perjuries,"[2] so the Mexicans baptised their children and pronounced them to be "born anew" by the rite.[3]

Again, throughout the Pagan world a forty days' lenten or spring fast was held, and it is still held by the people inhabiting ancient Assyria, the Yezidis, or devil worshippers of Koordestan.[4] It was held in Egypt in honour of the Sun god Osiris,[5] and in Rome to commemorate the sorrows of Ceres.[6] So also in Mexico "three days before the vernal equinox," says Humboldt, "began a solemn fast of forty days in honour of the Sun."[7]

Moreover, just as Apollo, Horus, Thor and the Indian Chrishna are represented as crushing the head of the serpent who is the genius of evil, so Humboldt writes, "The serpent crushed by the great spirit Teotl when he takes the form of one of the subaltern deities is the genius of evil."[8]

It is worthy of remark also that both the god *Pan*, who was one of the forms of the Pagan god in Greece and Rome, and the goddess *Maia* were well known in Mexico under those very names, and Pan was adored throughout Mexico and Central America.[9]

Finally, the statement of Francis Nuñez de la Vega clearly proves the origin of the Mexican religion. "According to the ancient traditions collected by Bishop Francis Nuñez de la Vega, the Wodan of the Chiapenese (Mexicans) was the *grandson* of that illustrious old man, who, at the time of the great Deluge in which the greater part of the human race perished, was saved on a raft together with his family. Wodan co-operated in the construction of the great edifice which had been undertaken by men to reach the skies; the execution of this rash project was interrupted; each family received from that time a different language; and the great spirit Teotl ordered Wodan to go and people the country of Anahuac (Mexico)."[10]

[1] Prescott, Appendix, part i. p. 465 ; compare *infra*, chap. x.

[2] Tertullian, vol. i. p. 1204.

[3] Humboldt's *Mex. Res.*, vol. i. p. 185 ; Prescott's *Conq. of Mex.*, Appendix, part i. p. 495 ; Hislop, pp. 132, 133.   [4] Layard's *Babylon and Nineveh*, p. 93.

[5] Wilkinson's *Egyptian Antiquities*, vol. i. p. 278, and Landseer's *Sabæan Researches*, p. 112.

[6] Julius Firmicus, *De Errore*, p. 70 ; Arnob., *Adv. Gent.*, lib. v. p. 405.

[7] Humboldt, vol. i. p. 404 ; H., p. 105.   [8] *Ibid.*, p. 228 ; Hislop, p. 60.

[9] Abbe Brasseur de Bourbourg's Introduction in Landa's *Relacion*, quoted in Kennedy's *Atlantis*, p. 145.

[10] Humboldt, *Mex. Res.*, vol. i. p. 320 ; H., p. 134.

This tradition, preserved by a people separated by long ages from the people of the old world, comes to us like a voice from the dead, not only corroborating the Mosaic account, but showing that the human original of the god worshipped as Buddha and Woden was indeed Cush, the grandson of Noah, and that, as indicated by the Greek tradition, he was chiefly responsible for the attempt to build the tower of Babel.[1]

Prescott has objected to this tradition as too much in accordance with Scripture, but this is no real objection, and the entire absence of artificiality about it obliges one to reject the idea that the author invented it; nor could any reason be conceived for his doing so at the time, and under the conditions, in which he lived. But besides this, it evinces a knowledge which has only come to light within the last few years; for how could the author have known, or conceived, that the original of the Gothic and Scandinavian god was Cush, the grandson of Noah? But the authenticity of the tradition is placed beyond doubt by the fact that, like the Goths and Scandinavians who called Wednesday, Wodansday, and like the Buddhists who call it Buddha's day, so the Mexicans call it after the name of their ancestral deity, Wodan.[2]

It will be observed that, although their gods Hu and Wodan associate the Mexicans with the Buddhist races, their other gods, and their language, ritual and customs, and the form of their temple towers, connect them more intimately with the Phœnicians and Babylonians, while their festival of the dead on November 17th[3] is more especially Egyptian.

The Peruvians, like the Mexicans, were worshippers of the Sun and fire, and Prescott describes the magnificent temple of the Sun at Cuzco in which was a representation of the Sun, consisting of a human countenance on a burnished plate of gold, studded with precious stones, and so arranged that the rays of the rising Sun fell directly upon it and lighted up the whole temple.[4] The sacred fire was tended, as at Rome, by vestal virgins, who, like those of Rome, were bound to perpetual virginity, and, like them also, were punished by being buried alive for any violation of their chastity. So also, as at Rome, the sacred fire, being regarded as an emanation from the Sun god, was kindled anew from the rays of the Sun by means of a polished metal mirror.[5]

[1] *Ante*, pp. **32, 33**.   [2] Humboldt, *Mex. Res.*, vol. i. p. 319.
[3] See *ante*, p. 5.   [4] Prescott, *Conquest of Peru*, bk. i. chap. iii. p. 41.
[5] Compare Lemprière, *Vesta and Vestales*; and Prescott, *Peru*, bk. i. chap. iii. pp. **46, 47**.

The Egyptian monarchs, being regarded as sons of the Sun, were only permitted to marry their sisters, and this was the custom of the Ptolemies down to the time of Cæsar. This was equally the custom with the Incas of Peru, who were also regarded as children of the Sun.[1] So also, as in the case of the Egyptian monarchs, the bodies of the deceased Incas were embalmed and placed in the great temple of Cuzco.[2] A yet more striking evidence of their connection with Egypt was their name for the Sun, namely, "*Ra*," while they called the great festival of the Sun "*Rami.*"[3] As in the case also of the festival of the Egyptian Sun god Osiris, it was preceded by three days' mourning.[4]

As in Pagan Rome, so also in Peru, there were Augurs who professed to foretell events by examining the entrails of the sacrificial victims.[5] These and many minor details of their religion as collected by the author of *Atlantis*, together with their festival of the dead on November 2nd,[6] show that they must have separated from the old world at a time when the religious system of Paganism was fully established and before it had commenced to decay, and that they must have been especially connected with the Egyptians.

. . . .

It is not necessary to pursue this portion of the subject further. It might be shown, as Mr Faber and others have done, that clear evidences of the same religion existed in New Zealand, Otaheite and among the islands of the Pacific Ocean, and even among the more barbarous tribes of Africa and South America, although, as might be expected, their greater ignorance and degradation and long separation from civilisation has obliterated any intelligent remembrance among them of its meaning. The large islands of the Eastern Archipelago are generally Buddhist, although in some cases leavened by Mahommedanism. The latter, however, has never entirely replaced the previous system, most Mahommedans being still worshippers of the Sun, Moon, etc.

[1] Prescott, *Peru*, bk. i. p. 8, note.
[2] *Ibid.*, p. 14.
[3] *Ibid.*, chap. iii. pp. 44, 45.
[4] *Ibid.*
[5] *Atlantis*, p. 144.
[6] See *ante*, p. 5.

PART II

ORIGIN AND NATURE OF PAGAN IDOLATRY

CHAPTER VIII

THE TEACHING OF HERMES—MAGIC

A VERY interesting point in our present inquiry, the importance of which has hitherto been insufficiently recognised, is the true character and essential nature of the ancient Paganism, and the way in which it first arose. This we now propose to consider.

We have seen that Cush, or Hermes, was the master mind and originator of this idolatry. His books were held in the highest estimation in Egypt, and the similar books attributed to the various deified forms under which he was known in other countries were equally honoured. The teaching of Hermes has, in short, been recognised in all ages as the great authority on the nature and mysteries of Paganism.

It is true that he and his son did not establish their own worship, and that anthropomorphic gods were not introduced until later. For, as Epiphanius says, "It was not until a considerable time afterwards that Cronus, Rhea, Zeus, Apollo, and the rest, were esteemed as gods." [1] But in all essential points it is evident that the religion which he taught during his lifetime must have been the same as that contained in the Hermetic books, which in after ages constituted the recognised authority on all matters of religion.

It would seem, indeed, that the worship of the Babylonian monarch and his father was merely the stepping-stone for the re-establishment of the religion they had themselves instituted. For although all who have studied the records of ancient Egypt and Assyria are agreed that the primitive religion of those countries consisted of the worship of the Sun, Moon and Stars and the powers of Nature; yet, as we have seen, the human originals of the Pagan gods were identified with these material objects and powers, and were regarded as their incarnations or human manifestations.

In short, the history and characteristics of Belus, Hea, Nin, Nebo, Merodach, Nergal, etc., and those of the Babylonian goddess are so essentially personal and human, that we must conclude that they

[1] Cory's *Fragments*, "Epiphanius," p. 55

did not come into existence until the deification of their human originals, and that the primitive religion of the Cushites or Accadians was simply the worship of the Sun, Moon and Stars and the powers of Nature, the latter being represented by a multitude of spirits supposed to be possessed of various powers for good or evil, whose aid, by means of certain arts, sorceries, or incantations, could be obtained, or their power controlled.

Everything points to the fact that "the thrice great Hermes," or Cush, who was the author of the first form of Paganism, was a man of no ordinary mental capacity, deeply versed in the secrets of Nature, and the author of the far-famed wisdom of the Chaldeans. The question is, What was the nature of this wisdom which gave him, as "Hea," the title of "the Lord of Understanding," "the Teacher of Mankind," "the All-Wise Belus"? Hermes is said to have "arranged in order and in a scientific manner those things which belong to religion and the worship of the gods," and as the oldest form of this worship was that of the Accadian people, who were the primitive Cushite inhabitants of the valleys of the Euphrates and Tigris, we may conclude that it chiefly consisted of the Magic, Sorcery, Demon and Nature worship of the Accadians, the texts and incantations of which, in the Accadian tongue, were carefully preserved and adopted by their successors, the Assyrians. We have already referred to this worship as portrayed by M. Lenormant from the Assyrian tablets,[1] and there can be little doubt that it was identical with the Shamanism of the Ural-Altaic races, and with that of the Tartars and Mongols of Eastern Asia—that is to say, with the magic and necromancy practised by the Shamanas or priests of Buddhism.

It has also been shown that there are strong grounds for identifying the most ancient or mythological Buddha with Cush, *i.e.*, Hermes. In short, the votaries of Theosophy and Spiritualism, who draw their occult knowledge from the teaching of Buddhism, speak of it as "the teaching of Hermes." It is from their publications, therefore, that we may learn the nature of the knowledge which constituted the teaching of Buddha or Hermes, *i.e.*, Cush.

The tradition of the original Buddha is that he received "five holy Scriptures which gave knowledge of retrospection and ability of accomplishing the desires of the heart and means of carrying words into effect." Here is an assumption of vast knowledge and power which, as far as this world is concerned, might be supposed to make its possessor independent of God and of the limitations of

[1] *Chaldean Magic.*

human nature. It is, however, strictly in accordance with the teaching of modern Buddhism and Theosophy, and the first of these occult powers is evidently based on the belief, common to Brahminism and Buddhism, that every person has passed through a series of previous existences and will have to pass through a series of others, until he attains "Nirvana" or perfection. Buddhism professes to enable a person, by a course of asceticism and self-absorption, to recall the memory of these past forms of existence.

Theosophists declare the identity of their teaching with that "which was given to the initiate in the sacred mysteries of antiquity." "Now, as of old, these mysteries comprise two classes of doctrine, of which one class only, that which, being historical and interpretative, belongs to the Lesser Mysteries, may be freely communicated. The other known as the Greater Mysteries is reserved for those who in virtue of the interior unfoldment of their consciousness contain within them the necessary virtues."[1] This "unfoldment of the consciousness" is called the "Intuitional Memory," which is explained as follows: "The intuition then is that operation of the mind whereby we are enabled to gain access to the interior and permanent region of our nature, and there to possess ourselves of the knowledge which in the long ages of the past the soul has made its own."[2]

Speaking again of the soul, the writer says, "All that she has once learnt is at the service of those who duly cultivate relations with her;" and again, "It is not his own memory alone that, thus endowed, he reads. The very planet of which *he is the offspring* is, like himself, *a person*, and possessed of a medium of memory, and he to whom the soul lends her ears and eyes may have knowledge, not only of his own past history, but of the past history of the planet as beheld in the pictures imprinted in the magnetic light of which the planet's memory consists. For these are actually *ghosts of events*, manes of past circumstances, shadows on the protoplasmic mirror, which can be evoked again.[3] He, say the Hindu scriptures, who in his lifetime recovers the memory of all that his soul has learnt, is already a God."[4]

This, then, is the power of "retrospection" alluded to, and it will be observed also that the teaching accords with the general belief of Paganism, which held that the stars were "intelligences" and the

[1] "The Perfect Way," p. 13, from Pember's *Earth's Earliest Ages*, p. 405.
[2] *Ibid.*, pp. 3, 4 ; Pember, p. 406.
[3] *Ibid.*, pp. 8, 9. [4] *Ibid.*, pp. 22, 23.

abode of the gods. Moreover, as Mr Pember remarks, "It falls in with a common fancy, that on rare occasions some dim memory of a former acquaintance with persons or places has been known to flash across the mind;" and he quotes Rossetti and Mrs Hemans as expressing this,[1] which is probably the experience of many others also. If so, it is impossible to regard it as mere fancy, and its true significance will be considered later.

With regard to the next power—viz., that of "accomplishing the desires of the heart"—this also is explained by the teaching of Theosophy. The conditions imposed on the initiate into the ancient mysteries were a severe form of preparation, consisting of fasting, absolute chastity and solitude, and sometimes the drinking of some powerful potion. These are equally prescribed to the seeker for the powers and knowledge offered him by Theosophy. *Marriage, Alcohol* and *Flesh* are forbidden,[2] and to "cultivate relations with the soul" is that mental concentration and absorption by which the Buddhist ascetic attains his powers,[3] and is probably similar to that by which, it is said, some Indian fakirs are able to throw themselves into a trance, a process which must require no little resolution, as well as the stimulus of a strong desire, so that few perhaps are able to attain the result.

That result is described as to "so bring his body under the control of his own soul, that he can project his soul and spirit, and, while living on the earth, act as if he were a disembodied spirit." He who attains to this power is called an "Adept," and his powers are thus depicted: He "can consciously see the minds of others. He can act, by his soul-force, on external spirits. He can accelerate the growth of plants, and quench fire, and, like Daniel, subdue ferocious beasts.[4] He can send his soul to a distance, and there not only read the thoughts of others, but speak to, and touch, these distant objects; and not only so, but he can exhibit to his distant friends his spiritual body in the exact likeness of that of the flesh. Moreover, since the adept acts by the power of his spirit, he can, as a unitive force, create out of the surrounding multiplex atmosphere the likeness of any physical object, or he can command physical objects to come into his presence."[5] This is all in exact accordance with the powers laid claim to by the Buddhist Shamanas.[6]

[1] Pember, pp. 459, 460.   [2] *Ibid.*, p. 406.
[3] See *ante*, pp. 99, 101, 116, 118.
[4] Daniel, it may be remarked, is not said to have done this by his own power.
[5] Wild's *Spiritual Dynamics;* Pember, p. 252.
[6] *Ante*, p. 116.

Mr Pember remarks that, though the powers here mentioned may be exaggerated, yet "the existence in all times of the world's history of persons with abnormal faculties, initiates of the great mysteries, and depositaries of the secrets of antiquity, has been affirmed by a testimony far too universal and persistent to admit of denial."[1] The above, at anyrate, is the teaching of modern Buddhism and Theosophy, and may therefore be presumed to be a fair presentation of the nature of that power, the attainment of which the five holy books of Buddha claimed to teach.

It is also stated that this "wisdom of Hermes," by which these results are attained, "consists in the discovery of a certain pure matter, that is a divine element, which, being brought by art to perfection, converts to itself proportionately all imperfect bodies which it touches. This light, discovered and perfected by art, applied to any body, exalts and perfects it in its own kind, and that not only is man reputed able to discover the divine nature, but, in the forcible language of Asclepian dialogue, to effect it. It is the obtaining a divine essence."[2]

As regards the last feature of this teaching, viz., "the means of carrying words into effect," it would imply that by the utterance of certain words, or incantations, certain results would follow. This, of course, is the well-known method of the sorcerers and wizards of old, and is fully illustrated by the numerous Accadian incantations which have been found on the Assyrian tablets, as well as by the similar inscriptions on the monuments of ancient Egypt. The object sought, and professed to be obtained, by these means, were certain supernatural effects—such as the death of an enemy at a distance, or the direction of some person's actions, or the presence of some "familiar spirit," or other result,—to effect which the enchanter depended, not on his own volition, but on the efficacy of certain words uttered by him to set in motion certain spiritual agencies.

If, then, these were the powers which the sacred books of Buddha, or Hermes, claimed to reveal the means of acquiring, the question to be considered is,—how far we are to regard that claim to be worthy of credit?

Here we have the unequivocal testimony of Scripture to the reality of the powers possessed by the priesthood and magicians of Egypt, who, up to a certain point, were able "by their enchant-

[1] Pember, p. 252.
[2] *A Suggestive Enquiry into Hermetic Wisdom*, p. 68, from "The Computation of the Number 666," pp. 2, 3.

ments" to imitate the miracles performed by God at the word of Moses. It is evident that, in this case, the effects are represented as real, and not as the effects of conjuring or jugglery, and it is also clear that they were not produced by the personal volition of the magician, but by enchantments or incantations which set in motion other agencies, viz., the powers of their gods.

Now Augustine quotes Hermes Trismegistus as stating "that visible and tangible images, *i.e.*, idols, are, as it were, only the bodies of the gods, and that there dwell in them certain spirits which have been invited to come in them, and which have power to inflict harm, or to fulfil the desires of those by whom divine honours and services are rendered to them."[1]

This would imply that the knowledge by which Hermes or Buddha claimed to be able to "fulfil the desires of the hearts" referred to the means used to obtain the assistance of certain spiritual beings. This was also certainly the case with the magicians, wizards, necromancers, diviners, sorcerers, enchanters and persons with familiar spirits who were the priesthood of the Canaanitish nations, and whose religion was identical with that of Babylon and Egypt. The spirits whose assistance they sought were their gods, who are stated in the Old Testament and by the Apostle Paul[2] to be *devils*, literally "*daimonia*," or *demons*—a word which the Greeks used to denote those spirits of the dead who had become their gods, and which afterwards was used to denote any supernatural being,[3] as in the case of Socrates, who believed that he was guided by a good demon, or spirit.

In the case of the oracle of Delphi, the priestess, who was called "the Pythoness," after the god, "the Pythian Apollo," sat on a tripod over a chasm whence proceeded a peculiar vapour which threw her into a frenzy. In this frenzy she uttered predictions and was supposed to be possessed by the spirit of the god. The veracity of the oracle was so famous that its answers came to be used as "a proverbial term for certain and infallible truth," and Cicero argues, "Would that oracle at Delphi have ever been so celebrated and illustrious and so loaded with such splendid gifts from all nations and kings if all ages had not had experience of the truth of its predictions? Let this fact remain—which cannot be denied, unless we will overthrow all history—that that oracle has told the truth for many

[1] *De Civitate Dei*, viii. 23 ; Pember, p. 307.
[2] Lev. xvii. 7 ; Deut. xxxii. 17 ; Psa. cvi. 36-38 ; 1 Cor. x. 20.
[3] Smith, *Dict. of Bible*, "Demons."

ages."[1] The remarkable accuracy of its answer to Crœsus is well known, but it induced that monarch to consult it again, when it returned the ambiguous answer, "Crœsus if he crosses the Halys will destroy a great empire." It turned out, indeed, to be correct, for Crœsus, having interpreted the empire mentioned to be that of Persia, entered upon the war and thereby destroyed his own empire.

That "the Pythoness" was possessed by a real spirit is implied by the story in the Acts of the Apostles of the damsel possessed of "a spirit of divination," literally "*a spirit of Python,*" which was cast out by Paul, with the result that her powers of divination, which "brought no small gain to her masters," were lost. So also the Israelites were commanded to put to death wizards, witches and those possessed of familiar spirits, showing that it was no pretended, but a real intimacy with, or possession by, spirits of evil for which they were condemned.

From the testimony also of MM. Huc and Gabet and that of Marco Polo, which have been already quoted, it would appear that the Buddhists of Eastern Asia possess a full knowledge of the means of attaining these Hermetic powers.[2]

We have seen that the idolatry of the Pagan nations was professedly the worship of the spirits of the dead, and the rites of the Canaanites, for joining in which the Israelites were punished, are spoken of as "eating the sacrifices of the dead." But it does not follow that the spirits they invoked, and by whose agency wonders were performed, were really those of the dead. The dead are constantly spoken of throughout the Scripture as "asleep," "sleeping in the dust," and the righteous dead are said to be "at rest," "asleep in Jesus," etc. The resurrection is therefore spoken of as "awaking," "rising from the dead," and while this does not absolutely deny a state of consciousness, it is certainly opposed to one of active existence. The souls under the altar are represented in Rev. vi. 9 as crying out, "How long, O Lord," etc., and they are told that they must "*rest* for a little season, until their fellow-servants also and their brethren that should be killed as they were, should be fulfilled." But it may be remarked that this *cry* of the souls under the altar occurs in a prophecy which is professedly told in the language of metaphor, and it probably has the same significance as the words

[1] Cicero, *De Div.*, xix. ; Potter and Boyd's *Grecian Antiquities*, "Delphic Oracle," bk. ii. chap. ix. p. 273.
[2] See *ante*, pp. 116, 117.

addressed to Cain, "Thy brother's blood *crieth* unto me from the ground."

To suppose that the dead can take an active part in the affairs of the living is explicitly denied by the statement, "Neither have they any more a portion for ever in anything that is done under the sun, for there is no work nor device, nor knowledge, nor wisdom, in the grave whither thou goest" (Eccles. ix. *b*, 10). The isolated case of the appearance of Samuel by the especial permission of God is no proof to the contrary, while his reply to Saul, "Why hast thou *disturbed* me?" shows that his state had been one of *rest*—"where the wicked cease from troubling and the weary are at rest" (Job iii. 17).

The human originals of the Pagan gods were, at the most, three individuals, and in order to have been present at all the shrines of their numerous deified attributes all over the ancient world, they would have had to be omniscient and omnipresent. It is true that the priesthood believed, or professed to believe, that they were deified human beings, but what the people generally worshipped were certain beings clothed with certain characteristics, powers and attributes, whose spirits were supposed to inhabit certain images, shrines, temples or other places, and these, both the Old Testament and the Apostle Paul say, were devils, *i.e.*, "daimonia," or evil spirits,[1] similar to those which were cast out of many persons by Christ and the apostles.

It is clear also that the spirits primarily invoked by Hermes or Buddha, for obtaining the desires of the heart, were not those of the persons afterwards worshipped as gods, of whom he himself was one. If not, they must have been simply the same daimonia as those mentioned in the New Testament, namely, spirits of evil who produced in those they possessed various forms of disease or insanity; or who, as in the case of the man possessed of a legion of these spirits, endowed the person with superhuman strength, like the "Berserkers" among the Scandinavians; or who, through their human mediums, revealed hidden things, as in the case of the damsel out of whom Paul cast the spirit of Python. All these are spoken of as evil spirits, and their chief prince, recognised by both the Jews and Christ as Beelzebub, the name of the chief god amongst the Canaanites, was identified by Christ with Satan himself, "the Prince of the power of the air" (Matt. xii. 24-28).

[1] 1 Cor. x. 20. *See* also Levit. xvii. 7; Deut. xxxii. 17; Psa. cvi. 37; 2 Chron. xi. 15.

That these spirits may be possessed of vast powers, as far as earthly things are concerned, and be capable of bestowing them on their faithful worshippers, is not only conceivable, but is implied by Satan's remark to Christ when he showed Him "all the kingdoms of the world, and the glory of them." "*All these things,*" he said, "*are delivered unto me and to whomsoever I will I give them;*" and Christ did not deny his claim. It is these powers which are sought by the followers of modern Theosophy, who are reviving, in the present day, the so-called "Worship of the Dead," by which worship the ancient Pagans invoked the powers of the spirit world. Hence a recent writer says, "Unless we mistake the signs, the day is approaching when the world will receive the proofs that only ancient religions were in harmony with Nature, and ancient science embraced all that can be known. The cycle has almost run its course; a new one is about to begin, and the future pages of history may contain full evidence, and convey full proof, that if ancestry can be in aught believed, 'descending spirits have conversed with man and told him secrets of the world unknown.'"[1]

The early Christian writers testify to the same effect. Cyprian of Carthage, speaking of the Paganism of his day, says, "These spirits lurk under the statues and consecrated images. These inspire the breasts of their prophets with their afflatus, animate the fibres of the entrails, direct the flight of birds, rule the lots, give efficiency to oracles, are always mixing up falsehood with truth, for they are both deceived and they deceive. They disturb their life, they disquiet their slumbers. Their spirits also creeping into their bodies, secretly terrify their minds, distort their limbs, break their health, excite diseases, to force them to the worship of themselves, so that when glutted with the steam of the altars, and the piles of cattle, they may unloose what they had bound, and so appear to have effected a cure. The only remedy from them is when their own mischief ceases; nor have they any other desire than to call men away from God, and to win them from the understanding of the true religion to superstition with respect to themselves; and since they themselves are under punishment, to seek for themselves companions in punishment whom they may by their misguidance make sharers in their crime."[2]

---

[1] *Isis Unveiled*, vol. i. p. 38 ; Pember, p. 397.

[2] Cyprian on "The Vanity of Idols," from *Reflections on the Character and Spread of Spiritualism*, by Benjamin Wills Newton. (Boulston & Sons, Paternoster Buildings, 1876.)

So also Clement of Alexandria, speaking of the Pagan oracles, says, "It is evident, since they are demoniac spirits, that they know some things both more quickly and more perfectly (than men); for they are not retarded in their learning by the heaviness of a body, and therefore they, as being spirits, know without delay, and without difficulty, what physicians attain after a long time and by much labour. It is not wonderful therefore if they know somewhat more than men do; but this is to be observed, that what they know, they do not employ for the salvation of souls but for the deception of them, that by means of it they may indoctrinate them in the worship of false religion," etc.[1]

In the above quotations allusion is made to the healing of diseases. This was done in the Pagan "temples of health," of which there were many specially set apart for that purpose, and in which the patients had to observe certain rules and conditions. They had to fast for twenty-four hours, and abstain from wine for three days, after which they went to sleep in the temple lying upon the skin of one of the sacrificial victims, and received an answer by dreams.[2] In the temple of Isis at Busiris the goddess herself, according to Diodorus Siculus, appeared to the sleeper and prescribed remedies. "Numbers," he says, "are thus cured after they have, through the malignancy of their diseases, been given up by their physicians, and many persons who have been absolutely deprived of sight, or disabled in any other part of the body, are restored to their previous soundness as soon as they have recourse to this goddess."[3]   Cicero also speaks of the number of votive offerings to the shrines of the god and goddess as incontestable evidence of the reality of their powers. This "*temple sleep*" was a mesmeric trance induced by the priests, or by the fumes of a particular sort of incense, and the cures were thus in exact accordance with the cures effected by modern mesmerism, in which the mesmerised patient states the means to be used to effect the cure.[4]

Besides the divination obtained through the temple sleep, there were other diviners called "*Theomanteis*," who did not require to be mesmerised, but were free and unconfined, and able, after offering sacrifices and the performance of the usual rites, to prophesy anywhere. These, when they received "the divine inspiration," were possessed by a frenzy, swelling with rage, foaming and gnashing with

[1] *Reflections on the Spread of Spiritualism*, p. 26.
[2] Potter and Boyd, *Grecian Antiquities*, "Other Grecian Oracles," bk. ii. chap. xi.
[3] Diod. Sic., i. 25; Pember, p. 291.   [4] Pember, p. 289.

their teeth as if mad. Some used to eat the leaves of the laurel, which was thought to conduce to this state, from which it was called "the prophetic plant."[1] The same symptoms occurred in the case of the Pythoness of the Delphic Oracle, and as it is clear, from the notice in the Acts, that this was due to possession by a demon, we may conclude that the Theomanteis were similarly possessed.

"One sort of the Theomanteis," says Potter, "were possessed with prophesying demons which lodged within them and dictated what they should answer to those who inquired of them, or spoke out of the bellies or breasts of the possessed persons, they all the while remaining speechless. These were called '*daimono-leeptoi*,' 'possessed with demons.'"[2] They are referred to by the prophet Isaiah, whose words, according to the Septuagint Version, are, "And if they say unto you, seek unto them *whose speech is in their belly*, and those that speak out of the earth, those that utter vain words, that *speak out of their belly*, should not a people seek unto their God."[3]

"Others," says Potter, "called '*Enthousiastai*,' were not possessed by the demon, but only governed, actuated or inspired by him, and instructed in the knowledge of what was to happen." These are evidently those spoken of in Scripture as having a familiar spirit. A third sort, called "*Ekstatikoi*" (from whence our word "*ecstasy*") were cast into a trance where they lay as if dead, and on returning to themselves gave strange relations of what they had seen and heard."

Then there were the "dreamers of dreams," who fasted one day and abstained from wine for three days, as it was considered that no dreams which were affected by a full meal, or undigested food, were prophetic. Besides this, they used to sacrifice to Mercury, *i.e.*, Hermes, before going to sleep.[5] That these dreams did often foreshadow future events is implied by a notice in Deut. xiii: "If there arise among you a prophet, or a dreamer of dreams, and giveth thee a sign, or a wonder, and the sign or the wonder cometh to pass whereof he spake unto thee, saying, let us go after other gods which thou hast not known, and let us serve them," etc.

It is here implied that certain individuals might possess a prophetic faculty. It is plain, however, that this faculty did not consist of a power inherent in themselves of foreseeing the future, but of a capacity for receiving impressions, either sleeping or waking, from a

---

[1] Potter and Boyd, *Theomancy*, bk. ii. chap. xii.
[2] *Ibid.*, bk. ii. chap. xii. p. 290.   [3] Isa. viii. 19.
[4] Potter, bk. ii. chap. xii. p. 291.   [5] *Ibid.*, bk. ii. chap. xii. p. 296.

power outside themselves; for in all the numerous cases recorded in Scripture in which persons were warned or instructed in dreams or waking visions, the power producing those dreams and visions was the Spirit of God.[1]

Hence we must conclude that prophetic dreams and visions, which tend to support, or advocate, idolatry or other evils, as in the case mentioned in Deut. xiii., are the work of spirits of evil, and that this must have been the case with the dreamers of dreams among the Pagan nations who worshipped devils or demons.

It may be asked, "How can an evil spirit know the future?" To this it may be replied that they cannot always know it and may often be in error. But if their powers are such as are implied by Scripture they may largely influence future events, and be permitted to do so by God in the case of events affecting those who worship them and seek their aid. In this way they may produce the very events which they have before foretold. So also with the diseases of which they reveal the cure. Many of these diseases are ascribed by Scripture to the agency of evil spirits, who, as Cyprian says, are then able to "unloose what they had bound, and so appear to have effected a cure" in order to induce men to seek their aid.

It will be observed that the conditions required for attaining the prophetic faculty and the magical powers wielded by the Pagan priesthood and the Buddhist ascetics, are abstinence from *marriage, wine* and *meat,* and this we are told by the Apostle Paul was to be the teaching of the foretold apostasy from the Christian faith, and that the persons concerned in this apostasy would give "heed to seducing spirits and the doctrines of devils."[2] It is thus clear that this abstinence is a necessary preparation for communicating with the spirit world, and that it placed those who practised it under the control and guidance of these seducing spirits who by dreams, visions or other forms of communication would be able to lead their deluded votaries into every form of error. The beginnings of this apostasy may be traced as early as the second and third centuries of the Christian era, but it was not until after the purifying effect of persecution had ceased—that is, after Constantine and his successors had professed Christianity—that it became fully developed. Isaac Taylor, in his *Ancient Christianity,* has exhaustively portrayed from the writings of the so-called "Fathers" of that time the characteristics of this apostasy, which became fully developed in the fourth and fifth

[1] *See* also 1 Cor. xii. 9, xiv. 30.
[2] 1 Tim. iv. 1-4.

centuries, showing how celibacy and abstinence from meat were then insisted upon as the highest form of holiness, while at the same time the worship of the dead, *i.e.*, of the saints, was equally inculcated, the result of which, as is well known, was the gradual re-adoption, under the cover of Christian names and incidents, of all the other features of the ancient Paganism, so that the rites and ceremonies of modern Romanism are now practically identical with those of the old idolatry.

It is thus clear that this predicted apostasy was effected by the teaching of demons or spirits of evil, through the agency of men who, by the means spoken of, fell or placed themselves completely under the guidance or influence of these spirits; that when calling on the supposed spirits of the dead, who could not hear or answer them, they were replied to and deluded by beings who were identical with the devils or demons, cast out by Christ and the apostles from those possessed or afflicted by them; and that the prince of these demons was Beelzebub or Satan.

It would appear that the prophetic faculty or capacity for receiving mental impressions, either sleeping or waking, from agencies external to man, when not specially bestowed on a person by God, as in the case of Balaam,[1] is dependent on certain physical conditions which may be, either constitutional, or self-induced by the various methods employed by the magicians and ascetics of Paganism, in order to obtain communication with the spirit world.

But it is evident that individuals, without any intention on their own part, may happen to temporarily fulfil these conditions which seem to depend on fasting and great mental absorption, and under such circumstances may experience prophetic dreams and visions. There are, indeed, numerous well-authenticated cases of persons having such dreams and visions, some of which are only curious and even trivial, while others have proved to be remarkable warnings against temporal dangers or moral evil which the person has in consequence been able to avoid. We might presume that the latter were of God, but others only tend to produce superstition and a belief in dreams and occult agencies which are not of God. If, then, the heathen oracles constantly gave true replies in order to induce men to believe in them, so it may be with those prophetic dreams which beget in those who experience them a belief in the reliability of other dreams, by which, perhaps, their thoughts, opinions and actions are powerfully influenced. This, indeed, is the case with many, who, even without

---

Numb. xxiv. 15, 16.

any experience of prophetic dreams are strongly influenced by ordinary dreams.

The point, however, is this, that if a person's mental and bodily conditions are at any time favourable for the reception of these impressions from spiritual agencies during sleep, he may dream of certain events in his future life which perhaps are of no great importance, and which are forgotten on awaking. Nevertheless, when the events take place in accordance with his dream, the impression left by the latter is partially revived, and he is conscious of a strange conviction that he has passed through the same circumstances before, which begets in him that common impression, before alluded to, of some past existence.

That this, and nothing else, is the true explanation of the common experience which Theosophy has made use of in order to build thereon the theory of a past existence, is supported by the circumstances related below.[1]

There are other persons, perhaps, who may recognise the correctness of this explanation; but it is clear that, as a rule, the triviality of the events, together with the bustle and cares of everyday life, and perhaps the length of time which elapses between the dream and its fulfilment, would, in most cases, drive from the memory all but that faint impression of the dream which is revived by its fulfilment; for how constantly the most vivid dream is completely forgotten at the moment of awaking in spite of every effort to recall it, and yet perhaps is suddenly recalled a few hours afterwards.

But the effect might be very different if a person, by fasting and the arts practised in Paganism, placed himself in a state of receptivity

[1] The author can vouch for the truth of the following : A young man who for some time lived alone with hardly any other companions but his books had, during that time, several experiences of dreams coming true. In the midst of ordinary events he would suddenly become conscious of this strange impression of having passed through those events before, and then would recall the fact that they were the events of a dream which, a short time before, had made a stronger impression on his mind than usual. In some cases he could not thus identify them, and was only conscious of the strange impression referred to, but in other cases he could, not only recall the dream, but could remember the nature and sequence of the events in the dream, and although incredulous at first of their prophetic character, found them, to his surprise, literally fulfilled. The events were generally of an unimportant and trivial character, and, with the exception of one or two cases of greater interest than the rest, they soon passed from his memory. His experiences ceased when his solitary condition was changed for a more active life, in which the memory of such dreams, if he ever had them, would be speedily obliterated by other cares and interests.

to, and earnestly sought the influence of, spiritual agencies. Not only might the dreams produced by these spirits have a prophetic character like those of the Pagan seers, but after the dreamer's confidence in his dreams had by this means been established, the same agents might produce powerful and vivid impressions of events and scenes, and of converse with spiritual beings in another state of existence, which the dreamer would be only too ready to believe were the realities of the past thus revealed to him, according to the teaching of the Hermetic philosophy.

In modern "Spiritualism" we have an apparent revival of the ancient forms of necromancy and magic, and its rapid progress amongst all classes is a proof that it is not the mere imposture and trickery which some persons try to persuade themselves it is. *The British Quarterly* of 1876, pp. 456, 457, thus writes: " The revival in the nineteenth century of the long-disused practices of necromancy is a startling fact. Since the year 1848 the number of persons in the United States who have betaken themselves to what, in the language of the Pentateuch, is styled " Seeking after the dead," is stated to amount to three millions. In this country they may be estimated at many thousands. The pursuit under the appropriate name of Spiritualism has been promoted by an active propaganda— not only literature but art has been appealed to for the re-establishment of ancient sorcery. The development of the asserted phenomena has been more rapid in England than in America. The earliest observers told of muffled knocks or sharp electric crackles. Tables and other articles of furniture were endowed with motion, musical instruments sounded in the dark. To these, it is asserted, have now succeeded more direct appeals to the senses; faces, hands and figures, resembling those of departed friends, have been visible in subdued light; articulate sounds have been breathed through flexible tubes; medicines, tangible substances, manufactured clothing, and vigorous resistance to attempted violence, have been displayed by what is said to be a disembodied spirit." [1] The writer of the above has, however, probably underrated the number of adherents of Spiritualism both in England and America in the year 1876. At the present day it is said to influence a large proportion of the upper classes in this country.

Mr Wallace, the naturalist, and second only to Mr Darwin as an evolutionist philosopher, has carefully and scientifically examined and collected the phenomena of " Spiritualism," and has come to the

[1] Quoted from *Reflections on the Character and Spread of Spiritualism*, pp. 4, 5.

L

following conclusion : " My position, therefore, is that the phenomena of Spiritualism in their entirety do not require further confirmation. They are proved quite as well as any facts are proved in other sciences." Similarly Professor Challis writes : "The testimony has been so abundant and consentaneous that either the facts must be admitted to be such as are reported, or the possibility of certifying facts by human testimony must be given up." Mr Pember also quotes other learned and able men to the same effect, including a man of such legal acumen as Lord Brougham.[1] It would indeed be folly, in face of the evidence, to reject the reality of the phenomena, and those who do so will generally be found to be either ignorant of the facts, or else, through dislike, or fear of facing the conclusion to be drawn from them, they refuse to look into or listen to the evidence. There have also been, as might be expected, many instances of trickery which has been resorted to by persons who have pretended to exercise these powers as a financial speculation, but these have always been exposed directly they were really tested, and do not affect the reality of the phenomena that have stood such tests. Nevertheless, these instances of trickery form a sort of refuge for those who shrink from admitting the evidence, and enable them to dismiss the matter from their minds.

It may be observed, also, that were not this the case,—if all who now shrink from, and disbelieve, the phenomena of Spiritualism were convinced of their reality,—they would rise up against this new religion and invoke the strong hand of the law to crush it. Nothing is so potent an influence as fear, and there are many who, because they dread having the truth forced upon them, are filled with anger at the mere mention of supernatural phenomena. This was well illustrated in the case of the Davenport brothers, who, on their first visit to this country, were nearly torn to pieces by the people of Liverpool, merely because they implied that they were assisted by supernatural agency. So it would be also with even many of the present votaries of modern Spiritualism, were it not presented to the public as a mere harmless drawing-room amusement, with a suspicion of trickery about it which conceals its more sinister aspect.

But the principal means by which its true nature is concealed, and the fear and shrinking, which it might otherwise create, is effectually allayed, is the fact that the spirits invoked are supposed to be, and claim themselves to be, the spirits of departed relatives or friends, or of celebrated persons. Interviews with these, instead of

[1] Pember, p. 327 and note.

creating fear, would naturally be regarded with pleasure and interest, while some who had lost some dearly-loved relations would even ardently desire renewed communication with them.

Necromancy was regarded in a similar way by the ancient Pagans, and a passage from the *Clementine Homilies*, quoted by Mr Pember, very clearly shows what was generally believed at the time they were written. Clement, who is supposed to be the person of that name mentioned by the Apostle Paul, says that before he became a Christian he was perplexed with doubts regarding the immortality of the soul. "What then," he says, "should I do but this. I will go to Egypt and cultivate the friendship of the hierophants and prophets of the shrines. Then I will inquire for a magician, and when I have found one, induce him by the offer of a large sum of money to call up a soul from Hades, by the art which is termed necromancy, as though I wished to consult it upon some ordinary nature. But my inquiry shall be to learn whether the soul is immortal, and I shall not care to know the reply of the soul that it is immortal, from its speaking, or my own hearing, but simply by its becoming visible." [1]

This was the character of the magic taught by Hermes Trismegistus. The spirits invoked by the necromancers and the magicians were supposed to be the spirits of the dead, and this may have been the belief of the first great magician, Hermes himself. The whole system, in short, of the ancient Paganism was professedly the worship of the dead. In this, however, the ancients were clearly mistaken, and the error was the cause, in no small degree, of their delusion. The spirits who replied to their invocations were not the spirits of the dead, but the daimonia of Scripture, evil spirits, the messengers or angels of the prince of the demons; and if so, there was sufficient reason for this misrepresentation of their true character.

It is equally clear that the spirits who reply to the deluded votaries of Spiritualism, and personate the spirits of their dead relatives, are not the spirits of the dead, but identical in every respect with the daimonia of Scripture, and the demon gods of the Pagans.

In both cases we see the sinister wisdom of these spirits of evil. Their personation of the dead, and the teaching by which they support the imposture, is simply a means to quiet the alarms and attract the affections of mankind, in order to bring them under their

[1] *Clementine Homilies*, vol. i. p. 5; Pember, pp. 294, 295.

influence and power. It is what we might expect from those seducing spirits who are opposed to God, and their hostility to God is manifest. For, covered as their teaching may be by a thin veneer of truth and righteousness, it denies or explains away the leading doctrines of Christianity and advocates the salient features of the ancient Paganism.

The following, among the more important manifestations of Spiritualism, as tested by Mr Wallace, require a few observations :—

1. Sound, from a delicate tick to blows like that of a sledge-hammer. Altering the weight of bodies. Moving bodies. Raising bodies into the air. Conveying bodies to a distance, out of, and into, closed rooms. Preserving from the effects of fire. Writing and drawing without human agency. Playing on musical instruments without human agency. Spiritual forms, often visible and tangible to all present, clothed with robes, pieces of which have been cut off, but which melt away. Flowers, ditto. Other flowers which remain. Photographs of spirit forms, etc.

2. Manifestations by a medium who is either in a trance, or in a passive state, in which state the manifestations take place without the exercise of volition on his part—viz., Clairvoyance. Perceiving events at a distance, or through opaque substances. Predictions of future events, either by word of mouth or by a planchette, sometimes in a language the medium does not understand. Speaking also in unknown tongues, and the general manifestation of remark-able powers and knowledge which the medium personally does not possess.

It will be observed that the first class of phenomena is independent of human agency, although as a rule it is necessary, either that a medium should be present to invoke the spirits, or that several persons should jointly use the recognised methods of doing so. The second class is produced by means of the body of the medium who is in a passive state. The two classes are also sometimes combined, as in the case of Mr Home, who seems to have been more or less an "adept." He was raised into the air, floated out of windows, etc. in the presence of a committee of twelve gentlemen who were assembled to report upon the phenomena, and which report was pub-lished in the daily papers a few years ago.

The "*levitation*," as it is called, manifested by Mr Home, is remarkably in accordance with what is related of the ancient Chaldean magic. Cælius Rhodoginus says, "that, according to the Chaldeans,

luminous rays emanating from the soul do sometimes divinely penetrate the body, which is then of itself raised above the earth, and
that this was the case with Zoroaster,"[1] while the "disciples of
Jamblicus asserted that they had often witnessed the same miracle
in the case of their master, who when he prayed was raised to the
height of ten cubits from the earth."[2] When, therefore, it is remembered that the gods to whom the heathen prayed were daimonia,
supposed to be spirits of the dead, the identity of modern Spiritualism
with ancient magic will be evident.

The same effects have taken place with others, who, in more
recent times, have been worshippers of the dead and of images, and
who, the Apostle Paul says, are in reality worshippers of devils
(demons) — (1 Cor. x. 20). This was the case with the so-called
"saints," Francis of Assisi,[3] Petrus a Martina,[4] and Francis of Macerata,
the latter of whom was not only raised from the earth when he
prayed, but his body became luminous, "a flame resting on his
head."[5] Similar phenomena are reported in the case of St Philip
Neri. "Philip was often seen with his whole body raised in the air:
among others, Paulo Spondrato, Cardinal of St Cecilia, saw him
in prayer raised several spans from the ground, indeed almost to the
ceiling as he told Paul V. a little before his death." On one occasion
he "was praying in St Peter's at the tombs of the apostles (*i.e.*,
worshipping the dead), when his whole body was seen to rise suddenly
into the air with his clothes gathered up as they had been when
kneeling, and then to descend with equal suddenness. He was
repeatedly raised into the air when he was saying Mass. Sometimes
when saying Mass he was seen with rays of glory around his head.[6]
Cassandra Raidi says, "I reckoned Father Philip to be a saint because
the first time I went to St Giralmo to confess to him, before I had
said a word, he told me all my thoughts and everything that was in
my mind. He used even to tell me what prayers I had said, and
the intention for which I had said them."[7] Antonia de Pericollis also
says, "Two years before the holy Father died, while we were talking

---

[1] Eusebe Salverte, p. 37. The Zoroaster here referred to is the Chaldean
Zoroaster, not the Persian of that name.

[2] *Ibid.* Jamblicus was probably an "adept." He lived in the time of Constantine,
and wrote a book on the Egyptian Mysteries which is still extant, *vide* Lemprière,
Jamblicus.

[3] *Ibid.*   [4] Flores, *Seraphici*, p. 158.

[5] *Ibid.*, p. 391 ; Hislop, pp. 258, 259.

[6] *Life.* Translated from the Italian by Father Faber, pp. 295-297.

[7] *Ibid.*, p. 365.

together, he disclosed to me some of my thoughts which I never mentioned to him, or told even in confidence to anyone. Seeing my heart thus laid open before him I was overwhelmed with astonishment." She also goes on to say that "there was not one person who was intimate with Philip who does not affirm that he knew the secrets of the heart."[1] He is also said to have seen "things which happened at a distance."[2]

These phenomena would, in former days, have been discredited by many as fables invented to glorify a saint of the Church of Rome, but their exact accordance with the phenomena of modern Spiritualism and Theosophy, and with the powers of the ancient priesthoods of Paganism, not only prove their possibility, but make it exceedingly probable that they are accurately reported.

With regard to other phenomena of Spiritualism, such as causing heavy bodies to move of themselves, spirit forms and other magical appearances, the reader will recognise their resemblance to the powers of the Buddhist priesthood which made the Great Khan afraid to profess Christianity. So also Salverte says, "The Theurgists caused the appearance of the gods (*i.e.*, daimonia) in the air in the midst of a gaseous vapour disengaged from fire. The Theurgis Maximus undoubtedly made use of a secret analogous to this when in the fumes of the incense which he burned before the statue of ʻHecate,ʼ the image was seen to laugh so naturally as to fill the spectators with terror."[3] So also Psellus says that, when the priests used their magical powers, "the statues laughed and lamps were spontaneously kindled."[4] Similarly, the statue of Isis shook the silver serpent on her forehead and nodded assent to her worshippers.[5] Both Lucan and Virgil also speak of the images of the gods weeping as foretelling misfortune to the country :—

> "Tears shed by Gods our country's patrons
> And sweat from Lares told the city's woes."

And again :—

> "The weeping statues did the wars foretell,
> And holy sweat from brazen idols fell."[6]

---

[1] *Life.* Translated from the Latin by Father Faber, p. 365.
[2] *Ibid.*, p. 341, quoted from *Reflections on Spread of Spiritualism*, pp. 57, 58, and note.
[3] Eunapius, p. 73.
[4] Psellus on Demons, pp. 40, 41.
[5] *Juvenal Satires*, vol. vi. l. 537.
[6] Lucan, *Civ. Bell.*, lib. i. v. pp. 356, 357, p. 41 ; *Georgics*, bk. i. l. 480 ; Hislop, pp. 257, 258.

With regard to the phenomena of Spiritualism, it will be observed that the first class of effects which have been enumerated are clearly done by the direct agency of the spirits; yet the second class of effects, viz., those which take place in, and by means of, the body of a medium, must also be produced by the same agency. This might be inferred from the intimate connection of the two classes of phenomena, but it also follows from the character of certain of the second class of phenomena, viz., those in which the medium manifests a knowledge of languages, or of science, or philosophy, which he himself has no knowledge of whatever. The medium as he is naturally, and the medium under the influence of the spirit trance, or spirit power, are two different individuals. Numerous examples are given of this *duality* in the same individual in the histories of persons manifesting similar phenomena under the kindred influence of catalepsy, hysteria and somnambulism. It would take too long to quote such cases which have been collected by Mr Colquhoun in his two works upon the subject,[1] in which ignorant and uneducated persons have manifested a knowledge of language and science while under one or other of these states, but of which they are otherwise totally devoid. Nor have they had any remembrance afterwards of what they have said or done while in that state.

It would thus appear that the medium, who, by certain methods, makes himself susceptible to the power, and invites the aid of the spirits, becomes for the time the habitation of one who speaks and acts through, and by means of, his body to describe things at a distance, foretell the future, and work various wonders, in the same manner as the spirit of Python did in the Pythoness.

Certain conclusions appear to follow from this. If the clairvoyance and prescience of the medium are derived from a spirit, how are we to regard the person who is simply mesmerised and who, it is well known, manifests in various degrees *the same phenomena?* The general belief, as the word "clairvoyance" implies, is that the spirit of the mesmerised person, freed from the veil of the flesh, is able to perceive events taking place at a distance, or that it can leave the body and pass in a moment of time to a distant place, and describe accurately what is passing there. It is, however, more difficult to explain on this assumption how it can, in this state, perceive the past history of other persons and even, in some cases, foretell the future. The Pagans believed that it was the spirits of their gods,

[1] *Isis Revelata*, published in 1836, 2 vols. 8vo; and *Magic and Witchcraft*, published in 1851, 2 vols. 8vo.

the daimonia of Scripture, who spoke in their oracles; and, as it was a real spirit who spoke by the Pythoness, it seems quite impossible to suppose that in the case of ancient magic and sorcery these powers should be due to the agency of daimonia, and in the one exception of the mesmerised person should be due to that person's own spirit!

Mesmerism is, in fact, often used to entrance the spiritualistic medium; it was also used to produce the temple sleep by the Pagan priesthood; and was one of the most ordinary practices of the ancient magicians, and, as we have seen, it is still used by the Buddhist priesthood. Tertullian writes: "Moreover, if even magicians produce apparitions and bring into evil repute the spirits of men who are now dead; if they *mesmerise* boys to obtain an oracular response; if they perform many wonders in sport by their conjuring illusions; if they even send dreams by the aiding power of angels and demons who they have summoned to their assistance, through whose influence also demons[1] and *tables* have been made to divine, how much more will that Satanic power be zealous to do with all its strength, of its own will, and for its own purposes, that which it does to serve the ends of others."[2]

The above passage, quoted by Mr Pember, gives a good idea of the methods of magicians in the age of Tertullian. Mr Pember also quotes a passage from Apuleius in which the practice of mesmerising boys by certain spells is spoken of as a well-known method of obtaining occult knowledge from them while in that state.[3] Kingsley also, speaking of the Neoplatonists, who were great magicians, in his book *Alexandra and Her Schools*, describes similar methods: "So they set to work to perform and succeeded, I suppose, more or less, for now one enters into a whole fairyland of those very phenomena which are puzzling us nowadays—ecstasy, clairvoyance insensibility to pain, cures produced by the effects of what we now call mesmerism. They are all there, these modern puzzles, in those old books of the long bygone seekers for wisdom. . . . But again their ecstasies, cures and so forth, brought them rapidly back to the old priestcrafts. The Egyptian priests, the Babylonian and Jewish sorcerers, had practised all this as a trade for ages, and reduced it to an art. It was by sleeping in the temples of the deities, after due

[1] The word used by Tertullian is "seirim," *i.e.*, "satyrs," a word used, as pointed out by Mr Pember, to denote a certain order of demons. "Satyr is evidently the same as the Chaldee 'Satur'—'hidden god.'" See Hislop, *Saturn*, p. 269.

[2] Tertullian, *Apol.*, xxiii.; Pember, pp. 301-303.

[3] Apul., *De Magia*, xliii.; Pember, p. 303, note.

mesmeric manipulations, that cures were even then effected. Surely the old priests were the people to whom to go for information. The old philosophers of Greece were venerable. How much more those of the East, in comparison with whom the Greeks were children! Besides, if these demons and deities were so near them, might it not be possible to behold them? They seemed to have given up caring much for the world and its course:—

> ' Effugerant adytis templisque relictes
> Di quibus imperium steterat.'

The old priests used to make them appear—perhaps they might do it again."[1]

If then mesmerism was one of the arts, or spells, by which the Pagan priests and magicians obtained answers from their gods, or demons, through the medium of a human being, it is clear that the mesmerised subject becomes the temporary habitation of a spirit. It will be observed that there are different stages in the mesmerised state, and that the first one of simple sleep is not accompanied by any phenomena, but that as the sleep, or state of unconsciousness, becomes deeper, so does a new state of consciousness become apparent, and finally the person, although insensible to pain, can yet speak and reply to questions. It was in this state that questions were put to the Pythoness, or to other persons mesmerised by the Pagan magicians, and the conclusion to be drawn, therefore, is, that until the mind and will of the person is in a state of complete subjection, the alien spirit cannot so entirely take possession of the body as to use it as its own. It may also be observed that all the appearances of death take place in the completely mesmerised person, the face taking the peculiar grey pallor of death, as if the connection between the true spirit and its body was for the time completely severed.

It is popularly supposed that the mesmeriser's power is merely a natural power inherent in himself, due to superior psychical energy asserting itself over persons who are naturally wanting in that energy, or who are exhausted or weakened by illness; for it is such persons who are most susceptible to the mesmeriser's influence; and consequently many mesmerisers seek to exhaust the psychical force, or nervous energy, of the persons they act upon, by making them gaze steadily at a bright light for a certain time, or at a disk of metal held in the hand, etc. It is to be observed, however, that by whatever means the natural powers are weakened, the person so

[1] From Pember, pp. 299-300.

weakened becomes more susceptible to spiritual influence, and that the conditions prescribed for holding intercourse with the spirit world are fasting, abstinence, solitude, etc., by which, either the psychical and mental forces are reduced, or the susceptibility increased. The body of man which veils from his sight the spirit world is also that which protects him from the influence of the spirit world, and the proverb, "Mens sana in corpore sano," will apply to preservation, not only from insanity, but from these kindred evils also.

In accordance with this, we find that persons of a certain physical constitution and susceptibility are able to throw *themselves* into a mesmeric trance by methods similar to those used by mesmerisers. Thus Apuleius relates that "when the inhabitants of Tralles were making inquiries by a magical process in regard to the issue of the Mithridatic War, a boy, who was gazing upon the reflection of a statue of Mercury in the water, uttered a prophecy of the future in a hundred and sixty rhythmical lines." [1] In other words, he threw himself, or fell, into a trance, or, speaking more correctly, by gazing steadfastly into the water he unconsciously did what mesmerists often require persons to do as a preparation for receiving the mesmeric influence. He simply placed himself into that state of susceptibility which is the preparation for spiritual influence, and the spirit of the god, or demon, entering into him, spoke by him.

Bernier says that voluntary somnambulism is frequent among the Indian Brahmins and Fakirs, and that even the means of producing it are taught. [2] Cardanus also states that he could voluntarily place himself in a state of ecstatic insensibility, [3] and Augustine relates the same thing of a priest called Restitutus. [4] Dr Cheyne also mentions the case of a Colonel Townshend, who was subjected to the most accurate medical observation. Colonel Townshend could, to all appearance, die at will, by composing himself on his back, and lying in that position for some time, during which his pulse gradually sank and his breathing decreased, until both heart and lungs became absolutely motionless, and the doctors were convinced that he had carried the experiment too far and had actually died. After some hours, however, life gradually returned as it had ebbed. [5]

With regard to some of the cases above-mentioned, especially that

---

[1] Apul., *De Magia*, xliii.; Pember, p. 302.

[2] *Ceremonies at Coutumes Religieuses*, tom vi. p. 188.

[3] *De Rerum Verietate*, lib. viii. cap. 43; Colquhoun's *Isis Revelata; Enquiry into Animal Magnetism*, vol. i. p. 146, note.

[4] *De Civitate Dei; Animal Magnetism*, vol. i. p. 147.

[5] Cheyne, *English Malady*, etc.; *Animal Magnetism*, vol. i. pp. 147-149.

of the Indian Fakirs, who are professed followers of the ancient Paganism, it is probable that the results obtained were largely due to those arts by which the magicians of old sought the aid of daimonia. It is asserted by those who have studied modern Spiritualism, that it is by no means an easy thing to become a medium, and that fasting, and the absorption of the mind and desires upon the end sought, are necessary before any relations with the spirits can be obtained. Hence, we may presume that where that relation has been established, and the person has become willingly and fully susceptible to the influence of a spirit, the state of trance may, at any time, be at once produced by the direct agency of the spirit, who takes possession of the body which is thus placed at his disposal. It would appear, in short, that a state of mesmeric trance may be produced independently of the aid of a mesmeriser, and that the state itself is in *no way due to the agency of the mesmeriser*, but to the possession by a spirit of the body of a person who has been brought into a state of susceptibility to the spirit's influence.

But if so,—if the mesmeric trance consists of nothing more or less than the temporary possession of the body of a person by a spirit,— how are we to regard the power which some men seem to possess of throwing certain persons into a mesmeric trance by a few waves of the hand. It is not the spirit of the mesmeriser that enters into the body and displaces the spirit of the mesmerised person, but a foreign spirit, which effects its entrance by means of the action of the mesmeriser. Since therefore mesmerism was one of the principal arts by which the magicians and necromancers of Paganism sought the aid of daimonia, the conclusion seems to be forced upon us that the mesmeric power itself was due to the agency of one of the spirits whose aid was thus sought, which spirit, entering into the mesmeriser himself, seemingly gave him abnormal powers, but really acted through, and by him, to subject the mind and will of another person, in order to possess completely the body of that person. It seems impossible to avoid this conclusion if, as is clearly the case, the mesmeric trance is due to the temporary possession of the mesmerised person's body by a foreign spirit.

The mesmeriser, moreover, would be wholly unconscious of this possession of himself, because the effects sought to be produced are wholly in accordance with his will, which would not be the case if they were opposed to it. This is seen, not only in cases of intermittent mania, in which the patient often struggles vainly against the strange desires which assault him, and is conscious of a dual spirit within him, but it is also seen in cases of "electro biology" and "hypnotism" in which the same struggle constantly takes place. In all such cases there is clear evidence of another spirit which is directly antagonistic to the person's natural character and inclinations. The New Testament, in fact, attributes mania, as well as many of the diseases to which the human race are subject, to the agency of daimonia, and it is well known that mania and the prophetic spirit were regarded by the Pagans as intimately connected, and that madmen were in consequence looked upon as divine, and as possessed by "the spirit of the Gods."

What part then does the mesmeriser play in producing the mesmeric trance, beyond the movement of his hands or by the use of other arts, acting as a preparation for the influence of the real mesmerising spirit? Probably none at all. Men of great force of will and energy of character, combined with the gift of oratory, a sonorous voice and histrionic talent, may powerfully influence a multitude whose minds are awed and subjected by this display of power. So also men of strong will when brought into contact with those of weaker will attain a power over the latter, who recognise their inability to oppose a resolution stronger than their own ; and this is often so marked that, after long association, a word or look from the stronger person is sufficient to reduce the weaker to obedience. But in all such cases the effect produced is on *the mind*, which is awed or cowed into submission, whereas the effect of mesmerism is wholly physical, or psychical.

It is certain also that the mesmeric power is not by any means proportionate to the psychical or will force of the mesmeriser ; for not only are there persons whose natural force of will exercises a powerful *mental* influence on those with whom they are thrown, who yet are incapable of producing the mesmeric sleep, but there are others who, although powerful mesmerists, are by no means remarkable for will or psychical force. In some also of no remarkable psychical energy, the power has come quite suddenly, without any seeking on their part, and to their own surprise; while in other cases it is only obtained after continued efforts and practice. This is just what we might expect. For while a few persons are from certain causes[1] naturally susceptible to spiritual influence, as in

[1] It would be interesting, but outside the scope of this inquiry, to consider more fully the psychical and physical conditions which are favourable to spiritual influence, but it may be noted that boys before the age of puberty and virgins were always selected as mediums of communication with the gods by the Pagan magicians.

the case of the subjects of mania, "electro biology," etc., yet the majority of mankind are protected against that influence, and it is only by assiduous efforts that some are able to break through that protection and establish relations with the spirit world.

If, however, the mesmeric power is due to the agency of a spirit of evil, it might be expected that, in many cases at least, its attainment would be intimately connected with certain *moral* characteristics. Mesmerism is the endeavour on the part of one person to subdue, or overcome, the spirit of another person, and an act therefore which, in itself, and apart from other moral and higher considerations which may actuate some mesmerisers, is of a malignant character. The lust of power, dominion, riches and position, or, in a word, of self-exaltation, has ever been a ruling passion in the human race, and this desire is most strongly manifested by persons of overweening pride, vanity and desire for self-assertion, who (more especially if they are wanting in other elements of superiority) would be the first to avail themselves of a power which gave them dominion over others. The spirit which actuates them is that very spirit of pride which we are told was the condemnation of him who is "the prince of demons" (1 Tim. iii. 6) and who, we may be certain, would be only too willing to gratify the ambition of those who seek to follow in his footsteps, and by so doing "give place" to him, or to his subordinate spirits to enter into them. Their abnormal powers may seem to be their own, but so does the superhuman strength of the maniac, like the one mentioned in Mark v., seem to be the result of his own volition, and in every case in which "seducing spirits" give their assistance to man, they will naturally seek to lead him on by flattering his pride with the idea that the powers which he wields are his own.[1]

Similarly, we must regard the reported powers of the "Adept" to be, not the result of the supposed "cultivation of the soul," as taught by the Theosophists, but the result of the inhabitation of a familiar spirit, for whose entry the Adept has prepared himself, and who carries out the desires of those who earnestly seek his aid. For the rigid abstinence enjoined on the would-be Adept, by which his natural inclinations and desires are weakened, are simply a means by which

[1] It may be noticed that just as an unhuman, malignant, wild-beast glare in the eye is the peculiar characteristic of madness, so there is often (but whether always we cannot say) a very similar appearance in the eye of the mesmeriser while exercising his art, which is perhaps startlingly foreign to his natural character. It is the expression we might expect from the presence of a spirit of evil.

the mind can be concentrated on the attainment of these occult powers. Such a state of intense and continual desire is like earnest prayer for the possession of these powers, placing the person in the same state of receptivity and relation to the daimonia, that earnest prayer for spiritual gifts places the Christian with regard to God; and it is doubtless true of one, as of the other, that "they which ask shall receive; they which seek shall find, and to him that knocketh it shall be opened."

The powers thus attained by the Adept may seem to be his own, but in this, as in every other form of man's alliance with spirits of evil, the latter will seek to blind their victim, and lead him to suppose that he is their master, instead of being, as he really is, their helpless captive with a seeming power for a very little while, and which power he holds entirely on sufferance.

Again, with regard to the allied phenomena of so-called "*Electro Biology,*" in which persons, being partially mesmerised by some method of exhausting the psychical energy, are made to do various absurd actions, and believe things opposed to the evidence of their senses, at the command of the "Biologist." They are not in a state of trance, but wide awake and seemingly in full possession of their faculties, and yet, when they recover from their biologised state, they are wholly unconscious of what they have been doing and of the delusions they were under. What they did was, not only without their consent, but opposed to their own wills, as is evident from the efforts made by many to resist the command of the Biologist. To all intents and purposes they were, for the time being, "out of their minds," and seemingly possessed by a spirit which was not their own.

The received explanation of these phenomena is that it is the will of the "Electro Biologist" which produces the result. But there are insuperable objections to this. In order to produce continuous and varied action there must be continued and varied action of the will, and, if so, then it is *not* the will of the "Biologist" which produces the result, for he has often five or more persons performing various sets of actions at the same time, to some of which he is paying no attention, and would be incapable of doing so to all at once. As a matter of fact, he exercises no volition on the subjects of the delusion after the delusion is effected. Moreover, although we speak of the effects produced as the result of *delusion*, it is not what we mean by delusion—that is to say, the effects produced are not the result of the delusion of the biologised person's *mind*. People in certain states of health may become possessed of strange and unreasonable fancies, but on recovery will recognise them as such, and similarly the events of a dream may appear vividly real and yet be recognised as absurd on awaking, but these and every other delusion of the person's mind are impressed upon the consciousness and memory. But in the *completely* biologised person, in spite of the often prolonged, violent and absurd actions which he performs, there is no consciousness or memory of what he has been doing, and in this respect the phenomena are identical with those of the mesmeric trance. When, therefore, it is considered that the methods of "Electro Biology" are similar to those of mesmerism and ancient magic, and that the phenomena produced by the latter are confessedly due to the agency of daimonia, it seems only reasonable to conclude that the similar phenomena of "Electro Biology" are produced by the same agency.

"*Hypnotism*" is merely a form of "Electro Biology," and if asked to decribe its effects we could not do so more exactly, or concisely, than by saying that they consisted of acts due to the presence of a spirit or influence in a person which was *not his own*, and by which he is made to act and to think in a manner entirely opposed to his own mind and spirit. To say that it is the spirit of the hypnotiser would be absurd, for no one pretends that the spirit of the hypnotiser is constantly present with the hypnotised person directing his thoughts and actions. Therefore, as there can be no effect without a cause, and the spirit which produces the effects is neither that of the hypnotiser nor that of the hypnotised person, it must be some other spirit.

The phenomena of Mesmerism, "Electro Biology," "Hypnotism," and the powers of "Mediums" and "Adepts," are merely the reproduction of the phenomena of ancient magic, produced by exactly the same arts as those by which the Pagan magicians, sorcerers, wizards, necromancers, etc., sought the assistance of the demons who they regarded as their gods; and the distinctive feature in the modern phenomena is that there is, in one and all, clear evidence of the presence and agency of spirits which can neither be those of the "Mediums," the "Hypnotisers," "Biologists," "Mesmerisers" or of the persons on whom they exercise their arts, and we are therefore forced to conclude that these foreign spirits must be the same daimonia as those which the ancient Pagans invoked by similar methods.

It is worthy of note also that even such methods of invoking the spirits as *table turning* and of receiving their answers by means of a *planchette* were equally methods of ancient magic. Tertullian, in the passage before quoted, speaks of the Pagans of his time "making *tables* to divine," [1] and a particular instance of this divination by tables is quoted by Mr Pember from Ammianus Marcellinus, in which two persons, Hilarius and Patricius, sought to ascertain the successor to the reigning Emperor Valens. The spirits spelled "Theod," and concluding that Theodorus was intended they made no further inquiry, but being found out, they were forced to confess, and, in consequence, Theodorus and other persons whose names commenced in a similar way were put to death. [2] Nevertheless, the spirits proved to be correct, for after the defeat of Valens by the Goths, *Theodosius* was proclaimed Emperor of the East. Mr Pember also quotes Zalman Zebi as defending table-turning in his day, 1615 A.D.; [3] and Mr Lillie says, "In China there is in front of many statues of Buddha a table on which an apparatus similar to a planchette is used for ghostly communications. This planchette has been known for many hundred years." [4] No doubt these methods have been handed down to the present time, and are merely revived by the followers of Spiritualism.

It is also worthy of notice that the teaching of Spiritualism and Theosophy remarkably accords with that of ancient Paganism, in the fact that, unlike the Christian Trinity of Father, Son and Holy Spirit, its Trinity consists of a Father, Mother and Son. The ancient Paganism, with its Father and goddess Mother, from whom proceeded a Son who was identical with the Father, also represented the Mother as herself proceeding from the Father, the Father being regarded as *Hermaphrodite*, or possessing within himself both male and female principles, so that each separate manifestation of the god, as the deification of his various attributes, had always a corresponding goddess who was his "manifestation"; [4] as in the case of Isis, who proclaimed herself to be "the first of the celestials and the uniform manifestation of the gods and goddess whose sole divinity the whole orb of the earth venerated." [5] So also in modern Theosophy and Spiritualism it is taught that "God is dual, He and She, Father and Mother. Hindu teachers obtained a golden glimpse of this impersonal truth." [6] In like manner it is said, "Man being made in the image of God is male and female," and as Christ is spoken of by the Apostle Paul as the second Adam, so it is taught by Theosophy that "there is yet to be expected a second Eve who is to be the Queen of Heaven

---

[1] *Ante*, p. 168.

[2] Ammianus Marcellinus, *Hist.*, xxix. i. 29 ; Pember, p. 305.

[3] Pember, p. 308.　　　　[4] *Buddha and Buddhism*, p. 39.

[4] Lenormant, *Anc. Hist. of East*, vol. ii. pp. 221, 222.

[5] Apuleius, *Wilkinson*, by Birch, vol. iii. p. 99.

[6] A. J. Davis's "Great Harmonia," from Pember, p. 353, note.

and to absorb the worship of the human race."[1] This is the more remarkable, because it is well known that the goddess mother of ancient Paganism eventually absorbed the worship of the Pagan world to the practical exclusion of the god.

In conclusion, it is important to allude to a class of supernatural phenomena which, although similar in many respects to those we have been considering, are not necessarily of demoniacal origin.

Scripture speaks of prophecy, or the power of foretelling the future, as a gift possessed by certain persons who were generally righteous men and the servants of God ; but this was not always so, and the case of Balaam, and the allusion in Deut. xiii. 1, etc., to prophets who, although able to foresee the future, made use of their power for evil purposes, are illustrations of the exception. This prophetic faculty appears to have been bestowed by God on certain persons, and on particular occasions, and its nature may be gathered from the account of Balaam's prophecy: "Balaam, the son of Beor, hath said, and the man whose eyes are opened hath said. He hath said which heard the words of God and knew the knowledge of the Most High, which saw the vision of the Almighty falling into a trance, but having his eyes open" (Num. xxiv. 15, 16). In this and other cases the future seems to have been revealed to the prophets, either by a vision or by the words of God heard by their minds, if not by their bodily ears. They also possessed at times "clairvoyance," as in the case of Elisha, when he perceived the messenger of the king of Israel coming to him before he entered his house (2 Kings vi. 32), or as in the case when his spirit witnessed the transaction between his servant Gehazi and Naaman, the Syrian (2 Kings v. 26).

But there are a multitude of well-authenticated cases of persons having possessed similar faculties in our own times. There are the cases, for instance, in which persons have seen a friend, or a relative, at the moment of the latter's death, perhaps thousands of miles away. There are also cases in which persons have received warnings of future danger by means of events or appearances, which were of a more or less supernatural character; and there are the well-known cases of "*second sight*" which used to be common in the Highlands of Scotland. These faculties of clairvoyance and second sight exercised by persons in full possession of sense and consciousness, although due, no doubt, to some spiritual influence, are quite distinct from the clair-

[1] "The New Revelation" and "The Perfect Way," quoted by Pember, Appendix B, pp. 377, 380.

M

voyance and other phenomena manifested by the mesmerised person, who is wholly unconscious and clearly possessed by a spirit which is not his own.

It is true that these abnormal faculties have been exercised by the Adepts of Buddhism and Spiritualism, and by the magicians and sorcerers of Paganism, but they were sought and obtained through magical art from the spirits or daimonia, whereas in the cases referred to above, the power, or faculty, has always come unsought. This does not, however, prove these faculties to be from God, for, unless prevented by God, an evil spirit might seize the opportunity, when a person is in the state susceptible to spiritual influence, to enter into him and give him these and other powers or faculties, in order to create a desire for them and produce a belief in powers independent of God.

Solitude and abstinence are conditions for producing this state of susceptibility, and these conditions are often satisfied by the people in the Highlands of Scotland and elsewhere. Great mental tension and absorption, such as that accompanying grief and anxiety, may produce a similar state, and this condition would also be fulfilled in some of the cases of clairvoyance referred to. But the state thus produced is equally susceptible to the influence of the spirit of God, and it would appear that Daniel, before his visions, was in this state of mental absorption, and that before one of his visions he had been fasting " three full weeks " (Dan. x. 2 and ix. 3).

Under these circumstances it would appear difficult to determine in every case whether these faculties are from God or due to daimonical agency. As a rule, however, their origin may be recognised by the following distinctions. The powers and faculties bestowed by God are given unsought, and although their object may not always be recognised, they are not conducive to evil. The powers obtained from the daimonia have been generally bestowed on their devoted worshippers, and have only served to exalt the pride and power of the recipient, and to increase the influence of superstition and idolatry, or they have been sought and obtained by persons of exceptional wickedness to enable them to satisfy their evil desires.

Other supernatural phenomena might be mentioned, such as apparitions and haunted houses, or localities, which have been the seat of former crimes, and are supposed to he haunted by the spirits of murderers or their victims. But if the daimonia personate the spirits of the dead in order to deceive their living friends and relatives, they may also do so in the case of haunted houses. Satan, the prince of the demons, is spoken of as the tempter, and Christians are warned not to " give place to him " ; that is to say, not to allow his suggestions and temptations to obtain a hold of the mind and affections, because having thus obtained a footing, he might possess the person, as in the case of Judas, of whom it is said, when he went out to betray our Lord, that " Satan entered into him."

It is thus implied that persons of exceptional wickedness, such as murderers, are possessed by an evil spirit, who dominates their minds and induces them to carry out their deeds of evil. Such spirits being wholly evil, glory in the evil they have brought about, and may be conceived to cling to the scene of their evil and be allowed by God to haunt it. This is implied by the statement, " For blood, it defileth the land, and there is no expiation for the land of the blood that is shed therein, but by the blood of him that shed it " (Num. xxxv. 33). The place, in short, is " accursed," and the evil spirit, permitted by God to haunt it, and, as in some cases, to rehearse before the eyes of the living the wicked deed, may be regarded as a sign and a warning of God that the blood of the murdered person still cries for vengeance.

A case in illustration of this was brought to my own notice when quartered at Athlone in 1879, in the vicinity of which, it is said, more murders have been committed than in any other part of Ireland. I had occasion to visit an out-station at some distance and was driving there accompanied by my sergeant-major, a most matter-of-fact and unimaginative man, who had been stationed at Athlone for some time previously. About four miles out, there was a police station, and some three miles further on was a gentleman's place called " The Doune," which, like many other places in Ireland, was let for a nominal sum, the owner refusing to live there. For a full mile before coming to " The Doune " the road was perfectly straight and level, but for a hundred yards, or so, before reaching the lodge gates of " The Doune," the road was dark and overhung with trees. While still in the open part of the road *before* reaching this spot the sergeant-major remarked,—

" A curious circumstance happened to me here, sir, a little time ago, at about this part of the road. I was *returning* from visiting the out-station to Athlone on an outside car, and had passed ' The Doune,' when I saw a car at some distance driving towards us on the same side of the road, and with four men and a driver on it. I thought very little about it at first until it was within a hundred yards or less. We were on our right side of the road, and I expected this car every minute to turn to its proper side, but instead of that it seemed as if it intended to drive right into us. I shouted to my driver to turn aside, but he took not the slightest notice and appeared to be completely dazed. I shouted again to him without result, and was preparing to jump off the car to avoid the certain crash which appeared imminent, when, just as the other car reached us, it completely vanished, and there was not a trace of it to be seen in any direction. At the same instant our horse, seemingly maddened with terror, ran away, nor could it be stopped until it pulled up streaming with perspiration at the police station. I there learnt that I had seen what was called 'The Doune' Murderers. It appeared that some years before, the owner of 'The Doune,' having incurred the enmity of certain people, was waylaid and murdered at the dark part of the road near his house by four men who drove there on an outside car and had *never been apprehended*, but that, at certain times since, different people had met with the apparition described, which disappeared just as it reached them. My driver's terror was due to the fact that he had heard of this apparition and recognised it."

Such was the sergeant-major's story, but I was not sufficiently interested at the time to take the trouble to verify it, which might have been done, for the driver was still in Athlone, and the people at the police station could have been questioned. But the little circumstantial incidents of the story, omitted for the sake of brevity, were so devoid of artificiality, and the driver's paralysed terror so unlike what would have been invented, and yet so true to nature, that the story has all the appearance of truth, and the narrator was not only the last person to invent such a story, but very unlikely to have told such an invention to his superior officer when it could have been easily proved to be false.

Moreover, there are many well-authenticated stories of a similar nature, which have all the appearance of truth, being wholly devoid of that systematic and artificial construction which always accompanies invention. In this case, the apparition was not of the murdered man, but of the murderers; some of whom were probably still living, and the apparition was not therefore produced by the spirits of the dead. The terror of the horse is also similar to that which, in the case of other apparitions, is said to have been produced on dumb animals. But, while there would be no reason for such terror if the apparition was the spirit of a human being, there would be every reason for it, if the apparition was produced by a wholly malignant spirit, "greater in power and might" than man.

The Scripture describes the dead as "asleep in the dust," that they "know not anything, neither have they any more a portion in anything that is done under the sun," and we must therefore conclude that these apparitions are not the spirits of the dead, but evil spirits who, for the reasons mentioned, are allowed to personate them.

Every effort, however, is being made at the present day to revive the Pagan belief in the powers and activity of the spirits of the dead, and their influence on human affairs, and thence, to introduce, under religious and other pleas, intercourse and relationship with them. The belief also that they are the spirits of dead friends and relatives, able and willing to aid the living, and reveal to them the secrets of the unseen world, together with their affectation of a certain righteousness and truth, exercises a fascination upon many. But, from an analysis of the phenomena, compared with the testimony of Scripture, it is evident that the intercourse with the dead by the modern votaries of Spiritualism and Theosophy is merely the revival of the old Pagan worship instituted by Hermes, whose teaching indeed they profess to follow, and that the beings who reply to them and show signs and wonders, although they personate and are supposed to be the spirits of the dead, are the same daimonia, or evil spirits, who were the real gods of the Pagans, and whose one desire is to obtain influence and control over the bodies and souls of men. It is also evident that the allied phenomena of Hypnotism, Faith-healing, etc., are equally revivals of the methods used by the Pagan magicians and sorcerers, and are due, not to any powers inherent in man, but simply and solely to the aid of the same daimonia.

But if so, it would seem that the Roman Catholic, or at least the *devotees* [1] of that religion, although they, like the Pagans, believe that the beings they invoke are the spirits of "holy men," must also be under the influence of daimonia; and that the spirits who reply to them and influence their minds and imaginations, and in some cases perform signs and wonders in order to confirm their faith in them, are not those of the Virgin and saints, but spirits of evil; and, as implied by the Apostle Paul, this would appear to be true of every worshipper of idols and the supposed spirits of the dead (1 Cor. x. 19, 20).

[1] See *infra*, chap. xvii.

CHAPTER IX

THE NEPHILIM

THE next point of our inquiry is the way in which the worship of and intercourse with evil spirits, supposed to be spirits of the dead, arose. How was it introduced to the human race?

Berosus, the Babylonian historian and priest of Bel, who is supposed to have lived in the time of Alexander the Great, has left us an account of the Deluge, and of certain features of antediluvian history. Allusion has already been made to his account of a being called "Oannes," "the Annedotus," partly human and partly fish, who appeared to the people of Babylonia and taught them "letters and science and every kind of art. He taught them to construct houses, to found temples, to compile laws, and explained to them the principles of geometrical knowledge. From that time, so universal were his instructions, nothing material has been added by way of improvement."[1] The mention here of an antediluvian Babylonia is probably only for the purpose of identifying the locality which, on account perhaps of its antediluvian associations, being close to the site of Eden, was selected to be the centre of the postdiluvian idolatry.

Berosus, like the historians of other Pagan nations, mentions *ten* kings as having reigned before the Deluge, just as the Mosaic account describes *ten* generations during the same period, and according to his history, as given by *Polyhistor*, this Oannes appeared in the reign of the first king, but according to *Apollodorus* in that of the fourth king. In addition to the first Oannes, Berosus mentions other Annedoti of a similar form who appeared in the reigns of other kings, and who "related to the people whatever Oannes had informed them of,"[2] that is to say, they instructed the people in the same knowledge. From these statements Berosus implies that the principles of idolatry were taught to mankind before the Deluge, and that Hermes, or Cush, therefore merely revived that teaching.

[1] Berosus, from *Polyhistor*, etc. ; Cory's *Fragments*, pp. 22, 23.
[2] Berosus, from *Polyhistor* and *Apollodorus*; Cory's *Fragments*, pp. 22, 30, 31.

In addition to these Annedoti, who are described as *semi-daemons*,[1] we learn from Sanchoniathon's history that the sixth descendant from "*Protogonus*," *i.e.*, "the first-born," or Adam, was "*Chrysor*," who, he says, is the same as Hephæstus. "He exercised himself in words and charms and divinations, wherefore men worshipped him after death as a god and called him Diamichius the great inventor."[2] Now Cush, or Hermes, who was the great teacher of the same knowledge after the Deluge, was in one of his deified manifestations, "Hephæstus," or Vulcan, and, according to Manetho, quoted by Syncellus, there were two Hermes, or Thoths, the one before, and the other after the Deluge.[3] Hence we may assume that just as the postdiluvian Hermes and Hephæstus were one and the same, so also the antediluvian Hermes was Hephæstus, or Chrysor, the sixth descendant from Adam, and that Chrysor was called by these names in after ages, because he was the chief teacher among the antediluvians of the knowledge taught by the second Hermes after the Deluge. For it must be remembered that the names under which Cush and his son were deified were not given them until long after their deaths.

We have suggested that the name "Oannes" was also given to Cush because he, like the first Oannes, was the teacher of this knowledge, but there seems to be no reason for identifying Chrysor with the Annedotus Oannes who, like the other Annedoti, is described as a *daemon*.

Chrysor, the antediluvian Hephæstus, having been worshipped as a god after his death, we may be certain that he would be also recognised as a god in the postdiluvian idolatry. Now Manetho's list of the god kings of Egypt begins with an Hephæstus, who is given a reign of 724 years,[4] a period which is not only irreconcilable with the reign of any king after the Deluge, but is in striking contrast with the reigns of other god kings which are of normal length. But these 724 years might perfectly accord with the lifetime of an antediluvian, and we may conclude therefore that the Hephæstus mentioned in Manetho's list is the antediluvian Hephæstus or Chrysor, the first Hermes, introduced by the priesthood as being the first human teacher of their religion.

All tradition points to the fact that the idolatry established by

---

[1] Berosus, from *Abydenus;* Cory, p. 32.
[2] *Sanchoniathon's History;* Cory's *Fragments*, pp. 7, 8.
[3] Cory's *Fragments*, pp. 168, 169.
[4] *See* Manetho's *Dynasties;* Cory's *Fragments*, p. 94.

Cush and Nimrod was a revival of antediluvian idolatry. Thus Berosus says that the knowledge obtained before the Deluge was carefully preserved, and that Xisuthrus, or Noah was directed to "commit everything to writing and bury the account in the city of the sun at Sippara," and that after the Deluge, having found these writings at Sippara, "they set about building cities and erecting temples, and Babylon was again inhabited."[1] Similarly, Manetho, the Egyptian priest, claims to have based his writings on certain inscriptions "engraved on columns by the *first* Thoth (*i.e.*, Chrysor) before the Deluge in the land of the Siriad."[2] This is probably the foundation, in part, of the statement of Josephus that the sons of Seth, in order that their scientific discoveries might not be lost, engraved them upon two columns, one of brick and the other of stone, and that the latter remains to this day in the land of Siriad (*i.e.*, Egypt). He has probably here confused the preservation of the antediluvian knowledge of idolatry with the knowledge, astronomical, cosmogonic and prophetic, which is recorded by the Great Pyramid.[3]

Again, Brahma is said to have written the Vedas, but they were stolen from him by the demon "Hayagriva" while "he slumbered in a prior world," *i.e.*, while shut up in the Ark. After which "Vishnu became a fish and recovered them from the bottom of the ocean."[4] This is simply a way of saying that they were recovered from the bottom of what had been the ocean. In other traditions the sacred writings came from heaven, as in the case of Buddha, who is said to have flourished at the time of the Deluge, "when the Earth poured forth the flood in order to assist him against the Assoors or giants,—five holy scriptures descended from above which gave knowledge of introspection and ability of accomplishing the desires of hearts and means of carrying words into effect."[5] This has already been referred to. So also "Maha Bad," "the great Buddha," who is said to have been the first monarch of Iran, "received from the Creator a sacred book in a heavenly language."[6] Again, Menu Satyavrata is represented as being saved with seven saints from the

---

[1] Berosus, from *Abydenus*, p. 33. The preservation of this knowledge thus attributed to Noah is characteristic of the methods of Paganism, which not only identified their gods with Noah, but made use of his name as the venerated father of the human race to obtain credit and respect for their religion.

[2] Cory, *Fragments*, p. 168.

[3] Josephus, *Ant.*, bk. i. chap. ii. It may be remarked that the name Seth is synonymous with Shem, who appears to be called Sheth in Numb. xxiv. 17.

[4] Faber, vol. ii. p. 150.　　　[5] *Ibid.*, p. 149.　　　[6] *Ibid.*

Deluge by Heri, the Preserver of the Universe, in the shape of a large fish (the Ark), and after the Flood he received a book of divine ordinances in the language of the gods.[1] The Druids have a similar tradition. They say that the Patriarch was saved with seven companions on a floating island with a strong door. They also speak of the sacred books of Pherylt, or the writings of Hu, or Prydain, of which Taliesen says that "should the *waves again* disturb their foundation he would conceal them deep in the cell of the Holy Sanctuary."[2]

Now it is, of course, utterly absurd to suppose that Noah, or anyone else, recorded and buried the principles of Pagan idolatry previous to the Deluge in order that they might be recovered and idolatry re-established after the Deluge. But, on the other hand, it is very probable that Cush, the originator of postdiluvian idolatry, may, like the votaries of modern Spiritualism, have received instructions from the spirits he invoked as gods, as to the means of communicating with them and enlisting their powers on his behalf;— or, in other words, the principles of magic and sorcery;—and that this was "the special revelation from the gods" said to be received by Buddha, Menu and other forms of the Pagan god. We may also presume that the uniform tradition of the recovery after the Deluge of the secrets of the Pagan religion has *some* foundation, and, taking into consideration the tradition of the first Hermes, or Hephæstus, and the first Oannes, as the primary teachers of idolatry, it implies that the worship of the gods, or communication with evil spirits, first originated in the antediluvian world, and was merely revived by the Hamite descendants of Noah from the traditional knowledge preserved by their father Ham.

It is necessary here to call attention to the fact that the traditions and histories bearing upon the subject are derived from writings dated 2000 years or more after the events of which they treat, and that they emanate from priests, or priestly castes, who represent them in accordance with their religious belief. Thus Bel, the chief god of the Babylonians, Osiris, the god of the Egyptians, and the Jupiter of the Greeks and Romans, are by these writers entirely removed from the events of human history, as being the supreme gods of these nations and the orderers and arbiters of those events. For instance, we find in the lately-discovered account of the Deluge on the Assyrian tablets that Bel, who was the first king in Babylon many years after that event, is represented as arranging the circumstances of the Flood

---

[1] Faber, vol. ii. pp. 113-116 and p. 149.   [2] *Ibid.*, p. 150.

as the supreme god. The same is the case with Osiris and Jupiter when they are spoken of in relation to the events of history. It is only in those myths which treat of the histories of the gods themselves that their true relations are revealed, although, for the causes before mentioned, their particular relationship to their human originals is sometimes misplaced.

We have also to take into consideration the dual character of Pagan idolatry. It consisted, as we have said, at first of magic, demon and nature worship, the worship of the Sun, Moon and Stars and the Phallic or generative principle; and afterwards the authors of this worship were themselves deified and identified with the demon and Nature gods they themselves had instituted, and therefore with the Sun as the Great Father and the Earth as the Great Mother. So also they were identified with the progenitors of the human race, and Belus, Cronus, Saturn, etc., being the Father of the Gods and of men, were therefore represented as, not merely the first rulers of Babylon and Egypt, but as Noah, and even Adam, whose histories were more or less interwoven with theirs.

In like manner the goddess Mother was not merely Rhea, the Earth and the Moon, but the Ark from which the human race had been reborn. So also she was Eve, "the Mother of all living," and hence was called "*Idaia Mater*" ("the Mother of Knowledge"[1]), that is, the woman through whom came the knowledge of good and evil. Again, because Eve was formed from Adam, and the Ark (the symbol of the goddess) was constructed by Noah, the goddess Mother is sometimes represented as the daughter as well as the wife and mother of the god, as in the case of Ila, who is both the daughter and wife of Menu, while, as the mother of the supposed reincarnation of the god, she is his mother as well, as in the case of Isis and Osiris.

The Greeks, knowing these things only in their allegorical form, and failing to understand their mystical import, turned them into a multitude of fanciful fables which, in a large number of instances, have completely obliterated their original significance. Nevertheless, by making due allowance for these confusing elements, the underlying truth may still be extracted from many of these myths by carefully comparing them with each other, and with the statements of ancient authors.

There is much in the antediluvian traditions of the various

---

[1] Called so from Mount Ida, "the mount of knowledge." Dymock's *Classical Dict.—sub voce;* Hislop, p. 111.

nations which is in accordance with the Scriptural account. M. Lenormant writes: "In the number given in the Bible for the antediluvian Patriarchs we have the first instance of a striking agreement with the traditions of various nations. In Chaldea Berosus enumerates *ten* antediluvian kings. . . . The legends of the Iranian race commence with the reign of 'ten Peisdadien kings, men of ancient law, who lived on pure Homa (water of life), who preserved their sanctity.' In India we meet with the nine Brahmadikas who, with Brahma, their founder, make *ten*, and who are called the *ten* Petris or Fathers. The Chinese count ten emperors, partakers of the divine nature, before the dawn of historical times, and finally, not to multiply instances, the Germans and Scandinavians believed in the *ten* ancestors of Odin, and the Arabs in the *ten* mythical kings of the Adites, the primordial people of their peninsula."[1] To this we might add the ten kings of the antediluvian Atlantis, the story of which was related to Solon by the Egyptian priests,[2] and also to the nine generations before Noah, mentioned by Sanchoniathon in his history, and to which we shall presently refer.

In the Scriptural account of the antediluvian world mention is made of "*giants*" who were the predisposing cause of the wickedness which led to the destruction of the world by the Deluge. The traditions of the Pagan nations are also in remarkable accordance with this. The Gothic legend speaks of a *first* world called "*Muspelsheim*," the abode of *Surtur*, which was destroyed by *fire*, and of a *second* world in which all the families of the *giants* were destroyed by a flood except one who saved himself and his household in a ship. His *three sons* born of a Cow, *i.e.*, the Ark,[3] were the gods of the Goths.[4] Another tradition mentions the giant "Ymer," whose blood destroyed all the other *giants* except one, Bergelmer, who escaped on board his bark. "Ymer" is represented as, in the first place, *the Earth*, from whose body (when "the fountains of the great deep were broken up") came the Deluge and who afterwards made the ocean.[5] He is evidently the same as "Typhon," the ocean, and the evil principle of the Egyptians.

The Celtic Hu, who is said to have lived at the time of the

[1] Lenormant, *Anc. Hist. of East*, vol. i. pp. 12, 13.
[2] Recorded by Plato, *The Critias*.
[3] "Theba" means both "cow" and "ark," and hence a cow was the symbol of the goddess Mother as a bull was of the god; Faber, vol. i. p. 21.
[4] Faber, vol. i. p. 133.　　　　　[5] *Ibid.*, pp. 215-219.

Deluge, and who is also called "Noe," is represented as the conqueror of the *giants* and "after patience in affliction became the father of all the tribes of the Earth." [1]

The Chinese tradition, although it does not speak of *giants*, yet attributes the Deluge to the moral evil of the human race. It mentions first a golden age, after which "men despised the Monarch of the Universe, disputes arose about truth and falsehood which banished eternal reason, in consequence of which they fixed their looks on terrestrial objects to excess, and became like them. Such was the source of all crimes. Then the pillars of heaven were broken, the Sun, Moon and Stars changed their motions, the earth fell to pieces and the waters enclosed within its bosom burst forth with violence and overflowed it." [2]   It will be remarked that the above attributes the moral evil which led to the Deluge to the loss of the knowledge of God and consequent disputes about truth and falsehood, the result of which was that men fixed their looks, *i.e.*, directed their attention, wholly to earthly things, or to the satisfaction of their natural lusts and inclinations, and the law of self, or selfishness, becoming thus predominant, the demands of righteousness would be ignored, which, as the tradition says, was the source of all crimes. As stated by the Mosaic account, "violence filled the earth."

Buddha, who, in certain aspects, is also Noah, is represented as living at the time of the Deluge, and it is said that the earth poured forth a flood to assist him against the Assoors or Asuras, who were *giants* and were the demons of Indian mythology. [3]

According to Hesiod, Neptune, or the Sea, shut up the Titans in a central cavity of the earth, surrounding them on all sides with the ocean, and overwhelmed the wicked race of Phlegyæ and their island beneath the sea. [4] This is an allegorical way of saying that "*the Titans*," the name by which Noah and his descendants

[1] Faber, vol. ii. pp. 305, 306. Hu is evidently in the above tradition identified with Noah, but, as in the case of Jupiter of the Aryans, he was afterwards identified with the Babylonian god just as the latter was often identified with Noah.

[2] Faber, vol. ii. pp. 139-141.

[3] *Asiat. Res.*, vol. ii. p. 386; Faber, vol. ii. p. 149. It is worthy of note that these traditions all speak of the earth and not the rain as the *chief* source of the waters of the Deluge, which is also in accordance with Mosaic account, which says that "the fountains of the great deep were broken up," or, in other words, the subsidence of the dry land gave vent to the subterranean waters. *See* also Appendix C.

[4] Faber, vol. ii. pp. 176, 177.

are spoken of in classical mythology, were shut up in the Ark and surrounded by the waters of the Flood which destroyed the wicked antediluvians.

The impious Phlegyæ were said by the Greeks to be descended from Mars and *Chrysa*,[1] while Phavorinus represents them to be Cushites.[2] The latter, of course, could not be the case, as Cush was not born until after the Deluge, but both traditions have a corresponding significance. The first seems to connect the Phlegyæ with the antediluvian *Chrysor*, who, according to Sanchoniathon, introduced magic and intercourse with evil spirits.[3] The second connects the Phlegyæ with the Cushite race, who resuscitated that magic and intercourse after the Deluge. The two traditions point, therefore, to a general recognition of the fact that this unholy intercourse with evil spirits was the cause of the wickedness which brought on the world the judgment of the Deluge.

If now we turn to the Scriptural account of "*the giants*," through whom it is implied that the human race became thoroughly corrupt and violence filled the earth, we find it stated that they were results of marriages contracted between the *sons of God* and the *daughters of men* (Gen. vi.) The popular interpretation of the statement is that the "sons of God" were the righteous descendants of Seth, and the "daughters of men" were the descendants of Cain. But it is manifestly absurd to suppose that the result of the marriage of the righteous with the unrighteous should be a gigantic race of men! Nor is there any precedent in the Bible for calling the unrighteous, "Sons or daughters of men," in contrast to the righteous, or people of God. Such an interpretation cannot be supported by any valid argument, and the rule of Biblical interpretation, namely that laid down by the Apostle Paul of comparing spiritual things with spiritual,[4] or of considering the meaning which Scripture attaches to the terms used, in other passages, obliges us to interpret the passage in a very different way.

The term "Sons of God" is only used in the Old Testament to express *the angels*, or those beings who are the direct creation of God,[5] and it is thus applied in the New Testament to Adam[6] and to Christ. It is also applied in a spiritual sense in the New Testament

---

[1] Pausan., *Bœot.*, p. 597 ; Apoll., *Bibl.*, lib. iii. c. 5.
[2] Phavor., *Apud Steph. Byzant. de Urb*, p. 60 ; Faber, vol. ii. pp. 176, 177.
[3] *See* infra, *Sanchoniathon's History*, pp. 200, 201.
[4] 1 Cor. ii. 13.
[5] Job i. 6, xxxviii. 7.   [6] Luke iii. 38.

to those who are spiritually born of God, or regenerated, but in that sense it was unknown in the Old Testament, and cannot be made use of to explain its use of the term. Again the original word translated " giants " is not " giants " but " *Nephilim*," meaning " Fallen Ones," although it afterwards became a term to express giants, because the result of these marriages was a race of gigantic beings. The statement in Gen. vi. is therefore as follows:—" There were *Fallen Ones* in the earth in those days" (*i.e.*, before the Deluge), " and also *after that*, when the sons of God" (the angels) " came in unto the daughters of men and they bare children to them ; the same became mighty men which were of old, men of renown " (ver. 4). The result of this union of the human race with beings who are said to be " greater in power and might " [1] was a mixed race of fallen angels and men, and this race were of vast stature and strength, and wholly and irredeemably wicked. Various races of these giants are mentioned in Scripture as existing amongst the nations of Canaan.

There is, however, among many, a singular hostility to the admission of the possibility of the supernatural in anything which immediately affects the human race ; and this has led them to oppose the manifest conclusion to be drawn from the Scriptural statements, and to fall back on the weak and inconsequent hypothesis that " the Sons of God " were merely the more pious antediluvians. They will accept the miracles of Christ as a fact of the past which does not affect people living now, but the possibility of spiritual agents, such as the Nephilim, able to communicate with and influence mankind, disturbs their minds, and rather than admit the plain teaching of Scripture, they shut their eyes to the evidence. The same hostility is seen in the refusal to admit of spiritual agency in the phenomena of Spiritualism, Hypnotism, etc., and the endeavour to explain such things, however illogically, by natural causes which may be controlled by the aid of human knowledge and science. It is the old Sadducean spirit, which revolts against the idea of spiritual powers outside the knowledge and control of human power and wisdom. To attempt to combat this sceptical spirit is useless, and we can only point out the testimony of Scripture to those with whom that testimony has greater weight than the laboured and illogical explanations of others, who desire to explain away its meaning.

The intercourse of these " fallen ones " with the human race in the past and the possibility of its recurrence was the general belief of the Jews and the early Christian Church. Josephus states it as an

---

[1] 2 Peter ii. 11.

undoubted fact,[1] and Augustine speaks of the folly of doubting it.[2] It was also the general belief throughout the East, and the Persians say that "Djemschid" married the daughter of a dev, *i.e.*, a demon.[3] Now "Djemschid," or "Ghemschid," is stated to be the *fourth* king of Iran, and the ancient Iran extended from the Caucasus to the Indus, including the valley of Shinar—that is to say, it consisted of the empire conquered by Nimrod, who was the *fourth* from Noah. The Persian account says that the father of Ghemschid founded the cities of Babylon and Nineveh, which is in accordance with the various records of the dynasties of the Assyrian Empire. These nearly always place Belus or Cush as the first king, and Ninus or Nimrod as succeeding him. The *Zendavesta* says that "Ghemschid, that wonderful king of Iran, built a place of enormous extent in the form of a square, and within it was a tower or castle and also a conspicuous palace."[4] This is clearly Babylon, the beginning of the kingdom of Nimrod, showing that the Ghemschid, or Djemschid, of these traditions was Nimrod. In the Arabian traditions Djemschid would appear to be Cush,[5] but the history and subsequent mythology of the two deified kings are so interwoven, that the one is constantly confused with the other.

This tradition of the marriage of Cush or Nimrod with the daughter of a demon will be referred to again, and it is here quoted as a record of the union of the human race with demons, which, as we shall see, and as is implied in Gen. vi., took place *after* the Deluge, as well as before that event.

The original authors of this intercourse, the Sons of God or fallen angels mentioned in Gen. vi., would appear to be alluded to by the Apostles Peter and Jude as "the angels which *kept not their first estate but left their first habitation*"; for this is exactly what the Nephilim were guilty of, and their sin is likened to that of the inhabitants of Sodom and Gomorrah, who "*went after strange flesh.*" These fallen angels are said to be "reserved in chains of darkness unto the judgment of the great day" (Jude 5, 6). But if these "fallen ones" had thus established communication with man, it is not necessary to seek further for the original source of that knowledge of the spirit world and the means of invoking the assistance of its inhabitants, which has been handed down to the present day. In

---

[1] *Antiq.*, chap. i. p. 6.
[2] Smith's *Dict. of the Bible*, "Giants." [3] *Ibid.*
[4] *Zendavesta*, tom. ii. p. 275 ; *Compn.* 666, p. 312.
[5] See *ante*, chap. iv. pp. 75, 76.

fact, it is the tradition of the Hindus that the gods (*i.e.*, the daimonia) at first became *incarnate* and conversed with men, and taught them arts and science and the nature of the place where they were to go after an earthly probation.[1] The latter, it may be remarked, is the special subject of spiritualistic revelation at the present day.[2]

The Nephilim were thus spirits of evil, the same as the daimonia, whose prince was Satan, and who were the real gods of the Pagans, the beings who replied to their invocations. If, then, some of them had intercourse with the daughters of men, they would not fail to teach men the means also of communicating with them. It is said these "Fallen Ones" were "*in the earth* in those days," which plainly implies that their presence there was abnormal, and therefore that they were not human beings, but nothing is said in Scripture about their actual appearance, and it seems very unlikely that they had the power of taking the form of man, who is made in the image of God, and living amongst men as human beings. In modern Spiritualism the spirits have been known to take the form of some relative or friend of the person invoking them, but it is temporary and evanescent, and even then depends on certain peculiar and exceptional conditions. Had the Nephilim indeed lived among men as men, and been known by them by distinctive names, features and characteristics, we may be certain that they would have been worshipped by the idolaters under those names and characteristics as their chief gods, whereas Chrysor, who was worshipped after his death, was seemingly the first of the Pagan gods.

On the other hand, it does not follow that they were unable to take *any* material form in order to converse with men. Who was Oannes and who were the other Annedoti? Are we to dismiss the tradition handed down by Berosus as a fable without foundation? If so, the fable is puerile and objectless, and only worthy of the imagination of a child; and this, as we shall see, is not the character of the generality of the Pagan myths when they have not been encrusted with fable by the imagination of the Greeks, who did not understand their true significance. Now, Berosus speaks of Oannes and the Annedoti as "*dæmons*," which is but another name for the Pagan gods, and we find that Oannes was actually worshipped in after ages as one of the chief gods of Paganism under his own name, Oannes, or as Dagon, the Fish god.

If Satan assumed the form of a serpent in order to converse with

[1] Maurice, *Hist. Hindustan*, vol. i. p. 371 ; Faber, vol. ii. p. 15.
[2] Pember, pp. 359-368.

man and withdraw him from his allegiance to God, there would be nothing anomalous in the assumption of a form like that of Oannes by his angels, the Nephilim, for a similar purpose. It may be asked, why should the Nephilim have assumed these forms, and why did Satan assume the form of a serpent instead of that of a man, in which form, we might suppose, his arguments would have been listened to much more readily by human beings? In both cases the forms assumed give an air of fable and grotesqueness to the story, which, with many, may seem to impeach its credibility. But there may be a deep reason, arising from the very nature of things, for the assumption of these forms; and, if so, the aspect of fable and unreality is removed, and the tradition of Berosus is in accordance with what we expect from the statements of Scripture.[1] In short, we might well conceive that in the ages before the Deluge, when fallen angels allied themselves with men and a race of demon-born beings was the result, some of these Nephilim, or possibly Satan himself, did assume the shapes described by Berosus, in order to deceive mankind and communicate to men the knowledge of evil. Satan is said to be him who "deceiveth the whole world" (Rev. xii. 9), and the chief of these Annedoti, who in after ages was worshipped as O'annes, may well have been Satan himself. For "*O*" is the Greek article "The," and *O'annes* might be the Hellenised form of "*Ha Nahash*"[2]—"the Serpent," with whom the other forms of the Pagan gods, as we shall see, were eventually identified.

The Scriptures say that the gods of the heathen were devils (dæmons), and we shall see that both Chrysor and the other human originals of the Pagan gods were probably of Nephilim descent. If so, there was a deeper reason than the fact of their being the human originators of idolatry for deifying them after death; for they were in very truth the incarnation of the dæmon gods, and their descendants therefore may have rightly claimed to be the children of the Sun and Serpent god.

It will be observed that the intercourse of fallen angels and women is said to have occurred, not only before the Deluge, but "after that," or at some subsequent period, and that "sons were born unto them who were mighty men of old, men of renown." In accordance with this we read of certain strange races of *giants* in

[1] *See* Appendix B, where the question is more fully considered.

[2] Oannes is the Greek form of the name, and as *h* is not represented by a letter in Greek, *Ha Nahash* would become *anaas* or *anas*, and with the article Oanas, or Oanes. Moreover, Berosus says that Oannes *first* appeared in the reign of the *first* king, who we shall see was Noah, (*infra*, pp. 199-201).

N

Palestine, the *Rephaim, Enim, Anakim* and *Zuzim,* concerning whom the writer of the article on "The Giants," in Smith's *Dictionary of the Bible,* says, "They were not Canaanites, as there is no mention of them in the genealogies in Gen. x. 15-19."[1] This omission would be incomprehensible if they were descendants of Canaan in the male line, but it would not be so if they were the result of the intercourse of "the sons of God" with the women of Canaan. This would account for their gigantic stature and strength, and the existence of whole races of such giants cannot be explained on any other grounds.

The word "*Rephaim*" occurs in two other places in Scripture, in one of which it is said that the path of the woman "which forsaketh the guide of her youth, and forgetteth the covenant of her God," "inclineth to *the Rephaim*," and in the other that "the man that wandereth out of the way of understanding shall remain in the congregation of *the Rephaim.*"[2] In the A.V. the word is translated "*the dead,*" which, no doubt, conveys the general meaning, such persons being spiritually dead, *i.e.,* separated or alienated from God;[3] but the particular use of the word "*Rephaim*" in these passages implies that the state of the Rephaim was one of irredeemable evil, or a state of hopeless *spiritual death,* which is not that of men by nature, however wicked they may be in other ways. It would thus appear that, just as the state of the fallen angels is irreversible[4] so also is that of the Rephaim, and of men who have allied themselves with them. This also may account for the commands given to the Israelites to destroy them utterly, as being wholly evil themselves and the source of untold evil to the rest of the human race.

If Cush knew from antediluvian tradition, or from other sources, the means of establishing intercourse with the spirit world, we may be certain that he would not neglect the method of inviting their companionship by means of women, and that it would indeed be a salient feature of the unholy arts of Paganism, and if this was the case, it would fully account for the existence of the giant races of Canaan. This receives strong corroboration from the description of the Tower of Belus at Babylon by Herodotus. On the top of it was the temple of Belus in which was "a handsome couch and table of gold." "No mortal," he says, "*passes the night there, except one woman chosen by the god out of the whole nation.*" He adds that the priests

---

[1] Smith's *Dict. of the Bible,* "Giants."
[2] Prov. ii. 17, 18 ; xxi. 16.   [3] Eph. ii. 1 ; iii. 18.
[4] As implied by Peter and Jude, "God spared not the angels who sinned."

" assert that the god himself comes to the temple and reclines on the bed in the same manner as the Egyptians say happens at the temple of Thebes in Egypt, for there also a woman lies in the temple of the Theban Jupiter, and both are said to have no intercourse with men." So also he says that the priestess of the oracle at Pateræ in Lycia is "shut up during the night in the temple with the god."[1]

This shows that, both in Babylon and Egypt, the two great centres of Paganism, as well as in other places, this intercourse with dæmons was openly invited, even so late as the time of Herodotus; and it is well known that, among the followers of the revived magic and necromancy in modern times, spirit marriages are advocated and are said to take place.[2] These facts would seem to show that the Grecian mythology, which is full of accounts of the amours of the gods with mortals, may be founded on something more than fable.

The Persian tradition, before alluded to, which speaks of Djemschid's marriage with the sister, or daughter of a dev, or dæmon (by which we ought probably to understand a Nephilim-born woman), says that from this marriage sprang "the black and impious race."[3] The origin of the black colour of the Cushite or Ethiopian race has been long a source of conjecture. Men may become very dark from generations of exposure to a tropical sun, but the Hindus, who have probably lived three or four thousand years in India, are not only not black, but their dark colour is of a superficial character as compared with that of the negro, and fades in some degree, even during a lifetime in a colder climate, while the women are decidedly fairer than the men. This is not the case with the negro races, and their colour is entirely unaffected by climate, as implied by Scripture, "Can the Ethiopian change his skin?" (Jer. xiii. 23). Some of the lower castes of Hindus are no doubt black, but this may be easily accounted for by their marriage with the former Cushite inhabitants. Moreover, climate cannot account for the fact that Æthiops, or Cush, and his descendants were black from the first, although living in the same countries, and under precisely the same conditions, as the other descendants of Noah.

Nimrod is called in the Septuagint "Nimrod the giant," and

[1] Herod., i. c. 181, 182.

[2] Pember, pp. 385-390. The Chaldean incantations also refer to dæmons who were supposed to bring men and women into their embraces during sleep. They were called " Incubus and Succubus," or " The Lilith." *See* Lenormant's *Chaldean Magic*, p. 38.

[3] Smith's *Dict. of the Bible*, " Giants."

Osiris, *i.e.,* Nimrod, is always represented as black, while Orion, with whom Nimrod has been identified, was represented as a giant of such vast strength that he boasted that no animal on earth could cope with him. This is also the character of another form of the god, the Assyrian Hercules,[1] and this gigantic stature and strength implies therefore his Nephilim descent, while the cruelties related of Ninus to those who resisted him were inhuman, and quite in keeping with a demoniacal origin. Zohak is represented as equally inhuman. It is amongst the black or Cushite races of Africa, the land of Ham, that "Obi," or demon, worship, of which strange tales are told, is most fully established; and the word "Obi" is clearly cognate with "Ob," the Hebrew word for the demons,[2] with whom the magicians and necromancers of Canaan had communication; and among no races do we find such habitual and fiendish cruelty as amongst the Obi worshippers of Africa.

In connection with this subject, a suggestion of Bishop Cumberland, in his analysis of the *History of Sanchoniathon,* is, at least, worthy of notice. We are told that the intercourse with the Nephilim did not take place until "men began to multiply on the earth," and we may conclude that this unholy intercourse, and the wickedness it gave rise to, although extending to all, would be most fully developed among the godless descendants of Cain. Now it is remarkable that Moses, in recording the names of some of the descendants of Cain, should mention the birth of one woman, and one only, as of direct descent from Cain in the eighth generation, namely, "*Naamah,*" the sister of Tubal-Cain. This is a departure from the usual manner of recording genealogies in Scripture, which only mentions those daughters who became wives of men of some other family; and we can only suppose that this mention of Naamah is because she became the wife of some person of importance. Bishop Cumberland suggests that she was the wife of Ham, and quotes Plutarch, who says that the wife of Cronus was "*Nemaus,*" which would be just the Greek form of the Hebrew "Naamah."[3] Cronus was indeed one of the names of both Cush and Nimrod, but for the reasons before stated it was often applied to Ham.

We may presume that Naamah of the last generation mentioned of the descendants of Cain would be more or less influenced by the exist-ing Nephilim intercourse, and if she was the wife of Ham it would help to account for the transmission, through her, of the occult knowledge

---

[1] See *ante,* chap. ii. pp. 23, 24.   [2] *Ante,* chap. v. p. 131.

[3] Cumberland, *Sanchoniathon's History,* p. 107.

of the antediluvians, and also for the tendency in her sons Cush and Canaan to revive their unlawful practices, and repeat the sin which had brought on the world the judgment of the Deluge.

Now Semiramis, who was first the wife of Oannes, king of Syria, *i.e.*, Assyria, was said to be the daughter of the *goddess* "Derketo," or Atergatis,[1] which may either mean that she was the daughter of a Nephilim-born woman, or of a Nephilim and a woman, and therefore regarded as a goddess or daughter of the gods; and as she afterwards bcame the wife of Nimrod, this would confirm the Persian tradition that Djemschid, who was either Cush or Nimrod, married a woman of demon origin. But, as we have seen, Nimrod was himself a *giant*—*i.e.*, one of those beings which were the result of these Nephilim marriages, and in all probability the most powerful of them all. This would imply that he was of Nephilim descent, a supposition which is supported by the fact that Semiramis was first the wife of the Syrian chief Oannes, who was probably Nimrod's own father, Cush,[2] from whom he took her; the story being in exact accordance with the Grecian myth of Vulcan, Venus and Mars.[3] If so, Semiramis may have been the mother, as well as the wife, of Nimrod, which would not only make him of Nephilim descent and account for his gigantic strength, but, in accordance with the often-repeated statements of mythology regarding the various gods under whose names he was deified, it would make him in actual fact "The Son and Husband of the Mother."

Again, if Nemaus, the wife of Ham, was Naamah the descendant of Cain, and therefore thoroughly acquainted with the principles of Nephilim intercourse, it is at least possible, even although she herself may have been in no sense of Nephilim descent, that she may have invited or submitted to Nephilim intercourse. The name "Naamah" means "beautiful," and it was because "the Sons of God saw the daughters of men that they were fair," that they "left their first estate" and took them for wives. Is it possible then that Semiramis, celebrated for her beauty, was the daughter of the beautiful Naamah by a Nephilim father? Semiramis is said to be the daughter of the goddess "Derketo," and Derketo was the wife of Dagon, who is the

[1] Lucian, *De Dea Syria*, vol. iii. pp. 460, 461 ; Hislop, p. 86.

[2] See *ante*, chap. III. p. 67.

[3] Venus was first the wife of Vulcan (*i.e.*, Cush), and was taken from him by Mars (*i.e.*, Nimrod), *see* Lemprière, *Vulcan, Mars*, etc. If both Cush and Nimrod married a Nephilim-born woman, this perhaps would account for the fact that Djemschid, who married the daughter of a "dev," or dæmon, is, in the traditions, seemingly identified with both father and son.

same as Oannes. The name Oannes may have been applied to Cush for the reasons that have been stated, but Oannes and Dagon have a distinct personality of their own, and were probably worshipped as the dæmons who first taught mankind the principles of the Pagan religion. Hence the name Oannes, or Dagon, may have been given to a Nephilim husband of Naamah as being of the same nature as the antediluvian dæmon, and Naamah in consequence would be known in mythology as "Derketo," the wife of Dagon, Derketo being the feminine form of Dagon.[1] This is only a suggestion, but it accounts for the facts connected with the case, while in the face of the mutually supporting testimony of profane and sacred history, and the facts of Spiritualism, the general conclusions arrived at cannot be rejected.

If then Nimrod and Semiramis were of Nephilim origin and the progenitors of the Cushite or Ethiopian race, may it not be possible that the black colour of that race, characterised as they ever have been by dæmon worship, was the result of an ordinance of God, or of one of those natural laws which, by the foreordainment of the Creator, stamped the descendants of such an union as "children of *darkness*" and as the "seed of the Serpent"? We see, moreover, that just as those Scythian races, ancestors of the Anglo-Saxons, who were most free from the debasing idolatry of Cush and Nimrod, have become, in spite of their orginal barbarism, the highest type of the human race at the present day, so the Cushite descendants of Nimrod, in spite of their original wisdom and power, have become both morally, intellectually, and in their facial type, the most degraded.

If we now turn to the history of Sanchoniathon the Phœnician,[2] in which he describes the first generations of the human race, we find much that confirms the general conclusions arrived at.

Sanchoniathon lived a few years before the Trojan War, and compiled his history from the records kept in the temples of the gods in various cities. It was translated into Greek by Philo, a native of Byblus. The portions still extant are fragmentary and disjointed, and manifest the general confusion in the history and identity of the gods which is characteristic of mythology, but they are in strict accordance with the mythologies and cosmogonies of other nations

[1] Hislop, p. 264.
[2] "Hist. of Sanchoniathon," from Cory's *Fragments*. Some modern writers have sought to discredit this history by suggesting it to be a forgery, but the reasons they give for such a suggestion are weak and inconclusive, and their objections are probably dictated by the *animus* possessed by certain writers of modern times against anything which tends to confirm the human origin of the Pagan gods. *See* App. E.

and with the general testimony of the Pagan writers that have been quoted, while they confirm and explain much of the early history of the Old Testament.

He begins by saying that the first mortals were begotten by the wind, *Kolpia* and his wife, *Baau* or *Baaut*, signifying "Night." It has been suggested that Kolpia is the Hebrew "*Kol pi Yah*," "the voice, or the mouth, of Yah, or Jehovah,"[1] and the wind is the ancient metaphor for expressing the Spirit of God. This, therefore, would simply mean that creation was the result of the Word and Spirit of God bringing forth life out of *darkness* and chaos.

One of these first mortals was called "*Protogonus*," the Greek for "first-born." This must be Adam, and the other, *Æon*, is said to have "*discovered fruit from trees*," which is evidently a confused tradition of Eve's plucking the forbidden fruit. "*Æon*," "age," Greek, αιων, meaning "living, or existence, for a space of time,"[2] would be synonymous with "Eve," which means "living" or "existence."

"From these descended *Genus* and *Genea*." "*Genus*" or "begotten" has the same signification as "*Cain*," which means "increase by generation." "These in times of great drought stretched forth their hands to heaven towards the Sun, whom they supposed to be the only god, and called him '*Beel Samen*'" (the Phœnician for "Lord of Heaven"). It would appear that at first there was no rain and that the earth was only watered by night dews;[3] the consequence of which would be great drought except in the neighbourhood of streams and rivers, and the ground would not yield food except by extreme labour, which was the result of the curse pronounced by God. This is confirmed by the fact that the rainbow, which is caused by the Sun's rays reflected through rain, did not appear until after the Deluge, when it is also stated that the curse on the ground was removed.[4] Hence the Sun, as the cause of great drought, was worshipped as a god whose wrath was to be deprecated.

"To Genus were born '*Phos*,' '*Pur*' and '*Phlox*' (meaning 'Light,' 'Fire' and 'Flame'), who discovered the means of generating fire by rubbing together pieces of wood, and taught men the use of it (*i.e.*, fire). These begat sons of *vast bulk and height*, who gave their names to the mountains which they occupied—*Cassius, Libanus, Antilibanus* and Brathu." This is the first mention of *giants*, and it would appear

[1] *See* note, Hodge's *Cory*, p. 4. The names used, however, are generally the Greek equivalents of the Phœnician.

[2] Bullinger, *Critical Concordance of Greek Test*, " Age."

[3] Gen. ii. 5, 6.   [4] Gen. viii. 21, 22.

that they must have been in some way the result of Nephilim intercourse. What follows is significant and may explain this, for Sanchoniathon goes on to say, "These begat, by connection with their own mothers, *Hypsuranius* and (or) *Memrumus*; the women of those times without shame having intercourse with any men whom they might chance to meet." The names "Hypsuranius" and (or) "Memrumus" clearly refer to the same person, as they have the same signification, namely "*issue from above*" (*i.e.*, descended from the gods), the one being Greek and the other Phœnician.[1] The history also goes on to say that Hypsuranius had a brother "*Usous*," but no farther mention is made of "Memrumus."

The explanation of this appears to be as follows: The giants, although in the generation following that of Phos, Pur and Phlox, were not their sons, but the sons of their daughters by Nephilim fathers, and these sons again begot Hypsuranius and Usous by their own mothers. In forsaking God, and in supposing the Sun to be the only god, the race of Cain had become without moral restraint, as shown by the shamelessness of the women, and were thus defenceless against the temptations of evil spirits, and the women, having followed the paths which lead to the Rephaim, from which there is no return, would probably prefer as husbands their heaven-born sons to any who were merely men, more especially if, as implied by the Apostles Peter and Jude, their angel husbands had met with swift punishment for leaving their "first estate."

After some mention of Usous, who is described as a hunter, the history goes on to say, "When all these were dead, those that remained consecrated to them staves of wood, and worshipped stelæ, or pillars, and celebrated feasts in honour of them every year." This implies that these Nephilim-descended men were recognised to be something more than human.

"In times long after there were born, *of the race of Hypsuranius, Agreus* and *Halieus*" (*i.e.*, Hunter and Fisherman). The expression "of the race" would seem to imply that they were not the sons or descendants of Hypsuranius and Usous, but of the same Nephilim parentage, and that the Nephilim intercourse had therefore been continued or renewed. Of these were begotten two brothers, one of whom was *Chrysor*, who is called Hephæstus, and who would thus be of Nephilim origin. "He exercised himself in words and charms and divinations, wherefore he was worshipped after his death as a god."

[1] Cumberland, p. 261, and Hodge's *Cory*, p. 6, note.

This implies that Chrysor, like Hermes and Hea, was a magician and sorcerer skilled in the arts of invoking the spirits, and it seems probable that he was the means whereby a general intercourse with them was established, with the result that the numbers of the Nephilim-begotten race rapidly increased, and, being wholly wicked, filled the earth with violence. It seems evident that the Greek story of the impious Phlegyæ descended from *Chrysa* and who were destroyed at the Deluge is a traditional remembrance of this.[1]

"Of his race were born *Technites*," *i.e.*, "the artificer" (who, Bishop Cumberland suggests, corresponds to Tubal-Cain) and *Geinus Antochthon*. These invented bricks and tiling.

Of these were begotten *Agrus* and *Agroueros*, or *Agrotes*, meaning "husbandmen." Agroueros had a wooden statue which was much venerated, and "at Byblus, he is called by way of eminence the greatest of the gods."

This Agroueros belongs to the tenth generation from Protogonus, or Adam, counted as follows :—

1. Protogonos.
2. Genus.
3. Phos, Pur, Phlox.
4. Daughters of above.[2]
5. The Giants, or Nephilim race.
6. Hypsuranius and Usous.
7. Agreus and Halieus.
8. Chrysor, or Hephæstus.
9. Technites and Genus Antochthon.
10. Agroueros, the husbandmen.

The history proceeds to say that from Agrus and Agroueros, "husbandmen and such as hunt with dogs derive their origin," and that they are called "*Titans*, "or "*Aletæ*." Now the principal Titans are said to be "Saturn," *i.e.*, Ham or Cush, "Japetus" or Japheth, and "Typhæus" or "Typhon,"[3] who would therefore appear to be Shem. These are the three sons of Noah, and the Sibyl similarly speaks of the three sons of the Patriarch as "Cronus" or "Saturn," "Japetus" and "Titan,"[4] which would identify Titan, *i.e.*, Shem,

---

[1] The name "Phlegyæ" seems to indicate their character. It is probably derived from πλέγω, "to inflame with madness or violence," which is also the characteristic of those who are possessed by evil spirits.

[2] It is significant that it was in the reign of the *fourth* king that Berosus says "Oannes" the Annedotus appeared.

Lemprière, *Titanes.*   [4] See *ante*, chap. ii. p. 17.

with Typhon. The term "*Titans,*" which was a general term given in after ages to the sons of Noah and their immediate descendants means "earth-born," and was probably given to them as being unaffected by the Nephilim intercourse, and in contradistinction to those who were, whom the Pagans regarded as "heaven-born." Hence it was a term of contempt, and appears to have been given especially to Shem, who is called also by the still more opprobrious name of "Typhon," the name in Egypt given to the evil spirit as the enemy of the Pagan gods.

By this it would appear that Agroueros, "the *husbandman,*" the father of the Titans, was Noah, and Noah is particularly described as a husbandman in Gen. ix. 20. So also, because certain of the family of Ham became the originals of the Pagan gods, Noah, as their ancestor, became the first or father of the gods, and hence is sometimes identified with Saturn, and his history is interwoven with that of the gods. This will explain the statement of Sanchoniathon, that at Byblos, Agrueros is called "the greatest," *i.e.,* the Father "of the gods."

Sanchoniathon continues, "From these (*i.e.,* Agrus and Agroueros) were descended *Amynus* and *Magus* and by these were begotten *Sydyk* and *Misor.*" Misor is clearly Mizraim, the grandson of Noah, for Mizraim, the Hebrew name for Egypt, is in Arabic "*Misr* or *Misor.*"[1] "From Misor," says the history, "descended *Taautus* who invented the writing of the first letters. The Egyptians call him *Thoor,* the Alexandrians *Thoyth,* and the Greeks *Hermes.*" Now Thoth or Cush was not the son of Misraim who was the father of the Mizraimite Egyptians, but Sanchoniathon says afterwards that Cronus "gave all Egypt to the god Taautus or Thoth that it might be his kingdom"—that is to say, Nimrod, having conquered Egypt among other countries, made his father king over it, thus superseding Misor, or Mizraim, and Sanchoniathon therefore represents Thoth as the son, or *successor,* of Misor.

It will be observed that Sanchoniathon, or the priestly chronicles from which he obtained his information, make no mention of the Deluge which destroyed the Nephilim, or, according to Pagan ideas, the gods and god-descended men of the antediluvian world; for to have done so would have condemned their own gods. Instead of this, having traced the descent of Thoth, he breaks the narration and succession and proceeds: "Contemporary with these was one *Elioun,* called *Hypsistus* (that is, 'the Most High') and his wife

[1] Hodge's *Cory,* p. 9, note.

Beruth" (or Covenant).¹ "By these were begotten *Epigeus*, or Autocthon, whom they afterwards called *Ouranos* (Heaven), so that from him that element which is over us by reason of its excellent beauty is named Heaven, and he had a sister of the same parents called *Ge* (Earth), and by reason of her beauty the earth was called by the same name."²

Now "Ouranos" and "Ge," called in Latin "Cælus" and "Terra" were, like Agrueros, the father and mother of *the Titans*,³ and therefore were Noah and his wife, and Ouranos, or Epigeus, is therefore the same as Agroueros, as his name *Epigeus*, "from, or dependent on, the earth," *i.e.*, a "husbandman," implies. Moreover, Sanchoniathon afterwards relates an incident in the history of Ouranos which is evidently the same as that in the history of Noah mentioned in Gen. ix. 21-27.

Ouranos and Ge are stated to be begotten by Elioun, "The Most High," and by Beruth "The Covenant." This is simply the mystical way, usual to Paganism, of saying that they were "born again" in the new world by "*the covenant of God*."⁴ For throughout the Pagan world the Deluge was regarded as the re-generation of the world and the human race. Thus the Brahmans claim to be "twice born" because descended from Brahm, who was the father of the Hindu gods Brahma, Vishnu and Siva, whose human originals were the three sons of Noah.⁵

In the subsequent history there is much confusion consequent on representing these two Noahs, and their respective descendants, as distinct, but more especially from the number of different gods who are introduced, and to each of which a distinct history is given, but whose names are only different deified forms of the same human original. Thus the Sons of Ouranos are said to be *Cronus* or *Il* (*i.e.*, Saturn), *Betylus*, *Dagon* or *Siton*, and *Atlas*. Betylus, or *Baitulos*, is a surname of Jupiter. It was the name of the stone which Saturn is said to have swallowed in mistake for Jupiter, who was consequently called Baitulos.⁶ Dagon, or Oannes, has been identified with Saturn, *i.e.*, Cronus. Atlas is generally represented

¹ *Berith*, Heb. for "covenant." *Elioun*, "the most high." *El Elyon*, is the word translated in Gen. xiv. 18, "the most high God." Hodge's *Cory*, p. 10, note.
² It will be remembered that Euhemerus says that the name Ouranos was given to him because he was the first who honoured the heavenly gods with sacrifice. This is the more probable origin of the name, and it is in accordance with the statement in Gen. viii. 20.
³ Lemprière, *Cælus*.
⁴ Gen. vi. 18; ix. 9-17.
⁵ *Ante*, pp. 17, 18; Hislop, p. 136.
⁶ Faber, vol. ii. p. 375.

as a son of Japheth, but, as he is represented here to be the son of Ouranos, he is probably Japheth himself.

Cronus is said by Sanchoniathon to have begotten three sons, "*Cronus,*" "*Jupiter-Belus*" and "*Apollo,*" who are all different forms of the same god. Then we have *Æsculapius,* another form of the same god, mentioned as the son of Sydyk; so also *Hercules, Cupid, Rhea, Astarte, Minerva,* and others, are mentioned as contemporary with the above and in various relations with them. This is just what we might expect from an historian who collected the stories concerning them from various sources in which the same god or goddess was mentioned under different names. "*Typhon*" and "*Pontus*" are also mentioned as contemporary with these, and *Nereus,* the father of Pontus. As Pontus is the same as *Oceanus,*[1] who was a son of Cælus and Terra, this would make Nereus to be Noah, and the name "Nereus," which means "watery," is probably a name given to him in connection with the Deluge. If then Typhon is Shem, Pontus, or Oceanus, would be Japheth. By the Greeks, Japetus, their ancestor, was regarded as the father of mankind, and similarly Oceanus was called by them "the father of the gods," which is, of course, the same thing. Japetus also became a term for extreme old age, and Oceanus is also represented as an extremely old man.[2] The countries first inhabited by the descendants of Japheth were the shores of the Pontus Euxinus and Mediterranean, which constituted "the isles, or shores of the Gentiles." Hence the titles Oceanus and Pontus given to Japheth.

Sanchoniathon speaks of the elder Cronus as the son of Ouranos, whereas he was really his grandson. This is due partly to the tendency before alluded to, to confuse Ham and Cush together, and also to the custom among the ancients of speaking of all the direct descendants of any important person as his *sons.*

The rest of the history is principally concerning the war between Cronus and Ouranos, in which Thoth is represented as the counsellor of Cronus and as stirring up the allies of Cronus to oppose Ouranos. Here there is evidently a confusion of the first and second Cronus, as it would seem to be the elder Cronus who is here spoken of, and he is the same as Thoth, *i.e.,* Cush. Thoth was the counsellor of Tammuz and of Osiris, and both the latter are the same as the second Cronus, *i.e.,* Nimrod, which accounts for the mistake of Sanchoniathon or of Philo, his transcriber.

This war which the elder Cronus made against Ouranos or Noah

---

[1] Lemprière, *Pontus.*　　　　[2] *Ibid.—Japetus* and *Oceanus.*

requires notice. We have seen that the elder Cronus, or Cush, was the ringleader in the building of the Tower of Babel. That tower was not, as some have supposed, an attempt to erect a place of refuge against a future Deluge. At the most, it could only have afforded room for a few hundred persons, and if it had been intended for that purpose the builders would have chosen a mountain rather than the low-lying plains of Babylon. It was, as is evident from the description of it by Herodotus, for the purpose of idolatrous worship, or for seeking communication with the demon gods of Paganism,[1] by which they thought to "reach heaven" and become immortal. This is further proved by its name. "*Babel*" has now become a term for *confusion*, but it is well known that its original meaning is "*bab el*," or "*Bab il*," "the gate of God."

It was the custom among the Pagans to select "high places" and "every high hill" as places of worship,[2] from which it would seem that such places were supposed to possess special advantages for seeking the aid of the daimonia. Perhaps it was supposed that the higher regions of the atmosphere were more especially the abode of these spirits; and the expression used by the Apostle Paul, "the spiritual hosts of wickedness in *heavenly places*," and the title given to Satan, "The Prince of the power of *the air*,"[3] tends to confirm this view. But it is also probable that they were chosen on account of the solitude and secrecy they afforded.

The professed object of the builders of Babel,—"lest we be scattered abroad upon the earth,"—implies that, by the erection of a mighty central temple, it was thought to attract the worship of all and bring them together; but the real object of the proposer was probably to bring them under the dominion of the daimonia, and be himself the high priest of their religion. This receives support from his after history, when, having been foiled in his first attempt, he endeavoured, through the strength and military prowess of his son, to establish their worship and bring the world under their dominion.

The building of Babel for the purpose of idolatrous worship was an act of open rebellion against Heaven, which Noah would certainly have opposed, and being the first who offered sacrifices to Heaven, he would be *the representative of Heaven*, and it was this, rather than the reason given by Sanchoniathon, that was more probably the origin of his name "Ouranos," or "Heaven." For men were

[1] Herod., lib. i. cap. 181, 182.
[2] As in the case of the idolatrous Israelites (Ezek. vi. 13, etc.).
[3] Eph. vi. 12 ; ii. 2.

called after the name of their gods, as in the case of the Brahmins, Buddhists, etc., and the name "Heaven" probably originated in the fact that Noah worshipped the god of those heavens which had poured forth the Deluge on the earth, and against whom the idolaters rebelled.

The building of Babel, in which Cush (*i.e.*, Cronus or Saturn) was the ringleader, was no doubt the origin of the war of Cronus against Ouranos or Heaven described by Sanchoniathon. This war must be the same also as the war in Grecian mythology of the Titans, who were the descendants of Noah, against Ouranos, and in which war Saturn (*i.e.*, the elder Cronus) is said to have been the ringleader.[1] In the account given by Sanchoniathon, Cronus is represented as successful, and Ouranos was obliged to fly from his dominions. This may very well have been the case, for the building of such a tower as Babel could not have been undertaken while the Patriarch was supported by the bulk of his descendants. Thoth, it will be remembered, is mentioned as stirring up "the allies of Cronus," *i.e.*, the other descendants of Noah, to oppose Ouranos.

In the Greek story the war of Saturn and the Titans against Cœlus, or Ouranos, is represented to have been undertaken on account of the cruelty of Cœlus, who confined all his children in the bowels of the earth; while Sanchoniathon represents Ouranos as endeavouring to kill his children. This is the colouring given to the story by the idolaters, who have ever adopted the method of misrepresenting and vilifying the followers of the true God, as in the case of the early Christians, who were represented by the Pagan priesthood as enemies of the human race. Ouranos, or Noah, must have protested, as he did in the days before the Deluge, against the demon worship advocated by Cush (*i.e.*, the elder Cronus), and must have condemned the seeking of that occult knowledge which promised to enable men to obtain the satisfaction of their natural lusts and desires, and make them seemingly independent of God. This limitation to the conditions of earthly existence as ordained by God, and submission to Him who had destroyed the antediluvian world, was no doubt represented by Cronus, or by the priesthood who in after ages related the story, as confining men in the bowels of the earth and endeavouring to kill them.

Both Sanchoniathon and the Greek story agree in representing Cronus as mutilating Ouranos in order to prevent him having any more children. This may be an exaggeration of the incident related

[1] Lemprière, *Titanes* and *Saturnus*.

in Gen. ix. 21-24; but by the expression used in ver. 24 it would appear that *something* was done to Noah, and it also appears that he had no more children.

The next point of importance in the *History of Sanchoniathon* is the statement that Cronus slew two of his own children, and that the act created "great amazement," and that afterwards, "when a plague or mortality happened, Cronus offered up his only son as a sacrifice to his father Ouranos." This, as already pointed out, seems to have been the origin of human sacrifice.

We must here refer again to Porphyry's account of the origin of these sacrifices:—"It was the custom among the ancients in times of great calamity, in order to prevent the ruin of all, for the rulers of the city, or nation, to sacrifice to the avenging deities the most beloved of their children as the price of redemption; they who were devoted for this purpose were offered mystically. For Cronus, whom the Phœnicians call Il, and who after death was deified and installed in the planet which bears his name (Saturn), when he was king had by 'a nymph of the country,' called 'Anobret,' an only son, who on that account is styled 'Ieoud,' for so the Phœnicians call an only son, and when great danger from war beset the land, he adorned the altar and invested his son with the emblems of royalty and sacrificed him."[1] An example followed by the king of Moab.[2]

Great attempts, especially by Bryant,[3] have been made to prove that this mystical sacrifice was done to foreshadow the death of Christ, the only-begotten son of *God*, who in Hebrew is called *El*, while the name of the nymph "Anobret" is said by some to mean "Grace," in order to identify her with the Virgin Mary, who was addressed by the angel as "much graced." By Bryant the name "Anobret" is said to mean "fountain of light," implying thereby that she prefigured the Virgin, as she from whom came Christ, "the light of the world." But the suggestions are forced and unnatural. The terms mentioned are only found in the *New* Testament, and were therefore unknown at that time, and it supposes that the idolatrous Phœnicians had a special revelation of things to come, unmentioned in Scripture and unknown to the chosen people of God.

The name "Anobret" has probably a very different signification. Both Philo and Porphyry, from whom Eusebius obtained his history of Sanchoniathon, invariably give the Greek equivalents of Phœnician names. The name "Anobret" would therefore appear to be derived

---

[1] Sanchoniathon, from Porphyry, Cory, *Fragments*, pp. 16, 17.
[2] 2 Kings iii. 27 ; Micah vi. 5-7.   [3] Hodge's *Cory*, pp. 19, 20.

from "ἄνω," "heavenly," and "βρίτᾶς" or "βροτός." The word "βρίτᾶς" means "an image," and "the heavenly image" would signify "the image, or likeness, of the gods," according to Pagan ideas. It is quite possible, however, that the name has been altered in the several transcriptions from the original author, and that "Ano*brot*" was the real name. If so, the name would have a peculiar significance, for βροτός is "mortal," and Anobrot would therefore be "the heavenly mortal," which, according to Pagan ideas, would signify that she was the daughter of a Nephilim father. It is possible, however, that the name was given because, in accordance with the principle of Paganism, by the change of a letter it could be given this twofold meaning.

Now "Anobret," the wife of Cronus or Cush, must be Semiramis, who is said by Ctesias to have been "a foundling child" ("*a nymph of the country*"), the daughter of the goddess Derketo; and that Oannes (*i.e.*, Cush), governor of Syria, married her on account of her beauty, and took her with him when he accompanied Ninus to the Bactrian War. There she was seen by Ninus, who took her from Oannes and married her himself.[1] The name of the nymph Anobret, or Anobrot, thus tends to confirm the Nephilim origin of Semiramis.

The sacrifice of his son by Cronus, *i.e.*, Saturn, is the origin not only of the human sacrifices of the Phœnicians, Carthaginians, Hindus, Mexicans and Celtic nations, but of *cannabalism*. For Cronus was king of the Cyclops,[2] with whom the practice is said to have originated. In the Greek story Saturn is said to have obtained the kingdom of Cœlus, or Ouranos, by the consent of his brother, "Titan," *i.e.*, Shem, on condition that he did not bring up any more male children, and that, in order to conceal them, he *devoured* them as soon as they were born. Another account says that he devoured them because he had been informed by an oracle that they would avenge his cruelty on his father Ouranos.[3] We know that it was the universal custom for the priests to eat the sacrifices. "Are not they who eat of the sacrifices partakers of the altar?"[4] It would thus seem that the charge against Saturn was true, and that, in order to propitiate his demon gods, and probably in obedience to their teaching, he offered his sons in sacrifice to them, and, as sacrificing priest, ate the sacrifice thus offered. The author of *Nimrod* says, "The tyrant Zoroaster, of the line of Cham (Ham), was one of the founders of the Tower of Babel; he sacrificed innumerable victims to

[1] Lenormant, *Anc. Hist. of East*, p. 365.
[2] *Ante*, p. 34.
[3] Lemprière, *Saturnus*.
[4] 1 Cor. ix. 12, 13; x. 18.

the dæmons;"[1] and the same is recorded of Zohak.[2] This Zoroaster is plainly the Chaldean Zoroaster, who we have seen to be Nimrod, who might be expected, from his Nephilim origin, to surpass even his father in these bloody sacrifices. Hence we find that the sacrifice of the *first-born* to the Sun god Osiris, that is, Nimrod, was one of the most notorious of the Egyptian rites.[3] This gives a peculiar significance to the judgment of God on "*all the first-born*" in Egypt in a single night.

This was also the origin of the human sacrifices to Baal and Moloch, to whom *children* were especially acceptable, and we may presume that the priests of the Canaanitish nations were also cannibals. The fiendish character of all these sacrifices gives strong probability to the suggestion that they were the result of demon teaching; and yet, just as may be observed in the "spirit" teaching of the present day, which makes a pretence of righteousness and quotes the Bible, so it is probable that the former spirit teaching with regard to the sacrifice of children was mixed up with the original promise of the Redeemer, who was to be "the seed of the woman." For it was plain from that promise that, in overcoming the enemy of the human race, He was to suffer in so doing, and this, coupled with the institution of sacrifice for sin, recognised by God as such, may well have suggested, even to men, that the Redeemer would have to die in order to accomplish the redemption of man. How much more might this be known to the prince of the demons, who would be only too ready to make use of the knowledge to give an appearance of mystical sanctity to a sacrifice which has been the cause of such appalling suffering to millions of the human race!

The Greek story of Saturn devouring his children goes on to say that Rhea (*i.e.*, Semiramis), the wife of Saturn, in order to save her children, gave him a stone instead of Jupiter (*i.e.*, Nimrod), when he was born. Jupiter, or Diespiter, was the supreme god of the Aryan nations, but the Greeks, who subsequently adopted the religion of the Phœnicians and Egyptians, bestowed the attributes and history of the chief god of the latter on Jupiter, and called him, like Osiris, the son of Saturn, thus identifying him with Nimrod. Hence the story implies that Semiramis, when Nimrod was born and was about to be sacrificed to his gods by Cush, substituted a stone for him, and as the sacrifice was by burning after the child had been killed, it

---

[1] *Nimrod*, vol. i. p. 146; *Compn. of 666*, p. 25.
[2] Lenormant, *Anc. Hist. of East*, vol. ii. p. 22.
[3] *Transactions Victoria Institute*, vol. xiv. p. 113.

O

would not have been difficult to deceive the father, or the priest in charge of the sacrifice, by placing a suitably-shaped stone bound in swaddling clothes on the altar. Now this, according to Hesiod, is just what Rhea did. She presented her husband with a stone bound in swaddling bands to represent a child.[1]

This stone was called in Grecian mythology "Baitulos," and was a surname given to Jupiter.[2] "Betylus" was another name for this stone. In Rome, Jupiter was called "Jupiter the Stone" and "Jupiter Terminalis," "Terminus" being another name for the stone which Saturn is said to have swallowed instead of Jupiter.[3] "Terminus," a "boundary," was worshipped in Rome as a distinct deity, and was represented by a square stone. He was called "the god of boundaries,"[4] the idea being evidently based on the mistaken signification which the Romans gave to the *bands* with which the stone was *bound* in order to represent the "swaddling bands" of a child. From this it appears arose the worship of stones, which were the symbols of so many of the gods.[5] They were representations of the god, and of the means by which his life was spared. Hence also the name *Baitulos* given to the swaddled stone, which means "life restored child."[6]

In the Greek story, Titan, or Shem, is said to have allowed his *brother*[7] Saturn the empire of the world on condition that he reared no more male children, but that when the birth of Jupiter, *i.e.,* Nimrod, was concealed, he made war against him and overpowered him.[8] The actual facts were, as we shall see, that in consequence of the cruelties of Nimrod and the obscene idolatry and demon worship which he forced upon the nations whom he conquered, Shem obtained the condemnation and judicial execution of Nimrod in Egypt, of which country Nimrod had made his father king, and the latter had in consequence to fly to Latium in Italy.[9] The Greek story is manifestly a misrepresentation, inasmuch as it was *through* Nimrod that the empire of the world was obtained by the Cushites, and that empire, therefore, did not exist before his birth. But it would appear that the priesthood, in order to conceal the real truth, which would

[1] Hesiod, *Theogonia*, lines 485, etc., pp. 38, 41.
[2] Priscian, lib. v. vol. i. p. 189 note; and lib. vi. vol. i. p. 249; Hislop, p. 300.
[3] Faber, vol. ii. pp. 375-377.   [4] Lemprière, *Terminus.*
[5] Faber, vol. ii. pp. 375-377.   [6] Hislop, p. 300, and note.
[7] Saturn was really his *nephew,* but by the ancients such relationship was spoken of as *brother.*
[8] Lemprière, *Titan.*   [9] *See* chap. xii., "The Death of the Pagan God."

have thrown discredit on their religion, ascribed the action taken by Shem to the fact that the life of Nimrod was concealed or spared, which was true in a sense, because it was in consequence of the life of Nimrod and the idolatry propagated by him that Shem obtained his condemnation, and that Saturn or Cush lost his kingdom. Moreover, we may well conceive that Shem protested against the Nephilim intercourse instituted by Cush, and the rearing of a Nephilim race of beings, which had before brought upon the world the awful judgment of the Deluge.

The reason why Titan is represented as making war against Saturn, *i.e.*, Cush, rather than Nimrod, is because the overthrow of the latter and of idolatry was in Egypt, of which Cush was king.

The conclusions arrived at may be briefly recapitulated as follows :—

Idolatry, or the worship of spirits of evil, supposed by the idolaters to be the spirits of the dead, originated in antediluvian times, and seems to have been the result, in the first case, of the teachings of fallen angels, and possibly of Satan himself, which prepared the way for their intercourse with the daughters of men and the consequent production of a race of giants, who, being wholly wicked themselves, corrupted the rest of mankind and filled the world with violence. This idolatry was further advanced by Chrysor, who was the first Hephæstus, and the first Thoth or Hermes, and he was probably himself of Nephilim descent.

The same idolatry was revived after the Deluge by Cush, who was the second Thoth, the " Thrice Great Hermes," the " Inventor of Letters and the Worship of the Gods," " Meni," the " Numberer," " the All-wise Belus," " Hea, the God of Understanding," etc. That he obtained the knowledge, as tradition says, from writings buried before the Deluge is absurd, and this was probably invented in order to give the sanctity of antiquity to his teaching. It is more probable that he obtained it through, and was influenced by, his mother Nemaus, who, there is strong reason for believing, was the same as Naamah, the sister of Tubal-Cain.

As in one of his deified forms he was known as "Saturn," the father of the gods, who was the husband of " Rhea," that is, Semiramis, it seems certain that he was "Oannes," the first husband of Semiramis. Tradition seems to show that the latter, so celebrated for her beauty, her talents and energy, her lasciviousness and cruelty, was of Nephilim parentage, and that Nimrod was probably her son and was subsequently her husband. There also seems a strong probability that the blackness of the Æthiopian race was due to this Nephilim parentage, as stated by the Persian tradition, and was the result of a law of God by which He stamped them as "children of darkness" and "seed of the serpent." This would account for its *sudden* appearance in the human race, which would otherwise be unaccountable. That this first appeared in Cush, or "Æthiops," which means "blackness,"[1] is doubtful, for the name may have been given him merely because he was the father of the Æthiopians, or black race.[2] Nimrod was certainly black, and the blackness may have first showed itself in him as the son of a Nephilim-born woman.

The statements of Herodotus seem to show that it was a recognised custom of the Pagan priesthood to invite this Nephilim intercourse by means of especially selected women. Perhaps this was one of the conditions on which the priesthood obtained their unquestionable powers, and by which they obtained dominion of the rest of mankind. If also, as implied by Solomon (Prov. ii. 18, 19; vii. 24-27), unrestrained debauchery is the surest way of destroying all moral principle in man, and, therefore, of blinding him to the evil of the grossest idolatry, then the obscene Phallic worship, of which Cush and Nimrod were the originators, was doubtless also the result of demon teaching, as being the surest way of bringing mankind under their dominion. So likewise we must conclude that the cruel and unnatural human sacrifices which Cush instituted, and which were offered to the demon gods, were likewise the result of their teaching, and a condition on which their aid was purchased.

[1] Cruden, "Cush," "Ethiopia."   [2] See *ante*, p. 195.

CHAPTER X

THE SUN, THE SERPENT, THE PHALLUS AND THE TREE

THE daimonia, supposed to be spirits of the dead, the worship of and intercourse with whom was initiated by Hermes, were, as we have seen, the real gods of Paganism; but an equally important feature of the Hermetic teaching, and one which gave it a yet more sinister aspect, was the worship of the Sun and Serpent, with which were associated the Phallus and the Tree or Cross, and by means of which the idolaters were eventually led, by a gradual process of development, to worship the Prince of the demons himself.

Some writers have superficially concluded that the worship of the Sun is a spontaneous product of the human mind in the case of people in the state of barbarism, because this worship is found in most of the savage races at the present day. But it is evident to those who have studied the question that these barbarous races must have been emigrant offshoots of the great nations of antiquity, from whom, therefore, they inherited their religious ideas. This is proved by numberless peculiar and arbitrary habits, customs and religious rites, which they have in common with those nations and by the evidence of language and tradition. Their barbarism has been the natural result of centuries of isolation from the centres of thought and civilisation, and the absence of all stimuli for improvement; but their religion has been inherited and not invented.

The immediate descendants of Noah were not barbarous, but the possessors of the knowledge and civilisation of the antediluvian world which, according to tradition, in its great centres at least, must have been of a colossal character.[1] This, indeed, we might expect from the great longevity of antediluvian man; for what decree of knowledge might not be attained if, instead of the experience of some sixty or seventy years, each possessed in himself the knowledge and experience of centuries! Now, according to tradition, this knowledge was

---

[1] As in the story of Atlantis, related by the Egyptian priests to Solon, and recorded by Plato.

preserved by the postdiluvians, and Cush, the great Hermes, the all-wise Belus, was the author of the famous wisdom of the Chaldeans. Consequently we find that civilisation, as in the case of Egypt, was at its highest in the *earliest* period of its history.

The first descendants of Noah also possessed the knowledge of the true God ; and the fear of Him, which the destruction of the antediluvian world produced on their minds, and for long afterwards, is evidenced by the fact that the record of that event is preserved even to the present day by nearly all nations, including the barbarous nations before mentioned, which is a further proof that they were offshoots of the great nations of antiquity. It is absurd to suppose, therefore, that the worship of the Sun was the result of a general and spontaneous superstition on the part of the first descendants of Noah, while on the other hand everything points to the fact that the first form of Sun worship was the product of an ingenious and atheistical mind, using sophistry to persuade others to worship the powers of nature and withdraw men from the worship of the true God.

There are men now who, in spite of the evidences of the truth of Christianity, rebel against the idea of a God who is the moral governor of the world, and who seek to prove, and to propagate the belief, that the first cause of all things is a mere law, pursuing with undeviating regularity the course of nature, unheeding, and unaffected by moral considerations. So it may have been with Cush and Nimrod, the first great rebels of the postdiluvian world, against the authority of God.

For the better understanding of the subject it will be as well to give first a short summary of the teaching of Hermes with regard to the worship of the Sun and the Serpent.

The cosmogonies of the various Pagan nations all speak of a male and female principle in the production of the world, and in this they are so far supported by the letter of Scripture, which, in the account of Creation, speaks of the earth as if it were a mother "*bringing forth*" both vegetables and animals, and the waters, in like manner, as "bringing forth" the creatures which inhabit them. If then the earth was the great Mother, might not the Sun, without whose heat and light, life, both animal and vegetable, perishes, which seems to quicken the dead seed, and even to call into being innumerable forms of the lower orders of animal life—might not the Sun be the great Father and origin of all life ? We know indeed that there can be no life except as generated by previous life, and therefore that the first origin of all life must be "The Ever Living." But the above and similar arguments would not be without weight on those who "did not wish to keep God in their knowledge" (Rom. i. 28).

It would not have been possible, however, to lead men to reject the true God, and to regard the great planet as the Creator of all things, by merely representing him to be the author of natural life. The consciousness of sin and ill desert, and the apprehension of future evil, which burdens in a greater or less degree the whole human race, demands relief, and therefore, in order to meet this need of the human mind, the religious rites of Paganism purported to be for "the purification of sin," and the Sun god was represented to be the source of that purification.

The means by which men were persuaded to believe this is characteristic of the whole genius of Paganism.

The essential principle of its teaching was making use of the double meaning of words, a common weapon still in the arguments of sophistry, which by a sudden and unrecognised change of meaning leads the hearer to adopt entirely false conclusions. This double meaning of words is characteristic of all language; for spiritual and moral things are always expressed by words, the primary meaning of which relates to material things. Thus we speak of "eating," "digesting," "drinking in" knowledge, "growing in it," etc., and in no book is this metaphorical language more used than in the Bible, the great object of which is to teach the meaning of spiritual truth. To understand such language in the letter is entirely to lose its meaning; it is to substitute the material type for the spiritual reality. Hence the Apostle says that "the letter killeth but the spirit (*i.e.*, the spiritual meaning of the words) giveth life." The very metaphor of "the Sun" is used by Scripture for God, as in the case where Christ is called "The Sun of righteousness"; but to read such passages in the letter, would naturally lead men to worship the visible material Sun, instead of the unseen God.

Sun and Fire Worship.—By designedly confusing the material with the spiritual, the Pagans substituted the material for the spiritual. Everything with them had an "exoteric" or outward meaning, and an "esoteric" or inward meaning. The Sun was exoterically the supposed source of natural life, but esoterically it was represented to be the source of spiritual life. Hence fire, as the great purifier of material things, and regarded also as an emanation from the Sun, was represented to be also the purifier of the soul from sin. Fire is indeed used as a *material type* for spiritual purification throughout the Scripture, and, from the first, the typical sacrifices for sin were burnt by fire. It was doubtless the general recognition of this that afforded the originators of idolatry a basis on which to work, in order to persuade men that the material type was itself the source of spiritual purification. In this, as in others of its features, Paganism was based, not on error unsupported by truth, but on error founded on the perversion of recognised truth.

Thus in the rites of Zoroaster it was said that "he who approached to *fire* would receive a *light* from *divinity*," and that "through divine fire all the stains produced by generation would be purged away."[1] Hence the practice of passing children through the fire to Moloch. Among the Hindus the sacred fire, kept perpetually burning, is thus invoked: "Fire, thou dost expiate a sin against the gods, may this oblation be efficacious. Thou dost expiate a sin against man; thou dost expiate a sin against the Manes, thou dost expiate a sin against my own soul, thou dost expiate repeated sins, thou dost expiate every sin which I have committed, whether wilfully or unintentionally; may this oblation be efficacious."[2] The same sacred fire, kept always burning, and attended by vestal virgins, and kindled anew every year from the rays of the Sun, was, as already shown, a prominent feature throughout Paganism, and was regarded as divine, an emanation from the Sun, or Great Father, and as a source of spiritual life and regeneration. But although this spiritual aspect was given to the Sun, and to fire as the emanation from the Sun, in order to quiet the consciences of men, the real aspect of the Sun was as the source of natural life and natural generation. Hence the deification of the Phallus as the manifestation of that natural life and generation in the animal world.

In like manner the Sun as the source of natural *light* was represented to be the source of spiritual light and of divine wisdom and knowledge, which, as in the case of the Sun god Apollo at Delphi, and other oracles, was believed to be revealed at his shrines. It was under this aspect that the Sun was especially identified with the *Serpent*, the form which the Prince of the Demons took when he persuaded Eve to eat of the fruit of the tree of knowledge of good and evil, and the Serpent was thus represented in Paganism to be the bestower of knowledge and wisdom on man. But that knowledge and wisdom related only to the things of this world, the

---

[1] *Proclus in Timæo*, p. 805; Hislop, p. 120.

[2] Colebrook, "Religious Ceremonies of Hindus," in *Asiat. Res.*, vol. vii. p. 273; Hislop, p. 121.

knowledge by which Hermes taught men the means of attaining the natural desires of the heart, the wisdom which the Apostle speaks of as " earthly, sensual (psychical), devilish " (demoniacal)—(Jas. iii. 15).

Similarly the Serpent was identified with the Sun as the source of *life*, but the life of which the Serpent was said to be the source was, as we shall see, natural life and generation, the knowledge of producing which he is represented as revealing to man.

Finally trees, and the cross as the symbol of a tree, were held to be sacred as symbols of the Sun god, because the tree was regarded as the manifestation of the principle of life in the vegetable kingdom, just as the Phallus was regarded as the manifestation of that life in the animal kingdom.

The revived Hermetic teaching of the present day affords a fair illustration of its general character, and a few extracts from it will therefore be quoted.

Dupuis writes: " The religion of Zoroaster, which has given us the key of Genesis and the explanation of the enigma of the destroying serpent, is that also which gives the explanation of the *Lamb*, or the Sun triumphant over darkness. The vernal equinox being the time of the celebration of the festival of Hilaria, the Sun of Spring has the power of *attracting virtuous souls* towards himself. This gives the explanation of the following passage from the Gospel, 'I, if I be lifted up from the earth, will draw all things with me.'"[1]

This is the sort of modern teaching on the subject, and is an illustration of the method alluded to, by which the material influence of the Sun is represented as spiritual, and identified with that of Christ. So again, the author of "Sun Worship" quotes the Gospel of St John, "In him (*the Sun*) was life, and the life was the light of men."[2]

Again, the last author, speaking of the proposed liturgies for the worship of the Sun, says, "The second prayer should specially be an adoration of the Sun, the sermon, or discourse, after the singing of another hymn, would be varied as they now are in the churches, with the exception that the prophet of Nazareth would be delegated to his true position, and not appealed to or worshipped as God." He also says, "All the various deities, as Jehovah, Jupiter, Hercules, Mithras, Ammon, Adonis, Baal, Bel, Horus, Buddha, Chrishna, Jesus, and many others, are but different names, in

[1] Dupuis, pp. 33-35, quoted from *Compn. of* 666, p. 24.
[2] "Sun Worship," from *Compn. of* 666, p. 33.

various ages, for the Sun and his phenomena and various manifestations." [1]

Another modern Theosophist, speaking of the Rosy Cross of the Rosicrucians, says, "This (the Rosy Cross) is the Narutz, Natzir, or Rose of Ishuren, of Tamul, or Sharon, or the Water Rose, the Lily, Padma, Rema, Lotus, *crucified for the salvation of Man,*—crucified in the heaven at the vernal equinox."

To understand what follows, it must be remembered that the numerals of the Greeks and other nations were represented by the letters of their alphabets, and they in consequence represented their gods by the numerical value of the letters composing their names, which number was therefore called "the number of their names" [2] (*vide* Rev. xiii. 17) Certain numbers also had often a natural symbolic relation and significance as regarded their gods, and the letters expressing such numbers became also a symbol of the God.

The above writer goes on to say that, "The symbol of the Narutz or Rose was PΣΞ (RSX) = 360; and the ΞPΣ (XRS), or cross, or crs, or with the letter e (epsilon) added, the Rose = 365, in short the *god of day,* or *Divine Wisdom.*" [3]

It will be observed that this writer identifies *the cross* with the Sun. This is quite in accordance with the ancient Paganism, in which the cross was the symbol of the Sun god, the cross being the symbol of the tree, and the tree being the manifestation in the vegetable world of the life of which the Sun was the supposed source. [4]

The ode to the Sun of Martianus Capellus gives perhaps the best view of the ancient adoration. "Latium invokes thee, Sol, because thou alone art in honour after the Father the centre of light, and they affirm that thy sacred head bears a golden brightness in twelve rays, because thou formest the numbers of the months and that number of hours. They say that thou guidest four winged

---

[1] "Sun Worship," from *Compn. of* 666, p. 33.

[2] Lenormant remarks: "One of the tablets in the Library of Nineveh gives a list of the principal gods, each with his mystic number" (*Chaldean Magic and Sorcery,* p. 25).

[3] *Mankind: Their Origin and Destiny,* pp. 303, 304; *Compn. of* 666, p. 246. Ξ (xi) = 60: R (rho) = 100; Σ (sigma) = 200; total 360, the number of days in the Egyptian year, or with the addition of E (epsilon) = 5, 365. These numbers, denoting the real or supposed length of the solar year, were used by the Pagans as symbols of the Sun god, called by the writer "*the Divine Wisdom.*"

[4] See *infra,* p. 226.

steeds, because thou alone rulest the chariot of the elements. For dispelling darkness thou revealest the shining heavens. Hence they esteem thee Phœbus (Apollo), the discoverer of the secrets of the future, or because thou preventest nocturnal crimes. Egypt worships thee as Iscean Serapis, and Memphis as Osiris. Thou art worshipped by different rites as Mithra, Dis, and the cruel Typhon. Thou art also the beautiful Atys and the fostering son of the bent plough, Thou art the Ammon of barren Libya, and the Adonis of Byblos. Thus under varied appellations the whole world worships thee. Hail, thou true image of the gods and of thy father's face, thou whose sacred name, surname, and omen, three letters make to agree with the number 608." [1]

What these three letters were, we learn from the author of *The Origin and Destiny of Man:* "The Sun," he says, "had the mystic surname of Bacchus, I. H. S. This mystic name consists of three letters the numerical value of which is 608. This number, 608, is one of the cycles." [2]

The meaning of the above seems to be as follows :—I (iota) stood for Bacchus, called also *Iacchus,* or for *Isiris,* the Egyptian form of Osiris or Bacchus; H (eta) stood for *Helios* the Sun; and Σ (sigma) for *Zoro,* or *Zero,* the seed; [3] thus signifying "Bacchus," or "Iacchus," "the son, or incarnation of the Sun." But in using these three letters a double mystification seems to have been introduced. Their actual numerical value is only 218; for $I = 10$, $H = 8$, and $\Sigma = 200$; but the B, V and I were interchangeable with the Greek Υ (upsilon) [4] and as $Υ = 400$, the numerical value of ΥΗΣ would be 608. The letters I. H. S., which are here said to represent the mystic surname of Bacchus, appear to have been a sacred symbol in India, from the Cushite Rameses of which country the Egyptians seem to have obtained much of their later idolatry. The symbol has been found on coins of the Maharajah of Cashmere. [5]

The names of the Sun gods were given them so that, while the word expressed some supposed attribute of the god, its numerical value should be symbolic of the Sun, as in the case of the ΞΡΣ of the Rosicrucians. Thus the Sun god *Mithra,* or *Mithras,* was worshipped as the Mediator, and was symbolised by a Lion with a

[1] From *Compn. of* 666, pp. 152, 153.
[2] *Origin and Destiny of Man,* p. 580 ; *Compn. of* 666, p. 87.
[3] See *ante,* p. 26.
[4] *Compn. of* 666, pp. 332, 333.
[5] Bonwick's *Egyptian Belief and Modern Thought,* quoted by the author of *The Compn. of* 666, p. 87.

Bee in its mouth to identify him with "the Divine Wisdom"; for the Chaldee for "bee," *dabar,* signified both a "bee" and "The Word,"[1] and the numerical values of *Mithras,* sometimes written *Meithras,* are respectively 360 and 365.

The Sun was also connected with the number 666, which was a sacred number in Egypt, and Higgins, in his *Anacalypsis,* states that every heathen god had the name of 666, and that this number "was the name, or I ought rather to say, the designation, of every one of the planetary bodies."[2] This of course could only be the case by representing each by some mystic surname. This number 666 has also a special but very different import in Scripture, for it is the "number of the name" of the Antichrist, and it is well known that, throughout the Bible, numbers are used in a symbolic sense, which sense also is not arbitrary, but natural and essential. A short explanation of their symbolism in Scripture may be summarised as follows:—

1. Is the symbol of unity, and therefore of the Godhead, the Creator, the One God.
2. Is symbolic of union, of Christ who was both God and man, and therefore of the union of God and man.
3. Is symbolic of individual completion and individual action, of the threefold aspect of God to man as Father, Son and Holy Spirit, and of man himself as body, soul and spirit.
4. Is symbolic of the world, and nature, and of man by nature.
5. Is symbolic of imperfection, or incompletion generally.
6. Is symbolic of sin, of death natural, and of death spiritual, or eternal; which three aspects are united in the number of the name of the Antichrist, viz., 666.
7. Which equals $3+4$, is symbolic of the primary *moral* relation of God to man and the world. It is the number symbolic of the dispensation of the *Law* or of *Justice,* and it is the number symbolic of *judgment.*
8. Which equals 4×2, is symbolic of the intimate union of Christ and the Christian which is salvation. It is also $4+4$ and is thus symbolic of a twofold state of the world and man, the natural and the spiritual, and thus symbolises regeneration, or renewal and resurrection. Thus just as the name of the Antichrist, who is the destroyer of men's souls and bodies, is 666, so the name of the true Christ

[1] Hislop, p. 194.
[2] *Anacalypsis,* vol. ii. p. 241; *Compn. of 666,* pp. 33, 34.

in Greek is Jesus, Ιησους, the Saviour, the numerical value
of which is 888.

9. Seldom occurs in Scripture, but it is an important number
in Magic, and seems to symbolise idolatry, and the world
and man in a state of incompletion—4+5—that is without
God.

10. Is symbolic of natural perfection and completion in general.

12. Is symbolic of spiritual perfection and completion. It is
4+8, or the world and man renewed. It is also 4×3,
or the world and man in intimate union with God, and
it is 6×2, symbolic of Christ taking upon Him the
sin of man, and becoming subject to death for the sake
of man's redemption.

Illustrations of the use of numbers with the above signification
may be found throughout Scripture, and as the symbolism attached
to them is not arbitrary, but essential, the significance attached to
them by Paganism is the more important. Thus 6, the *evil* number
of Scripture, is the *sacred* number of Paganism, and the Egyptians,
in consequence, especially venerated the Crocodile and regarded it as
an image of their chief god, the Sun ; because they said that the period
of the gestation of its eggs was 60 days, the number of its eggs
was 60, they were hatched in 60 days, and its life was 60 years ;
also that the animal itself had 60 vertebræ, 60 nerves and 60
teeth.[1] "The number 6×6=36 was also called a sacred quaternion,
and 6 lay at the root of the symbol of a god."[2] This also gives a
special significance to the worship of the Sun god, whose symbolic
number was 360, which equals 6×6×10, indicating the fulness or
completion of sin and death.

In connection with this may be mentioned the remarkable magic
square composed of the numbers from 1 to 36 or 6×6, the total of
which makes 666.

1	32	34	3	35	6
30	8	27	28	11	7
20	24	15	16	13	23
19	17	21	22	18	14
10	26	12	9	29	25
31	4	2	33	5	36

[1] Wilkinson's *Egyptians*, vol. v. pp. 236, 237.
[2] *Transactions of Victoria Institute*, vol. xvi. p. 136 ; *Compn. of 666*, p. 23, note.

It was a symbol of the Sun and was called the "Sigillum Solis," or Solar Seal, and was mystically sacred. It will be observed that each of the six rows, whether taken horizontally or vertically, amounts to 111, and that the arrangement depends on the essential properties of numbers. Moreover, if we take the *cross* made by the two diagonals they also consist of two amounts of 111 each, which together equal 222, a number significant of Christ, and which added to 666 makes 888, the number of Christ as the Saviour from sin; thus seemingly symbolising the fact that sin crucified by Christ is salvation—a mystic symbolism of the square, and yet not at once apparent.

The Hermetic teaching with regard to the Sun as the Creator is thus described by Jean Marie Ragon: "It is not alone in that grand star, refulgent in the heavens, that is comprised all that the ancients tell us of the Sun. By this word hierophants and philosophers understood the latent cause of all creation, of all vegetation, of all motion. Their Sun is that life-giving fire, that principle of heat expanded throughout all nature, and without which matter would have remained eternally buried in chaos. Here is the explanation of their first principles upon the allegorical formation of the world which we find in the Hermetic philosophy: One single force, one single principle, one single active cause, could never have given energy and life to the universe. The generation of bodies is the result of the action and reaction of their constituent parts. She (Nature) works by fermentation, and fermentation supposes on the face of it two powers. The hierophants believed then, or at least pretended to believe, that two primitive principles had worked out the development from chaos; and, as they noticed that everything in the universe is only fire or water, humid or warm, they named these principles (the one fiery, male, active) Form, Heaven, or Sun, and the other (humid, female, passive) Matter, Earth, or Moon. These are the Osiris and Isis of the Egyptians, the Elyon and Beruth of Sanchoniathon, and the Uranus and Ge of the same author. You may recognise them under the names of Odin and Frigga, and of Aske and Emla, among the peoples of the North: of Adam and Eve amongst the Hebrews—in short, there is no theogony in which they are not clearly marked out.[1]

THE PHALLUS.—It will be seen that the Hermetic teaching, denying the existence of the One God, ascribed creation to a male and

[1] *Maçonnerie Occulte*, chap. on "The Sun," p. 202; from *Compn. of 666*, pp. 160, 161.

female principle—the chief manifestation of the former being the Sun, through which all things by a supposed natural evolution had come into existence. This male principle was therefore God, the being to be adored, together with all forms and manifestations of that principle. From this arose the worship of the *Phallus*, as the distinctive emblem of generation in man, and the similar worship of *trees* as its manifestation in the vegetable kingdom. Hence figures of the Phallus were always carried in the processions at the festivals of the Sun gods, Bacchus and Osiris, and the Lingam (its Indian name) was always found in the most holy places of the Indian temples.[1] Similarly the *cross*, as the symbol of the tree, was, as we shall see, equally sacred.

Besides the Phallus, the female emblem was also carried in the mysteries. " The three most sacred emblems carried in the Greek mysteries were the Phallus, I, the Egg, O, and the Serpent, Φ, or otherwise the Phallus, the Ione or Umbilicus, and the Serpent. The first in each case is the emblem of the Sun, or of fire, as the male or active generative power. The second denotes the passive nature or female principle, or the element of water. The third symbol indicates the destroyer, the reformer, or renewer, the uniter of the two, and thus the preserver, or perpetuater, eternally renewing itself."[2]

The deity was, in fact, regarded as both male and female, or *Hermaphrodite*, and the female was regarded, as in the case of Eve, to have been produced from the male. Similarly the Ark from which the human race were, so to speak, born again, was a symbol of the goddess mother, and yet, having been made by Noah, was represented as having been produced by him.

The author of " The Perfect Way " says, " The wise of old who, by exalting the woman in themselves, attained to full intuition of God, failed not to make recognition of her in the symbols whereby they denoted deity. Hence the significance of the combination, universal from the first, of the symbols I O, the unit and the cypher in the names designative of *deity*. For, as the line of force and the circle of comprehension and multiplication, these two represent at once energy and space, will and love, life and substance, father and mother; and, although two, they are one, inasmuch as the circle is but the line turning round, and following upon itself, instead

---

[1] Vide *Lexicon of Freemasonry*, p. 353 ; *Compn. of 666*, p. 75.
[2] Hargrave Jennings, *The Rosicrucians*, vol. i. p. 275 ; *Compn. of 666*, p. 336.

of continuing into the abyss to expend its force in vain. Sex, says the Kabbala, is the true Lord of hosts." [1]

These symbols, I O, as emblematic of the organs of generation, explain the well-known salutation to Bacchus, the *Phallic* God— "I O Bacchus." They had, moreover, a further meaning. For, in accordance with the principle of the double meanings attached by the Pagans to words and symbols, the O was the symbol of "the seed"; for "*Zero*" signified in Chaldee both the *seed* and a *circle*; [2] and zero is the modern term for the O, or cipher, which is explained by the fact that our system of numerals was obtained from the Arabians, the successors of the Aribah, the ancient Adite or Cushite race, the father of whom was famous as the inventor of astronomy and mathematics. [3] The circle, O, also represented the disk of the Sun, and was one of the principal recognised symbols of the Sun. Thus "I O Bacchus" signified both "Bacchus, the god of generation," and also "the seed, or incarnation of the Sun." The combination of the two in Φ (Phi), the symbol of the Serpent, will be referred to later.

The "*Asherah*" of the Hebrews was also the Phallus and its worship, and the erection of figures and obelisks of it in the grove or tree worship, with which, as we have seen, it was intimately connected, is referred to in many places in the Old Testament. [4] The Israelitish women are also mentioned as making gold and silver phalli. [5]

The obscenity and vice to which this worship gave rise are well known, and were the natural consequence of deifying these powers of nature, by which the sanction of religion was given to sexual immorality. Yet it will be observed that the symbolism and analogies made use of are by no means false in themselves, save in making the Sun the male principle in nature and ultimate origin of life. The Sun and the power of generation in the animal and vegetable kingdoms are *intermediate* causes of life, but, as in the case of the Sun, its rays cannot give life unless the principle of life is there to be

---

[1] "The Perfect Way," p. 59, from *Compn. of* 666, p. 108.

[2] Hislop, p. 18, note.

[3] *See* chap. iv. pp. 72-76. The Aribah, and pp. 86, 87. Cush, or Meni, the numberer.

[4] *Asherah* is translated in the A.V. "grove," but it was plainly an image symbolic of the Phallus and distinct from "the groves" which, however, were symbolic of the same principle. *See* 1 Kings xxi. 7; xxiii. 4-6, and Smith's *Dict. of Bible*—"*Asherah*."

[5] Ezek. xvi. 17. *See* margin.

quickened. But the chief fallacy lay in representing the natural to be also spiritual, in identifying natural life with spiritual life, and the material light of the Sun with the Divine wisdom, or spiritual light, and thus giving the sanctity of religion to that which is natural only.

THE TREE AND CROSS.—Man as born into the world is natural and a part of nature, although he alone of all things in nature has a capacity for becoming spiritual. But the natural and spiritual are diametrically opposed to each other, and man cannot obey the demands of the spiritual law without doing violence to his natural inclinations. For the law of nature is the law of self; it is the law by which "might" is "right," the law of "the survival of the fittest," by which the strong prey upon the weak, and the law therefore of continual struggle and warfare and consequent suffering, without which natural existence would be impossible. It is thus the law of natural destruction and reproduction of which, as we have seen, the Serpent in Paganism was the symbol. Where this law is supreme, its fruits are selfishness, self-assertion, pride, anger, envy, emulation, covetousness, etc., etc.; in a word it is the law of sin and moral evil, and this is what the religion of Paganism sanctified.

Christianity therefore required that the lusts and affections of the flesh should be *crucified*, nor can the natural man become spiritual unless he dies to those natural inclinations which are the cause of sin; in other words, the law of nature and of sin, of which the Serpent is the symbol, must be brought to the *cross*, as implied by the hidden symbolism of the Sigillum Solis, and as is equally implied by the symbol of the Serpent lifted up in the wilderness by Moses, which was the type of the cross of Christ, who in His own body bore our sins to the cross (1 Pet. iv. 24), dying unto sin (Rom. vi. 10), crucifying in His own flesh the body of sin. Sin crucified is Salvation, but it is only by one cross that the power to do so is obtained, and that cross is the cross of Christ; the Christian must die with Christ (2 Tim. ii. 11).

But the cross was, as we have said, a distinctive symbol of Paganism; it was the symbol of a tree, and was the original form of the letter T, the Greek T ("tau"), and from the references made to it in Paganism it is clear that the origin of the idea was the tree of life in Eden. Thus among the Buddhists the cross is called "the divine tree, the tree of the gods, and *the tree of life and knowledge*, and productive of whatever is good and desirable, and is placed in

P

the *terrestrial Paradise.*"[1]   Hence also, throughout Paganism, the gods had certain trees which were especially sacred to them, as the palm tree in Egypt, the fir tree in Rome, the oak among the Druids.[2]

The Tree, like the Phallus, was the manifestation of that natural life and generation, the supposed source of which was the Sun. Hence the cross as the symbol of the Tree, and therefore of the same natural life, was combined with the circle, the symbol of the Sun's disk, and both were united together in Paganism as the symbol of the Sun god, as in figures 1, 2, 3, or in the form of the Maltese cross,

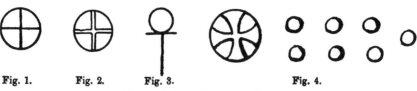

Fig. 1.   Fig. 2.   Fig. 3.   Fig. 4.

FIGS. 1, 2, 3, 4—CROSS AND CIRCLE.

as in fig. 4, which is a representation of the Sun and seven planets found on the Royal tablets discovered at Bavian by Layard.[3]

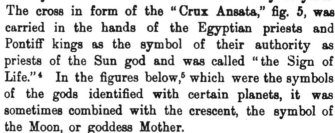

Fig. 5.
CRUX ANSATA.

The cross in form of the "Crux Ansata," fig. 5, was carried in the hands of the Egyptian priests and Pontiff kings as the symbol of their authority as priests of the Sun god and was called "the Sign of Life."[4] In the figures below,[5] which were the symbols of the gods identified with certain planets, it was sometimes combined with the crescent, the symbol of the Moon, or goddess Mother.

SATURN,   JUPITER.   MARS.   VENUS.   MERCURY,
Father of the Gods.   The Phallic God.

But the cross, although it was called "the Sign of Life," and was professedly a symbol of "the tree of life," was in reality a symbol

---

[1] Wilford's *Asiat. Res.*, vol. x. p. 124 ; Hislop, p. 200.   [2] Hislop, p. 97.
[3] Layard, *Babylon and Nineveh*, plate, p. 211.
[4] Wilkinson's *Ancient Egyptians*, vol. v. p. 283.
[5] From Deane's *Serpent Worship*, p. 148.

of the tree of *death*, "the tree of knowledge of good and evil," through eating the fruit of which death came into the world. For the life of which the cross was the sign, was the *natural* life of which the Sun was the supposed source, the full indulgence of which life leads to death, both natural and spiritual. The act of eating the forbidden fruit was an act by which our first parents cast off their allegiance to God and sought to become self-dependent, to be in short "*as gods*." But *self*-dependence, which is the antithesis of faith in God, is the very principle and law of all natural life; it is the principle of the law of *self*, of the law that "might is right," and it is thus the root of all moral evil, or sin, the wages of which is death. Thus the fruit of the tree of knowledge of good and evil, although "pleasant to the eye, and good for food" as far as natural life was concerned, was in reality the fruit of the tree of spiritual death, and the cross, as the symbol of natural life was the symbol therefore of the same spiritual death.

This natural life as the emanation and manifestation of the Sun god, was sanctified by Paganism. All therefore that conduced to it, and contributed to its fulness, became sanctified likewise. Power, riches, worldly honour, rank, position, dominion and earthly material and psychical pleasure, all that the Christian has to crucify, were therefore to be worshipped. This was the very spirit of Paganism, and the cross, as the symbol of the fulness of natural life, was therefore a fitting emblem of worldly power and success; and it was so regarded. From the cross-headed standards of ancient Rome, to its use as a badge of earthly honour and merit at the present day, the cross, throughout all nations, is the symbol of *worldly* power and success.

Some have claimed a special fitness in the cross to be the sign of natural life. Thus one writes: "Indeed it would seem that the cross is at the beginning and end of all the great phenomena of nature. Wherever Force is in connection with matter, and nature's products have been undisturbed, *i.e.*, where no destructive hand has been at work, whether in the animal, the vegetable, or the mineral kingdoms, wherever nature's grand formative power has been at work, there you may find the cross, that beauteous emblem of the life which proceeds from God, and which His mercy has employed in the death of His Son as the only means of making us perfect."[1]

There is a tendency here to confuse the natural and the spiritual, and it is not by any means clear that the cross is at the beginning and

[1] *Compn. of* 666, p. 228.

end of *all* phenomena. Many, indeed, of the illustrations which the writer gives of his statement appear to be laboured and far-fetched. Nevertheless the tree, of which the cross is the emblem, would appear to be a true symbol of natural life and natural generation. For the tree is the constant manifestation of this life and generation, *generating*, or producing, from itself *cross* branches, which again throw out, or *generate*, other *cross* branches, and "*a branch*," the product of this generation, has in consequence become throughout the world, ancient and modern, the synonym for "*a Son.*"

Moreover, the *idea* of the cross is in all natural life. For the law of natural life is the law of self, of struggle, warfare and death, the law by which the life and happiness of one is supported by the death and sufferings of others, and it is the law, therefore, by which the interests and happiness of each *cross* the interests and happiness of others. Even in the vegetable world this is exemplified; for the life of the tree and the plant is supported by the sustenance they obtain from the death and decay of other vegetation. This being the law, and the only possible law of natural life, the cross is the fitting emblem of that life, and it may be said that all natural existence is made up of either inflicting, or bearing the cross, the one tending to the advancement and fulness of natural life, the other to its extinction, or death. But the cross in its latter aspect comes sooner or later to all, and after a brief space, the life of those who have drunk most of the fulness of existence is itself crossed. Death is the fate of all things that are natural only, for death is the essential law of nature; and thus the cross, while the symbol of natural life, is equally the symbol of the death with which all natural life is inseparably connected; the symbol of the death which, by the law of God, is the necessary consequence of all moral imperfection; and this moral imperfection is the essential characteristic of all merely natural life.

Thus the cross may have a different aspect to different persons. To those with whom this world, and this life, with its honours, power, dominion and pleasure, is the highest good, the cross, as the symbol of that life, is honoured, and, like the "crux ansata" of the Egyptian priests, may be said, metaphorically, to be "carried in their hands," while it is actually worn by them as a badge of worldly honour, distinction, authority, or dominion. These are they who *honour* the cross. To others with whom the spiritual is the highest good, and who recognise that, in order to attain it, they must die to the natural, the cross is the emblem of that death, and therefore a thing of evil, to which, nevertheless, they must bow in order to attain the spiritual. These are they who *endure* the cross and who regard it, in its true aspect, as the symbol of that death which, by the law of God, is the consequence of all moral imperfection.

Nevertheless, to those with whom natural life is the only life and their highest good, who exalt the natural and despise the spiritual, the cross, which is their "sign of life," the symbol of the life they glory in, is really to them, though unperceived by them, the symbol of a double death. For it is the symbol of the physical death which must befall all that is natural, and the symbol also of that spiritual and eternal death which must be the fate of those who live for this life only.

These are the two aspects of the cross. To those who live for the present it is the symbol of earthly good. To those who do not it is a symbol of evil, the symbol of that which crucifies, and of that which has to be crucified. The one are the wearers of the material cross, the others are the bearers of the spiritual cross.

A modern Theosophist, speaking of Salvation, says, " The symbol of its triumph will still be the cross of Jesus, whether borne before him by, or in the name of, an Osiris, a Mithras, a Chrishna, a Dionysius, or a Buddha, or any other, who overcoming, by love, the limitations of matter, have been faithful unto death, mystically called the death of the cross, and thereby, attaining the crown of eternal life for themselves, have shown to man the way of salvation."[1] But while the cross of Christ was that which was *endured* by him, Ninus, or Osiris, seems to have been the first who *inflicted* death by it,[2] and the salvation spoken of, and the so-called "love" by which the limitations of matter are to be overcome and eternal life attained, are merely the means by which Hermes taught men to attain the desires of the heart, or the satisfaction of natural passions and ambitions, and led them, as the Serpent did with Eve, to fancy that they could become as gods and independent of God. Hence another writer says, " The religion which we profess is the law of *nature* which is the law of God, for Nature is God."[3]

In Romanism, which has retained, or readopted, the forms and principles of the old Paganism, there is the same tendency to make the cross the symbol of spiritual life, and to substitute the natural for the spiritual. It is the recognised symbol of the power and authority

[1] "The Perfect Way," 1882, p. 37 ; *Compn. of* 666, p. 38.
[2] *Ante.* p. 67.
[3] Mr Vaughan, from *Nimrod*, vol. iv. p. 516 ; *Compn. of* 666, p. 50, note.

of the priesthood of that religion, as it was before of the priesthood of Paganism, and the one, like the other, has sought, and claimed, and, for a time obtained, the dominion of the civilised world. We need not therefore be surprised at the following: "No images of the gods were reckoned by the ancients so sacred as the lingam, yoni, and phallic ones. . . . Even in the present day, in obscure parts of Italy and Spain, may be seen phallic amulets and charms against the evil eye, worn by village maidens and youths, and consisting of nothing, more or less, than representations of bisexual deities, or actual phalli carved in gold, silver, ivory, or other material. I myself saw in a village, not far from Naples, a young girl with a silver phallus hanging round her neck under which were carved the initial letters I.N.R.I. and which she devoutly kissed on passing a cripple, making at the same time the sign of the cross; and on another occasion, when passing a group of leprosy-stricken Arabs near the outer gate of the town of Tangiers in Morocco, I met a Spanish señora who, directly she perceived the lepers, commenced hurriedly to say her prayers, counting at the same time her beads, at the end of which hung a well-carved androgynus Christ nailed to a cross composed of four phali, and having the usual I.N.R.I. above and a conspicuous 'crux ansata' over the fork of the body thus ⚦."[1]

Here the cross and Phallus, the symbols of natural life and generation, are connected with Christ in such a way as to imply, at first sight, that He was the Phallic god and to associate the spiritual life, to give man which He died, with natural life, but in reality it represents Him as the victim of the Phallic god, crucified by him. The letters I.N.R.I., although the initial letters of the Latin part of the inscription which Pilate placed at the head of the cross of Christ, viz., "Jesus of Nazareth the King of the Jews," are probably, considering its connection with the Phallus, an ancient Pagan symbol, viz., that of the fire-worshippers, "Igne Natura Renovatur Integra," "By fire nature is renewed in its integrity";[2] fire, as we have seen, being regarded by the Pagans as *the male principle*, the source of the life and generation of which the Phallus was the symbol. For it was the policy of the teachers of the fourth, fifth and following centuries, in order to make Christianity palatable to the Pagans, to retain as far as possible the Pagan rites, ceremonies and symbols, and simply give them a Christian meaning, as in the case of Gregory's well-known instructions to his missioner Augustine, whom he sent to the Pagan

[1] Herbert Junius Hardwicke, M.D., quoted from *Compn. of* 666, p. 103.
[2] *Compn. of* 666, p. 70.

Anglo-Saxons, telling him to allow the latter to retain their ancient rites and customs, but that henceforth they were to do them in honour of Christ and the saints; which was, in effect, to retain the old Paganism and merely *call it Christian*. It is possible that the symbol I.H.S., to which a Christian significance is now given, but which is stated to have been a Pagan symbol, may also have been adopted in this way.[1]

THE SERPENT.—We have seen that the Serpent was the especial symbol of the prophetic god Thoth, Hermes, Hea, Buddha, etc., who was Cush, the great teacher of magic and demonology, and that the later Hermetic writers identify the Serpent of the Garden of Eden, whom Scripture speaks of as "the devil,"[2] with "the divine wisdom," or "logos," and the author of man's salvation, *i.e.*, with Christ. The worship of the Serpent appears to have been originated by Thoth, *i.e.*, Cush himself. The primary teaching of Thoth on the subject is thus stated by the Phœnician historian Sanchoniathon: "Taautus (*i.e.*, Thoth) first consecrated the basilisk and introduced the worship of the Serpent tribe, in which he was followed by the Phœnicians and Egyptians. For this animal was held by them to be the most inspirited (spiritual) of all the reptiles, and of a fiery nature, inasmuch as it exhibits an incredible celerity, moving by its spirit, without either hands or feet, or any of those external members by which other animals effect their motion. And in its progress it assumes a variety of forms, moving in a spiral course, and darting forward with whatever degree of swiftness it pleases. It is, moreover, long-lived, and has the quality not only of putting off its old age and assuming a second youth, but receiving at the same time an augmentation of its size and strength; and when it has fulfilled the appointed measure of its existence it consumes itself, as Taautus has laid down in the sacred books, upon which account this animal is introduced in the sacred rites and mysteries."[3]

In the later development of Paganism the Serpent was identified with the Sun, as the source of spiritual light or divine wisdom. "In the mythology of the primitive world," says Owen, "the Serpent is

[1] It has been supposed by some persons that the symbol represented the Egyptian Trinity, Isis, Horus, Seb, but there would have been no particular object in such a symbol, and if it was a Pagan symbol, it is more likely to have had the meaning given at p. 219, which was of important religious significance.

[2] Rev. xx. 2.

[3] Sanchoniathon, from Cory's *Fragments*, pp. 17, 18.

universally the symbol of the Sun."[1] Bunsen says, "In Egypt one of the commonest symbols of the Sun, or Sun god, is a disk with a serpent around it."[2] It was also represented combined with a winged disk of the Sun, as in the figure,[3] and this was a prominent

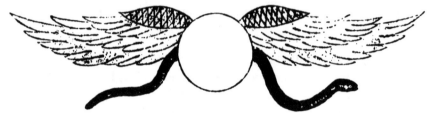

GLOBE WITH WINGS AND SERPENT.

symbol in the Persian, Egyptian and Mexican hieroglyphics.[4]

Kircher says of this symbol that in the teaching of Hermes, "The globe (*i.e.*, the disk of the Sun) represents the simple essence of God, which he indifferently called The Father, The First Mind, The Supreme Wisdom. The Serpent emerging from the globe was the vivifying influence of God which called all things into existence. This he called *The Word*. The wings implied the moving penetrative power of God, which pervaded all things. This he called Love. The whole emblem represented the Supreme Being as Creator and Preserver."[5] As the life and existence here referred to can only be *natural*, it is evident that the *love* spoken of is really that symbolised by the Phallus.

A similar figure without the wings was the symbol among the Greeks for a dæmon, or the Deity.[6]

Bryant remarks that the Serpent was "deemed symbolical of divine wisdom and creative energy and of immortality and regeneration."[7] These, it may be remarked, are the characteristics which the Bible ascribes to Christ, "The Word" and "the Wisdom of God"; and in this and other ways, which will be mentioned hereafter, the Sun and Serpent god became the false Christ of Paganism.

DISK AND SERPENT.

[1] Owen *apud* Davies, *Druids*, note, p. 437 ; Hislop, p. 227.
[2] Bunsen, *Hieroglyphics*, vol. i. p. 497.
[3] From Bryant ; Deane's *Serpent Worship*, p. 51.   [4] *Ibid.*
[5] Kircher, "Pamph. Obel. 399," from Deane's *Serpent Worship*, pp. 55, 56.
[6] Selden on Arundel Marbles, p. 133, cited by Stukeley ; *Abury*, p. 56 ; Deane, p. 53.
[7] Bryant, *Plagues of Egypt*, p. 200.

The modern Theosophist writers who seek to resuscitate the Hermetic wisdom, also glorify both the Serpent and the cross. Thus one writes : "The first Christians never perceived that not only was there no sin in this disobedience (of Eve), but that actually *the Serpent was the Lord God Himself*, who, as the Ophis, the Logos, or the bearer of divine creative wisdom, taught mankind to be creators in their turn. They never realised that the cross was an evolution from the tree and the Serpent, and thus became the salvation of mankind. By this it would become the very first symbol of creative cause, applying to geometry, to numbers, to astronomy, to measure and to animal reproduction." [1] This, although illustrating the character of the philosophy which seeks to substitute Satan for God, to exalt the natural and glorify the beginning of human sin, is clearly false. The power and instinct of generation is natural, and was implanted in both men and animals by the Creator, and not taught them by the Serpent.

"Æsculapius," one of the names given to the Babylonian Sun god, signified "the man-instructing Serpent," [2] and the Epidaurian snake, worshipped with the sacred fire in Rome, was regarded as the divine representation of Æsculapius,[3] who, in consequence, is represented as holding a staff with a serpent twining round it, and serpents were especially sacred to him.[4] Thus the Sun god Æsculapius was identified with the Serpent, who was the instructor of man in the knowledge of good and evil, implying by a confusion of the material and spiritual, that the Sun was the *enlightener* of men in the same sense as the Serpent was.

Macrobius, speaking of the mystic doctrine of the ancients, says that "Æsculapius was the beneficent influence of the Sun which pervaded the souls of man." [5] This also implies that the influence of the Sun god of Paganism, which can only be physical, was spiritual. Just also as the Sun was the supposed author of Life and Generation, so Æsculapius, the Serpent god, was "The life restorer "; [6] a belief which was no doubt based on the teaching of Hermes or Thoth regarding the supposed power of serpents of renewing their youth. The Greeks, not recognising the true esoteric doctrine, made Æsculapius merely the god of *healing*.

[1] "The Secret Doctrine," by H. P. B., 2nd edit. 1888, vol. ii. p. 215, from *Compn. of 666*, pp. 38, 39.

[2] *Ante*, p. 44.   [3] Ovid, *Metam.*, lib. xv. ll. 736-745 ; Hislop, p. 236.

[4] Lemprière, *Æsculapius*.

[5] Macrob., *Sat.*, lib. i. cap. 23 ; Hislop, pp. 278, 279, note.

[6] Pausanias, lib. ii., *Corinthiaca*, cap. 26 ; Virgil, *Æneid*, lib. vii. ll. 769, 773, pp. 364, 365 ; Hislop, p. 98.

EGG AND SERPENT.

The aspect of the Serpent as " the life giver," or god of generation, was likewise symbolised by an egg with a serpent twining round it; the egg being the symbol of the goddess, as " the Mother of Gods and Men,"[1] and the serpent being the Great Father, or the vivifying influence which gave them life.

Both the attributes of the Serpent god, viz., as " the life giver " and as " the revealer of wisdom," were recognised in the Mysteries, for the initiate, when he had passed the ordeal, had a golden serpent placed in his bosom as a token of his supposed spiritual regeneration, or new life,[2] and of his initiation into the hidden wisdom, or solemn secret, the "*Apporeta*," the revelation of which was punished by death. This is also the teaching of the modern Hermetic philosophy, which, as we have seen, boldly affirms that the Serpent of Eden was the divine logus, or wisdom, who, " by means of the tree, had become the salvation of mankind " and taught them to be " creators "; that is to say, he is represented as " the enlightener " and " the life giver."

The nature of the knowledge and life which the Serpent was supposed to have given to man was the knowledge of generation, or of producing natural life. This is represented by the symbol of the Serpent carried in the mysteries, viz., Φ, which is clearly the union of the I and O, the symbols of the Phallus and Yoni. The letter Φ (phi), is the root letter of the word "*Aphe*" and "*Ophe*," a serpent, the Hebrew "*eph*eh," "tze*pha*," "she*phiph*on," and the Coptic "Nou*phi*on," which have the same meaning, and Φ is said not to have been an original letter but to have been added afterwards,[3] probably to effect the symbolism; for it must be remembered that Thoth or Hermes was both the inventor of letters and the originator of idolatry, and we might expect therefore that they would be adapted to each other; while the Greeks obtained their letters from the Phœnicians and Egyptians.[4] The O being also a symbol of the seed, and of the disk of the Sun, the three symbols Φ, O, I, in their full esoteric meaning would signify " The Serpent, the incarnation of the Sun, the Phallic God."

[1] *Vide* Hislop on the Sacred Egg of Paganism, pp. 108, 109 ; and Faber, vol. i. pp. 175-190.

[2] Faber, vol. iii. p. 116.   [3] *Compn. of* 666, note, p. 356.

[4] Sayce, *Ancient Empires of the East*, pp. 189, 190 ; from *Compn. of* 666, p. 354. *See* also before pp. 8-10.

These symbols also occur in the word "ΦΟΙΝΙΚΕΑ," "Phœnicia," and it is evident that it is composed of "ΦΟΙ" and "ΝΙΚΕ," "victory," which looks as if the name was given to the country to indicate the triumph of the Sun and Serpent god; a name therefore peculiarly suitable to that country, and to the nations of Canaan generally.

The Sun god *Apollo* was identified with the Serpent *Python*, for although Apollo is represented as slaying the Python, the spirit of the god which entered into the Pythoness who revealed the oracles at Delphi was said to be the spirit of Python. But, according to the principle of Paganism, the term "slayer of the Serpent" had a double meaning. Mr Faber remarks that the word, which in its exoteric meaning is "slayer," is in its esoteric meaning "priest." Thus "*Argiphontes*," a title of Mercury, which in its exoteric meaning is 'slayer of Argus," is derived from "*arg*," "ark," and "*phont*," "priest," and thus meant esoterically "priest of the Ark."[1] Similarly, while Apollo was exoterically identified with the promised "seed of the woman" as the slayer of the Serpent, he was revealed to the initiated as the priest of the Serpent and therefore as the Serpent himself; for the priest was both the representative of, and identified with, the God he served. Hence at Delphi, Apollo was worshipped under the form of a python, and a hymn of praise was sung to it every seventh day.[2]

Bacchus, or *Dionuses*, is identified with the Sun by the Orphic poet in the line "The Sun, whom men call Dionusus as a surname," and he is also identified with the Serpent. The Greek myth represents him as begotten by Jupiter in the form of a serpent. The oracle of Apollo Clarius, speaking of the different aspects of the Sun god, declares that Iao, the highest of all the gods, is Aides in winter, Zeus in spring, Helius in summer, and Iao in autumn, while the Orphic poet substitutes the name of Dionusus for Iao in the line "One Zeus, one Aides, one Helius, one Dionusus,"[3] showing that the Sun god Dionusus was the same as Iao, and Iao by the Phœnicians was identified with the Serpent.[4] So also the Indian form of Dionusus, viz., *Deo Naush*, or *Deva Nahusha*, is fabled to have become a serpent,[5] and Deva Nahusha is clearly derived from *Deva*, "God," and *Nahash*, "serpent," and thus means "The Serpent God."

[1] Faber's *Mysteries of the Cabiri; Compn. of* 666, p. 355.
[2] *Protegomena to the Pythia of Pindar*, cited by Bryant; *Anal.*, ii. 147.
[3] *The Great Dionysiac Myth*, vol. i. pp. 44, 45; *Compn. of* 666, p 348.
[4] Cooper's *Serpent Myths*, p. 18; *The Great Dionysiac Myth*, Robert Brown, vol. i. p. 70; *Compn. of* 666, p. 347.
[5] Wilford's *Asiat. Res.*, vol. iii. pp. 450, 452.

Janus was worshipped in Phœnicia under the form of a serpent with its tail in its mouth, which was supposed to typify self-existence and eternity.[1] In Etruria he was called *Dianus* and was the husband of *Diana*, and appears to have derived his name from "*Ha Nahash*," "The Serpent." For, as already pointed out, Ha Nahash would pass in Greek into "*Ana'as*" or "*Anas*," the *h*, or aspirate, not being expressed by a letter, and "Anas," in which the article is combined with the word, would easily pass, according to varying dialects, into *Anus* or *Anes*. This, with the Greek article I or O again placed before it, as in "I'siris," "O'siris," would become "*I'anus*" or "*Janus*," and "*O'anes*" or "*Oannes*," and with "*Di*," "God," would become "*Dianus*." The latter name also, on the principle of the double meaning of words, served to identify Janus with the Sun, for "*Annus*" is the Latin for "year," and the Etrurian "*Dianus*" would thus mean "The God of the Year," the number of days in which was the usual symbol of the Sun; hence Janus or Dianus was called "The God of Day."

Janus was also called ΔΙΦΥΗΣ (Diphues), or geminus, the exoteric meaning of which is "twice born," or regenerated, which was also said of the initiate into the Mysteries. But the word is made up of ΔΙ (Di), god; Φ (phi) the symbol of the Serpent; and ΥΗΣ, the symbol of the Sun god; the whole word having thus the esoteric meaning of "The Sun and Serpent god."

The title also of Bel Nimrud the lesser, viz., "Hea," is evidently the same as the Arabic, or Adite, word "*Heya*," which means both "life" and "serpent,"[2] and the serpent was one of the principal forms of Hea.[3] By this name, therefore, the God, who was known as "The Lord of Understanding," "The Teacher of Mankind," and is the same as Æsculapius, "the man-instructing Serpent," was identified with the serpent who was regarded as "The Divine Wisdom" or "Logos," who taught man the knowledge of good and evil. Speaking of "Hea," Mr Rawlinson says, "He was figured by the great Serpent which occupied so conspicuous a place among the symbols of the gods on the black stones recording Babylonian benefactions. There are very strong grounds for connecting him with the Serpent of Scripture and with the Paradisiacal tradition of the tree of knowledge and the tree of life." He was known also as the star Kimmut, which was the same as "Draco," the Dragon, and was the father of Bel Merodach

---

[1] Macrobius, lib. i. chap. ix.
[2] Rawlinson's *Herod.*, vol. i. essay x. p. 600.
[3] Lenormant, *Chaldean Magic*, p. 232.

and Bel Nimrud.[1] Thus these first idolaters were represented to be in very truth "the seed of the Serpent."

The worship of the Serpent was general in Babylon, the central seat of the Cushite idolatry, as implied by the apocryphal book of Bel and the Dragon, where it is said, "In that same place was a great Dragon which they of Babylon worshipped." In short, as remarked by Bryant, the etymology of the word "*Ethiopian*" (Cushite) would appear to be "the race of Ophe," or "race of the Serpent," from "*ethnos*" or "*ethos*," "a collection of persons associating together from habit,"[2] and "*ophis*," "a serpent"; and the Arabians call the Ethiopians "*Nagashi*," *i.e.*, "serpents," from "*Nahash*" or the Indian "*Naga*," a serpent.[3]

In Egypt the Serpent of the Sun, called "*The Basilisk*," or "*Royal Serpent*," was regarded as "the type of dominion," and as such was worn on the head-dress of the Egyptian monarchs.[4] Hence the term "*Basilica*," "a Royal Palace," the form of which was adopted for Christian churches. The Sun, as identified with the Serpent, was called "*Pouro*," meaning at once "Fire" and "The King," thus identifying the Serpent with the God of Fire.[5] In Rome it eventually became the Imperial standard, which was a Dragon, or Serpent, elevated on a pole and coloured red to represent it as a symbol of fire.[6] The Egyptian god *Chnouphis*, the root of whose name is *aphe*, or *ophis*, "a serpent," was called *Agathodæmon* (the good dæmon), who was the son of Hermes,[7] and must therefore be Osiris or Nimrod. He is represented by a serpent with an egg in its mouth, while a serpent in a circle, and passing diametrically from circumference to circumference, was his distinctive symbol, and was the origin of the Greek Θ (*theta*).[8]

Chnouphis represented the creative power in the world, and as such was identified with Amenra, the Sun, who also represented the creative power, and with Khem, the god of generation.[9] The Serpent, as identified with the Sun, also represented the same creative power,

[1] Rawlinson's *Herod.*, vol. i. pp. 600, 601.   [2] *See* Donnegan, ἔθνος.

[3] Bryant, *Anal.*, ii. p. 206 ; Deane's *Serpent Worship*, p. 160.

[4] Wilkinson's *Egyptians*, vol. iv. p. 239.   [5] *Bunsen*, vol. iv. pp. 407, 457.

[6] Ammianus Marcellinus, lib. xvi. cap. xii., c. 39 ; Elliot, *Horæ Apocalypticæ*, vol. iii. p. 14, plate.

[7] Manetho from Syncellus ; Cory, p. 168.

[8] Kircher, *Ædip. Ægypt*, vol. iii. p. 46 ; Deane, p. 120.

[9] See *ante*, chap. ii. pp. 46, 47.

and, according to Horapollo, was the spirit which pervaded the universe.[1] All these attributes were given to Osiris in the later Egyptian mythology, and he became the chief Sun god and god of generation.[2] Now one of his titles was "*Onuphis*,"[3] which is plainly made up of "*On*," the name of the Sun at Heliopolis, and "*Ophis*," the serpent.[4] In short, Onuphis, which in modern Coptic is "*Nouphion*," signifies a serpent in that language.[5] "Chnouphis," which is the same as "Nouphis" with the K or Ch prefixed, as in the case of Kham for Ham,

THE CADUCEUS.

is merely a form of Onuphis, the Sun and Serpent god. In Herwart's table of Egyptian hieroglyphics, and also in the Isaic table, an Egyptian priest is shown offering adoration to a serpent, who was doubtless the Serpent god Onuphis, as Pausanius says that "in the Egyptian city of Onuphis they worship the asp."[6]

The "*Caduceus*," which is shown in the hand of Anubis and Mercury, was a winged wand entwined by serpents, as shown in the accompanying fig., so as to form a combination of the crescent, the circle and the cross, as in the symbol of Mercury.[7] It was regarded as powerful "for *paralysing the mind and rais-*

---

[1] *Wilkinson*, by Birch, vol. iii. p. 2, note. 　　[2] *See* App. A.
[3] *Wilkinson*, by Birch, vol. iii. pp. 307, 308.
[4] Wilkinson suggests a different etymology in order to accord with his ideal of Egyptian idolatry, but it is unsatisfactory. *See* App. A.
[5] *Ibid.*
[6] Pausanias, quoted by Kircher; Deane, p. 155. 　　[7] See *ante*, p. 226.

ing the dead," by which is probably meant *mesmerising* and calling up the supposed spirits of the dead, *i.e.*, the daimonia.[1]

The name of the Egyptian Vulcan, viz., "*Aphthah*," or "*Phthah*," the prefix being usually dropped, has for its root *Aphe*, "serpent." The title of the Egyptian kings—"*Pharaoh*," "*Phra*," or "*Aphra*," the "a" being quiescent, is also compounded of *Aphe*, "serpent," and *Ra*, "the Sun,"[2] by which they claimed descent from the Sun and Serpent god, while the serpent which they wore on their foreheads was the type of the power and dominion which they equally claimed in virtue of that descent. The name "Amenoph," by which some of the Theban kings were known, is also compounded of "*Amon*," or "*Amen*," the Sun god, and *Ophe*, "serpent."

The divinity attached to the serpent, and the claim, especially of the *Theban* kings, to be descended from the Serpent god, is explained by the fact that they were of the race called "Egyptian," *i.e.*, of Cushite or Ethiopian origin[3] (the race of Ophe), who were the originators of this idolatry. This claim on their part is also a strong proof, if other evidence was wanting, that the originals of those gods were human beings, men who claimed to be of Nephilim descent; for unless this was the case, there was nothing to suggest such a parentage. So intimately, indeed, was descent from the Serpent god associated with worldly power and dominion throughout Paganism, that we find Alexander the Great claiming, by means of an oracle, to be begotten by Jupiter Ammon in the form of a serpent, in order to give him the prestige of victory before undertaking the conquest of Asia.[4] So also Augustus pretended that he was the son of Apollo, and that the god had assumed the form of a serpent for the purpose of giving him birth.[5]

"*Beelzebub*," the god of the Canaanitish nations, was also represented by a serpent. Like the Indian Siva, he was worshipped, firstly, as the Destroyer, and then as the Renewer and Life Giver. The name "Beelzebub" signifies "the Lord of the fly,"[6] and the fly represented the god in both his aspects; for flies by their larvæ consume dead carcases, and in so doing produce life again in another form. Hence, as "Lord of the fly," he is represented in the woodcut

[1] Deane, *Serpent Worship*, pp. 135, 139.
[2] *Wilkinson*, by Birch, vol. iii. p. 44, gives a partly different etymology, but it is not so satisfactory as the above.
[3] *Vide* chap. iv.
[4] *Nimrod*, vol. i. pp. 364, 365.
[5] Suetonius, *Augustus*; Hislop, p. 277, note.
[6] Hislop, pp. 279, 280; Kitto's *Illustrated Commentary*, vol. ii. p. 217.

below [1] by the double figures of swallows pursuing flies and by serpents; the one representing the exoteric aspect of the god, the other his real or esoteric character.

THE LORD OF THE FLY.

SUN AND SERPENT GODS.

A somewhat similar double representation is given in another woodcut from *Pompeii*.[2] The two gods in the upper compartment, who are being sacrificed to by a priest, are shown by the rays around their heads to be Sun gods, while their black faces identify them with their Cushite originals.

In the lower compartment are shown two serpents, as in the other picture, to represent their true esoteric character.

"*Oph*," "*Ob*," "*Oub*" and "*Eph*" were the names given to the sacred Serpent among the Canaanites, and "*Oph*" is the same word as that used in Deut. xviii. 11 for a familiar spirit, while the Witch of Endor is called an "*Ob*" or "*Oub*."[3] "*Obion*," composed of "*Obi*," and "*On*," the name of the Sun in Egypt, is still the name of a serpent in that country.[4] It is well known that throughout Africa, which seems to have been peopled by the descendants of the Cushite and Canaanite races,[5] Obi, or Serpent worship, still exists. In Whidah and Congo the most celebrated temple is called "the Serpent's house," and the rites of the gods are performed by priests, priestesses and a pontiff. The priestesses call themselves "Children of *God*," and in token thereof mark their bodies with the figure of *a serpent*, thus claiming to be the "seed of the Serpent." Victims are daily brought

[1] From *Pompeii*, vol. ii. p. 141.
[2] *Ibid.*, p. 105.
[3] Deane, pp. 172-176.
[4] *Ibid.*, p. 176.
[5] The notice in Gen. x. 18, "afterward were the Canaanites scattered abroad" implies that at some period of the history, probably after the conquest of the country by the Israelites, they emigrated in large numbers, and Africa, as a comparatively unoccupied country, would naturally promise them great advantages.

to the god, and oracles required of him.[1] The Eboes, who worship
the Quana, say that the most acceptable offering to him is a human
victim. The Koromantynes, who worship a serpent which they call
"Oboni," also assert that when he is angry nothing will appease him
but a human victim.[2]

The gods of the ancient Mexicans were also identified with the
serpent, and a huge figure of a dragon was placed on the summit of
the pyramid temple on which human victims were sacrificed to the
Sun, which implies that their Sun god was also the Serpent god, as in
other Pagan countries.[3] The Spaniards, on first landing, found at
Campeachy a large serpent idol, still warm with the blood of human
victims,[4] and, according to M. Aglio, there was scarcely a deity who
was not symbolised by a dragon or serpent.[5] *Mexitli*, the Mexican
Creator, or "giver of life," was also represented in a similar way to
Æsculapius, "the life restorer," viz., as holding a staff with a serpent
twined round it.[6]

At Topira, in Peru, there was a temple with a vast image of a
serpent with its tail in its mouth, like the Egyptian representation of
the Serpent of the Sun. A man was sacrificed to it every year.[7]

In India, *Juggernaut* was sometimes worshipped under the form
of a seven-headed dragon, and the "*Naga*," or five-headed hooded
serpent, is constantly represented as the object of special adoration
in Indian sculptures.[8] *Siva Mahadeva* and the goddess *Parvati* are
represented with serpents about their necks and waists.[9] *Buddha*
was also represented by a serpent, and a serpent was the sign of his
worshippers.[10]

In China the great dragon was the banner of the Empire, and
indicated everything sacred in it. Like the basilisk in Egypt, it was
the stamp and symbol of royalty, and was sculptured in all temples.[11]
According to Cambry, "the Chinese delight in mountains and *high
places*, because there lives the great dragon upon whom their good

[1] Bosman on Guinea, *Acta Erud. Leip.*, 1705, p. 265 ; Deane, p. 165.
[2] Deane, p. 178, *vide* full account, pp. 160-180.
[3] Bernal Diaz de Castillo, quoted by Deane, pp. 295, 297.
[4] Peter Martyr, *De Orbe Novo*, p. 291 ; Deane, p. 298, 299.
[5] M. Aglio, *Mexican Antiquities ;* Deane, p. 299.
[6] Faber, vol. i. p. 270.
[7] *Purchas*, part iv. p. 1560 ; Deane, p. 302.
[8] Faber, vol. i. p. 452. *See* also plates in Ferguson's *Tree and Serpent Worship.*
[9] Moor's *Hindu Pantheon*, p. 22.
[10] Deane, p. 66. *See* also *ante*, chap. vi.
[11] Stukeley's *Abury*, p. 56 ; Maurice's *Hist. Hindustan*, vol. i. p. 210.

Q

fortune depends. They call him the father of happiness, and erect temples to him shaded with *groves*."[1]

Serpent worship was equally a distinctive feature of the Druidical religion. The Celtic *Hu* was called "The Dragon Ruler of the World," his car is represented as drawn by serpents, and his priests were called "adders."[2] In the sacrificial rites of "Uther Pendragon," the Dragon god Hu is invoked under the name of "Victorious *Beli*," a title which indicates its Babylonish origin.[3]

Sun, Serpent and Dæmon worship were thus integral parts of the same system, and constituted the substance of that Hermetic wisdom, the fruits of which were unbridled lust and cruelty, and which eventually spread over the whole earth from its centre, Babylon, and made the Prince of the Dæmons in very truth "The God of this World" (2 Cor. iv. 4).

The Sun and Serpent god of Paganism was also *morally* identical with Him whom the Scripture calls "The God of this World." The latter, in the form of a serpent, had, at the first, persuaded man to choose self-dependence, which is the principle of natural life, instead of faith and dependence on God, which is the principle of spiritual life, and had made it appear that this self-dependence was the only true life, and that those who ate of its fruit would be "*as gods.*" In like manner the Pagan god was the god of this natural life, and all that tended to exalt it and conduced to its satisfaction—"the lust of the flesh, the lust of the eyes, and the pride of life"—were regarded as his gifts.

Hence, when the Prince of the Demons, whom Christ identified with the Pagan god, showed Christ "all the kingdoms of the world and the glory of them," the tempter said to Him, "All these things will I give unto thee, *for that is delivered unto me, and to whomsoever I will give it.* If therefore thou wilt worship me, all shall be thine" (Luke iv. 5-7). Nor was the claim denied; and we therefore find that worldly power and dominion, which constitute the glory and satisfaction of this life, were possessed by those kings and priesthoods who served the Pagan god and his angels, the daimonia; and they wore *the cross*, his special symbol, and the emblem of this

---

[1] Cambry, *Monuments Celtiques*, p. 163 ; Deane, pp. 69, 70. The correspondence between the "high places" and "groves" of the Chinese and those of the Canaanite nations, adopted by the idolatrous Israelites, will be noted. "High places" were supposed to be especially the abode of the gods, and trees were symbolic of the gods.

[2] Davies, *Druids*, pp. 116, 122, 210.

[3] Owen's Dictionary ; Deane, pp. 254, 256.

worldly glory and power, as a token of their allegiance. On the other hand, *fire* and *the cross*, both of which were symbols of the god, and of natural life, were used to inflict death on the enemies of, or rebels against, the god and his servants. For the human sacrifices to the Pagan gods were not only made by fire, as in the case of those made to Moloch and Baal, but by the cross, and crucifixion and burning were the two forms of death throughout the Oriental world meted to offenders against the state or king, who was the earthly representative of the god.[1] These sacrifices consisted not only of malefactors, but of captives taken in war, or of those who had been spared and made slaves of, and crucifixion, instituted by the founders of Pagan idolatry, was not only the fate of the former, but of the latter also, if they rebelled. Thus the cross, the symbol of the Sun and Serpent gods, became the very altar of "The Prince of this World" (John xiv. 30).

Christ described Satan as a *liar*, and the Father, or originator, of lies, and as a *murderer* from the beginning (John viii. 44), and both characteristics were essential features of the Pagan system and its god. As "the Spirit who works in the children of disobedience" (Eph. ii. 2), "who deceiveth the whole world" (Rev. xii. 9), he was the real author of the whole system of Paganism, which constituted, therefore, those "works of the devil" which Christ was manifested to destroy (1 John iii. 8). That system was a system of lies, of doctrines founded on subtle perversions of truth, by which good was made to appear evil, and evil good—a system of which the essence was *mystery* and *deceit*, having an outward appearance of truth and righteousness which veiled a hidden and mystical evil, blinded men to its true character, and led them to substitute the fruit of the tree of knowledge of good and evil, or the tree of death, for that of the tree of life. So, also, it was a system of *murder*, which not only killed men's souls, but which, in the zenith of its power, demanded and obtained hecatombs of human beings as sacrifices to its gods, who could only be appeased by their tortures, by the shrieks of children devoted to Moloch, and the agonies of their parents and relatives.

Human sacrifices appear to have been a custom in Egypt. Porphyry, priest of Sebennytus, says that three men were daily sacrificed to the Egyptian Juno, after having been examined like clean calves chosen for the altar.[2] Plutarch says, "We are informed by Manetho

[1] Rawlinson's *Egypt and Babylon*, vol. i. pp. 190, 191.
[2] Porphyry, *De Abst.*, ii. p. 53.

that they were formerly wont in the city of Idithya, to burn men alive, giving them the name of "Typhos," and winnowing their ashes through a sieve."[1] Diodorus also states that it was formerly the custom to sacrifice men of a red complexion to Osiris, from their supposed resemblance to *Typhon.*[2]   Wilkinson remarks that this "could only have been at a very remote period and before the Egyptians had become the highly-civilised nation we know them from their monuments."[3]   But civilisation is no preventive of the cruelty which always accompanies superstition.   The Assyrians, an equally civilised nation, flayed their prisoners alive, or tore out their tongues with pincers,[4] and the burnings and tortures of the Inquisition in Spain occurred at a period when the Spaniards were the foremost among the civilised nations of Europe.   The fact that the victims were given the name of *Typhos* by the Egyptians proves that it must have been at a period when Set or Typhon, instead of being worshipped as a god as at one time, was hated and his name erased from the monuments.   This was not until after the advent of the Cushite Rameses from India,[5] under whom, and by whom, the great temples of the gods and principal monuments of Egypt were erected.

It is also a strong evidence of the existence of human sacrifices in Egypt, that the seal of the priests, with which they stamped the clay

affixed to the band round the neck of the animal destined for sacrifice, was a figure of a man with his arms bound behind him and a sacrificial knife pointed at his throat, as in woodcut, which is a copy of the figure found by Wilkinson in the

SEAL OF EGYPTIAN PRIESTS.

hieroglyphics of sculptures relating to the sacrifice of victims.[6]

Human sacrifices to the gods, it is well known, were common amongst all the principal Pagan nations and were only discontinued in Pagan Rome at a late period.   In Mexico it is said that 50,000 victims were sacrificed every year.[7]   Just as new-born babies were sacrificed to Moloch, so also in Mexico children were offered to the

[1] *De Iside,* s. 73 ; *Wilkinson,* by Birch, vol. iii. p. 30.
[2] Diod., i. p. 88 ; *Wilkinson,* by Birch, vol. iii. p. 143.
[3] *Wilkinson,* by Birch, vol. iii. p. 30.
[4] Layard's, *Nineveh and Babylon,* pp. 457, 458, and woodcuts.   [5] *See* chap. v. p. 95.
[6] Wilkinson's *Egyptians,* vol. v. p. 352.   Wilkinson says that Plutarch on the authority of Castor describes the same seal.
[7] Prescott, *Conquest of Mexico,* chap. iii. p. 26.

god Huitzilopochtli and their blood was mixed with the sacred cakes eaten by the worshippers; and in Lord Kingsborough's collection of Mexican antiquities, a group of Mexicans are represented adoring the cross, while a priest holds an infant in his arms as an offering to it.[1]

These gods were Serpent gods, and wherever Serpent worship has been pre-eminent, as among the ancient Phœnicians, and the Hamitic races of Africa at the present day, this system of Murder, or Human Sacrifices, has attained its fullest development.

It should be remembered, however, that the ancient idolatry had two phases or forms. The first was that instituted, and openly promulgated in all its evil, obscenity, and cruelty by Cush and Nimrod, but which received a speedy and world-wide overthrow, the history of which will be shortly described. The second form was that which it attained, after having been gradually and secretly resuscitated, in after ages, by a process of steady development, in the manner which will be hereafter described. In this form Cush and Nimrod were themselves worshipped as incarnations of the Sun and Serpent god. It would appear, however, that when the worship of the latter had been firmly established, and the god was identified with the Prince of the Dæmons, the human originals were kept out of sight of the common people, having served their purpose as stepping-stones, or a basis on which to build the ultimate development.

[1] "The Mexican Messiah," *Gentleman's Magazine*, Sept. 1888, pp. 242, 243. The author of this article suggests that the Mexican religion was a form of Christianity introduced by a Christian who they called Quetzalcoatl. His reasons for this conclusion are that the Mexicans, like the Roman Catholics, worshipped the cross, supposed their children regenerated by a water baptism, believed in a purgatory after death, ate sacred cakes like the Roman Catholic wafer which they believed to be the body of their god, had a celibate priesthood to whom the people made confession, inflicted penances, including flagellation and piercing the flesh with sharp thorns, etc. But all these were Pagan customs long before they were *adopted* by the Church of Rome, and although Quetzalcoatl may have been a Roman Catholic, yet as all the other customs of the Mexicans, including the worship of the Serpent and Human Sacrifices, were essentially similar to those of the Pagan nations of the East, it is pretty certain that all their religious customs were derived from the same source.

CHAPTER XI

THE WORSHIP OF THE STARS

IN concluding this portion of our inquiry a few remarks may be made on the worship of the seven stars and the twelve signs of the Zodiac, which, according to Maimonides, was instituted by Tammuz,[1] i.e., Nimrod.

There appears to have been little moral significance in this worship, beyond the fact that the planets were part of the solar system and satellites of the Sun, and might therefore be regarded as having some relation to the Sun. The Pagans merely called these by one or other of the names of their gods, Saturn, Jupiter, Mercury, Mars, etc. The Sun also passed through the signs of the Zodiac in the course of the year, while at the same time it had a slow retrograde movement by which it retired through them in the course of 25,827 years, or the period of the "precession of the equinoxes"; and if this was known to the ancients, the signs of the Zodiac would be regarded by them as having a special relation to the Sun. But these relations of themselves do not appear to have been the real reason of the original worship of the stars. Neither the signs of the Zodiac, nor the combinations of stars called "the constellations," have the remotest approach in form to that of the things by which they are called, such as the Scorpion, the Virgin, the Twins, the Balance, etc., and the suggestion that men by gazing at them thought they saw in them the forms of these things is therefore inadmissible. They are perfectly arbitrary names which have no relation whatever to the form of the constellations and signs themselves.[2] It is equally difficult to perceive any relation between their names and the moral significance of the religious system which has just been explained; it suggests no explanation for the arbitrary names by which they are known.

[1] More, *Nevochim*, p. 420.

[2] This applies of course only to the ancient names of the stars. Modern *popular* names have no doubt been given them on account of a certain rough resemblance to the things denoted by those names.

On the other hand it is stated in Scripture that GOD gave these constellations their names. " He telleth the number of the stars, He calleth them all by their names." [1] " Lift up your eyes on high and behold, who hath created these things, that bringeth out their host by numbers, He calleth them all by their names by the greatness of His might." [2] If, then, their names were given them by God, we may understand why their forms were made to have no relation to those names. It would have been the strongest temptation to worship them had their forms exactly portrayed the things after which they were named.

It has been pointed out by Mr Guinness that the allotted period of man's life, 70 years, plus the 40 weeks of gestation, is exactly 25,847 days, and that this number is probably the exact number of years of the precessional cycle; so that man's life, putting a day for a year, is a type of the precessional cycle. Moreover, the 25,847 solar years of the precessional cycle is equal to 26,640 lunar years, which equals 30×888, and also 40×666, numbers which have a special significance in Scripture, the one being significant of God and Redemption, the other of the world and evil; indicating that both enter into the history of the world, and, on account of the relation between the cycle and the life of man, that either may symbolise the history of the individual.

There are also certain eclipse cycles, the first consisting of 18 years and 10 to 11 days, in which 70 eclipses take place, and which recur in the same order in the next 18 years and 10 to 11 days; but on account of the extra days of the cycle, each eclipse will be those number of days later in each succeeding 18 years, until a period of 325 years has passed, when each eclipse will again take place on the same day as at first; and this will be the case again in another 326 years, or 651 years in all. Now, there are 1260 eclipses in the cycle of 325 years, and 2520 eclipses in the cycle of 651 years, and of these eclipses 666 are total, or annular, and 594 are partial. There is a final eclipse cycle of 5860 years which equals $2300 + 2520$ $(= 2 \times 1260) + 1040$ years. All these are also great cycles, and they are also the numbers of the great prophetic periods, which, if measured in years, are therefore exact astronomical cycles. The only interpretation of so exact a correspondence is that the prophetic periods are astronomical cycles.

The 2520 and 1260 years are multiples of 7 and 10, which are numbers expressing the completion of God's acts towards man; thus 1260 years $= 70 + 7 \times 10 + 490$; and the latter number which $=$

[1] Psa. cxlvii. 4.   [2] Isa. xl. 26.

7 × 7 × 10 enters into the history of the world and of the chosen people of God previous to the commencement of the prophetic periods. Thus, from the commencement of the building of the Ark and the preaching of Noah 120 years before the Deluge, to the Exodus, is 2 × 490 years, and from the Exodus to the Captivity is 2 × 490 years.[1] Again, from the Deluge to the Covenant with Abraham is 430 years, which equals 5328, or 666 × 8 lunar months, numbers symbolic of the growing evil and idolatry of the human race, followed by a new state of things, or the commencement of the first steps taken for the regeneration of mankind in the call of Abraham. A similar period of 430 years, or 666 × 8 lunar months, intervened between the Covenant and the Exodus, symbolic of the temporal evil undergone by Abraham and his descendants during their sojourning in a strange and hostile country, followed by their redemption.

It may also be remarked that there are various relations between the eclipse cycles and the geometrical properties of bodies, one of which is the following : The diagonal of a square exceeds its side by a number which, omitting fractions, is to the side as 12 to 29, or 29 to 70, or 70 to 169, etc., which form a series—allowing for the omission of fractions :—

$$12 : 12 + 17 : : 29 + 41 : 70 + 99, \text{etc.},$$

and these numbers, expressing the relation of the diagonal and side of a square, also express the relation of the various eclipses to each other. Thus in the first eclipse cycle there are :—

Total eclipses of the Moon . .	12
Partial „ „ „ . .	17
	—
	29
Eclipses of the Sun . . .	41
	—
Total . . .	70

Other remarkable relations might be mentioned, but these are sufficient to indicate the accuracy of the following statement : " All things are ordered by number, weight and measure ; God, as was said by the ancients, works by geometry : the legislation of the material universe is necessarily delivered in the language of mathematics. The stars in their courses are regulated by the properties of conic sections, and the winds depend on arithmetical and geometrical progressions of

[1] The exact date of the Exodus is slightly uncertain, but according to the corrected Scripture Chronology it was about 1570 B.C.

elasticity and pressure."[1] To this may be added that chemical combinations are based on similar mathematical laws, that harmony in form, harmony in sound and harmony in colour are all analogous and also based on similar laws;[2] that the phenomena of light, heat, electricity and sound depend on differentiation of force, and that even the structure and functions of the human body exhibit similar laws, as in the well-known case of the periodicity of vital phenomena, which are in multiples of 7×12 hours.[3] Hence the significance of Christ's remark, "But I say unto you that the very hairs of your head are *numbered.*"

These things show that there is no such element as *chance,* but that everything is the result of exact and pre-ordained *design.* Although we may not always be able to discover the significance of the exact relations which exist between geometry, natural phenomena, astronomy, and the history of man, it is sufficient to know that these relations do exist, and that the movements of the heavenly bodies and the events of human history have been so arranged as to have this exact relation to each other.

This being the case we have an explanation of the statement in Gen. i., that the Sun which marks the years, the seasons, and the days, and the Moon which marks the months, were not only appointed for these purposes, but were to be also for "*signs*" (ver. 14), that is to say, they were to mark the cycles which correspond with the great events of human history. But they are not sufficient in themselves to mark the date of events in human history. It is in combination with the changes which take place in the position of the constellations and signs of the Zodiac, in consequence, in short, of the "precession of the equinoxes," that they enable the astronomer to fix the date of those events exactly; as in the case of the Great Pyramid, the date of which is known by these means to be precisely 2170 B.C.

Thus the Sun and Moon, in connection with the Stars, are "signs," given by God to man; and as God also called the Stars by their names, then the names of the constellations and signs of the Zodiac must have a bearing on the events of human history.

Now the Apostle Peter, speaking of Christ, says, "Those things which God before had shewed by the mouth of all His prophets, that

[1] "Astronomy and General Physics with reference to Natural Theology," *Whewell-Bridgewater Treatises,* 7th edit. pp. 6, 7 ; *Compn. of* 666, p. 259.

[2] *Natural Principles of Harmony and their Analogy in Sound and Colour,* by Professor Hay.

[3] Guinness, *Approaching End of Age,* pp. 263-267.

Christ should suffer, He hath so fulfilled. Whom the heaven must receive until the time of the restitution of all things, which God hath spoken by the mouth of all His holy prophets *since the world began*" (Acts iii. 18, 21). The same thing is stated by Zacharias: "Blessed be the Lord God of Israel, for He hath visited and redeemed His people, and hath raised up an horn of salvation for us in the house of His servant David; as He spake by the mouth of His holy prophets since the world began" (Luke i. 68-70).

Thus it would appear that there was a continuous stream of prophecy, concerning Christ and the restitution of all things, from the beginning of the world; but beyond the promise of the seed of the woman, and the quotation by Jude of the prophecy of Enoch, we have no record of those prophecies. Yet Peter speaks of the ultimate destruction of the world by fire, which is also recognised in the various cosmogonies of the Pagan nations, as if it was a well-known thing. So also the Apostle Paul, speaking of the preaching of the Gospel to the Gentiles, and of the redemption of man, says, "Have they not heard? Yes, verily their sound went into all the earth, and their words unto the ends of the world" (Rom. x. 18.)—that is to say, he quotes Psalm xix. to prove that these things had already been preached throughout the world. That Psalm is as follows: "The heavens declare the glory of God; and the firmament sheweth His handiwork. Day unto day uttereth speech, and night unto night sheweth knowledge. There is *no speech nor language where their voice is not heard*. Their line is gone out through all the earth, *and their words to the end of the world*. In them hath He set a tabernacle for the Sun." Thus it is plainly taught, that the prophecy of a redeemer and of the restitution of all things had ever been preached by the signs in the heavens, or by those Stars which God had called by their names, and that their meaning was as plain as if uttered *in words* and *by voice*, and being seen all over the world there was no speech nor language where that meaning might not be recognised.

We may therefore presume that, in the absence of any written revelation, the prophets of these things, in the earlier ages of the world, pointed to and explained these signs in the heavens as prophetic, by the regular and foreknown changes in their position, of the varying events in the future history of the world. This also seems to be hinted by Josephus, who says that "the sons of Seth who were of good dispositions lived in the land without apostasising and in a happy condition. They were the inventors of that peculiar sort of wisdom which is concerned with the heavenly bodies and their

order. And that their inventions might not be lost before they were
sufficiently known, upon Adam's prediction that the world was to be
destroyed at one time by the force of fire and at another time by the
violence and quantity of water, they made two pillars, the one of
brick and the other of stone; they inscribed their discoveries on
them both, that in case the pillar of brick should be destroyed, the
pillar of stone might remain and exhibit those discoveries to mankind.
Now this remains in the land of Siriad (*i.e.*, Egypt) to this day." [1]

This ancient knowledge of astronomy is further confirmed by the
evidence of modern astronomers. "It is impossible to doubt," says
Cassini, "that astronomy was invented from the beginning of the
world; history, profane as well as sacred, testifies to this truth.
Bailly and others have asserted that astronomy must have been
established when the summer solstice was in the first degree of Virgo,
and that the solar and lunar Zodiacs were of a similar antiquity.
This would have been about 4000 years before the Christian era.
They suppose this science to have originated with some ancient and
highly-civilised people who lived at that time about latitude 40°, but
who were swept away by some sudden destruction, leaving, however,
traces of their knowledge behind them. Origen tells us that it was
asserted in the book of Enoch, that in the time of that Patriarch the
constellations were already divided and named. Volney informs us
that everywhere in antiquity there was a cherished tradition of an
expected conqueror of the Serpent, who was to come as a divine
person born of a woman, and he asserts that this tradition is reflected
in the constellations, as well as in all the heathen mythologies
throughout the world. Dupuis also and other writers of the same
school have collected ancient authorities abundantly proving that in
all the nations the traditions always prevailed that this Divine
person, born of a woman, was to suffer in His conflict with the
Serpent, but was to triumph over it at the last. He also asserts that
this tradition is represented in the constellations." [2]

The latter writer has indeed argued that both Christianity and
Paganism are nothing but astrological superstitions produced by the
imagination of ancient astrologers; but the fallacy of such a

[1] *Antiq.*, bk. i. chap. ii. It is evident that the stone one referred to here by
Josephus is the Great Pyramid, which is also a cosmogonic and prophetic record.
But it was not built in antediluvian but in postdiluvian times; and the mistake
of Josephus is probably due to his confusing Seth with Shem, the two names being
synonymous, both meaning "the appointed one," and Shem, as we shall see, was
the real builder of the Great Pyramid.

[2] *Primeval Man Unveiled* (Gall), pp. 204, 205.

conclusion is evident, when it is considered that there is no relation between the forms of the constellations and the names given to them. There must be a cause for every effect, and no reason can be discovered in Paganism for these names; for while it might be natural for the Pagans to call the planets and every other known star by the names of one or other of their deities, there is nothing in the nature of their religion which can suggest a reason for the arbitrary names given to the constellations and signs of the Zodiac.

But that religion being, as we have seen, founded on perversions of the truth, its founders would be certain, when perverting and incorporating that truth into their system, to make use of these recognised prophetic signs in the heavens to obtain a fictitious credit for their religion. Hence, instead of regarding them as signs by which God had revealed to man the future history of redemption, they associated them with their false gods, and thus hid from mankind their spiritual meaning. The principle of this perversion will be more fully considered when we come to treat of the subsequent development of Paganism.

Firstly, however, it is necessary to consider the history of the overthrow of the primeval form of idolatry as established by Cush and Nimrod.

PART III

OVERTHROW OF THE PRIMITIVE PAGANISM
AND ITS RELATION TO
THE EARLY HISTORY OF BABYLON AND EGYPT

CHAPTER XII

THE DEATH OF THE PAGAN GODS

FROM the various traditions of the conquests of "Ninus," "Osiris," "Sesostris," "Bacchus," "Dionusus," "Deva Nahusha," Hercules and the Arabian, or Adite, conqueror and sanguinary tyrant "Zohak," "the teacher of a monstrous and obscene religion," it appears that Nimrod extended his conquests and religion over the whole civilised world. The accounts limit his conquests by the Indus, beyond which were the so-called "deserts of India," and it is exceedingly improbable that, at that period, emigration had extended farther south, but that the Cushite race subsequently migrated there and formed the first inhabitants of Hindustan. To the eastward, these conquests extended to Bactria; to the north, to Thrace and Scythia, and Herodotus speaks of seeing some of the pillars of Sesostris in the latter country,[1] while the similar pillars of Hercules at the entrance to the Mediterranean Sea seem to show that his conquests extended westward to that point, including therefore those "shores of the Gentiles" colonised by the Japhetic race (Gen. x. 1-5). It would also appear that he established his religion in some at least of these countries, like Mahomet, by force of arms.

It is Egypt, however, which is chiefly connected with the later history of Nimrod. We have seen that he made his father king of that country, and accordingly we find both him and his father mentioned among the first of the god kings who ruled over Egypt in the lists of Manetho.[2] Of these the first, "*Hephæstus*," whose length of reign is given as 724 years, is probably the antediluvian Hephæstus, "Chrysor." The second is "*Helios the Sun*," probably Ammon, or Ham, who in early times was the Sun god of the Egyptians, and of them only. The third is "*Agatho-dæmon*," the name given to the good serpent in contradistinction to "*Kakodæmon*" the evil serpent. This Agatho-dæmon is plainly Nimrod, for he is stated by Manetho to be the son of the second Hermes,[3] *i.e.*, Cush.

---

[1] Herod., lib. ii. cap. cvi.   [2] Manetho's lists, Cory's *Fragments*, p. 92.

[3] Cory's *Fragments*, p. 173.

Then follows *Cronus* or Saturn, *i.e.*, Cush, and then *Osiris* and *Isis*, after which are the repetitions of these gods under the various other appellations by which their human originals were deified.

All tradition tends to prove that the first kings of Egypt were Æthiopian or Cushite. It is true that many of the monuments represent a brown or yellow race, with straight hair, and features very different from the Æthiopian type; but this is just what we might expect, for the first settlers in Egypt were the descendants of Mizraim, and were therefore the people conquered by Osiris or Ægyptus; while at a subsequent period, as we shall see, Egypt was for a considerable time delivered from the Æthiopian yoke "*by men of a different race.*"

Thus there were two races who alternately had the dominion, and the ancient historians, in consequence, distinguish between the kings of Mizraim origin, whom they call "*Mestraoi*," and those of Cushite origin, whom they call "*Egyptian*."

We have now to consider the circumstances which led to the overthrow of the Cushite idolatry in Egypt, and in a greater or less degree throughout the world, which overthrow, although only temporary, obliged its advocates to adopt other methods for propagating their religion, and consequently gave its subsequent development an entirely new aspect.

Ninus, according to Ludovicus Vives, was *torn in pieces*.[1] The same is said to have been the case with *Orpheus*, who is identified with the Egyptian and Babylonian god by Bryant and Hislop, and is called one of the Titans by Lucian.[2] A similar fate is recorded of *Lycurgus*,[3] whom the Phrygians identified with *Bacchus*.[4] In the rites of *Bacchus* a spotted fawn was torn in pieces in commemoration of the death of the god, and the spotted fawn was called *Nebros*, and was the symbol of *Nebrod*, the name of Nimrod in Greece. So also *Osiris* was cut in pieces, and the great feature in the rites of the god was the lamentation for his death at the solemn festival called "The disappearance of Osiris." Julius Firmicus says that "in the solemn celebration of the mysteries, all things in order had to be done, which the Youth either did or suffered at his death;"[5] therefore the initiates were required to cut and wound their bodies. This is what the priests of *Baal* did when they called on their god,[6] and the same

[1] *Commentary on Augustine*, lib. vi. cap. ix., note, p. 139; Hislop, p. 56, note.
[2] Bryant, vol. ii. pp. 419-423; Hislop, pp. 46, 55; Appollodorus, *Bibliotheca*, lib. i. cap. iii. and vii., p. 17; also Lemprière, *Titanes*, and Hislop, p. 124, note.
[3] Hyginus, Fab. 132, p. 109.   [4] Strabo, lib. x. cap. iii. p. 17.
[5] Julius Firmicus, p. 18; Hislop, p. 152.   [6] 1 Kings xviii. 28.

thing is still done by the devotees of Paganism in various parts of the world at the present day.[1] Herodotus speaks of the Carians doing the same.[2] The Egyptians who died were, in a manner, identified with Osiris, and were called by his name, and therefore their mourners also cut themselves. Hence the command to the Israelites: " Ye shall make no cuttings in your flesh for the dead."[3] There is thus a singular unanimity in the traditions with regard to the way in which the god met his death.

Orpheus, whose name, according to Hislop, is a synonym for *Bel*,[4] is said by Diodorus Siculus to have introduced the rites of Paganism into Greece,[5] and, like Bacchus and Osiris, to have been torn to pieces.[6] But he is also said to have perished by *lightning*.[7] *Æsculapius* is also said to have been killed by lightning for *raising the dead*,[8] that is to say, for invoking the demons who personated the dead. The same death by lightning is said to have been the fate of *Zoroaster*,[9] and some other forms of the god. "*Phæthon*," the child of the Sun, who can also be identified with Nimrod,[10] was likewise struck by lightning, and cast from heaven to earth when, it was said, he was on the point of setting the earth on fire,[11] the significance of which will appear later on. *Centaurus*, another form of the god,[12] was likewise struck by lightning for pride and presumption,[13] and *Orion*, the giant and mighty hunter, who boasted that no animal could compete with him, and who has also been identified with Nimrod, is said to have been killed by a scorpion for similar pride and presumption.[14] Death by lightning is probably a metaphorical form of expressing the judgment of heaven, but the death of Bacchus, Osiris, and other manifestations of the god point to a special form of that death.

[1] As witnessed by the author among the Malays.
[2] Herod., ii. 61. [3] Levit. xix. 20.
[4] Mr Hislop says that *Bel* signifies "to mix" or "confound," and that "*Orv*" in the Hebrew, which becomes "*Orph*" in Chaldee (hellenised into *Orpheus*), has a similar meaning ; Hislop, p. 124, note.
[5] *Bibliotheca*, lib. i. p. 9.
[6] Ludovicus Vives, *Commentary on Augustine*, lib. vi. cap. ix., note, p. 239 ; Hislop, p. 56, note.
[7] Pausanias, *Bœotica*, cap. xxx. p. 768 ; Hislop, p. 234, note.
[8] Ovid, *Metam.*, lib. xv. ll. 736-745 ; *Æneid*, lib. vii. ll. 759-773.
[9] Suidas, vol. i. pp. 1133, 1134 ; Hislop, p. 234, note.
[10] Hislop, p. 317. [11] *Ibid.*
[12] *Scholiast in Lycophron*, v. p. 1200 ; Bryant, vol. iii. p. 315, and Hislop, pp. 42 and 297.
[13] Dymock, *sub voce* "Ixion" ; Hislop, p. 297.
[14] Ovid, *Fasti*, lib. v. ll. 540-544 ; Hislop, p. 57, note.

R

Now "*Tammuz*," the name under which the god was more especially known and lamented in Syria and Palestine, suffered a *judicial* death. Thus Maimonides, deeply read in the learning of the Chaldees, writes: "When the false prophet, named Thammuz, preached to a certain king that he should worship the seven stars and the twelve signs of the Zodiac, that king ordered him to be put to a terrible death. On the night of his death all the images from the ends of the earth assembled in the temple of Babylon to the great golden image of the Sun which was suspended between heaven and earth. That image prostrated itself in the the midst of the temple, and so did all the images around it, while it related to them all that had happened to Thammuz. The images wept and lamented all the night long, and then in the morning they flew away each to his own temple again to the ends of the earth; and hence arose the custom every year on the first day of the month of Thammuz to mourn and weep for Thammuz."[1]

Now as Tammuz is Osiris, the conqueror of Egypt, the question is, who put him to death? This is explained by the Egyptian account of the death of Osiris, which is as follows: Typhon, the great enemy of their god, overcame him, "*not by force or open war*, but, having entered into a conspiracy with seventy-two of the leading men of Egypt, he got him into his power and put him to death, and then cut his body into pieces and sent the different parts to so many different cities throughout the country."[2] Egypt was divided into Nomes, each with a ruler or judge over it, and these judges in later times amounted to seventy-two. Of these thirty were the civil judges who had power over life and death, and decided the punishment of those who had been guilty of crime; while a further tribunal of forty-two decided whether those who had been found guilty should have burial or not.[3] The story thus implies that Osiris was condemned and judicially executed by the chief men in Egypt at that time. The cutting up the dead body and sending it to different cities was an ancient method of expressing both warning and command, as in the case of Saul when he cut up a yoke of oxen and sent the pieces to the twelve tribes of Israel with the message, "Whosoever goeth not forth with Saul and Samuel so shall it be done to his oxen."[4] This, it is plain,

[1] More, *Nevochim*, p. 426 ; Hislop, p. 62. The images, that is, the demon gods, are here represented as lamenting the death of Tammuz, implying that it was regarded as a most severe blow to their worship.

[2] Wilkinson's *Egyptians*, vol. iv. pp. 330-332.

[3] Diodorus, lib. i. pp. 48-58 ; Hislop, p. 64, note.

[4] 1 Sam. xi. 7.

is the origin of the characteristic feature in the funeral rites of the god in which a spotted fawn was torn to pieces.

Typho, or Typhon, the enemy of Osiris who accomplished his overthrow, was the name of the evil principle among the Egyptians, and was a word meaning pride or arrogance. Nevertheless, he is said to be the *brother* of Osiris,[1] and the term was applied to him therefore as a term of reproach by the incensed idolaters. Typhon was, as we have seen, one of the principal Titans, or sons of Noah, and identical with Titan or Shem. Typhon is said to be the brother of Osiris, and Titan is said to be brother of Saturn or Cush, who was the father of Osiris; but the ancients called all the parallel branches of a family "brethren," irrespective of their particular generation.

Just as Typhon overcame Osiris, so Titan is represented as making war against Saturn, *i.e.*, Thoth, or Cush, and we have seen that Thoth was made king over Egypt by his son, the second Cronus, *i.e.*, Osiris or Nimrod. In perfect accordance with this we are told, in the story of Typhon and Osiris, that the latter left Hermes, *i.e.*, Thoth, in charge of the kingdom of Egypt during his absence, and that Typhon, taking advantage of the absence of Osiris, raised sedition and inflamed the minds of the people against him, thus overcoming the influence of Hermes.[2] It is thus clear that the war of Titan against Saturn and that of Typhon against Osiris refer to the same event, and that Typhon is simply a term of reproach given to Titan, or Shem. This is confirmed by the name by which Typhon was commonly called, viz., *Set* or *Seth*,[3] which is synonymous with *Shem*, both meaning "The appointed one,"[4] and Shem is spoken of as *Sheth* in Numb. xxiv. 17. In short, exactly the same story is told of Set: "Set the brother of Osiris, rebelled against him and cut his body in pieces."[5] Birch says the name of the conspirator against Osiris was "Semu,"[6] the root of which is the same as Shem, or "Sem," as it is in Greek; and Plutarch also gives to Typhon the titles of "Seth" and "Smy," and the latter in Greek would be Smu, which is evidently the same as Semu.[7]

The Saite or Sethroïte Zone of Egypt, called so after Set, or

[1] Lemprière, *Osiris—Typhon.*   [2] *Ibid.*
[3] Epiphanius, *Adv. Hæres*, lib. iii.; Hislop, p. 65.
[4] Hislop, p. 65, note.   [5] Rawlinson's *Egypt and Babylon.*
[6] *Wilkinson*, by Birch, vol. iii. p. 138, note.
[7] *Ibid.* Wilkinson rejects all the traditions about Osiris and Typhon which represent them as human beings, but apparently he has no other reason for doing so except that they do not accord with his idealised view of Egyptian idolatry. *See* App. A.

Seth,[1] was, as we shall see, especially connected with him, and hence "Avaris" in that zone is said by Josephus to have been called in ancient theology a *Typhonian* City.[2] Typhon, which was also the name given to the ocean which destroyed the antediluvians, was represented by a hippopotamus among the Egyptians, and we consequently find Manetho saying that Menes, *i.e.*, Thoth, whose kingdom was, of course, overthrown at the death of Osiris, perished by a wound from a Hippopotamus.[3]

Set was worshipped as a god and was long held in the highest honour in Egypt, which would be only natural if he delivered the Mizraim Egyptians from the Cushite yoke. Bunsen says that he was regarded as one of the most powerful of their gods until the time of Rameses II., after which he was regarded as the foe of Osiris and all the gods of Egypt,[4] and was therefore given the name of Typhon, the principle of evil, and everything was done to blacken his memory The period of Rameses II. was that in which a new element of Cushite influence was received from the Cushites of India.[5]

It may be remarked that although Set, or Sutech as he is said to have been sometimes called, was worshipped as a god, it does not follow that in *all cases* of his reputed worship it was Shem himself who was so worshipped. There is no doubt that he was worshipped by the idolatrous Egyptians after idolatry had been restored, just as Cush and Nimrod were worshipped. But when we are told in the "Sallier Papyrus" that Apepi, the Pharaoh under whom Joseph was ruler, changed his religion and, rejecting the Egyptian gods, chose Set only as his god, we must conclude that it was *the God of Set* whom he chose, by whose servant Joseph he had been warned of the coming famine, and not only been enabled to provide against it, but through it had acquired unprecedented riches and power. But the idolatrous priesthood who recorded the fact in after ages, failing to recognise the distinction, would naturally represent the opponent of their gods and worshipper of the god of Set, as the worshipper of the god Set or Typhon, the great enemy of their own gods.

It would have been quite impossible for Shem to have overthrown the powerful Cushite race in the zenith of its power, by force of arms. But it is clear that he might have done so in the manner described, viz., by convincing the Egyptians of the deadly character

---

[1] *See* Manetho's fifteenth dynasty, from Africanus ; Cory, p. 114.
[2] Josephus, *Contra Apion;* Cory's *Fragments*, p. 177.
[3] Cory, p. 94.   [4] Bunsen's *Egypt*, vol. i. p. 456.
[5] *See* dynasties of Manetho by Syncellus ; Cory, p. 142.

of the idolatry advocated by Cush and Nimrod, and thus destroying their influence. He outlived all the Patriarchs of the antediluvian world, and with the weight and authority of centuries, and as the eye-witness of the terrible judgment that fell, as in a moment, upon the world which had despised the warnings of Noah, he could refer with startling force to the awful cataclysm that destroyed every living thing on the earth, and dwell on the cries and agonies of a perishing world when his own friends, relatives and acquaint-ances, with all "the kings of the earth, the great men, the rich men, and every bondman and every freedman," all who had hitherto scoffed and derided, were swept away by the flood of waters. He could solemnly and earnestly point to the crimes on account of which that judgment was sent, to the rejection of God, to the Nephilim intercourse and idolatry, and to the violence which, following in their train, covered the earth. He could refer to the prophecy of Enoch, which foretold that just as God had once destroyed the world by water, so yet again, in the future, he would destroy it *by fire;* while to prove that the god of whom he spoke was indeed the living God who could not be mocked or despised by man with impunity, he could refer to the recent confusion of tongues at Babel, as an earnest and warning of his power. Finally, he could show that the idolatry, the Nephilim intercourse and worship, and the unbridled lust and cruelty which accompanied it, and which were advocated by Cush and Nimrod, were simply a repetition of the crimes on account of which the old world had been destroyed. "Choose you therefore," he may have said, "whom ye will follow. If you will follow him under whose tyranny and cruelty you groan, and whose wickedness calls for judgment, and who is himself of this very Nephilim race which has been the cause of such untold evil, then be assured that the God of Heaven, who once destroyed the human race by water, will again take vengeance on such wickedness *in flaming fire.*"

That Shem did make use of these warnings and that the people whom he addressed fully believed that had the idolaters succeeded in firmly establishing the worship of the dæmon gods throughout the world, it would have been destroyed a second time by fire, is implied by the story of Phæthon, who was killed when on the point of *setting the world on fire.*

It is quite conceivable that such an appeal to the conscience, the fears and interests of his hearers might well have roused them to energetic action, and that on the return of Osiris, they seized him and condemned him to death. Yet it must be regarded as a wonderful triumph of truth, a victory gained by moral force over the mightiest king of the world. Doubtless a triumph gained by means, seemingly so feeble, as compared with the power against which they were arrayed, gave rise to the tradition that the god was slain, not by human hands, but by lightning, or the judgment of heaven, or power of God. This indeed was the case, inasmuch as the victory was gained by the power of truth, which is of God, and the power and efficacy of which depends on the spirit of God.

This overthrow of the god by the power of truth is mystically taught in the story of the death of Adonis or Tammuz. He was said to have been slain by the *tusk* of a *boar*.[1] A tusk in Scripture, and in ancient times, was called a horn,[2] and a horn was the universal symbol of *power*. Just, therefore, as a horn on the head was the symbol of physical and worldly power, so a horn in the mouth was a symbol of spiritual or moral power, the power of the mouth, or of words and arguments. Hence in the legends of Horus, Set is represented as having transformed himself into a *boar* in order to destroy the eye of Horus.[3] The *pig* was therefore an emblem of evil, and pigs were sacrificed in consequence to the Moon (Meni or Menes) and to Bacchus,[4] *i.e.*, to Thoth and Osiris. So also *boars* were sacrificed to the goddess who is represented as overcoming Typhon, *i.e.*, Set, and Diana is generally shown with a boar's head as an accompaniment, and as a token of her victory.[5] So also the continental Saxons used to offer a *boar* in sacrifice to the Sun, which with them was the goddess, in order to propitiate her.[6] In India likewise *a boar's* face is said to have gained such power through his devotion that he oppressed the devotees of the gods, who had to hide themselves.[7]

The same idea of moral power seems to be expressed in some of the characters given to Hercules. Hercules in later times became a synonym for *strength* or *power*, and the name was in consequence applied to others than Nimrod, and it would be quite in accordance with the ideas of the ancients that it should be applied to one who had overcome the great god of Paganism. This appears to have been the case in Egypt, where one of the names of Hercules was *Sem*,[8]

---

[1] Lemprière, *Adonis.*
[2] Ezek. xxvii. 15 ; Pausanias, *Eliaca*, lib. v. chap. xii. ; Hislop, p. 65, note.
[3] *Wilkinson*, by Birch, vol. iii. p. 298, note by Birch.
[4] *Ibid.*, p. 297.   [5] Lemprière, *Diana ;* Hislop, p. 100.
[6] Mallet, vol. i. p. 132 ; Hislop, p. 100.   [7] Moor's *Pantheon*, p. 19.
[8] Wilkinson's *Egyptians*, vol. v. p. 17 ; Hislop, p. 66, note.

i.e., Shem. He was also called *Chon,* and we find that Chon was also called *Sem.*[1] The meaning of "*Chon*" is "The Lamenter," which might well have applied to Shem, who witnessed this renewed apostasy of the human race, and who alone most fully recognised all that it threatened, while in all probability he lived to witness its partial revival, in spite of its temporary overthrow in Egypt. Just as Lot is said to have "vexed his righteous soul" at the iniquity of Sodom, so may the righteous Shem have lamented the growing apostasy of his kinsfolk and descendants.

The name "Chon," "The Lamenter," also tends to identify Sem, or Shem, the Egyptian Hercules, with *Hercules Ogmius,* "*Ogmius*" also meaning "The Lamenter." The latter is represented followed by multitudes with chains of gold and amber proceeding from his mouth to their ears, and he subsequently became known as the God of Eloquence.[2] A character so entirely opposed as this is to that of the Babylonian and Grecian Hercules could only apply to one whose power, like that of Shem, was moral, and was probably applied to Shem by those who worshipped Set, or the god of Set.

As a further proof that Typhon was Titan, or Shem, it is related by Plutarch that when Typhon was subsequently conquered, he fled away and begat Hierosolymus and Judæus,[3] that is, Hierosalem, or Jerusalem, and Judea. This is but the mystical way of saying that he was the founder of Jerusalem and the ancestor of the Jews. This tends to identify Shem with Melchisedek, whose name means "righteous king," and who was king of Salem or Jerusalem. As "priest of the Most High God"[4] he was evidently the origin of the name Jerusalem, or Hierosalem, "*Hieros,*" or "*Hiereus,*" meaning "priest."

Sha, an emblem of Seth.

Set or Typhon was represented in Egypt by a somewhat nondescript figure called "*Sha*" with long truncated ears and a tufted tail, bearing a strong resemblance to an ass (*vide* woodcut).[5] The same figure in a sitting position was the usual hieroglyphic for Set, as in the woodcut below.[6] The hieroglyphics, No. 1, read "*Nubti Set,*" and No. 2, "*Nubti Lord*

[1] Hislop, p. 66, and Lemprière, *Ogmius.*

[2] Sir W. Betham's *Gael and Cimbri,* pp. 90-93.

[3] Plutarch, *De Iside,* S. 31 ; Cumberland's *Sanchoniathon,* p. 108.

[4] Heb. vii. 1. It was a common tradition among the Jews that Melchisedek was Shem. *See* Smith, *Dict. of Bible,* "Melchisedek."

[5] *Wilkinson,* by Birch, woodcut, vol. iii. p. 311.

[6] Wilkinson's *Egyptians,* vol. vi., plate xxxviii.

of the Earth." It will also be seen that the figure of the god himself has a head similar to that of the Sha, and this is the way he is represented on other monuments.[1]

In the hieroglyphics, No. 4, a human figure in a sitting position with the head of the Sha is substituted for the Sha itself, and reads

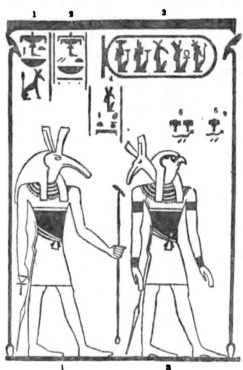

1   NUBTI SET, SON OF NUT.

"*Set son of Nut.*" A similar figure occurs in the cartouche No. 3, which reads, "*Osiris, Aroeris, Set, Isis, Nepthys.*" The figure of the other god with the double head is a combination of Hat Has, or Horus and Set. The title "*Nubti*" given to Set means "The Golden," and it is quite clear that at the time these monuments were erected, which was at least as late as the reign of Thothmes III., Set was worshipped as a god and the term Typhon had not been applied to him.

In later times, when a feeling of hatred had been fostered against him by the idolatrous priesthood, and he was identified with Typhon, the ass was regarded as an emblem of the evil deity,[2] probably on account of its resemblance to the Sha, the emblem of Set. So great was the detestation of the ass on this account, that the Coptites were in the habit of throwing one down a precipice as a mark of their hatred, while the inhabitants of Abydus, Busiris and Lycopolis scrupled to make use of trumpets because their sound was supposed to resemble the braying of an ass.[3]

The ass was also considered an appropriate emblem of Seth because it was usually of a red colour, and the complexion of Seth, unlike that

[1] Wilkinson's *Egyptians*, vol. vi., plate xxxix., where Set is shown instructing Thothmes III.

[2] *Wilkinson*, by Birch, vol. iii. p. 143.   [3] *Ibid.*, p. 300.

of the black Cushite Egyptians, was said to be red or ruddy,[1] which shows that he was "of a different race." For the same reason men of a red complexion, from their supposed resemblance to Typhon, were formerly sacrificed to Osiris, and on a similar principle they offered red oxen in their sacrifices.[2] It is also worthy of note that the Pagan opponents of Christianity in Egypt represented Christ as a man with the head of an ass, in order, no doubt, to identify him with Typhon.

Set or Typhon was also represented by a hideous deformed figure under the name of the god "*Bes*," who is shown with his mouth open, as if shouting or declaiming,[3] with the object, no doubt, of bringing into contempt that "power of the mouth" by which Set overthrew Osiris.

In Greek mythology, Typhon, who is also called *Typhœus*, was represented as a giant with a hundred heads like a dragon; the force of truth, or the power of his words by which he overcame the idolatry instituted by Osiris, was likened to "flames of fire darting from his mouth," and his words to "horrid yells like the dissonant shrieks of different animals."[4] "There is no new thing under the sun," and such misrepresentation was equally the weapon used by the idolatrous Jews against their own prophets;[5] by the same Pagans against the early Christians, and by their successors in more modern times against those who exposed their errors and superstitions. In short, just as Christ was accused of being possessed by a devil, and as being energised by the Prince of the Demons, so he who overthrew the head of the dæmons worshippers was represented as Typhon, the principle of evil.[6]

The story of Typhœus goes on to relate that the gods were so frightened that they fled away and assumed the shapes of various animals for concealment.[7] This refers to the manner in which idolatry was restored, when the dead king and his father were subsequently deified under various names, representing different attributes. But this had to be done secretly, by the use of words with double meanings and mystic symbols, and secret rites like "The

---

[1] *Wilkinson*, by Birch, pp. 143, 300.   [2] *Ibid.*, pp. 30, 143.

[3] *Ibid.*, pp. 148, 149, woodcuts.

[4] Lemprière, *Typhon* and *Typhœus*.   [5] Mat. v 11, 12.

[6] It is suggested by some that Set is the origin of the Hebrew "Satan," "an adversary." This would be possible, considering how completely Set became the name for the principle of evil throughout Egypt, and if it could be shown that the Israelites adopted the term from the Egyptians. But this is most unlikely, seeing that Set was honoured in Egypt until the time of the Rameses, their persecutors, and in whose time the Exodus took place.

Lemprière, *Typhœus*.

Mysteries," in order to avoid the exposure which would have followed, had this idolatry been openly taught while the memory of its exposure remained in men's minds. Now one of the principal ways by which the worship of the dead king was introduced was by representing him under the forms of different animals as symbolic of him. This was especially the case in Egypt, and accordingly we find, in another story, that when the gods fled and assumed the shapes of these animals, they went *to Egypt.*[1] Their assumption of this disguise we are told was by the advice of "Pan";[2] and the story would thus imply that it was *Cush* who devised this method for the secret resuscitation of idolatry.

Although Shem was the moral power by which idolatry was overthrown in Egypt, yet his advice was carried out, not only by the Egyptians, but by others also. For, in the war of Titan against Saturn, it is said that the former was assisted by *his brother Titans,* the name given to the descendants of Noah generally, from which we may conclude that the effect of the overthrow was by no means confined to Egypt. Hence, just as Shem was represented as *the giant* Typhœus with a hundred heads, so it would be natural that his brother Titans should be similarly represented. Accordingly we find an exact parallel of the conflict of Typhœus against the gods, in the war of "*the giants*" against the gods. These giants are represented as having fifty heads and a hundred arms, and, like Titan and Typhœus, they are described as of *Titan race* and *sons of Cœlus and Terra.* Just also as in the war of Typhœus against the gods, so in the war of the giants against the gods, the latter, terrified by the attack, fled to Egypt and assumed the shape of various animals, while, in both cases, Jupiter is represented as finally gaining the victory; just as in the war of Typhon against Osiris, Horus finally defeats Typhon.[3] This victory of the gods is merely the mystical way of saying that idolatry was finally triumphant.

Some have confounded another war, viz., the war of the Titans, with that of the giants, who were also Titans; but the war of the Titans was *against Cœlus* (*i.e.,* Ouranos or Heaven), who was Noah as the representative of Heaven, or of the True God; and Saturn, the father of the gods, was the ringleader of the Titans in this war;[4]

[1] Lemprière, *Gigantes.*   [2] *Ibid.—Pan.*
[3] Lemprière, compare *Gigantes, Typhœus, Typhon.*
[4] Lemprière, *Titanes.* The war of the Titans headed by *Saturn* or Cush against *Cœlus* is clearly the same as the war of *Cronus* against *Ouranos* mentioned by Sanchoniathon (*ante* p. 204-206), and evidently refers to the rebellion against *Heaven* at the building of Babel.

but the war of the giants was *against the heathen gods* and, therefore, against Saturn himself. The first was a war of the Titans against Cœlus or Noah, the second was a war of the Titans against the heathen gods, for the giants were Titans who, through the influence of Shem, now opposed the idolatry of the Cushite race.

One other feature in the description of the giants requires notice. They are represented as of terrible aspect, their hair hanging loose about their shoulders and their beards suffered to grow untouched. The Egyptians shaved every part of their bodies except their heads, and considered the appearance of the smallest hair a disfigurement, but the Patriarchs of the Semitic race and also many of the Japhetic race are represented with flowing hair and beards.

The giants are represented as piling Mount Pelion on Ossa in order to reach Heaven. This seems to imply that the *Titan* war, or the war against Cœlus or Heaven, in which Cush sought to build a tower " whose top should reach unto Heaven," has been mixed up with the war of the *giants*. It is very possible that the enterprise at Babel, which was frustrated by the God of Heaven, was advisedly associated with the war against the heathen gods, in order to throw the discredit attached to the former on the latter.

The overthrow of the chief and leader of the primitive idolatry is also a prominent feature in the traditions of other nations.

It seems to be referred to in the Chaldean legend of the war of the *seven* wicked gods against *the Moon* [1] (*i.e.*, against Meni or Cush), and which corresponds with the war of Titan against Saturn when Titan was assisted by his brother Titans, or the other descendants of Noah who in the various traditions are represented as *seven* in number.

In the Scandinavian traditions *Balder* was slain through the treachery of the god *Loki*, who, like Typhon, is the spirit of evil, while it is said that the *empire of Heaven* (*i.e.*, the empire of the Pagan gods) depended on the life of Balder. His father, Odin or Woden (*i.e.*, Cush), is said to have learned the terrible secret (*i.e.*, the means of establishing relations with the daimonia) from the book of destiny.[2]

In India it is said that a *giant* named *Durga* " dethroned Indra and the other gods, and abolished sacrifice. The Brahmans gave up reading the Vedas; fire lost its energy, and the terrified stars disappeared." [3] This is an exact parallel to the defeat of the gods in

---

[1] Lenormant, *Chaldean Magic*, chap. xiii. App. II. pp. 204-207.
[2] *Scandinavia*, vol. i. pp. 93, 94.
[3] Wilkins, *Hindu Mythol.*, pp. 247, 249.

Grecian mythology by the *giant* Typhœus or Typhon, which, in other words, was the overthrow of the worship of fire, and of the stars, and the practice of human sacrifices. The remainder of the story is in similar accordance; for just as Minerva is represented as slaying the giant *Pallas* in the war of the giants against the gods,[1] so the goddess "Parvati" slays the giant Durga and "the gods regained their former splendour."[2] Another account says that "*Mahesha*, king of the giants," overcame the gods in war and they had to wander about as beggars, but Vishnu formed a woman called "*Maha Maya*" (which is another name of Parvati), who slew Mahesha.[3] A third account says that Heaven was invaded by *men* who overcame the gods, and the latter were forced to wander about, and "sacrifices, ascetic practices and ordinances ceased." "*Ganesa*," son of *Siva* (who, we have seen, was identical with Osiris), was created by Parvati, and he advised the gods to allure men back to earth again by means of wives, children, possessions and wealth, and by these means restored the gods.[4] So also Isis is said to have restored the gods by means of her son Horus, the son of Osiris.

It will be observed in all these traditions, written long afterwards when the worship of the Pagan gods was firmly established, that the overthrow of the great king and his father, who were the originals of those gods, is represented as the conquest of *the gods*, although at the time of the overthrow their worship had not been instituted. Nevertheless, the death of Nimrod and flight of Cush was the overthrow of the worship of the daimonia instituted by them, and those daimonia were eventually identified with the gods of which Cush and Nimrod were the human originals.

The remarkable way in which all these traditions, preserved by different nations far removed from each other and related in different forms of allegory, mutually confirm and corroborate each other, is an incontestable proof of the reality of the event to which they refer. It is an evidence also that the myths of the ancients are not mere fables, for the invention of which there would have been no conceivable reason, but that they refer to real events related in the allegorical language of mythology.

All these traditions of the overthrow of the gods evidently refer to one and the same event, viz., the overthrow of Osiris or Nimrod, and his father Thoth or Cush, and of the idolatry established by them in Egypt, through the influence of Set or Shem, who was afterwards known as Typhon and Titan.

[1] Smith's Clas. Dict. *Athena.*   [2] Wilkins, *Hindu Mythol.*, pp. 247, 249.
[3] *Ibid.*, pp. 249, 250.   [4] *Ibid.*, pp. 272, 273.

But Set was *the first Shepherd king*, called *Saite*, or *Saites*, by the Greeks, and in an inscription on a tablet of red granite made by an officer of State in the reign of Rameses II., which was found among the ruins of Tanis by Mariette Bey, this Shepherd king is mentioned as having built the City of Avaris and founded there the temple of Set. In this inscription he is entitled "*King of Upper and Lower Egypt*," "*Set a a peh peh*" ("Set the powerful"), "*Son of the Sun*," "*Nubti Set*," and is done homage to as "*Set a a peh peh Son of Nut.*"[1]

The name of this Shepherd king is also found together with that of King Apepi, both partially erased on one of the Shepherd sculptures, and it reads like the above—"*Nubti Set a a peh peh*," or "*Set a a pehuti*," *i.e.*, "Nubti Set the powerful."[2]

Now these titles, "Nubti Set, son of Nut," are the exact titles given to *the god* Set, afterwards known as *Typhon;* while the City of Avaris, built by the Shepherd king Set, was called a *Typhonian* city, and the zone in which it was built to the east of the Bubastis Channel of the Nile was called the Sethroite zone.[3] There seems to be little doubt therefore that the Shepherd king Set was the human original of the god Set or Seth, and therefore the same as Typhon, or Shem, the enemy of Osiris or Nimrod.

Moreover, the story of the overthrow of the Cushite dominton and idolatry by the Shepherd kings exactly corresponds with the overthrow of Osiris by Set or Typhon, and with the story of the judicial execution of Tammuz as told by Mainonides.

"There was a king of ours," writes Manetho, "whose name was *Timaus.*" "This name," says M. Lenormant, "is an evident corruption of the Greek Copyists;"[4] and Bishop Cumberland has suggested, with much likelihood, that Timaus is a corruption of *Tammuz,*[5] in which case the king would be Osiris or Nimrod, who was overthrown through the influence of Set or Typhon.

Manetho proceeds, "Under him it came to pass, I know not how, that God was averse to us, and there came in a surprising manner men of ignoble birth out of the *eastern parts*, and had boldness enough to make an expedition into our country, and *with ease subdued it by*

[1] Lenormant, *Anc. Hist. of East*, vol. i. bk. iii. chap. ii. sect. iii. p. 221; Petrie, *Hist. of Egypt*, vol. i. p. 244; *Records of the Past*, vol. iv. pp. 33-36.
[2] Brugsch, *Hist. of Egypt*, vol. i. p. 238.
[3] Josephus, *Contr. Apion;* Cory, p. 177; and Manetho's dynasties, fifteenth dynasty, from Africanus.
[4] *Anc. Hist. of East*, vol. i. p. 219.
[5] Cumberland, *Hist. Sanchoniathon*, pp. 359, 360.

force, yet without our hazarding a battle with them." In this statement there is an evident anomaly. The country was subdued by "force," and yet apparently without the exercise of force! Nevertheless, it very exactly accords with the description of the overthrow of Osiris by Typhon, who overcame him, *"not by force or open war,"* [1] but through the moral influence exercised by him on the Egyptian people, and their consequent united judicial action. The account proceeds, "So when they had gotten *those who governed us* (*i.e.*, Tammuz, or Nimrod, and his father) *under their power*, they afterwards burned down our cities and *demolished the temples of the gods*, and *used all the inhabitants in a most barbarous manner*, nay, some they slew and *led their children and wives into slavery*. The whole nation was called Hyksos, that is, Shepherd kings." [2]

It might be expected that the idolatrous priesthood would exaggerate the power which overthrew their religion and misrepresent its subsequent action. The point to be observed, however, is that they *were Shepherds who came from the East*. Some have supposed that they were Philistines, and others have sought to identify them with the Hittites, because both Africanus and the Armenian call them "Phœnician kings"; but neither of these nations were shepherds, but dwellers in cities and followers of the same idolatry as the Cushites, and therefore the last people who would have been likely to oppose and overthrow it. On the other hand, those who were especially *shepherds*, with large flocks and herds *wandering from place to place*, were the Patriarchs of the Semitic race, who were particularly associated with Phœnicia, or Palestine, and who exactly answer the description of the Shepherds in the Armenian record of Manetho's seventeenth dynasty, viz., "*Wandering Phœnician kings*." [3]

The account goes on to say that the Shepherd king "chiefly aimed at securing the Eastern frontier, for he regarded with suspicion the increasing power of the Assyrians, who, he foresaw, would one day undertake an invasion of the kingdom. And, observing in the Saite zone, upon the east of the Bubasite channel, a city—called Avaris—and finding it admirably adapted to his purpose, he rebuilt it, and strongly fortified it with walls, and garrisoned it with a force of 250,000 men, completely armed." This was just what Set, who had

---

[1] *Ante*, p. 258.

[2] Manetho, from Josephus, *Contr. Apion*, lib. i. chaps. xiv. xv. ; Cory, *Fragments*, pp. 170, 175.

[3] *See* Manetho's dynasties ; Cory, p. 115.

overthrown the Cushite idolatry and put to death the king of the Babylonian Empire, might expect, and Avaris, which seems at first to have been more a fortified camp than a city, was situated exactly opposite the Isthmus of Suez, by which an army from Assyria would have to enter Egypt.

In after ages, when idolatry had been re-established and the Shepherd king, Set, as the overthrower of that idolatry and the enemy of the Egyptian gods, was identified with *Typhon*, the principle of evil, the priesthood called the city built by him a *Typhonian* city. This in itself is a clear proof that the Shepherd king Set was the human original of Set or Typhon. The hatred also of the idolaters to the memory of the Shepherds is implied by the statement in Genesis xlvi. 34, that "every shepherd is an abomination (*i.e.*, an object of religious hatred) to the Egyptians"; showing that the Shepherd Set, who overthrew Tammuz or Nimrod, and the idolatry established by him, was regarded with precisely the same religious hatred as was Set, the enemy and overthrower of Osiris.

The exact correspondence and mutual corroboration of these various stories make it clear therefore that the Shepherd king Set was the hated Set or Typhon who overthrew Osiris or Nimrod; that the overthrow of idolatry and of King Timaus or Tammuz by the Shepherd king Set, and the overthrow of Osiris by Typhon are one and the same event, and that Set, or Saites, was Seth, the synonym of Shem or Sem.

Manetho says that the Shepherds were finally prevailed upon to leave Egypt, which they did without molestation, and went to Judea, where they built the city of Jerusalem, and "that this people, who are here called *Shepherds*, in their sacred book are also styled *captives*."[1] It is clear that he here refers to the Israelites, whose history he associates and mixes up with that of the Shepherds. The Israelites were not only descendants of Shem, and would be regarded by the Egyptians as worshippers of the God of Shem, but they also were *Shepherds*. "Thy servants are Shepherds" they said to Pharaoh on their arrival in Egypt (Gen. xlvii. 3). This association by Manetho of the Shepherd kings with the Israelites is a further proof of the Semitic character of the former, and of the identity of their first king with Set or Typhon, who is also stated to have been "*the Father of the Jews and builder of Jerusalem*."[2] In short, Josephus, the Jewish historian, calls the Shepherds "*our ancestors*."[3]

[1] Josephus, *Contr. Apion*, lib. i. chap. xiv.; Cory, p. 173. [2] See *ante*, p. 263.
[3] Josephus, *Contr. Apion*, lib. i. chap. xvi.; Cory, p. 138.

"The study of the monuments," says M. Lenormant, speaking of the Shepherd kings, " proves the reality of the frightful devastation consequent on the invasion. With one single exception, all *the temples* built prior to that event have disappeared, and nothing can be found of them but scattered ruins, bearing traces of a violent destruction."[1] This was what might be expected from the servant of a God who afterwards commanded His people to " destroy the altars and break down the images, and cut down the groves, and burn the graven images with fire, and quite pluck down all the high places " of the heathen, "lest they should become a curse" to them.[2]

M. Lenormant continues, " Very soon after the first subjugation of the whole land by invaders, the native kingdom of the Thebaid was re-constituted and afforded refuge to all the patriots who had at first fled to *Æthiopia*."[3] We have seen, however, that those whom he calls " *the patriots*" were the *real invaders*, and those whom he calls the " *invaders* " were the *real patriots* of the race of Mizraim, who, through the influence of the Shepherd king, Set, threw off the yoke of the Cushites and the idolatry imposed by them. It would thus appear that it was the Cushite invaders who fled to Æthiopia, the natural refuge of their race and the place from which they had come. For Manetho, while he makes Menes the first king of a Memphite dynasty, and says that his son Athothes built the palace at Memphis, yet calls him " Menes, the Thinite," from This, or Abydos in the Thebaid, and similarly Eratosthenes calls him " Menes, *the Thebanite*," both Abydos and Thebes being in Upper Egypt on the borders of Æthiopia, and in all probability were originally part of African Æthiopia, or " Cusha dwipa without."

M. Lenormant adds, " We have finally, of the age of the Shepherds, only the remains of sculptures, but not one single architectural work ; the principal fragments, all in the Museum at Cairo, are first, a group in granite of most perfect execution, representing two personages in Egyptian costume, but with *a large beard and long hair*, absolutely unknown to the true Mizraite (or Egyptian) blood. Also four large Sphinxes, in diorite, bearing the name of Apepi, the king whom Joseph served. The sculptures of the Shepherd period represent moreover a race of radically different type to that of the Egyptians, a race evidently *Semitic*, with angular and

[1] Lenormant, *Anc. Hist. of East*, vol. i. p. 220.
[2] Numbers xxxiii. 52 ; Deut. vii. 5, 25, 26.
[3] Lenormant, *Anc. Hist. of East*, vol. i. p. 220.

sharply - cut features." [1]   Thus, everything tends to identify the Shepherd kings with the Patriarchs of the Semitic race, and it also suggests the reason why *the giants*, who overthrew the Pagan gods, were represented with *flowing hair and beards*.

Much mystery has hitherto surrounded these Shepherd kings, but that they were powerful Egyptian kings is clear, both from their complete conquest and dominion of Egypt, the high estimate in which Set was held for many ages, and from his title "Set Nubti," and "Set the Powerful." That they were the most powerful and celebrated of the Egyptian kings we hope to show in the next chapter.

[1] *Anc. Hist. of East,* vol. i. pp. 222, 223.   *See* also *infra,* chap. xiv., "Shepherd Sculptures."

S

CHAPTER XIII

THE SHEPHERD KINGS AND THE PYRAMID BUILDERS

THE evidence that has been brought forward appears to throw a new light on the earlier and more obscure periods of the Egyptian and Babylonian kingdoms. The conclusions arrived at may be briefly recapitulated as follows :—

The evidence seems to afford conclusive proof that the first kings of the Egyptian monarchy, viz., Menes or Mena, and Athothes or Athoth, were also the first kings of Babylon, and founders of the great Cushite Empire, viz., Cush or Belus, and Nimrod or Ninus, the latter being also known in Egypt as Osiris, Sesostris and Egyptus; that he, having conquered Egypt, made his father king over it, and that they and the Cushites were the progenitors of the black or Egyptian race, as distinguished from the descendants of Mizraim.

It has also been shown that they were afterwards deified, Cush being worshipped in Egypt as "Thoth" or "Hermes," "Anubis," "Cronus" and "Seb," "the Father of the Gods," "Phtath," "Meni the Lord Moon," etc.; and Nimrod as Osiris. In Babylon, Cush was known as "the All-wise Belus," the elder "Cronus," the elder "Bel Nimrud," "Hea, the Lord of Understanding and Teacher of Mankind," "the Prophet Nebo," the Moon God "Sin," and the Fish God "Oannes" or "Dagon"; and Nimrod as "Nin" or "Ninus," "Bel Nimrud the greater," "Bel Merodach," "Hercules," "Tammuz," "Dis," etc. In other countries Cush, keeping his character as "Father of the Gods," was "Saturn," "Cronus," "Vulcan," "Hephæstus," "Chaos," "Janus" and also "Æsculapius," "Mercury," "Buddha" and "Woden," while Nimrod was deified as "Bacchus," "Jupiter," "Mars," "Pluto," "Dis," and in India as "Siva," "Iswara," etc. These and other names given to each being titles representing them under various aspects and characteristics.

It has also been shown that "Semiramis," the wife and queen of Ninus, was the human original of the great goddess known as "Dea Myrionymus," "the Goddess with Ten Thousand Names."

We have also seen that, although the gods were eventually identi-

274

fied with the Sun and the male power in nature, and the goddess with the Earth and Moon and the female principle, yet they still retained much of their human character and personality, and that their human origin was fully recognised and admitted by the priesthood and the initiated.

We have further seen that the dominion of the two kings, Cush and Nimrod, who were the human originals of these gods, was overthrown in Egypt, Nimrod being put to death, and that the record and memory of his death were carefully preserved in every Pagan nation, and made use of for promoting his worship.

Finally, it seems to be clearly proved that the person by whose influence the Cushite power was overthrown in Egypt was "Set the Powerful," the first of the Shepherd kings, called in aftertimes by the priesthood and known in Grecian mythology as "Typhon," under which name he is shown by Manetho as the *immediate successor* of the God kings, "Cronus" and "Osiris," who we have seen to be Menes and Athothes, and that Set was identical with the Semitic Patriarch Shem, known also in mythology as "Titan," who overthrew Saturn, *i.e.*, Cronus or Cush. It follows, therefore, that these Shepherd kings must have been the *immediate successors* of Menes and Athothes. Yet, in spite of the fact that their dominion is said to have lasted 518 years, there appears to be no record of them on the monuments, save the notice in the reign of Rameses II., while according to the Greek copies of Manetho the only record of them is as a fifteenth or seventeenth dynasty, to which a duration is given of from 103 to 259 years.[1]

In the extract, however, from Manetho by Josephus,[2] these kings, although also called the seventeenth dynasty, are represented as *commencing* the Egyptian monarchy, and this is the case with other records, like "The Old Chronicle," in which the previous dynasties, except the one immediately preceding them, are represented to be those of *the gods*, and are therefore mythical.

But although this tends to confirm the conclusions we have arrived at, it affords no further light on their history, and the mystery which seems to surround these kings is admitted by all who have studied the subject.

Mr Nash writes, "The monuments bear no record of them, and we have the remarkable fact of a people, whose duration was nearly as long as the Romans, planting itself firmly on the soil of the most monumental country in the world, and leaving behind them no

[1] *See* Manetho's dynasties; Cory, pp. 114, 115. [2] Cory, p. 136.

monuments of their existence." Again he quotes Gliddon as saying, "It would be indifferent to me to sustain that the Hyksos once occupied Lower Egypt, or that they were never there at all. The latter view might result from the total absence of direct allusion to the Hyksos in the Hieroglyphics, and the necessity of interposing an immeasurable gap between the royal names 39 and 40 in the tablet of Abydos." Again, "In the period of 500 years, surrounded by Egyptian arts and civilisation, and what that must have been at the commencement, the grottoes at Benihassen inform us, subjected to softening and civilising influences, they must in that long period of time have become Egyptianised ; all history teaches us that it must have been so." Similarly Mr Kenrick writes, "Without the testimony of Manetho we should have been wholly ignorant of this most important event (the Hyksos invasion) in the history of Egypt."[1]

Yet the first Hyksos king, Set or Saites, is expressly mentioned on the inscription in the reign of Rameses II. as "Set the Powerful," and as a great Egyptian monarch, while Bunsen remarks that until the time of this Rameses, the god Set was one of the most powerful of the Egyptian deities,[2] implying that until then the influence of the Shepherds must have been more or less predominant.

Brugsch says that "the conclusions to be drawn from the monuments are, that Egyptian kings of the family of *Menti* (or *Menthu*) reigned for a long time in the Eastern Delta, or Saite zone, that they had Zoan and Avaris (the city of *Typhon*) as capitals, that they had the same customs and manners and the same official language and writing as the other Egyptians ; that they were patrons of art and erected statues and monuments in the same way, and that they worshipped the god Set or Sutech and constructed Sphinxes in his honour."[3] These Menti or Menthu are also identified as having been inhabitants of the land of Ashur, or Assyria, and this we know was the first home of the Semitic race until Abraham was called by God out of Ur of the Chaldees. Moreover, Apepi, or Apophis, is associated with the Menti, his name was engraved on four Sphinxes, and he is represented as the last of the Shepherd kings. This, therefore, tends to identify these Menti with the kings classed by Manetho as "Shepherd kings."

Apepi, or Apophis, was, however, different from the rest of the Shepherd kings. Unlike the others, numerous monumental records of him exist, and he is recognised to be one of the greatest of the

---

[1] Nash, *Pharaoh of the Exodus*, pp. 172, 180, 183, 184.   [2] See *ante*, p. 260.
[3] Brugsch, *Hist. of Egypt*, vol. i. pp. 236, 237.

Egyptian monarchs. He is different also from the others in that he seems to have *changed his religion*. A papyrus in the British Museum says, "The king Apepi chose the god Sutekh (*i.e.*, Set) as his Lord, and did not serve any other god in the whole land." [1] Now Syncellus says that it was a tradition, "received by the whole world," that Joseph ruled the land in the reign of King Apophis or Apepi, [2] and the evidence on the subject confirms this. If so, it would account for his rejecting idolatry in favour of the God of the shepherd Joseph, and which god would naturally be identified in later times with the god Set; for it was through the God of Joseph and Shem, or Set, that his kingdom was saved from famine, and he became the arbiter of the destinies of all Egypt.

This fact of his changing his religion distinguishes him from the rest of the Shepherd kings. Moreover, we learn that in his time, that is before Joseph was ruler, "Shepherds were an abomination to the Egyptians" (Gen. xlvi. 34). This, of course, would be the consequence of the destruction of the heathen temples and gods by the Shepherd kings, and the word "abomination" implies that the hatred, which would otherwise have been unmeaning, was of a religious nature. If, then, Apepi was the Pharaoh of that time, we must conclude that the idolatry destroyed by the Shepherd kings had been restored between their time and the reign of Apepi, and that the name of Shepherd had become by that time only a hated memory. We also learn from the "Sallier Papyrus" that Apepi, after his change of religion, endeavoured to force the worship of Set, and the repudiation of the Pagan gods, on all the Egyptians, [3] which further confirms the fact that previous to that time the worship of the Pagan gods had been general.

This shows that there was a great gap between the first Shepherds and Apepi. In short, the total length of the reigns of the Shepherd kings was, according to the highest estimate, only 259 years, while some records give them only 103 years, whereas the actual time from the first Shepherd king to the last is stated to be 511 or 518 years. This implies that there was a gap somewhere of at least 250 years, which is perfectly accounted for by the fact that Apepi was not at first a worshipper of the God of the Shepherds, but of the gods of Egypt, just as his predecessors had been for probably

[1] "Sallier Papyrus."   [2] Brugsch, vol. i. p. 260.
[3] Letter from Apepi to Skennen ra, or Ra Sekenen, vassal king of Southern or Upper Egypt, commanding him to repudiate his gods ("Sallier Papyrus"). Brugsch, *Hist. of Egypt*, vol. i. pp. 239-241.

centuries before him; but that, for the reason stated, he had repudiated idolatry and worshipped the god of Set, and by so doing had earned for himself in after ages the opprobrious title of "Shepherd king."

It is thus clear that Apepi must be distinguished from the other Shepherd kings, of whom, apparently, not a trace or record remains, but the notice in the reign of Rameses of "Set the powerful," and the statements of Manetho.

It is important, however, to remember the hatred with which the Shepherds were regarded in later times by the idolatrous priesthood. There is abundant evidence of this hatred, and of the fact that everything was done *to obliterate their memory*. It was indeed only to be expected that the priesthood, who were the sole recorders of their country's history, and custodians of its archives, would do their best to discredit and conceal the fact of the overthrow of their religion and the death of their God king. The Shepherd kings, as we shall see, were in reality some of the greatest Egyptian kings, kings who had made Egypt what it was, and for the priesthood to have admitted that it was they who accomplished this overthrow would have been a lasting and indelible disgrace on their gods and religion, tending to create constant doubt and suspicion of the whole system. If, then, they mentioned them at all in connection with the overthrow of their religion, it would be in terms of contempt and hatred. Thus we see Manetho describing them as "men of an ignoble race," just as, in Greek mythology, the giants who opposed the gods are described in terms of similar opprobrium.

In accordance with this, Mr Osburn has pointed out that the names given by Manetho to these Shepherd kings are really opprobrious epithets. Thus "*Salatis*" means "many lies," which is just the kind of epithet which would be bestowed by the idolaters on one who had overthrown their god by the force of *Truth*. "*Beon*" means "filthy fellow," and "*Apachnas*," "bond slave," [1] while *Apophis* appears to be an intentional corruption of Apepi, viz., *Ap*, and *ophe*, a serpent, to identify him with the malignant serpent Apophis slain by Osiris in his avatar as Horus. [2] These are the only names given in some of the copies of Manetho, and the other names recorded by Josephus are placed *after* Apophis, and appear to be intimately associated with him, while their names, "Staan," "Janias," etc., are also titles of contempt. Now it is very evident that we may in

[1] Osburn, *Monumental Hist. of Egypt*, vol. ii. p. 51.
[2] *Wilkinson*, by Birch, vol. iii. pp. 153, 154.

vain search the monuments for these names, and unless we can identify them by some other means it would be hopeless to discover them.

This being the case, it is a matter of some surprise that Apepi has been included among these Shepherd kings under the name by which he is known in the lists and on the monuments. There are plenty of evidences of the hatred with which the idolatrous priesthood regarded him. His name occurs in a vast series of tombs and grottoes, all of which are systematically mutilated, while in the same place those of the Theban kings of the twelfth dynasty are untouched.[1] Apepi was not, however, as we have seen, one of the original Shepherd kings but an Egyptian Pharaoh reigning at a time when the Shepherds had become a hated memory. The events of his reign made him of world-wide celebrity, and it was alike impossible to conceal his identity, or to ignore his change of religion ; all that the priesthood could do was to include him among the Shepherd kings, and thereby cover his memory with the opprobrium attached to them.

It may be remarked that Plutarch says that Apepi, or Apophis, was one of those who warred against Osiris.[2] Now, as the period from the first to the last Shepherd king is said to have been over 500 years, and Apophis was probably the last Shepherd king, he could have had nothing to do with the overthrow of Osiris by Set or Typhon. Nevertheless Plutarch's statement is of importance, because it shows that *the Shepherd kings* were recognised as identical with the *Typhonians*, and that the overthrow of Egyptian idolatry by the Shepherds was identical with the overthrow of Osiris by *Typhon*.

Brugsch says that the names of the Hyksos kings, or of some of the earlier kings before them, have been carefully obliterated, or chiselled out, on the life-size statue at Tel Mukkdam, on the lion found near Bagdad, the sacrificial stone in the Museum at Boulak, and the borders of the stand of the colossal Sphinxes in the Louvre, although in one case the names of Set and Apepi have escaped complete erasure.[3] Apepi was closely connected with the latter form of sculpture (sphinxes), and it is pretty certain therefore that these obliterated names were those both of himself and the other Shepherd kings. Wilkinson also observes that the name *Amunre* has been substituted for some other name on many of the oldest monuments, the latter name being

[1] Osburn, vol. ii. p. 81.
[2] Cumberland's *Sanchoniathon*, p. 165 ; Plutarch, S. 36.
[3] Brugsch, vol. i. pp. 237, 238.

erased with scrupulous care, and that these erasures were confined to monuments *preceding* those of Amenophis III. of the eighteenth dynasty.[1] Now it was in his reign, according to Syncellus,[2] that the Cushites from India came to Egypt, and that the Cushite influence, and therefore the influence of the Cushite gods, began to gain the upper hand. It would therefore appear that, as the name substituted for the erased name was that of Amun, the Sun god, the erased name was that of the rival god Set. The hatred to the Shepherds is also shown by the way in which the Egyptians always represented herdsmen and shepherds as dirty, unshaven, and of ludicrous appearance.[3]

These facts all tend to show that everything was done to obliterate the memory of the Shepherd kings, and to represent them as everything contemptible. If then they do appear in the lists and on the monuments as great Egyptian kings, every care will have been taken by the priesthood to dissociate these kings from the hated enemies of their god and religion.

The question then is—Is it possible, by any means, to identify, and learn the history of, these Shepherd kings?

We may learn something about the Shepherd kings by a consideration of the period at which their conquest took place.

It is sufficiently evident that Saites, or Set, the first Shepherd king who obtained the sovereignty of Egypt, after getting the then rulers of the country into his power, is Set or Typhon, who overcame Osiris or Nimrod. If then we can approximately ascertain the date of that monarch's death, we shall also know the date of the accession of Set. Now, there are a remarkable number of independent testimonies proving that the beginning of Nimrod's kingdom was about the year 2232-2234 B.C.

Firstly, there is the list of kings of the Assyrian Empire given by Berosus. The first of his dynasties, consisting of eighty-six kings reigning 34,080 years, may be regarded as similar to the reign of the gods in Egypt, to which a similar exaggerated period is given. The latter was composed of the human kings Menes and Athothes (*i.e.*, Cush and Nimrod), under their names as gods, viz., Agathodæmon, Cronus, Osiris, Horus, Ares or Mars, etc., to which are added the antediluvian Hephæstus or Chrysor, Helius the Sun, and some others, —the total length of their years added to those of the human kings being made up to be exactly 36,525 years, or twenty-five Sothic

[1] Wilkinson's *Egyptians*, vol. iv. p. 244.   [2] Cory, p. 142.
[3] Wilkinson's *Egyptians*, vol. iv. p. 126 ; Nash, p. 238.

cycles of 1461 years, to the Persian conquest.[1] It is evident that the reigns of these gods are purely fictitious, and merely added to make up this vast mythical period.

In like manner we find Evechius, the first king of the mythical dynasty of Berosus, given a reign of four *neri*, or 2400 years, and Comosbelus a reign of four *neri* and five *sossi*, or 2700 years, etc. It is evident that these are equally fictitious, and that the dynasty of 34,080 years is merely added to make a great mythical period, or an exact number of *sari*, each consisting of 3600 years.[2]

The first dynasty must therefore be regarded as entirely mythical, and the remainder stand as follows:—

Mythical dynasty,	34,080 years.							
8 Median kings,	.	224	,,	234 Marg. Arm.	} [3]	2458	B.C.
11 Chaldean ,,	.	(258)	,,	(2) 48 Marg. Arm.		2234	,,
49 Chaldean ,,	.	458	,,	.	.	.	1976	,,
9 Arabian ,,	.	245	,,	.	.	.	1518	,,
45 Assyrian ,,	.	526	,,	.	.	.	1273	,,
Canon of { Assyrian ,,	.	122	,,	.	.	.	747	,,
Ptolemy { Chaldean ,,	.	87	,,	.	.	.	625	,,
Overthrow of the Babylonian Empire by the Medes and Persians	.		.	.	.	.	538	,,

Total, 36,000 years.

The ancient home of the Cushite race was, as we have seen, Arabia, and the Babylonian portion of Nimrod's empire being previously occupied by Turanian races allied to the Medes who eventually threw off the Cushite yoke,[4] Berosus probably gave the name of this afterwards dominant race to the first inhabitants of Chaldea. The Median kingdom would thus represent the period when the country was occupied by these races before their conquest by the Cushites, and the first Chaldean kingdom must of course be that of Nimrod.

The number of years representing the duration of the first Chaldean kingdom in the canon of Berosus has unfortunately been

[1] "The Old Chronicle," Cory's *Fragments,* pp. 89-93.

[2] According to Berosus a *sarus* consists of 3600 years, a *neros* of 600, and a *sossus* of 60 years.

[3] Rawlinson, *Five Great Monarchies of the East,* vol. i. p. 151, note.

[4] Lenormant's *Anc. Hist. of East,* vol. ii. pp. 22, 23. *See* also Appendix D, "The Accadians."

erased, and the period given to it, viz., 258 years, is that deduced by Dr Brandis, as making up, with the other dynasties and the mythic period of 34,080 years, exactly a total of 36,000 years.[1] For the particular period which Berosus uses as the basis of his chronology is a *sarus* consisting of 3600 years,[2] and as he represents the reigns of the ten kings of Babylon before the Deluge as exactly 120 *sari*,[3] it appears certain that, like the Egyptian historians, he made the duration of the Babylonian monarchy after the Deluge, including the mythic period, to constitute an exact number of *sari*, which in this case could only be 10 sari, or 36,000 years.

The correctness of this period of 258 years also receives strong confirmation from Arabian history, which assigns to the first great empire of Western Asia founded by the Aribah, or Adite, conqueror Zohak, who has been identified with Nimrod, a period of 260 years.[4]

It receives also some further confirmation from the marginal numbers given by the *Armenian Chronicle* of Eusebius to the Median and first Chaldean dynasties (*see* table). It is evident that the period of 48 years given to the eleven kings of the latter dynasty is altogether too small and that the first figure must have been erased. The general accuracy of Berosus is proved by the fact that the Assyrian inscriptions give a list of exactly eleven kings as constituting the first Babylonian dynasty, and as the total of their reigns amounts to 292 years,[5] it is pretty certain the duration of the dynasty must have been between 200 and 300 years, and that the missing figure in the margin of the Armenian is "2," which would make the period 248 years. This is ten years *less* than 258 years, but it will be seen that the Armenian gives ten years *more* to the Median dynasty, indicating therefore that the total of the two dynasties was recognised to be the same as that given in the table; and as the 258 years is corroborated by Arabian history, it may be taken as the more correct period.

The only other point in the table which requires notice is this. Eusebius in the *Armenian Chronicle*, after enumerating the successive dynasties mentioned by Berosus to the end of the forty-five kings reigning for 526 years, proceeds, "After (or 'last of') whom he (Berosus) says that there was a king of the Chaldeans whose name

---

[1] Rawlinson's *Herod.*, vol. i. essay vi. pp. 433, 434.

[2] Berosus, from *Abydenus;* Cory, p. 32.

[3] *Ibid.*, p. 33.   [4] See *ante*, chap. iv. p. 76.

[5] *See* Appendix D. Berosus probably terminated his dynasty at a slightly earlier date than that given by the Assyrian inscriptions.

was Phulus, of whom also the historical writings of the Hebrews make mention under the name Phulus (Pul), who they say invaded the country of the Jews" (Euseb., *Arm. Chron.*, p. 39).

Phulus or Pul was the predecessor of Tiglath Pileser,[1] the commencement of whose reign (749 B.C.) corresponds with that of Nabonassar, the first king of Ptolemy's canon. It seems evident. therefore, that the object of the *Chronicle* in mentioning Pul was simply to bring down the chronology of Berosus to the recognised chronology of Ptolemy, and that Pul was the last king of the last dynasty mentioned.

The first Chaldean kingdom which follows the Median is manifestly that which was established by Nimrod, and the date of that according to this canon is 2234 B.C.

Concerning this date, Sir Henry Rawlinson writes: "We have here a fixed date of 2234 B.C. for the commencement of the great Chaldean Empire, which was the first paramount power in Western Asia; and this it must be remembered is the same date as that obtained by Callisthenes from the Chaldeans at Babylon for the commencement of their stellar observations which would naturally be coeval with the empire. Thus :—

" Date of visit of Callisthenes to Babylon .	331 B.C.
" Antiquity of stellar observations . .	1903 „
	" 2234 B.C.[2]

"It was the same date also which was computed by Pliny adapting the numbers of Berosus to the conventional chronology of the Greeks. Thus :—

" Greek era of Phoroneus . . .	1753 B.C.
" Stellar observations at Babylon before that time	480 „
	" 2233 B.C.[3]

"It is likewise probably the same which was indicated by Philo Byblius when he assigned to Babylon an antiquity of 1002 years before Semiramis (that is to say, the second Semiramis), who was contemporary with the siege of Troy. Thus :—

[1] 2 Kings xv. 19-29.
[2] Simplicius, *Ad Arist. de Cœlo*, lib. ii. p. 123 ; Rawlinson's *Herod.*, vol. i. pp. 422, 423.
[3] Pliny, H. N., vii. 56 ; Clinton, F. H., vol. i. p. 139.

"Siege of Troy, and Semiramis, whose reign
    probably began a year or two before   1229-1232 B.C.
"Babylon previous to this   .   .   .   1002   „
                                          _____
                                            "2234 B.C.[1]

Sir H. Rawlinson also shows that the chronology of Ctesias makes the beginning of the reign of Ninus (*i.e.*, Nimrod) 2231 B.C.[2]

The uniformity of this date deduced from five different calculations seems to place its general accuracy beyond question.

It is also strictly in accordance with the chronology of the Old Testament, which represents the date of the Deluge to be about 2430,[3] and as Nimrod, the grandson of Noah, was the sixth son of Cush, and is implied to have been born some time after the other sons of Cush, his birth may very well have been some 160 years after the Deluge, and the foundation of his empire 30 to 40 years later.[4]

Finally, the date appears to be remarkably confirmed by the records of the dates and reigns of Babylonian kings discovered on the Assyrian Tablets. *See* Appendix D.

Syncellus represents the reign of Ninus, or Nimrod, who is the same as Athothes, as 52 years, but Manetho gives Athothes a reign of 57 years, and Eratosthenes gives him a reign of 59 years. In his dynasty of God kings, Manetho also gives Agathodæmon, who is

[1] Steph. Byz., *ad voce* "βάβυλών."

[2] Rawlinson's *Herod.*, vol. i. essay vi. pp. 434, 435. The details of the last calculation are given in his *Notes on the Early History of Babylonia*, p. 7 *et seq.*

[3] The chronology adopted in our Bibles, which makes the Deluge to have been 2348, is that of Usher, but it is well known that he has omitted certain periods of the time of the Judges, which, according to St Paul, should be 450 years. This 450 years, however, appears to include the whole of Samuel's judgeship to his death, and of this period the last eighteen years, according to Josephus, was during the reign of Saul. *See* work by the Author, *The Great Pyramid and Its Builder*, chap. v., "Sacred Chronology"; which makes the date of the Deluge 2432 B.C.

[4] The tendency of scientific thought at the present day is to treat the chronology of Scripture with contempt, and to place greater reliance on the speculations of geologists, who affirm that the creation of man must have been thousands of years before the period assigned for it in the Old Testament. In support of this theory, modern archæologists have assumed that the numerous dynasties of Manetho, representing a period of over 5000 years, are *successive*, while some go so far as to assert that the mythical reigns of the Egyptian and Babylonian gods in the histories of Manetho and Berosus, represent periods of human history before the historical period. But both the speculations of geologists and the arguments of archæologists are based upon data which, upon examination, will be found to be capable of a very different explanation, nor do they afford any logical support for their conclusions, many of which are indeed mere assumptions. *See* Appendix C.

identified with Athothes, a reign of exactly 56½ years and 10 days, which would count as 57 years, and we may therefore take the period of 57 years as the true period of the reign of Ninus or Athothes. Taking then 2234 B.C. as the commencement of the empire of Nimrod, and deducting from it the length of his reign, the remainder will give the date of his death in Egypt :—

Commencement of empire	.	2234 B.C.
Reign of Ninus or Nimrod	.	57 „
		2177 B.C.

It may be observed, however, that the period from which this date is derived is the *establishment* of Nimrod's empire and the commencement of stellar observations at Babylon, both of which would necessarily be a few years subsequent to the commencement of the conquests of Nimrod, and it would be in accordance with the practice of the ancients to date his reign from the commencement of those conquests, which might be three or four years earlier. This would make the beginning of his reign about 2237-2238 B.C., and his death and the overthrow of the Cushite dominion in Egypt about 2180 B.C.[1]

This date is some ten years before the date of the Great Pyramid built by the Khufu, or Shufu,[2] of the monuments, the Suphis of Manetho's fourth dynasty, the Saophis of Eratosthenes, and the Cheops of Herodotus. This Pyramid, as proved by Piazzi Smyth, the Astronomer Royal of Scotland, records a certain conjunction of stars which took place at midnight at the autumnal equinox 2170 B.C., and which conjunction only takes place once in 25,847 years.

The conjunction is recorded by the particular position and angle of inclination of the first descending passage of the Pyramid, and as that position and angle of inclination could not have been determined before the conjunction actually took place and had been carefully observed, the Pyramid could not have been commenced until that event, and this portion of the plan of construction must have been designed to record it. Now the Pyramid could not have been commenced by Suphis until a certain period *after* his accession; and if we assume that period to be only ten years, it would make the date of his accession to be 2180 B.C. or exactly the date of the overthrow of the Cushite dominion in Egypt, by the Shepherd king Set.

[1] This date must be regarded as approximate only. It requires a certain small correction, which does not affect the conclusions drawn.

[2] In Lower Egypt Sh was substituted for the Kh of Upper Egypt.

But, if so, *the Pyramid king Suphis and the Shepherd king Set were both the immediate successors of Nimrod or Athothes, and of his father Cush or Menes.* In any case, it is quite impossible that the Shepherds who succeeded Menes and Athothes, and whose rule is said to have lasted from 103 to 518 years, could have intervened between that of the Cushite and Pyramid kings.

Is it possible then, that the Pyramid builders, who were among the greatest of the Egyptian kings, were identical with the Shepherd kings, but that the priesthood, for the reasons before mentioned, sought by every means to obliterate this identity? It would indeed seem to be so, and the evidence in support of it accumulates as we proceed.

If Suphis was "Set the powerful," nicknamed "Salatis," then the admission of Manetho, that "*he was arrogant to the gods*,"[1] is as much as we could expect. But the priests, his predecessors, who were consulted by Herodotus, were more communicative; "Cheops," *i.e.*, Suphis,[2] they said, "*plunged into every kind of wickedness.* For that, having *shut up the temples*, he first of all *forbade them to offer sacrifices*, and afterwards he *ordered all the Egyptians to work for himself.*" Then follows the description of the building of the Great Pyramid and the preparation of the stone for it. He says that, "they worked to the number of a hundred thousand at a time, each party during three months. The time during which the people were thus harassed with toil lasted ten years on the road which they constructed, along which they drew the stone, and in forming the subterraneous apartments on the hill on which the Pyramid stood," and he says that "twenty years were expended in erecting the Pyramid itself."[3]

Is not the above an exact parallel of the acts of the Shepherd kings, who are described as "*demolishing the temples of the gods*," and *reducing the inhabitants to slavery?*[4]

Cheops, says Herodotus, was succeeded by his brother Chephren (*i.e.*, Suphis II.),[5] who followed the same practices as his predecessor, both in other respects and in building a Pyramid, and that during their two reigns, amounting to 106 years, "the Egyptians *suffered all*

---

[1] *See* table of Egyptian dynasties; Cory's *Fragments*, p. 102.

[2] *Cheops* is a corruption by the Greeks of the Egyptian name *Shufu* or *Khufu.*

[3] Herod., ii. c. 124.   [4] See *ante*, p. 270.

[5] Suphis II., or Num Shufu, the successor of Suphis I., was also known by the name of *Shefra* or *Khefra*, and just as Shufu or Kuphu I. was hellenised into *Cheops*, so was Khefra changed into *Chephren.*

kinds of calamities, and for this length of time *the temples were closed and never opened."* [1]   In other words, all idolatry was suppressed during that period.

This is the account of the idolatrous priesthood centuries after the event, who of course would do all they could to cast reproach on the enemies of their religion, by accusing them of cruelty.   On the face of the account itself this cruelty is greatly exaggerated. Herodotus says that he himself saw an inscription on the Pyramid of the amount expended on the food provided for the workmen, *who were not slaves*, but only worked three months out of the twelve. [2]

Speaking of Cheops and Chephren, Herodotus says, "From *the hatred they bear them* the Egyptians are not very willing to mention their names."   Thus there is the same hatred evinced towards the Pyramid builders as to the Shepherd kings, and as to Set or Typhon. There are the same accusations of cruelty and oppression.   There is the same overthrow of idolatry in both cases; and the period of the commencement of their rule in Egypt would appear to *synchronise exactly*.

Again, like the Shepherds, the Pyramid kings are said to have been "*men of a different race*."   But there is no mention of them being foreign *conquerors*, and this exactly accords with the story of Set or Typhon.   For it was the judges or rulers of the different nomes who condemned and executed Osiris or Nimrod, by the advice of Set or Typhon, and Manetho, speaking of the Shepherd kings, says that after they had destroyed the temples they chose one of their number (*i.e.*, Saites or Set), to be king, who, it is clear, was the Shepherd prince Shem, the righteous king of Salem, who, with his flocks and herds and followers, went to Egypt to warn the people against the wickedness and idolatry of their tyrant conqueror.   In exact accordance with this, Herodotus says, "From the hatred they bear them (Cheops and Chephren) the Egyptians are not very willing to mention *their names* but call *the Pyramids* after *Philition, a shepherd*, who at that time kept his cattle in those parts." [3]   Now from the inconsequence of this statement it looks as if there was some error. If they called *the Pyramids* after the name of a shepherd, how would it enable them to avoid mentioning the names of the kings who built them?   Unless indeed they spoke of them as *built by this shepherd;* which would be equivalent to saying that *Cheops was that*

[1] Herod., ii. c. 128.   [2] *Ibid.*, c. 125.
[3] *Ibid.*, ii. c. 128.

shepherd. But it is certain that the Pyramids were never called after Philition the shepherd, and it is more probable that what the priests really said to Herodotus was, "The Egyptians call *them*" (i.e., *the kings* who had built the Pyramids, and *not the Pyramids* themselves), "after Philition, a shepherd," or, in other words, they called those kings (*i.e.,* the builders of the Pyramids), "*Shepherd kings.*" [1]

The fact also that Manetho describes these Pyramid kings as "*of a different race,*" [2] which was just what the Shepherds were, implies that their accession was the result of some kind of revolution.

Here then we have two sets of powerful Egyptian kings, both of a different race to the other kings; both ascending the throne in consequence of a revolution; both overthrowing the worship of the gods; both accused of reducing the inhabitants to slavery; both doing these things at apparently exactly the same period of Egyptian history; both regarded with the same hatred, while from the notice of Herodotus, it would seem that, at one time, the Pyramid kings were actually called "Shepherd kings."

How is it possible to avoid the conclusion that the hated Pyramid kings are the same as the hated Shepherd kings, the evidences of whose identity the priestly historians have taken such care to obliterate?

If Manetho had never told us the story of the Shepherd kings yet a careful examination of dates and the recognition of the identity of the first two Egyptian kings, Menes and Athothes, with the founders of the Babylonian Empire, together with a comparison of the story of Typhon and Osiris, and of Titan and Saturn, and that of the Pyramid builders related by Herodotus, would have forced upon our minds the fact that these stories related to the same events. But the story of the Shepherd kings, related to cast upon foreigners the wickedness of having overthrown the idolatrous religion supported by the priesthood, is just what was required to make this conclusion certain, and explain the exact nature of the event.

The reigns of the Shepherd kings are given by Josephus as follows :—

Salatis	.	.	19 years.
Beon	.	.	44 years.
Apachnas	.	.	36 years and 7 months.
Apophis	.	.	61 years.

---

[1] "*Philition*" is evidently a Greek word composed of "*Philo*" and "*itius*," meaning "a lover of rectitude or right"; a fit name for "the righteous king."

[2] *See* Manetho's dynasties, Cory's *Fragments*, p. 102.

and Manetho gives the reigns of Suphis and his successor as follows :—

Suphis	. . .	63 years.
Suphis II.	. .	66 years.

Now the names of Suphis or Shufu, and of Num Shufu or Suphis II., are found together in the monumental inscriptions with the symbol significant of reigning conjointly, and both are found in the Great Pyramid,[1] showing that they must have been contemporary, and that the first Suphis must have made his son, or successor, co-regent with him at some period of his reign. A portion of the 66 years of the Suphis II. must therefore be included in the reign of Suphis I. If, then, the Shepherd king Set, or Saites, was Suphis I., the second Shepherd king Beon must be Suphis II., who reigned conjointly with him, and the length of the two reigns of Saites, 19 years, and Beon, 44 years, exactly equal 63 years, the length of the reign given by Manetho to Suphis I.

Moreover, as it was only Suphis I. and Suphis II. (*i.e.*, Cheops and Chefren), who suppressed idolatry, they would be the only two kings besides Apepi to whom the hated name of "Shepherd" would be applied. Hence we may presume that the third Shepherd king Apachnas, which is only a nickname, is the name given to the second Suphis to represent the period when he reigned alone, it being the usual custom to give a king some special title or titles when he ascended the throne. Thus :—

FOURTH DYNASTY

Pyramid kings		Shepherd kings	
Suphis 33 } 63 years		Saites 19 } 63 years	
Suphis II. co-regent 30 }		Beon 44 { 14 / 30 }	
Suphis II. alone 36 years		Apachnas 36 years	

The extra 14 years given to Beon over and above that given to Suphis II. may represent the period previous to the latter's actual co-regency, during which period his father may have made him his coadjutor at Memphis without giving him a separate jurisdiction; for his name by which he is called on the monuments, viz., Shefra (Greek, Sephres), appears as one of the kings of the fifth, or Elephantine, dynasty of Upper Egypt, which, from this time, had always a separate king or viceroy. On account of

---

[1] Osburn's *Monumental History of Egypt*, vol. i. pp. 279-281.

T

the distance of the two seats of government from each other, and of each being the point at which attack from without might be feared, the necessity of a viceroy for one was obvious.

There is a further confirmation that the Shepherd kings were among the first rulers of Egypt. We have seen that Josephus places them as the *first* kings of Egypt, calling them the seventeenth dynasty; and similarly *The Old Chronicle* places the seventeenth dynasty as immediately succeeding the sixteenth dynasty of Tanites, previous to which are the mythical dynasties of gods.[1] These Tanites appear to represent the period during which Mizraim and his descendants possessed the northern part of the country about the Delta, where Tanis is situated, before Nimrod's conquest. *The Old Chronicle* gives this sixteenth dynasty a period of 190 years, and the seventeenth, which it calls *Memphites*, after Memphis, their seat of government, 103 years. Similarly, in the Armenian canon of Manetho, the sixteenth dynasty is given a period of 190 years, while the seventeenth dynasty, which follows it, is called *Shepherds*, and given also a period of 103 years.[2]

The period of the Shepherds is also given by Eusebius as 106 years,[3] showing that there was a more or less general recognition of a period of 103 to 106 years connected with *the Shepherd rule*. Now this latter period of 106 years is exactly that assigned by Herodotus to *the Pyramid builders*, Cheops and Chephren, (*i.e.*, Suphis I. and Suphis II.), during which the temples were closed and the worship of the gods suppressed.[4]

In the face of all this evidence it seems impossible to doubt that the Pyramid kings of the *Memphite*, or fourth, dynasty of Manetho were the Shepherd kings of the seventeenth dynasties of Josephus, the Armenian, and *The Old Chronicle*, both of which are also called *Memphites*, and that the Shepherd king "Set the Powerful" was the Shepherd Philition and the Pyramid builder Suphis I.

Herodotus says the successor of Cheops and Chefren, viz.,

---

[1] Cory's *Fragments*, p. 90.   [2] Cory; compare pp. 90 and 115.

[3] *Ibid.*, 115. This period of 103 or 106 years does not exactly agree with the period given to Saites, Beon and Apachnas, viz., 99 years, but Herodotus speaks of this period as that during which the temples were closed during the reigns of Cheops and Chephren, and this would naturally extend into the reign of their successor, Mencheres, who re-opened them, for we might expect that he would wait a few years before he made so great a religious revolution.

[4] Herod, ii. c. 128.

"Mycerinus," who is the "Mencheres" of Manetho's fourth dynasty and "Menkara" of the monuments, re-opened the temples and restored the worship of the gods. It is also stated that no open idolatry was ventured upon in Babylon until the reign of Arioch, the grandson of Semiramis.[1] Now the restoration of idolatry in Babylon would be the signal for its restoration in Egypt also, and if Set, the overthrower of Ninus or Nimrod and the idolatry instituted by him in Egypt, is Suphis, then the reign of Mencheres in Egypt would *exactly synchronise with that of Arioch in Babylon.*[2] This is a further remarkable confirmation of the fact that Set was the Pyramid king Suphis.

Under Set or Suphis, and his successor Suphis II. or Chefren, Egypt was probably the most powerful kingdom in the world and the idolaters would not venture on any open attempt to restore their religion during their lives, but directly the restraining influence of these kings was removed, steps would naturally be taken both in Babylon and Egypt to do so.

Mencheres, who is credited with having restored the worship of the gods in Egypt, received the name of Horus, and he is also spoken of as " born of Neith," the goddess of Sais, called Minerva by the Greeks, and who was also a form of Isis. This would seem to imply that he was the human original of the god Horus, the son of Isis, who is the same as Neith, and who by his aid is said to have overcome Typhon. Neitocris also, whose name is a compound of Neith, and is translated by Eratosthenes as " Minerva Victris,"[3] is associated with him. For Manetho says that she was the builder of the third Pyramid, while Herodotus says it was built by Mencheres or Mycerinus, the successor of Chefren.[4] Nitocris is said by Herodotus to have been queen of Babylon and *also queen of Egypt*, and that she revenged her brother's death, *who was king of Egypt and had been put to death by his subjects.*[5] This clearly identifies her with Isis, or Semiramis, the wife of Ninus or Osiris, and Manetho says that, like Semiramis, she was celebrated for her beauty. Semiramis is said to have quelled a rising rebellion among

[1] Cedreni, *Compendium*, vol. i. pp. 29, 30.

[2] The reigns in Babylon after the death of Nimrod, or Ninus, were—1st, Semiramis ; 2nd, Ninyas, or Zames ; 3rd, Arius or Arioch. The reigns in Egypt were—1st, Suphis I. ; 2nd, Suphis II. ; 3rd, Mencheres. *See* Manetho's dynasties, and *Dynasty of Assyrian Kings*, by Africanus and Eusebius ; Cory's *Fragments*, pp. 70, 71.

[3] Cory, *Eratosthenes*, p. 86.   [4] Herod., ii. c. 134.

[5] *Ibid.*, ii. c. 100.

her subjects by her beauty on suddenly appearing before them, and that a statue was erected to her in Babylon to perpetuate the memory of that beauty which had so fascinated them.[1]   Nitocris was also said to have been of a florid complexion with golden hair, and the goddess mother is always represented by the classical writers as fair with yellow hair.[2]   Herodotus, on the information of the priests, ascribes many of the great works constructed by Semiramis to Nitocris, being led to suppose that she was a different queen,[3] but it is evident that, like Neith and Athena, Nitocris is only another name for Isis or Semiramis, who, as we shall see, was the founder of the revived idolatry.[4]   Hence as the overthrower of the influence of the hated Set, the god of the Shepherds, Nitocris was placed by Manetho, or the Greek copyists, at the end of the sixth dynasty, after Apepi, which was the termination of the Shepherd rule.

It must be remembered that these are stories told by the priests ages after the event, and the statements that Mencheres was born of Neith, and that he re-opened the temples and restored the worship of the gods, are manifestly false.   For neither Neith, nor any other of the gods and goddesses afterwards worshipped, had as yet come into existence.   It is evident, therefore, that the title of " Horus the son of Neith " or " Isis " must have been given to Mencheres long after his death, in commemoration of his having been the first to restore idolatry in Egypt, and that the monuments thus describing him were erected by his successors in after times.

Reference has been made to the numerous obliterations of the names, and mutilation of the statues and monuments of the Shepherd king Apepi, and of those who were hateful to the idolatrous priesthood, and we might expect that similar attempts would be made to mutilate and obliterate the names of the Pyramid kings. This is the case, for in the list of kings found in the chamber at Karnak, at Abydos and elsewhere, the *earliest* names have all been more or less obliterated.

Again, Mencheres, following the example of Cheops and Chefren, also built a Pyramid, but while the Pyramid of Mencheres remained untouched until comparatively modern times, the two built by Cheops and Chefren (Suphis and Sephres) were early desecrated and their casing stones torn off, showing, as Mr Osburn remarks, that the

---

[1] Valerius Maximus, lib. ix. cap. iii. leaf 193, p. 2 ; Hislop, p. 74 and note.
[2] Hislop pp. 85, 86.   Mr Hislop quotes Ovid, Anacreon, Homer, etc.
[3] Herod, i. c. 185.
   See chap xv.

memories of Suphis and Sephres were "*execrable in ancient Egypt.*"[1] Statues of Shefra, or Chefren, have also been recently found thrown down a well in an underground building near the Great Sphinx.[2]

In spite, however, of this systematic obliteration of names, done to prevent identification, a record has been found of the titular name, or prenomen, of the first Shepherd king. That name according to the Turin Papyrus and the list of Chenoboscion, is "*Nufreka.*"[3] This title enters into the composition of many of the prenomens of the earlier Memphite kings, but hardly ever into those of the Theban kings of Upper Egypt, the original seat of the Cushite power.[4] As it was the custom of the kings of Egypt to adopt titles derived from a predecessor whom they especially honoured, or from whom they claimed descent, this of itself suggests the conclusion that Saites was one of the earliest kings of Egypt. The title "Nufreka" is also singular in the fact that it is without the Ra which terminates the prenomen of every recognised Pharaoh and which follows this prenomen in nearly every other case, and it has been observed by many, that while the names of the Egyptian gods Ra, Amon and Phtah enter into the composition of the names of nearly every other Egyptian king, they do not form part of those of Suphis and his successor Num, or Noh Suphis.

"Ra," the Sun god, with Aph, the Serpent, is "Aphra" or "Phra," the Egyptian for Pharaoh, and it is thus distinctive of every recognised Egyptian king. The prenomen of Saites being without the Ra, it is the distinguishing mark of that king by which he may be identified, and, as Mr Poole remarks, it indicates that the compilers of these lists refused to recognise Saites as a true Egyptian king, which is just what we might expect from the hatred bestowed on his memory in later times. When the worship of the Sun and Serpent god had been fully re-established, the "ra," or the name of some other Sun god, would, as a matter of course, be added to the title of every Pharaoh recognised as such, and not identified with one of the hated Shepherds. If, then, any recognised Pharaoh ever had a prenomen which was without the ra, it would only be found on monuments of the time of his reign, or immediately subsequent to it. Now, a monument does

[1] Osburn, vol. i. p. 324.   [2] Brugsch, vol. i. p. 78.

[3] Poole's *Horæ Ægypticæ*, part ii. sect. iii. p. 133. It is the title of the first king of a dynasty corresponding to Manetho's fifteenth dynasty which is that of the Shepherds.

[4] See *List of Abydos*, Poole, part ii. sect. iii. p. 101.

exist which records this very title "*Nufreka*" and it is *the title of Suphis I.*

This title "Nufreka" occurs in the mention of an estate of a Prince Cephrenes (75 Ghizeh), and as it was the regular custom of Egyptian notabilities to call their children after the reigning king, Prince Cephrenes must have lived during the reign of Suphis II. or Chefren. The reference in the inscription is to the king "*Shufu Nufreka.*"[1] Therefore, as nearly all the Egyptian kings have been identified by their titular names, this exceptional title, common to both, is an additional evidence, although not in itself conclusive, of the identity of Set the Powerful, and the great Pyramid king Suphis I.

With regard to the predecessor of Suphis I. in Manetho's fourth dynasty, viz., *Soris*, it is evident that he should be Nimrod, or his father (*i.e.*, either Athothes or Menes). Soris would be the Hellenised form of *suro* or *soro*, "the seed" or "son," and as this was the title especially given to the deified monarch,[2] we may conclude that Soris represents Osiris (*i.e.*, Athothes or Nimrod). This is confirmed by the monuments. In a tomb which is said to be of the time of the fourth or fifth dynasties the names *Shura*, *Nufrekara* and *Num Shufu* are found together, and in another tomb *Shura*, *Nufrekara* and a third king are found together.[3] Now, as *Num Shufu* is Suphis II. and *Nufrekara* is the prenomen of Suphis I. with the ra, as the title of a Pharaoh, added, *Shura* would be Soris, and as the Greeks always put "S" for "Sh" and substituted their own termination—as in "Suphis" for "Shufu"—*Soris*, or *Suris*, would be exactly the Hellenised form of *Shura*. It is very possible that these tombs are later than the fourth or fifth dynasties, but even if they are of that period, the *ra*, by which the Egyptian kings claimed to be descended from the Sun god, would be added to the prenomen of every recognised Pharaoh after the time of Mencheres, the successor of Num Shufu, inasmuch as Mencheres reopened the temples and restored the worship of the gods.

Mr Osburn mentions the following notices of Soris or Shura: In one inscription he is spoken of as "Lord of festivals, king of Upper and Lower Egypt, Soris (Shura) everlasting." Another inscription is: "The priest and chief of the scribes to the Pyramid of Soris (Shura) in the land of *Sho*,"[4] and as the Sh and Kh are interchangeable, it is

---

[1] Osburn, *Monumental Hist.*, vol. i. p. 278.

[2] *See* ante, chap. ii. pp. 23, 26, 31, 36, and chap. xv.

[3] Poole, *Horæ Ægypticæ*, pp. 106-111, and Plate n Appendix, where the cartouches of the above kings found on these tombs are shown (Figs. 1 and 2).

[4] Osburn, vol. i. pp. 268, 269.

probable that the Pyramid referred to is that mentioned as built by *Ouenephes* of the first dynasty near Khokhome, which might be written "*Sho Shome.*"[1] No one of the name of "Ouenephes" can be identified on the monuments, but it has every appearance of being a corruption of *Onuphis*, a title of Osiris. Neither can any place of the name of Khokhome or Shoshome be identified now, but Mr Birch says that at Sakkarah there is a Pyramid built in terraces like the tower at Babylon, and that this is the oldest monument in Egypt.[2] This would be just the description of building erected by the king of Babylon, and may therefore very well have been the Pyramid of Soris. It is also significant that Shura or Soris is the first God king mentioned in the tombs of Ghizeh. He is called God, and is represented as vanquishing enemies, and addressed as "Horus the divine and great," who strikes all enemies and "subdues all countries."[3] All this is completely in keeping with the characteristics of Osiris or Nimrod. Finally, Soris is given a reign of *twenty-eight* years by Manetho, and Osiris is stated by Plutarch to have also reigned *twenty-eight* years in Egypt.[4]

It should here be remarked that, although the Egyptian priest Manetho places the Pyramid king Suphis in a *fourth* dynasty, yet— with the exception of Menes and Athothes, who head the first dynasty, and the mention of the giant Sesochris, who appears to be Sesostris (*i.e.*, Nimrod or Athothes), together with the names Sethenes (Seth or Set ?), Souphis and Nufrekara (Suphis I.) and Sephuris (Sephres ?)— the other names in the first three dynasties cannot be identified on the monuments. It is evident that everything was done by the priestly historians to conceal the identity of the Shepherd kings, and some of the subsequent dynasties of Manetho are plainly repetitions of the kings of other dynasties representing them in different relations. In short, the interpolation by Manetho of dynasties of Shepherd and other kings between the twelfth and eighteenth dynasties is absolutely at variance with the older monumental lists of Seti and Rameses II. at Abydos, whose authority must be regarded as far superior to that of Manetho. These monumental lists show that there were *no* dynasties between the twelfth and eighteenth dynasties, but that the kings of the latter dynasty immediately succeeded those of the former.[5]

---

[1] *See* Manetho's dynasties, Cory, p. 96.
[2] Birch, *Hist. of Egypt*, p. 25.   [3] Osburn, vol. i. pp. 268-270.
[4] Plutarch, *De Iside*, S. 41; *Wilkinson*, by Birch, vol. iii. p. 80.
[5] *See* Appendix C.

This is in exact accordance with the evidence here brought forward which proves that the Shepherds were *not subsequent* to the kings of the twelfth dynasty, but the immediate successors of Menes and Athothes, and identical with the first kings of the fourth dynasty.

This evidence of repetition and interpolation makes it probable, therefore, that the kings in the first three dynasties are also repetitions of kings under one or other of the numerous titles which were assumed by the Egyptian kings.

There is a feature in the names of Suphis I. and Suphis II. which tends to further identify them with the Shepherd kings. Shufu, or Shuphu, the Egyptian form of their names, means "*much hair*," [1] a characteristic which distinguishes them in a radical manner from the Egyptians proper, who carefully shaved. Similarly Eratosthenes calls Suphis, "Saophis *Comastes*," which is the Greek for "long-haired." This was a distinguishing characteristic of the Semitic Patriarchs and Shepherd kings, and Shepherds were always represented by the Egyptians with ragged locks and unshaven. It seems extremely probable, therefore, that the group in granite, stated to be of *the Shepherd period*, now at the Museum of Cairo, of two persons with *long hair and flowing beards*, are these two kings, Suphis I., or Set, and Suphis II. (*See* Plate I.). The group is said to be of the most perfect execution [2] and this alone tends to identify it with the *Pyramid* era, the sculptures of which far exceed in perfection everything which followed it. [3] This question and the identity of the Tanis Sphinxes are discussed in the next chapter. If these figures are of Suphis I. and Suphis II., then one of them was probably, when first executed (it is now much shattered) a faithful representation of the antediluvian Patriarch Shem himself, while the other would be his son, or other relative, [4] whom he made co-regent at an early period, in order that, by preparing him for the sovereignty, he might himself resign and return to Jerusalem. The Shepherds are said to have made one of themselves king after the conquest of the country, and it is certain that he, by whose wisdom and influence the tyranny and

[1] Osburn, *Mon. Hist.*, vol. i. p. 275.
[2] Lenormant, *Anc. Hist. of East*, vol. i. pp. 222, 223.
[3] *Ibid.*, pp. 208, 209.
[4] Suphis II. is generally regarded as the son of Suphis I., but Herodotus calls Chephren the brother of Cheops, which would be equally the term given to a nephew, or grand-nephew, and it is quite possible that Suphis II., or Cephren, may have been a son of Mizraim.

idolatry of the Cushite invaders were overthrown, would be asked by the Mizraimites to rule over them until the kingdom was established, after which, as implied by the notice of Set or Typhon, he went to Jerusalem.[1]

Finally, the character of the Great Pyramid, built by Suphis I., shows that it could only have been constructed by one who, like Set or Shem, was not only a worshipper of the One God, but a priest and a prophet of that God.

Mr Flinders Petrie, the Egyptologist, has written a book on the Great Pyramid, with the object of overthrowing the conclusions of Mr Piazzi Smyth, regarding the sacred and cosmogonic significance of its construction; but, although Mr Petrie has given the world many valuable measurements of the building, his arguments against its sacred and cosmogonic significance are based on incorrect assumptions and reasonings and leave that significance entirely unshaken.[2]

✝ The Great Pyramid is a building the measurements of which symbolise the exact length of the solar year, the variation from a true circle of the earth's circuit of the sun, the precession of the equinoxes, the length of the earth's polar axis, the weight of the earth, its distance from the sun, the length of the sacred cubit used in the construction of the Ark and the Temple, besides various mathematical and other laws; and the knowledge of these things was not only absolutely unknown to the ancients, but the astonishing thing is that these things, many of which seem to have no relation or connection with each other, are symbolised by the relations to each other of, at most, two or three simple measurements,—a result which no human prescience could have conceived to be possible. ✕ It shows that there is one form of Pyramid, and one only, which possesses this remarkable significance, and even if the measurements of Mr Piazzi Smyth and others, who have discovered this significance, had been proved to be wrong, there would still remain the unexplained miracle that they had discovered, *by accident*, a Pyramid whose theoretical proportions possessed this astonishing significance!

In addition to this, the interior galleries of the Pyramid, when their symbolism is interpreted in accordance with the principles laid down in Scripture, represent exactly the length of the Jewish

[1] *Ante*, p. 263.
[2] *See* by the Author, *The Great Pyramid and Its Builder, with an Analysis of Professor Petrie's Measurements.*

and Christian dispensations, the latter terminating in the second coming of Christ at a period in strict accordance with the termination of the great prophetical periods, and in the 6000th year of the world's history according to Scripture chronology.[1]

Finally, the Great Pyramid, whose "top-stone" or "head corner-stone" is *missing*, is the only building which answers to the description of that spiritual building of which Christ is the "head corner-stone"; and which Head-stone is yet to be "brought forth with shoutings, crying grace unto it" (Zech. iv. 7). Moreover, standing as it does in *the midst* of the land of Egypt, and yet on its *border*, towards the desert, it also answers the description of the prophet, "In that day shall there be an altar to the Lord, in *the midst* of the land of Egypt, and a Pillar at *the border* thereof, and it shall be for a sign and a witness unto the Lord in the land of Egypt" (Isa. xix. 19, 20).

But if so, then no human wisdom or prescience could have designed it, and its constructor, Suphis, must, like Moses in the construction of the Ark and Tabernacle, have received his instructions from God, and, like Moses, must have been a priest and prophet of God. Such characteristics can apply to no Egyptian king, except to the Shepherd king, "Set the Powerful," who was Shem, the righteous king of Salem, and "priest of the Most High God."

We may here briefly recapitulate the evidence in proof of the Shepherd kings being the Pyramid builders, Suphis I. and Suphis II.

Firstly, it has been shown that Menes (*i.e.*, Mena or Meni), the first king of Egypt, is identical with Thoth or Meni, whom the second Cronus, or Nimrod, made king of Egypt, and that Thoth is identical with the first Cronus or Belus, who was also the first king of Babylon, viz., Cush.

Secondly, that Athothes, the son of Meni or Thoth, is identical with Osiris, the son of Saturn or Belus, and that Osiris was the first Cushite conqueror of Egypt, and the same as Egyptus and Sesostris, and identical with Nin or Ninus, the son of Belus, and with Bel Nimrod, or Nimrod the son of Cush, and the founder of the first great empire of the world. Therefore, that the Babylonian and Egyptian kingdoms commenced at, or about, the same time, and the first two kings of the one were also the first two kings of the other.

Thirdly, that the overthrow of Osiris by Set or Seth, whose name is synonymous with Shem, and who in after ages was

[1] See *The Great Pyramid and Its Builder*, etc.

identified by the idolatrous priesthood with Typhon, the Evil Principle, is the same event as the overthrow of Saturn by Titan or Shem, and the same as the conquest of Egypt by the Shepherd king, Set or Saites, who is also identified with Typhon, and with Shem, the founder of Jerusalem, while his memory was equally abhorred. Therefore, that the Shepherd kings were the immediate successors of the Cushite kings, Menes and Athothes, and they are in consequence represented as the first rightful kings of Egypt, by Josephus.

Fourthly, that the story of the Shepherd kings, their overthrow of idolatry and their supposed oppression of the people, is identical in every respect with the story of the Pyramid kings by Herodotus.

Fifthly, Herodotus implies that these Pyramid kings were actually called *Shepherds*.

Sixthly, the fact that Apepi, although a pure Egyptian king, who came to the throne long after the first Shepherd kings, and at a time when their memory was held in abhorrence—and was yet *called a Shepherd king*, because he changed his religion and suppressed the worship of the Egyptian gods—is a further powerful evidence that Suphis I. and Suphis II., who also suppressed the worship of the gods, must have been also regarded as Shepherd kings. Manetho, moreover, says that, like the Shepherd kings, the Pyramid kings were of "*a different race*" (*i.e.*, from their predecessors), showing that their accession, like that of the Shepherd kings, had been accompanied by some revolution.

Seventhly, the Pyramid kings, as shown by Herodotus, were held in the same abhorrence as the Shepherd kings by the Egyptian priesthood of later times.

Eighthly, the date of the Great Pyramid proves that the Pyramid kings, like the Shepherd kings, must have been the *immediate* successors of Menes and Athothes, and that the Shepherd and Pyramid kings must therefore be identical.

Ninthly, the period during which Egyptian idolatry was suppressed under the first two *Pyramid kings* is the same as that given to the *Shepherd kings*, and the respective lengths of their reigns, excluding the co-regency of Suphis II., is seemingly identical with those of the first two Shepherd kings.

Tenthly, the prenomen of the first Shepherd king is the same as that of the first Pyramid king.

Eleventhly, the Pyramid kings were distinguished by being long-haired and bearded, a thing unknown in the kings of pure Egyptian race, but a special characteristic of the Shepherds and of the Semitic Patriarchs.

Twelfthly, the sacred and cosmogonic character of the Great Pyramid built by Suphis I., and the profound knowledge it reveals, is an evidence that the builder could only have been a prophet, inspired by God—such as Shem, the righteous king of Jerusalem, and one, therefore, who, like the Shepherd king Set and the Pyramid king Suphis, would be the stern opponent of idolatry.

Considering, therefore, that the Shepherd kings can never be identified under the nicknames given to them by Manetho, and that they were nevertheless some of the most powerful of the Egyptian kings, and *must therefore be identical* with certain of the more famous kings whose true names are known to us, there seems to be no question that they were the Pyramid kings Suphis I. and Suphis II.

CHAPTER XIV

THE SHEPHERD SCULPTURES

THE evidence of the hatred of the priesthood for the Pyramid king Suphis or Set is probably the reason why no sculptures appear to remain of him. For the sculptured likeness of nearly every other king of any importance has been carefully preserved. This hatred is, of itself, the strongest evidence that the two figures in granite of the Shepherd period shown in Plate I. were Set or Suphis and his successor Shefra. It is perfectly clear that the features of both have been wilfully and violently destroyed—broken away by iron hammers —for the rest of the figures are as smooth and finely chiselled as on the day they were completed and show no signs whatever of disintegration by weather. An enlarged photograph of the left-hand figure is given in Plate II., and it will there be seen that one side of the head, the lower part of the forehead, the eyebrows and the eyes, with the exception of their lower lids, and the nose and upper lip, have been completely smashed and destroyed, indicating a vindictive malice which nothing but religious hatred can explain.

There is no record of such hatred, except in the case of the Shepherd and Pyramid kings, and as these figures have also the long hair and beards peculiar to the Shepherd and Pyramid kings, and to them alone, there are strong grounds for concluding that they are the figures of the first two of these kings, during whose reigns idolatry in Egypt was wholly suppressed.

The hieroglyphics between the supporting columns read as follows :—

" Life to the perfect God Amen Ra, Son of Mut Lady of Asher, King of Upper and Lower Egypt, Aa Kheper Ra, Sotep en Amen, Son of the Sun Mer Amen."

The inscription has nothing to do with the two figures themselves, and is evidently an after addition. It is a dedication to the god Amen by a king whose prenomen in the oval reads Aa Kheper Ra, or, according to Osburn, whose reading is confirmed by the Greek renderings of this and other prenomens, Aa Cher ra. It is the prenomen of Amenhotep II. of the eighteenth dynasty, and the other figures in the oval are probably a variation of his nomen "Amenhotep."

The dedication of this sculpture to the Sun god Amen by Amenhotep, king of Upper and Lower Egypt, indicates that it was uninjured at that time (Set being still at that time highly honoured), and that the persons it represents were regarded as of great importance, which is a further evidence that they were the famous kings whose memory was so hated by the priesthood of later times.

But, although the features of these figures have been nearly destroyed, there are other sculptures in good preservation which, it is almost certain, represent the features of the great Shepherd and Pyramid king, Set the Powerful, or Suphis. These are the Sphinxes or human-headed lions, discovered at Tanis (Plate III.), and the reason why these have escaped the vindictive malice of the priesthood is probably because Tanis was so far removed from the central seat of idolatry at Thebes.

Sphinxes were the particular form of sculpture associated with the Shepherd kings, and were constructed *in honour of Set,* while the Great Sphinx seems to be especially associated with the Great Pyramid built by Suphis, and as the Tanis Sphinxes are unmistakably the likeness of one particular individual, it seems certain that they represent the features of the first great Shepherd king, Set the Powerful, the overthrower of the mighty king of Babylon.

The nose of the nearest Sphinx is slightly broken, but with this exception the features of all three are identical. The sculpturing is of high excellence, the features admirably chiselled, and they are evidently a truthful likeness of the person they portray. It is a kingly face, truly leonine in its calm dignity and massive strength, bearing the expression of conscious power combined with benevolence and rectitude.

The features also present a type which, in its full strength and virility, is seldom, if ever, met with at the present day, and the features of the later Egyptian kings, as delineated in their statues, are weak and puerile compared to those of these Sphinxes. The great development of bone, the massive nose, jaws and chin, breadth of head and cheek-bones, indicate, to use a phrenological term, great "vitativeness" and physical stamina, more especially as all the features are admirably proportioned and clearly cut, vigorous without coarseness.

If, then, these heads are likenesses of the great Shepherd king Set, they represent the exact features of the antediluvian Patriarch Shem, and we behold in them something of the type of primeval man as he first came from the hands of God, possessed of a vitality that could endure for nigh upon a thousand years. It is also just such a face as we might expect to see in one who was not only of the mighty antediluvian stock, but the sole and fearless witness for God amidst the surrounding idolatry, the overthrower of the dominion and tyranny of the powerful and merciless Cushite monarch, and afterwards the guardian of the Truth he had restored. In representing him, therefore, as a lion with a human head, there was a certain fitness, and the idea was probably borrowed from the Cherubim, the form of which seems to have been generally known.

It is also remarkable, and not what we should expect to find in the sculptured effigy of a great king, nor is it seen in the sculptured figures of any other Egyptian king, that the face is slightly turned upward, and there is a far-away look in the eyes, as if appealing from earth to heaven. This also is fitly representative of one who overcame "not by might nor by power," but by the Spirit of God.[1]

The fact that Sphinxes were peculiarly characteristic of the Shepherd kings, and were representative and constructed in honour of Set, is a feature which intimately associates them with the Pyramid kings. For there can be little doubt that the Great Sphinx lying under the shadow of the Great Pyramid was constructed by one of the Pyramid kings, and that it was therefore the first original Sphinx on the model of which the Tanis Sphinxes were constructed. This is the conclusion of all who have carefully examined it, as in the case of Belzoni, who says, "It appeared to me that the Sphinx, the Temple and the Pyramid were all three erected at the same time, as they appear to be all on one line, and of equal antiquity."[2] In short, the Great Sphinx has been supposed to have represented the features of Shefra (Suphis II.),[3] from his name being found on it in a dedicatory inscription by Thothmes IV.;[4]

---

[1] It may be remarked that the hieroglyphics contained in the existing part of the oval, at the bottom of the breast of the left-hand Sphinx, are the same as the concluding portion of the title of Amenhotep II. on the pedestal of the two figures previously mentioned, viz. "(Son of) the Sun Mer Amen." They were probably inscribed by that king. The hieroglyphics higher up probably read "The good god." One is partially obliterated.

[2] Belzoni's *Travels*, vol. ii. p. 405.   [3] *Wilkinson*, by Birch, vol. iii. p. 310, note.

[4] Colonel Howard Vyse, *Pyramids of Ghizeh*, vol. iii. pp. 114, 115.

but in another inscription it is shown to have been already in existence in the reign of Shefra,[1] and considering its position in relation to the Great Pyramid built by Shufu (Suphis I.), it is evidently far more probable that it represented the features of the latter king. It appears to have been originally exactly similar to the Tanis Sphinxes. It has the same lion's body, and although its features are now nearly obliterated, they are described by ancient observers as having the same *calm dignity* as we see in those of the Tanis Sphinxes, and Abdollatiph, in whose time the Great Sphinx was entire, says that "the admirable proportions of its features excited his astonishment above everything he had seen in Egypt."[2] The beard has now disappeared, which has led some persons to suppose that it was the face of a woman; but the portions of its enormous beard were found lying beneath its chin by M. Caviglia,[3] showing that in this respect also it was similar to the Tanis Sphinxes. The general proportions and massive breadth of the features, and the curves of the cheeks, and contours round the mouth, are also identical with those of the Tanis Sphinxes, and there is the same upturned position of the face.

But if the features of the Great Sphinx representative of Suphis I. were originally the same as those of the Tanis Sphinxes, then the Pyramid king Suphis and the Shepherd king Set are *one and the same person.*

Now it is not a little remarkable, and it tends to confirm this conclusion, that the Sabæans believe the Great Pyramid to be the tomb of *Seth*[4] or Shem, for this shows how closely tradition connects the Pyramid king with the Shepherd king Seth, and it is just the sort of tradition which would arise if Set or Shem, having completed the Pyramid, abdicated the throne and disappeared, having retired to Jerusalem.

If again, in the last days, the Great Pyramid was to be "an altar to the Lord in the midst of the land of Egypt, and a pillar at the border thereof to the Lord, for a sign and a witness to the Lord of Hosts in the land of Egypt," there was a remarkable significance in this memorial of its builder, the great king and prophet and priest of the Most High God, placed like a watchful guardian by its side, in the form of a great human-headed lion, as if emblematic of that Spirit of God, symbolised by the Cherubim,

---

[1] Brugsch, *Hist. of Egypt*, vol. i. p. 80.
[2] Russell's *Egypt Ancient and Modern*, p. 125.   [3] *Ibid.*, p. 119.
[4] Uri's *Cat.*, MS. 785 ; Vyse, *Pyramids of Ghizeh*, vol. ii., Appendix, p. 364.

and of which Set was the mouthpiece and manifestation. For, in spite of the violence of man and his desecration of the Great Pyramid by tearing off the polished white casing stones that covered it, an act which in itself may be symbolic,[1] the building was yet to preserve the secrets of its structure in their integrity until the time came for their revelation.

The Sphinx was regarded by the Egyptians as emblematic of the union of intellect and power,[2] but the various forms of Sphinxes with heads of women and of rams and other animals adopted by the idolatrous Egyptians of later times shows how degraded the idea ultimately became.

If, now, we compare the features of the Tanis Sphinxes with those of the left-hand figure in Plate I., an enlarged view of which is given in Plate II., it will be seen that the proportions of the face in each are identical. There is the same breadth of face, massive cheek-bones and jaw, precisely the same curves round the mouth, the same proportionate height and breadth of head, while the full lower lip, which alone remains, is in every way identical with that of the Tanis Sphinx. The only difference is that the conventional long hair characteristic of Set or Suphis has been replaced in the Tanis Sphinx by the lion's mane.

The right-hand figure, although possessing the same broad, full eye and massive cheek-bones as in the Tanis Sphinx, is of inferior type. The forehead is neither so high nor so broad, nor is the jaw so massive. There is indeed a general likeness, such as might exist between persons of near relationship, but the features indicate a man of weaker and less commanding character. This is just what we might expect if they are those of Shefra or Khefra, and if we compare them with those of this king in Plate IV., it will be seen that, as far as their injured condition admits of comparison, there is a striking resemblance. There is the same broad eye and massive cheek-bones in each, but in both the face narrows towards the lower part, while the forehead in each is of similar proportions.

There is, therefore, every reason to conclude that they are figures of the two hated Shepherd kings, the one on the left hand being Set or Suphis, and the one on the right hand Num Shufu or Shefra.

[1] If, as seems to be the case, the Great Pyramid is symbolic of the earth and man, then the white casing stones by which it was covered, like the white raiment of Rev. iii. 18, xix. 8., etc., may be emblematic of the purity of man when first created in the image of God ; but which purity man himself, through sin, has torn off and desecrated.

[2] *Wilkinson*, by Birch, vol. iii. chap. xiv. p. 309.

U

From the fact that the human sacrifices offered to Osiris, and especially selected to represent the hated Typhon or Set, are described as being men of red or ruddy colour,[1] it would appear that the Shepherd king Set, or Shem, and possibly the Israelites also, who were regarded as the same race, were, unlike the black Egyptians or Cushites, of a ruddy or fair complexion. For while persons of a dark complexion only turn darker, those of a fair complexion become *red* in a hot climate. It seems also that Shem must have had red or auburn hair, for the Egyptians had the same hatred and contempt for people with red hair, and evinced this dislike by representing them in humiliating positions,[2] just as, in a similar way, they expressed their hatred of shepherds.

This is certainly opposed to our usual idea of the Semitic type, as represented by the Jews in Europe. But from the incidental mention of Sarah, Moses, David and Esther as being exceptionally fair, it would appear that it was not an uncommon type amongst the ancient Israelites.[3] In Holman Hunt's great picture of "Christ in the Temple," he has represented our Lord with auburn hair and blue eyes, and he did so because, after the most careful observation and inquiry, he ascertained that this was the most prevalent type among the Jews in the East, although, like the Creole descendants of English and French parents in the United States of America, a residence for generations in the warmer climate has given a darker tint to their complexion.

This is confirmed by Sir Gardner Wilkinson. He says, "The Jews of the East to this day often have red hair and blue eyes, with a nose of delicate form and nearly straight, and are quite unlike their brethren of Europe, and the children in modern Jerusalem have the pink and white complexions of Europeans. It is the Syrians who have the large nose that strikes us as the peculiarity of Western Israelites. This prominent feature was always a characteristic of the Syrians, but not of the ancient nor of the modern Jews of Judea."[4]

The authority of this learned traveller and archæologist is a proof that Holman Hunt was correct, and that red or auburn hair

---

[1] See *ante*, chap. x. pp. 243, 244.

[2] *Wilkinson*, by Birch, vol. iii. p. 403.

[3] Eusebius quotes Artahanus, a Jew who lived in the first century before Christ, as stating that Moses was of a ruddy complexion with white hair (Eusebius, lib. x.); Cory, p 189.

[4] Wilkinson's *Egyptians*, vol. ii. p. 198.

and blue eyes was an ordinary type among the Jews, and may have been still more marked among the other tribes, the type of the European Jew being evidently due to intermarriage with Syrian or other races. It is, therefore, confirmatory of the fact that it was the original Semitic type as represented by Set or Shem.

Now this is remarkable. For this type at the present day is confined to the British or Anglo-Saxon and Scandinavian races, and it has always been characteristic of those races. Gibbon remarks of the ancient Germans and Scandinavians, who by successive waves invaded or peopled Britain, "Almost the whole of modern Germany, Denmark, Norway, Sweden, Finland, Livonia, Prussia and the greater part of Poland were peopled by the various tribes of one great nation, whose complexion, manners and language denoted a common origin and preserved a striking resemblance." [1]

Tacitus says of them, "I concur in opinion with those who deem the Germans (*i.e.*, the ancient Germans) never to have intermarried with other nations, but to be a race pure, unmixed and stamped with a distinct character. Hence a family likeness pervades the whole, although their numbers are so great; eyes stern and blue, ruddy hair large bodies," etc.[2]

Strabo also describes the people of Belgica, who in the days of Cæsar had occupied the southern portion of Britain, and were the people who resisted his invasion, as being of great stature and yellow hair, from which it is evident that they were not Kelts as commonly supposed, but of the same race as the Germans. In short, Strabo says that in every respect they were similar in nature, laws and customs to the Germans east of the Rhine;[3] while Cæsar represents them as of quite a different race to the Kelts of Gaul,[4] and that they told him that they had "*sprung from the Germans*" and were the fore-

---

[1] Gibbon, chap. ix. p. 85 ; 8vo. edition in one volume.

[2] *Manners of Germans*, chap. iv. It should be remembered that, although many of the ancient Germans remained behind, both in North Germany and Scandinavia, yet the principal portion of them went to England and Scotland, and that the English and Scots are now the purest representatives of the ancient race, and possess its leading characteristics—fair complexion, red or yellow hair and great stature. This is not the case with the modern Germans, who, it is well known, are largely descended from Tartar races, Sarmatians, Huns, Sclavonians, etc., who at different periods occupied Central Europe after the departure of the bulk of the ancient Germans. As a consequence of this, although many of them are fair, the prevalent type in modern Germany is the broad head and moderate stature of the Tartar race.

[3] Strabo, bk. iv. chap. iv. pp. 2, 3 ; book iv. chap. v. p. 3.

[4] *See* Cæsar, bk. i. chap. :.

most of the German tribes who had crossed the Rhine and dispossessed the Kelts in Belgica.[1]

These Belgæ eventually spread over the greater part of Britain, for we find Caractacus, king of the Silures in South Wales, who fought against Suetonius, A.D. 51, recalling to his followers the fact that they were the people who had resisted Julius Cæsar a hundred years before;[2] and a large portion of them seem to have crossed over and conquered Ireland. The Iceni, also in Norfolk, who were defeated by Suetonius, were evidently of the same race, as their queen, Boadicea, is described as of great stature, with yellow hair.[3] The Caledonians and the Albanians, who came from Germany to Scotland, and constituted the chief portion of its population,[4] the latter giving their name, "Alban," to the country are also described as yellow-haired.[5]

It seems clear, therefore, that a fair complexion and red or yellow hair were the distinguishing characteristics of those ancient German and Scandinavian races, who were the ancestors of the British, and that it was not a Keltic characteristic; although the fair Belgæ, because they occupied a part of Keltica, formerly inhabited by the Gauls, are incorrectly spoken of as Kelts by Strabo, an inaccuracy on his part which has given rise to much misconception, and which is entirely denied by the more accurate Cæsar. The true descendants of the ancient Gauls or Kelts are the French, who are generally of a dark or sallow complexion, and the only exceptions to this are to be found among the Bretons and the people of Normandy. But the former are the descendants of a portion of the Belgic Britons, who, driven by the Saxons to the west of Cornwall, emigrated to Brittany, the ancient Armorica, which they called "Little Britain"; while the latter are the people of a part of France originally occupied by the Normans, a Scandinavian race, and which for many generations was a British possession. These exceptions only emphasise the fact that the true Kelts, as represented by the bulk of the French, were of a dark complexion. They claimed to be descended from Dis or from Hercules,[6] whom we have seen to be one and the same person—viz, Nimrod, the son of Cush. From these traditions it would appear that

[1] *Ibid.*, bk. ii. chap. iv.

[2] Lynam's *Roman Emperors*, vol. i. pp. 334-336.

[3] *Ibid.*, vol. i. pp. 406-410.

[4] Davies, *Welsh Triads*, vol. ii. p. 154 ; *Celtic Researches*, vol. ii. p. 204.

[5] Gaelic Poem of the Eleventh Century (Wilson, *Archæology of Scotland*, part iv. p. 463).

[6] Cæsar, bk. vi. chap. xviii. ; Toland's *Druids*, p. 129.

the Kelts were of a mixed Cushite and Japhetic race, which would account for their dark complexion.

It is probable, therefore, that the term " Keltic," as applied to the different dialects called by that name, may really be a misnomer, and, as the French and Iberians are the purest descendants of the ancient Kelts, that the French and Spanish languages, although largely leavened with Latin, should be regarded as more truly representative of the ancient Keltic.

It would also seem that the British may be of nearly pure Semitic origin, and although the features of Set or Shem are more massive than any now met with, yet it is evident that they more nearly resemble the Anglo-Saxon type than that of any other race.

It is clear, however, that there was a Keltic race in Britain before the arrival of the Belgic British, and that the latter may have inter-married with them, and have adopted many of their customs. Cæsar speaks of a race different from the Belgic Britons as inhabiting the interior of the island, and says that they were " born in the island," *i.e.*, that they were aborigines; and it is well-known that Britain was, originally, a principal seat of the Druidical religion, which was essenti-ally Celtic and quite distinct from that of the Germans. (*See* Cæsar, bk. v. chap. xii.; bk. vi. chaps. xiv.-xxi.) As the number of the Belgic British increased and they spread over the island, they seemed to have driven the Kelts to the extreme west and north of Wales—the people of Anglesey defeated by Suetonius, A.D. 61, being evidently of that race, as proved by their human sacrifices, which were an es-sential feature of the Keltic religion. (*See* Lynam's *Roman Emperors*, vol. i. p. 486; Cæsar, bk. vi. chap. xvi.)

PART IV

THE RESUSCITATION AND DEVELOPMENT OF PAGAN IDOLATRY

CHAPTER XV

THE RESUSCITATION AND DEVELOPMENT OF PAGAN IDOLATRY

WE have now to consider the character of the ancient idolatry as it was resuscitated after the death of Nimrod, and the methods by which it was developed.

On the death of Nimrod, his Cushite followers are said to have fled to Æthiopia, but Saturn (*i.e.*, Menes or Cush) is said to have fled to Italy,[1] and not only do the ruins of the two cities, Saturnia and Janicula, mentioned by Virgil,[2] attest to the fact, but Latium is also said to have received its name from "*latere*," "to lie hid," because Saturn was supposed to be hidden there.[3]

Latinus or *Lateinos*, the ancient king of Italy and father of the Latins, seems also to be the human form of Saturn. For *Saturn* signifies "the hidden one," and this also is the meaning of "*Latinus*," which is evidently derived from "*Latere*," which is itself derived from the Chaldee "*Lat*," "the hidden one."[4] Æneas represents Latinus to be the grandson of Saturn,[5] but this may only be the natural consequence of regarding him as a human king, and, therefore, distinct from the god Saturn, and a similar distinction between the gods and their human originals may be observed in other cases. Latinus was also deified as a son of the Sun god,[6] and this, together with the fact that Saturn, Latinus and Latium have all the same signification and that Italy was formerly called "The Saturnian Land," seems to indicate that the ancient Latins were a Cushite colony founded by Cush. The fact also that the Etrurians, the most ancient people of Italy, seem to have been of Accadian or Cushite origin tends to confirm this.[7]

The fact that Cush was obliged to conceal himself implies that the moral effect of the overthrow of idolatry in Egypt extended to the Japhetic people occupying the shores of the Mediterranean.

[1] Lemprière, *Saturn.*   [2] *Æneid*, lib. viii. ll. 467-470, vol. iii. p. 608.
[3] Ovid, *Fasti*, lib. vii. l. 238, vol. iii. p. 29 ; *Æneid*, lib. viii. l. 319, etc., p. 384.
[4] Hislop, p. 270, note.
[5] *Æneid*, lib. vii. ll. 45-49 ; Hislop, p. 271, note.
[6] Dryden, *Virgil*, bk. xii. ll. 245, 248, vol. iii. p. 775.   [7] See *ante*, p. 10.

The statement also that Titan (*i.e.*, Shem), in his war against Saturn, was assisted by his brother Titans,[1] implies that some of the descendants of Japhet combined with Set, or Shem, and the descendants of Mizraim against the Cushite idolaters, and that Cush, the originator of that idolatry, was therefore in as much danger of his life as his son. The complete defeat also of Semiramis by the king of India and the destruction of her army prevented any assistance from Babylon.[2]

It is manifest, therefore, that any attempt to restore idolatry could only have been made secretly at first. We are told that the gods, when they were overthrown by Typhon, fled to Egypt, where, by the advice of Pan, that is, Cush, they assumed the shape of various animals to conceal their identity,[3] which implies that the resuscitation of idolatry was in a great measure due to methods devised by Cush. Its ultimate triumph, however, is represented as due to Isis (*i.e.*, Semiramis), with the assistance of her son Horus. On the death of Osiris she is said to have collected the various portions of her husband's body, and erected a statue to each, and then to have established a priesthood, bound to secrecy and celibacy, whom she endowed with lands to support them, to pay divine honours to him. Each body of priests was to represent the god under the form of such animal as they chose; by which we may conclude that she acted under the advice of Cush. One portion of the body, the Phallus, she failed to discover, and therefore made a wooden representation of it, and paid it special honour.[4] In consequence of this there were many burial-places of Osiris in Egypt, at each of which a shrine was erected containing one of the relics, or supposed relics, of the god.[5]

It would thus appear that Isis, or Semiramis, was the founder of a priesthood for the purpose of resuscitating the fallen idolatry, and especially the Phallic worship, and that this worship was initiated in Egypt by representing the dead monarch under the form of certain animals to which a secret homage was paid; the result of which was that animal worship became the distinguishing feature of the subsequent idolatry in that country.

[1] Lemprière, *Titan.*   [2] *Ante*, p. 68.
[3] Ovid, *Fasti.*, lib. i. ll. 393-404; Diod., *Bibl.*, lib. i. p. 16; Hyg., *Poet. Astron.*, lib. ii. cap. xxviii.; Hyg., Fab. 196; Eratos., *Catast.*, cap. xxvii.; Faber, vol. ii. p. 406; Lemprière, *Typhon, Pan, Gigantes.*
[4] Lemprière, *Isis, Phallica.*
[5] There were several cities in Middle Egypt called "Busuris," meaning the burial-place of Osiris; Osburn, vol. i. pp. 328, 329.

In Egypt the worship of the true God and the suppression of idolatry appears to have continued in full force for over a century, and must have had a powerful effect on the minds of the people. Moreover, the worship of the Pagan gods was again suppressed in the reign of Apepi, and this, with the influence of Joseph and the Israelites, and the judgments of God at the Exodus of the latter, could not fail to have deepened the effect previously produced, and it is therefore probable that there were always a certain number of the descendants of Mizraim who clung to the purer religion. In short, it is recorded that Tnepachtus, the father of Bocchoris the Wise, who is called a "Saite," or follower of Set, and who reigned as late as the twenty-fourth dynasty, protested against the idolatry established by Menes,[1] and was burnt alive by the Cushite king Sabacon, who appears to have dethroned him.[2]

There was thus a necessity for a caution and reserve in the propagation of idolatry in Egypt which did not exist elsewhere, and which obliged its propagators to take every means to associate it with the purer religion, and to give it an outward appearance of a righteousness which was wholly foreign to it. "*Mystery*" was in consequence the prominent feature of Egyptian idolatry, and it was in Egypt that the celebrated "*Mysteries*," the object of which was the revelation of the god to the initiated, were first instituted.

This also accounts for the highly metaphysical character of Egytian theology, and it was by this means and by the use of allegory, metaphor, and the double meaning of words that its true nature was concealed.

The idolatry of Egypt was therefore very different to that of Babylon. Speaking of the magic, or worship of spirits in Chaldea, M. Lenormant says, "The belief in spirits is seen there in its most ancient form, without any philosophical refinements as to the divine substance, without any allusion to the vast number of mythological legends which fill the Egyptian formulæ. They (the magical formulæ of Chaldea) contain *no mysteries*, and the sacerdotal secret, if there was one, consisted in the precise knowledge of the exact forms of the incantations, sacred from their antiquity, and no doubt also from the idea that they were of divine origin."[3]

For the same necessity for reserve and secrecy did not exist among the kinsfolk and descendants of the dead monarch in Babylon. They were the supporters of the idolatry established by him, and the

---

[1] See *ante*, chap. iv. p. 85.   [2] Manetho's dynasties, Cory, p. 126.
[3] *Chaldean Magic and Sorcery*, chap. viii. p. 109.

glamour produced on their minds by his vast prowess and conquests would have prepared many of them to pay homage and honour to his memory, and eventually to regard him as a god. But even with them this belief would make but little progress while the memory of his overthrow and death was still fresh, and we are told that no open idolatry was ventured upon in Babylon until the reign of Arioch, the grandson of Semiramis,[1] a king who was apparently the contemporary of Mencheres, the restorer of idolatry in Egypt. We are also told that it was not until "long after their death that Cronus, Rhea, Zeus, Apollo and the rest were worshipped as gods,"[2] although, no doubt, the Accadian worship of spirits and Nature gods established by Nimrod and his father continued in force among the Cushites of Babylonia. It is evident, however, that the other descendants of Noah, who had been instrumental in overthrowing the cruel dominion and obscene idolatry established by Nimrod, would only hold him in abhorrence, and that special means would be necessary to remove the opprobrium attached to his memory, Nor could any world-wide success in resuscitating idolatry be hoped for until the true story of his judicial execution as the enemy of God had been lost sight of, and the lapse of generations had weakened the memory of the evil he had wrought.

The first and principal means by which, in after generations, the abhorrence attached to his memory came to be obliterated, was by representing his death to have been voluntarily suffered for the good of mankind, and that he was none other than the promised "*seed of woman.*" This was the foundation of the whole system, and was, no doubt, the real origin of the avatars and anthropomorphic gods of Paganism, and which suggested the idea of representing them as having become incarnate, and to have lived as men upon the earth.

The promise of the Messiah, and of the restitution of all things through Him, had not only been "foretold by holy prophets since the world began," but, as we have seen, the heavens themselves had revealed it to all ages and nations. The prophecy of Enoch is recorded by Jude, and both this, and the statement of Job, is evidence that the promised Redeemer was recognised, not only as the seed of the woman, but as the Son of God also. "I know," says Job, "that my Redeemer liveth, and that he shall stand at the latter day on the earth and after I shall awake, though my body shall be destroyed, yet in my flesh shall I see *God*." [1] Job here asserts that his Redeemer is God himself, and yet that He is one who should stand as *a man* upon the earth in a material form, visible to the eyes of the flesh.

It is in the last degree improbable that the idea of the Creator taking human form should have suggested itself to the mind of man. All the ancient cosmogonies recognise a primary creator of all things, but what is there in creation that could have suggested the idea that the Creator Himself should become created ? It is wholly opposed to every conclusion based upon the knowledge of the things which are seen. Man was so evidently merely a higher animal, a partaker with them of the same nature and instincts, that, looking only on the material side of things, and the numberless gradations of life from the vegetable to man, evolution became the natural conclusion. But the more the unity of man with nature was recognised, the more improbable would it have seemed that the Creator should become incarnate, and allied, like man, to the lowest organisms of nature. And yet it was amongst those who were essentially materialists, and who regarded nature, and the life of nature, as everything, that we first find the realised idea of an incarnate God.

It is true that the discoveries of modern science in geology, comparative anatomy, biology, etc., show that all nature manifests the steady and continuous evolution of *an idea ;* inasmuch as the lower organisms which precede are prophecies of the higher organisms which follow them, each of the former possessing the rudiments of organs of no possible use to itself, and for the existence of which it is absolutely impossible to discover a *natural* cause, but which in a more perfect development are necessities to higher organisms.[2] From this point of view, Nature herself demands a further evolution beyond man, with all his imperfections and evil, an evolution which a race allied to man, as man is to the animals, and yet partaking of the moral perfections of the Creator, would satisfy. But geology is a science of modern growth, and the data for such a conclusion were therefore absolutely wanting to the ancients. Hence, as every effect demands a cause, we are forced to seek a cause for their

[1] Revised rendering of Job xix. 25-27.

[2] This fact, while it emphatically implies the existence of *intention* in a creative power outside, and distinct from, the organism itself, is absolutely fatal to a belief in *natural* evolution. For how could an organ be evolved *naturally* without a *natural* cause ? The doctrine of chance might be invoked by some to account for one or two such evolutions, but not when they can be enumerated by the million and are all parts of one ruling idea.

ideas of avatars and incarnations of the Deity outside of nature.

Such a cause, according to Scripture, existed in the prophecies of the Redeemer, who was to be the seed of woman and the Son of God, and who was to be the destroyer of the serpent, and to suffer in so doing. These prophecies, known throughout the world, were just suited to the purpose of the advocates of the new idolatry, for no better method could be devised for recommending that idolatry to the world, than by representing the dead monarch to be the true seed of the woman, the hoped-for Redeemer who was to destroy the serpent and suffer in the conflict.

Therefore, one of the names given to the god in Babylon was *Zoroaster* or *Zeroaster*.[1] This name in its secret or esoteric meaning signified "Fireborn," or "seed of fire," from "*zero*," "seed," and "*ashta*," "fire;" but "*ashta*" also signified "woman," and the name was thus made use of in its exoteric sense to pretend that the god was the promised "seed of the woman." Zoroaster was also known as *Zaradas* and *Zeroastes*,[2] and in the Parsi religion he is called *Zoroadas* and *Zarades*, signifying "the one, or only seed,"[3] a title which could only apply to the promised Messiah. The great reformer in the Parsi religion is also called *Zarathustra*, a word of Chaldean origin meaning "the delivering seed,"[4] which is equivalent to the title given to Phoroneus, "the emancipator."

It would thus appear that *zar*, *zoro* and *zero* are variations of a word which means both "the seed" and "a circle," and is derived from the Chaldee "*Zer*," to "encompass" or "enclose,"[5] from whence is derived the Chaldean "*Sarus*" (so called by the Greeks), meaning "a circle or cycle of time," and it is also clearly the origin of the Hindu word "*Sari*," the name of the long scarf used by Hindu women for *encircling*, or winding round the body.[6] The Greek word "*Seira*," "a noose" or "*encircling* band," appears to be derived from the same root, and as kissos was a title of Cush,[7] the chaplet of ivy called "Seira Kissos," which the worshippers of Bacchus wore, would, in its esoteric meaning, signify "the seed, or son of Cush."[8] The name also of the second person in the Phœnician Trinity, viz., "*Chusorus*"[9] has

[1] *Ante.* p. 35.
[2] Johannes, *Clericus*, tom. ii. ; *De Chaldæis*, sect. i. cap. ii. pp. 191, 194; Hislop, p. 59, note.
[3] Wilson's *Parsi Religion*, p. 400 ; Hislop, p. 59.
[4] Wilson, p. 201 ; Hislop, p. 59, note.   [5] Hislop, p. 50, note.
[6] *Chambers's Dictionary*, "Sari."   [7] See *ante*, p. 39.
[8] Hislop, p. 50, note.   [9] Wilkinson's *Egyptians*, vol. iv. p. 191.

evidently a similar signification viz., *chus-sorus*, "the seed of Cush." *Zero*, the circle, also represented the disk of the sun, which was the especial emblem of the Sun god, and thus, while Zoroaster appeared to be exoterically the seed of the woman, he could be revealed to the initiates as the Sun and Fire god.

The name "*Asar*," by which Osiris is designated on many of the monuments, and the title "*Sarapis*" or "*Asar-apis*," appear to be also derived from the Chaldean *Zar* or *Zer*, and, as suggested by Mr Hislop, O'siris, or He'siris, may have the same signification, viz., the "seed,"[1] while in India Osiris was known as Esar, Iswar and Eswara, which appear to be also compounds of Sar or Zar. Hence the enemy of Osiris "the seed of the woman," was represented as Typhon, the evil principle, and Apophis, the evil serpent.

The names of the god in Babylon, "Nin" or "Ninus," "the Son," and "El Bar," "the Son of God," and the titles "the eldest son," "the first-born," "the only son," and those of the Goddess Mother, "Semiramis," "the branch bearer," and "Zerbanit," "Mother of the Seed," have the same doctrinal signification.[2]

This aspect of the god, as "the Son," or promised seed of the woman, was therefore constantly kept before the minds of the worshippers, by representing him as a child in his mother's arms. Thus, in Babylon, the image of the Goddess Mother is represented with a child in her arms.[3] In India, Indrani, the wife of Indra, is similarly represented.[4] In Egypt, although Horus was the son of Isis, yet being the same as Osiris, the Goddess Mother, represented with a child in her arms, were worshipped under the names of Isis and Osiris.[5] In Asia, mother and child were worshipped as Cybele and Deoius.[6] In Rome, as Fortuna and Jupiter puer, or Jupiter the boy.[7] In Greece, as Ceres, the Great Mother, with a babe at her breast,[8] or as Irene, the goddess of peace, with the boy Plutus at her breast.[9] In India to this day as Isi and Iswara,[10] while in Thibet, China and Japan the Jesuit missionaries found the counterpart of the Roman Catholic Madonna in the Holy Mother, Shing Moo, with a child in her arms and a glory round her.[11]

[1] Wilkinson's *Egyptians*, vol. iv. p. 103, note.
[2] See *ante*, chaps. ii., iii.
[3] Kitto's *Illustrated Commentary*, vol. iv. p. 31.
[4] *Asiat. Res.*, vol. vi. p. 393.
[5] Bunsen, vol. i. pp. 433-438.
[6] Dymocks *Clas. Dict.*, "Cybele," "Deoius."
[7] Cicero, *De Divinatione*, lib. ii. c. xli.
[8] Sophocles, *Antigone*, v. 1133.
[9] Pausanias, lib. i. ; *Attica*, cap. viii.
[10] Kennedy's *Hindu Mythol.*, p. 49, and p. 338, note.
[11] Crabb's *Mythol.*, p. 150. The above are quoted from Hislop, pp. 19-21.

As the promised seed of the woman who was to bruise the serpent's head, the god, although slain in the conflict with Typhon, the principle of evil, was represented as becoming reincarnate in the person of Horus, Apollo or Chrishna, etc., in order that he might slay the serpent and restore true religion. "The evil genius," says Wilkinson, "of the adversaries of the Egyptian god Horus is frequently figured under the form of a snake, whose head he is seen piercing with a spear. The same fable occurs in the religion of India, where the malignant serpent Calyia is slain by Vishnu in his avatar of Chreeshna, and the Scandinavian Thor was said to have bruised the head of the great serpent with his mace."[1] Chreeshna or Crishna is also represented in India crushing the head of the serpent with his *heel*.[2] Similarly, among the Mexicans "the serpent crushed by the Great Spirit Teotl, when he takes the form of one of the subaltern deities, is the genius of evil."[3] So also in Babylon, Eugonasis, "the Serpent Crusher," described by the Greek poet Aratus, crushes the serpent's head with his foot,[4] and Izdubar is represented with a dead serpent in his right hand.[5] The Greeks also represented their Sun god, Apollo, as slaying the serpent Pytho.

In the case of Chrishna and Thor, the death of the god and the destruction of the serpent are combined, and the god is represented as dying himself after the conflict.[6] The death of the god was also represented to have been voluntarily undergone for the good of mankind. Zoroaster is said to have prayed to the supreme God to take away his life.[7] Belus commanded one of the gods to cut off his head, that from the blood thus shed by his own command and consent, when mingled with the earth, new creatures might be formed, the first creation being represented as a sort of failure.[8] Vishnu the Preserver was worshipped as the Great Victim, who offered himself as a sacrifice before the worlds were, because there was nothing else to offer.[9] So also it was in conflict with the serpent as the principle of evil, that others were slain, and Osiris, Bacchus and other forms of the god are always represented as the great benefactors of mankind, which enhanced the value of their death.

Hence, periodical lamentations for the death of the god were

[1] Wilkinson's *Egyptians*, vol. iv. p. 395.   [2] Coleman, *Ind. Mythol.*, p. 34.

[3] Humboldt's *Mex. Res.*, vol. i. p. 228.

[4] *See* the whole account in Hislop, pp. 60, 61, and note.

[5] *Ante*, p. 56.   [6] Hislop, pp. 60, 61.

[7] Suidas, tom. i. pp. 1133, 1134.

[8] Berosus, from Bunsen's *Egypt*, vol. i. p. 709.

[9] Kennedy, *Hindu Mythol.*, pp. 221, 247, and note.

instituted, and when his worship had become general, the rites were invariably funeral rites in commemoration of his death.

Maimonides describes in metaphorical language the consternation and grief at Babylon on receiving the news of the death of the false prophet Thammuz (*i.e.*, Nimrod). "The images of the gods," he says, "wept and lamented all the night long and then in the morning flew away each to his own temple again to the ends of the earth, and hence arose the custom every year on the first day of the month of Thammuz to mourn and weep for Thammuz."[1] The same lamentations took place in Egypt for Osiris, and "his wife and sister Isis" is also represented as lamenting her brother Osiris. The name "Bacchus," the Greek Osiris, referred to its original Chaldean source, means "The lamented one," from *Bakkah*, "to weep," or the Phœnician *Bacchos*, "weeping."[2] Just also as Isis wept for Osiris, so did Venus for Adonis, and throughout Scandinavia there were similar lamentations for the death of the god Balder.[3] There is the same thing even in China, at the dragon boat festival, when the people go out to search for Watyune, which, Gillespie says, "is something like the bewailing of Adonis, or the weeping for Tammuz mentioned in Scripture."[4]

These lamentations were accompanied by singing, and especially by "the dirge of *Linus*," who is the same as Bacchus and Osiris.[5] This dirge is said to have been singularly sweet and mournful, and, according to Herodotus, was sung in all countries.[6] Nothing could have been better calculated to excite an emotional sympathy and sentimental reverence for the slain god, and to invest his memory with a false sanctity; for when the emotions have been powerfully excited by such means, people do not stop to inquire whether they are based on truth and righteousness, but will rather turn with anger against anyone who ventures to cast a doubt upon the justice and reality of that which evoked them.

The rites with which the god was worshipped were also represented to be for the purification of the soul from sin,[7] and thus the idolatry in its revived form appealed to that consciousness of sin and ill desert and fear of future retribution which is general in man, and

---

[1] More, *Nevochim*, p. 426. [2] Hesychius, p. 179; Hislop, p. 21.
[3] *Scandinavia*, vol. i. pp. 93, 94; Hislop, pp. 57, 58.
[4] Gillespie, *Sinim.*, p. 71; Hislop, p. 57.
[5] Hislop, p. 22, note, and p. 156, note. [6] Herod., ii. c. 79.
[7] Ovid, *Fasti*, lib. iv. ll. 785-794; Colebrooke, "Religious Ceremonies of Hindus," in *Asiat. Res.*, vol. vii. p. 273; Servius in Georg., lib. i. vol. ii. p. 197; and *Æneid*, lib. vi. vol. i. p. 400.

X

its followers were set free from this burden by the supposed efficacy of its rites to obtain forgiveness and purify the soul from sin. Hence the initiated into "The Mysteries" were declared to be "Emancipated,"[1] and this was the effect for which these rites were designed, and which they tended to produce on the minds of the devotees, who, by participating in them, were more or less emancipated, or set free, from the fear of God as the punisher of sin. Spiritual effects which are wholly future cannot be disproved, and men are always ready to believe on the slenderest evidence in any source of forgiveness which will relieve their conscience, and to think they are freed from the guilt, while still under the power, of sin.

But not only was the chief god of Paganism made, by these means, a false, or anti, Christ, but the events of the Deluge were made use of, and connected with the death of the god, in order to further recommend his worship.

The Ark was recognised as a divine symbol throughout Paganism, and it is so recognised, even at the present day, in countries where remains of the old Paganism still exist, as in the case of many of the North American tribes.[2] We may therefore conclude that its sacred symbolism was known and understood from the first. In Scripture the Ark is a symbol of Christ. Hence Israel, being a type of the people of God in all ages, were led in all their wanderings and undertakings by "the Ark of the Covenant."[3] It was carried in their front to battle, and was borne before them in their passage through Jordan, the waters of which rolled back at its presence, and as if to show that it alone had effected the result, it was directed to be placed in the midst of the bed of the river until all Israel had passed over, and not until it also had passed did the waters return.[4]

The sanctity of the Ark was such that Uzziah was slain for presuming to touch it,[5] and the men of Bethshemesh for looking into it.[6] Dagon, the god of the Philistines, fell down at its presence,[7] while the same presence was a blessing to the house of Obed Edom,[8] and all places were holy where it had been,[9] just as the presence of

---

[1] Hence the name Phoroneus, "The Emancipator," from *Pharo*, to "set free," which was given to the god. The goddess Pheronia, or Feronia, was similarly "the goddess of *liberty*," but it was a liberty which was practically licentiousness and lawlessness ; Hislop, p. 52, and note.

[2] *See* Catlin's *North American Indians.*

[3] Numb. x. 33-36.

[4] Joshua iii. 13-17 ; iv. 18.

[5] 2 Sam. vi. 6, 7.

[6] 1 Sam. vi. 19.

[7] *Ibid.*, v. 3-5.

[8] 2 Sam. vi. 11.

[9] 2 Chron. viii. 11.

God before Moses and Joshua made the place where they stood "holy ground." [1]

Solomon, in his prayer to God for Israel, beseeches His presence, and that of "*the Ark of his strength*"—"Thou and the ark of thy strength." [2] The term used has evidently a similar meaning to "the arm of his strength," [3] "the rock of thy strength," [4] and "the rod of thy strength," [5] all which refer to Christ. The simple word "strength" is also used with a similar signification, "Let him take hold of my strength that he may make peace with me," [6] and the same word is used to denote the Ark, "Thou didst divide the waters by thy *strength*," referring to the passage of Jordan. [7]

From this we perceive the meaning of the expression, so often used in the New Testament, to be "*in* Christ," as denoting salvation. It is evidently a metaphor taken from the Ark which saved Noah, who, it is said, "Prepared an ark to the saving of his house." [8] Just also as it is stated to be necessary for the Christian to "die with Christ" to the present world, so did Noah die to the world in which he lived; and just as the Christian is said to be "baptised into the death of Christ," and to receive a new life thereby, so Noah, in the Ark, passed through a symbolic baptism of death, and he and the Ark emerged again from that symbolic death to a new life, when, on the first reappearance of the new earth out of the waters of death, the Ark rested on Mount Ararat on the seventeenth day of Nisan. [9] This was three days after the Passover, which was on the fourteenth, and the seventeenth was therefore the very day on which Christ rose from the dead. [10] Thus the history of the Ark and the Deluge was symbolic of Christ in His relation to the Christian, and it is so recognised by the Apostle Peter, [11] while "the Ark of the Covenant" was a clearly recognised type of Christ, and of salvation through Him.

It is also clear that something of the sacred symbolism of the Ark was recognised throughout the postdiluvian world. But whatever was known concerning the typical character of the Ark, it was perverted to the service of the revived idolatry. Thus the Goddess Mother was identified with the Ark as that from which the human race had been "born again." Nevertheless she was also

---

[1] Exod. iii. 5 ; Joshua v. 13-15.
[2] 2 Chron. vi. 41.
[3] Isa. lxii. 8.
[4] *Ibid.*, xvii. 10.
[5] Ps. cx. 2.
[6] Isa. xxviii. 5.
[7] Ps. lxxiv. 13.
[8] Heb. xi. 7.
[9] Nisan, which had been the seventh month, was made the first month at the institution of the Passover (Exod. xii. 2). Compare Gen. viii. 4.
[10] Smith's *Dict. of Bible*, "Passover."
[11] 1 Peter iii. 20, 21.

identified with the earth and the female principle in nature, the passive source of that natural life which Paganism glorified instead of spiritual life, and she was regarded in consequence as the goddess and patron of sexual lust. In this way, the Ark, the type of Christ, through whom man was to be redeemed, became the type of woman through whom man fell, and was associated with that sexual immorality which is a prominent feature of human sin, while all the attributes of the true Christ as the friend and saviour of sinners, and mediator between God and man, were bestowed on the goddess.

Similarly, the god was identified with Noah, of whom Osiris and then Horus were supposed to be reincarnations. Therefore, as Noah was "born again" out of the Ark, the title "Ark born" was given to many manifestations of the god, as in the case of Bacchus, who was called "Thebe genus," or "Ark born," and his heart, the "sacred Bel," was carried at his festivals with the other sacred emblems of the god in a box which was called "the Ark." [1]

The name of the city Thebes, or *Thebe*, appears to have been given to it to identify it with the Ark. Wilkinson says that the name was derived from "*Taba*," which at Memphis was pronounced "*Thœba*," converted into "*Thebai*" by the Greeks, and that it had no connection with the Hebrew "*Thebh*," "the Ark." But in this he is incorrect. He says that "*Thaba*," or "*Taba*," was the name of the guardian goddess of Thebes; that it was derived from "*Ape*," or "*Aph*," which, with the feminine article T prefixed, becomes "*Tape*," pronounced "*Taba*" or "*Thaba*"; and that "Ape," or "Aph," was "the mother of the gods," [2] whom we have seen was identified with the Ark, as the house, or habitation, from which the gods were born. In the same way Thebes was called "*Amunei*," the abode or habitation of Amon, and was therefore called by the Greeks *Diospolis*, "the City of God," and the Hebrew name for Thebes, viz., "*No amon*," had the same meaning.[3]

Thus "*Thaba*" was the name of the mother of the gods, and the mother of the gods was identified with the Ark, or Thebe. Therefore, although the etymologies of "*Thaba*," the "*Ape*," or "*Aph*," and "*Thebh*," or "*Thebe*," the Ark, are different, yet in accordance with the Pagan principle of giving double significations to words, it would seem that the name was chosen in order that, as "Thebe," it should exoterically mean the Ark, or house of God, while its

[1] Faber's *Pagan Idolatry*, vol. ii. pp. 265-267.
[2] *Wilkinson*, by Birch, vol. iii. pp. 210, 211.
[3] *Ibid.*, p. 211.

secret esoteric meaning should be "Thaba," the "Aph," *i.e.*, the female Serpent, under which form the Egyptian goddess is constantly represented, as in the case of "Rannu," "the great producer," or mother of the gods.[1]

The death also of Osiris was represented to have been on the seventeenth day of the second month, by which it was identified with the symbolic death of Noah,[2] which was a type of regeneration, and recognised as such throughout the ancient world. For, both among Jews and Pagans, baptism by water was the rite of regeneration, and the initiates into the lesser mysteries of Paganism were plunged underneath the waters[3] in imitation of the death of the god, and were then pronounced to be "regenerate and forgiven all their perjuries."

It seems probable that, quite apart from the idolatry instituted by Cush and Nimrod, the Deluge was held in solemn remembrance by the postdiluvians, both in memory of those who had perished and as a thanksgiving for their own preservation. For, as we have seen, its memory is preserved by nearly every nation under the sun. If so, it was important for the revivers of the primary idolatry to connect their own religious rites with it, and thus make use of it, and of the reverence in which it was held, as a basis on which to gradually rebuild that idolatry. Hence the Ark was introduced into the mysteries, it was identified with the goddess, and Osiris, as an avatar of Noah, obtained the respect with which the latter was regarded, while his death, like that of Noah, was represented to be the necessary preparation for his regeneration and reincarnation as Horus, the restorer of the worship of the gods.

Thus the revived idolatry appears to have been wholly founded on the Patriarchal faith and religion, which it gradually perverted.

The god was called also by many of the same titles as the true God. For "Baal" and "Adon" were merely Phœnician terms for "The Lord," which was the ordinary expression for God among the Israelites. So also "Baal Shaman," "The Lord of Heaven," was a title equally applied to the true God, and "Baal Berith," "The Lord of the Covenant," was a title which unquestionably had reference to the God who had made the covenant of mercy with Noah; for Baal

---

[1] *Wilkinson*, by Birch, vol. iii. pp. 212-214, Plate XLV. and Plates XL. and XLI.

[2] *Ante*, p. 46.

[3] Hence *immersion* was the distinguishing feature of Pagan baptism.

Berith is represented as seated on a rainbow, the sign of that covenant.[1] So also in Egypt, Cnouphis was called "the Creative Spirit," Phthah was called "Lord of Truth,"[2] and Osiris was entitled "the manifestation of good," and said to be "full of goodness, grace and truth."[3] But this did not prevent the latter being recognised as the Phallic god, and identified with, and worshipped as, an animal, the type[4] of natural life and generation; or from being a god of cruelty to whom human victims were sacrificed.[5] Nor need it be said that the "goodness" ascribed to him was goodness according to the Pagan idea, which sanctified natural life and the good of this world, and that the "truth" was a belief in idolatry and superstition. These titles and epithets constituted that garb of outward righteousness with which error ever clothes itself in order to quiet the conscience of those whom it seeks to deceive, and wanting which, it would have little success.

It was not in these names and outward characteristics that the true God could be distinguished from the supreme God of Paganism, but in those actual moral characteristics which made the former a God of mercy, of truth and of righteousness, and the other a God of vindictive cruelty, falsehood, mystery and false righteousness, and which caused his most devoted followers to become like him.

In other respects, in its ritual and superficial aspect, the revived idolatry was not dissimilar to the Patriarchal worship. There were the same sacrifices by fire for sin, the only difference being that human victims, as well as animals, were offered on the Pagan altars, which gave the ritual of Paganism a still more solemn and efficacious aspect. Sacrifice by fire was the recognised mode of seeking the favour and mercy of the true God, and it was natural that many should content themselves with, and put their trust in, the mere performance of the outward rite, as if it had some occult spiritual efficacy in itself. Such persons would be easily persuaded by the priesthood of idolatry that this spiritual efficacy lay in the fire itself, and that the offering "purified by fire" was made acceptable to God. Thus, like everything in the revived idolatry, the sign was substituted for the thing signified by it, the material type for the spiritual reality.

The outward similarity of ritual between the true and the false

---

[1] *See* illustration of Baal Berith from Thevenot, *Voyages*, partie ii. chap. vii. p. 514; Hislop, p. 70.

[2] *Wilkinson*, by Birch, vol. iii. p. 2 and p. 15.   [3] *Ibid.*, p. 69.

[4] Herod., ii. c. 48.   [5] See *ante*, pp. 243, 244.

religion was, of course, much greater when the ritual of the Israelites had been ordained, but the existence, previous to the ordainment of that ritual, of a priesthood and of temples among the Pagans, instead of detracting from the Pagan ritual, gave it an appearance of greater awe and solemnity.

We find also that Apepi when converted to the true God erected a temple to Him,[1] while Joseph made special provision for a priesthood who could only have been for the services of the same God.[2] Thus the principal features of the two rituals were the same. Each believed in a Redeemer, the only difference between them being that the Pagans represented him to have already lived and died and become re-incarnate, and asserted that he might be beheld by those who duly prepared themselves by fasting and self-denial. This fasting and self-denial was equally recognised in the Jewish and Patriarchal faith as a necessary preparation for invoking the assistance of God on great and solemn occasions.

It seems probable also that the winged lions and bulls with the heads of men, which were symbols of the Deity in Paganism, were in their exoteric aspect derived from the Cherubim, the form of which appears to have been generally known, and recognised as a sacred emblem. The triune form also of the Godhead was imitated by the Pagans in their god and goddess and the re-incarnation of the former, and in vesting a woman with the divine nature they had the seeming warrant that she, who was the mother of a god, must be herself divine. In other respects, the solemnity and mystery of the Pagan ritual, which far exceeded the simple worship of the the Patriarchs, and even that of the Israelites, and the undoubted powers possessed by their magicians, wizards and necromancers, seemed to be unanswerable evidence of the power and majesty of their gods.

Thus Paganism, while it strongly appealed to the senses and imagination, had also so many features based on what all recognised as truth, that it was eminently calculated both to attract and deceive. It was, in short, a subtle perversion of that truth, and yet based upon it, and the repeated lapses of the Israelites, who constantly succumbed to its influence in spite of every warning and chastisement, and in spite of the striking evidences of the power of Jehovah, are a sufficient proof of its fascination. It is a proof also that although other nations may have at first rejected the gross idolatry of Cush and Nimrod, yet that succeeding generations, without the warnings

[1] *See* the "Sallier Papyrus"; Lenormant, *Anc. Hist. of East*, vol. ii. p. 223.
[2] Gen. xlvii. 22.

and punishments received by the Israelites, must have speedily fallen under its power, when revived in this more insidious and deceptive form.

The conclusions arrived at may be briefly recapitulated as follows : It would seem that the first step taken was merely a homage paid to the relics of the dead monarch.   Then it was pretended that he had died for the good of mankind, and that he was really none other than the promised Redeemer, the seed of the woman ; and when this point had been attained, and the lapse of several generations had obliterated the memory of his true character, the growing reverence for his memory would naturally develop into the belief that he was the Son of God and God Himself.   At the same time, the solemn events of the Deluge were subtly interwoven with his worship, and the reverence with which it and the Patriarch Noah were held was made use of to give a sanctity to the worship.

In Egypt, however, the revival appears to have taken a different form from that in Babylon.   It was in Egypt that the Cushite king was overthrown and condemned to death by the people themselves, and the knowledge of the true God implanted by Shem must have been preserved in the minds of the people for at least two or more generations.   It is therefore probable that, while the people still worshipped the god of Set, who, we know, was honoured to a late period, a priesthood was instituted, as in Babylon, and temples for the secret worship of the dead monarch, but that this was done at first under the plea of doing honour to his supposed relics, as a re-cognition of his great achievements and a protest against the suggested injustice of his death ; that his actual worship was con-ducted under the cover of words and symbols having a double meaning, and that he was represented by various animals, each of which was supposed to typify one or other of his attributes ; that when this religion of mystery had excited the curiosity and imagina-tion of many, they were cautiously initiated into the secret, the dead monarch being represented to them as in reality an incarnation of the Supreme God and the promised seed of the woman ; that gradually, as the mystery and solemnity of the worship appealed to the religious sentiments of the pious, the numbers of its adherents steadily increased, while its growing magnificence, and the number and piety of its devotees, overawed the senses and imagination of others and impelled them to follow in their footsteps, until at last, while still retaining its principle of mystery which so powerfully impresses the imagination of men, the worship of the dead monarch, under various names, became general.

When, therefore, this worship had become established, those kings who could claim descent from the god were recognised as his representatives on earth, and as vice-gods, and were therefore always the High Pontiffs, or chiefs of the priesthood, were spoken of as "His Holiness," and were also worshipped after their death.

Similar methods would be followed by the propagandists of idolatry in other countries. It seems probable that the Japhetic races at first worshipped the true God under the name of "Dius piter," "Jupiter," or "Heaven Father," and that they subsequently, in after ages, identified Him with, and ascribed to Him the characteristics of, the Babylonian god. This, and the fact that some of their sacred writings, such as the Vedas, although encrusted with subsequent error, evince more or less knowledge of the true God, is further evidence that the development of error was gradual.

The tradition quoted by Epiphanius describes the different forms of religion as—1st, Barbarism up to the time of the Deluge, by which is meant probably religion without specific religious forms; 2nd, Scythism, from Noah to the building of Babel. This was probably something of the same nature as that which is termed barbarism; 3rd, Hellenism, which, according to Cedrenus, consisted, at first, only of honouring celebrated warriors and leaders with statues, and tendering them a kind of religious veneration, but afterwards their successors "overstepping the intention of their ancestors, honoured them as gods, following forms of canonisation and inscribed their names in their sacred books and established a festival to each." According also to Epiphanius, the Egyptians, Babylonians, Phrygians and Phœnicians were the first who made images and introduced the mysteries.[1] We may therefore suppose that the way was first prepared for idolatry by merely suggesting the duty of honouring the memory of heroes and celebrated men, which would gradually be developed into a religious homage paid to their statues and shrines, and a belief that their spirits were able to watch over and protect the interests and destinies of their faithful votaries. Then, when the worship of the dead had thus been established in principle, it would be easy to introduce the worship of the mighty Nephilim Prince of Egypt and Babylon, as the incarnation of the Supreme God and the promised Redeemer of man.

But what must have chiefly favoured the propagation of idolatry

[1] Epiphanius and Cedrenus, Cory's *Fragments*, pp. 53, 55, 56.

among the nations, is the fact that it was in accordance with the natural desires of man. The Apostle Paul, speaking of the development of idolatry among the heathen, ascribes its initial principle to the fact that they "*did not like to keep God in their knowledge,*" that "when they knew God they glorified him not as God, neither were thankful; but became vain in their imaginations, and their foolish heart was darkened—and changed the glory of the uncorruptible God into the image of corruptible man and birds, and four-footed beasts and creeping things."[1] The consciousness of sin and consequent sense of ill-desert and apprehension of future evil causes men, as in the case of our first parents, to shrink from God, and seek to forget Him. At the same time the consciousness of sin is a burden which demands relief, and a religion which seems to promise him forgiveness and righteousness by means of material agencies and ritual acts under the will and control of man, and which thus avoids the necessity of seeking them from God, is therefore readily accepted.

This was the character of the revived Pagan idolatry which assured its followers of all spiritual good through the agency of material and created things, the result of which was that they quickly lost all true knowledge of God. Then, having come to regard material agencies as of divine efficacy, they were easily persuaded that material representations of God had a divine sanctity, and thence to associate Him with these representations, and to regard Him as inhabiting in some special manner the consecrated image, temple, shrine, or even animal.

Such must have been the moral causes which, beginning in the race of Cain before the Deluge, eventually led to a general idolatry, and finally to the intercourse with and worship of the Nephilim. In the case of Cush and Nimrod there seems to have been a bolder unbelief and rebellion against God (a heritage probably of antediluvian teaching) which led them to openly advocate the same worship and intercourse, and this was probably also the case with their adherents after their overthrow, and with the priesthood ordained by Semiramis. But amongst the other nations of the world the process would be gradual, each generation adopting one or more of the errors and superstitions offered for their acceptance, while each error, as accepted, would darken their hearts and consciences, and prepare the way for their acceptance of other and grosser superstitions. At the same time it must not be forgotten that, as implied by Scripture and confirmed by profane tradition, there must have been

[1] Rom. i. 21, 23, 28.

an active propaganda emanating from the central seat of idolatry at Babylon, which, acting on the receptive spirit of human nature, gradually established idolatry throughout the ancient world (Jer. li. 7).

Together with the gradual introduction of the worship of the dead monarch there was the restoration of the Sun and Nature worship instituted by Cush. There was no natural connection between these two forms of idolatry, or between the personal and human attributes of the gods and the powers of nature with which they were identified,[1] and neither was dependent on, or gave support to, the other. They must therefore have had a separate mode of propagation. Yet they were always the two distinguishing features of idolatry.

Sun worship, according to Sanchoniathon, was the initial feature of antediluvian idolatry, and the antediluvians also worshipped the spirits of those whom they believed to be of Nephilim origin. The idolatry instituted by Cush and Nimrod appears to have been similar. Tammuz, that is Nimrod, was put to death, according to Maimonides, because he taught the worship of Sun, Moon and Stars, and allied to this was the worship of the Phallus as the manifestation in the animal world of the life and generative power of which the Sun was the supposed source. But one of the principal features of the primary Accadian worship, which must have been that initiated by the Cushites, was also the worship of spirits, whose guidance and assistance they sought in every time of need, and with whom they invited sexual intercourse. In both this and the antediluvian idolatry, the spirits whose aid and communion were sought do not appear to have been merely the supposed spirits of dead men, but spirits of the same nature as the Nephilim—beings whom they had reason to believe were possessed of vast powers, the inhabitants of the spirit world, and identical with the daimonia, or devils, of Scripture.

In the case of the revived idolatry, the worship of Nimrod and his father was probably suggested because of their Nephilim origin or associations, and these two, being afterwards worshipped under a variety of names, each representing some different attribute, came to be regarded as so many different gods. It was the same with the goddess, although it was fully recognised by the initiated that they were only so many forms of the persons of a Trinity, consisting of father, mother and son. But the worship of the Sun, Moon and

[1] *See* remarks of Professor Rawlinson, *ante*, chap. ii. p. 19.

Stars, which was equally a feature of the revived idolatry, had this difference from the previous form of idolatry, in that it was combined with the worship of the above Trinity, all the gods being ultimately recognised as the Sun or incarnation of the Sun, while the goddess was identified with the Moon and the Earth.

Sun worship was a prominent feature of the Hermetic philosophy, which explained all phenomena by supposing that they were due to the action of a male and female principle in nature; the Sun, Fire and Force in general being the manifestation of the male principle, and the Earth, Water, etc., the manifestation of the female. This teaching, therefore, must have been cautiously and gradually revived, simultaneously with the homage paid to the memory of the dead king. It seems evident also that it was supported by certain perversions of truth.

The divine institution of sacrifice for sin by fire must be regarded as the foundation of the supposed spiritual efficacy of fire to purify the soul, the material type being substituted for the spiritual meaning. The supposed spiritual efficacy of fire was recognised throughout Paganism. Continual fires were kept burning before all the altars of the Sun god, and, in the case of the Incas of Peru, were kindled anew every year from the rays of the Sun by means of a concave mirror of polished metal.[1] In the rites of Zoroaster it was stated that "He who approached to the fire would receive a light from divinity,"[2] and again that "Through fire all the stains produced by generation would be purged away."[3] "Fire," says Ovid, "purifies both Shepherd and Sheep."[4] So also in the sacred books of the Hindus fire is thus addressed, "Thou dost expiate a sin against the Gods, thou dost expiate a sin against the Manes (departed spirits), thou dost expiate a sin against my own soul, thou dost expiate repeated sin, thou dost expiate every sin which I have committed whether wilfully or unintentionally; may this oblation be propitious."[5]

The supposed spiritual efficacy of fire and the apparent connection between Fire and the Sun as the source of the world's heat would furnish an argument for Sun worship. For if fire, as an emanation from the Sun, was divine, then the Sun was the source of all that is divine, and therefore God Himself, the source of spiritual life and regeneration. The Sun is also used in Scripture as the material type

[1] *Conquest of Peru*, chap. iii. p. 46.   [2] Taylor's *Jamblichus*, p. 247.
[3] *Proclus in Timæo*, p. 805.   [4] *Fasti*, lib. iv. ll. 785-794.
[5] Colebrooke's "Religious Services of Hindus," in *Asiat. Res.*, vol. vii. p. 260.

of God, and the general recognition of the type was no doubt made use of to give authority to the belief that the type was the reality. Now, when the Sun had come to be regarded as the manifestation of God, the dead king, as the promised seed of the woman and the incarnation of God, would, of course, be identified with the Sun, and the two forms of idolatry would be combined.

It was also a natural consequence that when Nimrod was worshipped as a god, his wife should be regarded as a goddess, and that if he, as Osiris, was identified with the Sun, she, as Isis, or Rhea, the Goddess Mother, should be identified with the Earth, or with the Moon. Moreover, if the Sun had become once incarnate as Osiris, so might he become again. Hence, for the purpose of overcoming Typhon, he was supposed to become re-incarnate as Horus, the son of Isis, and Isis is represented as saying, "I am all that has been, or that is, or that shall be. No mortal has removed my veil. The fruit which I have brought forth is the Sun." [1] For as the Son was the re-incarnation of the Father, he was identified with him, and hence the term given to him, "the Husband of the Mother."

This combination of the worship of the dead king and queen with that of the Sun and powers of Nature gave a human personality to the latter, and in place of an abstract power, or law, unaffected by the necessities and desires of man, the gods were regarded as having passions and feelings like men, and therefore able to sympathise with, and willing to aid them in the attainment of their desires.

It would be absurd to suppose that the ultimate form taken by the revived idolatry was the result of a scheme carefully prepared and premeditated from the first by evil men, and gradually carried out by their successors from generation to generation. It must rather have been the work of the guiding spirit of evil, viz., of him " who deceiveth the whole world " (Rev. xii. 9.), " the spirit which worketh in the children of disobedience " (Eph. ii. 2), who either directly, or through his ministers, the daimonia, led those who sought their aid and guidance, from error to error. It was a work of gradual development carried out by men who were probably ignorant of the ultimate tendency of their errors, each of which became the basis for a further development. This has been the history of error in Christendom, in which, from little beginnings, we can trace the gradual resuscitation

[1] Bunsen's *Egypt*, vol. i. pp. 386, 387. Wilkinson argues that Osiris was not identified with the Sun or Isis with the Moon. It seems probable that this was not the case at first, but it is quite certain that they were so eventually, a fact which might be expected from what has been said. *See* Appendix A.

of the same idolatry by a process of "*development*," the initiators of errors in one age often opposing and protesting against the errors which were fully adopted in a later age, but of which errors their own were the foundation.

So also it must have been with the ancient Paganism, and it would seem that the anthropomorphic character given to the gods of Paganism was merely in order to introduce and recommend the worship of the Sun and the powers of Nature, which was the ultimate object of the system. For it was through Sun and Nature worship that men were led to sanctify sin, and finally to worship the Prince of Evil.

The Sun, to whom a human personality had thus been given, was the supposed source of natural life and generation, and therefore of the honour and glory of this world, and of all those things which the natural man seeks to attain. So also he was the God of the Phallus, which became one of his distinctive emblems, and a huge image of which was carried by the priests in the rites of Osiris, as related by Herodotus.[1] Similarly, the Yoni was a distinctive emblem of the goddess, and it was an essential feature in her worship to prostitute virgins in her honour. This sanctification of vice tended, no doubt, to blind the conscience and prepare the way for a more sinister worship, as well as to make the resuscitated idolatry attractive to many, as in the case of the Israelites who worshipped Baal Peor.[2]

Finally, the god was ultimately identified with the Prince of Evil. We have seen that, although, at the outset, the Pagan god was identified by name, and in other respects, with the true God and the promised Messiah, that his moral characteristics were wholly different from those of the latter. An unseen God can only be known by his moral characteristics, and a person who believes in a Christ to whom he attributes moral characteristics and offices which are opposed to those of the true Christ, believes in a false Christ, and this was the case with the Pagan worshipper. He worshipped a false Christ or Messiah. For not only as the Phallic god did the god of Paganism sanction immorality and vice, but as represented by his priesthoods throughout the world, he was the approver of cruelty, tyranny and deceit, and men sought his favour by inflicting without remorse the most terrible sufferings on their fellow-men. He was the god of

---

[1] Herod., ii. c. 48.

[2] Numbers **xxv**. Baal Peor, to the worship of whom the Israelites succumbed, was the Phallic god of Canaan.

murder and falsehood, and these are the two salient characteristics by which Christ has especially identified the Prince of Evil.[1]

These also must have been the moral characteristics of the Pagan god from the first, and those who worshipped became like him. The system, with all its lust and cruelty, was in full force, and had evidently been long established in Canaan when the Israelites came there ; while the mention of the Rephaim, Zuzim and other Nephilim races, as early as the time of Abraham,[2] shows that it was then well established, and that full intercourse with the daimonia must have been long carried on. Nations who were thus under the guidance of spirits of evil would rapidly adopt all the worst features of the system, and this was evidently the case with the Canaanites, who are said to have been guilty of "every abomination."[3] Yet the remark made by God to Abraham, namely, "The iniquity of the Amorites is not yet full,"[4] shows that the ultimate result was reached by a process of *development*, each error being the foundation for the introduction of other and worse delusions. Hence we may conclude that, just in proportion as the god became more and more identified with the Prince of Evil, so were these nations conformed to the image of the god they worshipped.

The principle of this development has already been noticed, and it may be briefly defined as the materialisation of spiritual truth, putting the sign for the thing signified, interpreting every spiritual symbol according to "the letter which killeth," instead of seeking the spirit of its meaning.[5] Thus the material fire of the burnt sacrifice was supposed to be itself of spiritual efficacy; then the Sun as the supposed source of the purifying fire became the manifestation of god; then as the source of natural life and natural light he was regarded as the source of spiritual life and light, or "the divine wisdom," and the natural and spiritual being thus confused, the natural, which was wholly in accordance with men's inclinations and desires, became the only object of attainment, and the satisfaction of the lusts of the flesh received the sanction of religion; while the god, as the source and approver of everything which pertained to natural life, became the god of lust and of worldly power and ambition.

Similarly, the Serpent was introduced at first as a symbol only of life and regeneration, and then as the symbol of the Sun, the supposed source of life and generation, and thence became identified with the Sun. Then as the source of natural light he was regarded as the

---

[1] John viii. 44.   [2] Gen. xiv. 5, 6.   [3] Deut. xii. 31.
[4] Gen. xv. 16.   [5] 2 Cor. iii. 6.

source of divine wisdom, the great enlightener of men, and finally was identified with him, who in the form of a serpent had given to man the fruit of the tree of knowledge of good and evil. But although, when this was the case, the Pagans openly worshipped him whom Scripture calls "Satan, that old Serpent" (Rev. xii. 9.), and who is the adversary and enemy of both God and man, yet as moral characteristics are the principal evidence of the identity of a God, the Pagan god was, from the first, morally identical with the Prince of Evil.

It does not appear that the Serpent was formally worshipped in Rome until a comparatively late period, when, at the time of great pestilence, Æsculapius, the Child of the Sun, was brought to Rome in the form of a huge serpent and became its guardian deity.[1] But in Pergamos, whither the Chaldean priesthood had fled on the capture of Babylon by Cyrus, Æsculapius had ever since been worshipped under the form of a serpent.[2] Hence the significance of the statement in Rev. ii. 13 with regard to Pergamos, viz., "*Where Satan's seat is.*" In the great centres also of idolatry, Egypt, Babylon and Phœnicia, the Serpent seems to have been worshipped from an early period.

In consequence of the worship of the Serpent god in Rome, serpents became sacred, so that in nearly every house a serpent of a harmless sort was kept, and they multiplied so fast that they became a nuisance.[3]

In the time of Tertullian, so firmly was the worship of the Serpent established, that there were many who sought to combine it with Christianity. "These heretics" (the Oppiani), he says, "magnify the serpent to such a degree as to prefer him even to Christ Himself, for he, say they, *gave us the first knowledge of good and evil.* It was from a perception of his power and majesty, that Moses was induced to erect the brazen serpent to which whosoever looked was healed. Christ Himself, they affirm, in the Gospel imitates the sacred power of the serpent when He says that as Moses lifted up the serpent in the wilderness even so must the Son of Man be lifted up.[4] They introduce it when they bless

[1] Ovid, *Metam.*, lib. xv. ll. 736-745 ; Lactantius, *De Origine Erroris*, p. 82, and lib. ii. c. 16, p. 108 ; Hislop, pp. 236, 237, 280.

[2] Barker and Ainsworth's *Lares and Penates of Cilicia*, chap. viii. p. 232 ; Hislop, p. 278, 279.

[3] *Pompeii*, vol. ii. pp. 114, 115 ; Hislop, p. 237.

[4] It may here be remarked that the brazen serpent was not a symbol of Christ in itself, but of sin crucified by Christ. The serpent was the author of human sin and the symbol of evil, and Christ, in dying, is said to have "died unto sin" (Rom. vi. 10), and to have borne "our sins in his own body on the tree" (1 Pet. ii. 24).

the Eucharist."[1]   If this was done by professed Christians, it is no wonder that, in the Octateuch of Ostanes, it is laid down that "*Serpents were the supreme of all gods and princes of the Universe.*"[2]

This shows clearly how the Serpent, and indeed Satan himself, was regarded in the Pagan world, and how the idolatry eventually developed into his worship, thus verifying the statement of the Apostle that he was in truth "the god of this world."[3]

[1] Tertullian, *De Prescrip adv. Her.*, cap. xlvii. vol. ii. pp. 63, 64 ; Hislop, p. 278.
[2] Euseb., *Præparatio Evang.*, lib. i. vol. i. p. 50.
[3] 2 Cor. iv. 4.

Y

CHAPTER XVI

GENERAL FEATURES OF THE REVIVED IDOLATRY

IN consequence of the number of different attributes under which Nimrod and his father were deified, Paganism became the worship of "gods many and lords many," some of which were regarded as superior gods and identified with the Sun and the Serpent, and the others as inferior gods. In consequence also of the deification of these first monarchs, the custom arose of elevating other men, remarkable for their position or attainments, to the rank of demi-gods, their apotheosis being decreed by the priesthood, or sacred college of pontiffs. They were regarded as mediators between men and the higher gods, and each person selected one or other of these demi-gods as their particular patron, whose power and mediation he implored in times of need and distress.

Thus the system became essentially and professedly the worship of the dead, although the beings who replied to the invocations addressed to them were, as stated by Scripture, the daimonia, or evil spirits, whose prince was Satan, and with whom the chief gods were identified.

It would seem, in short, that, by leading men to worship the dead Cushite monarch and his father under a multitude of deified attributes, and by adding to the number of gods and demi-gods the supposed spirits of other men, the master-spirit by which the development of the ancient Paganism was guided, used this worship as a stepping-stone to induce them to worship himself and his subordinate spirits. Man would have shrunk at the outset from intercourse with alien spirits, the servants of the great enemy of the human race, but it was very different when he believed that they were the spirits of his own race and ancestry, allied to him by the experience of common infirmities and common hopes and sympathies.

The powers of these beings, called into play by the diviners, observers of times, enchanters, wizards, sorcerers and necromancers of Paganism, although limited, were real, as clearly intimated by Scripture, and it was this, no doubt, that gave such influence to the ancient Paganism. It seemed to give the priesthood control over the powers of the unseen world and the powers of nature, enabling men through them to obtain the accomplishment of their natural lusts and desires, and to be seemingly independent of a God from whom the consciousness of sin caused them to shrink, to become in short that which initiation into the mysteries professed to make them, viz., "Emancipated," *i.e.*, from the fear of the true God.

These powers, being wielded by the priesthood, and confined to the temples and shrines of the gods, caused them to be regarded as second only to the king himself, who in Egypt, Babylon and Rome was their head, or chief Pontiff. Hence, any extraordinary diviner, like Daniel, was regarded as having in himself " the spirit of the holy gods" (*i.e.*, the heathen gods), and Daniel was exalted in consequence to be the third ruler in the Kingdom.[1]

The principal feature in the worship of the gods and daimonia of Paganism was that they were worshipped through, and by means of, their images, or other symbols and representations of them. Image worship, in short, was inseparably connected with the worship of the Pagan gods, and therefore, although the ancient Paganism was the worship of the spirits of the dead, it received the name of "Idolatry"[2] (*i.e.*, the worship of idols or images). This it was in its outward aspect, and the great mass of its followers so regarded it.

It is important to notice the real underlying reason of the construction of images for the worship of the Pagan gods, and in which the constructors acted, no doubt, under the guidance and teaching of the spirits they worshipped.

The Pagans denied that the images of the gods were the gods themselves, and asserted that they worshipped the god through the image, and that " the spirit of the god was called into the image by the divine" (*i.e.*, the priestly) "consecration." The spirits which they worshipped were neither omniscient nor omnipresent, and to have invoked their aid at all times and in all places would therefore have been useless. Hence the necessity for some local habitation for them, such as an image, a temple, grove, or sacred symbol, which, when consecrated by the priestly adept who had already established communication with them, might become the special abode of some

[1] Dan. iv. 9, 18 ; v. 11, etc.
[2] From *Eidolon*, "image," and *Latria*, "service," or "worship."

one spirit who would then be ever at hand to reply to those who sought his aid.

Hence it is asserted by the followers of modern Theosophy and Buddhism that the idol, or the symbol, which has once been the habitation of a god, or spirit, will always remain so, and may at any time evince its power. The same thing is also recognised by Spiritualists, who find that particular tables, chairs or planchettes, which have been once used as mediums of communication with the spirits, are always more susceptible to their influence than similar articles which have not been so utilised.

Augustine quotes Hermes Trismegistus as saying that, "Visible and tangible images are, as it were, only the bodies of the gods, and that there dwelt in them certain spirits which have been invited to come into them, and which have power to inflict harm or to fulfil the desires of those by whom divine honours and services are rendered them." [1]

This being the case, we might conclude that any country or place where the people are idolaters, and which therefore abounds in images and temples, would be more or less subject to those manifestations which are associated with Paganism and Spiritualism; and experience proves that this is the case. [2] It is, as before remarked, a difficult thing to establish communication with the spirits, but when once established, *"place is given to them"* (Eph. iv. 27), and they are loth to surrender the power of exercising the influence which is thus afforded them.

We may also deduce a further conclusion which has already been referred to, viz., that houses or places which have been the abode of persons of exceptional wickedness might become the scenes of similar phenomena. [3] For when men give themselves over to such exceptional wickedness, it is implied, as in the case of Judas, that an evil spirit enters into them and possesses them, and *"the place"* thus given to that spirit, and the relation established by it with the human race, is retained, and the locality, or house itself, becomes "accursed"— *haunted*, not by the spirit of the wicked dead, but by the evil spirit to whom their wickedness has given power.

The development of image worship seems to have been gradual. From the mention of the gods, when overthrown by Typhon, having

[1] *De Civ. Dei*, viii. 23.
[2] This is also illustrated by the fact that witchcraft and sorcery abounded before the Reformation, and since then have gradually disappeared.
[3] See *ante*, chap. viii. pp. 178-180.

taken flight and assumed the forms of certain animals, and the worship of the dead Babylonian king under similar forms, it is probable that these were regarded at first as symbols only of the god, and that they then were looked on as sacred, and eventually as special forms or manifestations of the god in one or other of his attributes. This was also the principle of the image or statue, which at first seems to have been regarded only as a memorial of the individual it represented, and afterwards was supposed to be inhabited, in some sense, by his spirit.

The same principle was involved in the case of images of the Sun, the special symbol of the Serpent god. There was a golden image of the Sun in the temple of Belus at Babylon,[1] and a similar image of gold was found in the temple of Cuzco, in Peru.[2] Brilliant metal reflectors, or " Sun Images," were placed over the altars of Baal, the Sun god of the Canaanites.[3] Similar disks of the Sun were also placed for worship in the Egyptian temples, and in a grotto near Babian, in Upper Egypt, a representation has been found of priests worshipping an image of the Sun placed above the altar.[4] The obelisks, or pointed columns of masonry, as well as minarets, and even the spires of Christian churches, were originally symbols of the Sun's rays, and also of the Phallus, as representing the same principle of generation.

The principle of the image is manifestly the same as that of the temples, shrines, sacred trees and groves of the gods, which were also regarded as their particular habitations. The principle was also extended to other material things symbolic of the gods, and supposed to be, in some sense, possessed by them, and were therefore regarded as amulets or charms, by which their assistance could be invoked. Thus, as the tree was divine, there was a virtue in the cross, its symbol. If the brilliant metal images of the Sun were worthy of worship, then a simple circle used in a religious sense was also holy. Consequently, the cross and circle, the former surmounting the latter, or inscribed in it, became, throughout the Pagan world, the sacred signs of the Sun god; and both were supposed to possess a divine efficacy.

From this also arose the "*tonsure*" of the priests, as servants

[1] "Maimonides," *More Nevochim*, p. 426.
[2] Prescott, *Conquest of Peru*, chap. iii. p. 41.
[3] 2 Chron. xxxiv. 4. *See* margin, " Sun Images."
[4] Maurice, *Indian Ant.*, vol. iii. p. 309; Hislop, p. 162. *See* also Wilkinson, Plate XXIII., where Amenophis III. and his family are represented worshipping an image of the sun.

of the Sun god, and the "*nimbus*," or glory, or circle of light, round the heads of images and other representations of the gods and demigods. Concerning the tonsure, Herodotus says, "The Arabians acknowledge no other god but Bacchus, and Urania, the Queen of Heaven; and they say their hair is cut in the same way as Bacchus' is cut. Now they cut it in a circular form, shaving it round the temples." [1] The priests of Osiris in Egypt likewise shaved their heads,[2] and so also did those of Pagan Rome.[3] Guatama Buddha directed his disciples to shave their heads, and did so himself in obedience to the command of Vishnu.[4] " The ceremony of tonsure," says Maurice, referring to the practice in India, " was an old practice of the priests of Mithra, who in their tonsures imitated the solar disk." [5] Reference is also made to the practice in Leviticus, where the Israelites are forbidden to make any baldness for the dead.[6] It was the recognition that the dead had passed into the hands of the Sun god, as was the case in Egypt, where the dead were always spoken of as "in Osiris."

The *nimbus* was also commonly placed, not only round the heads of the images of the gods and heroes, but round those of the Roman Emperors, to whom, after death, divine honours were paid. It was regarded as betokening the divinity of the person represented. Thus Virgil, speaking of Latinus, says :—

> "Twelve golden beams around his temples play
> To mark his lineage from the god of day." [7]

The author of *Pompeii*, speaking of one of the paintings representing Circe and Ulysses, says, " This picture is remarkable as teaching us the meaning of that ugly and unmeaning glory by which the heads of saints are often surrounded. This glory was called the nimbus or aureola, and is defined by Servius to be the luminous fluid which encircles the heads of the gods." [8] In India the infant Chrishna and his mother Devaki are both represented with a glory round their heads,[9] and throughout India and China, wherever

---

[1] Herod., lib. iii. c. viii.
[2] Macrobius, lib. i. c. xxiii.
[3] Tertullian, vol. ii., "Carmina," pp. 1105, 1106.
[4] Kennedy, "Buddha," in *Hindu Mythology*, pp. 263, 264.
[5] Maurice, *Indian Ant.*, vol. vii. p. 851.
[6] Levit. xix. 27, 28 ; xxi. 5 ; Deut. xiv. 1.
[7] Dryden's *Virgil*, book xii. ll. 245-248 ; vol. iii. p. 775.
[8] On *Æneid*, lib. ii. v. 616, vol. i. p. 165 ; Hislop, p. 87, note.
[9] Moor's *Pantheon*, Plate LIX.

Buddhism prevailed, both the god and goddess mother were similarly represented.[1]

The principle of the image and symbol was extended to other things. Thus, those objects, the names of which had a double meaning, and one of which referred to the god, were regarded as sacred. This is exemplified in the case of the worship of the Sacred Heart. The Roman youth wore a golden ornament suspended from their necks, called the "bulla." This was heart-shaped,[2] and was an especial symbol of the god. It is stated of Dionysius Eleuthereus, one of the names of Bacchus, that when he was torn to pieces, his heart was preserved by Minerva, and "by a new regeneration again emerged, and being restored to pristine life and integrity afterwards filled up the number of the gods."[3] Here is the old story of the death of the god and his re-incarnation by the aid of the goddess. From this arose the worship of "the Sacred Heart," as a distinctive symbol of the god. In Mexico, where the ancient idolatry seems to have been retained with little modification, the image of the great god wore a necklace of alternate gold and silver hearts, and the hearts of human victims were especially sacred and pleasing to him, being torn out from the living victim by the sacrificing priest, and waved aloft as an offering to the Sun and Serpent god.[4] Now the esoteric reason of the heart being thus reverenced, was that in Chaldee, the sacred language, the word for "heart" was "Bel,"[5] and on the principle of using words with a double meaning, under the veil of which the priesthood of Babylon introduced the revived idolatry, the heart became thus a symbol of the god, and the worship of the Sacred Heart was, to the initiated, the worship of Bel.

The value attached to *Holy Water* by the Pagans seems to have originated in the symbolism deduced from the Deluge. By that event the old world was purified of its wickedness and regenerated, so that the human race was, so to speak, "born again." The Apostle speaks of the event as a sign, or symbol, of Christian regeneration similar to that of baptism,[6] and it was regarded in a similar way throughout the ancient world. Bryant remarks, "In the Babylonian mysteries

[1] *See* illustrations given, *Rome Pagan and Papal*, by Brock, pp. 141-147.

[2] Kennet's *Antiquities*, 300, 301 ; Barker's *Lares and Penates of Cilicia*, p. 147 ; Hislop, pp. 189, 190.

[3] Taylor's *Mystic Hymns of Orpheus*, note, p. 88.

[4] Prescott, *Conquest of Mexico*, bk. i. chap. iii. p. 25 ; bk. iv. chap. ii. pp. 214, 215.

[5] Hislop, pp. 190, 191.   [6] 1 Pet. iii. 21.

the commemoration of the Flood, the Ark and the great events in the life of Noah were mingled with the worship of the Queen of Heaven and her Son. Noah, as having lived in two worlds, both before the Flood and after it, was called 'Diphues,' or 'twice born,' and was represented as a god with two heads looking in opposite directions, the one old and the other young."[1] In India, Vishnu the Preserver is celebrated as having saved one righteous family when the world was drowned, and he is also identified with Noah himself. For Vishnu is the Sanskrit form of "Ishnuh," "The Man Noah," or "The Man of Rest." The name of Indra, the king of the gods, is also found in precisely the same form, viz., as "Ishnu." Hence the Indian Brahmans, who represent and claim the prerogatives of the god, claim to be "twice born" or regenerated.[2]

The same idea is found in the rite of initiation into the Lesser Mysteries, which was a baptism by immersion, after which the initiate, "If he survived, was then admitted to the knowledge of the mysteries, and was promised regeneration and the pardon of all his perjuries."[3] In token of this he was clothed in white, a custom which has been imitated by Roman Catholics and Ritualists. The Pagan Anglo-Saxons baptised their new-born infants,[4] and the Pagan Mexicans did the same, and believed their children to be regenerated by the rite.[5] Thus water, in accordance with the genius of idolatry, came to be regarded, like fire, as having an occult spiritual efficacy. "Every person," says Potter, "who came to the solemn sacrifices was purified by water. To which end, at the entrance of the temples, there was commonly placed a vessel full of holy water."[6] Holy water was also used to sprinkle the dead, and to purify houses and temples, and in certain cases wells, which were called "holy wells," and rivers, as in the familiar case of the Ganges in India, were regarded as having a divine efficacy.

The sacrifices of the Pagans were of two kinds; those offered to the Sun god consisted largely of human victims, of which Cush seems to have been the originator. They were especially offered to Kronos and Saturn, under which names Cush was deified. New-born babes were also offered to Baal and Moloch, and in certain cases men immolated themselves.

[1] Bryant, vol. iii. pp. 21, 84 ; Hislop, p. 134.
[2] Hislop, pp. 135, 136.
[3] Tertullian, *De Baptismo*, vol. i. pp. 1204, 1205 ; Gregory Nazienzen, *Opera*, p. 245.
[4] Mallet on Anglo-Saxon Baptism, *Antiquities*, vol. i. p. 335.
[5] Prescott's *Conquest of Mexico*, bk. i. chap. ii. p. 21 ; Appendix, p. 465.
[6] Potter, *Greek Antiquities*, bk. ii. chap. iv. p. 223.

These sacrifices appealed to the consciousness in man that sin deserves punishment, and thence led him to conclude that suffering expiated its guilt, and that the greater the suffering the more the anger of the gods would be appeased. This idea was used, no doubt, to lead men to believe that the value of the sacrifices ordained by God consisted in the suffering of the animal put to death, and, if so, how much more efficacious might be the sacrifice of a human being! These victims, however, were usually confined to captives taken in war, slaves and criminals,[1] and in Greece and Rome human sacrifices were gradually disused. The Romans offered human sacrifices until the year of the city 657 (90 B.C.), when a decree was made by the Senate abolishing them. In spite of this, however, Augustus sacrificed 400 persons, who had sided with Antony, on the altar of Julius Cæsar, to whom divine honours were paid. Moreover, wherever the ancient religion remained in its original form, as in Mexico, the number of human victims sacrificed to propitiate the god was enormous, but, as with other nations, these were chiefly criminals and prisoners of war. These being regarded as enemies of the State, and therefore enemies of its god, were sacrificed, either as a propitiatory offering, or as a thanksgiving for victory, and the mode of death throughout the East was either crucifixion or burning.[2] This shows that death on the cross, or tree, which was a symbol of the Sun god, was a sacrificial death, the cross being the altar of the god; which may explain the fact that, in the Levitical law, the victims of such death were held to be accursed, or cut off from God. It was, in fact, the manifestation of their being wholly given over, as far as this life was concerned, to the power of the god of Paganism, who, as we have seen, was identified with Satan.

The sacrifices offered on the altars of the goddess were quite different. Her worship gradually superseded that of the god, and exercised an extraordinary fascination over the people, chiefly, no doubt, on account of her milder attributes, and as the Mediatrix for the sins of the people with her sterner husband, or son.[3] There were no bloody sacrifices allowed on her altars,[4] and the usual offering was *a round cake*, the symbol of the Sun. " The thin round cake," says Wilkinson, " occurs on all altars." [5] This round cake was, of course, a

[1] Smith's *Dict. of Bible*, "Moloch."

[2] Rawlinson's *Egyptian and Babylonian Hist.*, vol. i. pp. 190, 191.

[3] She was known as " *Mylitta*," " The Mediatrix," in Babylon. Herod., lib. i. cap. cxcix.; Hislop, p. 157, and note.

[4] Tacitus, *Historia*, lib. ii. cap. iii. vol. iii. p. 106 ; Hislop, p. 156.

[5] Wilkinson's *Egyptians*, vol. v. p. 353, note.

symbol, both of the Sun, and of his Son, or incarnation, for the circle represented both the Sun's disk and " The Seed." [1]

Isis was worshipped in Rome as Ceres, and was called " *The Mother of Corn.*" The reason of this was that she was known in Babylon as " *The Mother of Bar,*" Bar being a name of the god, and signifying " The Son." But " Bar" also meant "*Corn,*" which was its exoteric meaning.[2] Hence the round cakes made of *flour* which were sacrificed to the goddess represented in their mystic sense, " the Son," or " promised seed," the false Christ of Paganism. In Greece and Rome, whose religions were derived from Babylon and Egypt, much of the mystical sense was lost sight of, and Ceres was regarded simply as *the goddess of plenty,* or of the fruits of the earth generally, just as the cup and branch with which Bacchus was represented led them to regard him as the God of Wine.[3] In Egypt another symbol for " the Son " was a goose, which was regarded as the favourite offering to Osiris,[4] and Juvenal says that in Rome, Osiris, if offended, could only be pacified by a large goose or a thin cake.[5] As these were both symbols of a Son, it would seem that both god and goddess were supposed to be propitiated by the symbolic offering of the promised seed. The round cakes were also offered on all the Grecian altars, and were called "*Popana.*"[6] The Israelitish women are also spoken of as offering cakes to " the Queen of Heaven," known by them as " Ashtoreth."[7] In Rome they were called "*Mola,*" a word derived from *immolare,* " to sacrifice," which shows that, like the goose, they were a propitiatory offering, and in fact this sacrifice was said to " *efface the sins of the people.*" [8]

But though this unbloody sacrifice may have been sufficient to satisfy the conscience of the Pagan worshippers under ordinary circumstances, the whole spirit of Paganism was characterised by that perverted idea of sacrifice which led them to suppose that the anger of the gods could be appeased by the sufferings of human victims. They naturally concluded that if such sufferings could expiate sin, then the sufferings of the sinner after death would in time expiate his own sins. Hence Virgil, speaking of the after existence of sinners, says :—

[1] *Ante,* p. 224.   [2] Hislop, p. 160.
[3] *Ante,* p. 38.   [4] Wilkinson's *Egyptians,* vol. v. pp. 227, 353, note.
[5] *Satires,* vi. 539, 540.
[6] *Grecian Antiquities,* Potter and Boyd, bk. ii. chap. iv. p. 217.
[7] Jer. vii. 18.
[8] *Pollux in Onom,* lib. i. cap. i. s. 25 ; Ed. Seb. Francf., 1608, p. 9 ; Alex. ab Alex., lib. iv. cap. xvii. ; Lug. Bat., 1673, p. 1103.

> "For this are various penances enjoined,
> And some are hung to bleach upon the wind,
> Some plunged in water, others purged in fires,
> Till all the dregs are drained and all the rust expires.
> All have their manes, and those manes bear
> The few so cleansed to those abodes repair,
> And breathe in ample fields the soft Elysian air.
> Then are they happy when by length of time
> The scurf is worn away of each committed crime.
> No speck is left of their habitual stains,
> But the pure ether of the soul remains." [1]

So likewise Plato says, that of those who are judged after death "some must first proceed to a subterranean place of judgment where they shall sustain the punishment they have deserved." [2] The supposed existence of a Purgatory suggested, no doubt, the possibility of appeasing the anger of the gods by costly sacrifices made by the friends of the deceased person, or arranged to be made by the person himself before he died. "In Greece," says Suidas, "the greatest and most expensive sacrifice was the mysterious sacrifice called *Telete*.[3] This, according to Plato, "was offered for the sins of the living and dead," and was supposed "to free them from all the evils to which the wicked are liable when they have left this world." [4] "In Egypt," says Wilkinson, "the priests induced the people to expend large sums on the celebration of funeral rites. For, besides the embalming process, the tomb itself was purchased at an immense expense, and numerous demands were made upon the estate of the deceased for the celebration of prayers and other services for the soul." He adds, "These ceremonies consisted of a sacrifice similar to those offered in the temples" (*i.e.*, the sacrifice of the round cake), and "they continued to be administered at intervals as long as the family paid for their performance." [5] In India, in the services of "*The Sraddha*" for the repose of the dead, it is urged that "donations of cattle, land, gold and silver and other things" should be given by the dying man, or, "if he be too weak, by another in his name." [6] In Tartary also at the present day the *Asiatic Journal* says that "*The Gurgumi*, or prayers for the dead, are very expensive," [7] and, as we have seen, prayers for the dead are characteristic of all Buddhist countries.[8]

[1] Dryden's *Virgil*, bk. vi. ll. 995-1012 ; vol. ii. p. 536.
[2] Plato, *Phædrus*, p. 249, A.B. ; Hislop, pp. 167, 168.
[3] Suidas, vol. ii. p. 879, B.   [4] Plato, vol. ii. pp. 364, 365.
[5] Wilkinson's *Egyptians*, vol. ii. p. 94 ; and vol. v. pp. 383, 384.
[6] *Asiat. Res.*, vol. vii. pp. 239, 240.   [7] *Asiatic Journal*, vol. xvii. p. 142.
[8] *Ante*, chap. vi. pp. 113, 114.

Another belief, springing directly from the idea that suffering expiated sin, was that a man might expiate his own sins by undertaking voluntary suffering during his lifetime. The whole principle is very exactly expressed by Balak, king of Moab: " Wherewith," he says, " shall I come before the Lord and bow myself before the high God? shall I come before him with burnt offerings, with calves of a year old? Will the Lord be pleased with thousands of rams, or with ten thousands of rivers of oil? shall I give my first-born for my transgression, the fruit of my body for the sin of my soul?" [1] Here the idea expressed is that the greater the cost and suffering to the sinner, the more will the sacrifice propitiate God.

Hence it was that, throughout the Pagan world, men sought to propitiate the gods by self-inflicted penances and self-mortification. The Egyptians at the feast of Isis at Busiris, after the ceremonies of sacrifice, assembled themselves to the amount of many thousands and scourged themselves.[2] So also Callimachus, speaking of sailors who visited the shrine of Apollo, says, " Nor do the crew presume to quit thy sacred limits till they have passed a fearful penance, with the galling whip lashed thrice around thine altar."[3] Similarly, the priests of Baal, to propitiate their god, " cried aloud and cut themselves after their manner with knives and with lancets until the blood gushed out."[4] The Corybantes, or priests of Cybele, the priests of Bellona, and the Balusses in their nightly processions also scourged themselves."[5]

Speaking of the penances done by the "Fakirs" and "Sunayases" of India, Nightingale says, " Of the first, some vow to continue for life in one unvaried posture, others undertake to carry a cumbrous load, or drag a heavy chain, some crawl on their hands and knees for years, some swing during their whole life in this torrid clime before a slow fire, others suspend themselves with their heads down for a certain time over the fiercest flames. They imagine," he adds, " that the expiation of their own sins and sometimes those of others consists in the most rigorous penances and mortifications."[6] The Sunayases have their tongues and sides split, or hooks are placed through the skin of their shoulders, and by these they are suspended from a pole twenty or thirty feet high with a horizontal beam by which they are swung round. " This penance," says Nightingale, " is generally voluntary,

[1] Micah vi. 6, 7.
[2] Herod., lib. ii. cap. lxi.
[3] Callimachus, v. 318-321, vol. i. p. 137.
[4] 1 Kings xviii. 28.
[5] Lactantius, lib. i. cap. ii. p. 52 ; Hurd's *Rites and Ceremonies*, vol. iii. p. 251.
[6] Nightingale, *Religions and Ceremonies*, chap. x. p. 398.

in performance of some religious vow, or inflicted for the expiation of sins committed." [1]

So also in Pagan Rome, Juvenal, describing a woman seeking to expiate her sins, says, "She will break the ice and go down into the river in the depth of winter; she will dip herself three times in the Tiber and bathe her timid head in its very eddies, then naked and shivering she will go and crawl on bleeding knees over the whole extent of the Campus Martius." [2] So also Tibullus says, "I would not hesitate, if I had done wrong, to prostrate myself in the temples and to give kisses to the consecrated floors and thresholds. I would not refuse to crawl over the floor on my knees and to beat my wretched head against the holy door posts." [3]

The worship of the Serpent and the Prince of Evil himself seems to have been chiefly propagated through the celebrated *Mysteries*. They were the principal features of the resuscitated idolatry, and the secrecy and mystery which surrounded them, while it served to conceal their real significance when they were first established, at the same time tended to impress and awe the minds of the initiated. They were conducted with great solemnity, and were divided into "The Lesser" and "The Greater Mysteries," the former being the preparation for the latter, and consisting, as has been said, of a purification by holy water, or of a baptism by immersion, which was often of a dangerous character. [4]

Initiation into the Greater Mysteries was more solemn, and was preceded by fasting and by confession to the priest, which was an essential part of the rite. The first question put to the aspirant was whether he was fasting, this being considered indispensable before partaking of the sacred rite. [5] The other questions related chiefly to matters of sexual impurity, and were evidently designed to place the person in the power of the priest lest he should be tempted afterwards to divulge what he saw or heard. "All the Greeks," says Salverte, "from Delphi to Thermopylæ, were initiated into the mysteries of the temple at Delphi. Their silence in regard to everything they were commanded to keep secret was secured, both by the penalties threatened to a perjured revelation, and by the general confession exacted of aspirants before initiation, a confession which caused them

[1] Nightingale, *Religions and Ceremonies*, chap. x. pp. 379-385 and 399.
[2] *Satires*, vi. 522-526.
[3] Tibullus, i. ii. 83.
[4] Tertullian, *De Baptismo*, vol. i. p. 1204; Eliæ Comment in S. Greg. Naz., *Orat. IV.*; Gregorii Nazienzeni, *Opera*, p. 245; Hislop, p. 132.
[5] Potter, *Greek Antiquities*, bk. ii. chap. xx. ; *Eleusinia*.

greater dread of the indiscretion of the priest, than gave him reason to fear their indiscretion."[1]

The Greater Mysteries themselves were accompanied by everything calculated to awe the mind and impress the imagination of the initiate: "The place seemed to quake and to appear suddenly resplendent with fire, and immediately afterwards to be enveloped in gloomy darkness; sometimes thunders were heard, or flashes of lightning appeared on every side. At other times hideous noises and howlings were heard and the trembling spectators were alarmed by sudden and dreadful apparitions."[2] These things, preceded as they were by prolonged fasting in darkness, which broke down the mind and spirit of the initiate, could not fail to impress him powerfully, invest the rite with awe and solemnity, and prepare him for what was its chief object, the revelation of the god.

It seems evident that the "Apporeta," the carefully-preserved secret revealed in the Mysteries, was the revelation of the god in his ultimate aspect, as the Serpent who had brought sin and death into the world.[3] It was "the revelation of a God superior to all those worshipped by the masses,"[4] *i.e.*, a god different from those known as Jupiter, Bacchus, Osiris, etc. The initiate was bound by the most solemn oaths never to reveal it, and was put to death without mercy, however high his position, did he do so, and it is said that the secret has never been divulged. Herodotus, who was an initiate, refuses to mention the name of the god, and says it was unlawful to do so.[5]

The appearance of the god is thus described by an ancient initiate: "In a manifestation which *one must not reveal* . . . there is seen on the wall of the temple a mass of light which appears at first at a very great distance. It is transformed, while unfolding itself, into a visage, evidently divine and supernatural, of an aspect severe but with a touch of sweetness.[6] Following the teachings of a mysterious religion, the Alexandrians honour it as Osiris or Adonis."[7]

Here, while giving the name of the god as known to the general public, the writer takes care not to reveal the real secret.

The initiated were supposed to be made partakers of the nature of the god, and as a serpent was placed in the bosom of the person as

[1] Eusebe Salverte, *Des Sciences Occultes*, chap. xxvi. p. 428; Hislop, p. 9.
[2] Lemprière, *Eleusinia*, and Potter, *Eleusinia*.
[3] *Ante*, p. 234.   [4] *Compn. of* 666, "Apporeta," p. 329.
[5] Herod., lib. ii. cap. clxx., clxxi.
[6] This severe but sweet aspect, which might apply to "an angel of light," is quite in accordance with the statement of the Apostle, 2 Cor. xi. 14.
[7] Damascius, Apud Photium, *Bibliotheca*, Cod. 242, p. 343.

the token of initiation, it is evident that the god whose nature the person was supposed to receive, was the Serpent god. The initiated was also declared to be "enlightened" and "emancipated"; and considering the character of the god, it seems evident that the enlightenment referred to that knowledge of evil which was the subject of the Hermetic teaching, and which was symbolised by the fruit of the forbidden tree in Eden. Similarly, the initiate, being supposed to be freed from the consequences of sin, he was freed, or emancipated, from the fear of God as the Judge and Punisher of sin. Hence the significance of the title given to the Pagan god, " Phoroneus the Emancipator," "Jupiter the Liberator," and "Bacchus the Deliverer." [1]

It may also be remarked that in the rites of Bacchus a serpent was carried in a box as the great and mysterious symbol, while the worshippers carried a serpent in baskets with honey cakes marked with the sacred "omphalos," the symbol of the goddess, and small pyramids symbolic of the rays of the Sun. So also in the Mysteries a consecrated cup of wine was handed round, called "the cup of Agathodæmon" (the good demon), who was symbolised by a serpent. [2]

It is not necessary to allude further here to the augurs, diviners, magicians and necromancers, and other offices filled by the Pagan priesthood, and the various oracles through which they sought the aid and guidance of the gods, or the numerous temples of health under their direction, by which, through the same aid, they cured, or professed to cure, all diseases. These things have already been fully referred to in a former chapter, and, with what has been now said, is sufficient to indicate the general nature and character of the ancient idolatry.

[1] Pausanias, lib. i., *Attica*, cap. xliv. ; Bryant, vol. v. p. 25 ; Pausanias, *Attica*, cap. xx. ; Hislop, pp. 52, 53, and note.

[2] Nicola, *De Ritu Bacch.*, Apud Gronov., vii. p. 186 ; Deane's *Serpent Worship*, pp. 188, 189, 194.

CHAPTER XVII

THE MORAL ASPECT OF PAGANISM

REFERENCE has already been made to the numerous forms in which the ancient Magic, Sorcery and methods of the Pagan priesthood, and the consultation of the supposed spirits of the dead, are being revived at the present day. For, not to mention the Saint worship practised in the Church of Rome, there are the constantly-increasing numbers of those who follow modern Spiritualism and Theosophy, and who seek the aid and guidance of spirits, which, although asserted to be the spirits of the dead, can only be the same daimonia who gave the Pagan priesthood their powers; while the associated practices of Mesmerism, Faith-healing, Hypnotism, etc., are identical with the arts by which the ancient sorcerers and magicians sought the aid of these daimonia.

It may be therefore of some interest and importance to many if, in conclusion, we consider the true moral aspect of the ancient Paganism as it is regarded in both the Old and New Testament Scriptures.

The poets and classical authors of Greece and Rome have done much to cover the ancient Paganism with a mantle of romance, and to conceal its more sinister features; but both amongst the Greeks and the Romans, especially in the later periods of their history, the system had lost much of its pristine influence. In both peoples there was a recognition of the claims of justice and righteousness, which constantly placed the more thoughtful in a position of antagonism to their religion, and which led their rulers to check and modify the excesses of its priesthood, in much the same way as the kings and parliaments of England, from Alfred the Great to the Reformation, sought to check the excesses and abuses of the priesthood and religious houses who obeyed the See of Rome.

Nor are these characteristics in the Greeks and Romans difficult to explain, for it is impossible that the fame of the power, just laws and remarkable history of the people of Israel, who dwelt so close to Greece, and many of whom appear to have settled there, should not

352

have spread abroad those principles of righteousness and justice which appeal to the conscience of man, and by so doing have, not only raised the moral standard of Greece, and of Rome who obtained her laws from Greece, but prepared both peoples in later times to listen to and accept the precepts of Christianity.

It must be remembered also that the evil effects of a false religion are not seen in those who pay little attention to it, and are more or less indifferent to its demands, and consequently fail to come fully under its influence. It is rather those with whom it constitutes the business of their lives, its priesthood and devotees, who manifest its full evil. . This is illustrated by the whole history of the world, and especially by that of the Jews at the time of Christ, and that of Roman Catholics at the time of the Reformation.

In the former case the publicans and sinners and the common people heard Christ "gladly,"[1] and were open to receive the truth, but the Scribes and Pharisees and the priesthood, the devotees of a false righteousness and of the ritual and ordinances which they had made idols of, were not only deaf to the demands of truth and true righteousness, but were filled with a vindictive malice towards Him who told them the truth. So likewise in Reformation times, while the common people were only too glad to read the newly-printed Bibles and Testaments, and pitied and befriended the martyrs, the priesthood and devotees burnt every Bible they could seize, and without remorse tortured and burnt all who taught its doctrines.

This was equally true of the priesthood and devotees of Paganism, and its full evil must therefore be sought in those countries where it reigned supreme, and at those periods when it was still in the zenith of its power.

This was the case with the nations of Phœnicia or Canaan, when conquered by Israel, by which time the resuscitated idolatry appears to have attained full power. The Phœnician idolatry was pre-eminently one of blood, murder, and remorseless cruelty, and of every unnatural lust and crime,[2] and it was against this idolatry that the God of Israel so solemnly warned His people.

The stringency of the commands to Israel with regard to this idolatry and the idolaters is remarkable. Both were to be utterly consumed. Israel was commanded—"Ye shall utterly destroy all

---

[1] Mark xii. 37.

[2] It was probably much the same in Babylon and Assyria at the same period, and the tortures inflicted by the Assyrians on their prisoners exceed belief.

z

the places where the nations which ye shall possess served their gods,—and ye shall overthrow their altars, and break their pillars, and burn their groves with fire, and ye shall hew down the graven images of their gods and destroy their names out of that place" (Deut. xii. 2, 3.) "And when the Lord thy God shall deliver them before thee, thou shalt smite them and utterly destroy them. Thou shalt make no covenant with them nor show mercy unto them; neither shalt thou make marriages with them; thy daughter shalt thou not give to his son, nor his daughter shalt thou take unto thy son. For they will turn away thy son from following me: so will the anger of the Lord be kindled against you to destroy you suddenly. But thus shall ye deal with them. Ye shall destroy their altars, and break down their images, and cut down their groves and burn their graven images with fire.—Thou shalt not desire the silver or gold that is on them, nor take it unto thee, lest thou be snared therein; for it is an abomination to the Lord thy God. Neither shalt thou bring an abomination into thy house *lest thou become a cursed thing like unto it*, but thou shalt utterly abhor and detest it; for it is a cursed thing" (Deut. vii. 2-5, 25, 26).

So also the Israelites were told to destroy all the "*pictures*" of the idolaters, as well as their molten images, and "quite pluck down all their high places" (Numbers xxxiii. 52). Again they were commanded—"Thou shalt not plant thee a grove of any trees near unto the altar of the Lord thy God" (Deut. xvi. 21). This was on account of the sacred significance which the Pagans attached to these groves and to trees generally, as symbols of their chief god. The prohibition shows that the least symbol of idolatry was regarded as a danger.

So also with the *Ritual* of Paganism. Thus we read, "When the Lord thy God shall cut off the nations from before thee,—take heed to thyself that thou be not snared by following them after that they be destroyed from before thee, and that thou enquire not after their gods, saying, How did these nations serve their gods, even so will I do likewise. Thou shalt not do so unto the Lord thy God, for every abomination to the Lord which he hateth have they done unto their gods" (Deut. xii. 31).

Thus every symbol of idolatry was to be destroyed, not a feature was to be retained, not a single custom or rite was to be adopted and used in the service of Jehovah. The very presence of an idolatrous symbol might bring a curse, and the person in whose possession it was might become a cursed thing like unto it. What was the reason of this? Why was the idolater an *accursed* being, and even the senseless symbols of his idolatry "*cursed things*"?

The excuses made for idolatry and idolatrous piety at the present day are due, in no small measure, to the fact that "religiousness" has come to be more esteemed than righteousness, and, as in the case of the Pharisees of the Jewish Church, religious zeal, however misdirected, is regarded as the evidence of a person's holiness. Hence there are those who see no harm in adopting the ritual and many of the surroundings of idolatrous worship, and condemn and despise those who are more scrupulous. It is natural that such persons should be inclined to view the commands given to the Israelites as unnecessarily harsh and severe, and as representing God in a way which repels them, supposing that in commanding the destruction of the idolaters and pronouncing a curse against those who tampered with idolatry, He did so to satisfy His anger and offended majesty in the death and sufferings of the transgressors.

But if we consider the matter, we shall see that the judgments decreed and the curses pronounced against certain sins are not the arbitrary inflictions of an offended judge, but the necessary consequence of the sin itself.

The sin of a created being cannot affect Him "who dwelleth in eternity." "If thou sinnest, what doest thou unto him? or if thy transgressions be multiplied, what doest thou unto him? If thou be righteous, what givest thou unto him? or what receiveth he of thy hand? Thy wickedness may hurt a man as thou art; and thy righteousness may profit the son of man" (Job xxxv. 6-8.) "My goodness," says the Psalmist, " extendeth not to thee " (Ps. xvi. 2.)

It is true that God does sometimes visit sin in this world by direct punishment, yet this is rather the exception than the rule. The ordinary lot of the unrighteous in this world is prosperous: " They have more than heart can wish" (Ps. lxxiii. 7.) "Wherefore," asks Job, "do the wicked live, become old, yea, are mighty in power?" Job replies, "Have ye not asked them which go by the way, and do ye not know their tokens? That the wicked is reserved to the day of destruction? They shall be brought forth to the day of wrath" (Job xxi. 7, 29, 30).

If then a curse was pronounced on the idolater; and the Canaanite nations, having given themselves up to idolatry, were commanded to be destroyed,—and if the people of God were so solemnly warned against that idolatry, and so sharply and severely punished every time they fell under its influence, it implies that there must have been a proportionate evil in it to the souls of men, from which God, by solemn warning and chastisement, sought to preserve His people. God is said to be "the Preserver (sŏtĕr) of all men, especially of those who believe," *i.e.*, He keeps them from those innumerable dangers and temporal evils, to which they would be subjected by the malignity of the powers of darkness, did He not place a limit on that malignity. But to be "accursed," is to be cut off from this protecting power, to be "anathema," or given over to destruction; and this is the state of the idolater, who, by his own act, has separated, or cut himself off, from God.

It is a condition of the moral law, that just as weakness and need are attracted to power, so is power attracted to weakness. So also the pity and compassion, which are ever the accompaniment of goodness, are called forth by that weakness and need. Hence, the uniform testimony of Scripture is to the effect that God regards with especial favour the poor and needy, the broken in spirit, and those who tremble at His word. But there is nothing which so calls forth the pity and sympathy of perfect goodness towards need and suffering, as trust and dependence on the part of the sufferers. It is the most powerful evidence of sympathy, and therefore bond of union between moral beings, and a bond which, when perfect, eternally unites the creature to the Creator. Hence, just as unbelief is the characteristic and evidence of man's spiritual death or separation from God, so is faith the characteristic and evidence of eternal life and union with God.

Yet the greatest sinners, and the most irreligious, are not without some latent consciousness of their dependence on an unseen God, which, in times of earthly trouble and extremity, may be awakened. It is not until a person has transferred all his religious hopes and dependence to beings other than God, and whose aid and guidance he will therefore seek in times of trouble, that he can be said to be wholly cut off from God, and to have become "accursed." Hence, it is not only stated "cursed be the man who maketh a graven image" (Deut. xxvii. 15), but it is also written, "cursed is the man who trusteth in man, and maketh flesh his arm, and whose heart departeth from the Lord" (Jer. xvii. 5). And the followers of Paganism came under the condemnation of both.

The Pagan rites were regarded as a service done to the gods, as acts of homage which satisfied their demands and appeased their

anger, while they were rites also which were supposed to purify
the souls, and obtain pardon for the sins of the worshippers, who,
nevertheless, for the most part, were merely spectators of the ritual
performed by the priesthood. But no moral change in the sinner
was required, or even thought of, and a reverent credulity in the
efficacy of the ritual was all that was demanded, and men were
actually encouraged in sin by the ease with which the gods could
be propitiated.

In like manner, all dependence for assistance, both temporal and
spiritual, was transferred to visible, material or created things.
Holy water, relics, charms, images, signs, incantations and ritual
acts were the ordinary objects of dependence. Holy water purified
the sinner; the sacrifice of the round cake atoned for his sins;
charms, relics and holy signs preserved him from worldly danger;
righteousness consisted of ritual acts and ordinances or self-mortifica-
tions; auguries and oracles revealed the will of the gods; and if
he wished to pray to them, he did so by appealing to them through
their images. The special presence of each god was also connected
with the inhabitant of a mighty temple, the surroundings of which
impressed the worshipper's mind with the idea of a being of *material*,
but therefore of *finite*, grandeur and power, who, localised in that
temple, could be left at will.

For all guidance in religion, for instruction or advice, the pious
Pagan depended on a human priesthood, on whom also devolved
the whole performance of the ritual and the interpretation of the
oracles. The priesthood, in short, stood in the place of God to their
followers, as the sole channel through which all knowledge and
spiritual effects were to be obtained, and as mediators between the
gods and men. Hence they necessarily obtained the entire trust,
dependence and obedience of the people, and, as arbiters of their
spiritual destinies, practically obtained the dominion of the world.

Thus the mind and affections of the Pagan and his entire dependence were confined to created things; and this is the whole spirit
and principle of idolatry. It is "worshipping and serving the
creature rather than the Creator" (Rom. i. 25), seeking spirit from
matter, life from that which is without life (Isa. viii. 19), and placing
the dependence due to God on men and created things.

The Word of God and the Spirit of God appeal to the heart and
conscience and the moral and *spiritual* part of man, opening his
eyes to the truth, to the good of righteousness, to the promises of
the future, and to the mercy of God, changing thereby his mind

and affections, and producing in him hope in, and love towards
God. But the ritual of idolatry appealed only to the senses, imagination, and the *psychical* or *natural* part of man.

The word "*psychical*" is from ψυχικός, "the soul," or "natural life,"
and it is the term used by the Apostolical writers to distinguish that
which is "*natural*," or characteristic of man by nature, from that
which is *spiritual*, and it is usually translated in the New Testament
by the word "*natural.*" It refers to the passions, sentiments and
affections which are called forth by the things of *time* and *sense*,
and includes, not merely the grosser passions, but the feelings and
sentiments evoked by music and art and anything of merely *material*
beauty and grandeur. This was the character of the ancient
Paganism. It appealed solely to the *senses*. Its splendour and
magnificence, the stirring and solemn strains of its music, its
sumptuous surroundings, its air of mystery and awe, its mighty
temples, whose vast and silent aisles and "gloom impressive told
a god dwelt there,"[1] had a powerful effect on the senses and imagination, calling forth in the more religious those temporary emotions
and passing *sentiments of piety*, which men, at all times, have
mistaken for spirituality, but which are purely psychical feelings,
i.e., feelings produced, not by any appeal to the conscience and
moral faculties, which is the effect of religious *truth*, but entirely
by these appeals to the senses and imagination. Hence, not only
was the trust and dependence of the Pagan placed on material and
created things, but his mind and affections were absorbed in that
which was natural and sensual. His very piety was the outcome
of imagination and psychical feeling, and the greater his devotion
the more effectually did this false piety shut out from his mind
everything of a moral and spiritual nature, and blind him to the
demands of true righteousness.

The Pagan devotee was thus wholly separated from the true God,—
accursed, or cut off, from His guidance and protection; and Scripture
implies that there are legions of evil spirits ever ready to enter into,
or delude and pervert, the minds of those deprived of that protection,
and thus complete and confirm their separation from God.

But that which made the Pagan devotee still more hopelessly
accursed or cut off from God was the fact that the gods he worshipped and trusted in, and whose guidance and assistance he sought,
were those very evil spirits.

It is not to be supposed that the ancient Pagans, any more than

[1] Ovid, *Fasti*, lib. iii. ; Potter, bk. ii. chap. ii. p. 201.

modern Spiritualists, avowedly worshipped evil spirits, or that Paganism in its ultimate form, when its chief god was identified with the Prince of Evil, was the result of a deliberate and sinister design by a succession of wicked men, working with one accord from generation to generation with that purpose in view. Everything points to the fact that it was the result of a process of gradual development, in which men, ignorant of the true God, were led to adopt, little by little, the different features on which the system was built up; and that the guiding spirit, from first to last of this development, was him " who deceiveth the whole world," "the spirit which worketh in the children of disobedience,"[1] and who by this means obtained for himself the open worship of the bulk of the human race, and became in very truth, as stated by the Apostle, " the god of this world."[2]

The foundation of the system was manifestly the worship of the spirits of the dead, on the supposition that they were the active and powerful inhabitants of the unseen world, willing and able to assist their descendants in the flesh. This delusion was carefully inculcated to the last, and it was, without doubt, the device of the guiding spirit of the ancient idolatry. Men would have shrunk from seeking the aid of alien and unknown beings who might be spirits of evil. The memory of the deception of their first parents, and of the " Nephilim " or " fallen ones," who were " in the earth " in the the days before the Flood, and who, it is implied, were the cause of the wickedness which brought on the destruction of the antediluvian world, were sufficient warnings against such intercourse. In short, the existence of evil spirits, hostile to the human race, was fully recognised in the Pagan system, which consisted largely of incantations and other methods for averting their hostile influence. But it was very different with spirits which were supposed to be those of the human race, related to them, and possessed of common sympathies and experience, and whose aid might therefore be reckoned upon to avert the hostility of alien spirits.

But in seeking the aid of these supposed spirits of the dead, men forsook God, and placed their trust in that which was not God, and having thereby cut themselves off from His guidance and protection, they fell under the influence of evil spirits personating the supposed spirits of the dead who could neither hear nor aid them. The worship of the dead, thus became a stepping-stone for bringing the human race under the influence and guidance of evil spirits; the great enemy

[1] Rev. xii. 9 ; Eph. ii. 2.   [2] 2 Cor. iv. 4.

of man, knowing well that, once men could be separated from the guidance and protection of God, they could easily and rapidly be led to give their entire trust and dependence to himself and his subordinate spirits of evil.

Under the influence and teaching of these spirits of evil, the conscience and moral perceptions of the idolater became utterly darkened, and being "past feeling, they gave themselves over to lasciviousness to work all uncleanness with greediness," or, as God said to Israel, "Every abomination to the Lord which He hateth, have they done unto their gods"; that is to say murder, human sacrifices, fornication, prostitution and unnatural crimes were practised by them as an essential feature of the service of their gods. Hence the Apostle's description of them as "given over to vile affections, to a mind void of judgment (margin), to do those things which are not convenient; being filled with all unrighteousness, fornication, wickedness, covetousness, maliciousness; full of envy, murder, debate, deceit, malignity; whisperers, backbiters, haters of God, despiteful, proud, inventors of evil things, disobedient to parents, without understanding, covenant breakers, without natural affection, implacable, unmerciful" (Rom. i. 24, 32).

This description of the moral effects of the ancient Paganism is sufficient evidence of its evil, showing how completely it perverted the minds and destroyed the conscience of its followers. Their conscience became, in short, an "*evil conscience,*" leading them to regard the evil, which their religion demanded, as good, and to reject the demands of true righteousness as evil (Heb. ix. 14; x. 32).

But the most marked characteristic was the extraordinary fascination and strong delusion which this religion exercised over the minds of its followers; more especially in the case of its *devotees*, who would, of necessity, fall most completely under the influence of the beings they worshipped. Even amongst the Greeks and Romans, as well as other civilised but idolatrous nations, such as those of Christendom before the Reformation, it was remarkable with what blind tenacity and affection the people clung to their delusions, as in the case of the people of Ephesus, who, in their enthusiasm, cried out for upwards of two hours, "Great is Diana of the Ephesians." In fact, while every kind of sin was permitted, or condoned, the only unpardonable sin was speaking against the gods and the established religion, as was illustrated by the case of Socrates, condemned to death by the Athenians.

Nothing illustrates the power of this fascination or delusion more than the blind adoration bestowed by the idolater, whether Pagan or Romish, on the supposed spirits of the dead, and the images which represent them to his imagination. For it is well known that, while blasphemy against God would have been passed over, a word spoken against the Virgin or Saints in some Roman Catholic countries, a few years ago, would have aroused the fury of the populace, and endangered the life of the speaker.

The Scriptures therefore liken idolatry to *drunkenness* and *madness*: "Babylon hath been a golden cup in the hands of the Lord, to make all the earth drunken. The nations have drunken of her wine, therefore the nations are *mad*." Again, speaking of Babylon, the prophet says, "It is the land of graven images, and they are *mad* upon their idols" (Jer. li. 7 ; i. 38). The devotee of idols is thus beyond the reach of argument and reason. Truth and righteousness produce no effect upon him, and the Word of God which condemns his idolatry, only arouses his anger and hatred ; and this is true, not merely of those who have little capacity for reflection, but of the most intellectual. Hence the description of the prophet, "He feedeth on ashes, a deceived heart hath turned him aside, so that he cannot deliver himself or say, Is there not a lie in my right hand ?" (Isa. xliv. 20). In other words, the idolatrous devotee is completely *hypnotised* by spirits of evil, and no power on earth can prevail upon him to recognise and resist his delusions.

The fascination exercised by idolatry is not merely due to the influence of spirits of evil on the minds of its followers, but to the fact, already referred to, that it appeals to the natural inclinations of human nature. The exercise of faith has always been a stumbling-block to those whose interests and affections are absorbed by the things of time and sense, and such persons find it impossible to trust to the promises of an unseen God in time of danger, distress and perplexity. Man, it is said, "looketh on the outward appearance," and, in consequence, he demands something visible, tangible and sensible, on which to rest his hopes. So it was with the Jews. The *moral* evidence of Christ's righteousness and truth, which convinced His own disciples that He was the Christ, "the Son of the living God," carried no weight to their minds. They demanded of Him "a sign from heaven," some palpable and sensible evidence to convince them of His authority and mission ; and Christ said that this was the characteristic of all who sought the satisfaction of the lusts and desires of the flesh. "An evil and adulterous generation," He said, "seeketh after a sign." [1]

Hence, a religion of sacraments and signs, which professes to obtain spiritual results by physical acts and material means under human control, and a human priesthood which claims to be the visible and authoritative source of truth to which all may appeal, instead of having to seek the guidance of an unseen God, has always had a fascination to the majority of mankind who seek their portion in this world, and the sinner finds more satisfaction from the authoritative "*I absolve thee*" of the priest than from the most explicit promises of God to those who seek His mercy.

This, as we have seen, was the essence of the ancient Paganism. It appealed to the senses of men, assuring them of spiritual results through material agencies, and instead of having to seek the help of an unseen God, the Pagan had before him a visible and tangible image in which he believed, and not without reason, that the spirit of a god dwelt. Herein lay the danger of, and the attraction exercised by, the ancient Paganism to every unspiritual Israelite to whom faith was a stumbling-block.

Were these images at a distance, and not at once accessible, the effort required to seek their assistance might deter the person from doing so, but if in the very house, or room, there was one of these images which were believed to be inhabited by the spirit of a god, and to possess strange and remarkable powers, then in times of affliction and distress, when the mind is overwrought or unstrung, the thought that help might possibly be obtained from them would present a temptation, which those without true faith in God would certainly succumb to, and which, once fully yielded to, would separate them from the protection of God and render them defenceless against the influence of those spirits of evil which are ever ready to confirm the delusion. For if the Christian has to fight against "the hosts of wicked spirits in heavenly places," and to resist steadfast in the faith the suggestions and temptations which, as "fiery darts from the wicked one," assail him in times of weakness and affliction, we may be certain that these spirits would seize the opportunity thus afforded them to delude and "hypnotise" the mind of one whose "heart had departed from the Lord" (Jer. xvii. 5).

There was a good and sufficient reason, therefore, for the remarkable

---

[1] The word "adulterous" seems to be used by Christ here in the sense in which it is used in other Scriptures, to denote those who forsake God, the fountain of living waters, for false religions, or the interests and pleasures of this world, and who are guilty of spiritual adultery with regard to God.

prohibition of God—" Bring not an abomination into thine house lest thou become a cursed thing like unto it, for it is a cursed thing." " Facilis descensus est Averni." Men's lives are moulded and decided by thoughts, words, or circumstances which appear trivial at the time, although, like the stone which has just commenced to roll slowly down a hill, but which gradually gets swifter and swifter, their fate is from that moment decided, unless they are arrested by some power external to themselves. This is rigidly true of all spiritual evil, and especially of idolatry. It is the first step, the first act, the first word, the first admission of the mind that determines all that follows, and once that step is taken the Rubicon is passed, and there is no return or recovery from that state of strong delusion which overtakes those who have fallen under the influence of spirits of evil.

The Israelites were also forbidden to adopt any portion of the *Ritual* of Paganism in their worship of Jehovah. Wherever there is want of faith in God, men have a tendency to trust in the outward ordinances of religion, and those who do so suppose that their performance of these ordinances makes them more righteous in the sight of God and satisfies His demands. This was the case with the majority of the Israelites; they made idols of their own ordinances, and in so doing accepted the very principle of idolatry. For it was to suppose that they could obtain spiritual good from that which was not God, or that God would " be worshipped " (" done good to," *therapeuetai*) by men's hands, as though he needed anything " (Acts xvii. 25), and that there was some spiritual efficacy in material and created things. Such persons would be peculiarly susceptible to the influence and fascination of idolatry.

It must be remembered also that there was the same outward resemblance between the ritual of the Israelites and Pagans, which there is between Romanism and true Christianity, and that, like Romanism, which is a perversion of Christianity, Paganism professed to be based on the same original truth and revelation which were acknowledged by the Israelites. The impressive and magnificent ritual of Paganism might well, therefore, have led the pious but unspiritual Israelite, like the unspiritual Protestant with regard to Romanism, to think that in adopting some of its features he might improve on his own ritual, give greater honour to Jehovah, and do more good to his own soul. But the Pagan ritual was polluted, because associated with every abomination which God hated, and just as the presence of one of the symbols of idolatry might make its possessor accursed, so also with equal certainty the adoption of the idolatrous ritual would do so likewise.

The retention of an idol, or symbol, of Paganism was the evidence that some value was attached to it, and so also the adoption of any portion of the ritual of Paganism implied the idea that some spiritual good might be obtained by so doing. But once that principle had been admitted the descent to Avernus had commenced, and it was certain that he who had fallen under this delusion would adopt more and more of that ritual and the doctrines which attributed to it this spiritual efficacy.

For *symbolism* was the essence of Pagan idolatry, and every act and posture and sacred emblem had its mystical meaning, and in adopting any portion of the Pagan ritual, the Israelite, who had thus commenced to withdraw himself from the guidance and protection of Jehovah, was certain to be led through the ritual to the doctrines it symbolised.

It cannot be doubted also that every sophistry by which the force of God's commands could be turned aside, evil made to appear good and falsehood truth, would be used by the priesthood of Paganism to propagate their religion amongst the Israelites, and to bewilder the minds of those who were already the subject of its fascination. In short, the ease with which, even in modern times, we see people perverted to Romanism, a religion the errors of which their forefathers died to repudiate, is an illustration of the way in which the Israelites may have been just as easily beguiled by the idolatry of the Canaanites, to which, in spite of repeated warnings and punishments, they again and again succumbed.

Considering, then, the strong delusion, the destruction of conscience and moral judgment, and the entire separation from God, which is the Nemesis of idolatry, we can fully perceive the solemn necessity for the stringent prohibitions against it, and God, in commanding the destruction of the idolaters, and in promptly punishing His people for every participation in their idolatry, kept many from falling under the power of the Pagan gods and brought others to repentance.

This, then, is the real evil of idolatry and the worship of the supposed spirits of the dead. It makes those who succumb to its influence accursed, or cut off from the protection of God, and places them under the guidance and dominion of spirits of evil, who constitute those " principalities and powers "—the real " rulers of the darkness of this world "—" the wicked spirits in heavenly places " (Eph. vi. 12) against whom the Christian has to fight, and whose one object is to delude and destroy the souls of mankind.

Therefore, the Apostolic writers renew the exhortations of the Old Testament, and urge their hearers to "flee from idolatry," "to come out and be separate" from it, and not even to "*touch* the unclean thing"; implying, as in the commands of God to Israel, that there was a danger in the least of its symbols and ritual observances. For the Apostle Paul asserts that the weak or ignorant Christian, who was tempted to "eat meat offered to idols," supposing that there was some occult efficacy in so doing, might thereby "perish." For such an act implied want of faith in Christ, and rendered the person liable to fall under the influence of the demon gods. "Eating meats offered to idols" was a representative act of idolatry,[1] and the Apostle's warning, therefore, extends to every feature of idolatrous worship, which, if participated in, would, but for the restraining power of God, gradually engulf those who did so in the mælstrom of idolatry, out of which, humanly speaking, there is no return.

[1] "Meats offered to idols." The victims sacrificed to the Pagan gods were supposed to be representative of the god to whom they were offered, and those who partook of the sacrifices were believed to receive the spirit of the god. Hence, "eating meats offered to idols" was an act of trust and dependence in the god, and is used as a representative term for idolatrous worship, as in Rev. ii. 3.

APPENDIX A

SIR GARDNER WILKINSON ON EGYPTIAN RELIGION

THE immense value of Sir Gardner Wilkinson's researches among the monuments of ancient Egypt naturally gives considerable weight to all his statements and opinions on the subject. But the deductions he has drawn from the facts, and the reasons by which he supports them, must be distinguished from the facts themselves, and may be legitimately questioned when they appear to be open to objections.

Like many other persons, he was naturally impressed by the stupendous labour, the high art and civilisation which are evinced by the monumental remains of Egypt, and considering that a people with the qualities necessary to perform such great works must have a religion of corresponding excellence, he has been inclined to idealise their idolatry and to give it a moral and spiritual aspect to which it has no real claim.

He argues that the Egyptian idolatry was not that of Sabæanism, or the Sun and Nature worship of the Cushite race, but that the attributes of the Egyptian gods were metaphysical conceptions of the true God, and he implies that Osiris, in particular, may have been a preconception of Christ.[1]

In support of this view he repudiates the idea that the originals of the gods were human beings, and rejects the evidence of Pagan authors when they do not agree with his ideal.

This much may be said in seeming support of his ideal, that after the primary overthrow of idolatry in Egypt,[2] the Misraimite people had, for a time, a knowledge of the true God, a knowledge which was again revived in the reign of Apepi, and this knowledge must necessarily, for a long time afterwards, have influenced the religious thought of the people. But it has been shown that the Cushite (*i.e.*, the Egyptian), as distinguished from the Misraimite element, was in later times predominant in Egypt,[3] and it is from the priesthood of the former, or Egyptian race, that we obtain our knowledge of Egyptian idolatry. On the other hand, the effect of the knowledge of the purer religion would be to retard the progress of the Cushite idolatry, and oblige it to assume an outward aspect of righteousness which it had not in reality. It would appear, in short, that there was, for a long time, more or less conflict between the adherents of the god of Set, and those of idolatry

---

[1] There is, of course, an element of truth in this, inasmuch as Osiris was *the false Christ* of Paganism. *See* chap. xv.

[2] *Vide* chap. xii.   [3] *Vide* chap. iv.

whose god was Osiris ; and that although, amongst the majority, the former worship eventually became degraded into the worship of Set himself, there was a similar opposition between his followers and those of Osiris. But it is quite certain that the latter triumphed in the end, and that Set, once known as "Set Nubti," was subsequently identified with Typhon, the principle of evil.

It was the opposition from the adherents of the purer religion which, no doubt, was the cause of that *mystery* and *reserve* which distinguished the Egyptian idolatry from the Babylonian. The advocates of the Egyptian idolatry had to overcome and quiet the scruples of the believers in the true God, and for this purpose they adopted a language of words having a double meaning, the exoteric sense of which would not offend the conscience of the scrupulous, while the revelation of its esoteric meaning was reserved for the initiated. It was also necessary for their success that their god should outwardly, and in name, be given the attributes of the true God, or be made to appear as "an angel of light," and "his ministers as ministers of righteousness," which has ever been the method by which error has been propagated and men deceived since the beginning of the world (2 Cor. xi. 13, 15). Hence also the establishment of the celebrated "Mysteries" which appear to have been initiated in Egypt, and the final act of which was the revelation of the god in his true character.

That this "mystery," which is so attractive and suggestive to the imagination, together with the outward appearance of righteousness which characterised Egyptian idolatry, should deceive one who was only too ready to believe good of a people of such high civilisation as the Egyptians, is perhaps natural, but the cause of, and necessity for, this mystery and outward righteousness, viz., the previous existence of a purer religion, must be taken into consideration, and the facts prove that the adherents of the latter were regarded with the most bitter hatred by the idolaters, and apparently put to death without mercy, showing that, in spite of the benevolence attributed to the Egyptian gods, their idolatry was as cruel and vindictive as in Babylon, Phœnicia and other countries.

The latter end of the eighteenth dynasty appears to be the period when the final change of religion commenced,[1] but it is sufficiently evident from the sculptures, that the religion of Set had, before that period, become degraded, and that he was only one of the many gods worshipped under the form of various animals.[2] This is in accordance with all history. Religious truth known in one generation becomes quickly leavened with error, and in a few generations is lost, even though it may still exist in name.

Wilkinson says, "If the Egyptians, like some other Eastern people,

---

[1] The title Set or Seth was taken by more than one of the earlier kings after Rameses I., showing that the influence of Set was not at once overthrown.

[2] Vide *Wilkinson*, by Birch, vol. iii. pp. 136-138, and Plate **XXXI.**, where Set is figured as an animal-headed god and represented as the instructor of Thothmes III. *See* also *ante*, chap. xii. pp. 263, 164.

adopted at first a Sabæan mode of worship, and afterwards *substituted for it*
the deification of the various attributes of the Deity himself, there would
be reason to suppose that the Sun once held the first place in their Pantheon,
and was not removed from it until *they had learnt* to consider the divine
mind superior to the works he had created."[1] But when did any nation,
of itself, ever develop the knowledge of the true God *out of idolatry*, as
Sir G. Wilkinson suggests?   On the contrary, as in the case of the
Israelites, nations have a constant tendency to pervert the truth and
return to error.

Sir G. Wilkinson, in the above passage, implies that Sun worship *may
have once been* the religion of the Egyptians, but that they ultimately
rejected it for a purer faith.   But everything shows that Sun worship was a
central feature of the *later* Egyptian religion, while the deified attributes
which were worshipped were Nature gods and constituted the very Nature
worship of Sabæanism.

The principal monuments, portraying the religion and gods of the
Egyptians, are those of the eighteenth and following dynasties, and Wilkinson
gives a Plate of Bekenaten, or Amenophis III., of the eighteenth dynasty,
worshipping an image of the Sun with rays "emblematic of its demiurgic or
creative power."[2]   These rays were called the "Aten Ra," and the Aten is
described as "the sunlight which is the Amen of Thebes and the maker
of all beings, the great living Aten, Lord of the Sun's Orbit, the Disk, Lord
of the Heaven, Lord of the Earth."[3]   The god Amen Ra, the Sun god of
Thebes, is also described in the hymns of the eighteenth dynasty as,—"the
creator of men, animals and plants; they identify him also with Khem
(the god of physical generation), and ally him in all respects to the Sun."[4]
What is this but the Sun and Nature worship of Sabæanism?

On an obelisk from Heliopolis, the Sun is described as addressing King
Rhamestes: "I, the Sun, the Great God, the Sovereign of Heaven, have
bestowed on you life.   Horus, the brave Lord of the Diadem incomparable,
the Sovereign of Egypt that has placed the statues of the Gods in this Palace
and has beautified Heliopolis in like manner as he has honoured the Sun
himself, the Sovereign of Heaven.   I, the Sun, the God and Lord of Heaven,
have bestowed strength and power over all things on King Rhamestes," etc.,
etc.[5]   If this is not the Sun worship of Sabæanism it would be difficult to
say what is.   Sir G. Wilkinson himself says, "It appears that the Egyptians
made of the Sun several distinct deities; as the *intellectual* Sun, the physical
orb, the cause of heat, the author of light, the power of the Sun, the
vivifying cause," etc.[6]   In other words they worshipped the Sun.

[1] Vide *Wilkinson*, by Birch, vol. iii. pp. 47, 48.
[2] *Ibid.*, Plate XXIII. *N.B.*—Modern Egyptologists make Bekenatem or Kuenatem to
be a fourth Amenophis. This, however, is opposed to the testimony of the two tablets
of Abydos, and there are other reasons for questioning the conclusion.
[3] *Ibid.*, p. 52, note by Birch.   [4] *Ibid.*, p. 13, note by Birch.
[5] "Ammianus Marcellinus," Cory's *Fragments*, pp. 170, 171.
[6] *Wilkinson*, by Birch, vol. iii. p. 53.

2A

Chnoumis, or Cnouphis, was also the creative power, and is likened by Sir G. Wilkinson to "the spirit of God which moved upon the face of the waters."[1]   But, as he remarks, "Amenra, like most of the gods, frequently took the character of other deities, as those of Khem, Ra, and Chnoumis";[2] that is to say, the latter were identified with Amenra, the Sun, as the creative cause, and as gods of physical life and generation.   What is this but the worship of the powers of Nature, of which the Sun was supposed to be the supreme source and cause?[3]   In addition to this, the Egyptians worshipped their gods under the forms of animals, beasts, birds and reptiles, which they regarded, as in the case of the bulls Apis and Mnevis, as the very gods themselves and adored them accordingly.[4]   The only effect of this was to associate the gods with the principles of natural life and generation of which such animals were the manifestation.

So also they portrayed the gods as human beings with the heads of beasts, birds, serpents, etc.   Thus, as the Apostle says, "they became vain in their imaginations and their foolish heart was darkened, professing themselves to be wise they became fools, and changed the glory of the incorruptible God into an image made like unto corruptible man, and to birds and four-footed beasts and creeping things.   Wherefore God also gave them up to uncleanness through the lusts of their hearts.   Who changed the truth of God into a lie, and worshipped and served the creature rather than the Creator."[5]

Sir G. Wilkinson tries to excuse the worship of animals by suggesting its origin to their utility;[6] but the excuse is lame.   For if they worshipped them for their utility, they would not have selected such creatures as wolves, serpents and beetles, and would not have excluded such useful animals as the horse and the camel; but it is also sufficiently evident that the animals worshipped were chosen, not because of their utility, but because they were regarded as manifesting the physical, or nature attributes of the gods.[7]

He further tries to distinguish Egyptian idolatry from the Sabæan worship, by pointing to what he calls "the metaphysical nature of their religion."   He says, "The existence of an early Sabæan worship in Egypt is merely possible, while the metaphysical nature of their religion is proved both by the ancient writers and the monuments."[8]

It is true that, except for a brief period at the beginning, when the Cushite idolatry was implanted in Egypt, the early Egyptians had a knowledge of the true God,[9] but it was quickly perverted into that very Sun, Nature and Animal worship which Sir G. Wilkinson tries to distinguish from Sabæanism.   The metaphysical character which he attributes to their religion consists in the titles given to certain gods, as "The Lord of Truth" given to Phthah,[10] the "Manifestation of Goodness" given to Osiris, who, he

---

[1] *Wilkinson*, by Birch, vol. iii. p. 2.   [2] *Ibid.*, p. 9.
[3] *See* chap. x. "Sun and Serpent Worship."
[4] *Wilkinson*, by Birch, vol. iii. pp. 89, 91, 92.   [5] Rom. i. 21-25.
[6] *Wilkinson*, by Birch, vol. iii. p. 251.   [7] *Ibid.*, p. 256.
[8] *Ibid.*, p. 48.   [9] *See* chap. xv.
[10] *Wilkinson*, by Birch, vol. iii. p. 15.

says, " is described as full of goodness, grace, and truth." [1]   So also he says that Amenra, in one of his aspects, is "the intellectual Sun." [2] *i.e.*, the source of wisdom, which was an especial aspect of the Sun and Serpent god.

We might as well ascribe intellect and wisdom to the rocks and earths of which the earth is constituted, as to the Sun, but this was the principle on which Paganism acted. It advisedly confused the spiritual with the physical, and the teaching of Hermes, the author of Egyptian idolatry, represented the material light of the Sun as also spiritual light, and the Sun and Serpent god of Paganism was in consequence identified, eventually, with the Divine Wisdom, or Logos. [3]

Men do not accept religious error because it is error, but because it is presented to them in the garb, or outward appearance of truth, and Christ therefore warned His disciples that false teachers would come to them clothed outwardly in the garb of His true followers, while the Apostle says that the ministers of Satan are transformed into ministers of righteousness. [4]   So it was in Egypt where the Cushite idolatry had to contend with a greater or less knowledge of the truth. It was therefore necessary that such titles as " Lord of Truth" and " Manifestation of Goodness " should be given to the Egyptian gods, in order to blind and deceive the people.

But the question is, what was really meant by this "truth " and " goodness " ? The "truth " was the truth as recognised by idolatry, and the " good " was that material good and worldly power which the god of this world bestows on his worshippers. The titles in themselves were mere words, but the gods on whom they were bestowed were Nature gods. Phthah, the "Lord of Truth," like Amenra, Cnouphis and Khem, was the creative power, the source of which was supposed to be the Sun, and he was identified with the Greek Vulcan or Hephæstus. [5]   The later texts ally him to the Sun, [6] and the scarabeous beetle, which was his particular emblem, was the emblem of the Sun and its supposed creative power. [7]

Osiris, the " Manifestation of Goodness," was also identified with the Sun. That he was not so identified at first is wholly in accordance with the way in which Egyptian idolatry was developed as described in this book ; [8] but the evidence of ancient authors is conclusive that he was so regarded in later times. Diodorus says that the Egyptians imagined that there were two chief gods, the Sun and the Moon, the first of whom was called Osiris, and the other Isis. [9]   Macrobius also calls Osiris the Sun, and Isis the Earth or Nature. [10]   Plutarch says that Osiris represented " *Mas-*

---

[1] *Wilkinson*, by Birch, vol. iii. p. 69. [2] *Ibid.* p. 11.
[3] *Vide* chap. x. " Sun and Serpent Worship," pp. 232, 233.
[4] Matt. vii. 15 ; 2 Cor. xi. 15. [5] *Wilkinson*, by Birch, iii. p. 16.
[6] *Ibid.*, p. 20, note by Birch. [7] *Ibid.*, pp. 15 and 345, 346.
[8] *See* chap. xv.
[9] Diod., i. 11 ; *Wilkinson*, by Birch, vol. iii. p. 46. The god Thoth was also the Moon, and in consequence of Isis being eventually identified with the Moon, the Egyptians regarded the Moon as both masculine and feminine (Plut., *De Iside*, S. 43).
[10] Macrob., *Saturn*, i. 26.

culine nature, or the prime cause " (that is, the creative power which the Egyptians regarded as the Sun), and that Isis represented the earth, " *the feminine part of nature*, the second cause or the receptive power." [1]

Sir G. Wilkinson objects to these statements, but his only reason for doing so is that they do not agree with his erroneous ideal. He does not recognise also the gradual development of Egyptian idolatry, and that its later aspect, as it was known by the above authors, was not necessarily the same as it had been at a previous period. The intimate acquaintance and intercourse of the Greeks, in later times, with Egypt, from whom they received their religion, and where they went to be initiated into the Mysteries, oblige us to accept the statements of the Greek authors, which, if so utterly incorrect as Wilkinson tries to make out, would have been denied at the time.

The Sun was called "the Lord of Heaven," and Isis, the wife of Osiris, was called "the Lady of Heaven," [2] while Horus, the son of Osiris and Isis, was regarded as the incarnation of the Sun, and was symbolised by the Hawk, the emblem of the Sun. [3] Horapollo says that Horus is the Sun, [4] and Isis is represented as saying, "No mortal has raised my veil, the fruit which I have brought forth is the Sun," [5] that is, the incarnation of Osiris. Horus was therefore supposed to be born at the time of the winter solstice, December 25th, when the Sun first begins to regain its power. [6] Osiris, as identified with Apis, the sacred bull, was worshipped as "Asar Apis," or " Sar Apis," [7] who was identified with the Sun, [8] and numerous Greek dedications to Sarapis are inscribed, "To Pluto the Sun, the great Sarapis." [9]

Again, 360, the number of days in the solar year before the epact was added, was a symbol of the Sun throughout the Pagan world, [10] and at the Sepulchre of Osiris at Philæ, priests especially appointed for the purpose filled daily 360 cups with milk, uttering a solemn lamentation, and the most solemn oath taken by the inhabitants of the Thebaid is to swear by Osiris who lies buried at Philæ. [11] This is a clear proof that Osiris was recognised as the Sun god. Osiris was also the judge of the dead. He was supposed to receive them after death, and they were said to be "in Osiris." Hence the invocation to the Sun on behalf of the deceased can only apply to Osiris, who was the chief god of the Egyptians : "O thou Sun our sovereign Lord, and all ye Deities who have given life to man, receive me and grant us an abode among the eternal Gods." [12]

The Sun was also identified with the Serpent, which was the particular

[1] Plut., *De Iside*, S. 38, S. 56 ; *Wilkinson*, by Birch, vol. iii. p. 101.
[2] *Wilkinson*, by Birch, vol. iii. p. 100, Plate XXVI.
[3] *Ibid.*, p. 314.   [4] Horapollo, i. 317 ; *Wilkinson*, by Birch, vol. iii. p. 125.
[5] Bunsen, vol. i. pp. 386, 387.   [6] Plut., *De Iside*, vol. ii. pp. 377, 378.
[7] *Wilkinson*, by Birch, vol. iii. pp. 87, 89.
[8] Macrobius, *Saturn*, i. 25 ; *Wilkinson*, by Birch, vol. iii. p. 97.
[9] *Wilkinson*, by Birch, vol. iii. p. 97.   [10] *See* chap. x., "Sun and Serpent Worship."
[11] Diod., i. 22 ; *Wilkinson*, by Birch, vol. iii. p. 85.
[12] *Wilkinson*, by Birch, vol. iii. p. 479.

symbol of the Sun throughout Paganism,[1] and one of the titles of Osiris was "Onuphis"[2] from *On* (which was the name of the Sun at Heliopolis, called On by the Egyptians), and *ophe*, "serpent." Wilkinson indeed derives Onuphis from *ouon nofre*, the "opener of good."[3] This derivation, however, is not only far less satisfactory than the other, and is probably suggested by him in order to accord with his ideal of Osiris, but as Onuphis was symbolised by a serpent, and this name, or its Coptic equivalent, is still the term for a serpent, it is evident that it was given to Osiris as the Sun and Serpent god.[4]

Osiris, as the Sun, was of course the creative power of which the Phallus was the symbol. Hence he was the Phallic god, and at his festivals huge figures of the Phallus were carried in procession.[5] Plutarch also says that the festival of Pammylia in honour of Osiris resembled the Phallophoria, or Phallic festival, in Greece, and adds that "from the manner of celebrating it, it is evident that Osiris is in reality the great principle of fecundity."[6]

It is thus evident that Osiris, the Manifestation of Goodness, was in every way identified with the Sun and Serpent, and with the obscene Phallic and Nature gods of Sabæanism, and, as in their case, there is ample evidence to show that in ancient times human sacrifices were offered to him.[7]

The latter is repudiated by Wilkinson as inconsistent with the *civilisation* of the Egyptians![8] But civilisation is no restraint to the most cruel bigotry and superstition. The Assyrians were as highly civilised as the Egyptians, but that did not prevent them flaying their prisoners alive and tearing out their tongues;[9] nor did the high civilisation of the Pagan Romans in the time of the Emperors prevent them from torturing and burning alive the early Christians; nor did the high civilisation of the Roman Catholic Spaniards, Italians, and others, prevent them from torturing and burning Protestants as a religious duty, in obedience to the dictates of a false Christianity.

The argument here used by Sir G. Wilkinson is an illustration of the erroneous pleas by which he defends his ideal, and there are therefore no reasonable grounds for rejecting the statements of ancient authors which show that, in times *subsequent* to the eighteenth dynasty, when Set had come to be hated and regarded as Typhon, human sacrifices called *Typhos* were offered to Osiris, just as similar sacrifices were offered to the Pagan gods in other countries.[10]

But just as Set, the name given to the god of the Shepherds and Israelites, was subsequently identified with Typhon the devil, and symbolised by an ass, just in short as Christ was called a devil by the Jews, and in later times symbolised by the Pagans as a man with the head of an ass to

---

[1] Chap. x. pp. 231-242.   [2] *Wilkinson*, by Birch, vol. iii. p. 308.
[3] *Ibid.*, p. 70.   [4] *See* chap. x. p. 238.   [5] Herod., ii. 48, 49.
[6] Plut., *De Iside*, S. 12, S. 36 ; *Wilkinson*, by Birch, vol. iii p. 83.
[7] *See* chap. ix. p. 209 ; chap. x. pp. 243, 244.   [8] *Wilkinson*, by Birch, vol. iii. p. 30.
[9] Layard's *Babylon and Nineveh*, pp. 457, 458.
[10] It is said that human sacrifices were discontinued in the reign of Amosis, the first king of the eighteenth dynasty, which implies that they existed also before that time, but that through the influence and vast power exercised by Apepi, they were for a time put a stop to.

identify him with the same Typhon,—so, on the other hand, Osiris, the Sun and Serpent and Phallic god, who was worshipped under the form of an animal, was "transformed into an angel of light" and called "the Manifestation of Goodness," "full of goodness, grace and truth!" In short, Osiris, like others of the Pagan gods, was represented to be the promised "seed of the woman," the destroyer of the Serpent and the redeemer of man,[1] while the rites of Bacchus, the Greek name of the Phallic god Osiris, in which the worshippers indulged in sensual excesses, were said to be for the "*purification of souls!* "[2] "There is no new thing under the Sun" (Ecc. i. 9).

Sir G. Wilkinson says further, "Osiris in his mysterious character was the greatest of all the Egyptian deities, but little is known of those undivulged secrets which the ancients took so much care to conceal. So cautious indeed were the initiated that they made a scruple even of mentioning him, and Herodotus, whenever he relates anything concerning this deity, excuses himself from uttering his name."[3] And again he says, "If their metaphysical doctrines, divulged alone to the initiated, are not within our reach, sufficient is shown to convince us that the nature of the great God was not derived from mere physical objects."[4]

It is evident from the above that Sir G. Wilkinson considers that if we only knew the secret of the Mysteries, we should be astonished and impressed at the moral and metaphysical attributes of the god revealed to the initiated. But the name of that god was not, as he supposes, Osiris, which was the name by which the god was *popularly* spoken of; nor did Herodotus hesitate to mention the name of Osiris, for he expressly does so, and says that he is the same as Bacchus.[5]

So far, the secret name of the god has never been divulged, but it is sufficiently clear that the Pagan gods, who were recognised by the initiated to be merely different forms of one and the same god, were identified with him whom Christ called the Prince of the Demons; that he was worshipped under the form of the Serpent; that this was the god revealed in the Mysteries; and that the betrayal of this dark secret, called the "Apporeta," was punished with immediate death.[6]

If the god revealed had been the God of righteousness and truth, there would have been no need to conceal the fact, but the revelation of a god which would shock the conscience, and alarm the minds of men before they had been gradually and cautiously prepared to receive the secret, necessarily required to be guarded and concealed with the utmost care from the general public. Men whose "deeds are evil love darkness rather than light, for everyone that doeth evil hateth the light, neither cometh to the light lest his deeds should be reproved; but he that doeth truth cometh to the light that his deeds may be made manifest that they are wrought in God."[7]

[1] *See* chap. xv. pp. 316-321.   [2] *Wilkinson*, by Birch, vol. iii. p. 70.
[3] *Ibid.*, p. 65.   [4] *Ibid.*, p. 48.
[5] Herod., ii. 42 and 144. *See* also *ante*, chap. ii. pp. 36, 37.
[6] *Vide* chap. x. p. 234.   [7] John iii. 19, 21.

Mystery and *darkness* are the fitting accompaniments of "the kingdom of darkness."

This, then, was the ultimate character of the god revealed in the Mysteries, and the way for this revelation was prepared by identifying him with the Sun and powers of Nature, by representing him as the god of the Phallus, and by adoring him as an actual beast of the field; for by these means the minds and consciences of his worshippers were blinded and degraded, for they directed them to that which was wholly earthly and sensual, and the sanction of religion was given to the things of the world and the lusts of the flesh. At the same time, in order to quiet their scruples, the god, in his superficial aspect, was made to appear as "an angel of light,"[1] by calling him "the pure and holy Osiris," "the Manifester of Good, full of grace and truth," by representing him as the promised seed of woman, the Overcomer of the Spirit of Evil, and by pretending that his rites were "for the purification of souls!"

It has been shown in the earlier chapters of this book that the originals of the gods of Paganism were human beings, which gave them the attractiveness consequent on their supposed human sympathies, and served as a basis on which to build up their ultimate development as Sun and Nature gods.

It was natural, however, that Sir G. Wilkinson, regarding only the superficial and pretended goodness of the Egyptian gods, should reject the evidence in proof of the fact that the original of Osiris was a human being;[2] for to have admitted this would have denied the view that Osiris represented the goodness and truth of the true God. Here again he rejects the evidence of the ancient authors which oppose his view, and only accepts those which support it.

Thus Plutarch relates the story of the capture and death of Osiris by Typhon, the cutting up of his body and search after, and collection of, the pieces, except the Phallus, which, in consequence, was specially consecrated, etc. But the Pagan author, in defence of his religion and in order to repudiate the death of Osiris, attempts to allegorise the story.

He says Osiris, who *in other places* he called "*the first creative cause*," represents *the Nile!* The conspiracy of Typhon, who the Egyptians identified with *the ocean*, he says represents the force and power of *drought!* Isis, the irrigated land; Horus, the offspring of Osiris and Isis, who overcame Typhon, he represents as the exhalation from the irrigated land! The box in which the body of Osiris was placed, the banks of the Nile! His death on the seventeenth day of Athyr (the seventeenth day of the second month) as the time when the moon begins to wane; which of course is not the case, as it varies from month to month, etc., etc. Other allegorical interpretations are given by Plutarch,[3] but one and all are so puerile, absurd and contradictory, that it is surprising that anyone could give them any consideration. But Wilkinson, rather than admit that Osiris may have been an actual

---

[1] 2 Cor. xi. 14. [2] *Wilkinson*, by Birch, vol. iii. p. 73.
[3] *Ibid.*, iii. pp. 75-80.

human king, regards them with approval, in spite of the fact also that they represent Osiris as a sort of *minor Nature god*, and therefore contradict the assumption that he represented the true God![1]

It was natural that the Pagan priesthood in later times, after it had served its purpose, should endeavour to conceal from the vulgar the human origin of their gods, which, if admitted, would then have diminished their aspect of importance and power. Augustine refers to the care taken by the Egyptian priesthood in later times to conceal or deny the human origin of Serapis or Osiris. He says, "They made a law that whoever should say he had been a man should die the death. And because that in all the temples of Isis and Serapis there was an image with the finger laid upon the mouth as commanding silence—this was, says Varro, to show them that they must not say that those two were ever mortal."[2] The secret was only revealed to the initiated, and, as shown by the letter of Alexander to his mother, was kept until a late period, but the testimony of facts and the statements of ancient authors are conclusive evidence of its being eventually the recognised belief.[3]

Sir G. Wilkinson, however, asserts that "no Egyptian deity was supposed to have lived on earth and to have been deified after death as with the Greeks and other people." He alludes to the statement made to Herodotus by the Egyptian priests, that no god had lived upon the earth as a man.[4] But he totally ignores the reason for this statement and what the priests afterwards told Herodotus. The account of Herodotus is as follows :—

The Greek historian Hecatæus when he visited the Egyptian priests on a previous occasion had claimed to be descended from a god. The priests regarded the Greeks as mere children compared with themselves, and this claim on the part of a Greek they therefore refused to admit, and in support of their argument they denied that a man could be born from a god. Nevertheless they were perfectly aware, as shown by Wilkinson himself, that the gods had not only wives and children like other men, but that every Egyptian king, who was also Pontifex Maximus and head of the priesthood, was believed to be descended from the gods, that their particular title was "Sons of the Sun god," and that they were in consequence worshipped as gods.

Moreover, Plutarch, whom Sir G. Wilkinson extensively quotes, says that the Egyptian priests expressly taught that all their principal deities were once mere men who had reigned upon earth.[5] This is also in exact accordance with what the priests *afterwards admitted* to Herodotus, viz., that *their gods had once been kings of Egypt and that the last God king was Horus, the son of Osiris, who had deposed Typhon.*[6] In addition to this there is the plain fact that Ham, the son of Noah, was worshipped in Egypt under his own

---

[1] It is a question whether the attempted allegorisation of the story of Osiris by Plutarch does not belittle him more than the admission of his human origin.

[2] *The Citie of God*, translated by J. Healey (1642), vol. ii. p. 165.

[3] *Ante*, chap. ii. pp. 13-20.   [4] *Wilkinson*, by Birch, vol. iii. p. 68 ; Herod., ii. 142, 143.

[5] See *ante*, chap. ii. p. 14.   [6] Herod., ii. 144.

name as Ammon, the Sun god, and as Khem, the god of generation. Set or Typhon is also referred to in the reign of Rameses II. as a former king of Egypt.

The conclusions of Sir G. Wilkinson are often self-contradictory, and they are at variance with the facts which he himself furnishes. His arguments are, in most cases, little more than assertions, and, at the most, rest upon these ascriptions of good and truth by which the Egyptian priesthood sought to give their idolatry, and their gods, a superficial veneer of righteousness. In this respect he is a fair illustration of many other writers, who, fascinated by the art and magnificence which is the unfailing accompaniment of idolatry, are ready to give credence to every assertion and excuse made by its adherents in its defence, and to ignore or reject the evidence which reveals its true nature.

APPENDIX B

OANNES AND THE ANNEDOTI

It will be observed that, throughout creation, every living creature has its own proper body, which is the *manifestation* and *expression* of its own particular character. The law of "expression" is uniform. Cunning, ferocity, courage, generosity, loyalty, love, hatred, etc., have all their proper forms of expression, which all mankind, and even some of the higher animals, instinctively, and at once, recognise. Physical characteristics are also expressed by distinctive form and shape. The elephant, the tiger, the ox, the horse, the snake, and the various forms of birds and reptiles, have each their distinctive form which enable us at once to determine their distinctive characteristics. The outward form of each, from the noblest of mankind to the lowest animal, is the exact expression of its individual spiritual, or physical, capacity and characteristics. As is the spirit of each, so is the flesh which clothes it.

So absolute is this law, that changes in the moral and intellectual characteristics of races of men, and even of individuals during their lifetime, are reflected in their bodily form and expression. Hence we must conclude that *spirit* is the determining cause of all material form. Between the embryo of the man and the embryo of the lowest animal there is no outward difference, and yet it is impossible for the embryo of the man to become anything else but a man, or for the embryo of the animal to become anything but the one particular animal of which it is the seed. There is manifestly a spiritual principle in each which determines the growth and development of each, and the particular form which each minute accretion of matter shall take during that growth. This has all the appearance of being one of those essential laws which have their origin in the very nature of things and of God.

If, then, there is no exception to this law, it would appear that spiritual beings, like the angels, if they took a material form, would be obliged to take one expressive of their true character. What, then, would be the form of a fallen angel?

"Greater in power and might" than man, their material form would probably express that power and might; but in every moral respect they have fallen far below the level of man, who is made in the image of God.

We are told that men who, after they have received the knowledge of the truth, have rejected it, are incapable of repentance, or change of mind, and therefore incapable of redemption. The same would appear to be the case with fallen angels, who, as purely spiritual beings, have the power of perceiving the truth at once without the necessity, as in the case of men in the flesh, of going through the process of gradually learning it. Therefore, if they fall, they fall irredeemably, because they sin against the full knowledge of the truth. Hence it is written that "God spared not the angels who sinned." They had no longer any moral principle, or moral capacity, but having wilfully separated themselves from, and rejected, righteousness and truth, they were for ever cut off from God, and were morally on the same level as the animals, who are ungoverned, and uninfluenced, by moral considerations.

Hence we may conclude that Satan and the first angels which fell, being wholly separated from God, and without conscience, or the recognition of righteousness as that which is good, and of wickedness as that which is evil, would become like ferocious animals, solely governed by the desire to assert and manifest their power in the destruction of others; as we see in the case of such animals as the tiger, to whom the sufferings and cries of its victim seem to afford the keenest pleasure, because they are a tribute to, and expressive of, its superior power.

If, then, it be asked, Why did not Satan, when he tempted Eve, take the form of a man, which would certainly have been far the fittest to have obtained her confidence?—the reply is that it was probably because he could not take the form of man, which is declared to be the image of God, the expression of the wisdom and righteousness of God. Instead thereof, he had to take the form of a serpent, which most perfectly expressed his true character of malignity and subtlety.

Similarly, in the case of those angels who left their first estate in order to co-habit with the daughters of men. They being actuated merely by sensual, or animal, lust, the forms which would best express their characteristics would be that of animals; and it is possible that this may explain the statements so constantly met with in the Greek mythology, which are otherwise inexplicable, that the gods (*i.e.*, the demons), in their amours with mortal women, invariably assumed the form of some bird, beast or reptile.

On the other hand, if fallen angels, or Satan himself, wished to draw fallen men yet farther from God and induce them to worship themselves (*i.e.*, the daimonia), and made use of all the resources of natural knowledge in order to recommend their teaching, then they might well be represented by the form of the annedoti, combining that of a man with that of a voracious fish. In short, if Satan once took the form of a serpent in order to deceive man, so might he, or other fallen angels, take the form of an annedotus for a similar purpose. It would indeed have been strange if, in those early days, he did not take some such measures for the purpose of communicating to mankind the principles of that idolatry by means of which he would be enabled to carry on and complete the ruin he had commenced.

In connection with this subject it may be worth while to allude to another statement of Berosus. Reference has been made to the various traditions of a former world which was destroyed by *fire*, and the records of geological research have many evidences of a former world, in which those mighty Saurians and sea monsters, some of the skeletons of which exist in our museums, flourished and were lords of creation, but all, or nearly all, of which have been destroyed. By what means this destruction was effected geological science does not determine; but as these inhabitants of the sea could hardly have been destroyed by *water*, it may have been by great heat, which, while obliterating all trace of many, left the remains of some, as records of their existence. It is certain that some were suddenly destroyed, for, like the antediluvian mammoth, individuals have been found with un-digested food in their stomachs.[1]

Now Berosus, in his history, speaks of such a former world, inhabited by sea monsters, and the shapes of these monsters he describes. But, no doubt, by that time, tradition and imagination had greatly exaggerated and altered their form. He says they were presided over by a woman named "Omoroca," or "Thalath," which means "the sea"; in other words, they were inhabitants of the sea, and many appear to have been amphibious, which was the case with many of the extinct Saurians. But the point to be observed in his statement is that representations of all of them were preserved and por-trayed on the walls of the Temple of Belus at Babylon.[2] This implies that they were either objects of worship, or of religious veneration, by the Baby-lonians, and therefore, in some way, allied to the gods, or daimonia, whom they worshipped.

Is it possible, then, that these mighty Saurians were the bodily forms which the first angels who rebelled against God were condemned to take, in order that, in them, they might manifest their true characteristics, and that this was known to those who first worshipped and sought intercourse with the Nephilim? This is but a suggestion, but it receives some support from

[1] *See* Kin's *Moses and Geology*, chap. viii. pp. 282, 283.
[2] Cory's *Fragments; Hist.*, Berosus, pp. 23, 24.

the fact that the Powers of Evil are spoken of in the Scripture under the terms of "Dragons" and "The Leviathan," and that the description of the latter, although not unlike some of the extinct sea monsters, corresponds to no living creature known to man (Job xli.). Just also as the Scripture speaks of the Prince of Evil as "The Old Serpent," the form of which he took, so he is likewise spoken of as "The Great Dragon" and "Leviathan" (Isa. xxvii. 1; Rev. xx. 2), which, although metaphors also of the world powers wielded by him, may have the same fitness of application to him as "the Serpent."

APPENDIX C

SPECULATIONS REGARDING THE ANTIQUITY OF THE HUMAN RACE

It is impossible within our present limits to do more than notice a few of the arguments which are used to prove the great antiquity of the human race.

As an example of geological speculation, we may mention the periods calculated from the thickness, in inches, of stalagmite deposits covering traces of human existence. It having been found, in certain stalagmite deposits during the historical period, that the rate of deposit must have been at an infinitesimal rate per hundred years, it is argued that other deposits must have been at a similar rate, and therefore that the human remains covered by them represent a period ages before the hitherto supposed creation of man.

But such a conclusion entirely ignores the fact that under favourable conditions, such as the extreme moisture, etc., which must have succeeded the Deluge, these deposits may be produced of many inches in thickness in a very few years, and can indeed be artificially produced in that time. Under such conditions, the greater portion of the stalagmite covering human remains may have been produced very rapidly, and when these conditions ceased, the subsequent addition in thickness would be at an infinitesimal rate. To build a theory on such data is therefore most illogical.

Much weight is also attached to the remains of what is termed "the Stone Age" of man, when flint was used as knives, arrow-heads, etc., as indicating a period long before the "Bronze," and still further remote from the "Iron" Age. But it is quite evident that such a Stone Age may have existed in remote countries far removed from the centres of civilisation, simultaneously with a Bronze or Iron Age in other countries. Where men have left the centres of civilisation and penetrated to remote regions cut off from communication with other people, they are not only forced to improvise tools and weapons from flint or fish-bones, but after a few generations of isolation they lose all traces of civilisation and become barbarous. Such people existed a couple of centuries ago in remote regions, and were contemporary with the highly-civilised nations of Europe. It is clear, therefore, that traces of people who used stone implements is no evidence of their antiquity.

But the supposed sheet-anchor of the geological theory consists in the evidence of a glacial period, which at one time covered not only the Arctic and Alpine regions of the earth but a portion of the Temperate regions. It is argued that æons of years must have passed during its formation, and further æons of years during its gradual subsidence; and yet human remains have been discovered which, it is shown, must have existed prior to it commencement. Now, Sir H. H. Howarth has clearly proved that a very large proportion of the supposed traces of glacial action have been due to the action of vast volumes of water carrying the largest rocks and other *débris* over the surface both of the lowlands and of the highest hills, and that these are mixed up with the traces of glacial action and must be distinguished from them.[1] They are, in short, just what would have been produced by such an universal Deluge as that described in Scripture, when not only torrential rains descended upon the earth, but "the fountains of the great deep were broken up"; by which it is implied that the surface of the earth sank and the vast volumes of water stored up beneath its superficial crust—"the waters under the earth"—were forced out and rushed in mighty torrents over its surface.

The vast volumes of water that may be stored up beneath the immediate surface of the earth is strikingly illustrated by Mr Catlin, in his interesting book, *The Uplifted and Subsided Rocks of America.* He there shows that of the whole prodigious rainfall on the Rocky Mountains, not one-tenth is carried off by rivers to the sea. The Mississippi and Missouri and other rivers are as large 1000 miles from their mouth as lower down. The mighty floods which often fill the valleys in which they run produce no effect; 200 miles further down they have disappeared. In like manner, in the Rocky Mountains, he speaks of ravines full of rushing water from a flood, and yet half a mile down there is not sufficient for a horse to drink. All passes into the bowels of the earth. He also mentions instances of torrents pouring into clefts in the face of cliffs, and *sub-montagne* torrents, cataracts and cascades, hundreds of which are known in these mountains, and from some of which smoke and watery vapour ascend, as in the case of the Falls of Niagara. Sometimes there is an overflow of these subterranean waters, and a roaring torrent issues from them inundating the surrounding country and forcing the Indians to fly for their lives, while after its subsidence multitudes of *eyeless* fish are left behind, showing that they must have been bred in the darkness.

The subterranean reservoirs which contain these waters are clearly of volcanic origin. Mountain ranges are thrown up in this way, and it neces-

[1] *The Glacial Nightmare.*

sarily follows that after their upheaval, when the igneous masses have cooled, vast spaces are left beneath them which form these reservoirs. But it is not merely under the Rocky Mountains that these reservoirs exist. The whole of North America is *uplifted*, and gradually rises from the sea-coast to the foot of the Rocky Mountains, indicating that these cavernous spaces between the upper and lower crusts of the earth may extend over the whole continent. That such is the case is proved by the existence of the subterranean sea in the mammoth caves of Kentucky, which was traversed for 20 miles without finding any limit, and similar subterranean lakes or seas have been discovered at the base of the Rocky Mountains.[1]

But if these subterranean reservoirs receive year after year, and century after century, the greater portion of the prodigious rainfall, then, vast as they may be, they must in time overflow. This is exactly what happens. Mr Catlin has pointed out that if the rock masses which support mountains of volcanic origin were by any interior convulsion broken down, the mountain would sink back, but it would no longer fill the same space that it did before its upheaval; for thousands of ages of exposure to rain and frost would have continually disintegrated its rocks and reduced its bulk. Therefore, instead of merely sinking back to the general level of the surrounding land, it would form a vast depression. This is the character of the depressions which now constitute the great chain of lakes in North America. They are of volcanic origin, and the gneiss and granite boulders which in past ages rolled down the mountains, which once occupied their sites, are still strewn round their shores. Isle Royal, on Lake Superior, shows a scarp of stratified rock over 600 feet high, and the same rock appears on the opposite side of the lake, showing that the mass which once connected them has sunk down, as might be expected from its volcanic origin.[2]

These great lakes are all on elevated ground which falls *from* them in all directions, as is evident from the great rivers which have their rise in their vicinity. The only exception to this is for 10 or 15 miles round their shores, where the ground falls towards them, and the ridge of the watershed thus formed evidently marks the edge of the subsidence. (*See* diagram).

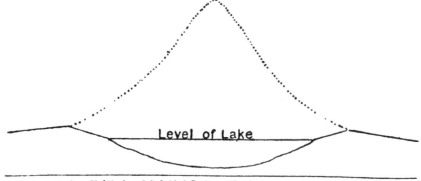

Level of Lake

[1] Catlin, *Uplifted and Subsided Rocks of North America.*   [2] *Ibid.*

It follows from this that little or no water falls into these lakes. The great rivers which feed other inland seas or lakes, as in the case of the Caspian, are only sufficient to supply their loss by evaporation ; but no great rivers flow into the North American lakes, and the small streams which do flow into them would be wholly insufficient to supply their loss by evaporation. Yet these great lakes are the source of the St Lawrence, one of the greatest of the world's rivers, and the volumes of water which are hourly carried by it to the sea would quickly drain them if they had no other source of supply. The only conclusion forced upon us is that they are supplied from subterranean sources, and form one of the great outlets of the ever-accumulating waters in the abysses beneath the uplifted crust of North America.

The other great outlet for these surplus waters would appear to be the Gulf Stream, which has its rise in the Gulf of Mexico. Some have supposed that the equatorial currents were the source of the Gulf Stream ; but not only do they sometimes flow for weeks to the south, but their waters are of the same character as the rest of the sea, and *wholly different* to the waters of the Gulf Stream, the volume and peculiar characteristics of which never change, nor do its waters mix with those of the ocean. The Gulf Stream is a mighty ocean river, 32 miles broad, 1200 feet deep, with a current of some 4 miles an hour, and its waters are not only much salter and of greater density than the rest of the ocean, but its colour is of a deeper blue, while its high temperature, which it preserves with but little diminution throughout its course up the east coast of North America, and across the Atlantic until it strikes the shores of Scotland, is many degrees higher than that of the ocean through which it flows, and sufficient to modify the general climate of England and Scotland. It also issues *suddenly* in its full volume, heat, force of current and other characteristics, from the western shore of the Gulf of Mexico, just where the Andes begin and the Rocky Mountains end.

If, then, it is necessary that some outlet should exist in order to explain the enormous perennial overflow of the waters in the subterranean reservoirs of the American Continent, the Gulf Stream—presumably supplied by numerous streams issuing at the bottom of the sea from the foot of the great mountain chains, and warmed by contact with the heated rocks of that volanic region—exactly meets the conditions ; and its extreme saltness and deep indigo colour are precisely similar to the waters of the Great Salt Lake, which Mr Catlin has shown to be of volcanic origin.

But if the mere overflow of the subterranean reservoirs is of such volume, what may not be the volume of water in the reservoirs themselves ! We have only to suppose the masses of rock which now support the uplifted rocks and strata of the American Continent to be overthrown by some convulsion of the earth's surface, and the whole land would sink, and the imprisoned waters, rushing forth, would bury it beneath their surface.

The peculiar circumstances which reveal the presence of these subterranean waters beneath the North American Continent do not exist elsewhere; but the evidence of their existence there forces us to conclude that similar subterranean waters exist beneath the uplifted strata and mountain ranges of other continents, and that they constitute those "fountains of the great deep," "the waters under the earth," which, on the subsidence of the land, rushed forth and submerged the whole of the dry land at the Deluge.

It is the fashion at the present day to deny the fact of an universal Deluge, although nothing can be more explicit than the statement that it covered "every hill under the whole heaven," and destroyed "every living thing" upon the earth that God had made (Gen. vii. 19-22).[1]   Moreover, evidences of this destruction exist in all parts of the earth.   Throughout Siberia and North America the carcases of the mammoth, preserved to this day, young and old, many with undigested food in their stomachs, is a proof of a sudden destruction, which, as Sir H. Howarth shows, could only have been by water.   The Pampas of South America are also a reservoir of the bones of countless animals which nothing can explain but a sudden destruction by water, and Australia and other parts of the world furnish similar evidence.[2]

But if there was this universal Deluge, then it would appear to be certain, as pointed out by Mr Geikie, that *a glacial period must have immediately succeeded it.*   For the surface of the earth is the great reservoir of the sun's heat, and the air heated by this means in tropical climates is constantly passing to the temperate zones to modify the cold which would otherwise exist there.   If, then, the source of this heat was completely cut off, not only because the dry land was covered with water, but because the rays of the sun were unable to penetrate the masses of cloud and vapour which for months must have enveloped the earth, the most intense cold would follow, and an arctic climate would prevail in parts which had before been temperate, or even semi-tropical.   Moreover, there is ample evidence to prove that such a glacial period did succeed the great Deluge.

It is well known that at one time a much warmer climate existed both in the Arctic and Temperate zones, the *flora* and *fauna* of temperate climates being found in the former, and that of semi-tropical climates in the latter. It is proved also by the food found in the stomachs of the mammoth that, at the time of their existence, Siberia had a temperate, and in parts a semi-tropical, climate.   But no sooner were the multitude of mammoths inhabiting Siberia, Northern Canada and America drowned, and before decay had commenced, than they were *instantaneously frozen*, and they have been preserved in that condition embedded in the frozen soil of Siberia to this

[1] Objections to the universality of the Deluge, such as those based on the difficulty of understanding how the various animals preserved in the Ark were assembled together from all parts of the world, and how, after the Deluge, they returned to the very places from which they came, are weak and superficial when regarded from the point of view that the Deluge was a special act of judgment and interposition of God. We might as well ask how the beaver, the ant and the bee obtained their marvellous instincts.

[2] Sir H. H. Howarth, *The Mammoth and the Flood.*

day. What occurred there must have taken place in other parts of the Northern Hemisphere. A glacial period must have set in, and have continued for centuries; for the excessive moisture in the atmosphere converted into snow would speedily cover and add to the thickness of the ice formed in arctic and present temperate regions, and aid in resisting the effects of the sun's rays.

Gradually, in the course of centuries, these ice masses would give way before the renewed heat of the sun. The ice on the low-lying plains in temperate zones would first disappear, and then the ice sheets clothing the lower hills and mountains in those regions would begin to descend their sides, producing in their descent those "*striæ*" which are the evidence of their action; while in the Arctic zone and the higher Alpine regions the ice masses would remain unmelted. How long this melting process took we cannot theoretically determine, nor do we know what thickness of ice had to be melted; but it would not of course be anything like the depth of the huge glaciers of the Alps, nor would such a weight of ice be necessary to produce the *striæ* which the ice sheets in temperate zones made in descending to the lower ground. In Scotland and Ireland, where there are so many traces of this glacial action, the influence of the Gulf Stream must have hastened the process, and there is no reason whatever to suppose that in the more temperate zones, where glacial action may be traced, the ice sheets could have resisted the renewed heat of the sun for any vast period.

There are many evidences, however, that the remains of this glacial period existed 2000 years ago, and that both the climate of Europe and North America was much colder at that time than it is now. Herodotus describes the southern part of Russia, which has now a moderate winter and a hot summer, as so cold that it was impossible to penetrate very far north of the Black Sea. The winter even at the Black Sea itself was eight months long, or longer than it now is at St Petersburg, and the Sea of Azoff was frozen over every year, while the country to the north of the "Issedones," a Scythian tribe, appears to have been under snow the whole year.[1]

Diodorus Siculus, who wrote as late as 45 B.C., says that the winter season in Gaul was so severe, that all the rivers were frozen over and able to bear the passage of armies with their baggage and chariots, that during its continuance no rain but only snow fell, and that "on account of the excessive coldness of the climate, there being scarce an interval of mild temperature, the *country produced neither vines nor olives.*"[2] It is thus clear that the climate of Europe was of an almost Arctic character 2000 years ago. Moreover, this accounts for the fact that, while the human race spread abroad in every other direction, they failed even to attempt

[1] Herod., lib. iv. cap. xxxi.
[2] Diodorus, quoted by Sir W. Betham, *Gael and Cimbri*, pp. 177, 178. The climate of Britain, although more to the north, and at the present time colder than that of France, was then warmer than France, owing, no doubt, to the influence of the Gulf Stream.

2B

to penetrate the northern portion of Europe and Asia until a little over 2000 years ago, and seem to have confined themselves to southern countries and those bordering on the Mediterranean.

The traditions of the Indian and other races inhabiting Central America and the southern portion of North America point to a similar condition of things in the Western Hemisphere.

The Thlinkeets of British Columbia have a tradition of the Great Deluge, and say that "after the waters went back and the dry land appeared" the world was still in darkness, "without sun, moon, or stars, very dark, damp, and chaotic."[1] The Miztecs of Mexico also speak of a time when the world was in "great darkness and chaos"; when "the earth was covered with water and there was nothing but *mud and slime* on the face of the earth."[2] The *Popul Vuh*, the national book of the Quiches of Tulan in Central America, speaks of a time when they "waited for the return of the sun"; when "they kindled fires on account of the cold"; a time of "general *dampness and cold,* for the earth was *moist,* there being yet no sun."[3] "At last the face of the ground was dried by the sun. Before the sun appeared, muddy and wet was the surface of the ground, and it was before the sun appeared, and then only the sun rose like a man, but his heat had no strength. It is not indeed the same sun that appears now."[4] The Aztecs of Mexico also have a tradition when their ancestors suffered from famine and "trembled with cold," "though they stay by a fire they find little heat."[5] The Toltecs likewise speak of a time lasting 104 years when they suffered from nakedness, hunger and cold.[6]

Such a state of damp, cold and darkness, consequent on the watery mist and clouds which enveloped the earth and shut out the light and heat of the sun, is just what we might expect to have been the case after the Great Deluge, and if the cold was so great even in tropical and semi-tropical America, what must it have been in the north, although, even in Canada now, there is an almost tropical summer. It is evident that a glacial period must have prevailed throughout Northern America at the period of which these traditions speak.

The fact also that the arctic conditions which existed in Europe just previous to the commencement of the Christian era have gradually abated up to the present day, is an indication of the far more intense cold which must have existed 2000 years and more before that era, and is a proof that 4000 years ago a glacial period must have prevailed in countries which are now temperate with warm summers. It is also evident that the climate of northern countries has become, in consequence of this glacial period, and the increased masses of ice in Arctic and Alpine regions which have been left behind, permanently colder, and incapable of producing the *flora,* or of sup-

[1] Bancroft's *Native Races,* vol. iii. p. 98.
[2] *Ibid.,* pp. 71-73.   [3] *Ibid.,* p. 46.
[4] Abbé Brasseur de Bourbourg, from Tyler's *Early Hist. of Mankind,* p. 308.
[5] Bancroft's *Native Races,* vol. iii. p. 204.   [6] *N. Americans of Antiquity,* p. 240.

porting the life of the *fauna* which we know existed in those countries previous to the glacial period.

But if such a glacial period succeeded the Great Deluge, then, of course, we may expect to find the evidence of human life previous to its existence, but instead of being æons of ages ago, these human remains would merely be antediluvian. The glacial theories of geologists are based on the assumption that the ice masses of that period were of the same extent and thickness as those which now exist in Alpine and Arctic regions, and that both their formation and disappearance must have therefore taken hundreds of thousands of years. But it is evident that all the conditions of the case are perfectly satisfied—firstly, by a glacial period in which the ice masses formed in those temperate regions and low-lying lands from which they have now disappeared were of moderate thickness, and secondly, by a glacial period the commencement of which was almost instantaneous, while its gradual disappearance in temperate zones until they arrived at their present condition need not have occupied more than four or five thousand years, which the evidence of history and tradition implies was the extreme limit of its duration; its remains being still evident in those portions of Arctic and Alpine regions which had previously a temperate climate.

Although the great principles of geology are founded on solid data and reasoning, yet it is not an exact science like astronomy, and many of the speculations of modern geologists are like a pyramid supported on its apex, which the slightest external influence may overthrow. This applies to other theories besides that of the glacial period, and such a cataclysm as the Great Deluge, and the breaking up of the fountains of the great deep, and the consequent disorder that may have been introduced in some of the upper strata of the earth, together with the vast masses of clay, sand, rock and other *débris* mixed with evidences of human existence, uprooted and carried about by the waters, and deposited by them on their subsidence under a multitude of varying conditions, are factors which may introduce error into the most plausible theories.

.   .   .   .

In conclusion, we may briefly refer to the speculations of some modern archæologists, which, like those of geologists, are often based on insufficient and slender data, and in many cases are mere assumptions or guesses, dominated by the desire to prove the great antiquity of the human race. Hence historical statements and traditions, however respectable their authority, are suggested by them to be forgeries, not to be depended upon, or to be viewed with suspicion whenever they appear to support Old Testament history and chronology, while those which tend to support a more ancient chronology are accepted without question.

We have seen that the dynasties given by Berosus of Babylonian kings, subsequent to the Mythic dynasty of the gods, shows the first Chaldean kingdom to have commenced 2234 B.C., previous to which was a Median dynasty of 224 years, which may well represent the period between the Deluge and the empire of Nimrod, during which period Babylonia and Assyria were occupied by the Medes, Bactrians and other nations subsequently conquered by him. This would make the date of the Deluge very nearly the same as that of Old Testament chronology.[1] But such a corroboration of Scripture chronology, being opposed to their views, the testimony of the historian Berosus is ignored by these modern archæologists, and Babylonian chronology is made to depend upon an isolated statement of Nabonadius, the last Babylonian king, which speaks of the reign of a certain king, Naram Sin, as having been 3200 years before his time (555 B.C.), or about 3750 B.C., which would make the date of Sargon, or Sargani, his predecessor, about 3800 B.C. The records of some other ancient kings have also been found, and as it is *assumed* that they preceded Sargon, the commencement of Babylonian history is placed about 5000 B.C., or nearly 3000 years before the date of the Deluge according to the chronology of Berosus and of Scripture. But to reject these two exact and detailed chronologies, which not only corroborate each other, but are corroborated by numerous other profane testimonies, for an isolated statement like the above, seems very unscientific.

The ancient priesthoods were the sole custodians of their countries' archives, and it was their one idea to add to their glory by magnifying the antiquity of their race. Moreover, the great cities of ancient Babylonia had each its own *patesi* or priest king, who without question at the time of Ammurabi (the Amraphel of Scripture) were contemporary rulers ; but nothing would have been easier for the priesthood, by representing these contemporary dynasties as successive, to greatly exaggerate the antiquity of an ancient king, and as Nabonadius must have obtained his information from the priesthood, this may very well account for the great antiquity assigned by him to Naram Sin. In like manner, modern archæologists, following the example of the ancient priesthood, have still further added to the antiquity of the kingdom by regarding other dynasties as successive and anterior to Sargani, although a careful examination seems to show that they also were contemporary. This subject is, however, more fully treated in Appendix D, "Tht Accadians and Nimrod."

Much dependence is also placed on the dynasties of the Egyptian priest Manetho by those who wish to prove the great antiquity of man. The dynasties of Manetho are lists of kings whose seats of government were at one or other of the great cities of Egypt, Memphis, Elephantine and Thebes, the names of such kings and the length of their reigns being given with exactitude. In addition to these, other dynasties are mentioned of kings who reigned at the less important cities, but neither their names or the length of their reigns are stated. They were considered, apparently, of not sufficient importance, and only the total duration of each dynasty is given. The duration of all these dynasties, if added together, on the assumption

---

[1] The chronology given in the margin of our Bibles is that of Archbishop Usher, but it is well known that he has omitted from 80 to 100 years of the time of the Judges which ought to be included.

that they were successive to each other, represents the beginning of the Egyptian monarchy, like that of the Babylonian, as some 3000 years before the Scriptural date of the Deluge.

But in the first place, by regarding these dynasties as successive to each other, the evidence is totally ignored that Egypt was divided into Upper and Lower Egypt, each having separate kings reigning contemporaneously, and that the Theban kings of Upper Egypt are proved to have been, at certain periods previous to the eighteenth dynasty, subordinate to, and viceroys of, the Memphite kings. It is also proved that there were other contemporary kings reigning over the more important cities or nomes into which Egypt was divided, such as the Heracleopolite kings of Manetho's ninth and tenth dynasties, but these being of secondary importance their names are not mentioned by Manetho.

In the second place, Manetho enumerates no less than five dynasties between the twelfth and eighteenth dynasties, among which are the Shepherd kings under their false names, while the rest are nameless. But the two tablets of Abydos, constructed by Seti Manephthah and Rameses II. of the eighteenth dynasty, 1000 years before Manetho's time, represent the kings of the eighteenth dynasty as the *immediate successors*, of those of the twelfth dynasty, and thus deny the existence of any kings between the twelfth and eighteenth dynasties. Which are we to believe,—the kings of the eighteenth dynasty, who had no reason to conceal or pervert the truth, or the idolatrous priesthood of later ages who, as we have seen, have erased the names and done everything to destroy the identity of the hated Shepherds ?

But some of these interpolated dynasties are manifestly mere repetitions of kings in other dynasties under certain relations. Thus, the sixteenth dynasty of Shepherds reigning for 518 years is plainly given as a record of the whole period from the first to the last Shepherd king, and this period is corroborated by Josephus. So also it is equally clear that the seventeenth dynasty of Shepherds and Thebans reigning together for 161 years is given to record the period of their joint reign, and is a proof, by Manetho himself, that many of the kings of Upper Egypt and Lower Egypt were contemporary. In like manner, certain other dynasties may equally have been interpolated to record the kings of previously mentioned dynasties in certain particular relations.

All this is totally ignored by those who wish to make out that the human race has existed for some thousands of years longer than stated by the Hebrew Scriptures. But it is evident that the conclusions and assertions of men, however learned they may be, and however valuable their facts and important their archæological discoveries, cannot be regarded as trustworthy while they are dominated by this desire, a desire which leads them to ignore every testimony which conflicts with their aims, and to disregard even the authority of the monuments themselves.

There are many who will regard the authority of the ancient monuments and the Old Testament Scriptures as of much greater value than that of an idolatrous priesthood who had every reason for misrepresenting facts which were hostile to their religion. But it is quite possible that Manetho never intended that his dynasties should be regarded as successive. In recording contemporaneous dynasties, it was necessary to record them successively, and it was probably the Greek copyists who, being ignorant of the earlier Egyptian history, added up the totals of each dynasty and recorded these totals at the end of each of Manetho's three books on the supposition that they were all successive.

On the other hand, it is to be remembered that the desire to enhance their nation's glory by attributing a vast antiquity to it was characteristic of the ancient priesthoods, as seen by the vast periods given by those of Babylon and Egypt to the reign of the gods. In the words of Ragozin, "they loved to magnify them by enshrouding them in the mystery of innumerable ages. The more appalling the figures, the greater the glory."[1] This being the case, we are justified in receiving with caution dates and periods of years emanating from these sources, and it would be equally wise to subject to a careful analysis the grounds on which are based the assertions and conclusions of those modern writers who are animated by a similar desire to extend the antiquity of the human race.

APPENDIX D

THE ACCADIANS AND NIMROD

M. LENORMANT has shown that the Accadian magic and worship of Nature gods was practically identical with that of the Ugric and Altaic tribes, the Finns, the Mongols and other Turanian races,[2] and the intimate relation of the Accadian religion with the Buddhist religion of China and Thibet has been shown in Chapter VI. of this book.

M. Lenormant has also shown that the language of these races is intimately allied to that of the ancient Accadians, while, on the other hand, he has pointed out that the people of Babylonia, the beginning of Nimrod's empire, used a Semitic language for centuries previous to the advent of the Semitic Assyrians, and that the Accadian language was confined to the southern provinces bordering on the Persian Gulf, the land of Shumir or Shinar.[3]

From this it has been argued that the language of the Cushite conquerors, under Nimrod, was really Semitic, and that the Accadians were Turanians conquered by Nimrod and not Cushites.

In support of this, it is also asserted that the Canaanites, who were of

---

[1] Ragozin, *Hist. of Chaldea*, p. 196.
[2] *Chald. Magic*, chaps. xiv.-xvii.
[3] *Ibid.*, chaps. xviii.-xxiii., and chap. xxv. pp. 332, 333.

Hamitic race, spoke a Semitic dialect, and therefore that the language which has hitherto been called Semitic is really Cushite or Hamitic.

M. Lenormant has moreover pointed out that the Chaldean Babylonian religion,—in its form as afterwards adopted by the Assyrians,—was first established by Likbabi (or Lugal kigub) and the ancient kings of Ur; that the name of Likbabi is found on all the bricks at the base of the Pyramid temples of Chaldea at Ur, Ereck, Nippur and Larsa, and that there is no trace of any sacred monument previous to these; that this religion was that of the Cushites, and M. Lenormant supposes that it superseded that of the Accadians, and that the latter had no temples or fixed public worship.[1]

These facts would at first sight seem to prove that the Accadians were quite distinct from the Cushites, and that the latter spoke what is known as a Semitic dialect. The conclusion is, of course, directly opposed to the evidence which shows that the Cushites, or the ancient Aribah, or Adites, of Arabia, spoke the language, and were the originators of the cuneiform writing and the religion of the Accadians.

But there are several points which have not been sufficiently taken into consideration :—

1. Nimrod, when he established his dominion over Central Asia, found various races in possession of the country. Berosus mentions a Median kingdom as preceding the first Chaldean kingdom, and as the latter must have been that of Nimrod, the Median kingdom must represent the period previous to his conquest when the Tigris and Euphrates valleys were inhabited by other races. M. Lenormant has shown that Media was inhabited, previous to its conquest by the Iranians, by a people whose language was closely allied to the Turco-Tartaric and Mongolian on the one hand and to the Accadian on the other.[2] We may presume that these Turanian people were the original Medes, the descendants of "Madai," a son of Japhet, and that they gave their name to the country, which ever afterwards retained it, and there were doubtless similar tribes associated with them. We may conclude also that these Medes, or a portion of them, were the primitive Turanian inhabitants of Babylonia to whom Berosus therefore gave the name of "*Medians*" as representing the occupiers of the country previous to the Cushite conquest. Moreover, as the Turanians eventually spread over Eastern and Northern Asia, it is quite possible that the Turanian Medes of Babylonia subsequently migrated to Media and settled there.

From the Scriptural accounts and the traditions of Ninus, Osiris, Bacchus, Zohak, and certain other conquerors with whom Nimrod may be identified, it is plain that he established his dominion over the whole of the tribes inhabiting Babylonia, Assyria, Media, etc., who at that period could only have been few in number and widely scattered, and it seems quite inconceivable that any portion of these should have imposed their language and religion on their powerful Cushite conquerors.

---

[1] *Chald. Magic*, chap. xxiv. pp. 318, 321-323.   [2] *Ibid.*, chap. xv. p. 217.

M. Lenormant refers to the fact that the Greeks spoke of the Cushites as the "*Cephenes*," or people of "*Cepheus*," the son of Belus (*i.e.*, Cush), and he suggests that the Turanians were the ancient Chaldees and distinct from the Cushites, because Hellanicus says that there were *Chaldees* inhabiting Chaldea before the Cephenes.[1]   But it does not follow from this that these Turanians, although called "Chaldees" by Hellanicus, were the people known in their own country as "Chaldees."   It was the custom among the ancients to call all the different peoples who successively inhabited a region after the recognised name of the country, and Hellanicus, when speaking of a people of Babylonia before the Cephenes, would therefore call them "Chaldees," simply because Chaldea was the general name of the country among the Greeks. In the same way some people might speak of a "British" people in Britain prior to the arrival of the Britons who opposed Julius Cæsar, to whom the name properly applied, and who were quite distinct from the aborigines.   It is a loose and inaccurate way of speaking, common to both ancient and modern writers, as in the case of Strabo, who speaks of the Belgae as Kelts because they occupied a portion of the country known as Keltica, although Cæsar, who wrote from personal acquaintance with them, expressly states that they were an entirely distinct people from the Kelts.[2]

M. Lenormant further suggests that the cities of Babel and Ereck, Accad and Calneh in Chaldea were in existence previous to the arrival of Nimrod, and implies that they were records of the previous Turanian civilisation.[3] But from the statement in Genesis that they were the *beginning* of Nimrod's kingdom it seems evident that they were founded by him.   It is true that Babel or Babylon had been previously commenced, but the building of it had been stopped, and all tradition represents Nimrod as the founder of the great city as it was afterwards known.   Nor is it possible that these cities could have been built by the fourth generation after the Flood, and while the human race was few and scattered,[4] without the forced labour which would be used by a conqueror.   On the other hand, all tradition speaks of the Cushites as great builders, and the fact that it is expressly stated that Nimrod built the mighty cities of Nineveh, Rehoboth, Calah and Resen in Assyria, is an additional proof that he built those in Babylonia also; nor can we have any doubt that for the purpose he employed the labour of the conquered peoples.

The Cushites had little consideration for the people they subdued, and we may be certain that they imposed their language and religion on the Turanians, and not that the Turanians imposed their language and religion on them.   This is in accordance with all historical experience, and it is quite impossible for the contrary to have been the case.

But as these prolific Japhetic races increased in numbers they would

---

[1] *Chald. Magic*, p. 338.

[2] Cæsar, lib. i. cap. 1 ; *see* also *ante*, chap. xiv.   [3] *Chald. Magic*, p. 339.

[4] In order to get over this difficulty some have suggested that the Turanians were the descendants of Cain, who, being more wicked than the rest of mankind, were carefully preserved from the destruction of the Flood, together with righteous Noah !

naturally migrate to other countries, and the way westward being closed by the Cushite empire, they would spread toward the vast unoccupied regions of Eastern Asia, carrying with them the Cushite language and religion, and thus form the nucleus of those multitudinous Turanian races, some of whom eventually spread northward and from there westward to Europe.

This seems the only natural and reasonable conclusion. Similarity of language and religion does not prove identity of race. The Hebrew is a Semitic dialect closely resembling the Phœnician, and the Israelites, in spite of every endeavour to prevent them, constantly adopted the religion of the Canaanites, who were a totally different race. But similarity of language and religion in two separate nations is an evidence that at one time there must have been intimate association and social relations between the two, and it is clear that this must have been the case with the primitive Turanian inhabitants of Chaldea and their Cushite conquerors.

This perfectly accounts for the fact that the Turanian races possess a language and religion similar to that of the Accadian, and at the same time perfectly accords with the evidence that the cuneiform writing and the Accadian language and religion were of Cushite origin.

It is admitted that the Accadians possessed a remarkable state of civilisation and knowledge of astronomy,[1] and to suppose that the slow-thinking, stolid, unenterprising Turanian race should be the originators of the civilisation, the writing and learning, which made the Chaldeans so famous in after ages, and that the same heavy-witted, conquered people should have been inventors of a religion which was accepted by the most powerful nations, who regarded it with such reverence that they even carefully preserved the language of its authors, is so utterly improbable that nothing but overpowering proof can warrant its acceptance.

This is the opinion of M. Renan. He says, " It does astonish us to see that ancient substruction of the learned civilisation of Babylon assigned to the Turkish, Finnish and Hungarian races ; in one word, to races which have never done anything but pull down, and have never created a civilisation of their own. If anyone can prove to us that the Turks, Finns and Hungarians founded the most powerful ante-Semitic and ante-Aryan civilisations we will believe it. But the force of the proofs must be in proportion to the improbability of the result." [2]

M. Lenormant, however, objects to these remarks as too severe upon the Turanian race, and he points to the intelligence, chivalry and eloquence of the present Hungarians in support of his objection. But, in taking the Hungarians as representative of the Turanians, M. Renan was hardly correct. No doubt, the original Hungarians were of the same race as the Turks, but not only have centuries of intercourse with the civilisation of the West greatly modified their previous character, but they have a very strong intermixture of Gothic and German blood. That part of Europe was for centuries occupied by Gothic races, many of whom must have remained

---

[1] *Chald. Magic*, pp. 354, 364 365, and note.   [2] *Ibid.*, p. 372.

there; but besides this, many thousands of captives from other European countries were imported by the Hungarians, and lastly the honours and estates of the country were bestowed on German nobles by the Hungarian king Geisa, who had married a Bavarian princess.[1]

We must, therefore, look to the pure Turkish, Tartar and Mongolian races before being brought into contact with Western civilisation, for the proofs of M. Renan's contention, and they show that he is absolutely correct, and that it is impossible that such races could have been the originators of the learning and civilisation of the Chaldees.

2. With regard to the question of *language*. Although it is evident that a portion of the primary inhabitants of Chaldea were Turanian, yet it is certain that Assyria and Babylonia was the original seat of the greater portion of the Semitic race. Genesis xi. speaks of Terah, Abraham and Lot, the descendants of Arphaxad and Peleg, coming out of Ur of the Chaldees, where, it is evident, therefore, their forefathers must have settled. It was the gathering point of all the descendants of Noah shortly after the Deluge, and it would appear that the descendants of Shem, viz., Elam, Asshur, Aram and Arphaxad, had remained there after the confusion of tongues. This is also implied by Joshua when he speaks of the ancestors of Abraham living "beyond the flood," a term for the river Euphrates.[2] Abraham was the tenth generation from Arphaxad, and considering the long lives of the Patriarchs of this family, and the consequent number of children begotten by each, the descendants of Arphaxad by this time must have been a numerous and rapidly-increasing race; Joktan, the brother of Peleg, being the only one of the family who seems to have migrated to Southern Arabia (Gen. x. 27-30). Asshur had settled more to the north, and his descendants eventually became the dominant race there, the country being called after them "Assyria," while the Elamites were in Eastern Chaldea, and the Aramaeans, or descendants of Aram, in Syria and Mesopotamia adjoining the Assyrians. These Semitic races, living in the heart of the Cushite Empire, although tributary to the Cushites and worshipping their gods,[3] must have constituted the main population of the country, and were probably far more numerous than either their rulers, or the Turanians of Chaldea, while, considering the influence exercised by the Semitic race upon other races, we may conclude that, by the time of Abraham's departure to Canaan, the influence of the Semitic language must have been predominant in Northern Chaldea and Assyria.

Arabian tradition says that the empire founded by Zohak lasted 260 years, and as this appears to be almost exactly the period assigned by Berosus to the first Chaldean kingdom, it is probably the correct duration of the first Cushite Empire.

Now as the Median kingdom of Berosus, which lasted 224 years, must

---

[1] Gibbon, chap. lv. p. 1025.   [2] Joshua xxiv. 2.

[3] *Ibid.* The "other gods" worshipped by the ancestors of Abraham could only have been those of their Cushite rulers.

represent the period from the Flood to the Cushite conquest, the end of the Cushite Empire would be 484 years after the Flood, and as Abraham left Harran and came to Canaan 427 years after that event, it would be some 57 years before the close of the Cushite power when decay had begun to set in.

This is proved by the account in Genesis, when, a year or two after Abraham's arrival in Canaan, we read of Amraphel, king of Shinar or Babylonia, with Chedorlaomer, king of Elam (the Kedor-Laghamar of the inscriptions), Arioch, king of Ellasar (Larsa), in South Babylonia, and Tidal, king of Gutium,[1] the country to the north of Babylonia, making war against five kings of Canaan. Professor Sayce suggests from this that Amraphel, the "Ammurabi" or "Hammurapi," of the inscriptions, was a vassal of Chedorlaomer. But the account does not imply this, but rather that he was an independent king, and an ally of Chedorlaomer, for the inscriptions show that his daughter had just previously married a prince of Elam, while a few years later he made war with and defeated Chedorlaomer in battle. The account in Genesis, however, shows that the Cushite Empire of Nimrod had been completely broken up, that the kings of Babylon had rule over only a portion of Babylonia, and were only just able to hold their own against the Elamite kings. Moreover, Arioch, the "Eriaku" of the inscriptions, king of Larsa, is shown by the inscriptions to have been a son of an Elamite king, Kedor Mabug, implying that the Elamite kings had already established their power over part of Babylonia.[2] We may also conclude from this that the capture of Erech and the overthrow of the first Babylonian kingdom by the Elamite king, Kedor Nahkhundi, which is referred to on an inscription of Asshur-banipal, did not take place until some years after this. Professor Sayce supposes that the conquest of Babylon by Kedor Nahkhundi was previous to the reign of Amraphel, but this seems very improbable, as Ammurabi, or Amraphel, was evidently an independent and powerful king, and the overthrow of Babylon must have been at the end and not in the middle of the first Babylonian dynasty.

The decay of the Cushite Empire is probably largely accounted for by the fact shown in Chapter V., that at an early period there was a considerable migration of the Cushites to India. It must be remembered also that only a certain portion of the Cushite race came to Babylonia and established the empire of Nimrod there. The greater proportion evidently remained in Arabia, and those in Babylonia and Assyria, after the emigration of many of them to India, would be completely outnumbered by the Semites and gradually succumb to their power and influence. Hence, while the apathetic Turanians of Babylonia, few in number as compared with the Semites, might be expected to fall completely under the influence and adopt the language of the Cushites, and eventually, following their nomadic tendencies, migrate to the north and east—the Semites, remain-

[1] "Tidal, King of *Nations*," or "Goyim," a probable misreading for "Gutium." *See* Sayce, *Fresh Lights*, p. 56.

[2] Sayce, *Fresh Lights*, p. 55.

ing in the country and possessed of an energy and enterprise entirely wanting in the stolid, heavy-witted Turanians, would speedily make their influence felt, and in proportion as they increased, and the Cushites decreased, in numbers and power, so would the Semitic language replace that of the Cushite, in much the same way as the Anglo-Saxon in Britain has replaced the French of the Normans.

This, therefore, may fully account for the fact that in the time of Amraphel, when the Cushite Empire had been broken up, the Semitic language should have become predominant, although the Cushite, or Accadian, was still used, and the Cushite religion being retained, the Cushite or Accadian language was especially preserved as the sacred tongue.

Again, it is argued that the language of Canaan, which was Semitic, was the language of the Hamitic Canaanites, and therefore that what is called Semitic was really Hamitic. But here again the influence of the Semitic races has not been sufficiently taken into consideration.

The Hamitic Canaanites were surrounded by, or intermingled with, powerful Semitic races who had conquered considerable portions of the country. There were the Semitic Moabites, Ammonites and Edomites in Eastern Canaan, the Aramæans in Northern Syria, and the Ishmaelites, Midianites, and other descendants of Abraham to the south, and finally the Israelites conquered the remainder of the country, and destroyed or dispossessed the remaining Hamitic peoples.

In Genesis x. we read that " afterwards were the Canaanites scattered abroad," and this would be the natural effect of the Israelitish conquest, so that by the time of David and Solomon the remaining Hamitic inhabitants could only have been very few in number. This would quite account for the fact that the language of Canaan, as it is known to us in the form of Phœnician and Hebrew, is Semitic, but it does not prove that the previous Hamitic peoples spoke Semitic. On the contrary, we know that the most powerful of them all, the Hittites, used a language closely allied to the Accadian or Cushite,[1] and although some of the Northern Amorites are said to have used a Semitic dialect, this may be fully accounted for by their association with the Aramæans, or, what is more probable, that the people supposed to be Amorites were really Aramæans who had occupied their country, and were therefore called by their name. For this is a contingency which must always be taken into consideration. A country receives its name from its first inhabitants, and the name thus received is in nearly every case retained, so that when the first inhabitants have been dispossessed by another race, the surrounding nations continue to speak of the new inhabitants by the same name as the former ones. This is the case with the modern Germans, a large proportion of whom are descended from the Huns, Slavs, and other Tartar tribes, while the bulk of the ancient Germans, who gave their name to the country, probably passed over to Britain.

[1] *The First Bible*, by Colonel Conder, LL.D., M.R.A.S., R.E., pp. 72-74.

It is possible that the language of the Israelites in the time of Moses may have been influenced by their long sojourn with the Hamitic Egyptians, but the words of Psa. lxxxi. 5, " Where I heard a language that I understood not"; and again, Psa. cxiv. 1, " When Israel went out of Egypt from a people of a strange language," show that it was not the same as the Egyptian, and therefore *not Hamitic*. The language of Abraham and his immediate descendants must have been Semitic, which was the predominant language of Chaldea when Abraham left that country, and both Abram and Sarai are Semitic names, and we may therefore conclude that the language of the Israelites was Semitic. Colonel Conder has shown indeed that the cuneiform writing was in use throughout Western Asia and in Egypt, and must have been used by the Israelites in the time of Moses,[1] but this proves nothing as regards the language, as this writing was used both by the Semites and by people like the Hittites speaking the Accadian language. Hebrew letters appear to have come into use about the time of Solomon, although the cuneiform writing still continued to be used.[2] No doubt the language of the other nations of Canaan underwent several modifications before it arrived at the form in which we know it as Phœnician, but the whole tendency of such changes would be to Semitise it through trade and association with the Semitic Israelites, Assyrians, Aramæans, etc.

3. M. Lenormant makes a distinction between the Chaldean-Babylonian *religion*, as established by the kings of Ur, and that of the Accadians. He admits that the gods worshipped and the essence of the religion were the same, but he draws attention to the elaborate forms, the temples and ritual of the kings of Ur, and these, he assumes, were wanting in the original Accadian religion. But what do we know of any Accadian religion previous to and distinct from that of the kings of Ur? What evidence is there that such a religion existed previous to that of the kings of Ur? The only reason for such a supposition is that the Turanian races, in subsequent ages, have been found to possess similar Nature gods and magic to those of the Accadians, but without the temples and elaborate forms of the latter, and, on the assumption that the Turanians were the Accadians, it is concluded that their religion was the primary religion of Chaldea.

But there is no ground for this assumption, and if the Turanians were the people conquered by the Cushite Accadians, and had adopted their language and religion, and afterwards migrated to Eastern and Northern Asia, then the absence of elaborate religious forms and temples among them in later ages is just what we might expect. Such temples and elaborate religious forms, which would be natural with a highly-civilised and settled race like the Cushites, would be quite inconsistent with the general characteristics and nomadic tendencies of the Turanian races.

There is nothing, therefore, to prove that there was an Accadian religion previous to, or distinct from, that of the kings of Ur. If the Accadians were the Cushites, then the Accadian religion was that established by the

---

[1] *The First Bible*, pp. 5 and 93. [2] *Ibid.*, pp. 51, 80-84, 93, 94.

Cushites, and, as we shall now point out, there is every reason to conclude that the first king of Ur, whose temples and monuments are the oldest known, was himself the founder of the Cushite Empire and religion.

4. Later Assyriologists are now asserting that the Cushites never conquered Babylonia and Assyria, and in spite of the consentient testimony of antiquity speak of "the legend of Nimrod" as a probable myth. Assuming the Accadians to have been Turanian and not Cushite, and recognising that their language and power was succeeded by that of the Semites, there was evidently no room for a great Cushite Empire between the fall of the one and the rise of the other. But the evidence that the Accadians were the Cushites, and that the Turanians were only a conquered race associated with them, seems to be conclusive.

Professor Sayce, however, who seems to lean to the modern theory, remarks that no evidence has been found on the monuments of Babylonia and Assyria of any such person as Nimrod.

It is most unlikely that there would be any record of him under that name. "*Nimrod*" is Semitic-Babylonian, or later Chaldee, and means "The Subduer of the Leopard." It was merely a *sobriquet* by which he was popularly known in after times. His actual Accadian name must have been quite different, and the first king of Accad—"Sargon," "Sharrukin," "Sargina" or "Sargani"—answers in every respect to him.

If the Cushites were Accadian, and Nimrod, who is stated to have been the founder of Accad, was their first monarch, then he was the first king of Accad, and *Sargani Sar Ali* was that king. Sargani Sar Ali was called by the later Babylonians "The Founder," "The World King,"[1] and is spoken of as the conqueror of Elam, while in an inscription he is made to say of himself, "The mighty king, the King of Accad am I." Like Ishdubar, he is the lover of the goddess Ishtar, a relationship which not only tends to identify him with the gods of Babylon, whose characters accord with that of Nimrod, but also indicates the human origin of those gods. The inscription goes on to say, "For forty-five years the kingdom I have ruled, and the black head (or black) race I have governed. In multitudes of bronze chariots I have rode over rugged lands. I *governed the upper countries* (Assyria, etc.) Three times to the sea I have advanced." He is also stated to have made successful expeditions to Syria and Elam, and that with the conquered peoples of those countries he peopled Accad, and built there a magnificent palace and temple, and that on one occasion he was absent three years when he advanced to the Mediterranean, and, like Sesotris, Hercules, etc., left there memorials of his deeds, returning home with immense spoils.[2]

The fact that Sargani brought conquered peoples to inhabit Accad implies that it was a city *newly built* by him, that he was Nimrod, its founder, and that, as king of the black race, he was a Cushite, while his expeditions and conquests and empire exactly correspond with those of Nimrod and with the traditions of Ninus, Zohak, Osiris, Sesostris, etc. If,

---

[1] *The First Bible*, Appendix, p. 217. [2] Ragozin's *Chaldea*, pp. 205-207.

then, the Accadians were Cushites, there appears to be every reason for concluding that Sargani was Nimrod, the founder of the Cushite Empire.

It has been shown that many of the Egyptian dynasties were those of contemporary kings, ruling either in Upper or Lower Egypt, or over the more important of the different nomes into which Egypt was divided. The same must have been the case in Babylonia and Assyria. Nimrod, in order to secure his conquests, built great fortified cities at various points of his dominions, by which, with a comparatively small garrison in each, he could hold the surrounding country in subjection, and, as the founder of these cities, he was the first king of Accad, of Erech, of Ur and of Babylon, although the titles given to him as the respective king of each may have been different.

In Professor Sayce's list of Babylonian kings, the first king of Ur is called " *Lugal Kigub*," and this name associates him with " *Lugal Zaggisi*," the first king of Erech, who is recognised as the founder of the Babylonian Empire,[1] and should therefore be Nimrod, or Sargani, the first king of Accad. Now, Colonel Conder has shown that this first king of Erech *is* Sargani, the first king of Accad. For the first part of the name " *Lugal*," or " *Ungal*," is the Accadian for " Great Lord," and is equivalent to the Semitic " *Sarru*," " King." The second sign is more properly read " *Sar*," and the third, " *gi*," has also the sound of " *kanu*," and may be rendered " *gina* " or " *gana*." Hence, *Lugal Zaggisi* is " The Great Lord (or King) Sargina " or " Sargani."[2]

There is a long inscription in his honour, written in Accadian, in a temple at Nippur. It speaks of him as " The mighty man, *son of the god Ea*, (Hea, or Cush), prince of the moon god, begotten of Tammuz and Ishtar." This, of itself, indicates that he was the human original of the Babylonian gods, who are entitled " The Eldest Son," " The First-born of the Gods," " The Only Son," although as a human king he is spoken of as the son of Tammuz instead of being Tammuz himself.

The inscription goes on to say that the god Enlil " had made him the grant of royalty on earth, allotted to him in the sight of the world, the hosts of the land being obedient to him from east and west. He has added every land by conquest."

" From the Upper Sea (which can only mean the Mediterranean), the Tigris, Euphrates, down to the Sea of Elam (the Persian Gulf) the multitudes have been allotted to him."

He is also called " Patesi (*i.e.*, priest king) of the royal city of Accad, powerful ruler of the city of Erech, he has obtained a throne not to be removed. Being chief ruler of Erech, he wields henceforth the power of them of Ur."[3]

He is thus the king of Accad as well as of Erech, while his conquests exactly correspond with those of Sargina, king of Accad. There can be no

[1] Sayce, *Early Israel and the Surrounding Nations*, Appendix II., p. 280.
[2] *The First Bible*, note xvii. pp. 217, 218.   [3] *Ibid.*, p. 218.

reasonable doubt, therefore, that The Great Lord Sargina, the first king of Erech, is Sargina, the first king of Accad, while it seems equally certain that he ruled over and was the first king of Ur, and was therefore the same as *Lugal Kigub*, "The Great Lord Kigub."

The conquests and dominion of Sargina of Accad, Erech and Ur, the first founder of the Babylonian Empire, exactly correspond with the conquests and dominion of Nimrod, and, like Nimrod, Sargina was deified. In the inscriptions quoted above, the mention of the Assyrian goddess Ishtar implies that the inscription, while written in the sacred Accadian language, was made when Assyrian influence and power had displaced the Babylonian or Cushite. In this inscription Sargina, although intimately connected with the gods, is yet, as a human king, distinguished from them. This distinction may be also observed in other inscriptions. In a very rude archaic inscription in Accadian, on an ancient door socket in the same temple, his name reads "Ungal Sargin nil ul ul," "King Sargina the illustrious," while a later text on the same door socket, in Semitic, reads "The divine Lord, the great King, King Sargina, the illustrious King, the just, the King of Agade (Accad)." So also a seal found in Cyprus, supposed to be about the date 2000 B.C., has an inscription in which the writer, Abilsar, calls himself a worshipper of "The divine Sargani, the illustrious King." Another Semitic text reads "The divine Sargani, the illustrious King, a son of Bel the just, the King of Agade and of the children of Bel." [1] In this last text he is clearly identified as a son of Bel or Belus (*i.e.*, Cush), and king of the children of Bel, or the Cushites.

Thus we see that, in these later Semitic texts, Sargani, the first king of Accad and Erech, is deified and identified with those gods who are represented as the son of the first Belus or Hea, and there can be little doubt, therefore, that Sargina is Nimrod, the founder of the Babylonian Empire.

Again, Lugal Kigub, the first king of Ur, called by Professor Rawlinson "Urukh" as a tentative name, is the oldest king of whom any architectural remains exist. His bricks are found in a lower position than any at the foundations of buildings, and the inscriptions on them are the most simple and archaic. He is known to us as a builder of gigantic works, and the basement platforms of the temples at Ur, at Calneh, at Erech and Ellasar, were all built by him, [2] implying that he must have been the founder of these cities, and therefore the same as Nimrod or Sargani of Accad and Erech. In short, he calls himself "King of Ur and of Kienge Accad"; [3] and as M. Lenormant has shown that "Kienge" is the equivalent of "Sumir," "Kienge Accad" would therefore mean "Sumir Accad," the name constantly used to describe the whole of Babylonia, the kingdom of Nimrod. [4]

It is worthy of notice also that just as Ninus, or Nimrod, was succeeded by Semiramis, who was the human original of the Babylonian goddess, so

[1] *The First Bible*, note xvii. pp. 219, 220.
[2] *Five Great Monarchies*, vol. i. pp. 155, 156.   [3] *Ibid.*, p. 159.
[4] *Chald. Magic*, Appendix, "Sumir and Accad," pp. 399-402.

one of the immediate successors of Lugal Kigub is a Queen Gula, and Gula is one of the names of the Babylonian goddess.

Professor Sayce also mentions another king who is ruler of Kienge, or Sumir, and whose name he gives as "*En Sag Sagana.*" But from the remarks of Colonel Conder on the name "Lugal zag gisi," which should read "Lugal Sargani," we may conclude that "En Sag Sagana" should read "*En Sar Sargana,*" or *Sargani,* and that he also is the same as Sargani Sar Ali of Erech and Accad.

On these grounds, the first kings of Erech, Kienge, Accad and Ur must be regarded as one and the same person, viz., Nimrod, the founder of these cities and of the Babylonian Empire. (*See* Table of Kings).

It is also to be noted that the most ancient Accadian king of Nipur, whose texts in the Accadian language have been discovered, is called "*Tur-cus-u,*" and as *tur* is the Accadian for "son," the name would read "Son of Cush" (*i.e.*, Nimrod).[1]

But Babylon was the chief city of Babylonia and the beginning of Nimrod's kingdom, and its first ruler must also have been the same as the first ruler of Erech, Accad and Ur. It is, however, probable that Cush, as the first originator of the Tower of Babel and the city which was commenced at the same time, would be shown as the first king of Babylon on the monumental lists, as in the case of the dynastic lists preserved by the Greeks, where Belus is the first king and Ninus the second. This seems to be indicated by the names of the first two kings on the monumental lists, where the first king is called "*Sumu Abi,*" and the second "*Sumu la Ilu.*"

"*Sumu*" is an Accadian term, and the name of the god of the sky, or heaven, corresponding with the Hittite "*Sumu,*" the god of storm, and with the Semitic "*Rimmon,*"[2] while "*Abi*" is the Accadian for "father,"[3] and Sumu Abi might, therefore, very well apply to Cush, or the elder Belus, who was deified as the father of the second and more important Belus, and hence as the father of the gods. The second Sumu is called "la Ilu," and "ilu" was the general Accadian name for "god," corresponding to the Semitic "el," and the name would, therefore, especially apply to the deified king Sargina or Nimrod. Moreover, the successor of Sumu la Ilu is a king called "*Zabu,*" and the successor of Ninus or Nimrod and Semiramis in the Greek lists of Babylonian kings is a king called "*Zames.*" Now, as the Egyptians and Greeks appear to have substituted "*m*" for "*b*" (as in the name Nebrod for Nimrod) Zabu would be written "*Zamu,*" which, with the Greek termination, would be "*Zames.*" This, therefore, is a strong confirmation that Sumu Abi, Sumu la Ilu and Zabu are the Belus, Ninus and Zames of the Greek lists.

It will also be noted that this first Babylonian dynasty consists of *eleven* kings, and this corresponds with the first Chaldean dynasty of Berosus, which

[1] Conder, *The First Bible*, pp. 156, 157.
[2] *Ibid.,* note xiv. p. 214 ; note xviii. p. 224.
[3] Lenormant, *Chald. Magic*, p. 300 ; Sayce *Isra* *and the Surrounding Nations*, p. 212.

2C

402 THE WORSHIP OF THE DEAD

also consists of *eleven* kings and which must be that of which Nimrod was the founder. The duration (292 years) is rather longer than the 258 years of Berosus, but it is very possible that the overthrow of the Babylonian kingdom by the Elamites, which would be the natural termination of the dynasty, took place at the beginning, or during the reign of the last king, and that this was taken by Berosus as the termination of the dynasty, in which case the length of the two dynasties would practically be the same. Colonel Conder says that this first Babylonian dynasty and the second or *Sisku* dynasty also are both "*Kassite*,"[1] a term which M. Lenormant identifies with "*Cissian*" or "*Kissian*,"[2] which is clearly the same as the "Kissioi" of the Greeks, one of the names by which the people of Chusistan, or the land of Cush, were known. Hence it would appear that the Elamite conquest was only temporary, as the Cushites continued to rule in Babylonia, the seat of government being merely removed to Sisku, so that there was no real break in the succession. (*See* Table).

Now a boundary stone recently found at Nippur states that the interval between the accession of the Kassite king of Sisku, "*Gulkisar*," and the death of *Nebuchadnezzar I.* was exactly 636 years,[3] and it can be proved that the date of the latter's death was about 1140 B.C., which would make the date of Gulkisar 1776 B.C., and that of Samu la Ilu 2234 B.C., in exact agreement with the date of Berosus for the beginning of the first Chaldean Kingdom or Empire of Nimrod. (*See* Table.) This, therefore, is a further confirmation that Samu la Ilu and Samu Abi are Nimrod and his father, the founders of the first Cushite Empire and the same as Lugal Sargina, the first king of Erech, Kienge, Accad and Ur.

As these dynasties of Erech, Accad, Lagas, Ur, etc., must be regarded as contemporary, it will account in part for the exaggerated estimate of the date Naram Sin by Nabonidus. No doubt he, or the priesthood, assumed all these dynasties to be successive and added the totals together. Moreover, if the first dynasties were contemporary, it is possible that other dynasties were also contemporary or partly so; as, for instance, the third Kassite dynasty may have been partly contemporary with the second Kassite or Sisku dynasty. For, if we estimate the period between the accession of Gulkisar and the death of Nebuchadnezzar I. according to the number of kings in the second and third Kassite dynasties and the length of their reigns, supposing the two dynasties to be successive, it will be found to be considerably in excess of 636 years. It will be seen that the length of the reigns of twenty-two of the kings of the third Kassite dynasty are unknown, and, excluding the abnormally brief reigns of those of two or three kings, the average length of the remainder would appear to be about 16 years, and, taking this as the average length of the unknown reigns, it will give 352 years to be added to the total of the known reigns from Gulkisar to Nebuchadnezzar. Thus :—

[1] *The First Bible*, chap. ii. p. 27.   [2] *Chald. Magic*, pp. 327, 410, and note.
[3] *The First Bible*, note vi. p. 203.

Sisku dynasty from accession of Gulkisar,	.	187 years
Kings of third Kassite dynasty to death of Nebuchad-		
nezzar I., ...	.	285 „
Add kings without reigns, . .	.	352 „
		824 years

This is 188 years in excess of 636 years, and suggests the probability that the third Kassite dynasty was partly contemporary with the Sisku dynasty, possibly from the time of Gulkisar, which appears to have been a marked epoch. For, if we suppose that Gandis, the first king of the third Kassite dynasty, was contemporary with Gulkisar, the period from Gandis to the death of Nebuchadnezzar would be almost exactly 636 years. Thus :—

THIRD KASSITE DYNASTY.

Length of known reigns to death of Nebuchadnezzar,	.	285 years
Length of unknown reigns, . . .	.	352 „
		637 years

This contemporaneous period, regarded as successive, would further help to account for the excessive estimates of Nabonidus. (*See* Table).

There is also great uncertainty with regard to the the exact position of some of the kings, which in certain lists are confessedly not in the proper order of succession,[1] and Professor Rawlinson remarks that, although the order of some of the earlier kings may be determined by the position of the bricks, the records of other kings are so "scattered and unconnected" that their relative order "rests on little more than conjecture."[2] This is the case with Ammurabi or Amraphel, who is placed in the middle of the first Babylonian dynasty. He and his son Samsu Iluna are neither connected with the kings before them nor with the kings which follow, and there are reasons for suspecting that they should be placed at the end of the dynasty. In the Greek lists, Ninus or Nimrod is shown to have been succeeded by Semiramis, who reigned for 42 years, and her death must therefore have taken place some 70 to 80 years after the foundation of the empire in 2234 B.C. Now, it seems impossible that within 40 years after the death of this powerful queen the great Cushite Empire should have been completely broken up, as it is shown to be in the days of Ammurabi or Amraphel. Such a state of things, showing as it does the growing power of the Elamites in Babylon, would be the natural precursor of the Elamite conquest, but not of a period 100 years before that event.

Ammurabi's expedition to Canaan as the ally of Chedorlaomer appears to have been in the thirtieth year of his reign, and his quarrel with the Elamite king in the thirty-second year, previous to which they were on the most friendly terms, a daughter of Ammurabi having married a prince of

---

[1] *The First Bible*, p. 152. [2] *Five Great Monarchies*, vol. i. p. 165.

Elam.[1] Is it not possible, therefore, that this quarrel with Elam was the beginning of the war with that country, and that, although Ammurabi at first defeated Chedorlaomer, it resulted in the temporary overthrow of the kingdom by Kedor Nakhunta a few years later? In this case, Ammurabi and Samsu Iluna would be the two last kings of the first Babylonian dynasty, and the thirtieth year of Ammurabi when he accompanied Chedorlaomer to Canaan would then be 2005 B.C. (*vide* Table of Kings), which would be almost exactly the date of Amraphel's expedition to Canaan according to corrected Scripture chronology; this expedition being a year or two before the covenant with Abraham. Thus :—

Abraham's departure to Canaan	2005 B.C.
Second Expedition and Defeat of Amraphel—	
Covenant with Abraham	2002
Period of 215 years	
Jacob and his Sons go to Egypt	1787
Israel in Egypt 215 years	
Exodus and giving of the Law	1572
Israel in Wilderness 40 years	
Entrance to Canaan	1532
Period of Judges—450 years, less 18 years of Samuel during reign of Saul } 432 years	
Accession of Saul	1100
Reign of the kings of Judah to—	
The First Capture of Jerusalem by Nebuchadnezzar two years before he came to the throne	608
Final Capture of Jerusalem	589
Capture of Babylon by Cyrus and accession of Darius the Mede	538
Accession of Cyrus	536

(Covenant with Abraham to Exodus bracketed as 430 years)

Some have supposed that Israel's sojourn in Egypt was 430 years; but this is quite impossible as it was to be only for four generations— Levi, Kohath, Amram and Moses (*see* Gen. xv. 16), and the whole period from the Covenant to the Law is stated to be exactly 430 years (Gal iii. 17), while from the Covenant to the arrival in Egypt was exactly half that period.

The period of the Judges is stated to have been "about 450 years" (Acts xii. 20). But Samuel, the last of the Judges, who is said to have "judged Israel all the days of his life" (1 Sam. vi. 15), did not die, according to Josephus, until the eighteenth year of Saul's reign, and these 18 years must therefore be included in the 450. This period also corresponds very exactly with the total of the different periods of rest and captivity given in the Book of Judges, although there is one brief period between the death of Joshua and the first captivity which has to be estimated.

---

[1] *See* chronological record of Ammurabi's reign, *The First Bible*, pp. 204, 205.

If the capture of Erech by Kedor Nakhunta, mentioned by Asshur-banipal, took place in the last years of Ammurabi's reign or in the first year of his successor, then, according to the arrangement of kings on the monumental list given by Professor Sayce,[1] it would have taken place in the year 2094 B.C., but Asshur-banipal says it was 1635 years before his time (645 B.C.), which would make it 2280 B.C. This discrepancy would, however, be accounted for if, as suggested, the third Kassite dynasty was partly contemporaneous with the second for a period of 180 to 190 years, and that Asshur-banipal regarded them as successive. For if we subtract 186 years from 1635 the period would be only 1449 years, which, added to 645, would be exactly 2094 B.C.

These are only suggestions, and with the present imperfect lists of kings and the uncertainty as regards their actual order of succession, it is impossible to arrive at any certain conclusion; but no doubt further discoveries will elucidate the question. The date, however, of Gulkisar's accession in 1776 B.C., and that of Samu la Ilu in 2234 B.C. seems to be fairly certain, and the apparent identity of the latter king with Nimrod, whose empire is proved by various testimonies to have commenced 2234 B.C., confirms this.

There are also certain other dates in the accompanying list of kings which, as explained in the Notes on the Chronological Table, appear to be fairly well established.

5. In connection with this subject we may notice the modern theory, or *assertion*, that Gen. x. is not a genealogical description of the descendants of Noah, but simply an enumeration of certain countries from which the people inhabiting them took their names, while some go so far as to say that the sacred historians invented progenitors of these different races, calling them by the names of these races in order to account for those names. Professor Sayce supports this theory. He asserts that Canaan was not a son of Ham whose descendants were cursed by Noah, but that, as it is a name meaning "low," it meant "low-lands" and was first given to the plain country near the coast of Palestine and afterwards extended to the whole country! But there is no evidence whatever that this was the case. So also he says that when we are told that Canaan begat Zidon his first-born, all that is meant is that the city of Zidon is to be found in the country called Canaan.

In like manner, he implies that Cush and Mizraim are not to be regarded as sons of Ham, but the countries Ethiopia and Egypt; that Elam was not a son of Shem, but a word meaning "high" or "exalted" given to the mountainous country on the east of the Lower Euphrates. Arphaxad he derives from Arpha Chesed, meaning "bordering on Casdim," or Chaldea, and says that it only signifies the country of Chaldea.

---

[1] *Early Israel*, Appendix II., p. 281. In this list Ammurabi and Samsi Iluna are shown as succeeding Sin Muballidh, in which case the beginning of Ammurabi's reign would be 2137 B.C., and the first year of his son, Samsi Iluna, 2094 B.C.

He endeavours to explain the origin of some other names in a similar way, and sums up by saying that Gen. x. "lays no claim to being an ethnological record. On the contrary, it tells us as plainly as language can speak that with ethnology it has nothing to do."[1]

This is like telling a person to his face, who says a thing is white, that he clearly means by his words that it is black. For if language has any meaning, the intention of the writer of Gen. x. is to record the descendants of Noah. He is speaking of *persons* and not of *places*, and when he speaks of the latter he clearly distinguishes between them and the persons inhabiting them.

Professor Sayce asserts that in speaking of these supposed countries as *sons* of Shem, Ham and Japhet, Scripture merely follows the usual Semitic method of calling colonies "*daughters*" of a mother nation. But, in the first place, while it is still a common form of speech to speak of colonies as "*daughter* nations" of a mother country, there is no precedent for the term "*son* nations"; and in the second place, when the term "daughter" is used, it is *the people* who have sprung from a *mother people*, and not the places they inhabit that is intended. The term "daughter" is strictly descriptive of a colony which has sprung from a mother nation, but to say that a certain tract of land has sprung from, or is the daughter of, a nation, or an individual, is clearly absurd.

Moreover, the language used by the sacred writer will not admit of Professor Sayce's interpretation. Shem, we are told, begat Arphaxad two years after the Flood. Did he beget *the country* Arphaxad in those two years, and did *the country* Arphaxad at the age of thirty-five years beget *the country* Salah, and, after that, beget sons and daughters or numerous other *countries, male and female?* And did *the country* Salah after thirty years beget *the country* Eber and numerous other *male and female countries?* Apparently also each of these *countries* lived so many years and then died, or ceased to exist! On the same principle also we must suppose Terah to be *a country* and that Terah took *the country* Abram and *the country* Lot, and the *female country* Sarai, and that these *countries* left the country of Chaldea and came and dwelt in the country Haran!

But if the absurdity of this interpretation shows that the writer is speaking of persons and not of places, it is clear that the other sons of Shem are persons and not places which are plainly distinguished from the persons inhabiting them; as when it is said of the sons of Joktan that "their dwelling was from Mesha as thou goest into Sephar a mount of the East."[2]

The chapter closes with the words, ' These are *the families* of *the sons of Noah after their generations* in their nations,"[3] and these words can only apply to people and would be unmeaning if applied to countries.

---

[1] *Fresh Lights*, pp. 40-42; *The Races of the Old Testament*, chap. iii. pp. 40, 68.
[2] Gen. x. 30.
[3] Gen. x. 32.

Moreover, with a few exceptions, it has always been the custom of the human race to call countries after the name of the people inhabiting them, as in the case of Gaul after the Gauls, Germany after the Germans, Britain after the British (originally Brythons), Scotland after the Scoti, etc., or in some cases after the discoverer, as in the case of America and numerous islands and places discovered during the last three centuries. This was equally the custom in ancient times—"They call the lands after their own names" (Psa. xlix. 11), and we may therefore be perfectly certain that the districts inhabited by the various tribes and families of the descendants of Noah, each of which was distinguished from the other tribes by the name of its particular progenitor, would be called by the names of the tribes inhabiting them, and that those names would not be relinquished for totally new ones based upon some superficial characteristic of the country, such as the people of the "high country," or the people of the "low country," which could only produce hopeless confusion, as the terms would be equally applicable to numerous other districts inhabited by quite distinct races.

The only exception to this would be when some celebrated city like Babylon, or Accad, was founded on the first occupation of the country, although, even in this case, the country was also known by the name of its inhabitants, the Kaldi or Chaldeans.

The origin given by Professor Sayce of names such as "Canaan" "*low*," hence "lowlands"; "Elam," "*high*," hence "a mountainous district"; Arphaxad, or "Arpha Chesed," "*bordering on chesed*," hence "the land of Chaldea," are very forced and unnatural. The only excuse for the theory is that in one or two cases the people inhabiting a country have been found to speak a language, or possess characteristics, different from those of the people by whose name they are called. But it should be remembered, as pointed out by Professor Sayce himself, that language is not of itself a proof of race, and that countries, although still retaining the name of the people who first occupied them, may have been inhabited later by a totally different race who were yet called after the original name of the country.

Thus some of the people called Amorites, who were descendants of Canaan, spoke a Semitic language and are represented by the Egyptians as of a brown complexion with brown hair and blue eyes, but this exception to the general character of the Canaanitish nations may be due, as pointed out, to the occupation of the country of the northern Amorites by the Aramæans, or other Semitic tribes, who were called by the Egyptians after the original name of the country they occupied.

The most marked instance, however, is that of the Elamites, who are said to have spoken an agglutinative language similar to the Accadian, while the racial type was similar to that of the primitive inhabitants of Babylonia,—*round, broad head*, low receding forehead, prognathous jaws, frizzly hair, *short stature* and *very little hair on the face*,[1] a type which

[1] *The Races of the Old Test.*, pp. 137, 138.

The arrangement of the other kings is in accordance with certain dates fixed by the inscriptions :—

1. Sagarkti Buryas is stated by Nabonidus to have reigned 800 years before him,[1] and as the elements of error which led Nabonidus to fix the date of Naram Sin 3200 years before his own reign, do not exist in later periods, the statement may be taken as more or less accurate.[2] Therefore as Nabonidus began to reign 555 B.C., the date of Sagarkti Buryas would be 1355 B.C. This date is confirmed by another inscription.

2. Sennacherib, in a rock inscription at Bavian, states that in his tenth year he recovered certain images of the gods from Babylon which had been taken there by Merodach Nadin Akhi, king of Babylon, after his defeat of Tiglath Pileser, king of Assyria, 418 years before.[3] Sennacherib's date of accession is taken as 703 B.C., and his tenth year as 693 B.C., but the grounds for this conclusion are doubtful. The exact chronology of the Bible makes his expedition against Hezekiah to be in the fourteenth year of the reign of the latter, or 713 B.C., and there seems to be no reason for questioning the date. If then we suppose that the expedition was made by Sennacherib in the first year of his accession, which would also be in accordance with the usual custom, it would then be 713 B.C., and his tenth year would be 703 B.C., and 418 years before this bring us to 1121 B.C., which is three years before the death of Merodach Nadin Akhi, according to the dynastic lists.[4]

The date of Nebuchadnezzar I. is taken by Colonel Conder as 1154 B.C.,[5] and the dates of the kings between Nebuchadnezzar and Sagarkti Buryas are in accordance with the known lengths of their reigns, the only uncertainty being the four kings whose names are missing to whom it is necessary to give a period of 97 years, or an average of 24 years each, which is high but not excessive. It will be noticed that the date of the termination of the third Kassite dynasty by Bel sum iddin, agrees almost exactly with the date of the termination of the corresponding dynasty of Berosus, which therefore tends to confirm its accuracy.[6]

3. The dates before Sagarkti Buryas are in accordance with the known lengths of the reigns to Kurigalzu III., but the reigns of the 18 or 20 kings previous to him have not been ascertained and can only be estimated. But even at the low estimate of 14 years for each king, it makes the first king of the dynasty to have been the contemporary of Gulkisar as already suggested.

4. Professor Sayce has made Kadasman Bel the successor of Kara-indas, but this is clearly incorrect, as shown by an Assyrian tablet which records a succession of five Babylonian monarchs as contemporary with certain

[1] *Early Israel*, Appendix II. p. 282.
[2] The 800 years would appear to be a round number, and the actual period may have been a few years more or less.
[3] *Five Great Monarchies*, vol. i. p. 164.
[4] Sayce, *Early Israel*, p. 232. *See* also Chronological Table.
[5] *The First Bible*, p. 203. *See* also Sayce, *Early Israel*, Appendix II. p. 282, and note.
[6] See *ante*, p. 281.

Assyrian kings with whom they were on terms of friendship. Kara-indas is the first, and concluded a treaty of alliance with Ashur bel nisi su, and this treaty is renewed by the Buzur Ashur, the successor of Ashur bel nisi su with Burna Buryas, the successor of Kara-indas. Burna Buryas continues the friendship with the successor of Buzur Ashur, viz., Ashur Upallit, and marries the daughter of the latter. The issue of this marriage is a Prince Kara-khardas, who on the death of Burna Buryas, succeeds to the throne of Babylon, but is murdered by a certain Nazi-bugas, who usurps the throne, whereupon Ashur Upallit invades Babylon, kills the usurper and places Kuri-galzu, a younger son of Burna Buryas, upon the throne.[1] This, therefore, is the true succession (see Table), and as Kara-khardas was murdered and the usurper was quickly deposed, the interval between Burna Buryas and his son Kuri-galzu was probably under a year and need not be taken into consideration.

There is nothing to show the position of Kadasman Bel, but as the succession is continuous after Kuri-galzu I., Kadasman Bel must have been previous to Kara-indas. Kadasman Bel was a contemporary of the Egyptian king Amenophis III., by whom the persecution of the Israelites appears to have been begun, and as the Exodus was in the reign of Menepthah, 80 to 100 years afterwards, it would imply that Amenophis III. reigned 80 to 100 years before 1572 B.C., which is the date of the Exodus according to corrected Scripture chronology. Both Scripture and Babylonian chronology are therefore completely at variance with the assumed Egyptian chronology, upon which very little dependence can be placed.

4. It will be seen that the contemporary Assyrian kings, from Ashur bel nisi su to Tiglath Bir, the contemporary of the Babylonian king Rimmon sum uzur, are very few as compared with the number of Babylonian kings during the corresponding interval, while the kings after Tiglath Bir to Asurdan I., the contemporary of the Babylonian king Zamana sum iddin, are much too numerous for the very short interval of 45 years. So also there is only one king between Assurdan I. and Assur ris isi, the contemporary of Nebuchadnezzar I., which is wholly inconsistent with the interval, which could not have been less than 125 years. Therefore, as the dates of the Babylonian kings are fairly well established, it implies that the succession of the Assyrian kings is considerably out of order, and that some of the earlier kings are probably missing.

5. There is one other date which can be approximately fixed, viz., that of Isme Dagon, king of Isin. Tiglath Pileser I. states that he rebuilt a temple which had been taken down 60 years before, after it had lasted for 641 years from its erection by Shamas Vul, a son of Isme Dagon.[2] The rebuilding must have been at the beginning of Tiglath Pileser's reign before his defeat by Merodach nadin akhi, or about 1130 B.C., and its first erection would therefore be $1130 + 60 + 641 = 1831$ B.C., and, as we must

[1] *Five Great Monarchies*, vol. i. p. 169.
[2] *Ibid.*, vol. i. p. 164.

suppose that Isme Dagon began to reign not less than 30 years before, it would make the date of his accession about 1860 B.C.[1]

APPENDIX E

"HISTORY OF SANCHONIATHON"

SANCHONIATHON was an ancient Phœnician historian who lived about the time of the Trojan War. He is referred to by Athenæus, by Porphyry, Theodoret, Suidas, and by Eusebius. His history was translated into Greek by a Pagan writer called Philo Byblius, who wrote at the end of the first century A.D., but both the original and translation are lost, and the only existing remains of the history are portions of the translation quoted by Eusebius and his Pagan opponent Porphyry.

But certain modern writers have tried to discredit this history by suggesting that it was a forgery by Philo Byblius. We naturally ask, however, What evidence is there of such forgery? An invention would show evidence of system and artificial arrangement. But there is nothing of the kind in this history. It is a statement of dry facts such as would be made by a person who, having collected them from various sources, recorded them without even understanding their true relation and significance.

Again, What object could Philo Byblius have in constructing a forgery which could only tend to bring his religion into contempt before the Christians?

The latter is evidently a crucial question, and felt to be so by the opponents of the history. It is, therefore, suggested by some that it was forged out of enmity to the Christians, in order to prove that the Pagans had something to show of equal antiquity to the books of Moses. Such a suggestion is weak and absurd. The history, so far as it goes, corroborates the Mosaic account, and the only effect of the forgery would, therefore, be to support the religion they hated.

Again, the Jesuit Father Simon suggested that it was forged to support Paganism, by expunging from the latter its mythology and allegories. But it does not even do this, and, as the writer of the article in the *Encyclopedia Britannica* remarks, the Christians did not object to the Pagan allegories,

---

[1] Professor Sayce represents Isme Dagon as a high priest distinct from the king Isme Dagon. He does this, no doubt, because to admit that he was king of that name would completely upset his arrangement of kings, which is constructed to give colour to the exaggerated date of Naram Sin by Nabonidus. No doubt the king Isme Dagon was a high priest, for all the early Babylonian kings were "patesis" or priest kings, and heads of the priesthood, or high pontiffs, which tends to prove that Isme Dagon, the high priest, was Isme Dagon the king.

but to the immorality of the Pagan gods and goddesses, which this history has done nothing to remove. This suggestion is equally forced and weak.

There are others again who assert that Philo was a particular adherent of Euhemerus, who, as we have seen, is stated to have searched the archives of numerous Pagan temples, and, on their authority, to have represented the originals of the Pagan gods to have been men who had lived upon the earth as human kings. It is asserted that Philo, in order to support the teaching of Euhemerus, forged the history and pretended that it was taken from the history of Sanchoniathon. These are mere assertions unsupported by evidence. It is a wholly groundless assertion to say that Philo was a special disciple of Euhemerus (another pretended forger), for we have seen that the teaching of Euhemerus was the common belief throughout the Pagan world, that it existed long before his time, and in countries which he had probably never seen, and that it is supported by a multitude of incidental and perfectly undesigned corroborations by numerous ancient writers.

The assertion that the human origin of the gods was invented by Euhemerus is not only disproved by these facts, but, as before remarked, it would have been impossible for anyone to have invented a theory wholly opposed to the previous belief of Paganism without calling forth a storm of opposition, of which ample records would have remained in contemporary and subsequent literature, together with ample evidence that it was fully recognised at the time to have been invented. There are no such records, because, although Euhemerus might be charged with impiety for publishing matters only revealed in the Mysteries, they were recognised as true by every initiate of those Mysteries.

In like manner with the history of Sanchoniathon. How is it that it was not opposed at the time and represented to be a forgery by those most interested in opposing it and best able to judge of its authenticity? If it had been a forgery for the purpose of misrepresenting the general Pagan belief, it would certainly have been opposed at the time and its authenticity questioned. The history of Sanchoniathon was well known at the time, and if Philo Byblius had forged his translation, the deception would have been quickly recognised and exposed. But instead of this, it was accepted at the time as genuine by both Pagans and Christians.

How is it again that Pagans, some of whom evince the greatest respect for their religion, should be the very people who insist on the human origin of their gods, which, if false, could only tend to lower the estimation in which they were held? Instead of the charge of invention and forgery being brought against them at the time by their co-religionists, who were most interested in the question and the best able to judge of its truth, it is not until quite modern times that these charges have been brought by people who have nothing but assertion to support their indictment.

There could be no motive for Pagans who believed in their own religion *inventing* the human origin of their gods.

On the other hand, when we see modern writers defending Paganism against the Pagans themselves, and, without any just grounds, calling every ancient document which admits the human origin of the gods an invention or forgery of the writer, one cannot help suspecting that an underlying animus is the cause of such charges. This suspicion is increased when we see that, in cases where one motive for the supposed forgery seems to be insufficient, another is suggested, as if there was a determination to use any and every means in order to throw discredit on the testimony.

In the case of Sir Gardner Wilkinson, it would seem that, fascinated by the art and grandeur of ancient Egypt and the outward attributes of righteousness given to its gods, he refused to admit any evidence which tended to lower his ideal, although his theories were often directly opposed to his own admissions.

In like manner, the halo of romance and antiquity, which surrounds the ancient Paganism, exercises an undoubted fascination over many classical scholars and might naturally create in them a feeling of antagonism to evidence which tends to dispel or diminish it; and this may lead them to accept, without sufficient inquiry, the suggestion that such evidences were forgeries. The attributes also given to the Pagan gods and their identification with the great powers of nature may seem to justify them in refusing to believe that these gods were merely the supposed spirits of the dead. In this they are so far right, for, as we have shown throughout, the gods eventually worshipped retained little identity with their human originals, who merely constituted the stepping-stone on the basis of which the system was ultimately developed.

But the originators of these charges of forgery will be probably found elsewhere. The worship of the dead is the central feature of the Roman Catholic religion and of those allied cults which are gaining such a hold upon the upper classes in this and other countries, and it must be expected, therefore, that the advocates and propagators of these creeds, and all who admire or lean to them, will be the chief opponents of evidence which, by identifying their doctrines with those of the ancient Paganism, throws discredit on their teaching.

In spite, however, of the opposition that must be expected from these sources, the accumulative evidence in proof of the human origin of the Pagan gods will, no doubt, convince many of its truth and lead them to conclude that the portions of Sanchoniathon's history which have been preserved are, in all probability, the genuine statements of that writer.

INDEX

415

2D

Printed in the USA
CPSIA information can be obtained
at www.ICGtesting.com
LVHW011507301023
762551LV00021B/1399